For Mies Paul
with our good wish

[signature]

4 May 2005

[handwritten note/signature]

SPUDASMATA

Studien zur Klassischen Philologie und ihren Grenzgebieten
Begründet von Hildebrecht Hommel und Ernst Zinn
Herausgegeben von Gottfried Kiefner und Ulrich Köpf

Band 67

WILLIAM M. CALDER III

Men in Their Books

Second Edition

2002

GEORG OLMS VERLAG HILDESHEIM· ZÜRICH· NEW YORK

WILLIAM M. CALDER III

Men in Their Books

Studies in the Modern History
of Classical Scholarship

Edited by
John P. Harris and R. Scott Smith

Second Edition

2002

GEORG OLMS VERLAG HILDESHEIM· ZÜRICH· NEW YORK

Die Deutsche Bibliothek – CIP-Einheitsaufnahme

Calder, William M.:
Men in Their Books : studies in the modern history of classical scholarship /
William M. Calder III. Ed. by John P. Harris and R. Scott Smith.-
Hildesheim ; Zürich ; New York : Olms 2002 / Second Edition
(Spudasmata ; Bd. 67)
ISBN 3-487-10686-8

∞ ISO 9706
© Georg Olms Verlag AG, Hildesheim 2002
Alle Rechte vorbehalten
Printed in Germany
Umschlagentwurf: Prof. Paul König, Hildesheim
Gedruckt auf säurefreiem und alterungsbeständigem Papier
Herstellung: Digital Druck AG, 96158 Birkach
ISSN 0548-9705
ISBN 3-487-10686-8

Robert Ackerman

Shaye Cohen

Howard Jacobson

David Konstan

Jacob Stern

John Vaio

Robert Wallace

olim discipulis

nunc collegis

semper amicis

d.d.d.

auctor

Denn die emsige und laute Betriebsamkeit der sogenannten
Wissenschaft mit ihren Zeitschriften, Enzyklopädien und
Massenversammlungen war von jeher nichts als der verlängerte
Schatten weniger großer Forscherpersönlichkeiten gewesen.

Werner Jaeger

Table of Contents

Preface

Twenty-one papers published in scattered places are gathered here in honor of their author's sixty-fifth birthday. The title seeks to translate *Wissenschaftlergeschichte als Wissenschaftsgeschichte*. All concern the modern history of classical scholarship but with a pronounced biographical *Richtung*. Obvious *errata* when detected have been corrected. Occasionally references to later relevant literature have been added. Very occasionally and in brackets brief additions have been inserted. An *index nominum* seeks to make details easily available to specialists. Thanks are given to editors and publishers of the original contributions for permission to republish them here. A bibliography of the author's writings since 1983 is included. This continues the bibliography for 1955-1983 earlier published at *Antiqua* 27 (Naples 1984) 269-298. Thanks are made to the William Abbott Oldfather Research Fund of the University of Illinois at Urbana/Champaign and to the Alexander-von-Humboldt-Foundation, both of which have made the editing and publication of this volume possible. The papers are arranged chronologically by date of composition. The English original of "Die Rolle Friedrich Althoffs bei den Berufungen von Ulrich von Wilamowitz-Moellendorff" is published here for the first time. The editors hope that this volume will further stimulate interest in a challenging field.

John P. Harris
R. Scott Smith

University of Alberta
University of Illinois at Urbana/Champaign

William M. Calder III
Bibliography 1984—1997

The items below are arranged by year in the order: Books, Articles, Reviews. The numbering continues the numbers of the complete bibliography (1955–1983) extending through the silver jubilee of the Chicago doctorate and published at *Antiqua* 27 (Naples 1984) 269–297.

1984

315. "Studies in the Modern History of Classical Scholarship," *Antiqua* 27 (Naples 1984). Pp. xii + 327.

   Review: A. Motte, *RD* 64 (1986) 110-113.

316. "Studies presented to Sterling Dow on his Eightieth Birthday," *Greek Roman and Byzantine Monographs* 10 (Durham 1984). Pp. xxxvi + 336. (Editor and Contributor).

317. "Ulrich von Wilamowitz-Moellendorff to Kekule von Stradonitz on Friedrich Gottlieb Welcker," *Studi italiani di filologia classica* NS 3.2 = 77 (1984) 116–133.

318. "Secreti loquimur: An Interpretation of Seneca's *Thyestes*," *Seneca Tragicus Ramus Essays on Senecan Drama,* ed. A. J. Boyle (Berwick, Australia 1983; published 1984) 184–198.

319. "Seneca *Thyestes* 101–106," *Classical Philology* 79 (1984) 225–226.

320. "A Scholar's First Article," *Classical World* 77 (1983/84) 361–366: see Marilyn B. Skinner *CW* 79 (1985/86) 183; E. Badian, *CW* 79 (1985/86) 184–185.

321. "Foreword," *Classica Americana: The Greek and Roman Heritage in the United States,* by Meyer Reinhold (Detroit 1984) 9–12.

322. "A Fragment of Anaxagoras in Thucydides?," *Classical Quarterly* NS 34 (1984) 485–486.

323. "An Echo of Sappho Frag. 16 L-P at Aeschylus, *Agamemnon* 404–19?," "Apophoreta Philologica Emmanueli Fernandez-Galiano a Sodalibus oblata," *Estudios Classicos* 36, 87–88 (Madrid 1984) 215–218.

324.   "Gold for Bronze: *Iliad* 6. 232–236," "Studies presented to Sterling Dow on his Eightieth Birthday," *Greek Roman and Byzantine Monograph* 10 (Durham 1984) 31–35.

325.   Review: *Sophocles, Oedipus Rex,* edited by R. D. Dawe (Cambridge 1982). Pp. viii + 260. *Classical Journal* 79 (1983/84) 367–368.

326.   Notice: John V. A. Fine, *The Ancient Greeks: A Critical History* (Cambridge/London 1983) xiv + 720. *Religious Studies Review* 10 (1984) 172.

327.   *Historical Dictionary of Archaeology,* ed. Nancy de Grummond: Advisory Editor for the History of Archaeology in the X1X and XX Centuries.

328.   *The Adventure of Archaeology.* National Geographical Society. Advisory Editor for X1X and XXth Century Germany.

329.   *Greek Roman and Byzantine Studies* 24 (1984) Editorial Board.

330.   *Philologus* 128 (1984) Advisory Editor and Referee for USA and Canada.

1985

331.   *Wilamowitz nach 50 Jahren,* edd. William M. Calder III, Hellmut Flashar, Theodor Lindken (Darmstadt 1985) xviii + 802. Editor and Contributor.

Reviews: Herbert Bannert, *WS* 109 (1996) 322-323; F. Bertolini *Athenaeum* 66 (1988) 647-649; Bourel, *RMM* 92 (1987) 562-563; Bernhard vom Brocke, *Historische Zeitschrift* 243 (1986) 101–136; R. L. Fowler, *CJ* 82 (1986/87) 67–72; Siegfried Jäkel, *Gräzer Beiträge* 17 (1990) 298-312; Rudolf Kassel, *Göttingische Gelehrte Anzeigen* 239 (1987) 188–228; Hugh Lloyd-Jones, *CR* NS 36 (1986) 295–300 with the corrections of W. M. Calder III, *CR* NS 37 (1987) 337; reprinted without corrections in Sir Hugh Lloyd-Jones, *Greek Comedy, Hellenistic Literature, Greek Religion, and Miscellanea: The Academic Papers of Sir Hugh Lloyd-Jones* (Oxford 1990) 399-406; A. Motte, *RD* 64 (1986) 110-114; Beat Näf, *SZG* 37 (1987) 205-206; Holger Thesleff, *Arctos* 20 (1986) 245.

332. *HYPATIA: Essays in Classics, Comparative Literature, and Philosophy presented to Hazel E. Barnes on her Seventieth Birthday*, edd. William M. Calder III, Ulrich K. Goldsmith, and Phyllis B. Kenevan (Boulder 1985). Editor and Contributor.

333. *The Adventure of Archaeology published by the National Geographic Society*, ed. Carol Bittig Lutyk, et al. (Washington D.C. 1985). Advisory Editor (see p. 361).

334. (with Renate Schlesier) "Wilamowitz on Mommsen's *Kaisergeschichte*," *Quaderni di storia* 21 (1985) 161–163.

335. "The Lion Laughed," *Nietzsche-Studien* 17 (1985) 357–359.

336. "The Political and Literary Sources of Sophocles' *Oedipus Coloneus*," *Hypatia* (Boulder 1985) 1–14.

337. "Ulrich von Wilamowitz-Moellendorff to Hermann Sauppe: Two Unpublished Letters," *Philologus* 129 (1985) 286–298.

338. "Wilamowitz' Call to Göttingen: Paul de Lagarde to Friedrich Althoff on Wilamowitz-Moellendorff," *Studi italiani di filologia classica* NS 3 (1985) 136–160.

339. "The Welcker Symposium," *Gnomon* 57 (1985) 100.

340. "Ecce homo: The Autobiographical in Wilamowitz' Scholarly Writings," *Wilamowitz nach 50 Jahren* (Darmstadt 1985) 80–110.

341. "The Provenance of the Documents," *Wilamowitz nach 50 Jahren* (Darmstadt 1985) 589–590.

342. Review: Anthony Grafton, *Joseph Scaliger: A Study in the History of Classical Scholarship. 1: Textual Criticism and Exegesis* (Oxford 1983). *Classical World* 78 (1985) 606.

343. Review: Francis West, *Gilbert Murray: A Life* (London/Canberra/ New York 1984). *Gnomon* 57 (1985) 313–316.

344. Review: Peter Rosumek, *Index des périodiques dépouillés dans la collection de bibliographie classique et index de leurs sigles* (Paris 1982) and Jean Susorney Wellington, *Dictionary of Bibliographic*

Abbreviations Found in the Scholarship of Classical Studies and Related Disciplines (Westport/London 1983).
Classical Journal 80 (1984/1985) 162–163.

345.   *Greek Roman and Byzantine Studies* 26 (1985) Editorial Board.

346.   *Philologus* 129 (1985) Advisory Editor and Referee for USA and Canada.

1986

347.   (with Robert L. Fowler) "The Preserved Letters of Ulrich von Wilamowitz-Moellendorff to Eduard Schwartz. Edited with Introduction and Commentary." *Bayerische Akademie der Wissenschaften Philologisch-historische Klasse Sitzungsberichte Jahrgang* (1986) Heft 1. Pp. 116.

Review: Nicholas Horsfall, *CR* NS 38 (1988) 191.

348.   *Myth, Scandal and History: The Heinrich Schliemann Controversy and a First Edition of the Mycenaean Diary,* edited by William M. Calder III and David A. Traill (Detroit 1986). Pp. 215. Editor and Contributor.

Reviews: Robert Ackerman, *Victorian Studies* (Autumn 1987) 136–137; J. K. Anderson, *Classical Journal* 86 (1990) 79-81; W. Geoffrey Arnott, *LCM* 12.8 (1987) 122–126; Justus Cobet, *Frankfurter Allgemeine Zeitung* (29 April 1987) 35–36; J. T. Hooker, *Journal of Hellenic Studies* 108 (1988) 258–259; William A. McDonald, *Religious Studies Review* 13 (1987) 258–259; C. G. Thomas, *American Historical Review* 92 (1987) 946.

349.   "Friedrich Gottlieb Welcker: Werk und Wirkung," *Hermes Einzelschriften* 49, edd. William M. Calder III, Adolf Köhnken, Wolfgang Kullmann, Günther Pflug (Wiesbaden 1986). Pp. x + 293. Editor and Contributor.

Reviews: Giovanni Benedetto, *Maia* 43 (1991) 256-259; R. Chevallier, *Revue Belge de Philologie et d'Histoire* 67 (1989) 171–172; F. W. P. Dougherty, *Nuncius* 2 (1987) 253–255; H. Lloyd-Jones, *CR* NS 37 (1987) 294–296; C. Robert Phillips III, *AJPh* 110 (1989) 636–657.

350.   "A New Picture of Heinrich Schliemann," *Myth, Scandal, and History* (Detroit 1986) 17–47.

351.   "F. G. Welcker's *Sapphobild* and its Reception in Wilamowitz," *Friedrich Gottlieb Welcker: Werk und Wirkung*, 131–156.

352.   "A Scholar's First Article," *RE:ACE* (DeKalb 1986) 1, 3, 5–6. An unauthorized reprint with omissions and minor changes of No. 320 above.

353.   "Schwester Hildegard von Wilamowitz-Moellendorff, Meine Erinnerungen beim Lesen der Erinnerungen meines Vaters," edited with notes by William M. Calder III, *Quaderni di storia* 24 (1986) 121–126.

354.   "Heinrich Schliemann: Ein neues Bild," *Journal für Geschichte* (Januar/Februar 1986) 14–25.

355.   "A Word on Scholarly Wills," *American School of Classical Studies Newsletter* (Spring 1986) 14.

356.   (with Christhard Hoffmann) "Ulrich von Wilamowitz-Moellendorff on the Basel Greek Chair," *Museum Helveticum* 43 (1986) 258–263.

357.   "Elucidation" [ad No. 341 above], *Gnomon* 50 (1986) 383.

358.   Review: J. P. Sullivan, *Literature and Politics in the Age of Nero* (Ithaca/London 1985).
Classical Journal 81 (1985/86) 263–265.

359.   Review: Hellmut Flashar, *Grundriss der Geschichte der Philosophie. Die Philosophie der Antike* vol. 3: *Ältere Akademie Aristoteles-Peripatos* (Basel/Stuttgart 1983). Pp. xxii + 645.
Classical Journal 81 (1985/86) 359–360.

360.   *Greek Roman and Byzantine Studies* 27 (1986) Editorial Board.

361.   *Philologus* 130 (1986) Editor and Referee for USA and Canada.

1987

362.   "The Nineteenth Century Rediscovery of Euripides" = *GRBS* 27 (1986) 334–430 (Editor and Contributor).

See Jan Ross, "Lumpenpoet und später Gewinner: Epochen der wechselvollen Wirkungsgeschichte des Euripides," *Frankfurter Allgemeine Zeitung* 21 October 1987 Geisteswissenschaften.

363. "The Nineteenth Century Rediscovery of Euripides: An Introductory Note," *GRBS* 27 (1986) 334.

364. "Ulrich von Wilamowitz-Moellendorff, Sospitator Euripidis," *GRBS* 27 (1986) 409–430.

365. "The Riddle of Aeschylus, Persae," *Athlon: Satura Grammatica in Honorem Francisci R. Adrados II*, edd. P. Bádenas de la Peña, A. Martínez Díez, M. E. Martínez-Fresneda, E. Rodríguez Monescillo (Madrid 1987) 129–134.

366. "Vir bonus discendi peritus," *American Journal of Philology* 108 (1987) 168–171.

367. "Golo Mann on Ulrich von Wilamowitz-Moellendorff," *Quaderni di storia* 26 (1987) 137–139.

368. "Why did Wilamowitz leave Bonn? The New Evidence," *Rheinisches Museum* 130 (1987) 366–384.

369. "Correspondence," [Reply to Hugh Lloyd-Jones on *Wilamowitz nach 50 Jahren*] *CR* NS 37 (1987) 337.

370. Two photographs: "Laufende eleusinische Gottheiten und Gelagerter (Dionysos?) vom Ostgiebel des Parthenon in Athen, 5. Jh. v.u.Z. London Britisches Museum" and "Aphrodite und Peitho (?) vom Ostgiebel des Parthenon in Athen, 5 Jh. v.u.Z. London Britisches Museum," in Wolfgang Schindler, *Mythos und Wirklichkeit in der Antike* (Leipzig 1987) plates 72, 73.

371. Review: F. A. Wolf, *Prolegomena to Homer 1795*. Translated with Introduction and Notes by Anthony Grafton, Glen W. Most and James E. G. Zetzel (Princeton 1985). Pp. xiv + 266.
The American Historical Review 92 (1987) 121–122.

372. Review: Seneca, *Medea*. Translated and with an Introduction by Frederick Ahl. (Ithaca/London 1986). Pp. 116; Seneca, *Phaedra*. Translated and with an Introduction by Frederick Ahl. (Ithaca/London 1986). Pp. 122; Seneca, *Trojan Women*. Translated and with an Introduction by Frederick Ahl. (Ithaca/London 1986). Pp. 122.
Vergilius 33 (1987) 139–142.

373. Notice: Pierre Ducrey, *Warfare in Ancient Greece,* translated by Janet Lloyd (New York 1986). Pp. 315 with 32 full color and 158 black-and-white illustrations, 12 line drawings and 4 maps. *Religious Studies Review* 13 (1987) 348.

374. Summary: *Myth, Scandal and History. The Heinrich Schliemann Controversy and a First Edition of the Mycenaean Diary,* edited by William M. Calder III and David A. Traill (Detroit 1986). *History & Theory* 26 (1987) 235–236.

375. *Greek Roman and Byzantine Studies* 25 (1987) Editorial Board.

376. *Philologus* 131 (1987) Editor and Referee for USA, Canada, and Cuba.

1988

377. "Otto Brendel 1901–1973," *Archäologenbildnisse: Porträts und Kurzbiographien von Klassischen Archäologen deutscher Sprache,* edited by Reinhard Lullies and Wolfgang Schiering (Mainz 1988) 283–284.

378. "Fünf Briefe von Ulrich von Wilamowitz-Moellendorff an Friedrich Leo," *Antikerezeption, Antikeverhältnis, Antikebegegnung in Vergangenheit & Gegenwart Eine Aufsatzsammlung* III, edd. J. Dummer and M. Kunze (Stendal 1983; published 1988) 723–732.

379. "Eva Sachs on Ulrich von Wilamowitz-Moellendorff," *Illinois Classical Studies* 13.1 (1988) 203–216.

380. "Hadas, Moses," *Dictionary of American Biography: Supplement 8 (1966–1970),* edited by John A. Garraty and Mark C. Carnes (New York/London 1988) 235–237.

381. "An Open letter to Professor Rudolf Kassel," *Quaderni di storia* 28 (1988) 221–225.

382. "Vita Aeschyli 9: Miscarriages in the Theatre of Dionysos," *Classical Quarterly* NS 38 (1988) 554–555.

383. "Wilamowitz' Bimillenary Essay on Vergil," *Vergilius* 34 (1988) 112–115.

384. A Translation: Ulrich von Wilamowitz-Moellendorff, "Vergilius: On the Occasion of his 2000th Birthday," *Vergilius* 34 (1988) 115–127: see Nicholas Horsfall, "Afterword," *Vergilius* 34 (1988) 128–130.

385. "The Eduard Meyer Symposium," *Gnomon* 60 (1988) 668–669.

386. "Correspondence," [A. E. Housman's and Edgar Lobel's knowledge of Greek] *Liverpool Classical Monthly* 13 (1988) 160.

387. Review: R. J. Tarrant, "Seneca's *Thyestes,* Edited with Introduction and Commentary," *American Philological Association Textbook Series* 11 (Atlanta 1985). Pp. xii + 269. *Classical Journal* 83 (1987/88) 341–344.

388. Notice: *The Cambridge History of Classical Literature* I *Greek Literature,* edited by P. E. Easterling and B.M.W. Knox (Cambridge 1985; reprinted 1986). Pp. xvi + 936. *Religious Studies Review* 14 (1988) 246.

389. Notice: Ward W. Briggs Jr. and Herbert W. Benario (Editors), "Basil Lanneau Gildersleeve: An American Classicist," *AJP Monographs in Classical Philology* 1 (Baltimore/London 1986). Pp. xii + 115. *Religious Studies Review* 14 (1988) 374.

390. *Greek Roman and Byzantine Studies* 29 (1988) Editorial Board.

391. *Philologus* 132 (1988) Editor and Referee for USA, Canada, and Cuba.

1989

392. (with Alexander Košenina) *Berufungspolitik innerhalb der Alterumswissenschaft im wilhelminischen Preußen. Die Briefe Ulrich von Wilamowitz-Moellendorffs an Friedrich Althoff (1883– 1908)* (Frankfurt/Main 1989). Pp. xiv + 190.

Reviews: Jürgen Hönscheid, *Gnomon* 69 (1997) 382-384; Nicholas Horsfall, *CR* NS 41 (1991) 525–526; Johannes Irmscher, *Deutsche Literaturzeitung* 113 (1992) 168-172; Hans Kloft, *Historische Zeitschrift* 255 (1992) 139-140; E. Mensching, *Latein und Griechisch in Berlin* 34 (1990) 145–147 = *Nugae zur Philologie-*

Geschichte IV (Berlin 1991) 120–122; Hartmut Leppin, *Das historisch-politische Buch* 39 (1991) 158–159; Domenico Mugnolo, *Quaderni di storia* 32 (1990) 209–218; Edgar Pack, *Quaderni di storia* 33 (1991) 191–230, 34 (1991) 235–284; Klaus Rosen, *Bonner Jahrbücher* 192 (1992) 781-782; Otto Schönberger, *Gymnasium* 98 (1991) 190–191; Wilt Aden Schröder, *GGA* 242 (1990) 211–236.

393. Ulrich Goldsmith, *Studies in Comparison,* edited by Hazel E. Barnes, William M. Calder III and Hugo Schmidt, *Utah Studies in Literature and Linguistics* 28 (New York/Bern/Frankfurt am Main/Paris 1989). Pp. 493. Editor.

Review: Robert Kramer, *German Studies Review* 14 (1991) 184–185.

394. "The Authenticity of Seneca, *Thyestes* 336–338," *Mnemosyne* NS 4, 42 (1989) 107–109.

395. "A little garden little Jowett made," *American Notes & Queries* NS 2 (1989) 50–52.

396. "Werner Jaeger," *Einzelveröffentlichungen der Historischen Kommission zu Berlin* Band 60: *Berlinische Lebensbilder,* edited by Wolfgang Ribbe Band 4 *Geisteswissenschaftler,* edited by Michael Erbe (Berlin 1989) 343–363.

397. "The Dramaturgy of Sophocles, *Inachus,*" "Satyrspiel," edited by Bernd Seidensticker, *Wege der Forschung* Bd. 579 (Darmstadt 1989) 134–153 [= reprint of No. 11 *supra* with addenda and corrigenda].

398. "Ulrich von Wilamowitz-Moellendorff on the Importance of Greek for England," *Liverpool Classical Monthly* 14.4 (1989) 51–53.

399. "An Unpublished Emendation of Wilamowitz on *Anthologia Palatina* 7.50.3," *Classical Philology* 84 (1989) 234–235.

400. "The Members of Wilamowitz' Graeca," *Quaderni di storia* 29 (1989) 133–139.

401. "Ulrich von Wilamowitz-Moellendorff to Sir Alfred Zimmern on the Reality of Classical Athens," *Philologus* 133 (1989) 303–309.

402. "The Otto Jahn Symposium," *Gnomon* 61 (1989) 380–381.

403.   (with Alexander Košenina) "Ein Heide im Gespräch mit einem Christen: Ulrich von Wilamowitz-Moellendorffs Briefwechsel mit Adolf Jülicher," *Zeitschrift für Kirchengeschichte* 100 (1989) 85–100.

404.   "The Westminster Epigram on Dean Liddell," *Classical Journal* 84 (1988/89) 265–266.

405.   A translation: "Aubade [Carm. Pop. 853 Page]," *Classical Outlook* 66.4 (May–June 1989) 111.

406.   A translation (with A. G. Calder): Wolfgang Schindler, A Review of Paul Zanker, *The Power of Images in the Age of Augustus* (Jerome Lectures–Sixteenth Series), translated by Alan Shapiro, Ann Arbor. The University of Michigan Press 1988: 385 pp. 259 illustrations.
Vergilius 35 (1989) 146–149.

407.   Review: C. O. Brink, *English Classical Scholarship: Historical Reflections on Bentley, Porson, and Housman* (Cambridge/New York 1985). Pp. x + 243.
Mnemosyne NS 4, 42 (1989) 256–262.

408.   Review: Norman Yoffee and George M. Cowgill, *The Collapse of Ancient States and Civilizations* (Tucson 1988). Pp. xii + 333.
The International History Review 11 (1989) 119–120.

409.   Review: Seneca's *Phaedra* with introduction, text, translation and notes by A. J. Boyle. "Latin and Greek Texts 5." (Liverpool 1987) *New England Classical Newsletter & Journal* 17 (1989) 42–43.

410.   Notice: *Epiploke: Rhythmical Continuity and Poetic Structure in Greek Lyric.* By Thomas Cole. (Cambridge/London 1988). Pp. v + 267.
Religious Studies Review 15 (1989) 260.

411.   Notice: *Callimachus Hymns, Epigrams, Select Fragments translated with Introduction and Notes.* By Stanley Lombardo and Diane Rayor with a Foreword by D. S. Carne-Ross (Baltimore/London 1988). Pp. xxvi + 123.
Religious Studies Review 15 (1989) 170.

412.   *Greek Roman and Byzantine Studies* 30 (1989) Editorial Board.

413.   *Philologus* 133 (1989) Editor and Referee for USA, Canada, and Cuba.

1990

414.   *Classical Scholarship: A Biographical Encyclopedia*, edited by Ward W. Briggs Jr. and William M. Calder III (New York 1990) 520pp. Editor and Contributor.

Reviews: Thomas W. Africa, "The Owl at Dusk: Two Centuries of Classical Scholarship," *The Journal of the History of Ideas* 54 (1993) 143-163; Paul Cors, *American Reference Books Annual* 22 (1991) 452; H. D. Jocelyn, *CR* NS 42 (1992) 174–77; J. H. C. Leach, *Times Literary Supplement* (April 27–May 3 1990) 440; Michael di Maio, Jr., *CW* 84 (1990/1991) 318; Alessandra Bertini Malgarini, *La Cultura* 29 (1991) 340-345; Stephen T. Newmyer, *Classical Outlook* 68.3 (1991) 108; Meyer Reinhold, *New England Classical Newsletter & Journal* 18 (1990) 43–45; Jeffrey Rusten, *BMCR* 1.2 (1990) 45–46; Robert P. Sonkowsky, *The Key Reporter* 57 (Spring 1992) 11.

415.   *Eduard Meyer: Leben und Leistung eines Universalhistorikers,* edited by William M. Calder III and Alexander Demandt (Leiden 1990). Editor and Contributor.

Reviews: Jan Burian, *Eirene* 30 (1994) 198-200; Karl Christ, *Frankfurter Allgemeine Zeitung* (11 January 1991); Karl Christ, *Gnomon* 64 (1992) 569-572; Peter Kehne, *Hist.-Pol. Buch* 40 (1992) 80-81; Hans Kloft, *Historische Zeitschrift* 257 (1993) 134-135; Anne Lagny, *Archives de Philosophie* 58 (1995) 158-159; Burkhard Meissner, *Journal of Roman Studies* 82 (1992) 309-310; Meyer Reinhold, *BMCR* 5 (1991) 270–274; Klaus Rosen, *Bonner Jahrbucher* 92 (1992) 782-785.

416.   *Heinrich Schliemann nach hundert Jahren*, edited by William M. Calder III and Justus Cobet (Klostermann Verlag, Frankfurt am Main 1990) Pp. 460. Editor and Contributor.

Reviews: W. G. Arnott, *Classical Review* NS 42 (1992) 178-180; A.A. Donohue, *BMCR* 3 (1992) 434-439; Beat Näf, *Gnomon* 65

(1993) 258-265; Roy Arthur Swanson, *Religious Studies Review* 20 (1994) 59.

417.   "'Credo gegen Credo, Arbeit gegen Arbeit, Anschauung gegen Anschauung:' Ulrich von Wilamowitz-Moellendorff contra Eduard Meyer," *Eduard Meyer* (Leiden 1990) 41–73.

418.   "Apocolocyntosis: The Biographers and the Archaeologists," *Schliemann nach 100 Jahren*, (Frankfurt am Main 1990) 360–378.

419.   "Werner Jaeger (30 July 1888–19 October 1961)," *Classical Scholarship: A Biographical Encyclopedia*, (New York 1990) 211–226.

420.   "Usener und Wilamowitz Ein Briefwechsel 1870–1905: Index personarum and Index locorum antiquorum," *Quaderni di storia* 32 (1990) 219–222.

421.   "The Heinrich Schliemann Symposium," *Gnomon* 62 (1990) 383–384.

422.   "The Later Letters of Ulrich von Wilamowitz-Moellendorff to Michael I. Rostovzev," *Philologus* 134 (1990) 248–253.

423.   "Otto J. Brendel 1901–1973," in Otto J. Brendel, *Was ist Römische Kunst?* (Köln 1990) 149–150.

424.   "Harvard Classics 1950–1956: Reminiscences of H. Bloch, S. Dow, J. P. Elder, J. H. Finley, W. C. Greene, Werner Jaeger, A. D. Nock, Joshua Whatmough and C. H. Whitman," *Festschrift für Ernst Vogt* (Munich 1990).

425.   "To the Editors," [Lucan 9. 510], *The New York Review of Books* (October 25 1990) 68.

426.   "The Werner Jaeger Symposium," *Gnomon* 62 (1990) 669–670.

427.   (with Dietrich Ehlers, Alexander Košenina and Wolfgang Schindler) "Katalog der Handbibliothek von Ulrich von Wilamowitz-Moellendorff, nach einer Anonymen Bearbeitung Herausgegeben," *Philologus* 134 (1990) 254–285.

428.   (with Alexander Košenina) "Poesie, Philologie und Politik: Ulrich von Wilamowitz-Moellendorffs (1848-1931) Briefwechsel mit Robert Friedlaender (1874–1950)," *Antike und Abendland* 36 (1990) 163–186.

429.   A translation: Ernst Vogt, *Friedrich Ritschl,* Briggs-Calder, *Classical Scholarship: A Biographical Encyclopedia* (New York 1990) 389–394.

430.   A translation: Joachim Wohlleben, "Homer in German Classicism: Goethe, Friedrich Schlegel, Hölderlin and Schelling," *Illinois Classical Studies* 15 (1990) 197–211.

431.   Review: Sander L. Gilman, Carole Blair, David J. Parent, *Friedrich Nietzsche on Rhetoric and Language With the Full Text of His Lectures on Rhetoric Published for the First Time* (New York/Oxford 1988). Pp. xxviii + 273.
       German Studies Review 13 (1990) 553–554.

432.   Notice: *The Making of Homeric Verse: The Collected Papers of Milman Parry* (Oxford 1987). Pp. lxii + 483.
       Religious Studies Review 16 (1990) 70.

433.   Notice: *The Ambition to Rule: Alcibiades and the Politics of Imperialism in Thucydides.* By Steven Forde. Ithaca/London: Cornell University Press. 1989. Pp. x + 216.
       Thucydides The Peloponnesian War Book II. Edited by J. S. Rusten. (Cambridge 1989). Pp. x + 261.
       Religious Studies Review 16 (1990) 249.

434.   Notice: *The Guernica Bull Studies in the Classical Tradition in the Twentieth Century.* By Harry C. Rutledge. (Athens/London 1989). Pp. xv + 154.
       Religious Studies Review 16 (1990) 340.

435.   Notice: *Rediscovering Hellenism. The Hellenic Inheritance and the English Imagination.* Edited by G. W. Clarke with the Assistance of J. C. Eade. (Cambridge 1989). Pp. xiv + 264.
       Religious Studies Review 16 (1990) 340.

436.   *Greek Roman and Byzantine Studies* 31 (1990) Editorial Board.

437.   *Illinois Classical Studies* 15 (1990) Editorial Board.

438.   *Philologus* 134 (1990) Editor for Canada, Cuba and USA.

1991

439.   *Otto Jahn (1813-1869): Ein Geisteswissenschaftler zwischen Klassizismus und Historismus*, edited by William M. Calder III, Hubert Cancik and Bernhard Kytzler (Stuttgart 1991). (Editor and Contributor).

Reviews: Bolonyai Gábor, *Helikon* 3 (1996) 368-369; Hans Kloft, *Historische Zeitschrift* 259 (1994) 120-121; Friedhelm Krummacher, *Die Musikforschung* 50 (1997) 246-247; Hans Lenneberg, *Notes* (September 1992) 105-106; Manfred Mayrhofer, *Kratylos* 39 (1994) 181-183; Franz Verhaeghe, *L'Antiquité classique* 63 (1994) 659-661; Gerhardt Wirth, *Bonner Jahrbücher* 195 (1995) 870-872.

440.   "The Cambridge Ritualists Reconsidered," edited by William M. Calder III *Illinois Classical Studies: Supplement Volume* 2 = *Illinois Studies in the History of Classical Scholarship* I (1991) xiii + 295 (Editor and contributor).

Reviews: W. Geoffrey Arnott, *CR* NS 42 (1992) 418-420; Cristiano Grottanelli, *Quaderni di storia* 38 (1993) 205-211; Richard Jenkyns, *JHS* 113 (1993) 235; J. H. C. Leach, *Times Literary Supplement* (February 21 1992) 24; Annabel Robinson, *Phoenix* 47 (1993) 367-370; Jon Solomon, *Religious Studies Review* 18 (1992) 229; Daniel P. Tompkins, *BMCR* 3 (1992) 9–20.

441.   (with Michael Armstrong and *Wolfgang Buchwald) *Ulrich von Wilamowitz-Moellendorff Bibliography 1867–1990* Revised and Expanded after Friedrich Freiherr Hiller von Gaertringen and Günther Klaffenbach by Michael Armstrong, *Wolfgang Buchwald, and William M. Calder III (Hildesheim 1991) xii + 166.

Reviews: Hans-Ulrich Berner, *Gymnasium* 100 (1993) 561-562; Enzo Degani, *Eikasmos* 3 (1992) 351; Robert L. Fowler, *BMCR* 2

(1991) 197–199; Nicholas Horsfall, *CR* NS 42 (1992) 492-493; Luigi Lehnus, *Paideia* 47 (1992) 142-147; Alain Martin, *L'Antiquité Classique* 62 (1993) 610; P. G. Naiditch, *The Classical Bulletin* 68 (1992) 13-20.

442.   *The Prussian and The Poet: The Letters of Ulrich von Wilamowitz-Moellendorff to Gilbert Murray (1894–1930)*, edited by Anton Bierl, William M. Calder III and Robert L. Fowler (Hildesheim 1991). Pp. xvi + 144.

Reviews: Ward W. Briggs, *CR* NS 43 (1993) 464-465; Mariella Cagnetta, *Quaderni di storia* 36 (1992) 193-196; J. H. C. Leach, *Times Literary Supplement* (April 17 1992); James O'Donnell, *BMCR* 3 (1992) 94–96 cf. *BMCR* 3 (1992) 244–247; Henning Ritter, *Frankfurter Allgemeine Zeitung* (27 May 1992) Nr. 123 p. N 5.

443.   "What did Ulrich von Wilamowitz-Moellendorff learn from Otto Jahn?," *Otto Jahn: (1813–1869)* (Stuttgart 1991) 195–203.

444.   "Jane Harrison's Failed Candidacies for the Yates Professorship (1888, 1896): What did her Colleagues Think of Her?," "The Cambridge Ritualists Reconsidered," *Illinois Classical Studies: Supplement Volume* 2 (1991) 37–59.

445.   "How did Ulrich von Wilamowitz-Moellendorff read a Text?" *Classical Journal* 86 (1990/91) 344–352.

446.   "Moses Hadas (1900–1966)," *The Classical Outlook* 69 (1991) 8–9.

447.   "Paul Maas on IG II² 2940, 13199," *Mnemosyne* NS 4,44 (1991) 439.

448.   "Die Rolle Friedrich Althoffs bei den Berufungen von Ulrich von Wilamowitz-Moellendorff," *Wissenschaftsgeschichte und Wissenschaftspolitik im Industriezeitalter: Das 'System Althoff' in historischer Perspektive*, edited by Bernhard vom Brocke (Hildesheim 1991) 251–266.

449.   [Letter to the Editors on the Value of Independent Discovery],
        Liverpool Classical Monthly 16.5 (1991) 67.

450.   (with Anton Bierl) "The Tale of Oblomov: Tycho von
        Wilamowitz-Moellendorff (1885–1914)," *Eikasmos* 2 (1991) 257–
        283.

451.   (with Anton Bierl) "Instinct against Proof: The Correspondence
        between Ulrich von Wilamowitz-Moellendorff and Martin P.
        Nilsson on *Religionsgeschichte* (1920–1930)," *Eranos* 89 (1991)
        73-99.

452.   (with Dietrich Ehlers) "The German Reception of J. G. Frazer: An
        Unpublished Document," *Quaderni di storia* 33 (1991) 135–143.

453.   (with Dietrich Ehlers) "Wilamowitz to Max Pohlenz on Eduard
        Schwartz," *American Journal of Philology* 112 (1991) 111–114.

454.   (with Alexander Košenina) "Geschichtsschreibung als Mythisierung
        der Vergangenheit: Eine ungedruckte Korrespondenz zwischen
        Ricarda Huch und Ulrich von Wilamowitz-Moellendorff," *Studien
        der Ricarda-Huch-Gesellschaft* 3 (1991) 107–113.

455.   Review: Stephen V. Tracy, *Attic Letter-cutters of 229 to 86 B.C.*
        (Berkeley 1990). xvi + 291. 39 Figures + 29 Plates.
        New England Classical Newsletter & Journal 18 (1991) 41–42.

456.   Review: Sandra J. Peacock, *Jane Ellen Harrison: The Mask and the
        Self*, (New Haven/London 1988). XVIII + 282. Eight Illustrations.
        Gnomon 63 (1991) 10–13.

457.   Review: Guido Avezzu, *Il ferimento e il rito. La storia di Filottete
        sulla scena attica, studi e commenti* 7 (Bari 1988). 187 S.
        Andreas Schnebele, *Die epischen Quellen des Sophokleischen
        Philoktet. Die Postiliaca im frühgriechischen Epos.* Dissertation
        zur Erlangung des akademischen Grades Doktor der Philosophie der
        Fakultät für Kulturwissenschaften der Eberhard-Karls-Universität
        Tübingen. (Karlsruhe 1988). 194 S.
        Gnomon 63 (1991) 358–360.

458.   Review: Marinus A. Wes, "Michael Rostovtzeff, Historian in Exile: Russian Roots in an American Context," *Historia Einzelschriften* Heft 65 (Stuttgart 1990), xxxi + 106 (13 plates). *BMCR* 2 (1991) 158–162.

459.   Review: Robert Ackerman, *The Myth and Ritual School: J.G. Frazer and the Cambridge Ritualists* (New York & London 1991). Pp. xiv + 253. *BMCR* 2 (1991) 259–261.

460.   Review: Shelley Arlen, *The Cambridge Ritualists: An Annotated Bibliography of the Works by and about Jane Ellen Harrison, Gilbert Murray, Francis M. Cornford, and Arthur Bernard Cook.* (Metuchen/London 1990). Pp. x, 414. Four Illustrations. *BMCR* 2 (1991) 195–197.

461.   Review: Robert Eisner, *Travelers to an Antique Land: The History and Literature of Travel to Greece.* (Ann Arbor 1991). Pp. xiv, 304. *BMCR* 2 (1991) 343–345.

462.   Review: John O'Meara. *The Singing-Masters.* (Dublin 1990). Pp. viii,115. *BMCR* 2 (1991) 325–327.

463.   Review: Carl Werner Müller, *Otto Jahn Mit einem Verzeichnis seiner Schriften* (Stuttgart/Leipzig 1991). 87 pp. *BMCR* 2 (1991) 429–431.

464.   Notice: *The Stoic in Love. Selected Essays on Literature and Ideas.* By A.D. Nuttall. (Savage, MD 1989). Pp. xii + 209. *Religious Studies Review* 17 (1991) 65.

465.   Notice: *Pausanias' Guide to Ancient Greece.* By Christian Habicht. (Berkeley 1985). Pp. xvi + 205. *Religious Studies Review* 17 (1991) 66.

466.   Notice: *The Birth of Athenian Democracy: The Assembly in the Fifth Century B.C.* By Chester G. Starr. (New York/Oxford 1990). Pp. 86. *Religious Studies Review* 17 (1991) 359.

467.   Notice: *Pericles of Athens and the Birth of Democracy.* By Donald
        Kagan. (New York 1991). Pp. ix + 287.
        Religious Studies Review 17 (1991) 359.

468.   *Greek Roman and Byzantine Studies* 32 (1991) 619. Editorial
        Board.

469.   *Illinois Classical Studies* 16 (1991) Editorial Board.

470.   *Philologus* 135 (1991) Editor for Canada, Cuba and USA.

471.   *Biographical Dictionary of North American Classicists* Editorial
        Board.

472.   *American National Biography,* Advisory Editor for Classics.

1992

473.   (With Daniel J. Kramer) *An Introductory Bibliography to the
        History of Classical Scholarship Chiefly in the XIXth and XXth
        Centuries.* Pp. xiv + 410 (Hildesheim 1992).

        Reviews: Anonymous, *Sileno* 19 (1993) 612; J. B. Trapp, *CR* NS
        44 (1994) 421-422; Robert Ackerman, *Victorian Studies* 37 (1994)
        492-493; Mariella Cagnetta, *Quaderni di storia* 38 (1993) 249-250;
        Jean Irigoin, *REG* 106 (1993) 682-683; Alessandra Bertini
        Malgarini, *La Cultura* 32,1 (1994) 171-173; Luigi Lehnus, *Maia*
        48 (1996) 91-94; James J. O'Donnell, *BMCR* 3 (1992) 496-497;
        Hélène Perdicoyianni, *Révue des Études Classiques* (1993) 257.

474.   "Werner Jaeger Reconsidered: Proceedings of the Second Oldfather
        Conference, Held on the Campus of the University of Illinois at
        Urbana-Champaign, April 26–28, 1990," edited by William M.
        Calder III, *Illinois Classical Studies: Supplement Volume* 3 =
        Illinois Studies in the History of Classical Scholarship 2 (1992)
        xiv + 325 (Editor and contributor).

        Reviews: Anonymous, *New Testament Abstracts* 38 (1994) 111-
        112; Z. Phillip Ambrose, *New England Classical Newsletter and
        Journal* 20 (1993) 41-42; W. Geoffrey Arnott, *CR* NS 44 (1994)

187-189; Charles Rowan Beye, *BMCR* 3 (1992) 340-347; Mariella Cagnetta, *Quaderni di storia* 38 (1993) 199-204; Lawrence A. Tritle, *CW* 89 (1996) 237-238.

475.   "12 March 1921 The Berlin Appointment," "Werner Jaeger Reconsidered," *Illinois Classical Studies* Supplement Volume 3 (1992) 1–24.

476.   "Was Aristotle a Myth? (DL 2.63)," *Mnemosyne* NS 4, 45 (1992) 225.

477.   "The Refugee Classical Scholars in the USA: An Evaluation of their Contribution," *Illinois Classical Studies* 17 (1992) 153-173.

478.   "The Unpublished American Diaries of Heinrich Schliemann (1865; 1867–68)," *Heinrich Schliemann: Grundlagen und Ergebnisse moderner Archäologie 100 Jahre nach Schliemanns Tod* edited by Joachim Herrmann (Berlin 1992) 23–28.

479.   "Morton Smith," *Gnomon* 64 (1992) 382-384.

480.   "Arthur Darby Nock 1902–1963," *Classical Outlook* 70 (1992) 8-9.

481.   (with Anton Bierl) "Friedrich Nietzsche, Abriß der Geschichte der Beredsamkeit: A New Edition," *Nietzsche-Studien* 21 (1992) 363–389.

482.   (with Anton Bierl) "Recollections of Scholars I have Known," by †Otto Skutsch, edited by Anton Bierl and William M. Calder III, *Harvard Studies in Classical Philology* 94 (1992) 387-408.

483.   (with Anton Bierl and R. L. Fowler) "Bierl-Calder-Fowler on O'Donnell on Bierl-Calder-Fowler," *BMCR* 3 (1992) 244–247.

484.   (with Sven Rugullis) "Ulrich von Wilamowitz-Moellendorff on Wilhelm Dilthey: His Letters to Georg Misch (1914-1928)," *Illinois Classical Studies* 17 (1992) 337-345.

485.   A translation: Wolfgang Schindler, "An Archaeologist on the Schliemann Controversy," *Illinois Classical Studies* 17 (1992) 135–151.

486.   Review: David Sox, *Bachelors of Art: Edward Perry Warren & The Lewes House Brotherhood.* (London 1991). Pp. xii + 290. *BMCR* 3 (1992) 81–82.

487.   Review: Karl Christ, "Geschichte und Existenz," *Kleine Kulturwissenschaftliche Bibliothek* 34. (Berlin 1991). Pp. 89. *BMCR* 3 (1992) 100-104.

488.   Review: Michael P. Steinberg, ed., "The Presence of the Historian: Essays in Memory of Arnaldo Momigliano," *History and Theory: Studies in the Philosophy of History* Beiheft 30. (Wesleyan University 1991). Pp. 64. *BMCR* 3 (1992) 222–226.

489.   Review: *Seneca The Tragedies,* vol. I, edited and translated by David R. Slavitt (Baltimore 1992). Pp. xvi + 207. *New England Classical Newsletter & Journal* 20 (1992) 42-43.

490.   Notice: *The Traffic in Praise: Pindar and the Poetics of Social Economy.* By Leslie Kurke. (Ithaca/London 1991). Pp. xvi + 288. *Religious Studies Review* 18 (1992) 228.

491.   *Greek Roman and Byzantine Studies* 33 (1992) Editorial Board.

492.   *Illinois Classical Studies* 17 (1992) Editorial Board.

493.   *Philologus* 136 (1992) Editor for Canada, Cuba and USA.

494.   *Biographical Dictionary of North American Classicists* Editorial Board.

495.   *American National Biography,* (Oxford University Press) Advisory Editor for Classics.

1993

496. Editor: David A. Traill, "Excavating Schliemann," *Illinois Classical Studies Supplement Volume* 4 (Atlanta 1993). Editor's Preface, pp. xi-xii.

    Reviews: Susan Heuck Allen, *AJA* 101 (1997) 598-599; D. F. Easton, *Antiquity* (1994) 455-456; David Gill, *BMCR* 5 (1994) 57-64; Donald L. Jennermann, *Religious Studies Review* 21 (1995) 50; Olivier Masson, *REG* 108 (1995) 593-600.

497. "*Nuda Veritas*: William Abbott Oldfather on Classics at Columbia," *Illinois Classical Studies* 18 (1993) 359-378.

498. "Harvard Classics 1950-1956: Reminiscences of S. Dow, J. P. Elder, J. H. Finley, W. C. Greene, Werner Jaeger, A. D. Nock, Joshua Whatmough and C. H. Whitman," *Miscellanea di Studi in onore di Ernst Vogt = Eikasmos* 4 (1993) 299-308.

499. Πῶς διάβαζε ἕνα κείμενο ὁ Wilamowitz, *ΦΙΛΟΛΟΓΟΣ* 72 (1993) 83-95.

500. "Correspondence" [The Englishness of J. K. Newman], *CR* NS·43 (1993) 214.

501. "Symposium on the Twenties," *Gnomon* 65 (1993) 763-764.

502. (with Thomas A. Suits) "J.F.C. Richards, *In Memoriam*," *American Philological Association Newsletter* 16 No. 2 (April 1993) 15.

503. Review: D. W. Blandford. *Pentekontaetia: The Virgil Society 1943-1993: Proceedings of the Virgil Society* Vol. XXI Supplement (London 1993). Pp. vi + 145.
    Vergilius 39 (1993) 97-98: see Herbert H. Huxley, *Vergilius* 40 (1994) 154-155.

504. Notice: *Alexander the Great: The Invisible Enemy: A Biography.* By John Maxwell O'Brien (London/New York 1992). Pp. xxii + 336.
    Religious Studies Review 19 (1993) 349.

505.   Notice: *'Reading" Greek Culture, Texts and Images, Rituals and Myths.* By Christiane Sourvinou-Inwood (New York/Oxford 1991). Pages viii + 315. *Religious Studies Review* 19 (1993) 353.

506.   *Greek Roman and Byzantine Studies* 34 (1993) Editorial Board.

507.   *Illinois Classical Studies* 18 (1993) Editorial Board.

508.   *Philologus* 137 (1993) Editor for Canada, Cuba and USA.

509.   *Biographical Dictionary of North American Classicists* Editorial Board.

510.   *American National Biography*, (Oxford University Press) Advisory Editor for Classics.

1994

511.   Hermann Dieterich and Friedrich v. Hiller, *Usener und Wilamowitz: Ein Briefwechsel 1870-1905* Second Edition with Epilogue, Corrigenda, Addenda and Indices by William M. Calder III (Leipzig/Stuttgart 1994).

512.   *Further Letters of Ulrich von Wilamowitz-Moellendorff,* edited by William M. Calder III (Hildesheim 1994) xii + 261pp.

Reviews: Anonymous, *Quaderni di storia* 41 (1995) 227; Hans-Ulrich Berner, *Gymnasium* 102 (1995) 381; Karl Christ, *AnzAlt* 48 (1995) 43-47; James W. Halporn, *Religious Studies Review* 21 (1995) 231; Bernhard Kytzler, *BMCR* 6 (1995) 17-18; Olivier Masson, *REG* 108 (1995) 631-632; Hans Schwabl, *WS* 109 (1996) 323-324.

513   "Autobiographical Remarks," *Harvard Class of 1954: Fortieth Anniversary Report* (Cambridge 1994) 34-35.

514.   "'Aquila in Nubibus': Ulrich von Wilamowitz-Moellendorff in his Letters to Eduard Norden (1893–1931)," *Eduard Norden (1868-1941): Ein deutscher Gelehrter judischer Herkunft,* edited by

Bernhard Kytzler, Kurt Rudolph and Jörg Rüpke *Palingenesia* 49 (Stuttgart 1994) 173-189.

515. (with J. M. Bremer) "Prussia and Holland: Wilamowitz and Two Kuipers," *Mnemosyne* NS 4 (1994) 177-216.

516. "Ulrich von Wilamowitz-Moellendorff's Obituary for Himself," *Philologus* 138 (1994) 353-358.

517. "Ulrich Graf von Gaure: The Origin of Wilamowitz' Preoccupation with Drama," *Orchestra Drama Mythos Bühne Festschrift für Hellmut Flashar anläßlich seines 65. Geburtstages*, edited by Anton Bierl and Peter von Möllendorff (Stuttgart/Leipzig 1994) 371-376.

518. "Πῶς διάβαζε ἕνα κείμενο ο Wilamowitz," in Tadeuz Zielinski, *HMEIΣ KAI OI APXAIOI*, translated by Ioannes Sukoutres with introduction and appendices by J. N. Kazazis (Thessaloniki 1994) 261-278.

519. (with Michael Armstrong) "The *Damnatio* of Vergil in Th. Mommsen, *Kaisergeschichte*," *Vergilius* 40 (1994) 85-92.

520. "Warren Everett Blake," *Biographical Dictionary of North American Classicists* (Westport 1994) 46-47.

521. "Richard T. Bruère," *Biographical Dictionary of North American Classicists* (Westport 1994) 68-70.

522 "Carl Darling Buck," *Biographical Dictionary of North American Classicists* (Westport 1994) 70-72.

523. "Edward Capps," *Biographical Dictionary of North American Classicists* (Westport 1994) 84-85.

524. "R. E. Glanville Downey," *Biographical Dictionary of North American Classicists* (Westport 1994) 141-143.

525. "Edward Fitch," *Biographical Dictionary of North American Classicists* (Westport 1994) 181-182.

526. "Hermann Fränkel," *Biographical Dictionary of North American Classicists* (Westport 1994) 197-199.

527. "Paul Friedländer," *Biographical Dictionary of North American Classicists* (Westport 1994) 200-202.

528. "E. Adelaide Hahn," *Biographical Dictionary of North American Classicists* (Westport 1994) 248-249.

529. "Gertrude Mary Hirst," *Biographical Dictionary of North American Classicists* (Westport 1994) 285-286.

530. "A. A. Howard," *Biographical Dictionary of North American Classicists* (Westport 1994) 291-292.

531. "James Loeb," *Biographical Dictionary of North American Classicists* (Westport 1994) 368-370.

532. "John Andrew Moore," *Biographical Dictionary of North American Classicists* (Westport 1994) 424.

533. "Morris Hickey Morgan," *Biographical Dictionary of North American Classicists* (Westport 1994) 425-427.

534. "Edward North," *Biographical Dictionary of North American Classicists* (Westport 1994) 448-449.

535. "Ben Edwin Perry," *Biographical Dictionary of North American Classicists* (Westport 1994) 494-496.

536. "Howard Newton Porter," *Biographical; Dictionary of North American Classicists* (Westport 1994) 504-505.

537. "J. F. C. Richards," *Biographical Dictionary of North American Classicists* (Westport 1994) 522-523.

538. "Michael I. Rostovtzeff," *Biographical Dictionary of North American Classicists* (Westport 1994) 541-547.

539. "Morton Smith," *Biographical Dictionary of North American Classicists* (Westport 1994) 600-602.

540. "Classical Scholarship in the United States: An Introductory Essay," *Biographical Dictionary of North American Classicists* (Westport 1994) xix-xxxix.

541. Review: M. L. West, *Greek Lyric Poetry: The poems and fragments of the Greek iambic, elegaic, and melic poets (excluding Pindar and Bacchylides) down to 450 BC* (Oxford 1993). *New England Classical Newsletter and Journal* 22 (1994) 128-129.

542. Review: Christopher Stray, *The Living Word: W. H. D. Rouse and the Crisis of Classics in Edwardian England* (Bristol 1992). *Quaderni di storia* 39 (1994) 297-298.

543. Review: Rudolf Kassel, *Kleine Schriften* (Berlin/New York 1991). *Classical Journal* 89 (1993/94) 431-433: see Reinhold Merkelbach, "Entgegnung an William M. Calder III," *ZPE* 110 (1996) 311-312.

544. Review: John Boardman et al., eds. *The Cambridge Ancient History* Volume III, pt. 2 *The Assyrian and Babylonian Empires and Other States of the Near East from the Eighth to the Sixth Centuries BC* (Cambridge 1991). Pp. xix, 906. *The International History Review* 16 (1994) 114-115.

545. Notice: *Athenian Economy & Society: A Banking Perspective.* By Edward E. Cohen. (Princeton 1992). Pp. ix + 288. *Religious Studies Review* 20 (1994) 52.

546. Notice: *Oxford and Empire: The Last Lost Cause?* By Richard Symonds (Oxford 1991). Pp. xxiv + 368. *Religious Studies Review* 20 (1994) 59.

547. Notice: *Aidos: The Psychology and Ethics of Honour and Shame in Ancient Greek Literature.* By Douglas L. Cairns. (New York/Oxford 1993). Pages viii + 474. *Religious Studies Review* 20 (1994) 146.

548. *The Best of the Argonauts: The Redefinition of the Epic Hero in Book One of Apollonius' "Argonautica."* By James J. Clauss (Berkeley 1993) Pp. ix + 238. *The Argonautica of Apollonius Rhodius: Literary Studies.* By Richard Hunter. (New York 1993). Pp. ix + 206.

Apollonius of Rhodes Jason and the Golden Fleece (The Argonautica), translated with Introduction and Explanatory Notes by Richard Hunter. (Oxford 1993). Pp. xxxiii + 175 with three maps.
Religious Studies Review 20 (1994) 334.

549. *Greek Roman and Byzantine Studies* 35 (1994) Editorial Board.

550. *Illinois Classical Studies* 19 (1994) Editorial Board.

551. *Philologus* 138 (1994) Editor for Canada, Cuba and USA.

552. *Biographical Dictionary of North American Classicists* Editorial Board.

553. *American National Biography*, (Oxford University Press) Advisory Editor for Classics.

1995

554. (With Max Braun and Dietrich Ehlers) *Philology and Philosophy: The Letters of Hermann Diels to Theodor and Heinrich Gomperz* (Hildesheim 1995). Pp. xxi + 202.

Reviews: C. J. Classen, *Historische Zeitschrift* 264 (1997) 139-140; Luc Dietz, *FAZ* 31 (6 February 1996) Feuilleton; Robert L. Fowler, *BMCR* 9 (1998); Jackson P. Hershbell, *RSR* 23 (1997) 64.

555. (With Max Braun and Dietrich Ehlers) *"'Lieber Prinz': Der Briefwechsel zwischen Hermann Diels und Ulrich von Wilamowitz-Moellendorff (1869-1921)*, Unter Mitarbeit von Stephen Trzaskoma (Hildesheim 1995). Pp. xxiv + 353.

Reviews: Hans-Ulrich Berner, *Gymnasium* 104 (1997) 578-579; C. J. Classen, *Historische Zeitschrift* 264 (1997) 139-140; Robert L. Fowler, *BMCR* 9 (1998).

556. "Filologia Klasyczna w Ameryce," *Meander* 7/8 (1994; publ. 1995) 379-398.

557.   "'Pionier der ersten Stunde:' Wolfgang Schindler and the Modern Study of Heinrich Schliemann," *Modus in Rebus: Gedenkschrift für Wolfgang Schindler*, edited by D. Rößler and V. Stürmer (Berlin 1995) 19-25.

558.   "William Abbott Oldfather and the Preservation of German Influence in American Classics 1919-1933," *Altertumswissenschaft in den 20er Jahren Neue Fragen und Impulse*, edited by Hellmut Flashar (Stuttgart 1995) 403-421.

559.   "Margarete Bieber," *Dictionary of American Biography* Supplement 10 *1976-1980*, edited by Kenneth T. Jackson, Karen E. Markoe and Arnold Markoe (New York 1995) 38-40.

560.   (with Maximilian Braun) "Dorothea Freifrau Hiller von Gaertringen, geb. von Wilamowitz-Moellendorff and Hermann von Wilamowitz-Moellendorff on their Father," *Eikasmos* 6 (1995) 297-308.

561.   "Karl Otfried Müller Symposium," *Gnomon* 67 (1995) 382.

562.   Review: Jon Solomon (ed.), *Accessing Antiquity: The Computerization of Classical Studies* (Tucson/London 1993) Pp. xii + 187. *Quaderni di storia* 41 (1995) 141-147.

563.   Review: *Virgil and the Moderns.* By Theodore Ziolkowski. (Princeton 1993). Pp. xvi + 274. *Journal of English and Germanic Philology* 94 (1995) 588-591.

564.   Review: Alston Hurd Chase, *Time Remembered.* (San Antonio, 994). Pp. viii + 444. *New England Classical Newsletter & Journal* 22 (1995) 178-179.

565.   Review: Hugh Lloyd-Jones, *Sophocles I Ajax Electra Oedipus Tyrannus LCL 20*; *Sophocles II Antigone The Women of Trachis Philoctetes Oedipus at Colonus LCL 21* (Cambridge/London 1994). Pp. viii + 483; viii + 599. *New England Classical Newsletter & Journal* 23 (1995) 75-76.

566.   Review: Alfred Burns, "From Austria to Hawaii: Odyssey of a Classicist," *Hawaii Classical Studies* 1 (New York/Washington/Baltimore etc.: Peter Lang, 1994) Pp. 292. *International Journal of the Classical Tradition* 2 (1995) 309-311.

567.   Notice: *The Metamorphoses of Antoninus Liberalis: a Translation with a Commentary.* By Francis Celoria. (New York 1992). Pp. x + 241.
        Religious Studies Review 21 (1995) 51.

568.   Notice: *Innovations of Antiquity.* Edited by Ralph Hexter and Daniel Selden. The New Ancient World 5. (New York/London 1992). Pp. xvii + 584.
        Religious Studies Review 21 (1995) 50.

569.   Notice: *Xanthus: Travels of Discovery in Turkey.* By Enid Slatter. (London 1994). Pp. v + 362.
        Nicholas Biddle in Greece: The Journals and Letters of 1806. Edited by R. A. McNeal. (University Park, PA 1994). Pp. vii + 243.
        Religious Studies Review 21 (1995) 132-133.

570.   Notice: *Euripides Phoenissae.* Edited with introduction and Commentary by Donald J. Mastronarde. Cambridge Classical Texts and Commentaries, 29 (Cambridge 1994). Pp. viii + 673.
        Religious Studies Review 21 (1995) 327.

571.   Notice: *Aristophanes Birds.* Edited with Introduction and Commentary by Nan Dunbar (Oxford 1995). Pp. xix + 782.
        Religious Studies Review 21 (1995) 327.

572.   Notice: A New History of Classical Rhetoric. By George A. Kennedy (Princeton 1994). Pp. xi + 301.
        Religious Studies Review 21 (1995) 328.

573.   *Greek Roman and Byzantine Studies* 36 (1995) Editorial Board.

574.   *Illinois Classical Studies* 20 (1995) Editorial Board.

575.   *Philologus* 139 (1995) Editor for Canada, Cuba and USA.

576.   *American National Biography*, (Oxford University Press) Advisory Editor for Classics.

1996

577.   (with Stephen Trzaskoma) *George Grote Reconsidered: A 200th Birthday Celebration with a First Edition of his Essay "Of the*

Athenian Government," edited by William M. Calder III and Stephen Trzaskoma (Hildesheim 1996).

Reviews: Myles Burnyeat, *TLS* (20 June 1997) 3-4; Lee Pearcy, *BMCR* 8 (1997) 516-518.

578.   "Aeschylus, *Prometheus*: A DDR Interpretation," *Worte, Bilder, Töne: Studien zur Antike und Antikerezeption Bernhard Kytzler zu ehren* edited by Richard Faber and Bernd Seidensticker (Berlin 1996) 323-329.

579.   "The Seuthopolis Inscription *IGBR* 1731: a New Edition," *Transitions to Empire: Essays in Greco-Roman History, 360-146 B.C., in honor of E. Badian,* edited by Robert W. Wallace and Edward M. Harris (Norman 1996) 167-178.

580.   "Drei Briefe Wilhelm Diltheys an Ulrich von Wilamowitz-Moellendorff (1908-1910)," *Polyhistor: Studies in the History and Historiography of Ancient Philosophy Presented to Jaap Mansfeld on his Sixtieth Birthday,* edited by Keimpe A. Algra, Pieter W. van der Horst, and David T. Runia (Leiden 1996) 407-417.

581.   "What Werner Krenkel and the DDR taught me about Antiquity," *Satura Lanx: Festschrift für Werner A. Krenkel zum 70. Geburtstag,* edited by Claudia Klodt (Hildesheim 1996) 1-9.

582.   "Sophocles, *Antigone* 687: An Emendation," *Scripta Classica Israelica* 15 (1996) 44-45.

583.   "George Grote Conference," *Gnomon* 68 (1996) 381.

584.   "Sterling Dow†," *Gnomon* 68 (1996) 572-574.

585.   "Seneca, *Thyestes* 593: A Defence of the Elizabethan Translation," *Rheinisches Museum* 139 (1996) 367-368.

586.   "Friedrich Althoff," *Encyclopedia of Modern German History,* edited by Dieter K. Buse (New York forthcoming).

587-629.
          43 articles on the following persons and subjects in Nancy Thomson de Grummond (ed.), *An Encyclopedia of the History of Classical Archaeology* 2 vols. (Westport, Connecticut 1996):

W. Amelung; Paul Arndt; Sir John Beazley; W. A. Becker; Otto Benndorf; Hugo Blümner; W. von Bode; August Böckh; H. Braun; O.J. Brendel; Heinrich von Brunn; Ernst Buschor; Conrad Cichorius; Alexander Conze; Ernst Curtius; Ludwig Curtius; Friedrich von Duhn; Adolf Furtwängler; Augustus Hare; Hiller von Gaertringen; Carl Humann; Otto Jahn; Reinhard Kekule von Stradonitz; H. Kiepert; Robert Koldewey; James Loeb; Monumental Philology; K. O. Müller; M. P. Nilsson; Charles Eliot Norton; A. W. Pickard-Cambridge; Carl Robert; Georg Rodenwaldt; Erwin Rohde; Sir John Sandys; Scenic Antiquities; E. S. Strong; Franz Studniczka; Totalitätsideal; E. P. Warren; F. G. Welcker; Theodor Wiegand; Ulrich von Wilamowitz-Moellendorff.

630.   "Brief von Prof. Dr. William Calder III anläßlich seines Besuches im Frühjahr 1996 in Ankershagen," *Heinrich-Schliemann-Gesellschaft Ankershagen e.V. Informationsblatt* 6 (1996) 18.

631.   "The balance of power," Letters to the Editor, *Times Literary Supplement* (September 13 1996) 17.

632.   A lascivious limerick, *CA News* Number 15 (December 1996) 11.

633.   (with Anton Bierl) "The Tale of Oblomov Tycho von Wilamowitz-Moellendorff (1885-1914)," in Tycho von Wilamowitz-Moellendorff, *Die dramatische Technik des Sophokles*[4] (Olms/Weidmann 1996) 381-409.

634.   (with Maximilian Braun) "'Tell it Hitler! Ecco!': Paul Friedländer on Werner Jaeger's *Paideia*," *Quaderni di storia* 43 (1996) 211-248.

635.   (with Maximilian Braun) Paul Friedländer, "Some Remarks on Research in Classics: The Twenty-fifth Annual Faculty Research Lecture," *Classical Journal* 92 (1996) 39-55.

636.   (with J. M. Bremer) "Prussia and Holland: Wilamowitz and the Two Kuipers A Postscript," *Mnemosyne* NS 4, 49 (1996) 191-195.

637.   Review: Christoph Ulf, *Griechische Antike und deutsche Geschichtswissenschaft in biographischen und bibliographischen Daten: Von der Französischen Revolution bis zum 2. deutschen Kaiserreich 1871* (Berlin 1995).

International Journal of the Classical Tradition 3 (1996) 581-583.

638. Review: Marinus A. Wes, *Classics in Russia 1700-1855 Between two Bronze Horsemen = Brill's Studies in Intellectual History* 33 (Leiden 1992). Pp. viii + 366.
Scholia NS 5 (1996) 148-150.

639. Notice: Reading Greek Death to the End of the Classical Period. By Christiane Sourvinou-Inwood. (New York/Oxford 1995). Pp. xii + 489.
Religious Studies Review 22 (1996) 61-62.

640. *Greek Roman and Byzantine Studies* 37 (1996) Editorial Board.

641. *Philologus* 140 (1996) Editor for Canada, Cuba and USA.

642. *American National Biography*, (Oxford University Press) Advisory Editor for Classics.

1997

643. (with Bernhard Huß) *"Sed serviendum officio...": The Correspondence between Ulrich von Wilamowitz-Moellendorff and Eduard Norden (1892-1931)* (Hildesheim 1997). Pp. xxii + 287.

644. Editor (with Renate Schlesier) *Zwischen Rationalismus und Romantik: Karl Otfried Müller und die antike Kultur* (Darmstadt 1997).

645. Editor (with Judith P. Hallett) Special Double Issue of *Classical World* 90, 2-3 (1996/97): 81-224: "Six Women Classicists."

646. "Introduction: Six North American Women Classicists: Historical Perspective," *Classical World* 90 (1996/97) 83-90.

647. "Gertrude Hirst (1869-1962)," *Classical World* 90 (1996/97) 149-152.

648. "Wissenschaftlergeschichte als Wissenschaftsgeschichte," *Das Altertum* 42 (1997) 245-256.

649.   "Heinrich Schliemann: Erinnerungen an den 150. Geburtstag,"
        Heinrich-Schliemann-Gesellschaft Ankershagen E.V. Informations-
        blatt 8 (May 1997) 6.

650.   "'Tripe and Garbage:' William Abbott Oldfather on the Limits of
        Research," *Qui Miscuit Utile Dulci: Festschrift Essays for Paul*
        Lachan MacKendrick, edited by Gareth Schmeling and Jon D.
        Mikalson (Wauconda 1997) 87-93.

651.   "Martyr and Maecenas James Loeb (6 August 1867-27 May
        1933)," *America's Classical Greece, IJCT Supplement =*
        Festschrift for Meyer Reinhold.

652.   "Deutsche Philologen im amerikanischen Exil—Eine Analyse ihrer
        Wirkungen," *Philologus* 141 (1997) = *Festschrift* for Jürgen
        Werner.

653.   "A Believer's History of the Literature of Ancient Greece: Carl
        Otfried Müller 150 Years Later," *Zwischen Rationalismus und*
        Romantik: Karl Otfried Müller und die antike Kultur edited by
        William M. Calder III and Renate Schlesier (Hildesheim 1997).

654.   "Summer Reading," *Inside Illinois* 16,23 (June 19, 1997) 1.

655.   (with Max Braun), "Hermann Diels, the Gomperzes and
        Wilamowitz: A Postscript," *Quaderni di storia* 45 (1997) 173-184.

656.   Review: Kurt Weitzmann, *Sailing with Byzantium from Europe to*
        America: The Memoirs of an Art Historian (Munich 1994).
        Quaderni di storia 45 (1997) 231-236.

657.   Notice: *A Historical Commentary on Arrian's History of*
        Alexander. By A. B. Bosworth. Volume II Commentary on Books
        IV-V. (Oxford 1995). Pp. xviii + 381.
        Religious Studies Review 23 (1997) 62.

658.   Notice: *Palaephatus ΠΕΡΙ ΑΠΙΣΤΩΝ on Unbelievable Tales*
        Translation, Introduction and Commentary by Jacob Stern. With
        notes and Greek text from the 1902 B.G. Teubner edition.
        (Wauconda 1996). Pp. viii + 167.
        Religious Studies Review 23 (1997) 291-292.

659.   Notice: *Cleisthenes the Athenian: an Essay on the Representation of Space and Time in Greek Political Thought from the End of the Sixth Century to the Death of Plato.* By Pierre Lévêque and Pierre Vidal-Naquet. Translated from the French and edited by David Ames Curtis. (Atlantic Highlands, NJ 1996). Pp. xxxvi + 216. *Religious Studies Review* 23 (1997) 294.

660.   Notice: *The Greeks and Us: Essays in Honor of Arthur W. H. Adkins.* Edited by Robert B. Louden and Paul Schollmeier (Chicago 1996). *Religious Studies Review* 23 (1997) 292-293.

661.   Notice: "Alexis The Fragments: A Commentary." By W. Geoffrey Arnott. *Cambridge Classical Texts and Commentaries* 31 (Cambridge 1996). Pp. xxii + 886. *Religious Studies Review* 23 (1997) 401.

662.   Notice: "Reflexe früher und zeitgenössicher Lyrik in der Alten attischen Komödie." By Christoph Kugelmeier. *Beiträge zur Altertumskunde* 80 (Stuttgart 1996). Pp. xii + 379. *Religious Studies Review* 23 (1997) 401.

663.   Notice: *Hestia und Erigone: Vorträge und Aufsätze.* By Reinhold Merkelbach. (Stuttgart/Leipzig 1996). Pp. x + 501. *Religious Studies Review* 23 (1997) 403.

664.   Notice: *Theodor Mommsen und Adolf Harnack: Wissenschaft und Politik im Berlin des ausgehenden 19. Jahrhunderts mit einem Anhang: Edition und Kommentierung des Briefwechsels.* By Stefan Rebenich. Berlin and New York. Walter de Gruyter, 1997. Pp. xxii + 1018. *Religious Studies Review* 23 (1997) 404.

665.   Notice: *Down from Olympus: Archaeology and Philhellenism in Germany, 1750-1970.* By Suzanne L. Marchand. (Princeton 1996). Pp. xxiv + 400. *Religious Studies Review* 23 (1997) 396.

666.   Notice: "Die Entstehung von Ordnung: zur Bestimmung von Sein, Erkennen und Handeln in der späteren Philosophie Platons." By Michael Hoffmann. *Beiträge zur Altertumskunde* 81 (Stuttgart/ Leipzig 1996). Pp. 348. *Religious Studies Review* 23 (1997) 398.

667.   *Greek Roman and Byzantine Studies* 38 (1997) Editorial Board.

668.   *Philologus* 141 (1997) Editor for Canada, Cuba and USA.

669.   *American National Biography*, (Oxford University Press) Advisory
       Editor for Classics.

Wilamowitz' Call to Göttingen: Paul de Lagarde to Friedrich Althoff on Wilamowitz-Moellendorff

I. Introduction

I suppose that for his biographer Wilamowitz' (1848-1931) most embarrassing friend was the brilliant orientalist and *Kulturphilosoph*, Paul de Lagarde (1827-1891).[1] In 1869 he succeeded Heinrich Ewald (1803-1875)[2] as Ordinarius for Oriental Languages at Göttingen, for eight years (1883-1891) he was Wilamowitz' colleague there, and, thanks to Wilamowitz' effort, was himself succeeded by Julius Wellhausen (1844-1918),[3] one of Wilamowitz' closest friends and his last teacher. The number, breadth, and excellence of Lagarde's publications, particularly his work on the text of the Septuagint, have secured him an enviable place in the history of his discipline. I am not competent to evaluate his contribution but refer to one who has.[4] He was benefactor of the Göttingen Scientific Society.[5] His

---

[1] For early work on Lagarde see Götz von Selle, *Die Georg-August-Universität zu Göttingen 1727-1937* (Göttingen 1937) 382-83. Most recently see Jürgen Schriewer, *NDB* 13 (Berlin 1982) 409-12. I find especially useful: Alois Brandl, *Zwischen Inn und Themse: Lebensbeobachtungen eines Anglisten: Alt-Tirol/England/Berlin* (Berlin 1936); Anna de Lagarde, *Paul de Lagarde: Erinnerungen aus seinem Leben für die Freunde zusammengestalt* (Göttingen 1894); Robert W. Lougee, *Paul de Lagarde 1827-1891: A Study of Radical Conservatism in Germany* (Cambridge 1962); Ludwig Schemann, *Paul de Lagarde: Ein Lebens und Erinnerungsbild*[3] (Leipzig 1919); Fritz Stern, *The Politics of Cultural Despair: A Study in the Rise of Germanic Ideology* (Berkeley/Los Angeles/London 1961; repr. 1974) 3-94; Ulrich von Wilamowitz-Moellendorff, *Erinnerungen*[2] *1848-1914* (Leipzig 1929) 230-36. I shall cite these works within by author's name.

[2] Like Lagarde a violent polemicist: see Horton Harris, *The Tübingen School* (Oxford 1975) 43-48.

[3] See "Julius Wellhausen and his Prolegomena to the History of Israel," ed. Douglas A. Knight, *Semeia* 25 (Chico 1982); Alfred Jepsen, "Wellhausen in Greifswald: Ein Beitrag zur Biographie Julius Wellhausens," *Der Herr ist Gott: Aufsätze zur Wissenschaft von Alten Testament* (Berlin 1978) 254-70; Rudolf Smend, "Wellhausen in Greifswald," *Zeitschrift für Theologie und Kirche* 78 (1981) 141-76. Wilamowitz, *Erinnerungen*[2], 188-91.

[4] For a judgment *sine ira et studio* see D. Winton Thomas "The Textual Criticism of the Old Testament," *The Old Testament and Modern Study: A Generation of Discovery and Research*, ed. H.H. Rowley (Oxford 1961) 243-45, 250-55. For Paul Wendland's praise of Lagarde to Hans Lietzmann: see *Glanz und Niedergang der deutschen Universität: 50 Jahre deutscher Wissenschaftsgeschichte in Briefen an und von Hans Lietzmann (1892-1942)*, ed. Kurt Aland, (Berlin/New York 1979) 172 (letter of 27 December 1897): "Lagarde ist der einzige gewesen, der klar gesehen hat..."

[5] Lagarde in Anna de Lagarde, 162-89; Stern 24 n.; Usener, *apud* Aland, 180-81; Wilamowitz, *Erinnerungen*[2], 235. For the difficulties involved in the complicated will see Wilamowitz to Mommsen (7 August 1892), *Mommsen und Wilamowitz Briefwechsel 1872-1903*, edd. Friedrich and Dorothea Hiller von Gaertringen, (Berlin 1935) 461 and Ulrich Schindel, "Wilamowitz in den GGA," *GGA* 234 (1982) 1-12.

magnificent library was sold for 30,000 marks to New York University.[6] His wholehearted devotion to scholarship inspired the best of his younger contemporaries.[7] But there was a darker side. It has eclipsed the blazing light of that intellect.

Lagarde was a Prussian, proud of his country and of his people. Such pride still demanded courage among the provincial Whelfs of Lower Saxony.[8] A doctor of theology in the Philosophical Faculty, he treated the Judaeo-Christian religion with an objectivity remarkable for his time. He was in fact a philologist in the service of theology. His intense nationalism warped his thinking. He was not anti-semitic. That would have made him typical of his time and place. He was a rabid Jew-hater. A.H. Sayce reports:[9]

> Ewald's successor in the chair of Hebrew was...De Lagarde, who had all his Hebrew books bound in pigskin in order, as he said, "to keep the dirty fingers of the Jews from off them."

He seriously proposed that all Jews be resettled in Madagascar.[10] Shortly before his death he found an erratic but devoted disciple in the *Rembrandt-Deutscher*, Julius Langbehn (1851-1907), a pupil of Heinrich Brunn, whose anonymous *Rembrandt als Erzieher* was even attributed to Lagarde.[11] The influence of his popular publications grew considerably in the first third of this century.[12] Houston Stewart Chamberlain compared his political genius with that of Bismarck.[13] Alfred Rosenberg set him among Nietzsche, Wagner and Chamberlain, as prophet of the Third Reich.[14]

---

[6] Stern 24 n., adding "...it was maintained as a separate unit—the Lagarde Library—until recently. It constituted one of the best Oriental libraries in America." Anna de Lagarde, 148, Schemann, 95 and Schriewer, 411 are ambiguous ("Universität der Stadt New York"). New York University, a private foundation, not the City University of New York, a municipal institution, bought the library.

[7] E.g., Hans Lietzmann: see Aland, 342-43, where Lietzmann in July 1914 writes: "Seit ich als Primaner Untersuchungen Paul de Lagardes zu lesen begonnen, ist mir mit der Verehrung für diesen Mann auch das Verständnis für die Eigenart und die hohe wissenschaftliche Bedeutung der gelehrten Gesellschaft, die seinem Lebenswerk die Basis gab, gekommen und stetig gewachsen." His schoolteacher, Hermann Halfmann, was a Lagarde pupil: see Aland, 4.

[8] See Schriewer, 410: "im noch preußenfeindlich gesinnten Göttingen" and Wilamowitz, *Erinnerungen*², 198-200.

[9] A.H. Sayce, *Reminiscences* (London 1923) 53. See further Lougee, *Lagarde*, 210-15; 245-52.

[10] See Luciano Canfora, *Intellettuali in Germania* (Bari 1979) 121 with n. 251 (the suggestion was considered by Heinrich Himmler) and Schriewer, 412.

[11] See Stern, 94 (which I have rephrased), 106, 109 n.

[12] See Stern, 82-94 and Canfora, *Intellettuali*, 121-22.

[13] H.S. Chamberlain, *Politische Ideale*⁶, (Munich 1926) 114, cited by Canfora, *Intellettuali*, 122 n. 257.

[14] Alfred Rosenberg, *Gestaltung der Idee* (Munich 1936) 11-12, cited by Canfora, *Intellettuali*, 122 n. 254.

George Foot Moore, the Harvard Semiticist, manfully sought to exculpate Lagarde.[15] Like Th. Mommsen,[16] Lagarde considered Jews divisive and subversive. They were rootless and anti-nationalistic. That an Old Testament scholar could so detest the heirs of ancient Israel strikes a modern American as bizarre. But even so temperate and simple a man as Wellhausen drew a sharp distinction between Israel and *Judentum*, the ancient Hebrews and the modern Jew.[17] The view also infected German Hellenism. It explains Ernst Buschor's interpretation of the German invasion of Greece in 1941 as the rescue of Greece by the true Greeks.[18] Modern Greeks were *Mischwesen*, in anthropological terms, "a remnant culture."

II. What was it about Lagarde that appealed to Wilamowitz?

Alois Brandl (1855-1940) knew both men well and stated the paradox.[19] "Lagarde was friend and at the same time the opposite of Wilamowitz." The decisive document is the *Rede...am Sarge*, delivered by Wilamowitz on 25 December 1891 in the cemetery at Göttingen. He published it immediately and repeatedly reprinted it in his *Reden und Vorträge* and in his *Erinnerungen*.[20] Brandl observed of this remarkable address that of all Wilamowitz' writings it probably revealed "the most personal mirroring of his innermost character."[21] Wilamowitz saw a distorted portrait of himself in Lagarde. First there was "das stille Heldentum der Arbeit,"[22] Lagarde's wholehearted, fanatical devotion to his work, his scholarship, that formed the center and purpose of his life. Next there was his vast erudition, more particularly philological erudition: "there is, I suppose, here no one who can

---

[15] G.F. Moore, *apud* Anna de Lagarde, 157: "...his antagonism to the existing churches, his animosity toward Judaism, springing from the feeling that they divide and weaken Germany, that they make impossible the full development of the national character and the achievement of the mission and destiny of the German people."

[16] See Karl Christ, *Von Gibbon zu Rostovtzeff: Leben und Werk führender Althistoriker der Neuzeit*[2] (Darmstadt 1979) 91-92.

[17] See Lou H. Silbermann, "Wellhausen and Judaism," *Semeia* 25 (1982) 75-82.

[18] See my remarks at *CP* 76 (1981) 168 with n. 3. Compare Niebuhr's appalling view on Italians. Mommsen was different.

[19] Brandl 223: "Freund und zugleich Gegenpol von Wilamowitz war Lagarde." For Brandl see Fritz Wölcken, *NDB* 2 (Berlin 1955) 527-28.

[20] Ulrich von Wilamowitz-Moellendorff, *Rede gehalten im Auftrage der königl. Georg-August-Universität am Sarge des Geheimen Regierungsrates Professors D. Dr. Paul de Lagarde am 25. December 1891* (Göttingen n.d.). He published this in early editions of his *Reden und Vorträge*[3] (Berlin 1913) 91-97 with the important 91 n. 1 (details of the funeral). He last published it in slightly revised form in *Erinnerungen*[2] 231-35. I shall cite the first and last publication.

[21] Brandl 224: "die innerste Spiegelung seines Charakterkerns."

[22] Wilamowitz, *Rede* 3 (= *Erinnerungen*[2] 232). Lagarde's death is dated at *Erinnerungen*[1] 228 (= *Erinnerungen*[2] 230) 22 December 1890. At *My Recollections 1848-1914*, translated by G.C. Richards (London 1930) 277, it is dated 22 December 1900. The correct date is 22 December 1891, Wilamowitz' 43rd birthday.

spell all the languages in which he has edited texts." His devotion to work and his learning brought him his loneliness. "To many of his colleagues he remained distant; only a very few did he approach and remain with them."[23] Wilamowitz had two close friends at Göttingen, Felix Klein and Friedrich Leo. The older he grew the more he lamented *die Einsamkeit meines Lebens*. Only posterity can judge what is lasting in de Lagarde's work. That is recompense for the world's hatred of excellence.[24] They shared a teacher. Lagarde sought to put the philological method of textual criticism into the service of the sources of Christianity. "That comes from Lachmann."[25] Both shared Yeats' "the fascination of what's difficult." The enormity of the task that Lagarde had undertaken, the establishment of the text of the Old Testament on a scientific basis, just because it was impossible, proved the Herculean greatness of the man.[26] "A more difficult and therefore more beautiful task of textual criticism does not exist anywhere."[27] It was a task that would have daunted Lachmann and that men of 1891 would not dream of undertaking. Only an organized team ("eine organisierte Arbeitsgemeinschaft") could carry on the superhuman effort of that one man. Wilamowitz is thinking of the Göttingen Academy.[28]

There is a pause and then a sentence of greatest import. "Aber der Entschlafene war nicht nur Gelehrter, ja es ist damit der Kern seines Wesens gar nicht getroffen." "He was more than a scholar." He was a prophet. Wilamowitz continues: "As prophet he has raised his voice on State and Church, on the education of youth and the worship of God, on society and morality. Nor did it disturb him that the voice of the one crying remained in the wilderness: for he felt himself as a prophet. He had a right to that; for his was a prophetic nature."[29] Wilamowitz compares him with the prophets of the Old Testament, with Heraclitus, Parmenides, St. Augustine, Giordano Bruno, Rousseau and Thomas Carlyle. Eight years later, on the 150th birthday of Goethe, Wilamowitz wrote:[30] "Was Religion ist, das lerne, wer es nicht weiß, bei Carlyle oder bei Lagarde." Wilamowitz does not mean what these men wrote about religion. He means the intensity of conviction

---

[23] *Rede* 4 (= *Erinnerungen*[2] 232): see Stern 23.

[24] Compare "Ulrich von Wilamowitz-Moellendorff, Selected Correspondence 1869-1931", edited by William M. Calder III, *Antiqua* 23 (Naples 1983) 301 with n. 19. He felt a kinship with Lagarde.

[25] *Rede* 5 (= *Erinnerungen*[2] 233). For Wilamowitz' indebtedness to Lachmann see *AuA* 27 (1981) 43 with n. 54 (= *Antiqua* 27 [Naples 1984] 156 c.n. 54).

[26] For Wilamowitz who saw himself as a Herakles of Wissenschaft see my "Ecce Homo: The Autobiographical in Wilamowitz' scholarly Writings," *Wilamowitz nach 50 Jahren*, edd. William M. Calder III, Hellmut Flashar, Theodor Lindken (Darmstadt 1985) 80-110.

[27] *Rede* 5 (= *Erinnerungen*[2] 233).

[28] For Wilamowitz' interest in the Göttingen Academy see *Erinnerungen*[2] 236-38 and for the Berlin Academy, *ib.*, 308-10.

[29] *Rede* 5-6 (= *Erinnerungen*[2] 233).

[30] Ulrich von Wilamowitz-Moellendorff *Griechische Tragoedien* II[5] (Berlin 1907) 6.

in their writings, their acknowledged mission to better the world. One cannot but recall Wilamowitz' later ambiguous dismissal of Nietzsche:[31]

> Er hat getan, wozu ich ihn aufforderte, hat Lehramt und Wissenschaft aufgegeben und ist Prophet geworden, für eine irreligiose Religion und eine unphilosophische Philosophie.

In contrast is the earlier declaration of 1889:[32] "We philologists as such have nothing of the poet nor of the prophet...Contrarily we ought to bear in us something of the actor." The philologist in the sense of Diderot is the skilled actor who sacrifices his individuality to revive a figure of the past, as an actor becomes a character in a play. I think that Wilamowitz envied the prophet in Lagarde, even in Nietzsche. The effort that *Griechisches Lesebuch* cost him,[33] the importance he placed in the face of public opposition on his translations from Greek tragedy and their staging,[34] his emphasis on popular public lectures, all reveal his wish to be "nicht nur Gelehrter." Brandl knew the prophet hidden in Wilamowitz' own breast but described as Lagarde's.[35]

Brandl recorded other similarities.[36] Each stood for Bismarck and Moltke, Lagarde at the same time for every other German in the world. Both composed verses, but Wilamowitz only in translation from the Greek dramatists. Here Brandl erred.[37] Both were reformers, but Wilamowitz with more caution. Lagarde sometimes unfortunately reformed without sufficient knowledge of the circumstances. If one needed help in some university matter, Lagarde would say: "For that you have to go to Wilamowitz. He has a party behind him." They both worked extraordinarily hard until their last days. Lagarde literally went from his desk to the operation table.[38]

---

[31] *Erinnerungen*[2] 130. Compare now Wilamowitz' letter of 1 July 1920 to Ernst Howald, edited by Jaap Mansfeld, *Maatstaf* 10-II (Amsterdam 1983) 121 on men without scholarship who pretend to be scholars (he speaks of Nietzsche): "Die sind Propheten; man muß ihnen glauben. Auf das Katheder gehört der Prophet so wenig wie der Publizist." See further *Nietzsche-Studien* 15 (1986) 41-58.

[32] Ulrich von Wilamowitz-Moellendorff, *Euripides Herakles* I[3] (Darmstadt 1969) 257. For Diderot see *AuA* 27 (1981) 48 with n. 92 (= *Antiqua* 27 161).

[33] See Luciano Canfora, "Wilamowitz und die Schulreform: Das griechische Lesebuch," *Der altsprachliche Unterricht* 25 (1982) 5-19 (= *Wilamowitz nach 50 Jahren* 632-48).

[34] For the staging of Wilamowitz' translations see Hellmut Flashar, "Aufführungen von griechischen Dramen in der Übersetzung von Wilamowitz," *Wilamowitz nach 50 Jahren*, 306-57 and for the attack of the George Circle on the translations see Ulrich K. Goldsmith, *ibid.*, 583-612.

[35] One may compare Erwin Rohde to Friedrich Nietzsche on first reading Lagarde in a letter of 20 May 1873 (= *KGB* II. 4 [Berlin/New York 1978] 255): "Lagarde habe ich erst jetzt gelesen mit großer Stärkung, in dem sehr kräftigen, ja austeren Aposteltone und Ernste." See also Crusius, *Rohde* 68.

[36] Brandl 224. The paragraph summarizes Brandl.

[37] For Wilamowitz' original poems in Greek and Latin see Ulrich von Wilamowitz-Moellendorff, *Elegeia*, ed. Wolfgang Buchwald (Berlin 1938) with the review of A. Koerte, *Gnomon* 15 (1939) 46-53. For the German poem to Wellhausen see *Erinnerungen*[2] 189 and W. Kranz, *Gnomon* 11 (1935) 511. For Lagarde's depressing poetry see Stern 25-26.

[38] For details see Anna de Lagarde, 117 with Wilamowitz' admiring remarks at *Erinnerungen*[2] 230-31.

I should add a telling similarity. Wilamowitz' avoidance of professional gatherings is known. Lagarde once attended a meeting of German philologians and orientalists. He writes his wife on 1 October 1851:[39]

> What was most repulsive at the meetings was the stench of the guild (*Zunft*), which assailed me everywhere: intellectual proletariat, that labors on its humdrum articles in the sweat of its brow, that does not know that science is to make one free and happy.

Wilamowitz could never have shared Lagarde's strident anti-semitism.[40] On the other hand in spite of his adoration of Jacob Bernays,[41] he shared Theodor Gomperz' view that Jews must integrate thoroughly into German culture,[42] and considered the extremes of orthodoxy childish superstition.[43] Wilamowitz belonged to the *Septima*, a group of seven men who met every fortnight at the home of one of them for dinner, paper, and discussion. I know only five members:[44] Brandl, Lagarde, W. Meyer, Wilamowitz and the baptised Jew, Friedrich Leo.[45] That Lagarde's brand of anti-semitism did

---

[39] See Anna de Lagarde, 20-21. The translation is that of Stern 12 n. 3.
[40] For his disgust with Nazi anti-semitism see *Quaderni di storia* 18 (1983) 276.
[41] *Selected Letters* 158-60.
[42] Compare *Selected Letters* 158 n. 37 with *Erinnerungen*[2] 38-42.
[43] See Ulrich von Wilamowitz-Moellendorff, *Der Glaube der Hellenen* I[2] (Basel 1956) 27 n. 1.
[44] See Brandl 219; Anna de Lagarde, 117; Wilamowitz, *Erinnerungen*[2] 230.
[45] See Anna de Lagarde, 117. The *Septima* met at Leo's on 16 December 1891. On the 19th Lagarde was operated upon for intestinal cancer. Years later another Jew thanked Lagarde publicly for the kindness shown him: see Adolf Erman, *Mein Werden und mein Wirken: Erinnerungen eines alten Berliner Gelehrten* (Leipzig 1929) 263. Two letters survive (Göttingen *Nachlaß* No. 509) of the Jewish journalist and reformer, Maximilian Harden, born Witkowski (1861-1923), editor of the *Die Zukunft*, to Wilamowitz. Harden requests (4 August 1893) a contribution from Wilamowitz on Lagarde. He writes:

> Die Angelegenheit des literarischen Denkmals, das Paul de Lagarde gesetzt werden soll, scheint, was Alles was diesen großen Deutschen betrifft, nicht annährend das verdiente Interesse zu finden. Deshalb gestatte ich mir die höfliche Anfrage, ob Sie nicht geneigt wären, über den Toten, der Sie seinen Freund nannte, uns über die Stiftung in meiner Wochenschrift ein Wort zu sagen, von dem ich mit Bestimmtheit die...Wirkung erwarte.

Wilamowitz promptly replied in a lost letter of ca. 7 August, refusing. Harden already sided with "Kollege Bismarck" against Wilhelm II. That may have deterred him. He recommended Roethe. Harden replied on 10 August 1893:

> Für Ihren sehr gütigen Brief habe ich bestens zu danken. Ich bedaure freilich sehr, daß Sie nicht in der Lage sind, meinen Wunsch zu erfüllen; vielleicht ergäbe sich dazu ohne Namensnennung doch die Möglichkeit.
> Indessen will ich, Ihrem freundlichen Rath gemäß, im Interesse der guten Sache mich nun an Herrn Professor Roethe wenden. Ganz besonders gütig wäre es, wenn Sie—im Falle, daß dieser Herr zum Schreiben bereit ist—ihm die so liebenswürdig in Aussicht gestellte thatsächliche Auskunft ertheilten, so weit er derer noch bedarf.

For Harden see Harry F. Young, *Maximilian Harden: Censor Germaniae* (The Hague 1959), and Gerhard Masur, *Imperial Berlin* (London 1971), 179-86. For Harden's

not deter Leo from becoming one of his closest friends would not have gone unnoticed by Wilamowitz.

III. The New Text

In spring 1883, Hermann Sauppe (1809-1893)[46] inquired of Wilamowitz whether he wished to come to Göttingen as successor of the vegetable-gardener, Ernst Ludwig von Leutsch (1808-1887).[47] Wilamowitz did and gratefully named his second son Hermann. The call was not official until July.[48] By October 1883 he had removed to Göttingen[49] to begin the happiest period of his life.[50] Little is known (to me at least) of the politics behind the call. For whatever reason remarkably little contemporary documentation survives. Ed. Schwartz later observed that Wilamowitz ought earlier to have succeeded Wachsmuth but the jealousy of the second-rate thwarted good.[51] Wilamowitz tarried too long at Greifswald. On 4 May 1883 Wilamowitz was still unsure of the outcome.[52] In a recently published fragment from a letter of Th. Mommsen to his brother Tycho, dated May 1883, Mommsen sums up the matter:[53]

> Es ist im Werk Wilamowitz nach Göttingen zu berufen; und ich hoffe, daß es dazu kommt. Augenblicklich wird er dadurch mehr verlieren als gewinnen: hübsche Wohnung, leidlichen Verkehr, anerkannte Stellung, gewöhnte Verhältnisse gibt er auf und das *settling down* ist nirgends bequem. Aber es ist doch der Fortschritt von einer kleinen Universität zu einer großen und eine Änderung, die für ihn um so mehr

---

"shockingly admiring" review of Julius Langbehn see Stern 159-60. The point that must be stressed for moderns is that neither Harden (also baptized) nor Leo considered themselves Jews but German Lutherans. And Lagarde would have allowed them to handle his books.

[46] See Ulrich von Wilamowitz-Moellendorff, "Gedächtnisrede auf Hermann Sauppe," *Kleine Schriften* VI, ed. Wolfgang Buchwald (Berlin 1972) 3-10 and for the barest facts J.E. Sandys, *A History of Classical Scholarship* III (Cambridge 1908) 163-64.

[47] For Leutsch's gardening ability see Wilamowitz' scornful remarks at *Erinnerungen*[2] 205-06. B.L. Gildersleeve, contrarily, esteemed the man: see *Selections from the Brief Mention of Basil Lanneau Gildersleeve*, ed. C.W.E. Miller (Baltimore/London 1930) 250.

[48] See *Erinnerungen*[2] 197 where Sauppe's letter is also attested. One ought not to forget that the Bonn *Philologenkrieg* began over Jahn's wish to appoint Sauppe. The veneration of Sauppe and Wilamowitz for Jahn would have been a further bond. [For details of the call see now W.M. Calder III, *Wissenschaftsgeschichte und Wissenschaftspolitik im Industriezeitalter*, ed. Bernhard vom Brocke, (Hildesheim 1991) 255-260.]

[49] Wilamowitz writes from Greifswald to Mommsen on 18 August 1883; from Göttingen on 27 October 1883; see *Briefwechsel* 159 (No. 140), 160 (No. 142).

[50] So Wilamowitz calls it at *Erinnerungen*[2] 239.

[51] Eduard Schwartz, *Gesammelte Schriften I: Vergangene Gegenwärtigkeiten* (Berlin 1938) 372: "Die Georgia Augusta wagte 1877, als Wachsmuth sie verließ, noch nicht, W. zu berufen; erst 1883 überwand sie ihre Bedenken."

[52] See Mommsen-Wilamowitz, *Briefwechsel* 153-54 (No. 132). Wilamowitz modestly confesses that he had not thought a Göttingen appointment possible.

[53] See Lothar Wickert, *Theodor Mommsen: Eine Biographie IV Grösse und Grenzen* (Frankfurt/Main 1980) 252.

wert ist, als er—nicht durchaus ohne eigene Schuld—zahlreiche und recht laute Gegner hat.

The Dean of the Philosophical Faculty that spring was Paul de Lagarde.[54] All known of the later friendship between Lagarde and Wilamowitz led me to suspect that Lagarde had eagerly supported the appointment. He was a great enough scholar not to be threatened by a classicist 21 years younger than himself. However, a remarkable letter written by Lagarde in his capacity as Dean to the all-powerful Prussian Ministerialrat, Friedrich Althoff (1839-1908)[55] proves the contrary. I doubt that Wilamowitz ever read or even knew about the document. I first learned of it by reading a footnote in Fritz Stern, *The Politics of Cultural Despair*. There Stern writes:[56]

> Of course, Wilamowitz could not have known that Lagarde had opposed his call to Göttingen; in a letter to Friedrich Althoff, powerful councillor of the Prussian Education Ministry, Lagarde wrote: "Wilamowitz is not the right man for us...and that for a very definite reason," which remained unspecified. Letter of April 4, 1883, Lagarde Archive.

I applied to that tireless friend of scholars Dr. K. Haenel of the Manuscript Department of the Göttingen Library. He generously located the document and sent me a copy with permission to publish. I am most grateful. The text (fortunately) is not in Lagarde's difficult hand.[57] It is a copy written in a copperplate hand by an amanuensis. The original (in Lagarde's hand?) presumably had been sent to Berlin. I do not edit the whole letter, which elsewhere concerns matters in which I have no competence. It is dated "Goettingen 4. 4. 1883." Althoff had called on Lagarde, who was not at home. Therefore, Lagarde is writing what he would have said. He has nothing to say about himself. He next discusses a library matter concerning the lending of manuscripts. He then turns to the revision of university statutes concerning the awarding of the doctorate. The revision will be delayed. Only in the last paragraph does he turn to Wilamowitz. The text follows.

---

[54] In his letter of 4 April 1883 to Althoff edited below, Lagarde remarks: "Als Dekan bitte ich..."

[55] The authoritative biography remains Arnold Sachse, *Friedrich Althoff und sein Werk* (Berlin 1928), approved at Wilamowitz, *Erinnerungen*[2] 249. For a brief statement of facts see Franz Schnabel, *NDB* I (Berlin 1953) 222-24. The great modern study is: Bernhard vom Brocke, "Hochschul- und Wissenschaftspolitik in Preußen und im Deutschen Kaiserreich 1882-1907: das 'System Althoff'," *Preußen in der Geschichte*: I *Bildungspolitik in Preußen zur Zeit des Kaiserreichs*, ed. Peter Baumgart (Stuttgart 1980) 9-118.

[56] I cite Stern 23 n. 2.

[57] Two notes of Lagarde to Wilamowitz survive at Göttingen (Wilamowitz-Nachlaß No. 768), dated 13 October 1889 and 19 February 1891. The first attests Lagarde's reading in *Herakles* and refers to the local big-shots as *führende Lemüren*.

In den Akten des Ministeriums beruht [*sic*] eine von mir und Genossen[58] zu Gunsten des Professors Alfred Schoene[59] in Paris gemachte Eingabe. Ich halte diesen Gelehrten für sehr geeignet, an die Stelle des Herrn von Leutsch[60] zu treten, wie ich andrerseits überzeugt bin, daß Herr von Wilamowitz, der einzige, auf den wir greifen könnten, da Hartel[61] aus Wien nicht weggelassen werden wird, der rechte Mann für uns aus einem ganz bestimmten Grunde[62] doch nicht ist. Ich erlaube mir die Frage, ob die Berufung Alfred Schoenes von dem Herrn Minister principiell abgelehnt werden würde: in disem Falle würde ich sie hier gar nicht zur Discussion stellen. Zu weiterer Aeußerungen bin ich bereit, falls solche zu thun mir ausdrücklich befohlen werden sollte.

In schuldiger Ehrerbietung
Prof. P. de Lagarde
Doctor der Theologie.

IV. What have we learned?

We can reconstruct what today we should call the list. It seems to have been:

1) Wilhelm Ritter von Hartel (*aet.* 44)
2) Ulrich von Wilamowitz-Moellendorff (*aet.* 34)
3) Alfred Schöne (*aet.* 47)

[58] For speculation on the identity of the comrades see *infra*.

[59] For Alfred Schöne (1836-1918) see Rudolf Ehwald, *BiogJahr* 181 (1919) 87-112; Otto Baumgarten, *Zum Gedächtnis an Alfred Schöne* (Kiel 1928) (with portrait); and Volbehr-Weyl-Bülck-Newiger, *Professoren und Dozenten der Christian-Albrechts-Universität zu Kiel 1665-1954* (Kiel 1956) 152 No. 136.

[60] See *supra* n. 47.

[61] For Wilhelm Ritter von Hartel (1839-1907) see Augustus Engelbrecht, *BiogJahr* 141 (1908) 75-107; Brandl, 96-99; S. Frankfurter, *Wilhelm von Hartel: Sein Leben und Wirken* (Vienna/Leipzig 1912) esp. 93-95 (Göttingen call); Heinrich Gomperz, *Theodor Gomperz: Briefe und Aufzeichnungen ausgewählt, erläutert und zu einer Darstellung seines Lebens verknüpft* 1 (*1832-1868*) (Vienna 1936) 439 n. 3; Heinrich Gomperz-Robert A. Kann, "Theodor Gomperz: Ein Gelehrtenleben im Bürgertum der Franz-Josefs-Zeit: Auswahl seiner Briefe und Aufzeichnungen, 1869-1912, erläutert und zu einer Darstellung seines Lebens verknüpft," *ÖstAkdWiss philosoph.-hist Klasse Sitz* 295 (Vienna 1974) 412-13 (Theodor Gomperz' necrology of Hartel), 539 *s.n.* Hartel; Carl E. Schorske, *Fin-de-Siècle Vienna: Politics and Culture* (New York 1981) 238 n.; 237-45 (espousal of modern art and Freud's professorship), 253, 264. Not an original scholar, a diplomat, a courtier, a man of limitless ambition, son of a linen-weaver who became Austrian Minister of Education in 1900, knighted in 1882, he was decisive in opening university study to women. He defended Arthur Schnitzler and Sigmund Freud against anti-semitism. Schorske (238 n.) calls his career "exemplary for the cultivated liberal bureaucracy." He was Ordinarius for Classical Philology at Vienna, colleague of Theodor Gomperz. He could only have been asked *honoris causa*.

[62] The choice of phrase is revealing. It means "for a very definite reason." That is not a reason that would occur to one. Lagarde had wished to communicate orally with Althoff and declines to be explicit in writing.

Hartel proved to Berlin that the Georgia Augusta's reach far exceeded her grasp. Was there need to flatter Hartel? Or was his name a device, attested elsewhere, to stall for time? No one believed (least Althoff) that Hartel would exchange the Golden Age of imperial Vienna for rustic Göttingen.[63] Sauppe, Göttingen's leading classical scholar, wanted Wilamowitz. Presumably, *Aus Kydathen* had appealed to one who dealt with the Attic orators. The youthful author's savaging of Ernst Curtius may even have been welcome.[64] Leutsch, admittedly an elderly friend of Lagarde,[65] had no influence. An eccentric bachelor, his candidate remained a joker 45 years later.[66] Friedrich Bechtel (1855-1924), a youthful friend of Lagarde, had habilitated at Göttingen in 1878, and would not become Extraordinarius until 1884. He would not have been consulted.[67] The call required almost five months to become official. This means a divided faculty and hesitation by Althoff. Lagarde was impulsive. He was not a fool. He needed an ally within the *Fach*. There remains only one philologist unaccounted for. Lagarde refers to "comrades." Karl Dilthey (1839-1907) must have represented the local philological opposition to Wilamowitz. I shall pose three questions. 1. Why would Dilthey have distrusted Wilamowitz? Later *Zusammenarbeit* was amiable enough.[68] 2. Why would Lagarde have joined with Dilthey against Wilamowitz? 3. Why did Lagarde prefer Alfred Schöne?

1. Dilthey had corresponded with the *enfant terrible* since at least 3 January 1875 (the earliest preserved letter). After leaving Zürich for Göttingen in 1877 he languished under the shadow of Sauppe. Wilamowitz, when he left Greifswald, had a bibliography of 85 items of astonishing variety and brilliance and a big book on the way, *Homerische Unter-suchungen*.[69] It would be more painful to languish in the shadow of one

---

[63] The late Dorothea Freifrau Hiller von Gaertringen told me how Wilamowitz caused a scandal by serving Italian wine at a rectorial dinner (cf. *Erinnerungen*[2] 204-05). And for Gomperz Wilamowitz was provincial.

[64] Ernst Curtius' intense displeasure with *Aus Kydathen* is attested in his unpublished letters to his brother Georg at Leipzig. Wilamowitz only advanced to Berlin after Curtius' death.

[65] The friendship is attested in a letter of Lagarde to Schöne dated 14 March 1876, where Lagarde consoles Leutsch on the death of a favorite dog: see Schemann, *Paul de Lagarde*[3] 311 with n. 40.

[66] Leutsch naively confessed to Wilamowitz that he had supported August Luchs (a nonentity at Erlangen), "weil der etwas von Metrik verstünde" (*Erinnerungen*[2] 206). This is to the author of *Griechische Verskunst*!

[67] For Bechtel see Hans Hartmann, *NDB* I (Berlin 1953) 694 and Olivier Masson, "Friedrich Bechtel et l'anthroponymie grecque," *apud* Friedrich Bechtel, "Kleine onomastische Studien: Aufsätze zur griechischen Eigennamenforschung," *Beiträge zur Klassischen Philologie* 125 (Königstein/Ts. 1981) i.v (with portrait). For Bechtel as friend of Lagarde see Schemann, *Paul de Lagarde*[3] 91. Bruns similarly would not have been consulted.

[68] See the generous words of Wilamowitz at *Erinnerungen*[2] 206-07. But Wilamowitz also observes that he was a failure as a scholar and a teacher and that, in spite of all that Wilamowitz did for him, he bore a secret grudge against his benefactor.

[69] The book was controversial. Theodor Gomperz did not like it; see Gomperz-Kann 162-63 (*cf. Philologus* 122 [1978] 291-92 = *Selected Correspondence* 155-56). Contrast Th. Mommsen in his letter to Frau Helbig: Wickert, IV 252.

eleven years younger. After Wilamowitz' epiphany, Dilthey withdrew, often reported ill, and was granted repeated medical leave.[70] In autumn 1889 Wilamowitz arranged a solution. Friedrich Leo, after a year at Strassburg, became ordinarius at Göttingen, in effect, the successor of Dilthey, who soon thereafter (1893) succeeded an aged non-entity, Friedrich Wieseler (1811-1892), in the chair of archaeology. Here was no competition, only the memories of K.O. Müller and F.G. Welcker. A splendid example of kicking upstairs. Wilamowitz, against his better judgment, struggled to place Dilthey in the Academy. In spite of all done for him, Dilthey nursed a secret grudge against Wilamowitz which first surfaced after Wilamowitz' departure for Berlin in 1897.[71] Dilthey early became an embittered second-rater, colleague, brother, and brother-in-law of great men.

Dilthey's past had not prepared him for passionate friendship with Wilamowitz. At Naples in 1869 he had befriended Erwin Rohde (1845-1898). They lived together briefly and paid a memorable visit to Pompeii.[72] Rohde through excessive loyalty to a friend had defended a cause he knew to be wrong and his career suffered. He lacked the magnanimity to blame himself and remained the lifelong enemy of Wilamowitz, who had driven Nietzsche from classics.[73] There was a more sinister intimate than Rohde. Lilly Dilthey (1846-1920), Karl's sister, had since 1866 been the wife of Hermann Usener (1834-1905).[74] The youthful friendship of the Dilthey

---

[70] Wilamowitz, *Erinnerungen*[2] 206-07. For K. Dilthey, Konrad von Krosigk cites Laura Koepp, *Die Familie Dilthey* (Wiesbaden 1906) 23-34.

[71] Wilamowitz, *Erinnerungen*[2] 208.

[72] See O. Crusius, *Erwin Rohde: ein biographischer Versuch* (Tübingen/Leipzig 1902) 34, 262, where in a letter of 20 August 1869 Rohde writes:

> Zunächst ging ich nach Pompeji, und bin dort, in Gesellschaft eines sehr angenehmen Kameraden, Dilthey, 4-5 Tage geblieben, in idyllischer Einsamkeit in der kleinen Kneipe 'zur Sonne' eingemiethet.

[73] For details see my "The Wilamowitz-Nietzsche Struggle: New Documents and a Reappraisal," *Nietzsche-Studien* 12 (1983) 214-54, esp. 246-47 (= *Antiqua* 27 [1984] 183-223, esp. 215-16).

[74] For Usener I have found the following most helpful: Hermann Dieterich and Friedrich v. Hiller, *Usener und Wilamowitz: Ein Briefwechsel 1870-1905* (Leipzig/Berlin 1934) with the notices of Ed. Schwartz, *DLZ* 42 (1934) 1978-86 and Alfred Körte, *Antike* 11 (1935) 211-35 [the edition was reprinted in 1994 with my *Nachwort*]; Hans Joachim Mette, "Nekrolog einer Epoche: Hermann Usener und seine Schule," *Lustrum* 22 (1979-80) 5-106; Arnaldo Momigliano, "New Paths of Classicism in the Nineteenth Century," *History and Theory Beiheft* 21 (Wesleyan 1982) 33-48; id. "Premese per una discussione su Hermann Usener," *apud Aspetti di Hermann Usener filologo della religione*, edd. G. Arrighetti et al., (Pisa 1983) 9-21; Hans Herter "Die Klassische Philologie seit Usener und Bücheler," *Bonner Gelehrte: Beiträge zur Geschichte der Wissenschaften in Bonn: Philosophie und Altertumswissenschaften* (Bonn 1968) 165-77; Albert Henrichs, *apud Wilamowitz nach 50 Jahren* 263-305. Because so much panegyric is written of Usener attention should be drawn to Paulsen's frank report of his lectures on the history of Greek literature at Bonn summer semester 1869: see Friedrich Paulsen, *An Autobiography*, translated and edited by Theodor Lorenz (New York 1938) 188-89. For Mommsen and Wilamowitz on Usener see further Jürgen Dummer, *Studia Byzantina* II (Berlin 1973) 370 n. 5. Wilamowitz headed his blacklist of those from whom he had learned nothing with Usener: *AuA* 27 (1981) 48 (= *Antiqua* 27 [Naples 1984] 161). [See now Roland Kany, *Mnemosyne als Programm* (Tübingen 1987) 11-128.]

brothers with Usener has been described elsewhere.[75] Karl habilitated under his brother-in-law at Bonn *ca.* 1870.[76] The friendship endured. Usener dedicated his greatest book, *Götternamen* (1896) "den Brüdern Wilhelm und Karl Dilthey seinen Freunden und Schwägern."[77] Momigliano calls the brothers Usener's "dearest friends."[78] There is ground in short to believe that Usener was in an excellent position to influence Karl Dilthey.[79]

I have elsewhere discussed Usener's ambivalence to Wilamowitz.[80] Momigliano recently has done likewise, although more from Usener's point of view.[81] Wilamowitz, the Bonn *mulus*, aged 19, admittedly was brilliant, arrogant, and probably a show-off. Not for nothing was he called the "brilliant beast" (*genialer Wildling*).[82] Usener, a young Ordinarius, never a great textual critic,[83] approved silly seclusions in Euripidean prologues, an author all of whom Wilamowitz had read.[84] He could not meet Wilamowitz' forcibly stated objections. There was a public quarrel. Wilamowitz seems to have written a satirical poem against his luckless instructor.[85] Usener was enraged. Bonn lost her best classical student to Berlin. Wilamowitz apologized indirectly in 1870.[86] Of especial interest for the present context is Usener's mischief in 1881.[87] Friedrich Heimsoeth (1814-1877) died in 1877 and a chair in classical philology became available at Bonn. He was succeeded on 1 April by Eduard Lübbert (1830-1889), a man who possessed

---

[75] See Clara Misch, *Der junge Dilthey: Ein Leben in Briefen und Tagebüchern, 1852-1870* (Berlin 1933).

[76] See Mette 29-30. The date is not given but in 1872 he was called to Zürich, a *terminus ante quem*.

[77] Hermann Usener, *Götternamen: Versuch einer Lehre von der religiösen Begriffs-bildung*[3] (Frankfurt/Main 1948), dedication. On 31 November 1905 W. Dilthey dedicated *Das Erlebnis und die Dichtung* (Berlin 1905) to Usener's memory (ob. 21 October 1905).

[78] Momigliano, *New Paths* 38.

[79] Karl Dilthey often joined his relatives for holidays. The friendship did not wither; see "Briefwechsel zwischen Wilhelm Dilthey und dem Grafen Paul Yorck v. Wartenburg 1877-1897," *Philosophie und Geisteswissenschaften* I ed. Sigrid v. d. Schulenburg (Halle 1923) 5, 31. Revealingly no extensive necrology of Karl Dilthey exists: see F. Leo, "Nachrufe auf W. v. Hartel, Karl Dilthey, Otto Benndorf," *NGG Geschäftliche Mitteilungen* (1907) 3-7. The date of his birth varies. I follow *NDB* with 1839.

[80] See *Selected Correspondence* 14, 301 n. 21.

[81] Momigliano, *New Paths* 34-36. I do not agree (35) that Wilamowitz left Bonn and took his degree at Berlin "because he had offended Usener by a satirical poem." He *tells* us he did so because Jahn had died: see *Selected Correspondence* 36 [and now *Further Letters*, 43-57].

[82] A. Körte, *Die Antike* 11 (1935) 219.

[83] See the excellent remarks of Momigliano, *New Paths* 39.

[84] See *Erinnerungen*[2] 91-92. The *Valediktionsschrift* proves his early familiarity with all Euripides.

[85] This is accepted by Momigliano, *New Paths* 35. The only unambiguous evidence is Ed. Schwartz *GS* I. 323 n. Cf. Herter, 165-66. [See now *Further Letters*, 57.]

[86] He sent a copy of his dissertation with a covering letter to Usener on 27 July 1870: see Usener-Wilamowitz, I (No. 1). One should be cautioned that the texts of these letters are not consistently accurate; see R. Kassel *ZPE* 45 (1982) 283 n. 59 (corrections to the text of No. 2).

[87] See my "Ulrich von Wilamowitz-Moellendorff to Kekule von Stradonitz on Friedrich Gottlieb Welcker," *SIFC* NS 3.1 (1984) 130 n. 104 (= *Further Letters*, 93 n. 104).

"an inner affinity to Pindar" and detected the influence of Terpander on Propertius. "Bonn fährt mit Lübbert elend genug," observed Wilamowitz tartly.[88] The bitterness confirms other sources. Wilamowitz had been considered for the post but discarded for a fool. Usener's opinion was decisive.[89] In 1880 Usener had successfully prevented Wilamowitz from leaving Greifswald. In 1883, through his pliant brother-in-law, he may have tried his luck again. As late as 1897, when writing of Wilamowitz now in Berlin, Wilhelm Dilthey, who knew a good deal about the matter, chronicles the end of a long rivalry.[90]

> Wilamowitz noch nicht gesehen...Seine öffentliche Vorlesung über das griechische Drama hat durch die anthropologische Grundlegung über Drama der Naturvölker große Begeisterung der Studenten erregt. Er nimmt mit Diels die Position einer ganz modernen Psychologie ein. Das Gegengewicht in Bonn wird schwächer: mein Schwager hat nun das eine Auge ganz verloren, das andre ruft bei jedem Gebrauch Schmerzen in dem todten hervor: so ist dies gewaltige Kraft gebrochen.

To sum up: Karl Dilthey's own incompetence provided reason enough to oppose Wilamowitz. His friendship with Rohde and closeness to Usener would have strengthened his determination. That Dilthey[91] and Usener[92] hastened to congratulate the victor is expected. Rohde was silent—and honest. There is one last bit of evidence. In a letter of 8 November 1891 to a young friend, Paul de Lagarde observes of the *Septima*:[93]

> Mit Wilamowitz, Leo, W. Meyer usw. habe ich jetzt alle vierzehn Tage einen philologischen Abend, an dem Heyne und Dilthey nicht Theil nehmen.

2. If the argumentation above is correct, Lagarde joined with Dilthey to prevent the appointment of Wilamowitz. Why? I have no evidence that Lagarde before 1883 had reason to dislike Wilamowitz. I cannot prove that they even corresponded before 1889.[94] Their later friendship and Wilamowitz' admiration, which the hypercritical Lagarde returned,[95] reveal no coolness that might suggest earlier hostility. Lagarde agreed to oppose Wilamowitz because of his loyalty to Schöne, which I shall document

---

[88] Mommsen-Wilamowitz, *Briefwechsel* 89.

[89] See *supra* n. 87.

[90] Dilthey-Wartenburg 239 (No. 151).

[91] An unpublished letter of Karl Dilthey to Wilamowitz, dated 27 July 1883. I publish it for the first time as Appendix I *infra*.

[92] Usener-Wilamowitz, 32-33 (No. 20). The date is precisely the same and suggests collusion. The effusion seems excessive. Notice that the letter is numbered *19*; but in fact is No. 20. The letter printed as No. 20 is in fact No. 19.

[93] Schemann, *Paul de Lagarde*[3] 373.

[94] See *supra* n. 57.

[95] See Schemann, *Paul de Lagarde*[3] 354.

below, and his hatred of Wilamowitz' father-in-law, Theodor Mommsen (1817-1903). Lagarde detested the man Mommsen for two reasons. The value of his work he grudgingly admitted.[96] Lagarde was politically conservative, while Mommsen, in Lagarde's eyes, was an irresponsible liberal, comparable perhaps to Virchow.[97] Mommsen reciprocated Lagarde's hatred. It is a pity that he expressed himself so virulently that his editors have censored the text.[98] Wilamowitz did not share Mommsen's political views. If anything, they embarrassed him.[99] But Lagarde in 1883 could not easily have known the young man's politics. Wilamowitz, it is often forgotten, was not blatantly political before 1914. A *Junker* who had deserted his class and married the bourgeois daughter of a liberal would be suspect.

Lagarde, a passionate man, had one special reason to be furious with Mommsen in 1883. On 12 July 1880, through Mommsen's carelessness,[100] fire had destroyed the library in his home on the Marchstraße, Charlottenburg. The details are available elsewhere.[101] The shattering loss proved Mommsen's resilience and the international collaboration to restore the library its fame.[102] I have seen no accurate report of the ancient manuscripts destroyed in the fire. Adelheid Mommsen reports that "two manuscripts on loan from Brussels and Halle" were destroyed.[103] In July 1880 Wilamowitz knew only of the Breslau MS of Jordanes.[104] A Trinity manuscript, MS 0.4.36 (1266), "a twelfth-century *Ethicus* and Antonine Itinerary" is reported by Montague Rhodes James as "Destroyed by fire in the house of Professor

---

[96] Lagarde writes to Alfred Schöne in a letter of 28 April 1876 cited by Schemann, *Paul de Lagarde*[3] 344 n. 10 (of Mommsen):

> Er ist ein bedeutender Gelehrter, vielleicht sollte ich sagen eine bedeutende Arbeitskraft und ein großer Anempfinder: als Mensch soll er mir weit ab von Halse bleiben.

Schemann considers this his "Dauermeinung über Mommsen."

[97] One need only recall Bismarck's libel suit against Mommsen: see Wickert IV. 94-122. The trial gained wide publicity in early 1882.

[98] See Mommsen-Wilamowitz, *Briefwechsel* 453 (No. 358): "In Lagarde steckte wohl manches, das einen rechten Mann gemacht habe würde; aber [...]."

[99] See *Selected Correspondence* 57-63.

[100] See Adelheid Mommsen, *Theodor Mommsen im Kreise der Seinen* (Berlin 1936) 54: "Im Juli war durch Unvorsichtigkeit des Vaters jener Brand ausgebrochen..."; cf. Wickert IV. 43: "durch das Verschulden des großen Mannes."

[101] See especially Wickert IV. 42-45, 263-65 to which should be added Wilamowitz to Usener of 15 July 1880 (Usener-Wilamowitz, 16-17) and Friedrich Nietzsche to Peter Gast of 18 July 1880 (*KGB* III. 1.29). The latter especially rewards attention for it reveals Nietzsche's respect for Mommsen. I am grateful to U.K. Goldsmith for alerting me to the text.

[102] Thus Wickert IV. 43.

[103] Adelheid Mommsen, *Theodor Mommsen* 54. She provides no further details. I assume the family sought to underplay the loss.

[104] Usener-Wilamowitz, 16 (No. 11): "Von Handschriften weiß ich sicher nur die Pfälzer, die mit Jordanes ja so viel Unika enthielt, außerdem interpolierte..." See further *Erinnerungen*[2] 181-82.

Theodor Mommsen, to whom it had been lent by the College."[105] There may have been others. The result of the fire was that European libraries refused henceforth to lend ancient MSS to private scholars. Lagarde's work on the Septuagint suffered considerably. He writes:[106]

> So oft ich das Ende von Mommsens Vorrede zum Jordanes in die Hand nehme, ergrimme ich darüber, daß dieser Gelehrte gar nicht wissen will, wie sehr er die Wissenschaft geschädigt hat. Meine Septuaginta hat er geradezu unmöglich gemacht. Ich verbitte mir alle ungezogenen Bemerkungen darüber, daß ich Handschriften des Auslandes nicht benutzt habe: aller Tadel dafür ist an Herrn Mommsen, und ist an die Regierungen und Bibliotheksverwaltungen zu richten, welche die verschiedenen casus Mommsen gegen alle Handschriften brauchende Gelehrten genutzt haben. Zu reisen, wie ich möchte, ermöglicht mir mein Einkommen nicht; nur wer vor sich trommeln und blasen heißt, bringt es in unsrer Zeit zu etwas, und die welche trommeln und blasen heißen, sind meist danach, keine Musik zu verdienen.

His biographer sums up the matter:[107]

> In Lagarde selbst hatte sich mit den Jahren ein leidenschaftlicher Zorn gegen Mommsen angesammelt, mit dem er ja auch mehrmals, wenn auch nie direkt, heftig zusammenstieß, wie in der Angelegenheit der Moabitica und in Personalfragen. Dem Fasse den Boden ausschlagen sollte die berühmte Brand- und Handschriftensache, die in ihren Rückwirkungen Lagarde aufs schwerste schädigte, und über die er sich auch öffentlich aufs ingrimmigste geäußert hat. Momentsaufwallungen, die bei ihm—auch brieflich—an der Tagesordnung waren, sollen hier am wenigsten festgehalten werden.

To sum up: there is no evidence that Lagarde disliked Wilamowitz personally before 1883 nor disparaged his scholarship. Lagarde, however, had long before 1883 intensely hated his father-in-law as a human being, had misgivings about his scholarship, and during 1882-1883 had suffered considerably in his own editorial work because of Mommsen's carelessness. Lagarde's "very definite reason" may have been that to import Wilamowitz would be to import Mommsen into Göttingen academic affairs with all that implied. That once Lagarde met Wilamowitz (he did not until after the

---

[105] See Richard William Pfaff, *Montague Rhodes James* (London 1980) 190.

[106] I cite Paul de Lagarde, *Mitteilungen* II (1887) 280-81, as cited in the transcription of Wolfgang Buchwald by Wickert IV. 265.

[107] Schemann, *Paul de Lagarde*³ 344 n. 10. His hatred of Mommsen survived his friendship with Wilamowitz, who himself was ambivalent. In a letter from Rome to "a young friend" dated 10 April 1885 Lagarde writes (Schemann, *op. cit.*, 371): "Und nun kommt Mommsen noch! Der fehlte mir gerade. Doch wird er meine Kreise nicht kreuzen." Again the censor prevents us from knowing what follows.

appointment and subsequent removal to Göttingen) he quickly discarded Dilthey, proves the lack of any personal animus.

3. Why did Lagarde and by implication his "comrades" prefer Alfred Schöne to the most brilliant Hellenist in Europe? Schöne had one indisputable advantage. He threatened no one on campus.[108] He loved music. He had served in the diplomatic corps and spoke fluent French. He was gentleman and bellelettrist. He had no enemy and was loved by all who crossed his path. His only remembered contribution to classical scholarship before 1883 was an incomplete edition of Eusebius edited with others some 15 years before. There had also been work on Jerome. He had long planned an edition of Thucydides but (like Lagarde's) his work remained *Vorarbeiten*. Hude did the edition which Schöne reviewed. He better deserved a chair in Germanistik or even musicology. He had edited several volumes of Lessing's correspondence and his *Bildende Kunst*. In 1898 he would publish his most lasting work, the edition of *Campagne in Frankreich 1792* for the Weimar edition of Goethe's opera. In imitation of his teacher's, Otto Jahn's, research on Mozart, Schöne edited in 1867 the letters of Beethoven to Marie Countess Erdödy and in 1871 those of Moritz Hauptmann, musical director at the Thomasschule in Leipzig, to Franz Hauser. He even composed and, what was worse, published 12 Lieder with pianoforte accompaniment. In 1880 Schöne, the German Montague Rhodes James, published a ghost-story, entitled "The Blue Veil," and good enough to be republished four years later by Paul Heyse (1830-1914), the eromenos of Jacob Bernays (Schöne was a Bonn man) and later Nobel prize winner.[109] Schöne died in 1918 but published nothing after 1901. In 1915 he plays a pathetic role in an abortive attempt by the incompetent Bickel to gain an *Ordinariat* for himself at Kiel. It was quashed by Jacoby.[110]

What was Schöne's career before 1883? He had habilitated in Leipzig in 1864, and taught there as Dozent while sharing in the musical life of the great city. In 1869 he succeeded H. Keil as Ordinarius for philology and ancient history at Erlangen. There was a scandal that Schöne never forgot.[111] Leave was arranged. He travelled to Rome in 1872 and resigned

---

[108] What follows derives from Rudolf Ehwald, *op. cit.* (*supra* n. 59). It would be cumbersome to provide a page reference for every assertion.

[109] See Paul Heyse, *Jugenderinnerungen und Bekenntnisse*[3] (Berlin 1900) esp. 93-109 ("Bonner Studien"). For Bernays' fascination with the young Heyse see Hans I. Bach, "Jacob Bernays: Ein Beitrag zur Emanzipationsgeschichte der Juden und zur Geschichte des deutschen Geistes im neunzehnten Jahrhundert," *Schriftenreihe wissenschaftlicher Abhandlungen des Leo Baeck Instituts* 30 (Tübingen 1974) 87-92 ("Der fazinierende junge Heyse").

[110] Details are preserved in an unpublished letter of Felix Jacoby (1876-1959) to Wilamowitz, dated Kiel 28 January 1915. Jacoby protrays Schöne as senile and Bickel as unscrupulous and incompetent. He calls the whole affair "das Satyrspiel."

[111] See Ehwald 93: "Doch sollte er in Erlangen nicht warm werden: ...es kam anderes hinzu, das den Erlanger Aufenthalt zur unglücklichsten Zeit seines Lebens machte." This is a cover-up. Some sort of unpleasantness had occurred. The evidence does not allow us to be more specific.

his post in 1874. After brief residence in Gotha, he served 1877-1884 as cultural attaché to the German Embassy in Paris. He was welcome at parties and greeted visiting scholars warmly. Among others he befriended Usener.[112] But the Parisian appointment was running out. "Schöne was deeply worried about his future."[113]

This man appeared on the same list with Hartel and Wilamowitz. Lagarde was prepared to argue his case to Althoff against Wilamowitz. Why? The answer lies in Lagarde's character. In published polemic he often seems brutal.[114] In fact those who best knew him concur that toward those whom he trusted he was loving, loyal, pathetically grateful for any kindness shown him. The pattern is not unknown. Lagarde had few friends. One was Alfred Schöne. Ehwald dates Schöne's friendship with Lagarde to Schleusingen (1866-68).[115] They certainly corresponded earlier. Schemann published a personal letter of Lagarde to Schöne (*aet.* 29), dated Berlin 11 October 1865.[116] I suggest that contact between the two may have begun when Schöne reviewed Lagarde's edition of Scaliger's poems in *Grenzboten* 2 (1864) 197. Lagarde early trusted Schöne as the revealing letter of 8 April 1866[117] proves. Eusebius, Jerome, Scaliger and music were common interests. Schemann calls him "one of the oldest and most loyal friends of Lagarde."[118] By 1883 they had known one another well for some twenty years. Lagarde had looked after Schöne in Paris and acquainted him with the French Assyriologist, J. Oppert.[119] He knew that Schöne desperately needed a permanent post in Germany with a pension at the end.[120] Lagarde's loyalty to a trusted friend warped his judgment. Brandl alleges that Lagarde had clout with Althoff.[121] Fortunately not clout enough for Althoff to allow Schöne over Wilamowitz. But it is no coincidence that on 1 July 1885 Schöne became University-Librarian at Göttingen, a post he held until

---

[112] Ehwald 95.

[113] Thus Ehwald 97 of Winter 1884. Schöne knew earlier that time had become a factor.

[114] Lagarde gathered critical reviews of his works into a volume which he published at his own expense adding vigorous rebuttals: see Paul de Lagarde, *Aus dem deutschen Gelehrtenleben: Aktenstücke und Glossen* (Göttingen 1880) and Stern 11-12. Wilamowitz could only have smiled.

[115] Ehwald 92.

[116] Schemann, *Paul de Lagarde*[3] 365-66.

[117] See Schemann 67 n. 47.

[118] Schemann 364. Here Schemann attests (365) that Schöne was long scholarly adviser and attaché at the German Embassy in Paris. Otto Lüders held the similar post at Athens.

[119] See Ehwald 95.

[120] Schöne wrote to Ehwald on 19 May 1884 (Ehwald 97, who seems to have misdated a letter of 1885):

> Aber ich muß fragen, ob ich ein Recht hatte, auf mehr zu hoffen, und ich will zufrieden darüber sein, daß ich endlich wieder ein Amt habe mit festen Pflichten und Rechten und Pensionsberechtigung, vor allem im preußenischen Staatsdienst und wieder in Deutschlang.

[121] Brandl 217: "vom mächtigen Lagardeverehrer Althoff."

1887, when he succeeded H. Jordan at Königsberg. In 1892 he migrated to Kiel.

Lagarde's loyalty to Schöne caused him to propose the lesser man. Althoff, supported by Sauppe, secured the chair for Wilamowitz.[122] Lagarde, however, exacted the library post for Schöne and two years later a chair in far off East Prussia. There was no friction between Wilamowitz and Schöne. Wilamowitz had always liked him.[123] He respected his more famous younger brother, Richard Schöne (1840-1922), General Director of the Royal Museums at Berlin, for whom Wilamowitz later delivered the memorial address at the Academy in Berlin.[124] Schöne, so far as I know, bore no grudge against Wilamowitz. His only published reference to the younger rival is laudatory.[125] The tale ends happily. Excellence for once received its due. The injustices of 1877 and 1881 were not repeated. Göttingen and classical philology, not only Wilamowitz, were the winners.

Appendix I

Karl Dilthey to Ulrich von Wilamowitz-Moellendorff

Göttingen 27 VII 83.[126]

Verehrter Herr Kollege

Endlich also die ersehnte Botschaft, und das Schifflein unserer Vorschläge durch alle Klippen glücklich hindurch gelangt. Für mich ist damit das Ziel mehr als dreijährigen Wünschens, Bemühens und Harrens erreicht. Als ich seinerzeit die Berufung nach Heidelberg hatte, die mich mehr lickte, wie Sie sich denken können, setzte ich bereits in Berlin ein mit

---

[122] Further grounds for Wilamowitz' loyalty to Althoff; see *Erinnerungen*[2] 249-51. For Althoff's trust in Wilamowitz see Brandl 219 where Wilamowitz at Göttingen in 1888 is "Der gewichtigste unter den vertrauten Ratgebern Althoffs am Orte."

[123] See *Erinnerungen*[2] 128, 147.

[124] For this great figure see Ludwig Pallat, *Richard Schöne Generaldirektor der königlichen Museen zu Berlin: Ein Beitrag zur Geschichte der preußischen Kunstverwaltung 1872-1905* (Berlin 1959), and Wilamowitz, *KS* VI. 68-70. Richard Schöne knew Karl Dilthey slightly: see Pallat 26, 38.

[125] See Alfred Schöne, *Über die Alkestis des Euripides: Rede zur Feier des Geburtstag Sr. Maj. des Deutschen Kaiser Königs von Preussen Wilhelm II gehalten an der Christian-Albrechts-Universität am 27. Januar 1895* (Kiel 1895) 19:

> Um so nothwendiger ist die eifrige Pflege der Euripideischen Studien, und um so erfreulicher ist es, dass die jüngste Vergangenheit für die Würdigung des Dichters wie einzelner seiner Tragödien eine Reihe bedeutender Leistungen gezeigt hat, welche vornehmlich U. v. Wilamowitz angehören, und deren Vorzüge auch der dankbar erkenne wird...

[126] Presumably on the morning of the 27th the appointment was announced in the press; for on the same day a similarly unctuous letter was penned by Usener: see *supra* n. 92.

meinem Verlangen einer Hülfe. Damals glaubte ich freilich meine Blicke auf Sie für erste nicht richten zu sollen und dürfen. Es handelte sich zunächst um einen Extraordinarius, und am Nächsten lag es, einen Latinisten zu begehren. Schon damals bezeichnete ich Göppert[127] Sie als denjenigen, der an Sauppes Stelle gehöre, wenn dieser einmal zurückträte.[128] Sobald ich mich vergewissert, daß in nicht zu langer Zeit ein Ordinarius erreichbar sei, verzichtete ich dann auf die nicht ohne Anstrengung durchgesetzte Concession, und zog vor, die höchst unvollkommenen und lästigen Verhältnisse lieber noch eine Zeit lang zu tragen, um einer möglichst befriedigenden Gestaltung der Dinge die Bahn offen zu halten. Endlich glaubte der Minister resp. Göppert[129] genügenden Anhalt zu haben Leutsch,[130] der längst ein στέλεχος,[131] bei Seite schieben zu dürfen. Auch da gingen—naturgemäß—Sauppe's und meine Gedanken zunächst auf einen Latinisten. Mir war keine der in dieser Richtung möglichen Lösungen ganz befriedigend. Eine günstige Wendung des Gespräches (S. hatte Kaibel[132] gennant, weil er im Universitätskalender gesehen, daß dieser ein Latinum angekundigt)[133] ermutigte mich, Ihren Namen zu nennen, was ich sonst— aus begreiflichen Rücksichten—nicht gewagt hätte—und nun waren wir schnell einig.[134] Es war gemeinsamer Abmachung entsprechend, daß S. dann an Sie scrieb,[135] und billig, daß ich ihm den Vortritt ließ. Sie sehen, verehrter Herr Kollege, wie sehr Ihre Voraussetzung, daß Ihr Kommen mit meinen Wünschen übereinstimmte, den thatsächlichen Verhältnissen entspricht. Mit herzlicher Befriedigung und voll der besten Hoffnungen heiße ich Sie zum Voraus bei uns willkommen. Ich hege die gute Zuversicht, daß wir, wie sehr verschieden auch unsere Naturen und zum Theil unsere Gewohnheiten sind, doch in gleichem Sinn und ernstem Willen an der Aufgabe, die uns zusammensführt, arbeiten werden: vor Allem, was ich als gutes Omen begreife und festhalte: in gegenseitigem *Vertrauen*.[136]

---

[127] Heinrich Göppert, since 1874 Ministerialrat, died in autumn 1882 and was succeeded by Althoff on 21 October 1882. The coincidence of the Göttingen vacancy and Althoff's translation to Berlin released Wilamowitz from Greifswald. Dilthey knew that Göppert was dead and his assertion could not be denied. For Göppert see Sachse 39 and vom Brocke 40.

[128] *Passim* Dilthey seeks to ally Wilamowitz with him against Sauppe. Fortunately Wilamowitz knew better.

[129] Göppert, like Althoff until 1897, was adviser to the Minister of Education, not Minister.

[130] See *supra* with n. 47.

[131] See Lysippos, frag. 7. 1 Kock = *CAF* 1. 702 (= 8. 1 K-A= *PCG* V. 621).

[132] The great Hellenist, Wilamowitz' close friend and later successor at Göttingen, Georg Kaibel (1849-1901): see W. Radtke, *BiogJahr* 123 (1904) 115-71.

[133] A gratuitous remark, meant to imply the superficiality of Sauppe's judgment.

[134] *Sc.* Dilthey, and not Sauppe, initiated Wilamowitz' call to Göttingen. Nonsense.

[135] Dilthey had to explain away Sauppe's letter of February 1883 (see *Erinnerungen*² 197). Sauppe had only been the tool of Dilthey, who, out of courtesy, had allowed the senior colleague to write. *Cras credam.*

[136] Dilthey had never met Wilamowitz but is an expert on his nature and peculiarities. As to the flattery and trust, methinks the lady doth protest too much.

Die Richtung unserer Wahl wird ja vielfach überraschen und kritisirt werden,[137] ja das Letztere ist schon reichlich geschehen, die Superfötation mit Gräzisten ist Vielen anstössig. Hätten wir Sie ins Lateinische übersetzt haben können, so müssten Sie zur Zeit uns noch willkommener sein.[138] Aber daß wir auch so Sie lieber gewollt, als irgend einen der habhaften Latinisten, mag Ihnen zeigen, wie ernst es uns ist und welchen Werth wir auf Ihre persönliche Kraft legen, und inbesondere ist für unser philologisches Studium die persönliche virtus des Lehrenden immer ungleich wichtiger erschienen, wie sein Repertoire. Sauppe ist im 75 Jahre; wenn er zurücktritt, wird ein Latinist eingepflanzt werden müssen. Hoffentlich ist auch dann diese Frage befriedigender, als jetzt, zu lösen. Einstweilen müssen wir nur ein wenig rücken (?), und wenn auch mit vorübergehenden Unbequemlichkeiten, zusammen das Bedürfniss zu decken suchen. Ich gestehe Ihnen aber offenherzig, daß ich Ihrer Natur und Ihren Jahren die grössere (?) Expansivkraft zutraue. Und so hoffe ich, daß wir gut zusammen am Strang ziehen werden, wenn auch Sie feuriger, als ich. Daß ich Ihnen ein gutes Theil meines Einflußes und meiner Betriebsamkeit werde abzutreten haben, weiß ich, und scheue ich nicht, da es zum Besten unserer philologischen Studien geschehen wird. Und ich bin eigennützig genug, auch daran zu denken, daß ich selber einer Auffrischung bedarf, wie die Göttinger Philologie seit Dezennien, und auch für mich nicht wenig von Ihnen zu erwarten.

Sauppe geht morgen als Deputirter nach Zürich zur Jubiläumsfeier; ich selber wollte den Mittwoch eben dahin reisen. Aber es ist mir wichtig und unbedingt nöthig, daß wir uns sehen, und sprechen, als daß ich, als supernumerarer Deputirter, in Z. erscheine.[139] Und auch bei der nicht leichten Aufgabe der Wohnungssuche kann ich Ihnen nützlich sein. Mein Entschluß, die Reise aufzugeben (am 2. und 3. August ist das Fest) war also so fort gefasst, als ich Ihren Brief empfing. Dafür bitte aber auch ich um eine Concession. Ich habe schon seit einiger Zeit meine Vorlesung duplirt—Seminar vergangenen Freitag geschlossen—um zeitig fertig zu sein. Ueber längstens Mittwoch hinaus habe ich hier Nichts mehr zu schaffen. Könnten Sie da nicht vielleicht schon am Freitag oder Sonnabend hier erscheinen? Freilich, sollten Sie am Sonnabend noch examiniren müssen, so wurde ich natürlich mich bis Sonntag oder Montag gedulden. Hierüber also bitte ich um freundliche Nachricht.

Was das Seminar betrifft, so hatten wir, da zur Zeit als der Katalog der Vorlesungen zu machen war, weder eine Berufung erfolgt war noch auch für

---

[137] A Hellenist had been preferred to the needed Latinist. But Dilthey also confirms the testimony of Th. Mommsen, Ed. Schwartz, and Wilamowitz himself (see *Selected Correspondence* 301 with n. 19) that his honesty and excellence had gained enemies among the second-rate.

[138] As soon as possible and with the appointments of Wilhelm Meyer and Friedrich Leo: see *Erinnerungen*[2] 207-08.

[139] A godgiven opportunity to speak alone to Wilamowitz with Sauppe safely in Zürich.

den Winter mehr zu erwarten schien, uns aufs Neue der freundlichen Mitwirkung von Dr. Bruns[140] versichern zu müssen geglaubt; er übernahm wiederum das Proseminar, und hat Seneca's Briefe als Interpretationsstoff gewählt. Nach unseren Statuten hat von den drei Direktoren des Seminars immer einer semesterweise das Proseminar zu leiten, während die zwei anderen die Interpretationen und Disputationen (über Arbeiten) im Seminar zu dirigiren haben. Da Sie nun als der Jüngste hinzutreten, läge es wohl am Nächsten, daß Sie jetzt das Proseminar übernehmen, im folgenden Sommersemester ich an Ihre Stelle trete, dann Sauppe. Indessen würde ebenso gern ich jetzt das Proseminar nehmen, wenn Sie irgend wie das vorziehen sollten.[141] Sauppe traktirt im Sommer Tacitus hist.; ich habe Hesiod angezeigt u. was die Kollegien angeht, so liest S. Epigraphik u. Terenz (2 Privatvorlesungen, wie er immer thut), ich griech. Tragoedie. Ich würde Ihnen vorschlagen mit einer Vorlesung einzutreten, die sogleich eine Lücke füllt, die länger empfunden wird, wie etwa Metrik. Irre ich nicht, so lasen Sie in Greifswald Metrik in Verbindung mit Interpretation der griechischen Lyriker.[142] Oder auch Geschichte der griechischen Prosa bis auf Demosthenes. Pindar interpretirt Leutsch, hat wenigstens angezeigt.

Lassen Sie mich bei diesem erfreulichen Anlaß eine alte zeitweilig drückende Schuld abtragen. Sie haben mich mit mancher werthvollen literarischen Gabe erfreut, die ich infecunditatis causa nicht zu vergelten vermocht. Ich bin ein sehr säumiger Briefschreiber, und tröstete mich mit der eitelen Hoffnung, meine Erkenntlichkeit durch Gegengaben an den Tag legen zu können. Dazu schien ich mir jedesmal nicht recht danken zu können, ehe ich das Innere des Geschenkes auch recht kennen gelernt, was nicht so schnell von Statten ging. Nicht wenig verdanke ich Ihrem Antigonos.[143] Ich bin schrittweise dieselben Gedankenpfade gewandelt, habe aber kein Kapitel Ihres Buches ohne Belehrung u. Anregung gelesen.[144] Und doch—die meiste Freude machte mir eigentlich das Widmungsblatt.[145] Sie

---

[140] Ivo Bruns (1853-1901) promoted at Bonn in 1877 under Usener and habilitated at Göttingen in 1880 under Sauppe. He remained at Göttingen until 1884 and would have had no say in the Wilamowitz appointment.

[141] Wilamowitz gave the proseminar in SS 1884 on Euripides, *Medea* and again in WS 1884-1885 on Cicero, *de optimo genere orationum.*

[142] Wilamowitz had offered *Metrische Übungen* at Greifswald SS 1882 and WS 1882-1883. He would at Göttingen SS 1884.

[143] Ulrich von Wilamowitz-Moellendorff, "Antigonos von Karystos," *Philologische Untersuchungen* 4 (Berlin 1881): see *Selected Correspondence* 297-304.

[144] Comparison with the replies of Wilamowitz to those who sent him their books proves what Wilamowitz must have thought of this. That anyone would wait three years to thank Wilamowitz for *Antigonos* is explicable only if he wished to humiliate its author.

[145] *I.e.,* "Hermann Usener gewidmet."

verstehen mich.[146] Dann überraschten Sie mich ganz kürzlich mit dem Kallimachos,[147] womit Sie mir eine Arbeit abgenommen haben.[148] Aber nun genug—mündlich mehr und viel mehr!

Ihr

K. Dilthey[149]

[146] With this gratuitous and intrusive reference to the youthful quarrel with Usener, Dilthey tastelessly reveals his hand.

[147] Udalricus de Wilamowitz-Moellendorff, *Callimachi Hymni et Epigrammata* (Berlin 1882). For praise of Dilthey's earlier work on Callimachus see Rudolfus Pfeiffer, *Callimachus* II *Hymni et Epigrammata* (Oxford 1953) xlvi.

[148] This sounds rude but in fact Dilthey had earlier promised an edition of all the fragments: see Pfeiffer, *loc. cit. (supra* n. 147).

[149] Dilthey's hand is extraordinarily difficult. Without the remarkable transcription of Ulrich K. Goldsmith, improved in a number of places by Albert Henrichs, I could not have read, much less edited, this document. The whole manuscript has been rigorously improved by R.L. Fowler (Waterloo), U.K. Goldsmith (Colorado), Albert Henrichs (Harvard) and M.H. Chambers (Los Angeles). I am most grateful. This article is an attempt to reconstruct what happened on the basis of evidence available to me. I am ready to modify my views should new documents warrant modification.

On 5 July 1984 I was able to examine the *Acta* concerning Wilamowitz' call to Göttingen in 1883, preserved in the University Archive there. I am grateful to Frau Bruns and Dr. Haenel for their help. The decisive document is a copy of a letter by Paul de Lagarde (Dean), dated 21 May 1883 (the day before Th. Mommsen's letter to his brother Tycho), to the Minister of Education at Berlin, von Gossler. The list there submitted was: 1. Hartel; 2. Rudolf Schoell (Wilamowitz' *bête noire*); 3. Wilamowitz. Schöne was vetoed by Althoff. The Latinist Schoell, friendly to the Ritschl group and safe, was inserted and Wilamowitz relegated to third place. To the credit of de Lagarde the assessment of Wilamowitz is eminently fair. I cite the pertinent passages:

> Er besitzt eine für sein jugendliches Alter höchst ausgedehnte Gelehrsamkeit und eine Energie der Forschung, die überall den Kern der Sache zu erfassen bemüht ist, in kühner Verbindung von Thatsachen und kecken Folgerungen nicht selten das Maß überschreitet, aber immer durch Scharfsinn und lebensvolle Behandlung fesselt und anregt...Aber besondere Hervorhebung verdient bei ihm die ausgezeichnete Art u. Weise, in welcher er die Studierenden zu selbstständiger Forschung anzuregen, mit Liebe zu angestranger Tätigkeit zu erfüllen und ihre Studien mit Hingebung zu leiten versteht, wie dies alle, die seine Wirksamkeit zu beobachten Gelegenheit haben, bezeugen und eine Anzahl von Promotionsschriften zeigt, die, seit er in Greifswald ist, dort erschienen sind. Die Gegenstände seiner Vorlesungen sind Homer, Pindar, Euripídes, Aristophanes, Thukydides, Catull, Ovidius; griechische Dialekte, Quellenkunde der griechischen Geschichte, grammatische Literatur der Griechen.

I am grateful to Dr. Renate Schlesier for aid in decipherment. I have further discovered and hope to publish Wilamowitz' reply to Sauppe's initial query. [See *Philologus* 129 (1985) 286-98 (= *Further Letters* 223-35).]

ECCE HOMO:
THE AUTOBIOGRAPHICAL IN
WILAMOWITZ'
SCHOLARLY WRITINGS

1. The Problem

Americans do not believe what they read in ancient authors. Germans did. The distinction is telling. Barthold Georg Niebuhr in summer 1822 wrote a famous letter, "an einen...Jüngling,...welcher Philologie studiren wollte." I cite only a revealing passage:[1]

> Homer, Aeschylus, Sophokles, Pindar, das sind die Dichter des Jünglings, das sind die, an denen die grossen Männer sich nährten, und welche, so lange Literatur die Welt erleuchet, die jugendlich mit ihnen erfüllte Seele fürs Leben veredeln werden...Zu jenen Dichtern und unter den Prosaikern zu Herodot, Thukydides, Demosthenes, Plutarch, zu Cicero, Livius, Cäsar, Sallust, Tacitus—zu diesen bitte ich Dich dringend Dich zu wenden, Dich ausschliesslich an sie zu halten. Lies sie nicht, um ästhetische Reflexionen über sie zu machen, sondern, um Dich in sie hineinzulesen und Deine Seele mit ihren Gedanken zu erfüllen, um durch die Lectüre zu gewinnen, wie Du durch das ehrerbietige Zuhören bei der Rede grosser Männer gewinnen würdest.

Wilamowitz attests that matters had not changed in the Pforte of his time. The boys read Tacitus with Rector Peter:[2]

> In der Tragödie der Kaiser des julisch-claudischen Geschlechtes, wie Tacitus sie gestaltet hat, sollte unser sittliches Empfinden und Urteilen gestärkt werden.

During his most impressionable years Wilamowitz learned from his beloved teacher an intensely personal approach to a text, to find something there that would make him better. This means to judge morally what the ancients said. It is a far cry from the historian that demands the interpreter become part of the first audience of Aristophanes, *Lysistrata*.[3] There is nothing of the delusion of an arid objectivity that ends in a text both trivial and remote. This same urgency enlivens the protreptic preface (1902) to *Griechisches*

---

[1] Johannes Classen, *Barthold Georg Niebuhr. Eine Gedächtnisschrift zu seinem hundertjährigen Geburtstage, den 27. August 1876* (Gotha 1876) 142.

[2] Wilamowitz, *Erinnerungen*[2], 76.

[3] Wilamowitz, *Lysistrate*, 5; *Briefe Stenzel*, 95-96; W.M. Calder III, *Antiqua* 23 (Naples 1983), 227 n. 99 (henceforth: Calder).

Lesebuch, the volume proved by the letters to have cost him more toil and doubt than any other. Greek authors will teach the boy to become a better citizen and—rather unexpectedly—win his soul for the Kingdom of God.[4] That requires belief. It is remarkably near to what eight years before he had vehemently criticized in Ernst Curtius' *Geschichte*, the aim "das edle zu loben, das schlechte zu tadeln," that is the use of Greek history to provide material for homilies.[5] Another example that proves Jaeger's point:[6]

> Zwei Seelen rangen in seiner Brust unaufhörlich miteinander: der Historiker, der nichts anderes wissen will als was gewesen ist, und der Humanist und Philologe, der anbeten und verkünden muß was groß und ewig ist.

On 3 June 1908 Wilamowitz revealed to an Oxford audience:[7]

> The tradition is dead; our task is to revivify life that has passed away. We know that ghosts cannot speak until they have drunk blood; and the spirits which we evoke demand the blood of our hearts. We give it to them gladly; but if they then abide our question, something from us has entered into them; something alien, that must be cast out, cast out in the name of truth!

This idea of revivification is fundamental to the Wilamowitzian conception of philology.[8] In part it is the influence of Anton Springer.[9] Professor Huxley has reminded us that Gilbert Murray cited these words in his inaugural address.[10] Sir Ernest Barker remembered them alone from the two Oxford lectures forty-five years later.[11] Arthur Darby Nock often repeated them.[12] A present Regius Professor will use them to title his collected

---

[4] Wilamowitz, *Lesebuch* I, viii. Wilamowitz was never a Christian: see *Latin Autobiography*, 42 with n. 41. A Platonic theist, he declared: *Fidem profiteor Platonicam*, Norden, 668. Hugh Lloyd-Jones wrongly calls him an atheist ("Rudolf Carl Franz Otto Pfeiffer", *Proceedings of the British Academy* 65 [1979] 771-81, at 773; repr. in: H. L.-J., *Blood for the Ghosts. Classical Influences in the Nineteenth and Twentieth Centuries* [London 1982] 261-70, at 263).

[5] Wilamowitz, *Aristoteles* I 377.

[6] Jaeger, cxxvi-cxxvii (219) (after Goethe, *Faust* I, v. 1112).

[7] *Greek Historical Writing*, in *Lectures*, 3-26, quotation 25 (= *Hellenistische Geschichtsschreibung*, in *Reden* II, 216-46, cf. 245).

[8] Wilamowitz, *Philologie*, 1, and *Trauerspiele*, 3 n. 18. Note the frequent use of 'lebendig' in his scholarly vocabulary.

[9] For a striking parallel compare Anton Springer *apud* Udo Kultermann, *Geschichte der Kunstgeschichte. Der Weg einer Wissenschaft* [Ullstein Sachbücher. 34054] (Frankfurt a. M. 1981) 214.

[10] *The Interpretation of Ancient Greek Literature* (Oxford 1909) 19.

[11] *Age and Youth. Memories of Three Universities and Father of the Man* (Oxford 1953) 79.

[12] In seminars and lectures: see also A.D. Nock, *Conversion. The Old and the New in Religion from Alexander the Great to Augustine of Hippo* (Oxford 1972[6] [1933[1]]) 270.

essays. The Victorians passionately agreed.[13] How splendid that the greatest German shared their view. Wilamowitz' words are the metaphorical confession of the essential subjective in his writings. When he informs Drachmann on 10 August 1929 that he could never study Demosthenes with care for the lawyer so disgusted him, we see in a negative way precisely the same admission.[14] That Wilamowitz was taught to believe the authors he read and that he recognized publicly the indispensable subjective in his interpretations should alert us to a personal concern in his work of a sort the modern "objective scholar" would claim to scorn. Not surprisingly Wilamowitz distinguished between books he had to write and books he wanted to write, between *Pflicht* and *Neigung*. He puts this beyond all doubt in a candid letter to the young Eduard Norden of 16 May 1903:[15]

> Entweder sind unsere Bücher etwas Fremdes, an dem wir arbeiten, wie eine Edition, oder sie sind Kinder: die kann man nicht noch einmal machen, die sind Fleisch von unserm Fleisch. Die leben aber, wenn sie geboren sind, ihr eigenes Leben.

It is these 'children' that absorb the biographer. Which are they? What do they reveal of their father?

2. Sorts of Books

Pflichtarbeiten are easy. Mommsen ordered Wilamowitz to edit the *Kleine Schriften* of his teacher, Moriz Haupt. He groaned but did it well and learned a lot.[16] He thought it a duty to edit or interpret new papyri that came his way. Aristotle, *Athenaion Politeia*, which entailed the welcome *Zusammenarbeit* with Kaibel, Bacchylides, Callimachus,[17] Menander, Sophocles, *Ichneutai*, which also interested Carl Robert, and Timotheus are the famous examples. The correspondence with Grenfell, Hunt, Körte, and Smiley demonstrates an intense collaboration, revealed only in part by scores of references in published volumes.[18] Professor Pintaudi's publication of the letters to Vitelli deserves notice here.[19] Then there were inscriptions,

---

[13] Frank M. Turner, *The Greek Heritage in Victorian Britain* (New Haven/London 1981) *passim*. Expurgation in Victorian classics reveals the intense effort to remake Greeks into themselves: see K.J. Dover, "Expurgation of Greek Literature," in *Les Études classiques aux XIX⁀ et XX⁀ siècles. Leur Place dans l'histoire des idées* (Entretiens sur l'Antiquité Classique 26) Vandœuvres/Genève 1979, 55-89.

[14] W.M. Calder III, "Wilamowitz on Demosthenes", *CW* 72 (1978-79) 239-40.

[15] Calder, 214.

[16] Wilamowitz, *Erinnerungen*², 176.

[17] Compare *Briefe Gomperz*, 296-98, with *Über die Hekale des Kallimachos*, NGG 1893, 731-47 (= *Kl. Schr.* II, 30-47).

[18] Notice entries MA (= *Mitarbeiter* in *Bibliographie, passim*).

[19] See *AnnPisa* 3, 3 (1981) 363-98.

whether new finds[20] or re-editing the known. How often is he cited in *IG*
XIV? Of course a special case for Kaibel was editor but not altogether
untypical. Certain texts had unsatisfactory editions and required attention.
Aeschylus, *Bucolici Graeci*, Callimachus, Euripides[21] are obvious examples. *Certamen Homeri et Hesiodi* is peculiar because here Nietzsche-
Polemik is a factor.[22] His books on the text-history of lyric and bucolic
poetry are works of duty rather than inclination. Most book reviews belong
here, although of course he was more attracted to some books than to
others, whether because of subject matter or author.

"Dies Buch ist eine Pflichtarbeit." So writes Wilamowitz of
Griechische Verskunst (1921).[23] Not entirely. The matter is dry but the
book proved that neither musician nor musicologist could write competently
of sung verse. This recalled the old quarrel with Nietzsche, a composer, who
had written of tragedy born from the spirit of music. Just so friendship with
the violinist Kaibel proved that not every musician need be an enemy.[24] The
book also was apolitical and could be dedicated without embarrassment to
two Danes, loyal friends but neutrals in the great conflict. I wonder if they
understood the date of the preface. 18 January 1921 was the fiftieth
anniversary of the proclamation of the Second Reich by Wilhelm I in the
Hall of Mirrors at Versailles, an intentional provocation under the Weimar
Republic, which Wilamowitz despised.

This volume leads to the second great division, works of inclination;
that is books that Wilamowitz chose to write for some other reason than
that they "needed doing." This "other reason" provides the subjective
element in their composition. It varies considerably in those works of which
it is an ingredient. For purposes of exposition I distinguish three degrees of
subjectivity. Of course there is give and take. Funeral or memorial orations
are occasioned by death (Vahlen, Böckh) but often deepened by friendship
(Kaibel, Leo). And Wilamowitz writes:[25] "Fast alles, was ich geschrieben
habe, ist durch einen äußeren Anlaß hervorgerufen, der mir dies und jenes
Objekt in die Hände warf."

A.

Those writings owed to the influence of a revered teacher, a respected friend,
and at least once a gifted student. Not unexpectedly most of these works are

---

[20] See *Kl. Schr.* V, 1, 243-494 and 545-46.

[21] Apart from his editions of selected plays see Wilamowitz' contributions to Murray's
apparatus criticus with *Briefe Loeb*, 324 with n. 37.

[22] See Ernst Vogt, "Nietzsche und der Wettkampf Homers", *A & A* 11 (1962) 103-13; and
for the text: N.J. Richardson, "The Contest of Homer and Hesiod and Alcidamas' *Mouseion*,
CQ 31 (1981) 1-10.

[23] p. v.

[24] *Briefe Schadewaldt*, 452-53; denied by Abel, *Gymnasium* 88 (1981) 401 n. 30,
unconvincingly.

[25] *Erinnerungen*[2], 7.

from the first Berlin and Greifswald periods, when the young scholar, not yet entirely sure of himself, remained susceptible to influence. One expects a dissertation to be of this sort but Wilamowitz' remains an anomaly. *Observationes criticae in comoediam graecam selectae* (1870) is dedicated to Peter not to *parentibus optimis*, an untruth, but Peter certainly did not suggest the topic. Wilamowitz tells us that Eupolis was second best. He would have preferred Euripides but feared a premature birth, "sonst arbeite ich an einer dissertation über Eupolis, den attischen komiker, von dem ich ein deutlicheres literargeschichtliches bild zu geben in stande zu sein hoffe."[26] There are traces of Springer's historicism.[27] Too the subject matter of Φίλοι (= fragg. 265-275 Kock) had entranced Wilamowitz since Pforte,[28] and would until oldest age.[29] It surely was a contributing factor. The brochures against Nietzsche (1872/73) owe their pathological intensity to the need to prove to Peter that Wilamowitz not Nietzsche was Pforte's best scholar. In this sense they belong here.[30]

The *Habilitationsschrift* (1875), *Analecta Euripidea*, dedicated to Theodor Mommsen, is a remarkable and revealing case. Wilamowitz was proud and eager to show Mommsen how he had mastered the disciplines of scientific philology and grasped a major thinker from a major period. *Mommsen...inde ab 1872 totum me cepit.*[31] This subservience (the *Fahneneid*) to Mommsen required the rebellious provocation of dedicating a book on Euripides to the great scholar who had publicly damned him. *Poetae...quem quantum contemneres non reticuisti.*[32] The words recall *Römische Geschichte* I of 1854.[33] Mommsen belonged to a generation that confirmed the strictures of Schlegel. Wilamowitz did not change his mind. In 1886 Mommsen retorted to the Rector of Lincoln, who had twitted him on the subject:[34] "If I were to write that passage again now,...I should put it still more strongly." The correspondence of 1891, consistently ignored by Euripidean scholars, reveals no change.[35] Provocation was a *Leitmotiv* of

---

[26] *Briefe Bormann*, 146 (4 December 1869).

[27] *Supra* n. 9 and the letter cited *supra* n. 26.

[28] Wilamowitz, *Platon* I², 758 (= I⁵), 602-03; *Erinnerungen²*, 65, proves as Pohlenz (review of *Platon*, GGA 183 [1921] 1-30, at p. 1; repr. in M.P., *Kleine Schriften* I, ed. H. Dörrie, [Hildesheim 1965] 559-88, at p. 559) saw, that the passage is autobiographical: see *Trauerspiele*, 13 with n. 56 and *Latin Autobiography*, 42 with nn. 38, 39.

[29] *Briefe Stenzel*, 92 with n. 91 (8 January 1928).

[30] See my study "The Wilamowitz-Nietzsche Struggle: New Documents and a Reappraisal", *Nietzsche-Studien* 12 (1983) 214-54, and M.S. Silk/J.P. Stern, *Nietzsche on Tragedy* (Cambridge 1981) 90-131, with my review at *Classical and Modern Literature* 3 (1983) 113-16.

[31] *Latin Autobiography*, 45.

[32] *Analecta*, iii.

[33] Theodor Mommsen, *Römische Geschichte* II (dtv. 6054) München 1976, 436-40 with the remarks of Wilamowitz, *Tragödien* III 165; IV 368.

[34] W. Warde Fowler, "Theodor Mommsen. His Life and Work", in W.W.F., *Roman Essays and Interpretations* (Oxford 1920) 250-68, quotation 251.

[35] W.M. Calder III, "The Riddle of Wilamowitz' Phaidrabild," *GRBS* 20 (1979) 219-36, esp. 226-29.

the book and Wilamowitz paid the price. *Nova docere volo, nota praefabor*[36] cost Wachsmuth's chair at Göttingen in 1877 and Heimsoeth's at Bonn in 1880 and extended the Greifswald exilium until 1883.[37]

Ad Ernestum Maassium Epistula (1880) grew from Wilamowitz' absorption in a gifted pupil's dissertation, that also touched on Friedrich Nietzsche's early writings on Diogenes Laertius for the dread Ritschl in *Rheinisches Museum*. The epistle was the seed of *Antigonos von Karystos* (1881). This book was inspired by the Bonn lectures of Jacob Bernays, writings of Eduard Zeller, and certain pages were written expressly for Usener, to whom, rather as a peace-offering, the book was dedicated. The details available elsewhere need not be repeated here.[38] Owed Bernays too had been *Phaidon von Elis* (1879).[39]

Next *Homerische Untersuchungen* (1884), the last product of the Greifswald period. The hazy, remote, largely legendary figure of 'Homer' held *per se* little attraction for Wilamowitz, who, with his strong inclination to biography, to Euripides, Plato, or Pindar *als Mensch*, preferred an author from the historical period with considerable, more or less trustworthy, dated documents. Some outer impulse was needed to provide the interest. At Greifswald he found for the first and only time a colleague, soon a friend, who commanded his full respect, the master of Hebraic, New Testament, and Islamic philology, Julius Wellhausen (1844-1918), a contemporary and his equal in brilliant historical intuition and in philological expertise.[40] Simply because Wellhausen was not a classical scholar but expert in a field close enough so that the methodology was applicable to Wilamowitz' own, the symbiosis worked and Wilamowitz could—for the last time—learn more from him than from anyone since Mommsen. He read all but the most technical that Wellhausen had written.[41] There were endless conversations and a long correspondence the utter loss of which is most to be regretted.[42] Ignorant Protestant orthodoxy drove Wellhausen in 1882 to resign his chair. Wilamowitz, enraged, convinced the philosophical faculty to grant him an honorary degree.[43] The parallel, Bible and Homer, imposed itself. There was "something revolutionary" about it that attracted Wilamowitz, the Wilamowitz who earlier had renounced his father and his noble heritage, the allurement of struggle against the "gewaltige macht der gewohnheit, des

---

[36] *Analecta*, 31.

[37] Schwartz, 33 (372), where for "am Anfang der Habilitationsschrift" read "S. 131". Schwartz cited from memory.

[38] *Briefe Zeller*.

[39] *Briefe Bernays*.

[40] Schwartz, 40 (371).

[41] *Latin Autobiography*, 46: *Wellhausen 1878 et vir et per libros cepit; inde ab 82 per libros*; cf. *Untersuchungen*, v.

[42] Calder, 215 with n. 38. For Wellhausen's letters to Mommsen see Ernst Bammel, "Judentum, Christentum und Heidentum: Julius Wellhausens Briefe an Theodor Mommsen 1881-1902", *Zeitschr. für Kirchengeschichte* 80 (1969) 221-54.

[43] *Erinnerungen*[2], 190 and *Latin Autobiography*, 47 n. 83.

aberglaubens, der trägheit."[44] "Im Kampf ist Leben," Usener had once written him.[45] Sometimes with Wilamowitz *Wissenschaft* becomes almost a military exercise. Theodor Gomperz' letter of 5 December 1884 to Otto Hirschfeld reveals how he disturbed the elder generation.[46] The nature of the challenge together with the injustice done his hero of the moment spurred Wilamowitz to complete the book. He dated the preface "Göttingen, 17. Mai 1884," the fortieth birthday of Wellhausen. The book honored the wronged friend and closed the Greifswald period on an heroic note.[47] In time Wilamowitz would arrange with Althoff that Wellhausen join him at Göttingen.

Three later items deserve notice here. *Aischylos, Agamemnon* (1885) is dedicated to the memory of two sisters-in-law (the wives of Hugo and Tello), prematurely deceased. More telling is the date of completion. 26 June 1885 is the eleventh anniversary of his mother's death, the death that brought most pain. The refrain, αἴλινον αἴλινον εἰπέ, τὸ δ' εὖ νικάτω evoked a profound response in Wilamowitz' soul and afforded the comfort of hope in darkest sorrow. That he invoked it after 1919 is revealing.[48] Bereavement elicited *Agamemnon*. In *Choephoroi* there is indication that he recalled Ulrike and the love he bore her.[49] A famous and influential study, *Asianismus und Atticismus*,[50] we know grew from Wilamowitz' reply to the young Eduard Norden, who had sent to him a copy of *Die Antike Kunstprosa*.[51] This began a long correspondence (293 letters to Norden survive) and productive friendship and led to Norden's eventual call to Berlin in 1906 as successor to the problematic Vahlen.

Wilamowitz had long distrusted the French. After 1914 distrust became conviction.[52] Ironically the only foreigner who elicited a book from Wilamowitz was a Frenchman.[53] Anonymous persons in that country used to send Wilamowitz pornographic novels, which, to his credit, he read.[54] Somehow he received a copy of "P.L., *Les chansons de Bilitis*, traduites du

---

[44] *Untersuchungen*, iv.

[45] *Briefe Usener*, 7, No. 5; cf. Alois Brandl, *Zwischen Inn und Themse. Lebensbeobachtungen eines Anglisten. Alt-Tirol/England/Berlin* (Berlin 1936) 221: "Den Feldzug von 1870 hat er nicht bloß mitgemacht, sondern durch sein ganzes Leben im Hörsaal weitergeführt".

[46] *Briefe Gomperz*, 291-92.

[47] One could document in detail Wellhausen's influence on *Untersuchungen*.

[48] "Die griechische Tragödie und ihre drei Dichter", in *Tragödien* IV, 233-302, esp. 301-02; cf. *Trauerspiele*, 14.

[49] *Opfer*, 27-28; cf. "Die beiden Elektren", *Hermes* 18 (1883) 214-63, esp. 227-28 (= *Kl. Schr.* VI, 161-208, esp. 174).

[50] *Hermes* 35 (1900) 1-52 (= *Kl. Schr.* III, 223-73).

[51] Calder, 218 with n. 52. [See now William M. Calder III and Bernhard Huss, *"Sed serviendum officio..." The Correspondence between Ulrich von Wilamowitz-Moellendorff and Eduard Norden (1892-1931)* (Hildesheim 1997).]

[52] *Latin Autobiography*, 35 n. 6.

[53] I omit English editors of papyri like Kenyon.

[54] *Sappho*, 63, n. 3.

Grec pour la première fois (Paris 1895)." Unexpectedly he reviewed Pierre
Louys' book at *Göttingische Gelehrte Anzeigen* 158 (1896) 623-638. More.
He reprinted the review with learned *addenda* at *Sappho und Simonides*
(Berlin 1913) 63-78. In modern terms Wilamowitz 'over-reacted'. The
interesting question is: why? The hoax of Dr. G. Heim of Leipzig irritated
him.[55] One did not joke with scholarship. But the book was "eine
fortgesetzte Blasphemie."[56] "Mir ist es um die Reinheit einer großen Frau
zu tun: da scheue ich mich nicht, herzhaft in den Kot zu fassen."[57] The
review is a spirited defence of Sappho against the charge of female
homosexuality. The tone is quite the opposite of the openminded introduction to *Lysistrate*,[58] where Wilamowitz disavows all prudery in order to
exegete *Lysistrate* honestly. Sappho was peculiar. Frederik Poulsen reports
Wilamowitz in Berlin WS 1902/03 defending the chastity of Sappho before
an international audience of hundreds. American women wept while South
European men smiled.[59] I sometimes think that in his mind he has confused
Welcker's Sappho with an idealized portrait of his mother. He triumphantly
delivers to us "eine vornehme Frau, Gattin und Mutter,"[60] as much Ulrike
as Sappho. No tribad here. The outburst was exceptional. The book the last
of its type.[61]

B.

Second are those works written by Wilamowitz because he considered their
matter apt to his own time. Although generally foreign to Anglosaxon
practice (Gilbert Murray's *Trojan Women* is an exception), the tendency of
Germans to elucidate ancient subjects as commentary on their own times is
well know and probably a sign of health if not carried too far.[62] Four items
indisputably belong here. Several others might be adduced. That only four of
some 800 publications belong here does credit to Wilamowitz' historicism.
Unlike, e.g., Drerup, he eschewed cheap parallels. The youthful (Wilamowitz was twenty-eight years old) *Von des attischen reiches herrlichkeit:
eine festrede*, delivered at Greifswald[63] on 22 March 1877, the birthday of

[55] *Sappho*, 63. Louys intended a pun, which Wilamowitz either missed or disapproved.
[56] *Sappho*, 70
[57] *Sappho*, 63. For the *Kot* of anger cf. *Zukunftsphilologie!*, 7 (30).
[58] *Lysistrate*, 7.
[59] *I det gaestfrie Europa. Liv og Rejser indtil Første Verdenskrig*, (Copenhagen 1947) 12-
13.
[60] *Sappho*, 73.
[61] Unless one includes "Oedipus auf Kolonos", in T.v.W.-M., "Die dramatische Technik
des Sophokles", *Philologische Untersuchungen* 22 (Berlin 1996⁴ [1917¹]) 313-76.
[62] See W.A. Oldfather, review of W. Nauhardt, *Das Bild des Herrschers in der
griechischen Dichtung*, (Berlin 1940), *CW* 35 (1941-42) 53-55, and my remarks at *CP* 76
(1981) 166-68 (review of V. Losemann, *Nationalsozialismus und Antike* [Hamburg 1977]).
[63] Not at Göttingen: correct *Bibliographie*, 4, No. 23. The address was five times
published. I cite the version in *Kydathen* (1-96): see *Erinnerungen*², 192 n. 1.

Wilhelm I, was a thinly veiled *Von des deutschen Reiches Herrlichkeit.*[64]
Reich not *Seebund* made the point.[65] Kimon, "der leutselige junker, von
gewinnenden formen und cavaliermäßiger moral, im felde der tüchtige soldat,
zu hause der gnädige herr, durchaus loyal, aber ein wenig beschränkt" and
Pericles "das ideal constitutioneller romantik" are described as contemporaries.[66] The cavalry is that of his brothers: "die reiterei hat durchaus den
charakter eines exclusiven corps von adlichen oder sich als adlich
aufspielenden jungen leuten."[67] The importance of the fleet and Athenian
control of the money market are stressed. So too the *phoros.*[68] One easily
recalls French reparations after the defeat of 1870/71 that provided capital for
the expansion of the *Gründerjahre.* The praise of Athens captures the
euphoria of 1877:[69]

> Denn das höchste und beste was Athen seinem volke schenkte war das
> was allezeit das höchste und beste ist. seine götter und seine helden,
> seinen glauben und seine ehre hat es dem Hellenenvolke wieder
> lebendig gemacht.

At the end Wilamowitz draws the parallel in a manner reminiscent of
Niebuhr's old equation of Demosthenic Athens with Germany, against the
Napoleon of Philip II,[70] both a contrast to the German tendency since Karl
Otfried Müller to see themselves as Spartans.[71]

The outbreak of World War I attracted Wilamowitz to Homer's *Iliad,* the
unsurpassed poetic expression of military heroism. He taught the *Iliad* WS
1914/15, WS 1915/16, SS 1918 (*Ilias* III).[72] His book, *Die Ilias und
Homer* (Berlin 1916), begins: "Der Krieg ist wenn nicht der Vater so der
Geburtshelfer dieses Buches."[73] But except for an occasional remark here and
there,[74] the book is a brilliant stylistic analysis of the epic free of
ideological preoccupation. Compare it, e.g., with Jaeger, *Paideia* I. Basil L.

---

[64] Hölscher, 17.

[65] *Von des attischen reiches Herrlichkeit,* 5 n. 5, and *Erinnerungen*², 192 n. 1.

[66] 2.

[67] 24.

[68] 31-33.

[69] 39; cf. Hölscher, 17.

[70] Karl Christ, "Johann Gustav Droysen", in K.C., *Von Gibbon zu Rostovtzeff. Leben und
Werk führender Althistorker der Neuzeit,* (Darmstadt 1979² [1972¹]) 50-67, esp. 50.

[71] Elizabeth Rawson, *The Spartan Tradition in European Thought* (Oxford 1969) 306-43
("Sparta in Germany").

[72] *Bibliographie,* 81.

[73] 1; cf. Eduard Schwartz, review of Wilamowitz, *Ilias, DLZ* 39 (1918) cols. 355-62, 379-
86, quotation col. 355; repr. in: E.S., *Gesammelte Schriften II: Zur Geschichte und Literatur
der Griechen und Römer* (Berlin 1956) 25-41, quotation 25: "...die Widmung an den
gefallenen Sohn legen Zeugnis davon ab, daß die längst ausgetragenen Gedanken unter dem
Druck des Krieges zu fester Form zusammenkristallisiert sind".

[74] Hölscher, 17 cites *Ilias,* 275. But there is nothing militaristic there. The exegete must
turn to the expert in the matter of the passage: see *Erga,* 125 for urinating on the march and
Briefe Stenzel, 90 (one must consult the astronomer, botanist, and shoemaker).

Gildersleeve, the defeated Confederate warrior and editor of Pindar, saw with a flash of insight what in 1922 would draw Wilamowitz to Pindar:[75] "...another requisite for the understanding of Pindar is the experience of a losing side..." Occasionally even the mask is drawn aside:[76]

> So redet ein ehrlicher treuer Mann nach dem Zusammenbruche des Vaterlandes. Er überwindet die Lähmung seiner Kraft, die ihn zuerst niederhielt, und kehrt zu seiner Kunst zurück. Hätte er die Freiheit verloren, er würde in seinem Gottvertrauen auch dann der Muse treu geblieben sein, wie unsereiner es zu tun versucht. Denn nur den Feiglingen, die ihre Ketten als Schmuck tragen oder in der Schande von Freiheit faseln, hilft kein Gott.

The sentiment is quintessentially Wilamowitzian. Schwester Hildegard tells us that he survived the death of Tycho only by working harder.[77] The passage recalls Euripides, *Herakles*, vv. 674-677, *ein Gelübde fürs Leben*, that he turned to repeatedly in crucial moments of his life.[78] His German version reveals what *Kunst* in *Pindaros* implies.

> Allzeit will ich zu holdem Vereine
> Chariten laden und Musen:
> Ohne die Kunst kein Leben
> Immer kränze mein Haupt der Efeu.[79]

The title of a last book decides its inclusion here. *Die Heimkehr des Odysseus* (Berlin 1927) concerns the return of the veteran Odysseus and recalls the fate of so many Berlin students and younger colleagues of the postwar period.[80] *Heimkehr* novels are almost a genre of German literature. In 1946 Schadewaldt purposely revived the title of his great teacher and predecessor in the Berlin chair. He later told us so:[81]

> Die hier folgende Nacherzählung der Homerischen *Odyssee* habe ich im Sommer 1946 auf die Bitte von Peter Suhrkamp geschrieben, der in

[75] *AJP* 34 (1913) 110; for Wilamowitz and Gildersleeve see W.M. Calder III, "B.L. Gildersleeve and Ulrich von Wilamowitz-Moellendorff: New Documents" *AJP* 99 (1978) 1-11; repr. in: Wilamowitz, "Selected Correspondence 1869-1931", ed. by W.M. Calder III, *Antiqua* 23 (Napoli 1983) 141-51.

[76] *Pindaros*, 198, on which see Erich Thummer, "Pindar: Die Isthmischen Gedichte II: Kommentar" (*Wissenschaftliche Kommentare zu griechischen und lateinischen Schriftstellern*) Heidelberg 1969, 126 n. 2: "Hier interpretiert der Interpret sich selbst, nicht den Dichter". Compare *Pindaros*, 413.

[77] *Trauerspiele*, 161. The pain of loss was intensified by Wilamowitz' conviction that he had underestimated Tycho. The family name Oblomov speaks volumes.

[78] Material at *Trauerspiele*, 24 n. 51.

[79] *Herakles* II (1959) 213.

[80] Did the title conceal an implied rebuke to one denied an *Heimkehr* by a post in Switzerland, Basel, the chair of Nietzsche? I mean the problematical Jaeger.

[81] "Die Heimkehr des Odysseus", in W.S., *Von Homers Welt und Werk. Aufsätze und Auslegungen zur Homerischen Frage*, (Stuttgart 1959³) 375-412, 486-88, quotation 375.

seinem für den damaligen Heimkehrer bestimmten *Taschenbuch für junge Menschen* das Bild der homerischen Urheimkehr nicht missen wollte.

In *Heimkehr* too there is little militarism,[82] rather a sharp analytical attack on the text, inspired by Schwartz' book to whom Wilamowitz dedicated his own.

I cannot examine here Imperial Birthday Addresses or War Speeches, both genres with their own rules. As Public Orator or Rector Wilamowitz could not avoid what admittedly was often a welcome task. He was a brilliant speaker of considerable histrionic talent. Like Wilhelm II, he was occasionally carried away. But of the scholarly works cited under this rubric, with the possible exception of several passages in the youthful effusion of 1877, which Wilamowitz himself later confessed were exaggerated; and he softened in later printings,[83] I doubt that the most determined critic could argue convincingly the view that Wilamowitz perverted ancient evidence for the purposes of political propaganda.[84] His devotion to truth forbade that:[85]

> Jede wissenschaftliche Trübung der Wahrheit aus Rücksicht auf Konfessionen oder Politik, auf Beifall oder Gunst oder Lohn, ist uns Felonie.

C.

Three books deserve especial attention in any discussion of the autobiographical, or more generally, of the subjective in Wilamowitz' work. They are *Hippolytos* (1891), *Herakles* (1889), and *Platon* (1919).[86] A profound personal affinity drew Wilamowitz to their subject matter. Their writing is not owed the suggestion of a friend or teacher. They are crucial precisely therefore. The need to write the books grew out of inner compulsion. With the exception of *Platon*, and that only in a special personal way, the books are not immediately relevant to their dates of composition in the sense of those just discussed. I shall call this third subdivision, "autobiographical documents in the guise of scholarly books." The genre should not be unfamiliar. Most Alexander books belong to it.

---

[82] Hölscher, 17, provides only an innocuous sentence from *Heimkehr*, 24.

[83] *Erinnerungen*², 192 n. 1.

[84] He was tempted to improve Mommsen's politics: W.M. Calder III, "Adolf Erman to Wilamowitz on Mommsen's Politics", *Quaderni di storia* 14 (1981) 151-57; repr. in: *Wilamowitz, Selected Correspondence*, 57-63.

[85] *Erinnerungen*², 320.

[86] Dover, *Expurgation of Greek Literature*, 88-89, remarks of Wilamowitz: "It seems obvious, too, that he sympathised greatly with Lysistrata and resented the frivolous treatment of her serious proposals." I wonder.

The titles might fruitfully label the three seasons of Wilamowitz' mature life: *Hippolytos* (1867-1883), *Herakles* (1883-1914), *Platon* (1914-1931).

3. Hippolytos

The date of publication is unimportant. Anyone who reads the *Valediktionsarbeit* of 1867 knows that ideas could incubate for fifty years. The *Valediktionsarbeit* attests that already aged 18 Wilamowitz admired Hippolytos:[87]

> Hippolytos ist noch ein Jüngling, erfüllt von idealem Streben nach dem Unausführbaren, ein Phantast, ein bei weitem mehr deutscher Character, das führt denn dahin, dass er zu weit geht und fällt.

More German means less Greek and more like me: the dreaming schoolboy, filled with an ideal yearning for the unobtainable, who goes too far only to stumble. By 1868 he had written out a translation of the play.[88] In 1869 he admits that *Hippolytos* is his favorite Euripidean tragedy (next *Bacchae*).[89] By October 1870 he had memorized the Greek text.[90] He discusses it in the *Habilitationsschrift* of 1875.[91] SS 1875 he taught the play at Berlin; SS 1881 and WS 1881/82 at Greifswald; WS 1886/87 at Göttingen. Then in 1891 the edition. Together some twenty-five years of attention. I have shown elsewhere that the view of Friedrich, Reinhardt, Lesky, and (seven times!) Lloyd-Jones that Ibsen's *Hedda Gabler* determined Wilamowitz' *Phaidrabild* is chronologically impossible. Rather he read into Phaedra the character of his aunt, Emma von Schwanenfeld (1800-1876).[92] This confirms in an unexpected way Landfester's insight that Wilamowitz interpreted characters of drama as though figures of history,[93] an intelligent variant, I suppose, of Waldock's "documentary fallacy."[94] Wilamowitz' lifelong association of Phaedra and Hippolytus with Tante Emma and himself of 1868 prepares us for the autobiographical in his *Hippolytos-bild*.[95] Because I find that philologists tend to take matters literally unless warned,[96] I stress that Hippolytus is *not* a self-portrait. It is a distortion of

---

[87] *Trauerspiele*, 114.

[88] See *Hippolytos*, 1 and 54 n. 1; *Tragödien* I⁴, 121 n. 1; *Erinnerungen*², 55 n. 1; Calder, *The Riddle of Wilamowitz' Phaidrabild, GRBS* 20 (1979) 221-22 (= *Antiqua* 27 [1984] 167-8).

[89] *Briefe Bormann*, 147 (4 December 1869).

[90] *Hippolytos*, 232 n. 1; *Kriegserinnerungen* (1914) in *Kriegszeit*, 39-73, esp. 51-52; *Erinnerungen*², 111-12.

[91] *Analecta*, 209-21.

[92] Calder, *The Riddle of Wilamowitz' Phaidrabild*, 219-36 (= *Antiqua* 27 [1984] 165-82).

[93] Landfester, 176.

[94] A.J.A. Waldock, *Sophocles the Dramatist* (Cambridge 1951) 11-24.

[95] See supra n. 88 and Calder, *The Riddle of Wilamowitz' Phaidrabild*, 235-36.

[96] I have just read B. Gentili, "Eric R. Dodds mentitore", *QUCC* NS 7 (1981) 175-76.

one. The parallel is a novelist's use of a friend as source of a character in fiction, a phenomenon endlessly documented. The crucial text follows:[97]

> Das wesen des Hippolytos lässt sich auf griechisch mit einem wort bezeichnen: es ist ἀνεπαφρόδιτον. Aphrodite ist für ihn der teufel, nicht weil er das so gelernt hat, sondern weil das in seiner natur liegt: ihm geht alles aphrodisische ab...freilich ist er ein kräftiger schöner jüngling, ergeben den ritterlichen vergnügungen und meister in diesen künsten. aber er hat ein herrisches wesen gegen jedermann und kann gar nicht anders als anmassend auftreten. dass sein gesinde und die genossen, die ganz unter seiner tyrannei stehn werden, ihn vergöttern...steht in keinem widerspruch dazu: denn hoffärtige und eitele jugend erzielt das mit noblen passionen und anmasslichem gebaren bei untergebnen und jungen mädchen noch heute...er ist sich selbst genug; das gefühl, anschluss zu suchen, zu lieben und geliebt werden zu wollen, in welchem sinne auch immer, ist ihm ganz fremd...er ist kein grübler und kein politischer streber, wie der vater ihm vorwirft. er hat das vorrecht, auf der wiese der Artemis blumen zu pflücken: mehr verlangt er nicht. nun tritt ihm von aussen der verbrecherische antrag entgegen, der sein wesen im kerne verletzt; er muss unschuldig wegen des verbrechens, das ihm am fernsten liegt, in die verbannung und den tod gehn. beides steigert seinen tugendstolz und macht ihn trotz allem mitleid, das er verdient und findet, nicht liebenswürdig. er ist frei von menschlicher schwäche: das mag ihm den himmel öffnen: auf die erde gehört er nicht, noch unter dieser götter regiment.

With "noch heute" Wilamowitz shows his hand. He exegetes an ancient text from personal experience, with what some, not I, would call "impertinente Familiarität."[98] For convenience I make three divisions.

1. Shared characteristics. Wilamowitz learned from no pastor nor parent to avoid women. He had a natural antipathy toward them. Except for mother and aunt and briefest references to Marie Mommsen what women appear in the pages of *Erinnerungen?*[99] This is not Wilhelmian scruple. Contrast the memoirs of his colleague, Adolf Erman.[100] There is not the slightest hint of an *affaire* in Wilamowitz' three and eighty years.[101] He wrote poems, as far as I know, only to men. Contrast the student Karl Marx! In contrast to Nietzsche, there is no evidence that Wilamowitz ever entered a

---

[97] *Hippolytos*, 51. I have necessarily abridged.

[98] Allegedly a phrase used by Nietzsche against Mommsen but I think apocryphal: see W.M. Calder III, review of H. Flashar/K. Gründer/A. Horstmann (eds.), *Philologie und Hermeneutik im 19. Jahrhundert* (Göttingen 1979), *CW* 74 (1980-81) 33-34.

[99] Cf. *Aristoteles* II, 100 n. 35, on history that stinks of female perfume.

[100] *Mein Werden und mein Wirken. Erinnerungen eines alten Berliner Gelehrten*, (Leipzig 1929).

[101] Interest in Eva Sachs and Esther Drachmann was purely innocent.

brothel, in Cologne or elsewhere. In war he shared a bed only with his adjutant.[102] For adultery he had no tolerance whatsoever.[103] Ihm geht alles aphrodisische ab. He was a strong, handsome youth and a master at riding.[104] He was always the leader: ein herrisches Wesen.[105] Among the friends of his twenties take Carl Bardt, Walter Bormann, Walther Engel, Georg Kaibel, Adolf Kießling, Otto Lüders (who dedicated his dissertation to the twenty-four year old Wilamowitz!), Carl Robert. They all stood "ganz unter seiner tyrannei;" and worshipped him. His pride and aloofness attracted them. Already in Schulpforte he was withdrawn and self-sufficient, the beginning of the famous "Einsamkeit meines Lebens."[106] He said what he thought (e.g., to Usener) and took the consequences. He was no politician like Hugo whom Arnold preferred. He had the right to pluck blossoms in the shrine of Athena or, as he sometimes said, the Goddess *Wissenschaft*. That is all he wanted.

2. Hippolytos attracted Wilamowitz because he persevered in spite of great hardship loyal to his ideals,[107] chastity and his oath. Wilamowitz' loyalty was to scholarship which led him to renounce his aristocratic past and marry a bourgeois woman, the first in his family to do so for over two hundred years.

3. This leads directly to a profound affinity with Hippolytos. Both young men suffered the curse of a father, Theseus and Arnold, and for what in neither's case was a crime. The Schulpforte Life makes this clear:[108]

> Ich will ein Jünger der Wissenschaft werden, freiwillig, scheel angesehen von Verwandten, Nahestehenden, verstossen aus den vermeintlich höheren Kreisen, in welche die Geburt mich gestellt hat. Wohl—es wird gehen, ich folge ungehemmtem Drange, verehrte Männer, die sich freundlich für mich interessieren, und wahre Freunde werden mir übervoll alles etwa verlorne ersetzen.

Arnold (Ulrike had died in 1874) did not attend Ulrich's wedding 20 September 1878 in Berlin (I do not know that any of his family was there) nor send a gift. Only years later at the request of Hugo he relented and bestowed the silver tea service. Typically at Arnold's death in a sanatorium

---

[102] *Erinnerungen*[2], 111.

[103] For the Jaeger case see *Trauerspiele*, 163. Letters reveal his disapproval of Susemihl's second marriage.

[104] *Erinnerungen*[2], 58-59.

[105] See Ed. Fraenkel (*Briefe Fraenkel*, 295) on his "unabhängiges Herrentum".

[106] *Trauerspiele*, 4-6.

[107] W.M. Calder III, *The Riddle of Wilamowitz' Phaidrabild*, 221 n. 6.

[108] *Trauerspiele*, 24.

at Wiesbaden 2 January 1888 only Ulrich was there: "Es ward mir schwer—es war aber doch gut und nötig, daß ich es tat."[109]

Natural superiority to friends, reckless devotion to ideals, unjust rejection by a father who could not understand him caused the isolation of the tragic hero, a matter well known to students of Greek tragedy. Wilamowitz' conviction that the world misunderstood him but that nonetheless he must persevere in his devotion to truth receives remarkable expression in the letter of 7 December 1881 to Eduard Zeller:[110]

> gewöhnt daß meinen arbeiten nichts als hohn und rancune gegenüber laut wird, ist mir nächst dem eigenen gewisssen die einzige beruhigung daß die männer, auf deren urteil ich den höchsten wert lege, das urteil der tageswelt nicht teilen.

It is no coincidence that these words were written at the very time he was teaching *Hippolytos*. Eduard Schwartz reports how shattered Wilamowitz was by Mommsen's critique of *Hippolytos*.[111] The reason is clear. He had put so much of himself into the book.

4. Herakles

Marcello Gigante has written that like Nietzsche Wilamowitz has no single *magnum opus*.[112] True, but Wilamowitz intended *Herakles* to be his. For this reason he published it in his fortieth year, in the ancient sense his *akme*.[113] He makes this clear:[114] "Bei Goethe und bei Platon macht allerdings das vierzigste Jahr Epoche: da erst sind sie fertig." "Bei mir auch," he thought. There is a puzzle about its inception. Wilamowitz published privately an early version (simply text and translation)[115] on 10 September 1879 as a gift for his father-in-law, Theodor Mommsen, on his silver wedding anniversary, which the Mommsens passed in Greifswald.[116] Earlier (1868) he had presented his brother, Hugo, with a translation of *Alcestis*, as a wedding present. That fit: the good Alcestis in the Platonic sense (*Symposium* 179b), the wife loyal to her spouse unto death. But out of over thirty surviving Greek tragedies why choose as a wedding anniversary gift

---

[109] *Autobiography*, 576 n. 63 (23 September 1893 to Hermann Peter).

[110] *Briefe Zeller*, 181.

[111] Schwartz, 32 (371); cf. Calder, *The Riddle of Wilamowitz' Phaidrabild*, 229 with n. 54.

[112] "Dal Wilamowitz al Pfeiffer. Storici della filologia classica", *La Parola del Passato* 29 (1974) 196-224, at 214.

[113] For the importance he attached to the *akme*, Dr. Buchwald cites *Aristoteles* I. 311.

[114] *Einleitung*, (1959) 18.

[115] *Euripides Herakles — als Manuscript gedruckt* (Berlin 1879).

[116] *Erinnerungen*[2], 183.

the one where a husband brutally butchers his wife and children? Even
Wilamowitz was not blind to the impropriety:[117]

> Der Held kann schwerlich dienen zum Exempel,
> Denn Wahnsinn reißt ihn fort zu blutgen Fakten.

The choice proves how little wife and children mattered. Mommsen was
Wilamowitz' *Herakles*, the θεῖος ἀνήρ.[118] The famous epigram easily
applies to Mommsen:[119]

> Mensch gewesen, Gott geworden; Mühen erduldet, Himmel erworben.

There was the *Grundbedeutung der Gestalt*. The progress of Mommsen from
Frisian to German to international figure parallels Herakles' progress from
Dorian to Panhellenic to barbarian and Roman figure.[120] Mommsen won
greatness through work[121] and like Herakles Mommsen too became (in the
Greek sense) a hero after death. On his hundredth birthday Wilamowitz urges
young men to turn to him:[122]

> Mit dem Loben und dem Danken ist es nicht abgetan, wenn man den
> Geist eines großen Toten aufruft...Helfen soll er uns, zu erfüllen, was
> unser Lebenstag von uns fordert. Er hat im Leben so vielen geholfen;
> diese Kraft besitzt er noch heute. Vertrauen Sie sich seiner Führung
> an...Dringen Sie durch bis zu seiner lebendigen Seele.

For Wilamowitz in 1879 Theodor Mommsen remained the Herakles of
Wissenschaft and, therefore, Wilamowitz presented him with text and
translation of the ancient poem that best incorporated the *Heraklesbild*. It
was a gift to the scholar not to the husband. We know how Wilamowitz'
adoration of Mommsen waned in later years.[123] He was *menschlich
allzumenschlich*[124] and at the end did more against *Wissenschaft* than for
it.[125] He betrayed Herakles. This turn from adoration to rejection parallels
Nietzsche's change toward Richard Wagner and Wilhelm II's toward

---

[117] *Briefe Mommsen*, 73.

[118] *Herakles* II (1959) 118.

[119] *Herakles* II (1959) 38. The language recalls the Creed.

[120] Compare *Herakles* II (1959) 18ff. with "Theodor Mommsen", *Internationale
Wochenschr. für Wissenschaft, Kunst und Technik* 1 (1907) cols. 263-70 (= *Kl. Schr.* VI. 11-
17).

[121] *E.g.*, "Theodor Mommsen", *Zeitschr. für das Gymnasialwesen* N.F. 6 (1918) 1-10, esp.
9 (= *Kl. Schr.* VI. 18-28, esp. 28).

[122] *Ibid.*

[123] Calder, 222-24; *Latin Autobiography*, 45-46 with nn. 73-78; J. Malitz, "Theodor
Mommsen und Wilamowitz," *Wilamowitz* 53-55.

[124] *Briefe Jaeger*, 320-21 with nn. (December 1917)

[125] Werner Jaeger, review of *Briefe Mommsen*, *DLZ* 57 (1936) cols. 271-81, esp. col 281;
repr. in W.J., *Scripta Minora* II (*Storia e letteratura*. 81) Roma 1960, 137-45, esp. 145.

Bismarck. Some biographers have thought it typical of the time, the darker side of heroworship. By 1889 Wilamowitz had dethroned Mommsen and himself become Herakles. Two facts conspired to make identification easier.

1. Wilamowitz did not treat Herakles as a modern might a figure of myth, Achilles or Hector. Rather he wrote a *biography* of Herakles, parallel to that of Euripides in his first volume. He discusses his parents, how he got his name, his birth and childhood, education and marriage, and so on.[126] It is the ancient manner. Plutarch had written a *Vita Heraclis* (= fragg. 6-8 Sandbach). More immediately Philipp Buttmann in 1810 to celebrate the birthday of Frederick the Great declared:[127]

> das Leben des Herakles ein schöner und uralter Mythos ist, darstellend das Ideal menschlicher Vollkommenheit, geweihet dem Heile der Menschheit.

Not Herakles but the *life* of Herakles. It is almost unavoidable for the "omniscient biographer" not to identify with the hero of his biography. It would be a poorer biography if he did not.

2. Wilamowitz documents carefully the habit attested in antiquity of drawing contemporary parallels with Herakles. Pindar[128] first drew a parallel between Herakles and an athletic victor. The comic poets may have seen Perikles and Aspasia as Herakles and Omphale.[129] Already in IV B.C. (Diodorus Siculus XVI. 44) Nikostratos of Argos appeared on the battlefield dressed as Herakles.[130] Commodos (Herodian I. 14. 8) believed himself Herakles.[131] The tradition of νέος Ἡρακλῆς would certainly not discourage Wilamowitz from seeing himself as part of it.

Aristotle in a remarkable passage (*Problemata Physica* XXX. 1)[132] describes Herakles along with Plato and Socrates as the type of the "melancholic man," that is a sort of unstable genius. In Wilamowitz'

---

[126] *Herakles* II (1959) 47ff.; so Nietzsche at Pforte wished to write a *life* of Prometheus: see *Kritische Gesamtausgabe. Briefe* I. 1, 60 (April/May 1859) No. 70.

[127] I know only the citation at *Herakles* II (1959) 106.

[128] *Herakles* II (1959) 82.

[129] *Herakles* II (1959) 71 ff. Wilamowitz vigorously argues that the Herakles-Omphale story is Hellenistic, i.e., decadent. Friedrich Cauer, "Omphale", defended a fifth century source (*RhM* 46 [1891] 244-49). Vengeance was swift (*Herakles* II [1959] 72 n. 128). Yet modern opinion favors Cauer against Wilamowitz: see Gertrud Herzog-Hauser, "Omphale" in *RE* 18, 1, (1939) cols. 385-96, esp. col. 389, 19 ff.; for Old Comedy esp. col. 390, 13 ff. Wilamowitz found the story distasteful and at any cost wanted it late. The violence proved how much was at stake. That interests me. [Compare Jane Harrison's downplaying of Orpheus' love for Eurydice: S.J. Peacock *ICSSupp* 2 (1991) 180.]

[130] *Herakles* II (1959) 94 n. 174.

[131] *Herakles* II (1959) 94. Iconographic evidence allows an earlier Alexander-Herakles.

[132] See the authoritative discussion by Hellmut Flashar, Aristoteles, *Problemata Physica* (*Aristoteles. Werke in deutscher Übersetzung.* 19) Berlin 1975² (1962¹) 711-27, where add a reference to Wilamowitz, *Herakles* II (1959) 92-93 with n. 170.

words Aristotle sets Herakles "in die Reihe der Heroen des Geistes."[133] That is there is Aristotelian precedent for Wilamowitz to see himself, a scholar, as a parallel to Herakles, as a νέος Ἡρακλῆς.[134]

> Wenn Herakles in die Reihe der Heroen des Geistes und der sittlichen Kraft eingeführt ist, so ist das in unserm Sinne keine Degradation, die Gewalt der alten Sagengestalt macht sich auch darin noch fühlbar.

We saw with Hippolytos how certain traits fitted to what I called "a distorted self-portrait." Others don't. Wilamowitz was not a matador. But they don't count. Herakles is not a farmer but a nobleman (*Adel*) who provides security that his farmers may farm peacefully.[135] Herakles amidst the prehistoric Dorians does precisely what Arnold or Hugo do for Poles at Markowitz. He is *unus e·nobis*. There is a dangerous fire in these melancholic men like Herakles:[136]

> Wir dürfen etwa sagen, daß in der Seele dieser Höchstbegnadigten unter den Sterblichen ein vulkanisches Feuer brennt; solange es nur in der Tiefe treibt und wärmt, bringen sie hervor, was reicher und köstlicher ist, als sonst ein Mensch vermag, aber wehe, wenn es durchbricht: dann verzehrt es alles und vernichtet sie selbst zuerst.

The unpleasantness with Usener[137] and the Nietzsche affair are only the obvious examples.

As with Hippolytos, I suggest that two aspects of the traditional Herakles appealed to Wilamowitz on a level far more profound than the amusement gleaned from coincidence.

1. Herakles dared to undertake tasks that would daunt the greatest contemporaries: the Nemean Lion (or the historical Euripides), the Augean Stables (or the Homeric Question), the Hydra (or the religion of the Greeks). Herakles was the exemplum, the man who attained Heaven through the distinctively Prussian ethic of hard work.[138] Du sollst arbeiten, bis Du stirbst. On his deathbed until the final coma Wilamowitz dictated *Der Glaube der Hellenen* II to Dorothea. After death he became a

---

[133] *Herakles* II (1959) 93.
[134] *Ibid.*
[135] 61.
[136] 93. I avoid contrasting Wilamowitz' *Heraklesbild* with Nietzsche's *Übermensch*. Both imply projections of their own personalities.
[137] Calder, 222, and A. Körte, Review of *Briefe Usener, Die Antike* 11 (1935) 211-35, esp. 218.
[138] Herakles appealed to Wilamowitz' practical nature in a way Jesus Christ did not.

god. Werner Jaeger by his own admission paid him *Heroenkult*.[139] In 1948 Eduard Fraenkel wrote:[140]

> To speak of Wilamowitz with any sort of detachment is as yet almost impossible: he is still so near to us, so immensely alive, that at times we do not seem to be fully aware that he is gone.

Intuitively at age 40 Wilamowitz saw to whom his epigram applied. As Lothar Wickert remarked in another context:[141] "er wußte schon damals, wer er war." The conviction only grew during the next forty years.[142]

> Mensch gewesen, Gott geworden; Mühen erduldet, Himmel erworben.

It is Wilamowitz' epitaph.

2. For Pindar, "the last prophet of the Dorians," Herakles meant the splendid incarnation of an aristocratic ideal drawn from a greater past that already had become an anachronism in the poet's time:[143]

> Pindar war der letzte Prophet des Dorertums und seiner Ideale; er war auch der letzte, der den Glauben an den echten Herakles ungebrochen bewahrte und verkündigte, mitten in einer Welt, die weder für ihn noch seinen Herakles mehr Raum hatte. Unschätzbar für uns, daß wir diesen Propheten noch hören können. Wie Nebel vor der siegreichen Sonne sinken irdische Fabeln vor der Erhabenheit des göttlichen Bildes, das er entwirft, eben da, wo er den Kindermord still ablehnt.

This conviction is profoundly Wilamowitzian. Eduard Meyer would call it more Wilamowitzian than Pindaric or Dorian.[144] The better for me. I have argued elsewhere that there was something of the revolutionary in Wilamowitz (therefore he turned to Euripides not Sophocles in the first place!); but at heart he remained a nobleman, loyal to his class, in the best sense conservative, convinced that an enlightened aristocracy of inherited privilege in spite of regretted defects provided a better government than any other. Since 1848 there had been encroachments on the old order. The death of the Old Emperor meant a ruler younger than Wilamowitz. Closer to home standards in school and university were

---

[139] Jaeger, CXXVIII (220).

[140] "The Latin Studies of Hermann and Wilamowitz", *JRS* 38 (1948) 28-38, quotation 29; repr. in: E.F., *Kleine Beiträge zur klassischen Philologie* II: *Zur römischen Literatur, zu juristischen Texten, Verschiedenes (Storia e letteratura. 96)* Roma 1964, 563-76, quotation 563.

[141] *Autobiography*, 577 with n. 67.

[142] Again *Herakles* II (1959) 38; it applies as well to Wilamowitz as to Mommsen.

[143] *Herakles* II (1959) 88.

[144] Eduard Meyer, *Geschichte des Altertums* III, ed. H.E. Stier (Darmstadt 1954³) 239 n. 1, and (against Pindar the Prophet) 242 n. 1.

dropping. As the older generation departed and genius increasingly isolated him from most contemporaries (the great students and foreign friendships were later), solitude (*Einsamkeit meines Lebens*) led him to ponder gloomily on an end to an epoch. An irrepressible sense for drama exacerbated the tendency. The finality of 1918 could never have been anticipated but later events confirmed rather than redirected earlier gloom, In this way Wilamowitz *depontanus* predated the Weimar Republic. As early as 1889 Pindar, prophet of a creed outworn, attracted him.[145]

Infanticide did not sully the ideal Dorian. There is a sharp division between traditional Herakles and Euripidean innovation.[146] What attracted Wilamowitz to *Der Herakles des Euripides*? Euripides, *Hercules furens*, vv. 674-677 (οὐ παύσομαι etc.) first did. He had cited the lines at the start of the *Valediktionsarbeit* of 1867. The same verses adorn the base of the dedicatory page of the editions of 1889, 1895, and 1907.[147] In the blackest hours of his seventieth birthday he cites them.[148] The mystical reverence in which he held them drew him to the play and to its author.[149] Their repetition in 1889 symbolized the fulfillment of the vow of 1867 to dedicate Almae Matri Portae his first great book.[150] His attraction to *Agamemnon* in 1885 because of several verses is similar.

As usual Wilamowitz shows his hand in depiction of character. Here is his description of Amphitryon:[151]

Amphitryon ist zwar ehedem etwas gewesen...Jetzt ist er Greis; er kennt das Leben und macht sich keine Illusionen mehr. Er hat nichts mehr zu fordern noch zu erwarten, darum aber auch nichts für sich zu fürchten. Er übersieht nicht bloß die Schwiegertochter und den Tyrannen, sondern auch die stürmische Unbedachtsamkeit des Sohnes. Dieser Sohn ist sein alles; Schwiegertochter und Enkel schätzt er nur um des Sohnes willen...Seine schwerste Prüfung ist der endliche Abschied von ihm, und daß er doch hoffen darf, die einzig geliebte Hand werde ihm die müden Augen zudrücken, wenn sie endlich brechen werden, ist sein letzter Trost. Amphitryon ist der Vater des Herakles.

---

[145] Aged 73 Wilamowitz writes, *Pindaros*, 445: "Als Pindar hochbetagt aus dem Leben schied, hat es die Welt kaum beachtet; er war ihr fremd geworden". Pindar in 1922 is little changed from 1889.

[146] *Herakles* II (1959) 108 ff. Wilamowitz argues three Euripidean innovations: 1. postponement of the infanticide from the middle to the end of Herakles' career with addition of Megara's murder; 2. introduction of Theseus and Herakles' *Lebensabend* at Athens; 3. invention of Lycos to avoid an unrelievedly evil Herakles.

[147] Three dates adorn the dedicatory page of the last two editions, 9 September 1867 (graduation from Pforte), 21 May 1889 (*Schulfest* and the birthday of Plato, 7 Thargelion), 22 December 1892 (his 44th birthday).

[148] *Platon* I², vi; cf. *Trauerspiele*, 24 n. 51.

[149] At *Herakles* II (1959) 132, Wilamowitz applies them to Euripides' life in a way that recalls his own.

[150] *Erinnerungen*², 62, further proof of the importance of the volume to its author.

[151] *Herakles* II (1959) 113-14.

Amphitryon is the foil to Theseus of *Hippolytos*. Theseus cursed his son; Amphitryon forgave his everything. That is: Theseus was the vigorous Arnold of Markowitz; Amphitryon the aged Arnold of Wiesbaden, who had died the year before, on 2 January 1888, alone with Ulrich. He had been something once. Now he is an old man who knows life and no longer has illusions. He neither demands nor expects anything more and so has nothing to fear for himself. He accepts daughter-in-law and the stormy temperament of his son. This son is everything to him. He approves daughter-in-law and grandchildren only for his son's sake. His most difficult test is the final parting from him; his last consolation the hope that the beloved hand of his son will close his weary eyes. Arnold is the father of Ulrich. A final touch clinches it:[152] "Um Amphitryon zu geben...ist die Mutter Alkmene ganz und gar ferngehalten..." Ulrike had died in 1874. Reconciliation with Arnold required her absence. One instantly recalls the influence of Emma von Schwanenfeld on Wilamowitz' *Phaidrabild*.[153]

There is a further revealing characterization. I explained how Wilamowitz saw himself in Pindar as well as in Pindar's Herakles. Just so he summons up the shade of Euripides with his own blood. Two citations must suffice. Euripides' composition of his *Herakles* parallels remarkably Wilamowitz' composition of his *Herakles*:[154]

> Dieses Werk, auf das er so viel Fleiß und Liebe verwandt hatte, dem er mit dem eigenen Herzblute Leben gegeben hatte, trägt denn auch nicht nur unter der dramatischen Hülle sein sophistisches Bekenntnis verborgen, sondern er hat sich nicht gescheut das Gelöbnis, trotz allem fortzuleben und fortzudichten, seinem Lebenswerke treu zu bleiben wie sein Heros, dem Chore geradezu in den Mund zu legen. οὐ παύσομαι etc.

Fleiß and *Liebe* are clear. *Herzblut* is "the blood of our hearts" in his Oxford lecture. The philologist's task to "grant life" to the past is Euripides' also. *Hercules furens* vv. 674-677 is Euripides' motto as well as Wilamowitz'. For both Herakles is hero and model. A bit later Wilamowitz sums up Euripides' genius:[155]

> Eine fieberhafte Hast, eine trostlose, friedlose, Götter und Menschen, Güter und Genüsse verachtende Stimmung und daneben eine Schaffenskraft und Kühnheit, ein unermüdliches Haschen nach neuen Aufgaben und neuen Lösungen, eine immer junge Empfänglichkeit für all das Neue, Gutes und Arges, das um ihn aufkommt—man kann sich nicht

---

[152] *Herakles* II (1959) 114.
[153] Calder, The Riddle of Wilamowitz' Phaidrabild, 234-35.
[154] *Herakles* II (1959) 132.
[155] *Herakles* II (1959) 133.

genugtun, um die Menschenseele zu schildern, der es möglich war, die
Reihe widerspruchsvoller Werke zu schaffen.

This could be from an obituary of Wilamowitz. In twenty years
Wilamowitz had moved from youthful distaste for the poet to identification with him.[156] One could trace similar involvement, although for
different reasons, in the anti-clerical A.W. Verrall and Gilbert Murray, the
pacifist and friend of G.B. Shaw.

5. Platon

In an odd way *Herakles* led to *Platon*. Already in *Herakles*, thirty years
before, there was the temptation:[157]

Platons entwickelung zu übersehen würde einen ähnlichen reichtum von
psychologischer belehrung bieten wie die Goethes.

But not too soon. To understand Plato one must grow old with him.[158]
Zeller had remarked:[159]

Es gibt nur wenige unter den alten Philosophen, deren Lebensver-
hältnisse uns so genau bekannt sind, wie dies bei Plato der Fall ist.

Wilamowitz had not forgotten Aristotle, *Problemata Physica* XXX. 1,
the remarkable passage discussed earlier, that set Herakles with Socrates and
Plato among "the heroes of the mind" and eased the comparison of himself
with them:[160]

In den aristotelischen Problemen steht, daß Platon ein Melancholiker
war; aber das sollen alle großen Dichter und Denker gewesen sein,
selbst Sokrates, auch Herakles.

And in a clever but unexpected way, he describes Socrates as bearer of the
same "eternal gospel of Hellenism," quite different from Christianity's, that
Herakles represented. He even cites from his earlier work to explain what
Socrates means for mankind:[161]

[156] For earlier aversion to Euripides see *Trauerspiele*, 95 with n. 200, and *Briefe Bormann*,
147.
[157] *Einleitung* (1959) 19. The parallel Plato-Goethe is revealing. Bruno Snell has drawn
attention to the Goethean coloring of *Platon: Platon* I⁵, 605.
[158] *Platon* I⁵, xv.
[159] Eduard Zeller, *Die Philosophie der Griechen in ihrer geschichtlichen Entwicklung* II,
1: *Sokrates und die Sokratiker. Plato und die alte Akademie*, (Leipzig 1922; repr. Darmstadt
1963) 389. For Wilamowitz' admiration of this book see *Philologie*, 67.
[160] *Platon* I⁵, 562 with n. 1.

Lebensbejahung, Lebensmut und Lebensfreude stecken in diesem Glauben. Das Leben ist kein Kreuz, und die sittlichen Forderungen, die allerdings erhoben werden, sind kein Joch, denn sie entsprechen dem, was im Menschen steckt, was er weiß und will, sobald er 'philosophiert', d.h. nicht aufhört zu lernen und für seine Seele zu sorgen, denn zu lernen hat er das eine, was not tut; darin lernt er freilich niemals aus. "Du bist gut geboren und kannst das Gute, so du nur willst. Auf deiner eigenen Kraft stehst du, kein Gott und kein Mensch nimmt dir ab, was du zu tun hast; aber deine Kraft genügt zum Siege, wenn du sie gebrauchst." So habe ich einst in Worte zu fassen gesucht, wozu die Heraklessage den Hellenen mahnte. Sokrates sagt im Grunde dasselbe: das ist das ewige Evangelium des Hellenentums. Antisthenes hat seinen besten Gedanken gehabt, als er Herakles zum Träger seiner Tugendlehre erwählte.

The passage also proves how fundamentally incompatible any Nietzschean idea of Greek pessimism remained. There is a further similarity. The Faust of flesh and blood is not at all the real Faust, who rather is a conception of popular imagination. Just so the Herakles of saga and poetry rather than any historical original claims our attention. So Wilamowitz had earlier argued.[162] So similarly Plato's great feat was through the affect of his teacher's death upon his *Dichterseele* to transmute the Athenian Socrates but not into one who (like Herakles!) became a god but who remained a human being and therefore was great.[163] This elevating and romantic notion runs through *Platon*. It is a legacy from *Herakles*. Did Wilamowitz conceive of his own book as doing for Plato what Plato had done for Socrates? One recalls the earlier parallel between himself and Euripides. Werner Jaeger may have thought so. He wrote Wilamowitz immediately after having read *Platon:*[164]

Ihr *Platon* hat ja so recht wieder gezeigt, dass man niemals aufhört, Ihr Schüler zu sein. Einmal durch die Fülle des Neuen, das er lehrt, dann aber auch durch den Trieb, den er erweckt, nun den Philosophen in Platon mit der Lebendigkeit zu erfassen, zu der Sie erst unser Sehvermögen erzogen haben, indem Sie den Menschen Platon der Welt zurückgegeben haben.

Through his art Wilamowitz had returned the human being Plato to the world. Through his art Plato had preserved the human being Socrates for the world.

---

[161] *Platon* I⁵, 83; cf. *Herakles* II (1959) 41.
[162] *Herakles* II (1959) 39.
[163] *Platon* I⁵, 124.
[164] *Briefe Jaeger*, 326 (21 December 1919).

Platon war der dritte Sohn seiner Eltern, von denen nur die Mutter aus
altem Adel stammte.[165]

Ulrich was the third son of his parents, of whom only his mother, Ulrike
née von Calbo, came from the old aristocracy. Plato's brothers were
Kavalleristen.[166] Hugo, Tello, and Georg were officers in the cavalry. When
Plato died, his brothers were already dead.[167] Ulrich survived all three of his
brothers. As a boy Plato memorized Homer.[168] As a boy Ulrich memorized
Voss' Homer.[169] Socrates, teacher of the noble youth, Plato, was "aus
einem gut bürgerlichen Hause."[170] Karl Ludwig Peter, Otto Jahn, and
Theodor Mommsen, teachers of the noble youth, Ulrich, were from good
bourgeois families. Plato regrettably lacked "ein herzliches Verhältnis zu der
Mutter.[171] But Ulrich had a deep affection for his mother. Socrates knew
nothing of music. Rather than a "Mangel an Erziehung," he probably lacked
the gift for it.[172] Ulrich knew nothing of music but only "das bleibende
bittere Gefühl eines Mangels in der ganzen Bildung."[173] Similar personal
associations colored Hippolytos, Phaedra, Herakles, Amphitryon, Pindar and
Euripides.[174] Such details prove the intensity of Wilamowitz' historicism,
the effort to make them like us. Alopeke, just a foreign word, becomes
Fuchsheim (Foxborough).[175] If, like the George Circle, you are out to make
fun of your betters, the game is easy. For *Protagoras* 311a (ἀναστάντες)
we find the following delightful note:[176]

Daß Sokrates sich, hoffentlich, gewaschen hat, wird nicht gesagt. Den
Mantel hat er zur Hand, denn unter dem hat er geschlafen, wie das Sitte
war. Schuhe trug er nicht. Viel Toilette war also nicht zu machen.
Gefrühstückt ward allgemein nicht; viele aßen bis zur Abendmahlzeit
überhaupt nichts.

---

[165] *Literatur*, 124. Thus he introduces Plato. He next describes the boy's military service.
[166] *Platon* I⁵, 26.
[167] *Platon* I⁵, 22.
[168] *Platon* I⁵, 34.
[169] *Erinnerungen*², 59.
[170] *Platon* I⁵, 69-70.
[171] *Platon* I⁵, 22.
[172] *Platon* I⁵, 71.
[173] *Erinnerungen*², 60.
[174] Margherita Isnardi-Parente, "Rileggendo il Platon di Ulrich von Wilamowitz-
Moellendorff", *Annali della Scuola Superiore di Pisa. Classe di lettere e filosofia*, Ser. 3, vol.
3 (1973) 147-67, esp. 153-54, first noticed autobiographical traces in *Platon*. I am grateful to
her for a copy of her valuable work.
[175] *Platon* I⁵, 67.
[176] *Platon* I⁵, 107 n. 1.

"Platon für Dienstmädchen!," cried Friedrich Gundolf.[177] "A historical novel" is the envious Paul Shorey's cheap jibe.[178] Wilamowitz sought to rescue the Greeks from a false classicism that made them remote and different, "etliche Heroen in einem fernen, schönen Weltenfrühling."[179] He did what he set himself to do splendidly.

Amusing details[180] should not detract us from notice that, as with *Hippolytos* and *Herakles*, there existed deeper, older reasons.

1. *Fidem profiteor Platonicam* proclaimed Wilamowitz in 1908.[181] But his conversion, the *tolle, lege*, was much earlier:[182]

> *Plato autumno 66 Symposio me initiavit, ψυχὴν ἔρωτι subdidit. religionem dedit, qua omnino carueram. Christiana cor meum numquam intravere. in dies magis me tenuit tenebit sed totus Plato, a Protagora ad Leges.*

This mystical moment in autumn 1866 at Schulpforte he describes in more lyrical terms at the end of *Platon*:[183]

> Da liegt ein Knabe unter einer Buche an einem sonnigen Herbsttage und lies das Symposion. Seine Wangen flammen, seine Augen leuchten, denn unter den Worten Diotimas steigt Eros empor und küßt seine Seele wach. Hinauf, hinauf strebt's; es schweben die Wolken abwärts, die Wolken neigen sich der sehnenden Liebe. Da hat Sokrates, hat Platon einen Jünger gewonnen, der nun weiß, wozu er auf Erden ist. Das ist Platons lebendige Wirkung; die ist mehr als alle Historie.

The convert Wilamowitz wrote with the passion of a believer of over fifty years the biography of his religious teacher, often in the vocabulary of Christianity (*Evangelium, frohe Botschaft*). One should compare a Christian's life of Paul.

---

[177] *Apud* K. Hildebrandt, *Erinnerungen an Stefan George und seinen Kreis* (Bonn 1965) 55 n. 11, and see contra E.R. Dodds, *Plato. Gorgias. A Revised Text with Introduction and Commentary* (Oxford 1959) 31 n. 2.

[178] *What Plato Said* (Chicago 1968[7] [1933[1]]), 2. Shorey continues to translate "Ein glücklicher Sommertag" as "a happy picnic day". He knew Wilamowitz meant "a fortunate summer's day". For Shorey's unfair view of Wilamowitz see *Briefe Stenzel*, 87 n. 40, and E.C. Kopff, "Wilamowitz and Classical Philology in the United States of America," *Wilamowitz*, 571-72. Against Shorey see Dodds, *Plato. Gorgias*, 31 n. 2.

[179] *Vorrede* in *Lesebuch* I, iii-viii, quotation iv, and *Briefe Schadewaldt*, 456-57.

[180] Once more: *Platon* I[5], 25: "...ein Junge...hatte für seine Unarten die heilsamen Ohrfegen der mütterlichen Hand zu gewärtigen." The evidence is *Lysis* 208d. Compare *Erinnerungen*[2], 42 n. 1: "...es war ein unheimlicher Gestus, wenn man sah, wie an der rechten Hand der Siegelring umgedreht wurde; das verschärfte die verdiente Ohrfeige mit raffinierter Kunst." He describes maternal discipline.

[181] Norden, 668.

[182] *Latin Autobiography*, 42.

[183] *Platon* I[5], 602-03. "Hinauf...Liebe" is Goethe, *Ganymed* 22-25 (= *Weim. Ausg.* I. 2, 79-80).

2. At eighteen Wilamowitz turned to the youthful idealist, Hippolytos; at forty to the vigorous, middle-aged Herakles. At seventy he sought a new hero. Like the nonagenarian Sophocles in *Oedipus Coloneus*, he turned to one his age, Plato. He writes:[184] "Die Bühne erzwingt einen raschen Schluß; das Leben ist grausamer; es geht auch nach dem fünften Akt weiter." That in a letter of the time to Eduard Norden he applies the epigram to himself[185] proves its autobiographical intensity. Plato surmounted triumphantly a cruel old age. Wilamowitz will in his old age do the same.

3. The cruellest blow for the aged Plato was the death of Dion in 353. "Platon war von dem Schlage im tiefsten Herzen getroffen."[186] He had loved Dion: "...noch als Greis hat er sein Verhältnis zu Dion einen rasenden Eros genannt..."[187] Death had removed the beloved successor. There was no one now. Whom did Wilamowitz see in Dion? He tells us in typical indirect fashion. We need only combine two bits of evidence. We are explicitly told: "Fünf Jahre hat Platon den Dion überlebt."[188] Under the brief notice of the second edition after the dedication is the date 15. X. 1919.[189] It is the *fifth* anniversary of the death of Tycho in victorious engagement at the Battle of Iwangorod.[190] By the cruellest of ironies this was also the seventy-fifth anniversary of the birthday of Friedrich Nietzsche. There was a streak of mysticism in Wilamowitz similar to that he admired in Socrates and Plato. He saw a parallel between Tycho's dying on Nietzsche's seventieth birthday and Dion's murder by Kallippos. He writes a threnos:[191]

> Dion ermordet, ermordet durch einen Athener, einen aus dem Kreise der Akademie.

Nietzsche a German, a German from the circle of the academy, a classical scholar, a fellow student at Schulpforte and at Bonn. In a strange way a curse, in a mystical way proof that Wilamowitz was the νέος Πλάτων.

---

[184] *Platon* I⁵, 517.

[185] See *Briefe-Norden*, 169 (24 October 1918) with n. 627.

[186] *Platon* I⁵, 509.

[187] *Platon* I⁵, 32; cf. 423. Of course the erotic epigrams had to be genuine: contrast Walther Ludwig, "Plato's Love Epigrams" *GRBS* 4 (1963) 59-82.

[188] *Platon* I⁵, 517, a typically Wilamowitzian way of saying that Plato died in 348. He colors the date by extracting its human poignancy.

[189] *Platon* I⁵, v. Snell regrettably omitted the note from his reprint.

[190] Ernst Kapp, *Vorwort*, in T.v.W.-M., *Die dramatische Technik*, v-viii, esp. v. The date appears on the dedicatory page of *Ilias*. On 15 October 1915 Wilamowitz delivered his Berlin rectorial address: *Bibliographie*, No. 523.

[191] *Platon* I⁵, 509. I assume Nietzsche's seventieth received public notice. But it would have been familiar to Wilamowitz since Pforte where birthdays were noted: see Nietzsche, *Kritische Gesamtausgabe: Briefe* I. 1, 92 No. 128.

4. The Sicilian voyages, of which Wilamowitz makes so much, had been the opportunity for the scholar Plato to apply his theory to international politics. "Nun rief ihn die Welt: wie sollte er nicht folgen?"[192] The adventure ended in catastrophic failure. The rectorate in 1915-16, visits to the front, possibly a diplomatic mission or two, for some brief intoxicating moments, had transported Wilamowitz from the study into the arena of international politics.[193] Like Plato's, Wilamowitz' effort had ended in catastrophic failure. This drew them together, *Leidensgenossen*. The seventieth birthday preface (Socrates had died at seventy) and Wilamowitz' letter to Jaeger of 26 November 1918 are the crucial documents for his despair at this period.[194]

5. This leads to Wilamowitz' obsession with Plato's last phase (353-348 B.C.): *Resignation*.[195] It was a productive resignation from which emerged the *Laws*, which Wilamowitz compared to Homer's *Odyssey* in Longinus' sense and to Goethe's *Wanderjahre* and the last parts of *Faust* II.[196] He wrote Drachmann that he hoped for a stroke. "Er hat nur abzusterben."[197] Suicide was a coward's choice:[198]

> O nein, zu leben ist unendlich schwere als das Leben fortzuwerfen: aber das ist Menschenadel und Menschenmut, den Schritt der Feigheit nicht zu tun.

He made the Heraclean and Platonic decision. There would be an "Absage an die Welt."[199] He learned precisely the disillusionment of Plato at *Epistulae* 7, 325c-326a, a document most certainly genuine. "Ich flüchte mich in die reinen Höhen der Wissenschaft, eklipsire mich sonst, so viel ich kann."[200] Solmsen's recollections do much to document the extraordinary last decade.[201] The bibliography for 1918-1929 lists 200 items and *Der Glaube der Hellenen* has not yet appeared. If this is owed the example of Plato, the debt is a great one.

6. Finally Wilamowitz detected in Plato's last years the lofty theme of a higher victory in defeat. *Philosophia* for Plato was not philosophy in the modern sense. "Platon war nicht bloß ein Professor der Philosophie, den

---

[192] *Platon* I[5], 423.
[193] Before 1914 Wilamowitz' political engagement was that of the intelligent, critical citizen. One speaks of Wilamowitz the politician as of Churchill the painter.
[194] *Briefe Jaeger*, 323-25.
[195] *Platon* I[5], 517-59, admittedly only part of a large biography.
[196] *Platon* I[5], 559; cf. p. 518.
[197] *Platon* I[5], vi (the seventieth birthday preface).
[198] *Herakles* II (1959) 130.
[199] *Platon* I[5], 158-82.
[200] *Briefe Jaeger*, 324 (26 November 1918).
[201] Solmsen, 115 (456), and further Abel, 389-408.

nur Kollegen verstehen können."[202] For then Wilamowitz could not
understand him.[203] With one Herculean blow Wilamowitz rescued Plato
from the philosophers. "Diese Philosophie macht dann Platon zu dem,
was wir Wissenschaft nennen..."[204] Plato, like Wilamowitz, was a
Wissenschaftler. In an eloquent final chapter on *Tod und Unsterblichkeit*
Wilamowitz sums up Plato's achievement in the context of subsequent
intellectual history. In a famous passage he speaks as much of himself as
of Plato:[205]

> Aber ein König im Reiche der Wissenschaft war er geworden. Der Same,
> den er in die Seelen seiner Schüler gestreut hatte, war aufgegangen und
> trug nun reiche Blüten und Früchte. Die Schule enthielt schon mehr
> Talente, als sie fassen konnte. Wir sagen, Platon war doch geworden,
> was zu werden in ihm lag. Was ihm in der Zeitlichkeit versagt war, hatte
> er für die Ewigkeit erreicht. Er empfand nicht so; bitterste Resignation
> lag darin, daß er sich dabei beschied, das Spiel des Lebens Gott wohl-
> gefällig zu spielen. Aber wenn dies die Lebensaufgabe des Sterblichen
> überhaupt war, so hatte er sie erfüllt. Auch so konnte er beruhigt
> scheiden.

The language is scriptural. *Reich* recalls the spirited address of 1877. *König*
is Prussia not Periclean Athens.[206] Wilamowitz took a famous phrase, that
had adorned August Böckh,[207] bestowed it on Plato and saw himself as "a
King in the Empire of Scholarship." The emphasis on students is typical.
Wilamowitz saw himself first as a professor and then as a scholar.[208]
Directly after Plato's death, Speusippos deified him and set him among the
heroes. Wilamowitz mildly disapproved.[209] But soon after his own death,
his students would do the same.
　　Gerhart Hauptmann observes:[210]

---

[202] *Platon* I[5], x.

[203] Werner Jaeger, "Die klassische Philologie an der Universität Berlin von 1870-1945,"
in: H. Leussink/E. Neumann/G. Kotowski (eds.), *Studium Berolinense. Aufsätze und Beiträge
zu Problemen der Wissenschaft und zur Geschichte der Friedrich-Wilhelms-Universität zu
Berlin* (*Gedenkschrift der Westdeutschen Rektorenkonferenz und der Freien Universität
Berlin zur 150. Wiederkehr des Gründungsjahres der Friedrich-Wilhelms-Universität zu
Berlin*) II, Berlin 1960, 459-85, quotation 473: "Plato hat er geliebt, das im engeren Sinne
Philosophische vermied er in richtiger Selbsterkenntnis. Wo es ihm in seiner reinen Gestalt
entgegentrat, wie bei Aristoteles, war es ihm wider die Natur".

[204] *Platon* I[5], 80.

[205] *Platon* I[5], 573.

[206] He avoids Mommsen's and Harnack's industrial metaphor, "the big business of
scholarship", see *Briefe Loeb*, 325 n. 26.

[207] See Ernst Curtius, *August Boeckh. Rede zur Säcularfeier von Boeckhs Geburtstag am
24. November 1885* (Berlin 1885) 26.

[208] *Erinnerungen*[2], 7.

[209] *Platon* I[5], 572.

[210] "Wilamowitz-Moellendorff" (May 1930) in: G.H., *Sämtliche Werke*, edd. H.-E. Hass/
M. Machatzke, XI: *Nachgelassene Werke, Fragmente*, (Frankfurt a.M./Berlin/Wien 1974)
1086-90, quotation 1090.

Schongauer und Dürer schneiden die Passion Jesu des Nazareners in Holz. Sie geben den Gestalten Gegenwartscharakter und ihr eigenes Zeitkostüm; die römischen Legionäre werden deutsche Landsknechte. Diese Art zu beleben und gegenwärtig zu machen finden wir auch bei Wilamowitz-Moellendorff, und zwar angewandt auf eine doppelte Passion: die des Sokrates, deren Ähnlichkeit mit der des Nazareners nicht zu übersehen ist, und die des Platon, die im Fehlschlag seines syrakusanischen Abenteuers und im Tode Dions gipfelt.

6. Questions without Answers

I have argued that with some give and take Wilamowitz' scholarly works may be arranged schematically into four categories:

I. Works of Duty

II. Works of Inclination
A. Works owed the influence of another person.
B. Works apt to their time of composition.
C. "Autobiographical documents"
1. *Hippolytos* 2. *Herakles* 3. *Platon*

I cannot imagine the most captious faulting works of duty or works owed the influence of another, usually a colleague. The Nietzsche pamphlets, admittedly, are a special case. The most rigorously objective may look down their noses at people who choose subjects from antiquity relevant to their own time. This implies that either classics can no longer be relevant or that, if relevant, others than experts, perhaps journalists, should make them so. This seems a counsel of despair. There is the danger of twisting ancient evidence to make it fit.[211] But with the possible exception of the youthful address of 1877, where Wilamowitz later admitted and corrected occasional exaggeration, I found no evidence of intentional perversion of ancient evidence by Wilamowitz. I believe that when a scholar turns to his subject to clarify the great problems of his time, he reveals the importance he attributes to it. This is a sign of vigor. Editing Manilius can become superior crossword.[212]

---

[211] Dover, *Expurgation of Greek Literature*, 82: "It is hard to imagine any classicist in 1979 suggesting that it is 'better to forget' any proposition about the Greeks which is supported by the evidence." I can readily make suggestions for Aristotle on natural slaves, Hippocrates on racism and abortion, St. Paul on women in church and homosexuals. Bowdlerism flourishes. The obscenities are different.

[212] Dover, *Expurgation*, 123-24, on "Housman as a disastrous influence on the classical scholarship of our time"; cf. W.M. Calder III, "Research Opportunities in the Modern History of Classical Scholarship" *CW* 74 (1980-81) 241-51, at 251.

That leaves *Hippolytos*, *Herakles* and *Platon*. Most criticism of Wilamowitz, apart from criticisms of detail,[213] centers on these books. I do not intend a detailed defense. Four charges seem to be often made. What do they come to?

1. Wilamowitz' committment sometimes causes him to push the evidence, e.g., for the authenticity of the Seventh Epistle and the erotic epigrams of Plato. I agree. Yet his views are nowhere lunatic and have been held by fine scholars not committed in the way he was. A notorious lack of evidence makes a certain push inevitable in classical studies, not least in questions of authenticity and chronology. It is a weakness endemic to the subject.

2. Wilamowitz sometimes goes "beyond the text" in such matters as, e.g., his characterization of Phaedra. Perhaps. Yet literary judgements are notoriously determined by personal inclination. There is no widely approved methodology. Conclusions find neither general or lasting acceptance. The charge could be made against most practitioners and, therefore, is weak when made *ad hominem*.

3. By stressing similarities rather than differences Wilamowitz makes us think that we understand the Greeks better than we do. The noisiest of this is simply the snobbism of German literati not Wilamowitz' match in scholarship (George, Gundolf, Mann, Hauptmann). The "vive la différence" critics must distinguish between what Wilamowitz ignores because he could not know it and where Wilamowitz wrongly used available evidence. The use of comparative material from other cultures, rare in Wilamowitz, enters here.

4. There are better approaches than Wilamowitz' biographical one to Euripides, Plato, and Pindar. That may be; but not best isn't all bad. The gospel of 1950's new criticism was sown among Anglosaxons by Harold Cherniss,[214] and David C. Young.[215] Has it given us more and better than biography does? The fanatics of Bundyism are not yet ready "umzulernen." But we are seeing in modern languages and in classics a return to historicism and biography which is a part of it.[216]

---

[213] On that see Ed. Fraenkel, *Aeschylus. Agamemnon* I (Oxford 1950) 60.

[214] "The Biographical Fashion in Literary Criticism" *University of California Publications in Classical Philology* 12 (1943) 279-92; repr. in: H.C., *Selected Papers*, ed. Leonardo Tarán (Leiden 1977) 1-13. Throughout the article attacks Wilamowitz' biographical method.

[215] "Pindaric Criticism" *The Minnesota Review* 4 (1964) 584-641, esp. 606 ff.; repr. in W.M. Calder III/J. Stern (eds.) *Pindaros und Bakchylides* (*Wege der Forschung*. 134) Darmstadt 1970, 1-95, esp. 52 ff.

[216] For a brilliant defense of the biographical approach against modern dogmatics see Gilbert Highet, "Masks and Faces in Satire" *Hermes* 102 (1974) 321-37.

I think that two unpopular truths deserve in fairness to be stated. Sometimes American and English criticism of Wilamowitz has been racist. Shorey and Scott treated Wilamowitz in the way Beloch might Jews.[217] That Wilamowitz was greatest of the Germans and stated strong views honestly caused him to draw most of the fire. Who cares what Constantin Ritter thinks about Plato? Or N. Wecklein about Euripides? Wilamowitz is a different story. The lasting damage has been that many young scholars who cannot read German only know Wilamowitz as one must Celsus through his detractors.

I do not see anything wrong about putting one's lifeblood into one's work. It is a metaphorical way of saying that one takes one's work seriously. In 1964 W.S. Barrett published an authoritative edition of Hippolytos.[218] It represents the best Oxford scholarship of its time in the subject. Barrett is "gross in Kleinarbeit," an expert in MSS, meter, language. No article will ever be written on "The Riddle of Barrett's *Phaidrabild*." The reason is simple. Barrett has no *Phaidrabild*. Nor is there anything in the book that explains why the play is worth editing. Wilamowitz' Euripides is important; Barrett's a text, accurately edited. In his Oxford Lecture of 1908 Wilamowitz called the blood in ghosts "something alien, that must be cast out, cast out in the name of truth!" I have drawn attention to it. I do not want to cast it out.[219]

[217] Paul Shorey, "Fifty Years of Classical Studies in America" *TAPA* 50 (1919) 33-61, and John Scott, *The Unity of Homer* (*Sather Classical Lectures.* 1), Berkeley 1921, are racist documents: see further E.C. Kopff, "Wilamowitz and Classical Philology." For Fitch's loyal attempts to divert the hysteria see *Briefe Fitch*, 387-88 with n. 94. Frank J. Frost, *Plutarch's Themistocles: A Historical Commentary* (Princeton 1980) xii-xiii, baldly states that he will not cite Wilamowitz. For the worst sort of English slander see Hugh Trevor-Roper, "Apologia transfugae" *Didaskalos* 4 (1974) 393-412. The remark attributed to Wilamowitz on Paris (397) is without any attestation whatsoever. I doubt that the author has ever read a book by Wilamowitz.

[218] I have reviewed the book at *CP* 60 (1965) 277-81. I have picked on Barrett because Bond's *Herakles* has not yet appeared and I know no modern Plato book worthy of comparison.

[219] I am grateful for the eighth time to the Fondation Hardt for the leisure in which I composed this paper. I thank especially M. Bernard Grange for obtaining books not in the library. I should like to draw attention to a recent excellent study similar to my own: see Fergus Millar, "Style Abides" *JRS* 71 (1981) 144-52. Millar isolates the autobiographical in the lifework of Sir Ronald Syme. I am grateful to Dr. Wolfgang Buchwald for valuable corrections.

F.G. Welcker's Sapphobild
and its Reception in Wilamowitz

I. The Problem

"Sappho was Welcker's love. Whether he ever had another does not appear. He was a bachelor all his days, and his famous vindication of Sappho, written in his early prime (1816), has made him her knight for all the ages."[1]

If Karl Marx is Welcker's most famous student,[2] B.L. Gildersleeve has claims to be his next most famous.[3] In a few well chosen words he states the case. Welcker's chivalrous rescue of Sappho (the phrase is his own)[4] sought to cleanse Sappho of the libellous stain of tribadism and restore to the world, in Wilamowitz' words,[5] "a noble woman, wife, and mother." His principal thesis has not found unanimous consent. The emancipation of women has even caused her inclinations to be welcomed.[6] Nonetheless, F.G. Welcker's "Sappho von einem herrschenden Vorurtheil befreyt" (Göttingen 1816) remains a book of abiding importance.[7] Its methodology makes it the first scientific study of Sappho.[8] She had become a figure of scandalous fiction and Welcker restored her to history.[9] His book became the model for subsequent treatments of poets' lives. Its concern with Sappho's proclivities caused the moral question to remain in the center of Sapphic

---

[1] B.L. Gildersleeve, *AJP* 34 (1913) 232 (= *Selections from the Brief Mention of Basil Lanneau Gildersleeve* ed. Charles William Emil Miller [Baltimore/London/Oxford 1930] 283).

[2] In WS 1835-36 Karl Marx heard Welcker on "Mythologie der Griechen und Römer." Welcker noted on his *Zeugnis* for 22 August 1836 "mit vorzüglichem Fleiße und Aufmerksamkeit." See *Die Promotion von Karl Marx—Jena 1841* edd. Erhard Lange, Ernst-Günther Schmidt, Günther Steiger, Inge Taubert, and Bolko Schweinitz (Berlin 1983) 186.

[3] For his role as founder of scientific philology in the United States see my "Studies in the Modern History of Classical Scholarship," *Antiqua* 27 (Naples 1984) 20-23.

[4] F.G. Welcker, *Kleine Schriften* II: *Zur griechischen Literaturgeschichte* (Bonn 1845; repr. Osnabrück 1973) 127: "der ritterliche Schriftstellerversuch."

[5] Ulrich von Wilamowitz-Moellendorff, *Sappho und Simonides: Untersuchungen über griechische Lyriker* (Berlin 1913) 73 (hence cited: *SuS*).

[6] See e.g., Susan Gubar, "Sapphostries," *Signs* 10 (1984) 46: "Sappho represents, then, all the lost women of genius in literary history, especially all the lesbian artists whose work has been destroyed, sanitized, or heterosexualized..."

[7] I cite throughout the revised version of *Kl. Schriften* II. 80-144.

[8] See Helmut Saake, *Sappho-Studien: Forschungsgeschichtliche, biographische und literar-ästhetische Untersuchungen* (München/Paderborn/Wien 1972) 18: "Mit Welcker erhebt zum ersten Mal ein kritischer klassischer Philologe seine Stimme im Streit um die Integrität oder Pervertiertheit Sapphos." Henceforth cited: *Sappho-Studien*.

[9] See Horst Rüdiger, "Sappho: Ihr Ruf und Ruhm bei der Nachwelt," *Das Erbe der Alten Zweite Reihe* 21, ed. Otto Immisch (Leipzig 1933) 33ff. This informative book is largely a history of the reception of Sappho in Germany.

scholarship as it had since Pierre Bayle (1695)[10] and has until Kirkwood (1974).[11] Further, Welcker convinced Wilamowitz, who was ready to be convinced, of his cause.[12] In *Sappho und Simonides* (Berlin 1913), Wilamowitz firmly asserted that his heroine was no tribade. A few eccentric and premature voices aside, not until D.L. Page, *Sappho and Alcaeus* (Oxford 1955) did the tide change. For almost 150 years Welcker had dominated Sapphic criticism. To phrase the matter provocatively, the personal view that Welcker and Wilamowitz held toward women for more than a century determined the scholarly reception of the greatest lyric poetess of antiquity. Finally, *Sappho* has been called Welcker's most subjective book.[13] There are contenders.[14] But *Sappho* as a biographical aid in understanding one of the four or five most influential philologists of XIX century Europe deserves notice.

I intend to say a word about Welcker's predecessor, G.E. Lessing. I shall then state in summary Welcker's case and seek to place it within the context of previous research and of Welcker's own interests. Then I shall discuss the famous attacks of Colonel Mure (1850, 1854), wrongly called an English dilettante by Wilamowitz,[15] Welcker's reply (1856) and Mure's savage but revealing rebuttal (1857). Next I shall treat Wilamowitz' famous reception (1913) of Welcker's Sapphobild and allude *en passant* to D.L. Page (1955) and Heinrich Dörrie (1975). I have chosen to limit myself to the great figures. In the end they alone matter.

---

[10] Rüdiger, *Sappho* 40ff.; cf. Wilamowitz, *SuS* 17-18.

[11] G.M. Kirkwood, "Early Greek Monody: the History of a Poetic Type," *Cornell Studies in Classical Philology* 37 (Ithaca/London 1974) 101-02, 242-43. That Kirkwood accepts Virbius Caudinus as Sappho's husband should not surprise us. He has written that there is no need today to read Wilamowitz carefully: *CW* 74 (1980/81) 34.

[12] See Wilamowitz, *SuS* 71:

> Aber mit voller Zuversicht bekenne ich mich zu dem Glauben, daß Welcker Sappho von einem herrschenden Vorurteil befreit hat, für alle die ihn hören wollen und verstehn können.

A *confessio fidei*. Welcker's title is not forgotten: see O. Schönberger, "Cornelius Nepos von einem herrschenden Vorurteil befreit," *Hermes* 96 (1968) 508-09.

[13] See Reinhard Kekulé, *Das Leben Friedrich Gottlieb Welcker's nach seinen eignen Aufzeichnungen und Briefen* (Leipzig 1880) 368:

> ...sein Herz sprach am lautesten mit bei Sappho, dem in früher Jugend gewonnenen Ideal, dem er stets treu blieb.

Kekulé's opinion is cited with approval by Rüdiger, 103. For Wilamowitz' view of Kekulé's biography see my "Ulrich von Wilamowitz-Moellendorff to Kekulé von Stradonitz on Friedrich Gottlieb Welcker," *SIFC* NS 3, 2 (1984) 116-33 (= *Further Letters*, 81-95).

[14] Obviously the Zoega volumes and *Tagebuch einer Griechischen Reise* (Berlin 1865); cf. Kekulé, *Welcker* 247-322.

[15] He was a Scot: see *infra* and correct Wilamowitz, *SuS* 71 and Rüdiger, *Sappho* 109.

II. Gotthold Ephraim Lessing: "Rettungen des Horaz"

Horst Rüdiger first suggested in 1933 that Lessing's rescue of Horace inspired Welcker's rescue of Sappho.[16] Lessing's "Rettungen des Horaz" (1754) is a work of surpassing intelligence and wit.[17] It anticipates much modern philological methodology and Eduard Norden rightly called it in 1929:[18] "eine Abhandlung, die bei den Philologen noch jetzt, nicht bloß um Lessings Namem willen, sondern wegen ihres Eigenwerts in Ansehen steht." Lessing rescues Horace from four charges: voluptuousness, homosexuality (*Knabenliebe*), cowardice, and casual piety. His thesis briefly put is that the charges are groundless because poems are not autobiographical documents and gossip must be treated as gossip (*Quellenforschung*). How does he assemble his proof?

Lessing discusses at length (550ff.) Suetonius, *Horatius* with the aim of proving unjust the slander:[19]

> Ad res Venerias intemperantior; nam speculato cubiculo scorta dicitur habuisse disposita, ut quocumque respexisset ibi et imago coitus referretur.

I summarize his remarkably sophisticated argument. The frail evidence for ascribing the life to Suetonius is noticed (550-51). The hearsay source is stressed: *traditur, dicitur*, "two fine words which by now many an honest man has to thank for the loss of his good name" (551). Over one hundred years separated Suetonius from Horace. Suetonius rejects Horace's *Elegia* and a prose letter as spurious. Why would the same scholar accept such slander? Lessing finds the passage out-of-place, its language un-Roman, and that it contradicts other passages in the biography. The mirrors do not prove (553) the charge of immoderate lust (*intemperantior*) but only of its attractiveness; and the evidence of Horace's poems show him too refined for such to be attractive.

---

[16] Rüdiger, *Sappho*, 102-03.

[17] For date and background see Erich Schmidt, *Lessing: Geschichte seines Lebens und seiner Schriften* I[3] (Berlin 1909) 234-42 and Volker Riedel, *Lessing und die römische Literatur* (Weimar 1976) 127-38. Although Riedel carefully discusses the reception of "Rettungen" by Latinists, he says nothing of its influence on Welcker. In the following discussion I cite the pages of Gotthold Ephraim Lessing, *Gesammelte Werke* III: *Frühe kritische Schriften*, ed. Paul Rilla (Berlin 1955) 547-94.

[18] Eduard Norden, "Lessing als Klassischer Philologe," *Kleine Schriften zum Klassischen Altertum*, ed. Bernhard Kytzler (Berlin 1966) 627.

[19] I cite the text of C.L. Roth, *C. Suetoni Tranquilli quae supersunt omnia* II[2]: *de Grammaticis et Rhetoribus deperditorum librorum Reliquiae* (Leipzig 1924) 298. 20-22, where *nam...referretur* are deleted without a reference to Lessing who in fact (559) first deleted them.

Lessing queries (554-555) the Latinity of *speculari* and for *speculatum cubiculum* he would expect *cubiculum speculis ornatum*. Although solving the difficulty differently, modern scholars have shared his doubts.[20] Finally, the slander is inconsistent (555) with Augustus' praise of Horace attested in the *vita*. He calls the poet *purissimum penem*. *Purissimum* means *Allerreinste* and a man *ad res venerias intemperantior* does not deserve the epithet. Lessing attempts emendation (555) but prefers (556-59) that the offending passage is an interpolation.[21] He brilliantly compares Seneca, *NQ* 1. 16, where a similar though more lurid tale is told of the degenerate Hostius Quadra,[22] whose murder by his slaves Augustus approved. How could the same Augustus approve a poet devoted to the same perverse exhibitionism? How could he hold Hostius *indignum vindicta* and Horace *purissimum penem* (558)? The proper names, both from Augustus' reign, are similar, but Horatius is far better known than Hostius. Horatius replaced Hostius in the scurrilous anecdote which thus became ascribed to the poet and a scribbler inserted the libel into Suetonius' text. The analysis proves the erudition and subtlety of Lessing's defense.[23]

In a memorable passage, Lessing anticipates modern *Topos-Forschung*. A poet does not mean what he says literally. Lessing writes of Horace's critics:[24]

> They cannot imagine how a poet can be angry without being angry; how he can be drunk with love without feeling it. They, who allow all passions to be aroused in themselves only by experience, know nothing of the secret of making them alive through random imagination...Because they do not know how the pain over the loss of a beloved might be expressed without having felt it, so a Neaera must have been faithless to him, when he wants to describe nature and her tempests on such an occasion.

Lessing will not (564) turn Horace into "a priest of chastity." Far from it. "He may always have been in love. I only plead for him that one ought not to use his odes against him and to turn the fancies of his wit into

---

[20] I note the standard text of F. Klingner, *Q. Horati Flacci Opera*[6] (Leipzig 1982) 3: *nam specula to<to> cubiculo [scorta] dicitur habuisse disposita*. There is no mention of Lessing in his apparatus.

[21] Roth (*supra* n. 19) deletes the passage. Contrarily Ed. Fraenkel, *Horace* (Oxford 1957) 21 remarks: "The time is past when scholars could feel justified in obelizing this section." He next stresses *traditur, dicitur* as indicating hearsay, and continues: "Lessing compared Seneca's very similar report about the rich Hostius Quadra, who lived under Augustus." He provides no reference to Lessing nor does he add that precisely because of the "similar report" Lessing deleted the passage. Has he Lessing second hand?

[22] See A. Stein *RE* 16 (1913) 2517. 8-19.

[23] I regret that his case has been forgotten by modern Horatians. In my opinion he has proved that *nam...referretur* are an interpolation. Werner Krenkel, "Skopophilie in der Antike," *Wissenschaftliche Zeitschrift der Wilhelm-Pieck-Universität Rostock* 26 (1977) 622, cites Lessing and uses Suetonius only to attest a *Spiegelzimmer*.

[24] Lessing, *op. cit.* 561.

confessions of his heart." The leads into Lessing's defense of Horace against the charge of *Knabenliebe* (566-74), from Welcker's viewpoint the most important passage in Lessing's essay. Lessing argues first that Horace *denies* such vice (*Sat.* 1. 2. 19: *non ego*). The appeal to Ligurinus (*Carm.* 4. 1. 33-40) is a topos. Ligurinus is "a thought of the poet" based on Anacreon's Bathyllos. Lessing compares *Ep.* 14. 9-12: "Horace was so moved by the loving tears of Anacreon that he decided to make them his own" (569). The source of *Carm.* 4. 1. 35-36 is Sappho in Catullus 51. 7-9. The citation of Sappho in the context of *Knabenliebe* and as a topos deserves especial remark (569-570). If this is not enough, Lessing adduces an historical argument. Augustus promulgated legislation against *Knaben-liebe*, the *de adulteriis et pudicitia* and the *de maritandis ordinibus*. Horace praises just these laws (*Carm.* 4. 5. 21-24).[25] He would not publicly have flaunted them. It is special pleading to hold that his peccadilloes preceded Augustus' legislation (573).

The defense against cowardice in battle runs that throwing away a shield is a Greek topos and that Horace would not have been promoted to tribune and honorably discharged had he been a deserter. *Carm.* 2. 7 is "nichts als ein Scherz" (577).[26] The defense against casual piety procedes on similar lines. It is impossible (580) to derive Horace's religious convictions from his poems. Then in unexpected anticipation of Mary Lefkowitz[27] Lessing writes: "aber nur selten ist das ich sein eigen ich" (580-81). *Carm.* 1. 34 is translated and interpreted with historical parallels and in the context of *Topos-Forschung*.

From Lessing, Welcker, also a pastor's son, learnt method and to defend a great ancient poet against the vile charge of homosexuality. There was a further bond, one that reappeared with Wilamowitz. Lessing remarked (562): "Niemand hat diese verhaßten Anwendungen weiter getrieben, als einige Franzosen." The slanderers of the ancients, those who invented their vices, were in both cases French, once the same man, Pierre Bayle (1647-1706).[28] Welcker had twice enlisted against the French.[29] Wilamowitz would in

---

[25] See lately L.F. Raditsa, "Augustus' Legislation Concerning Marriage, Procreation, Love Affairs and Adultery," *ANRW* II. 13 (Berlin/New York 1980) 278-339.

[26] R.G.M. Nisbet and Margaret Hubbard, *A Commentary on Horace: Odes Book II* (Oxford 1978) 113 (*ad* 2. 7. 10) accept Lessing's argument that Horace is writing "a poetical topic."

[27] I recall *HSCP* 67 (1963) 177-253.

[28] Rüdiger, *Sappho* 40-46. For a succinct account of Bayle's thought see Élisabeth Labrousse, "Pierre Bayle et l'instrument critique," *Philosophes de tous les temps* 16 (Paris 1965). For the dictionary see 36-39. It was translated into English and German in the eighteenth century (183).

[29] Welcker served as *Oberleutnant* in the campaign against France in 1814: see Kekulé, *Welcker*, 131-35. He re-enlisted in Berlin spring 1815 when learning of the return of Napoleon to France: Kekulé, *Welcker*, 137-38. Gildersleeve (*Brief Mention*, 324) numbers Welcker among "the glorious band of scholars who went forth to fight for the liberation of Germany—Boeckh, Welcker, Reisig, Lachmann, classicists all." Naturally their hatred of the French carried into their scholarship. Comparable is the anti-Germanism of Anglo-Saxon

1870. Nothing cements friendship like shared hate. Literary vengeance for political wrong united Welcker to Lessing, and later the both to Wilamowitz.

III. Welcker's Defense of 1816

"Sappho freed from a reigning prejudice" appeared as a small book, Vandenhoek and Ruprecht, Göttingen 1816. Epicharmus fragment 250 Kaibel ("remember to distrust") is the epigraph. Welcker begins with a programmatic statement worthy of Lessing (80):

> Because usually it is all too lacunose and self-contradictory, what is told of the life of famous poets by generations who write little and almost all of it poetry, wins in general little confidence. Most is only deductions from their works, often one-sided and wrongly interpreted and presented by ancient writers under the guise of the historical. Different generations have often expressed their own taste in varying opinions; and most confusion arises through the fact that so long as active and inventive saga and her sister allegory thrive and hold the field, the names of the poets themselves, to a certain degree, become the object of their attention.

That is we must treat our few unsatisfactory sources critically and be alert to the perversion of truth caused by a reception that has no commitment to historical veracity. Welcker stresses (80-81) the peculiar danger of comic poets whose distortions (*Zerrbilder*) can permanently replace in historical consciousness the figure they mock.[30]

Welcker, with impeccable method, seeks first (81-82) to isolate "was wir geschichtlich von der Sappho wissen" (81). With the exception of Ovid *Heroides* 15, which Welcker holds Ovidian and to be drawing on Sappho's own poems,[31] he accepts only Herodotus 2. 135, Marmor Parium 36 (= *FGrHist* 239 F36), and Plato, *AP* 9. 506, which Wilamowitz still held genuine.[32] Welcker (83 c.n.3) cites Pollux 9. 84 and Aristotle, *Rhetoric* 2. 23 (= 1398b 12-13) as proof that Mytileneans, proud of their citizen though

---

scholars after World War I (e.g., Lindsay, Murray, Scott, Shorey). Gildersleeve, Oldfather and Fitch remained loyal.

[30] Welcker had a predecessor who distinguished between the person and the tradition about her, Gottfried Olearius (*ob.* 1715) in his *Dissertatio de poetriis Graecis* (1708) and who also did not consider the poems obscene (*at nihil in eis obscoenitatis*). I know the book only from Rüdiger, *Sappho* 48-50.

[31] For the authoritative modern discussion of sources, authenticity and language see Heinrich Dörrie, "P. Ovidius Naso: Der Brief der Sappho an Phaon," *Zetemata* 58 (Munich 1975) (henceforth cited: Dörrie).

[32] Wilamowitz, *SuS* 41 with n. 1. More sceptical are A.S.F. Gow and D.L. Page, *The Greek Anthology: Hellenistic Epigrams* I (Cambridge 1965) xxii n. 2, who, however, do not commit themselves on *AP* 9. 506.

a woman, minted coins in her honor. In fact Aristotle is not relevant and Pollux refers to an imperial issue,[33] but the joining of literary and numismatic evidence in a philological context recalled Zoega and heralded a new age.

Then the evidence of the preserved fragments is considered. Welcker insists on interpreting them in the context of literary-history. Unlike Horace, Sappho is archaic; and her poetry lacks ambiguity and indirectness, what we might today call irony. It is "simple and straightforward" (*einfach und bestimmt*: 83). One finds in this early Doric-Aeolic poetry lofty adherence to nature (*Naturwahrheit*)[34] joined with the most subtle sense for art. Comparable only is the sculpture of the age of Phidias. Welcker approvingly cites the Elgin Marbles and Canova's opinion about them.[35] Again his argumentation is not limited to philological evidence. One sees the beginnings of monumental philology, the use of artifacts to elucidate texts, that would bloom later under Welcker's colleague, Otto Jahn, his student, Hugo Blümel, and later Carl Robert.[36] Welcker concludes (83) by stressing the unique historical problem caused by the fragmentary preservation of Greek poetry. It must be interpreted with use of all extant evidence: the *Totalitätsideal*.[37]

The next part of Welcker's study (84-105) is the most famous and treats the charge of homosexuality. Apart from the cogency of individual observations, attention must be drawn at the start to three techniques of argument, used by Welcker, that have exerted considerable and often welcome influence on subsequent scholarship.

---

[33] See Werwick Wroth, *A Catalogue of the Greek Coins in the British Museum: Catalogue of the Greek Coins of Troas, Aeolis, and Lesbos* (repr. Bologna 1964) lxx-lxxi.

[34] *Naturwahrheit* as a decisive criterion of excellence in art is found in Anton Springer and his students Kekulé von Stradonitz and Wilamowitz: see *SIFC* NS 3, 2 (1984) 121 with n. 39. It derives from Robert Wood, *Essay on the Original Genius of Homer* (1769) which in the German version *Versuch über das Originalgenie Homers* (Frankfurt/Main 1773) exerted extraordinary influence in Germany: see David Constantine, *Early Greek Travellers and the Hellenic Ideal* (Cambridge 1984) 72-80. An enthusiastic review by C.G. Heyne and praise by Goethe did much to insure its fame. See also Georg Finsler, *Homer in der Neuzeit von Dante bis Goethe* (Leipzig/Berlin 1912) 368-72. The reception of this book in nineteenth century Germany deserves a careful study.

[35] In welcome contrast to Thorwaldsen's readiness to mutilate the Aeginetan marbles, Antonio Canova declared that it would be sacrilege in him or any man to presume to touch the Elgin marbles with a chisel: see William St. Clair, *Lord Elgin and the Marbles* (London 1967) 152. Presumably Welcker heard of this while in Rome.

[36] See Wolfgang Schindler, "Die Archäologie im Rahmen von Wilamowitz' Konzeption der Altertumswissenschaft," *Wilamowitz nach 50 Jahren* edd. William M. Calder III, Hellmut Flashar, and Theodor Lindken (Darmstadt 1985) 241-62.

[37] By his example F.G. Welcker did most to popularize among scholars the *Totalitätsideal*. His inclination to work with fragments of cyclic epics, tragedies, or Sappho, did not allow confinement to a small corpus. But scholars before Welcker, particularly F.A. Wolf (1759-1824) and his teacher C.G. Heyne (1729-1812) had begun to think this way: see Anthony Grafton, "Prolegomena to Friedrich August Wolf," *Journal of the Warburg and Courtauld Institutes* 44 (1981) 103 with literature there cited.

1. Welcker judges Greek homosexuality in its historical context; and, although a pastor's son, he disregards scriptural injunctions (Leviticus and Paul) against its practice. He writes as Lessing did and Wilamowitz would entirely without prudery.[38] The elucidation of λεσβιάζειν as *fellationem facere* is regularly attributed to Wilamowitz.[39] In fact Wilamowitz took it silently from Welcker.[40] This wholly admirable attempt to see the Greeks as they saw themselves aroused the wrath of Colonel Mure and for 150 years was impossible in Anglo-Saxon scholarship.[41]

2. 50 years before its vogue, Welcker, by introducing material from other cultures, anticipated Sir James George Frazer's (1854-1941) use of anthropology to elucidate the classics.[42] In M.P. Nilsson's famous phrase:[43] "The chief value of analogies is to show what is possible and what may be reasonably expected; they do not prove anything in special or specified details." On the other hand, analogies are welcome in a subject where evidence is so scarce. Welcker (91) compares Herakles undertaking labors for love to a knight of the Middle Ages. He compares (91) to Dorians "pristine, simple Alpine people," whom perhaps he met while walking from Darmstadt to Rome in 1806. He cites an old Norse parallel for *Heldenbrüderschaft* (92). He compares (104) French and German Minnesingers for a sublime love that transcends sensuality. He invokes (105) the youthful Dante, who loved "non per libidine, ma per gentilezza di cuore." He holds (105) that Queen Christina of Sweden's interest in the Countess Ebba Sparre was innocent. "Still far more remarkable" (105 n. 49) are Shakespeare's sonnets to the fair youth. And (*ibid.*) he arouses our curiosity with a tantalizing reference to "what Prof. Vischer tells about the sentimental amorous friendship of boys in the lower Cloister at Blaubeuern." Occasionally the analogies may sound naive but their use is very modern. They also presuppose Wilamowitz'

---

[38] See especially Ulrich von Wilamowitz-Moellendorff, *Aristophanes Lysistrate* (Berlin 1927) 6-8. Wilamowitz could only have approved Welcker.

[39] Wilamowitz, *SuS* 73 n. 1.

[40] See Welcker, *Kl. Schriften* II. 86 n. 14.

[41] One need only recall how A.E. Housman was forbidden to publish *Praefanda* in England: see A.S.F. Gow, *A.E. Housman: A Sketch together with a List of his Writings and Indexes to his Classical Papers* (Cambridge 1936) 76 with n. 1. For the paper see *Hermes* 66 (1931) 402-12 (= *Classical Papers* 3 [Cambridge 1972] 1175-84). For English censorship of classics see K.J. Dover, "Expurgation of Greek Literature," *Les Études classiques aux XIXe et XXe siècles: leur place dans l'histoire des idées, Entretiens* 26 (Vandoeuvres-Genève 1979) 55-89.

[42] If one may trust her index, Welcker's name does not appear in S.C. Humphreys, *Anthropology and the Greeks*[3] (London 1983). Merkelbach, *Philologus* 101 (1957) 16 compares troubadours, Dante and Minnesingers without citing Welcker!

[43] Martin P. Nilsson, *Homer and Mycenae* (London 1933) 214. The passage was repeatedly cited with approval by A.D. Nock. Wilamowitz did not approve the use of such analogies and told Frazer so: see *Antiqua* 23 (Naples 1983) 118-19.

axiom that an ancient is "a man like you and I."[44] Both scholars assume sameness not difference.

3. Welcker, who had just been discharged from the army, elucidates antiquity from personal experience (92). "Adventurous campaigns and long confinements to barracks" (*Feldlagerungen*) encourage *Heldenbrüderschaft*. Wilamowitz also learned from military service to understand ancient authors.[45] Souda II. 683. 17-18 Adler supports Welcker. There were Italians (92 n. 34) "die κατ' ἀνάγκην στρατείας auf Männerliebe fielen."

He propounds an unexpected thesis. Male homosexuality was pure, beautiful, and good. He calls it *Heldenbrüderschaft* (92), *reine Männerliebe* (93), *die wunderbare Freundschaft* similar to fatherly love (95). Admittedly (94) some men are ready to yield to weakness when it can be hidden behind a greater virtue. In some cases (94 n. 37) even Platonic pederasty served as a mask for the sensual. Nonetheless, the modern vice is repeatedly lauded by the ancients and appears in their poetry, religion, and history. Female homosexuality contrarily was vile and abhorrent, confined to prostitutes and, therefore, called ἑταιριστρία (85; see Pl. *Smp.* 91e). Comparative material suggests it existed but aversion banished it from the sources. "Nowhere is the chaste love of women praised while on numberless occasions that of men is" (96). Sappho is treated as a paragon of womanly virtue in antiquity by such moralists as Socrates, Aristotle, and Plutarch. Lucian (*Imag.* 18) in a sycophantic work compares her character to that of Panthea, the favorite of Verus (102-03), which he surely would not have done were there the least taint of tribadism.[46] The Syracusans erected Silanion's statue of the poetess in their Prytaneum (104).[47] If she had been a tribade, she would have been vilified by posterity not adored. This is Lessing's defense of Horace against the charge of cowardice. If he had thrown away his shield, he would not have been promoted and honorably discharged.

Welcker reconciles the vice of tribadism and the repute of Sappho in an ingenious way. Sappho is an unicum. She alone of women loved her schoolgirls in precisely the blameless manner that Socrates and Plato did

---

[44] See Ada Hentschke and Ulrich Muhlack, *Einführung in die Geschichte der Klassischen Philologie* (Darmstadt 1972) 102: "Realismus und Aktualisierung—der Alltag des antiken Menschen und dieser Mensch als 'Mensch wie du und ich'—sind die hervorstechenden Merkmale aller großen Interpretationen Wilamowitz'."

[45] A parade at Tempelhof allows one to understand a Homeric simile: Ulrich von Wilamowitz-Moellendorff, *Die Ilias und Homer* (Berlin 1916) 275; urinating on the march in 1870-71 elucidates Hes. *Op.* 727-32: id. *Hesiodos Erga²* (Berlin 1962) 125. There are other examples. See his "Kriegserinnerungen," *Reden aus der Kriegszeit* (Berlin 1915) 39-73.

[46] The weakness of Welcker's argument is that he ignores the question of what sources were available to Lucian and the others. The view has been argued that by V B.C. no biographical information apart from her poetry survived: see Dörrie 15. The vases prove this.

[47] Cicero *In Verrem* 4. 125ff.: see Dörrie 14 with n. 2.

their students. He cites two passages in ancient literature to confirm this view. Plutarch, *Lycurgus* 18. 9 (= 51d) parenthetically refers in a discussion of male homosexuality to the chaste love of "beautiful and good" Spartan women for maidens (96). Further (97 with n. 41) Maximus of Tyre (18. 9a 230-31 Hobein = Testimonium 20 Campbell) redeems the love of Sappho for Gyrinna, Atthis, and Anactoria by comparing it to Socrates' for Alcibiades, Charmides, and Phaedrus. From this arises the tenacious thesis of the school-mistress Sappho (98). Myrtilos of Methymna (*FGrHist* 477 F 7c) records that Lesbian girls sang at festivals and funerals and shared in the art of the Muses (98). These are the sort of girls whom Sappho might have taught. In her own poetry (frag. 150 L-P) she refers to μουσοιτίλων οἰκίαν. That is (97): "ein Musensitz."[48] Once in a typical attempt to make antiquity less remote Wilamowitz calls Sappho's establishment "a girls' boarding school" (*ein Mädchenpensionat*). This is done with an apology and for lay-readers not for scholars.[49] Pöschl's criticism is in a word unfair.[50]

Welcker (105) next poses a crucial question. If it is agreed that female homosexuality was abhorred in antiquity and that Sappho's love for pupils was unsullied by sensuality, then how can we explain the origin of "the malicious rumor" (*das böse Gerücht*) that she was a tribade? Welcker's answer to this question (105-114) is an early masterpiece of scientific *Quellenforschung* that has determined the course of all subsequent work on Sappho-biography by informed scholars.[51] He concentrates not on the person Sappho nor the nature of the vice. The answer lies in *Überlieferungs-geschichte*. In the manner of a critical editor he seeks to isolate a conta-

---

[48] Wilamowitz, *SuS* 73: "...ihr Haus ist ein Musensitz."

[49] See Ulrich von Wilamowitz-Moellendorff, "Die griechische Literatur des Altertums," *Die griechische und lateinische Literatur und Sprache³*, *Die Kultur der Gegenwart* I. VIII (Leipzig/Berlin 1912) 41: "Wenn der moderne Ton nicht schreckt, mag das immer ein Mädchenpensionat nennen." Wilamowitz' boarding school for girls has recently received welcome support from *PKöln* II. 61 (Inv. 5860), where Sappho is described as "in peace and quiet teaching not only the noblest girls of the locals but of families in Ionia as well." Kallias of Mytilene is invoked. The papyrus is II A.D.

[50] See Viktor Pöschl, *Philologie und Hermeneutik im 19. Jahrhundert: Zur Geschichte und Methodologie der Geisteswissenschaften*, edd. Hellmut Flashar, Karlfried Gründer, Axel Horstmann (Göttingen 1979) 377:

Und schließlich—um nur ein bekanntes Beispiel zu nennen—den Kreis der Sappho als ein "Mädchenpensionat" zu beschreiben: das zeugt doch, gerade weil es ernst gemeint ist, von diesem völligen Mangel an historischer Distanz, was um so erstaunlicher ist, als der Historismus natürlich doch nicht ahistorisch war, es jedenfalls nicht immer sein muß.

Wilamowitz did not mean it seriously. He was drawing an amusing modern analogy for laymen. The origin of the analogy is in Welcker. Largely because of Wilamowitz' lively style the volume went through three editions and did untold good for Greek studies in German-speaking lands. R. Kassel, *ZPE* 45 (1982) 297, much to his credit, tries to see what Wilamowitz is doing. So earlier had Reinhold Merkelbach, *Philologus* 101 (1957) 4 n. 1.

[51] For allowance for the comic factor in ancient biographical tradition about Sappho see Wilamowitz, *SuS* 23 with n. 2; W. Aly, *RE* 2 A (1920) 2359. 51ff.; Wilhelm Schmid, *Geschichte der griechischen Literatur* I (Munich 1929) 422 with nn. 3, 4; Dörrie 14-18 (a magisterial treatment).

minated tradition. For the first time[52] he proves that tradition to be Attic Comedy. For Welcker's own development the pages are decisive. He first seeks here to reconstruct lost dramas from their titles, fragments, and testimonia. He reconstructs scenes from anecdotes in later authors (106 n. 50). This anticipates his later work on lost tragedy and epic. Because the venture is bold and pioneering, errors and omissions have been set right by later scholars. For some reason he overlooks Ameipsias, *Sappho*, which if genuine proves fifth century caricature.[53] Perhaps under Ovidian influence, he accepts the historicity of Phaon and introduces Kratinos and Plato Comicus, where scholars after Wilamowitz would not (105-07 with n. 50). He misses the comic origin of Sappho's husband. But this in no way dims the brilliance of his achievement.

He adduces (107 with n. 51) three middle and two new comedies which by their title "Sappho" must have concerned the poetess. They are:

I. Middle Comedy
A. Amphis frag. 32 (II. 246) Kock, only recently published (1814) at Bekker, *Anecdota* I. 89. 22.
B. Antiphanes, fragg. 196, 197 (II. 94-96) Kock. In the long fragment (Athen. 10. 450e) Sappho's father (196. 13 K) or an old man tries unsuccessfully to solve her riddle.
C. Ephippus, frag. 20 (II. 262) Kock, three and a half uninformative verses from Athenaeus 13. 572c.

II. New Comedy
A. Diphilos, fragg. 69, 70 (II. 564) Kock. Welcker assigns (107 n. 51) the two verse frag. 60 which contains the vocative Ἀρχίλοχε to Sappho. He skilfully expands (107) the comic possibility of frag. 70, the testimony from Athenaeus 13. 599d: "Diphilos, the comic poet, in his drama "Sappho" has made Archilochus and Hipponax lovers of Sappho." The chronological difficulties either did not occur to Welcker or he allowed comic licence.
B. Timocles, frag. 30 (II. 464) Kock, which because it mentions the *Lüstling* Misgolas is dated ca. 345 B.C.: see Geyer, *RE* 30 (1932) 2049. 20-33.

---

[52] Welcker, *Kl. Schriften* II.105:

> So natürlich und nothwendig richtet man hier sogleich den Blick nach der Komödie daß man nicht begreift, warum sie niemals in dieser Hinsicht in Betracht gekommen sey.

Rüdiger, *Sappho* 104 holds that Welcker owes the suggestion to A.W. Schlegel.

[53] Ameipsias frag. 16 (I. 674) Kock from Pollux 9. 138 (= II. 184. 31 Bethe), where for Ἀμειψίου I should with Kaibel correct to Ἄμφιδος. This removes the anomaly of a fifth century "Sappho" and a theme that differs considerably from Ameipsias' other titles.

Welcker draws two cogent parallels to support the charge of comic invention. He cites (108) an ancient source. Plutarch, *Pericles* 13. 9-12, who attests how grossly comic poets slandered Pericles. The second (109) is his own. If the Socratic dialogues were lost and we could only evaluate Socrates from Aristophanes and the scurra Atticus of a Roman (Cic. *ND* 1. 93 with Pease), what a different reputation he would have today. He wisely observes (108) that the utter lack of biographical information and the remoteness of the subject allow "contradictions, exaggerations, and inventions in large part to evolve from the free play of caricature-poetry."[54] This is an extraordinary insight for 1816. He first suggests (112-13) that the tradition of Sappho as a small negress has a comic origin, a view vigorously defended by Dörrie without citing Welcker.[55] He again reveals the influence of Lessing, when (112) he explains Menander's report (frag. 258 Körte) of Sappho's suicide-leap from the Leucadian cliff for love as a *topos*. He compares Stesichorus, frag. 277 Page and Anacreon frag. 376 Page.[56] His emphasis on Menander's λέγεται recalls Lessing on *dicitur*, *traditur* in Ps-Suetonius.

The least satisfactory part of Welcker's essay is his treatment (114-23) of Roman sources. This is not only because Welcker's interests lay elsewhere. Scientific investigation of the subject had not yet begun so that he necessarily relied on intelligent observation and general impressions. The irony was that although Roman sources were unimportant historically in comparison to Greek, yet their part in forming uncritical popular opinion was far greater. "Aber die moderne Welt bildete sich ihr Urteil an den Lateinern," remarked Wilamowitz pointedly.[57] Welcker begins (114) by excusing the Romans for their incapacity to distinguish between what was fun and what was serious among the Greeks. Further (115), the products of Greek art and culture are liable to misunderstanding. He turns first to the most damaging reference to Sappho, Horace, *Ep.* 1. 19. 28:

temperat Archilochi musam pede mascula Sappho.

He admits (115) an ambiguity (*Nebengedanken*) but the first meaning is "Sappho in her measure a man." To decide the meaning he cites a reminiscence of the passage at Statius, *Silvae* 5. 3. 154-55:

...saltusque ingressa viriles
non formidata temeraria Leucade Sappho...

---

[54] The same view is cogently stated at Dörrie, 15.

[55] See Dörrie, 16-17.

[56] In an *addendum* of 1845 (112-13) Welcker argues that "nach diesem Attischen Sprachgebrauch" later authors regularly call writers handsome, sc. a *topos*.

[57] Wilamowitz, *SuS* 17.

Wilamowitz vigorously endorsed his method and conclusion.[58] Ovid,
Heroides 15 remains the great indictment.[59] Welcker accepts its authenticity
(116 n. 65). Wilamowitz followed him.[60] The two embarrassing passages
are Ov. *Her.* 15. 15-20 and 199-206. The first is handled easily by reading at
verse 19 "*quas h i c sine crimine amavi*" rather than "*quas n o n sine crimine
amavi.*" There is manuscript support for both. The choice is largely one of
predisposition: and, as Arthur Palmer remarked *ad loc.*, "...little is gained by
reading *hic* for *non.*"[61] Certainly *amavi* is not changed. In spite of G.P.
Goold,[62] I should retain *non.* It is supported by verse 201 *Lesbides infamem
quae me fecisti amatae*, as Welcker reluctantly observes (119). He candidly
lists other passages equally incriminating in Ovid (119-120). Because he
cannot emend them away and because he does not like to change his mind
once made up,[63] he attributes them to the Roman's inability to grasp the
purity of Greek affection; or perhaps his poetic aim requires the ambiguity.
But even so Ovid suggests (*Her.* 15. 83-84) that her poetry rather than her
inclination may have damaged her reputation (120).[64] Martial simply proves
(121) how low Roman women had fallen (see Mart. 1. 90. 7 with Howell).
He traces the evil influence of Porphyrio's explanation of *mascula Sappho*[65]
upon the apostolic secretary, Domitius Calderinus (1447-1477) and
subsequent scholars, largely French (122). The verdict is the Scots' "not
proven." Welcker warns against the danger of interpreting a pair of
misunderstood sources "without wider examination in the whole field of
antiquity." Again the *Totalitätsideal*, one can only interpret the specific in
the context of the whole, not "by empty cleverness and superficially learned
discoveries" (122). He adduces a revealing *argumentum ex silentio*. No
church father accuses Sappho of tribadism, although always ready to
discredit a pagan on any count. Of course there is Tatian; but "in my

---

[58] Wilamowitz, *SuS* 17 n. 1.

[59] The two authoritative modern discussions are Dörrie, *op. cit.* (supra n. 31) and Howard
Jacobson, *Ovid's Heroides* (Princeton 1974) 277-99, especially in this context 291-95.

[60] Wilamowitz, *SuS* 17-22. Modern experts agree.

[61] *P. Ovidi Nasonis Heroides with the Greek Translation of Planudes* ed. Arthur Palmer
(Oxford 1898; repr. Hildesheim 1967) 427, and similarly Jacobson, *Heroides* 292.

[62] Grant Showerman, *Ovid Heroides and Amores* ed.², revised by G.P. Goold (Cambridge/
London 1977) 182. He retains Showerman's translation of *hic*: "...nor in the hundred other
maids I loved here to my reproach" (183). Read rather "without reproach." Wilamowitz, *SuS*
19 retains *non* rightly.

[63] We shall see further evidence of this in his reply to Colonel Mure. Professor Radt
(*Welcker* 168) observes in another context: "Selbstkritik war bei Welcker offensichtlich
nicht stark entwickelt."

[64] The passage is remarkable. I cite Palmer's text.

Sive abeunt studia in mores, artisque magistra
Ingenium nobis molle Thalia facit.

[65] See *Pomponii Porphyrionis Commentarii in Q. Horatium Flaccum* ed. G. Meyer
(Leipzig 1879) 306. 1-3: *mascula autem Sappho, vel quia in poetico studio est, in quo saepius
mares, vel quia tribas diffamatur fuisse.* See Nisbet-Hubbard *ad* Hor. *Carm.* 2. 13. 25.

opinion he would call Heloise a whore" (123).[66] He dismisses unconvincingly (123 n. 71) Didymus' query (Sen. *Ep.* 88. 31): *an Sappho publica
fuerit.*[67] Welcker discards the "two Sapphos" theory, already found in
antiquity and defended by Bayle (124-126). This requires that Menander knew
of a younger prostitute of the same name but not of the poetess (124).
Serious scholars agree.[68]

Welcker concludes (129) by recalling the epiphany of the poetess to the
Marchese Berio during a sleepless night (sc. not in a dream). She explained
satisfactorily difficulties the Marchese had encountered with an Etruscan vase
thought to portray Sappho unflatteringly. Not all of us have such luck:[69]

> So leicht war es allerdings uns nicht geworden und wir haben, um einen
> Zusammenhang herauszubringen verschiednerley Punkte, wie wir
> nemlich glauben, berichtigen und was hinderlich war entfernen müssen.
> (129)

Tracing the reception of Welcker's thesis by his contemporaries is eased
because Welcker (*Kl. Schriften* IV. 98-99) collected their opinions to prove
with satisfaction the extent of his success.[70] He presents the jury's vote: 6
against; 1 abstention; 30 for his view. A five to one victory in what
Welcker modestly calls (98) "one of the more difficult controversies within
the field of classical philology." Amusingly he can cite no Frenchmen either
way. Either they could not or they would not read him. There is a Dutchman
and a Pole and three Englishmen. The latter included Julius Charles Hare[71]
and Connop Thirlwall (1797-1875),[72] the translators of Niebuhr's *History*,
and the dictionary-maker, William Smith (1813-1893). All three men were
widely read in their time. Karl Otfried Müller (1797-1840), Welcker's
successor at Göttingen, immediately accepted in two famous books, both

---

[66] For the irrational anti-Hellenism of Tatian see Werner Jaeger, *Early Christianity and
Greek Paideia* (Cambridge 1961) 34-35.

[67] Contrast the sensible discussion of Dörrie, 21-22.

[68] See Wilamowitz, *SuS* 22-25; Dörrie, 22.

[69] Welcker is not ironic but regretful. That he firmly believed in dreams see Kekulé,
Welcker 278, noticed by Wilamowitz at *SIFC* NS 3,2 (1984) 125, 126. Karl Lehrs, *Kleine
Schriften*, ed. Arthur Ludwich (Königsberg 1902) 330-31, ridicules Welcker's belief in
dreams.

[70] For later examples of the "Tendenz der Ehrenrettung Sapphos" see Saake, *Sappho-
Studien* 20-21. For an amusing parody see Eduard Zeller, "Zur Ehrenrettung der Xanthippe,"
Vorträge und Abhandlungen I² (Leipzig 1875) 56-67.

[71] For his Germanophilia see his nephew's report, Augustus J.C. Hare, *The Story of My
Life* I (London 1896) 14: "Julius...already, during his residence with his mother at Weimar,
had imbibed that passion for Germany and German literature which characterised his after
life."

[72] See John Connop Thirlwall Jr., *Connop Thirlwall: Historian and Theologian* (London
1936). His *History of Greece* in both editions of which he accepted Welcker (1836, 1846)
was until Grote the standard English history. His translation of Schleiermacher almost ruined
his ecclesiastical career: see A.H. Sayce, *Reminiscences* (London 1923) 91 n., where Lord
Melbourne asks the newly made bishop: "Then what the devil made you translate
Schleiermacher?"

translated into English, Welcker's rescue of Sappho, in *Die Dorier* (1824)[73]
and in *History of the Literature of Ancient Greece* (1840).[74] The treatment
of Sappho in the latter is little more than an English summary of Welcker.
Müller holds (175) that the Aphrodite Ode (frag. 1 L-P) concerns the
poetess' love for a male[75] and (178) the *Longinus Ode* (frag. 31 L-P) is a
harmless one in which "the poetess expresses nothing more than a friendly
attachment to a young girl."[76] Like Wilamowitz later, chided by Page,
Müller omits from his translation the most embarrassing words: κὰδ δέ μ'
ἴδρως κακχέεται.[77] Müller, Smith, and Thirlwall made Welcker the
opinio communis for English-speaking peoples until Bowra.[78] Philip
Buttmann's death-bed repentence (1829) for his libel against Horace and
Sappho by taking *mascula* in Porphyrio's second sense is well known to

---

[73] K.O. Müller, *Geschichten hellenischer Stämme und Städte* II *Die Dorier* (Breslau 1824)
297. The English translation appeared in 1830. For Müller see recently Wolfhart Unte "Karl
Otfried Müller," *Schlesien* 25 (1980) 9-21 with the bio-bibliography at 19 n. 1 and Arnaldo
Momigliano, "K.O. Müllers Prolegomena zu einer wissenschaftlichen Mythologie and the
Meaning of Myth," *AnnPisa* 3, 13 (1983) 654-89. Of earlier work informative and readable
is Karl Hillebrand "Otfried Müller," *Unbekannte Essays* ed. Hermann Uhde-Bernays (Bern
1955) 184-241. [See now Wolfhart Unte and Helmut Rohlfing, *Quellen für eine Biographie
Karl Otfried Müllers (1797-1840)* (Hildesheim 1997).]

[74] The English translation appeared before the German original. The references are: K.O.
Müller, *History of the Literature of Ancient Greece* I (London 1840) 172-78 (= *Geschichte
der Griechischen Literatur bis auf das Zeitalter Alexanders* I⁴, edd. Eduard Müller and Emil
Heitz [Stuttgart 1882] 288-98).

[75] Compare Welcker, *Kl. Schriften* IV. 59: "Die erste Ode bezieht sich auf einen Mann."
English translators, with few exceptions, as late as Walhouse (1877) follow Müller and
Welcker: see Henry Thornton Wharton, *Sappho: Memoir, Text, Selected Renderings and a
Literal Translation* (London/Chicago 1885) 45-57. In a letter of 26 November 1866 John
Addington Symonds writes to Henry Graham Dakyns:

> Was said to me by a stranger at Lincoln's Inn Dinner "Swinburne—faugh! I can
> listen to a fellow talking Παιδεραστία—we understand that—but the Lesbian:—
> little beast!"

This shows beautifully the readiness of the English to accept Welcker: see *The Letters of
John Addington Symonds* I: *1844-1868* edd. Herbert M. Schueller and Robert L. Peters
(Detroit 1967) 680.

[76] Müller, *History* 178 (= *Geschichte* I⁴ 298): "nichts als eine freundliche Zuneigung zu
einem jüngern Mädchen."

[77] See Müller, *History* 178 (= *Geschichte* I⁴ 298) and Wilamowitz, *SuS* 56; against
Wilamowitz: Denys Page, *Sappho and Alcaeus: An Introduction to the Study of Ancient
Lesbian Poetry* (Oxford 1955) 32 n. 2 where he cites E. Bickel, *RhM* 89 (1940) 202 for the
matter.

[78] C.M. Bowra, *Greek Lyric Poetry from Alcman to Simonides*² (Oxford 1961) 179:
"Towards these girls Sappho felt what can only be called love." For a frank admission of the
defects of his own book see C.M. Bowra, *Memories 1898-1939* (London 1966) 263-64. The
English homosexuals, Bowra, Housman, Swinburne (the friend of Jowett), Symonds did most
to discredit Welcker's position. For Housman and Sappho see Paul Keyser, "A.E. Housman's
Variations on Sappho Frag. 52 Bergk⁴," *Classical & Modern Literature* 5 (1985) 315-22. The
work of Havelock Ellis (1859-1939) on sexual inversion sought to redeem Sappho but not, as
Welcker, by denying her inversion, rather by explaining it: see Phyllis Grosskurth, *Havelock
Ellis: A Biography* (New York 1980) 185. Symonds' close work with Ellis is well known: see
Grosskurth, 491 s.n.

English-speaking students through Ed. Fraenkel.[79] Among other influential German scholars who accepted the *Ehrenrettung* and are listed by Welcker (IV. 99) are Bernhardy, F.D. Bothe, Friedrich Schlegel, Schneidewin, and W. Teuffel.

Only one great German scholar was not convinced, the editor of Sappho, Theodor Bergk (1812-1881), friend of Welcker,[80] and later (1869-1881) professor at Bonn, and editor of *Rheinisches Museum*.[81] In his edition of Sappho (1843) Bergk at frag. 1. 24 Bergk⁴ for κωὐκ ἐθέλοισαν read κωὐκ ἐθέλοισα and in the apparatus remarked: *nam de puellae more agitur.* Examination in 1892 of the Laurentianus pl. 59 cod. 15 proved Bergk right[82] and, except for a foray by A.D. Knox in 1939,[83] subsequent scholars have followed Bergk. Welcker was angered and disappointed.[84] In 1856 (*Kl. Schriften* IV. 68-76) he replied and in 1861 reports that in a letter of 9 August 1857 Bergk withdrew his suggestion and in his lectures presented Welcker's Sappho ("in meinem Sinn").[85] Once Welcker was safely dead, however, Bergk returned to his ways. The posthumous third edition of *Lyrici Graeci* prints the dread participle in the nominative.[86] Bergk takes final leave of his friend:[87]

Welcker non dubitavit ad viri desiderium hoc carmen referre, non recte, si quid video: omnino enim Sappho a virorum amore abhorrebat.

There was a more formidable adversary, a "friend" too,[88] but not a German nor an Englishman.

---

[79] Eduard Fraenkel, *Horace* (Oxford 1957) 346 n. 3 and earlier Wilamowitz, *SuS* 71, trivialized by Nisbet-Hubbard *ad Hor. Carm.* 2. 13. 25. See Philipp Buttmann, *Mythologus oder gesammelte Abhandlungen über die Sagen des Altertums* II (Berlin 1829) 377 (I owe the reference to Dr. J. Dummer, Berlin, DDR). Welcker reacted at *Kl. Schriften* II. 116 n. 65.

[80] Kekulé, *Welcker* 186. They met in the house of Bergk's father-in-law, August Meineke, at whose school Bergk taught, during Welcker's visit to Berlin in 1839: see following note.

[81] See Rudolf Peppmüller, "Theodor Bergks Leben," *Kleine philologische Schriften von Theodor Bergk*, ed. Rudolf Peppmüller II (Halle 1886) xi-xcv. The facts seem to belie Peppmüller's description of the friendship of Bergk for Welcker (xxiv-xxv) which, he says, not the slightest disagreement ever clouded. The indignation of Welcker (*Kl. Schriften* IV. 69-70) proves disagreement.

[82] See Aeneas Piccolomini, *Hermes* 27 (1892) 10. L has ἐθέλουσα which insures Bergk's ἐθέλοισα.

[83] A.D. Knox, *SIFC* NS 15 (1939) 194 n. 3 where he would read κωὔ σε θέλοισαν.

[84] See *supra* n. 81.

[85] See *Kl. Schriften* IV. 70 n. 2. The Welcker-Bergk correspondence is attested at Peppmüller xxiv: "ein belebter, inhaltreicher Briefwechsel, welcher bis in Welckers letztes Lebensjahr hinein ununterbrochen fortgedauert hat."

[86] Th. Bergk, *Poetae Lyrici Graeci* III: *Poetae Melici*⁴ (Leipzig 1914) 86 (= ed.³ 1882).

[87] *Loc. cit.*, 86-87.

[88] Kekulé, *Welcker* 183: "Mure 'ein herrlicher Mann'."

IV. Colonel Mure

He was a Scot. William Mure (1799-1860), born on his ancestral estate, Caldwell in Ayrshire, Scotland, grandson of William Mure (1718-1776), baron of the Scots exchequer and friend of David Hume, received an excellent classical education at Westminster School and the University of Edinburgh.[89] He then (ca. 1820) studied at the new university of Bonn, where he presumably heard the professor for Greek, F.G. Welcker. In 1838 he toured Greece, visiting Korfu, Ithaca, Acarnania, Delphi, Boeotia, Attica, and the Peloponnese. He published, as later Welcker did his,[90] a "Journal of a Tour in Greece and the Ionian Islands" (Edinburgh 1842). His great work remains: *A Critical History of the Language and Literature of Antient Greece* 5 vols. (London 1850-57).[91] He treats epic, early lyric, Herodotus, Thucydides, and Xenophon only. There is nothing on, e.g., drama or oratory. Although a torso, the volumes remain the most ambitious and original history of Greek literature ever undertaken in the English language, the only one not a compendium of earlier (usually German) work. Mure is learned, controls German scholarship in a way the English could not but the Irish did, and writes with a pleasing historical rather than literary bias, which endeared him to D.L. Page.[92] That Mure visited Greece before writing his *History*, while Grote did not, gives him a practical advantage over the Englishman, whose work he often attacked.[93] He was Colonel of the Renfrewshire Militia. Two sons became officers. Mure quite naturally enjoyed polemic.[94] He married the granddaughter of the Archbishop of York and became, as his father and grandfather before him, Lord Rector of Glasgow University. His biographer calls him "a man of commanding presence, winning manners,

---

[89] I draw my facts from *DNB* 13 (Oxford 1937/38) 1227. I have not seen the 'kürzlich aufgefundenen Briefwechsel mit seinem englischen [sic!] Freunde, dem Colonel MURE, Schloßherrn von Caldwell": see Wolfgang Schmid, *150 Jahre Rheinische Friedrich-Wilhelms-Universität zu Bonn 1818-1968: Bonner Gelehrte: Beiträge zur Geschichte der Wissenschaften in Bonn: Philosophie und Altertumswissenschaften* (Bonn 1968) 129 (= *Ausgewählte philologische Schriften*, edd. H. Erbse and J. Küppers [Berlin/New York 1984] 698).

[90] One wonders whether the correspondence would confirm a deduction that Mure encouraged Welcker to see Greece, which Welcker did in the year that Mure published his journal.

[91] I cite vol. III² (London 1854) which contains his discussion of Sappho (272-326).

[92] Mure vigorously defended the historicity of Homer against Grote. Frank M. Turner, *The Greek Heritage in Victorian Britain* (New Haven/London 1981) 137 with n. 5, rightly compares Mure with D.L. Page, *History and the Homeric Iliad* (Berkeley 1959) 258. For Page's use of Mure on Sappho see *infra*.

[93] See William Mure, *Remarks on the Appendices to the second volume 3rd edition of Mr. Grote's* History of Greece (London 1851). Like Grote he was a Member of Parliament (for nine years) but unlike Grote a conservative.

[94] I have not seen his *National Criticism in 1858* (London 1858), which replies to a criticism of his *History*. For his criticism of Grote see *supra* n. 93 and Turner, *op. cit.* (*supra* n. 92) 136-37, 144-45.

and kindly disposition." How did this gentleman, scholar, and soldier become the great adversary of his teacher and friend?

Mure devotes 54 pages of his five volume *History* to a Sappho preserved only in the book fragments. Of these some 24 pages concern the moral question. Welcker's book of 35 years before remained authoritative for the Sappho biography and was arranged about the moral question. Mure simply did not accept the *Ehrenrettung*. One's attitude to Mure depends on one's predisposition to the Sapphic Question. D.L. Page recommends Mure against Wilamowitz as "still more fervid and outspoken, and with no lack of common sense."[95] Wilamowitz dismisses Mure airily:[96] "Er [Welcker] hat bei Lebzeiten nur gegen einen englischen [sic!] Dilettanten kämpfen müssen." Had Wilamowitz even read Mure? Mure's programmatic statement reveals the considerable influence of Welcker much of whose argument he accepts. He believes Welcker exaggerated comic influence. Because of the rarity of the book I shall cite Mure at some length:[97]

> To this celebrity of her genius may partly be ascribed the obscurity which involves her history. In addition to the popular tendency, in such cases, to engraft fabulous details on a comparatively slender stock of matter of fact, the controversies which arose relative to the merits or defects of her personal character, and the efforts made by the different sections of the critical public who took part in these controversies, to force the data at their disposal into harmony with their own peculiar views, interpose serious obstacles to the success of impartial investigation. There can be no better evidence of her surpassing fame and popularity, than the fact of her having figured as a favourite heroine of the comic drama of Athens, to a greater extent, it would appear, than any other historical personage upon record...there can be no doubt that, in the hands of such censors, her defects would be broadly caricatured. Nor could the judgement of so popular a tribunal fail to exercise influence upon that of posterity. This latter consideration, however, has led her more enthusiastic modern admirers and apologists into the opposite extreme, of ascribing all the less favourable features of her portrait to the above polluted source, in their efforts to convert her into an ideal model of purity and moral excellence. It will be the object of the following review of her life and character to steer a just medium between these two extremes, by an impartial analysis of the existing materials for guiding the judgement, whether supplied by herself or derived from other sources.

---

[95] D.L. Page, *op. cit. (supra* n. 77) 146 n. 1.

[96] Wilamowitz, *SuS* 71.

[97] Mure, *History* V. 274-75. The similarity to Welcker, *Kl. Schriften* IV. 80, cited in part above in English is noteworthy. They differed in fewer points than they agreed.

Let us look at his argument in the light of what he learned from Welcker. Mure accepts (309) the view of Welcker and Müller that the Aphrodite Ode concerns a man but will not see in it "the language of an innocent virgin, or a virtuous matron." He makes the astute observation (*ibid.*) that the poem reveals "that this love was not the first of the same kind." Page over 100 years later revived this observation, based on the thrice repeated δηὖτε, as a cornerstone of his famous interpretation of the ode.[98] Mure even introduces a stubborn error to Welcker that has persisted into our time. He alleges that Sappho (276) "was left an orphan when six years old."[99] He rightly discards, in anticipation of Wilamowitz, Sappho's "husband" as a comic fiction (278) and accepts Welcker's "association or club of ladies" (279) while warning that they were "devoted to the pursuit of every species of refined and elegant pleasure, sensual or intellectual." He later (306) calls them "a school not only of poetry and music, but of love and every variety of voluptuous pursuit." One finds nothing like that in Ayrshire. Phaon may be a real or fictitious name (282) but Mure, who had visited Acarnania, accepts the Leucadian suicide. He argues by defending the historicity of the practice and continues that because Sappho's leap is the best attested (286), it is wrong to discount it. One must pronounce (289) "the balance of evidence to be on the affirmative side."[100]

He proceeds (290) to "the most delicate and difficult element of the present inquiry." He must reluctantly (*ibid.*) "correct the fallacious point of

---

[98] D.L. Page, *op. cit. (supra* n. 77) 13-15. He does not cite Mure in this context oddly. Merkelbach accepts Page at *Philologus* 101 (1957) 6.

[99] Palmer's text of Ov. *Her.* 15. 61-62 is:

> Sex mihi natales ierant, cum lecta parentis
> Ante diem lacrimas osa bibere meas.

What Ovid says is: "My sixth birthday had passed when the gathered bones of a parent drank my untimely tears." *Parentis* singular means "her father, probably" (Palmer) but may as well mean *mother*. Palmer cites frag. 102 L-P to show that Sappho's mother was alive when she was a poetess. I do not think the evidence cogent that the word alone may refer to either parent. Ovid does not specify. In 1841 Welcker wrote (*Kl. Schriften* II. 81 n. 1) that at age six Sappho lost her father. In 1854 Mure (*History* III². 276) has her "left an orphan when six years old." In 1856 (= *Kl. Schriften* IV. 85) Welcker writes: "Ihre Eltern hat sie nach Ovid (61) im zwölften [!] Jahre verloren." Wilamowitz, *SuS* 20 cites Ovid, whom he does not believe, for Sappho early losing her father. He is followed without the doubt by W. Aly, *RE* 1 A (1920) 2363; Schmid *GGL* I² (1929) 417 n. 3 ("sagt nur Ovid"); and M. Giebel, *Sappho* 12 ("ihr Vater...starb früh"). D.L. Page, *op. cit. (supra* n. 77) 133-34 n. 1 writes: "She was six years old when her parents died" (Mure) and cites Ov. *Her.* 15. 61-62. M.L. West *Maia* 22 (1970) 328 seems to make the same error (from Page?). Finally in his great commentary Dörrie 25 writes: "Ovid berichtet—hierfür einziger Zeuge—die Eltern seien verstorben, als Sappho sechs Jahre alt war." Later (112) he varies this: "Die Eltern sind früh verstorben, als Sappho ein Kind von sieben Jahren war." The only scholar to have noticed the confusion is Jacobson, *Heroides* 279 who omits at his n. 10 Welcker, *Kl. Schriften* II, 81 n. 1. I agree with Wilamowitz, *SuS* 20 that the whole matter is *unbezeugt*: but one ought to be clear about what Ovid says.

[100] Contrast M.P. Nilsson, *Geschichte der griechischen Religion* I² (Munich 1955) 109, who calls Sappho's leap a "mythologischen Niederschlag" of the Leucadian pharmakos ritual.

view in which it has recently been placed by writers of deserved authority."
A note cites Welcker and his followers (290 n. 2). It includes the English
books of Müller and William Smith. These scholars give us (291-92): "a
model of perfection, physical and moral, such as was never probably
exemplified in woman, and least of all in the prioress of an association of
votaries of Venus and the Muses, in one of the most voluptuous states of
Greece." Because Mure has not read Lessing, he makes the cardinal error
(292) that the poems are autobiographical documents, "the infallible
criterion." Further he overestimates the historicity of Ovid's report (298; cf.
299 n. 1): "Among classical critics there were few who possessed a deeper
insight than Ovid into the spirit and habits of antient society." On the other
hand (299 n. 1) he dismisses Seneca-Didymus with an assurance that
Welcker and Müller lacked. Because he does not heed Welcker's parallel of
Socrates in *Nubes* and ignores Plutarch's allegation of comic distortion of
Pericles, cited by Welcker, Mure rules unconvincingly on comedy (300):
"Nor was it the custom of the Attic comedians to invest the objects of their
satire with attributes entirely different from those which belonged to them in
real life." That the poets had no idea what attributes belonged to Sappho in
real life does not occur to him.

Largely by treating 31 L-P as autobiography Mure rules (315) on "the
precise nature of the intercourse between Sappho and her female associates."
He has no patience with Müller's "friendly attachment" (317) and concludes
with a classic formulation of the predicament that faces an historian who
meets up with a *topos* (318):

> If Sappho did *not* mean or feel what she has expressed in the passages
> above quoted, then the most brilliant extant specimens of her muse
> become comparatively unmeaning rhapsodies; if she *did* so feel, her
> sentiments were not those of maternal tenderness or sisterly
> friendship.

This is precisely his defense of Homer against Grote, *Wahrheit* is better than
Dichtung. In both cases Page follows him.[101] On the other hand Mure's
aporia reveals how much Welcker had learned from Lessing.

Welcker's catastrophic mistake was to reply to Mure. The three
questions of the autobiographical content of Sappho's two poems, of Attic
Comedy's ability to ignore or pervert truth, and of the value of Ovid,
Heroides 15 as an historical source for the life of Sappho, had all been posed

---

[101] See D.L. Page, *History and the Homeric Iliad* (Berkeley/Los Angeles 1959) 258:

> It adds something to the appeal of Homeric poetry, to know not only that its subject
> is historical, but also that its leading people are, for the most part, real people,
> remembered and idealized figures of men and women who played no small part
> on the stage of history, living brilliantly and richly on the verge of the darkest night
> that was ever to fall over ancient Greece.

by Welcker and all available evidence set forth for answering them. Any reply, because of the nature of the available evidence, would have to be repetitious, a denial rather than a refutation. How many continental scholars read Mure? Benevolent neglect was the wiser course; for Mure, as Welcker learned, was a hot-tempered Celt not a complacent Englishman. He liked a good fight.

In "Ueber die beiden Oden der Sappho," *RhM* 11 (1856) 226-59 (= *Kl. Schriften* IV. 68-99), Welcker, aged 71, replied politely but firmly to Mure and Bergk. I have discussed Bergk. His reply to Mure (76-99) restates his case of forty years before and rightly draws attention to exaggerations (*e.g.*, 95-96 with n. 23) in Mure of the German apologists' case. Citation of G. Sand's autobiography as further proof of the non-sensual love of women (77-78 with n. 6) does little to help his cause. His naive criticism of Mure (78), who ignored "the pure Greek love of men for boys," would raise a fury. He suggests that Mure (79 with n. 7) may have been influenced by the rise of sensual female homosexuality "in various European capitals." He agrees with Mure (83) on the value of Ovid and clings to the view (84) that the Aphrodite Ode is directed to Phaon.[102] It does not prove, however, many loves but that Phaon was long inconstant (88). He reminds Mure that after all Sappho deserted her schoolgirls for love of a fellow (87). He does not think that Mure needed to have brought Maria Stuart (89) into the controversy. There is further discussion of the school, until Welcker wearily admits (92): "Gegen Windmühlen werden immer wieder Lanzen eingelegt." That he ends by counting jurors' votes (98-99) is both honest and revealing. There is nothing else to do.

William Mure, "Sappho, and the Ideal Love of the Greeks," *RhM* 12 (1857) 564-93, the most virulent polemic written against Welcker in his lifetime, appeared in a journal edited by Welcker (and Ritschl). After a nod (565) to "the friendly intercourse that had long subsisted between us," Mure removes his gloves (566):

> It has been my study through life, never wantonly to hurt the feelings of any man, either friend or adversary; but when so wantonly and ungenerously assailed, I shall not in self defence deal lightly with the aggressor.

No quarter is yielded for age or that Mure wrote in a language foreign to Welcker. He alleges that Welcker misunderstood him, misquoted him, attributed to him things he did not say,[103] and most disgusting of all

---

[102] Wilamowitz, *SuS* 74 n. 1, would later regret Welcker's stubborn adherence to the fabulous passion for Phaon and the trip to Leukas.

[103] Mure's case is convincing. The details are not worth disinterring. He concludes (575 n. 6): "I must beg the reader, generally, to put no faith in any quotation of my text by Welcker, unless verified by collation with the original."

attributed to him *French* words.[104] By citing (568-69) Müller, Bernhardy, Richter, Pauly, Bode and William Smith, Mure shows that Welcker was unfair to say that he had caricatured German opinion. He refutes (572-75) Welcker's unwise objection to his view of the prominence of amorous material in Sappho's "collective works" with a parade of ancient and modern authorities, including early Welcker.

Mure now reaches (575) his chief quarrel with Welcker. He states the matter in the most personal terms (576):

> The substance of the imputation against me is: that I am unable to appreciate ideal art, because I am not susceptible of the ideal paederastia of the Greeks...Welcker, I presume I am correct in stating, can appreciate ideal art, and therefore does possess that susceptibility. I readily concede to him this advantage over me; and am content that my claims to appreciate art, shall be judged by those, whose opinions are more akin to mine than to his on the subject of paederastia.

Welcker says that I cannot appreciate Sappho because I am not a homosexual. Welcker can appreciate Sappho and, therefore, is a homosexual. Mure substantiates his claim (577) by gathering those references in the *Ehrenrettung* (1816) "indulgent" to a vice which "all enlightened Christian men" view "with unqualified abhorrence."[105] Welcker becomes (578) "the living champion of the paederastian system" and Mure delivers a fiery and highly amusing tirade against the old man, the Platonic Circle, and (585) "the national curse of paederastia." With a thoroughly unfair *ad hominem* against the bachelor Welcker he writes (581):

> ...how stands the case between man and woman? It seems hardly credible that, in an elaborate commentary on that passion by a Christian writer, not an allusion should occur to the dreary, withering blight, which it [male homosexuality] shed on the best and dearest of all human connexions, the Connubial bond!

He dismisses, as remarkably no German had, Welcker's odd thesis that while male homosexuality was pure and beautiful its female counterpart was vile. Indeed it might not even have been so bad (585-86). When one considers (587) "the privations and indignities to which they were subjected by the

---

[104] See Mure, 575 n. 1: "He even forces on me scraps of his own French composition... with which I trust I never could have had the bad taste to disfigure my page."

[105] Some sixty years later on precisely the same grounds, Hans Blüher accused Wila-mowitz of homosexuality; see Hans Blüher, *Ulrich von Wilamowitz und der deutsche Geist* (Tempel-hof-Berlin 1916) 31:

> Und wüßte nicht, wie gut er es versteht, die griechischen Erasten-Verhältnisse zu schildern! Wie 'lebendig' klingt sein Euthydem-Kolleg! etc.

See further *Antiqua* 27 (Naples 1984) 184 n. 9.

heartless tyranny of the other sex," one cannot blame them for "solacing themselves by Sappho's 'eros lysimeles,' whatever it may have been." There is further savaging of Welcker. Mure concludes by denying Welcker's view that Sappho was married. He well states the case (591):

> My opponent and his fellow apologists everywhere assume that Sappho was married; on the ground chiefly that she had a daughter, and that the daughter of so exemplary a woman must necessarily have been a legitimate child.

Welcker never replied. Perhaps he did not understand Mure or better he saw that there was nothing more to say. Mure first criticized unwarranted assumptions and detected an unnoticed bias in Welcker's arguments of 1816, that had gone unchallenged by Germans. This is the "common sense" that later earned Page's praise. Whether Mure's accusation in *Rheinisches Museum* that Welcker was himself a paederast is true or not, published documents do not allow us to decide. The charge makes Gildersleeve's and Kekule's remarks on the *Ehrenrettung* easier to understand. They both knew Welcker personally. No matter. Welcker's great superiority to his Celtic foe consists in his exemplary, albeit occasionally naive, attempt to understand Greek homosexuality as the Greeks had rather than to judge it by the Pauline preconceptions of a fire-and-brimstone Scots preacher. Welcker wrote a scholarly book, a century before its time. Mure wrote a homily.

Mure died in 1860. Welcker died in 1868. Except for the third edition of Bergk's edition, nothing of importance happened in Sapphic studies until the *annus mirabilis* 1895. In that year the Committee of the Egypt Exploration Fund agreed to support an excavation at Bahnasa, Oxyrhynchus by A.S. Hunt and B.P. Grenfell[106] and in the same year Pierre Louys published "*Les Chansons de Bilitis traduites du Grec pour la première fois.*[107]

V. Ulrich von Wilamowitz-Moellendorff

If Welcker was the knight-errant who saved Sappho from libel, Wilamowitz was the one who saved Welcker from oblivion. Today most of us come to Welcker through Wilamowitz:[108]

> E philologis Welckerum amare sponte coepi 1868, sequi constitui statim, et veneror multumque feci ut alii venerarentur.

---

[106] See Sir Eric Turner, "The Greco-Roman Branch," *Excavating in Egypt: The Egypt Exploration Society 1882-1982* ed. T.G.H. James (Chicago/London 1982) 161-78.
[107] See H.P. Clive, *Pierre Louys 1870-1925: A Biography* (Oxford 1978) 110-12.

There was a personal connection of a sort that meant much to Wilamowitz. He never saw Welcker who died 17 December 1868 at 9 p.m. But he missed Christmas at Markowitz in order to follow his coffin to the grave. Otto Lüders (1844-1912), a close friend of the young Wilamowitz,[109] had been the last amanuensis of the blind *Greis*.[110] He told many stories of Welcker to Wilamowitz.[111] Jahn's and Mommsen's affection for Welcker would have helped.[112] That Usener assumed Welcker to have been superseded presumably inclined Wilamowitz to the opposite view.[113] He was the "forgotten unforgettable."[114] The day came when Hermann and Lachmann had nothing more to say to Wilamowitz.[115] Welcker's horizon was far broader than that of a *Wortphilolog*. His stupendous learning, his catholic interest, his poetic intuition, his daring reconstructions,[116] made him a formative influence on Wilamowitz in a way that Böckh and K.O. Müller never were. Their interests widely overlapped: epic, tragedy, lyric, monumental philology, and *Religionsgeschichte*. Wilamowitz was the heir of Welcker.

He dedicated *Sappho und Simonides* (Berlin 1913) "Dem Andenken Friedrich Gottlieb Welckers."[117] He tells us why:[118]

> Gehuldigt habe ich ihr [Sappho] oft: hier will ich versuchen, durch den Sagenkreis zu ihr selbst und von ihren Versen in ihre Seele vorzudringen, auf Welckers Spuren. Doch auf denen bin ich mir bewußt zu wandeln, wo immer ich von hellenischen Göttern oder Dichtern rede; darum habe ich dem Vergessenen, Unvergesslichen dieses Buch gewidmet. Im Leben habe ich ihn nicht mehr zu Gesicht bekommen; aber er war mir schon der Lehrer, der den Weg zur Seele der Hellenen wies, als ich hinter seinem Sarge ging. Das ist er geblieben.

---

[108] *Antiqua* 27 (Naples 1984) 156.

[109] *Antiqua* 23 (Naples 1983) 295 n. 11, 310.

[110] Wilamowitz, *Erinnerungen*[2] 89.

[111] See *SIFC* NS 3,2 (1984) 128: "meine vorstellung war zu sehr nach Lüders berichten von dem greise bedingt." For Lüder's shallow recollections of Welcker see *Im neuen Reich* 11. 1 (Leipzig 1881) 661-72, 711-25.

[112] For the many references in their correspondence to Welcker see *Theodor Mommsen-Otto Jahn: Briefwechsel 1842-1868* ed. Lothar Wickert (Frankfurt/Main 1962) 386 *s.n.* Welcker.

[113] For Usener on Welcker see Albert Henrichs, "Welcker's *Götterlehre*," *Welcker* 223-29.

[114] Wilamowitz, *SuS* 16.

[115] *Antiqua* 27 (Naples 1984) 156: *sed venit dies qui docebat, neutrum mihi satis facere.*

[116] See *SIFC* NS 3,2 (1984) 131: "...wie wir ihnen [Hermann and Welcker] für ihre conjecturen auf den Knien danken sollen und der Teufel uns holen soll, wenn wir conjicieren wie sie."

[117] Wilamowitz dedicated only *Sappho und Simonides* to Welcker. Correct F. Frh. Hiller von Gaertringen and G. Klaffenbach, *Wilamowitz-Bibliographie 1868 bis 1929* (Berlin 1929) 48 No. 490.

[118] Wilamowitz, *SuS* 16. [On 1 July 1920 Wilamowitz wrote to Ernst Howald: "kein anderer grosse Philologe hatte in Wahrheit mehr auf mich gemerkt als Welcker."]

There was a more specific reason for the dedication. Wilamowitz later writes:[119]

> Wenn es denn Tatsache ist, daß Sappho eine Tribade war, so werde ich der letzte sein, das zu beschönigen oder mit schillernden Phrasen zu verschleiern. Aber mit voller Zuversicht bekenne ich mich zu dem Glauben, daß Welcker Sappho von einem herrschenden Vorurteil befreit hat, für alle die ihn hören wollen und verstehn können.

Wilamowitz believed (*Glauben*) that Welcker had proven once and for all that Sappho was not a tribade. But Welcker's proof for Wilamowitz was of a different order than, say, proving the date of the Peace of Kallias. "Mir ist es um die Reinheit einer großen Frau zu tun: da scheue ich mich nicht, herzhaft in den Kot zu fassen."[120] "Und nun Sappho! Eine vornehme Frau, Gattin und Mutter..."[121] Frederik Poulsen heard Wilamowitz' lectures on the Greek lyric poets at Berlin, WS 1902/03. There were 800 hearers. The actor dominated the scholar. He reports:[122]

> Wilamowitz defended Sappho's virtue. German, American, and English women were moved to tears. Frenchmen and Italians shrugged their shoulders or bit their lips in order not to laugh. The sons of the Balkan folk looked even more gloomy than usual.

This was shortly after Pierre Louys. Why did Sappho's purity mean so much to Wilamowitz? Why was he drawn to Welcker's *Ehrenrettung*? Was there something that the two men shared and that somehow culminated in Sappho? I think there was, their attitude toward women. They adored the untouchable, that is the safe, woman. There are three women in Welcker's life as narrated by Kekule: his mother, "die hohe gestalt der Julie Dohna" as Wilamowitz described her,[123] and Karoline von Humboldt.[124] He knew them as he wanted Sappho's students to know her, with a pure love not stained by the sensual. In Wilamowitz' *Erinnerungen* there are two women,

---

[119] Wilamowitz, *SuS* 71.

[120] Wilamowitz, *SuS* 63.

[121] Wilamowitz, *SuS* 73.

[122] Frederik Poulsen, *I Det Gaestfrie Europa: Liv og Rejser indtil Første Verdenskrig* (Copenhagen 1947) 13. I am grateful for the reference and the translation to Jørgen Mejer (Copenhagen).

[123] See *SIFC* NS 3,2 (1984) 128. It is revealing that Wilamowitz noticed her role in Welcker's life.

[124] See *Karoline von Humboldt und Friedrich Gottlieb Welcker: Briefwechsel 1807-1826* ed. Erna Sander-Rindtorff (Bonn 1936). I should compare the friendship of Welcker's homosexual colleague and fellow librarian, Jacob Bernays, with the Fürstin von Wied: see Hans I. Bach "Jacob Bernays: Ein Beitrag zur Emanzipationsgeschichte der Juden und zur Geschichte des deutschen Geistes im neunzehnten Jahrhundert," *Schriftenreihe wissenschaftlicher Abhandlungen des Leo Baeck Instituts* 30 (Tübingen 1974) 97-100 and *passim*. For Welcker's idealizing view of Greek women Dr. Jan Bremmer acutely cites Welcker, *Cyclus* 2² 30-31.

his mother Ulrike and his aunt, Emma von Schwanenfeld, upon whom he later based his conception of Phaedra.[125] He was Hippolytus. He loved them with a pure love, not stained by the sensual.[126]

[125] See *Antiqua* 27 (Naples 1984) 165-82 and W.J. Slater *Classical Views* (= NS 1 [1982] 378-79 with n. 1). Attention should also be drawn to Wilamowitz' hymn on the love between mother and adult son at *Kleine Schriften* VI ed. Wolfgang Buchwald (Berlin 1972) 174-75, written clearly with autobiographical intensity.

[126] I am grateful to the Fondation Hardt where I began this paper and for its improvement to Jan Bremmer (Utrecht), Jürgen Dummer (Berlin DDR), R.L. Fowler (Waterloo), J.P. Hallett (Maryland), Wolfgang Schindler (Humboldt University), and Renate Schlesier (West Berlin). But I owe most to Albert Henrichs (Harvard).

Ulrich von Wilamowitz-Moellendorff:
Sospitator Euripidis

I begin with a word on achievement. Wilamowitz wrote on Euripides first in 1867,[1] last in 1931.[2] For 64 years he was concerned with Euripides. Athenian tragedy always remained a center of his interest. Within this center he wrote least on Sophocles,[3] more on Aeschylus,[4] but most on Euripides. The Hiller/Klaffenbach bibliography lists 45 items on Euripides, against 19 on Aeschylus and 18 on Sophocles.[5] Four great books, whose influence on subsequent scholarship in tragedy has been incalculable, are concerned wholly with Euripides: the Habilitationsschrift, *Analecta Euripidea* (1875); the two-volume *Herakles*, first published in 1889; the commentary, text, and translation of *Hippolytos* (1891); and the edition of *Ion* (1926). Marcello Gigante has written that neither Wilamowitz nor Nietzsche published a *magnum opus*.[6] Wilamowitz intended Herakles to be that, and completed it in his fortieth year—his acme in the ancient sense[7]—with a dedication to Schulpforte, meaning it to be the fulfillment of a vow taken as a schoolboy to become a scholar worthy of his *alma mater*.[8] His history of the text, from autograph to latest edition,[9] permanently altered critical method. One need only cite the reaction of August Nauck (1822-1892),[10] whom Wilamowitz considered most competent to judge.[11] His life of

---

[1] U. von Wilamowitz-Moellendorff, *In wieweit befriedigen die Schlüsse der erhaltenen griechischen Trauerspiele? Ein ästhetischer Versuch*, ed. W.M. Calder III (Leiden 1974 [hereafter *Trauerspiele*]) 95-148.

[2] *Der Glaube der Hellenen* (Berlin 1932) II 597f. *s.n.* 'Euripides'.

[3] For details see my "Ulrich von Wilamowitz-Moellendorff on Sophocles: A Letter to Sir Herbert Warren," *CalStudClAnt* 12 (1979) 51-63 (= *Ulrich von Wilamowitz-Moellendorff: Selected Correspondence, 1869-1931*, ed. W.M. Calder III, *Antiqua* 23 [Naples 1983, hereafter *Antiqua* 23] 279-91).

[4] For Wilamowitz' work on Aeschylus see Herwig Görgemanns, *Wilamowitz nach 50 Jahren*, edd. W.M. Calder III, Hellmut Flashar, and Theodor Lindken (Darmstadt 1985 [hereafter *50 Jahren*]) 142-45.

[5] F. Hiller von Gaertringen and G. Klaffenbach, *Wilamowitz-Bibliographie 1868 bis 1929* (Berlin 1929).

[6] *ParPass* 156 (1974) 214.

[7] Wilamowitz draws special attention to the notion that a great man is not ready until he is forty. He cites Goethe and Plato; a third is implied: *cf.* Euripides, *Herakles* (repr. Darmstadt 1959 [hereafter *Herakles*]) I 18.

[8] *Herakles* I vii.

[9] Originally published in the first edition (Berlin 1889) of *Herakles* I as ch. III of the "Einleitung in die attische Tragödie," of which I-IV were omitted from the second edition of 1895 but later reprinted separately as *Einleitung in die griechische Tragödie* (Berlin 1906ff); the three-volume Darmstadt reprint includes this material in volume I; II-III correspond to the two volumes of the edition of 1895.

[10] In a letter of 2 October 1889: *Antiqua* 23, 236-38.

[11] *Herakles* I 251.

Euripides[12] remains the most authoritative ever written, and is today plagiarized indirectly by monoglots unaware of their debt. His commentary was model and inspiration for Kaibel's *Electra* (1896), Ed. Fraenkel's *Agamemnon* (1950), and Norden's *Aeneis Buch VI* (1903, 1916[2]).[13] The introduction and commentary exemplified the *Totalitätsideal* that Wilamowitz had inherited from F.G. Welcker (1784-1867)—the conviction that the particular may only be elucidated by a knowledge of the whole. The interpreter's goal was to experience the play as its first audience had.[14]

Three times, excluding revisions, Wilamowitz discussed the entire oeuvre (1867, 1905, 1923).[15] Again and again he elucidated metrical, textual, and exegetical *cruces* in Euripides. Only eventual publication of the *index locorum Wilamowitzianus* will allow appraisal of the vast extent of this contribution. Hundreds of *loci* from other plays are treated in his edition of *Herakles* alone. Wilamowitz never edited all of Euripides because he believed that anything accurate or lasting in Gilbert Murray's *Oxford Classical Text* was his, even the collations. The sixty preserved letters of Wilamowitz to Murray put this beyond doubt, though not as sharply as a remark to Georg Kaibel:[16]

> My English friend, Murray, sends at least one drama a week of his Euripides. I am serious. What he does is almost sheer nonsense. A pupil of Verrall... The first proof will contain seven dramas, I think. I am not touching the Cyclops, because he has made so incredibly many stupid mistakes there.

If the proofs corrected and annotated by Wilamowitz still survive, they will likely confirm Murray's debt. Wilamowitz translated eight Euripidean plays into German verse—*Alcestis, Bacchae, Heracles, Supplices, Hippolytus, Medea, Troades, Cyclops*[17]—and affixed a lengthy essay to each. I shall discuss later the staging of these translations in the German-speaking world.

---

[12] *Herakles* I 1-43.

[13] *Cf.* the observation of G. Kaibel, *Sophocles, Elektra* (Leipzig 1896) vii, "dass aber v. Wilamowitz' Heraklescommentar zu den meist citirten Büchern gehört, wird jeder natürlich finden."

[14] See Wilamowitz' later words at *Aristophanes, Lysistrate* (Berlin 1927) 5; *cf. Antiqua* 23, 19 n. 99. For an evaluation of Herakles see Görgemanns, *50 Jahren* 138-42.

[15] See *Trauerspiele* 95-148 (where I draw attention in my notes to later discussions); *Die griechische Literatur des Altertums* (= *Die griechische und lateinische Literatur und Sprache. Die Kultur der Gegenwart* I.8[3], ed. Paul Hinneberg [Leipzig/Berlin 1912; first edition 1905; second 1907]) 78-82; "Die griechische Tragoedie und ihre drei Dichter," *Griechische Tragoedien* IV (Berlin 1923) 363-94.

[16] See *Antiqua* 23, 222 n. 37.

[17] They are easily available in U. von Wilamowitz-Moellendorff, *Griechische Tragoedien* I-IV (Berlin 1899ff).

In a teaching career spanning one hundred and eleven semesters (without sabbatical), Wilamowitz taught Euripides in seventeen of them.[18] The plays he taught included *Alcestis, Hecuba, Heracles, Hippolytus, Ion, Iphigenia in Aulide, Medea, Phoenissae, Troades*. He once taught the choral lyrics and once Euripides' *Life and Work*. No other author is represented on this scale. Plato, Homer, Aeschylus (all favorites) lag far behind. But of the eighty-eight dissertations directed by Wilamowitz, only three concern Euripides.[19] Of these the only one still read by specialists is von Arnim's of 1881, on the prologues,[20] a theme recalling Wilamowitz' youthful dispute at Bonn with Usener on interpolations in the prologues.[21] It is revealing that his students did not share his enthusiasm for the neglected poet.

The achievement is dazzling. No scholar of modern times—by which I mean since Friedrich August Wolf's matriculation at Göttingen in 1777—has done more for Euripides. Nauck, Murray, Verrall cannot be compared. Wilamowitz' books have endured as have none by his contemporaries on tragedy.[22] Yet his publications on Euripides constitute only a small fraction the *Lebenswerk*: six volumes, more or less, out of over seventy!

I. Why Euripides?

The achievement is undeniable. Si monumentum requiris, circumlege! Why did the Junker-scholar, unlike his teachers, friends, and students, lavish such attention on the Ishmael of classical Greek poetry? Chance and inclination, I suspect, rather than *Zeitgeist*. That is, the reasons are biographical, an approach that students of the history of ideas disapprove.[23] First, chance. Thanks to a suggestion of Koberstein, his German master at Pforte,[24] the schoolboy determined to write his senior essay on the subject: "How far are

---

[18] For the details of Wilamowitz' teaching see Hiller/Klaffenbach (*supra* n. 5) 75-83. For its influence see *QuadStor* 25 (1987) 151.

[19] See Hans-Ulrich Berner, "Index dissertationum Udalrico de Wilamowitz-Moellendorff promotore conscriptarum," *QuadStor* 15 (1982) 227-34.

[20] Hans von Arnim, *De prologorum Euripideorum arte et interpolatione* (diss. Greifswald 1881; publ: Jena 1881).

[21] See U. von Wilamowitz-Moellendorff, *Erinnerungen 1848-1914*² (Leipzig 1929 [hereafter *Erinnerungen*²]) 92, and for later implications my "Ulrich von Wilamowitz-Moellendorff to Kekule von Stradonitz on Friedrich Gottlieb Welcker," *StItal* N.S. III. 21 (1984) 130 n. 104.

[22] What Ed. Fraenkel writes of Wilamowitz' work on Aeschylus could be well applied to his Euripidean achievement (*Agamemnon* [Oxford 1950] I 61): "But what he has done is more than enough to encourage and enable his successors to fill some of the gaps he left. If the serious study of Greek survives, as we hope it will, then Wilamowitz' work on Aeschylus will maintain its stimulating and enlightening power for many generations to come."

[23] This is precisely why philosophers detest Wilamowitz' *Platon*: see E.N. Tigerstedt, "Interpreting Plato," in *Stockholm Studies in the History of Literature* 17 (1977) 47-50.

[24] On August Koberstein (1797-1870) see Elisabeth Frenzel, *Neue deutsche Biographie* 12 (Berlin 1980) 246f.

the ends of preserved Greek tragedies satisfying?"[25] Joachim Wohlleben has indicated the sources behind the young man's approach.[26] The choice of the topic itself caused Wilamowitz at age eighteen to do what very few other men in Europe had done in 1867: he read all the preserved tragedies of Euripides critically; and he memorized great stretches of text.[27] On turning to Euripides in this essay he writes:[28]

> From one of the first-class poets of the world [sc. Sophocles], certainly from two first-class tragedians [sc. Aeschylus and Sophocles], we descend to an average poet and a bad tragedian, Euripides.

He then proceeds through all the preserved plays and *Rhesus*, which he thinks too bad even for Euripides,[29] and provides scholarly and aesthetic judgments of great perspicacity on all of them. One need only contrast the eighteen-year-old schoolboy's ability to see Euripides historically with the embarrassing superficiality of Richard Porson's Latin inaugural of 1792 on *Hecuba* to see how far and how swiftly science had progressed.[30] Wilamowitz later tellingly observed that the great English critics never athetized or transposed verses:[31] they read word by word and could understand neither plays nor passages.

By 1869 Wilamowitz' opinion of Euripides had improved. He still thought little of him as a poet: he does not belong to world literature, but, as a representative of one of the most interesting periods of history, as a highly talented, reflective mind, Euripides now seemed to Wilamowitz to be "one of the most interesting persons of all literature."[32] Chance now intervened again. In January 1872 Friedrich Nietzsche published his first book, *Die Geburt der Tragödie aus dem Geiste der Musik*. The title alone was a provocation to a man who could never play a musical instrument.[33] In the text Nietzsche roundly condemned Socrates and Euripides. Rudolf Schöll (1844-1893) trapped Wilamowitz into reviewing the book. I have explored elsewhere the schoolboy rivalry that lay behind Wilamowitz'

---

[25] I discovered the essay still preserved at Schulpforte, and published it 1974 (*supra* n. 1).

[26] See Joachim Wohlleben, "Die Abiturient als Kritiker," *50 Jahren* 3-30, and Görgemanns, *ibid.* 132-35.

[27] See *Trauerspiele* 10.

[28] *Trauerspiele* 95.

[29] *Trauerspiele* 95-98. He taught it 1895/6.

[30] See *Ricardi Porsoni Adversaria*, edd. J.H. Monk and C.J. Blomfield (Cambridge 1812) 1-31; M.L. Clark, *Richard Porson: A Biographical Essay* (Cambridge 1937) 38: "Hastily written as it was, we may be grateful that it was preserved, if only because of the limitations it reveals."

[31] *Herakles* I 231. What attracted Porson to Euripides was his "nativa venustas et inaffectata simplicitas"!

[32] From a letter to Walter Bormann: *Antiqua* 23, 37, and Görgemanns, *50 Jahren* 135.

[33] *Antiqua* 23, 258ff.

savaging of Nietzsche.[34] Inevitably, therefore, Nietzsche's condemnation of Euripides, so ably investigated here by Professor Henrichs, demanded that the youthful and passionate Wilamowitz defend him. Hence the two polemical pamphlets of 1872 and 1873.[35] The appearance of *Geburt* during Wilamowitz' palaeographical, epigraphical, and archaeological *Wanderjahre* in Italy may be regarded as a spur to his collation of Euripides. Professor Pintaudi of the Biblioteca Laurentiana has discovered in the guest book of the Library for 11 September 1872 the entry, "Dr. U. v. Wilamowitz di Berlino." The result was *Analecta Euripidea*, which among much else contains a critical edition of *Supplices*—a work that would long appeal to Wilamowitz,[36] in part surely because of its patriotism—and an essay on the staging of *Hippolytos*. We shall see that the play exerted extraordinary influence on the youthful Wilamowitz. That he was already concerned with staging proves that he began early to insist on seeing plays as scripts, not simply as poems—anticipating the performance of his own translations, the *actio* of his *editio maior* of Aeschylus (1914),[37] and his son's epoch-making investigations of the dramatic technique of Sophocles.[38]

Analecta Euripidea is dedicated (iii) to Wilamowitz' future father-in-law, the brilliant, arrogant Theodor Mommsen.[39] Fifty-three years later, long after the disenchantment with Mommsen, Wilamowitz rationalized that the dedication was politic.[40] Mommsen was rector of the University (1874-75) and, since 16 March 1874, Secretary of the Academy. First Otto Jahn had died (1869); now, on 5 February 1874, Moriz Haupt. There remained only one patron. In two years Mommsen presented the *cliens* with the Greifswald chair. "From him I could count on a friendly reception; from him I could learn not only Roman studies, but above all scholarship" ("Wissenschaft überhaupt").

---

[34] See my "The Wilamowitz-Nietzsche Struggle: New Documents and a Reappraisal," *Nietzsche-Studien* [hereafter *NSt*] 12 (1983) 214-54 (= "Studies in the Modern History of Classical Scholarship," *Antiqua* 27 [Naples 1984, hereafter *Antiqua* 27] 182-223, 306f). A newly-discovered letter of Wilamowitz to Ernst Howald confirms much of the argument there: see Jaap Mansfeld, *NSt* 15 (1986) 41-58.

[35] They are available at *Der Streit um Nietzsches "Geburt der Tragödie": die Schriften von E. Rohde, R. Wagner, U. v. Wilamowitz-Moellendorff*, ed. Karlfried Gründer (Hildesheim 1969) 27-55, 113-35.

[36] *Analecta Euripidea* (Berlin 1875 [hereafter *Analecta*]) 73-130. Cf. *Griechische Tragoedien* I[4] (Berlin 1904) 285-369.

[37] *Aeschyli Tragoediae*, ed. Uldaricus de Wilamowitz-Moellendorff (Berlin 1914).

[38] Tycho von Wilamowitz-Moellendorff, *Die dramatische Technik des Sophokles* (= *Philolog. Unters.* 22 [Berlin 1917]). For an intelligent discussion of the book, with frequent comments by Ed. Fraenkel, see H. Lloyd-Jones, *Blood for the Ghosts: Classical Influences in the Nineteenth and Twentieth Centuries* (London 1982) 219-37. [See now Anton Bierl and William M. Calder III, *Eikasmos* 2 (1991) 257-83.]

[39] The preface (iv) is dated Berlin, 15 May 1875.

[40] On this rationalization, found at *Erinnerungen*[2] 170, see *AuA* 27 (1981) 45 f (= *Antiqua* 27, 158f).

There was a deeper reason. Not only the Schlegels and Nietzsche had condemned Euripides: so had Theodor Mommsen. In his widely read *Roman History* (1854-56), which won for him in 1902 the Nobel Prize for Literature, he damned the poet.[41] The historian Mommsen, as would later Eduard Meyer, conceded Euripides' prophetic insight, proven by his adulatory reception in Hellenistic and Roman times. Yet Mommsen made four criticisms of Euripides. The first two are Aristophanic and had been revived by the Schlegels. In Mommsen's opinion (170) Aristophanes' indictment was irrefutable:

> The criticism of Aristophanes probably hit the truth both morally and poetically; but poetry influences the course of history not in proportion to its absolute value, but in proportion as it is able to forecast the spirit of the age, and in this respect Euripides was unsurpassed.

By abandoning the grand character-types of his predecessors, Euripides was able to portray man as he is, through what Werner Jaeger later described as the introduction of bourgeois realism into tragedy.[42] But his retention of the external forms of tragedy—the use of masks, the chorus—made it impossible for him to delineate man in his entirety and to set these fully-realized individuals into higher poetic form. This, Mommsen held, only Shakespeare accomplished, and so (in a conclusion in part anticipating Nietzsche), "Euripides was able to destroy ancient tragedy, but not to create the modern" (167). The introduction of suspense and melodrama further cheapened the coin. So much for the literary criticism; now the moral. Mommsen, like Friedrich Schlegel, is offended by Euripidean women (168f.):

> Euripides is a master in what are called effects; these, as a rule, have a sensuously sentimental coloring, and often moreover stimulate the sensuous impression by a special high seasoning, such as the interweaving of murder or incest with subjects relating to love. The delineations of Polyxena willing to die and of Phaedra pining away under the grief of secret love—above all, the splendid picture of the mystic ecstasies of the Bacchae, are of the greatest beauty in their kind; but they are neither artistically nor morally pure, and the reproach of Aristophanes [*Thesm.* 547], that the poet was unable to paint Penelope, was thoroughly well-founded.

---

[41] *Römische Geschichte* II 436-40 (= *The History of Rome* III², tr. by W.P. Dickson [New York 1898] 166-70). I cite from Dickson's version, with occasional minor revisions. For the *Entstehungsgeschichte* of Mommsen's *History* see Karl Christ, "Theodor Mommsen und die 'Römische Geschichte'," *Römische Geschichte und Wissenschaftsgeschichte* III: *Wissenschaftsgeschichte* (Darmstadt 1983) 26-73.

[42] *Paideia*, tr. Gilbert Highet, I (New York 1945) 344ff.

His profound detestation of Phaedra survived into old age.[43]
Mommsen went further than the Schlegels. He adds two criticisms of
his own. Euripides was both subversive and anti-nationalistic (168f.):

> But, above all, poetic effect is replaced in the tragedies of Euripides by
> moral or political purpose. Without strictly or directly entering on the
> questions of the day, and having in view throughout social rather than
> political questions, Euripides in the legitimate issues of his principles
> coincided with the contemporary political and philosophical
> radicalism, and was the first and chief apostle of that new cosmopolitan
> humanity which broke up the old Attic national life. This was the
> ground...of that opposition which the ungodly and un-Attic poet
> encountered among his contemporaries...

Euripides was prophet of the *oikoumene*. This anticipates Mommsen's
criticism of the Jews in his *Roman History* III as "an effective fermentation
of Cosmopolitanism and national decomposition," a phrase later varied by
Joseph Goebbels and Adolf Hitler.[44] Mommsen never recanted. In 1886 at
Lincoln College, Oxford, when asked by the Rector whether he still held to
his view of 1856 on Euripides, Mommsen retorted sharply: "If I were to
write that passage again now, I should put it still more strongly."[45]
Wilamowitz never caused him to change his mind. I have already noted the
letter on Phaedra of 1891. Mommsen always attributed Wilamowitz'
weakness for Euripides to aristocratic decadence.

A need to disagree with authority—with his father, with Rector Peter
on Nietzsche, Usener on Euripides, Mommsen on Euripides—is typical of
the young Wilamowitz, certainly through the Greifswald period and in many
cases beyond. The first word of *Analecta* (iii) is "subirascere": you may
grow angry at my dedicating to you a book about a poet "quem quantum
contemneres non reticuisti." But the messianic task remains, expressed in
the provocation, later recalled by Eduard Schwartz:[46] "Nova docere volo;
nota praefabor" (131). Wilamowitz' later adoration of Julius Wellhausen

---

[43] For his letter of 17 September 1891, written when he was seventy-three, cf. Friedrich
and Dorothea Hiller von Gaertringen, *Mommsen und Wilamowitz: Briefwechsel 1872-1903*
(Berlin 1935) 425-29, fully discussed in *GRBS* 20 (1979) 226-29 (= *Antiqua* 27, 172-75).
Ironically, the plays most distasteful to Mommsen were Wilamowitz' favorites as early as
1869; see *Antiqua* 23, 37: "ich habe Hippolytus, auch Bakchai, die ich nur gegen in [sc. 'ihn']
herabsezte, stäts für grosse schöpfungen gehalten."

[44] *Römische Geschichte* V 216, on which see Karl Christ, *Von Gibbon zu Rostovtzeff*
(Darmstadt 1979) 91f. For the use of Mommsen's phrase by later anti-semites from Paul de
Lagarde to Goebbels and Hitler see Christhard Hoffmann, "Das antisemitische Schlagwort
vom 'Ferment der nationalen Dekomposition'," *Juden und Judentum im Werk deutscher
Althistoriker des 19. und 20. Jahrhunderts* (Leiden 1988) 96-103. Note especially: *Mein
Kampf* (Berlin 1939) 743.

[45] W. Warde Fowler, *Roman Essays and Interpretations* (Oxford 1920) 251.

[46] Cf. Eduard Schwartz, *Gesammelte Schriften* I: *Vergangene Gegenwärtigkeiten* (Berlin
1938) 372, who alleges that passages such as this caused Wilamowitz to remain longer in
Greifswald than expected.

(1844-1918),[47] the Old Testament scholar and Greifswald colleague, was fueled by seeing Wellhausen, as the philological martyr, betrayed by stupid orthodoxy.[48] In the *dedicatio* of *Homerische Untersuchungen* to Wellhausen on his fortieth birthday (17 May 1884) Wilamowitz writes that the philological problem of the analysis of Homer and the Old Testament is "etwas revolutionäres."[49] Everyone who has sought to solve it has to struggle (*kämpfen*) with the mighty power of tradition, of superstition, and of inertia. This "something revolutionary" in Wilamowitz drew him to the defense of Euripides, cast out by nineteenth-century German neo-classicism whose darling was Sophocles, especially his *Antigone*.[50]

This strain of the revolutionary or perverse—of what Solmsen happily called the *unus sed leo* in Wilamowitz[51]—drew him to a poet despised by the Establishment. But more than that, Wilamowitz was peculiarly attracted to two famous characters in Euripidean tragedy. This attraction, even identification, was so remarkable that one may speak of his youthful and middle periods as the *Hippolytus* and *Heracles* periods.[52] Still a schoolboy he wrote:[53]

> What is more, Hippolytus is a youth filled with an ideal striving for the unfulfillable, a phantast, a by far more German character, which leads to the point where he goes too far and falls.

More German means 'more like me'. It recalls also Niebuhr's conception of Germany as the New Greece.[54] By 1868 he had translated *Hippolytus*; between semesters that year at Bonn, while vacationing at his family estate in Posen, he visited his paternal aunt, Emma von Schwanenfeld (1800-

---

[47] For Wellhausen and Wilamowitz see *AuA* 27 (1981) 46f (= *Antiqua* 27, 158f), and Wilamowitz' letter of 18-19 March 1918 to Ed. Schwartz in W.M. Calder III and R.L. Fowler, "The Preserved Letters of Ulrich von Wilamowitz-Moellendorff to Eduard Schwartz," *SitzMunich* 1986. 1 78-84 (= no. 31).

[48] See for this episode in Wellhausen's life Alfred Jepsen, "Wellhausen in Greifswald: Ein Beitrag zur Biographie Julius Wellhausen," *Der Herr ist Gott: Aufsätze zur Wissenschaft vom Alten Testament* (Berlin 1978) 254-70. Wilamowitz arranged for the Philosophical Faculty to present him with an honorary doctorate on the occasion of Wellhausen's dismissal by the Theological Faculty: see *Erinnerungen*[2] 190.

[49] U. von Wilamowitz-Moellendorff, *Homerische Untersuchungen*, (= *Philolog. Unters.* 7 [Berlin 1884]) iv. Wellhausen in an unpublished letter of 20 October 1884 to his mother-in-law vigorously denies influence on Wilamowitz. I owe knowledge of the text to the kindness of Professor Dr. Rudolf Smend (Göttingen).

[50] At age eighteen Wilamowitz already found *Antigone* unsatisfactory: see *Trauerspiele* 77 and Görgemanns, *50 Jahren* 145. The influence of his Bonn teacher, Jacob Bernays (1824-1881), ought not to be underestimated: see *Herakles* II 147 n. 1.

[51] Friedrich Solmsen, *Kleine Schriften* III (Hildesheim/Zürich 1982) 446.

[52] See W.M. Calder III, "Ecce Homo: the Subjective in Wilamowitz' Scholarly Work," in *50 Jahren*, 91.

[53] *Trauerspiele* 114.

[54] See *The Life and Letters of Barthold George Niebuhr and Selections from his Minor Writings*, ed. and tr. by Susanna Winkworth, III (London 1852) 297: "...Greece fell, the Germany of antiquity." Attention should be drawn to his condemnation of Euripides (178).

1876), and read his translation aloud to her. Wilamowitz never forgot this meeting and the effect, almost a conversion, that it produced. Sixty years later he wrote of it in his autobiography.[55] Twice in scholarly publications he had earlier recalled it.[56] The power of lofty poetry had effected a change in a susceptible soul. The poetry was Euripides', and because it was in the transmuted version of Wilamowitz it elicited a powerful affinity. The importance of this early incident is underlined by the fact that later Wilamowitz based his influential portrait of Phaedra on his aunt.[57] He taught *Hippolytus* in 1875, 1881, 1882, 1886/7. In 1891 his great edition appeared.[58] For anyone familiar with the young Wilamowitz, his characterization there of Hippolytus is a distorted self-portrait (51):

> The quintessence of Hippolytus may be described in Greek with one word. It is *anepaphroditon*. Aphrodite is for him the devil, not because he was taught that but because it lies in his nature. Anything to do with Aphrodite is not for him... Of course he is a husky, handsome young man, given over to equestrian pleasures and master in these arts. He is a born leader and inevitably creates an impression of arrogance. That his comrades who will stand completely under his tyranny deify him is no contradiction... He does not brood, and has no political ambition, as his father would wish. He has the right to pluck blossoms in the meadow of Artemis. More he does not demand... He is free from human weakness. That may open heaven for him. He does not belong on earth, ruled by the gods who rule it.

Hippolytus attracted Wilamowitz because he persevered in spite of hardship and injustice, loyal to his ideals, chastity and the oath. Wilamowitz' loyalty was to *Wissenschaft* (he plucked blossoms in the meadows of Athene). This loyalty led him to renounce his aristocratic past, a military or diplomatic career, and marry a bourgeois woman, the first in his family to do so in over two hundred years.[59] This leads directly to a profound affinity with Hippolytus. Both young men suffered the curse of a father, Theseus and Arnold; and in neither case for a crime.

---

[55] *Erinnerungen*[2] 55 n. 1; cf. *GRBS* 20 (1979) 221 n. 12 (= *Antiqua* 27, 167 n. 12).

[56] For a translation of the latter of these, which appears in *Griechische Tragoedien* I[4] (Berlin 1904) 121 n. 1, see *GRBS* (*supra* n. 55) 221f.

[57] I have documented this in my "The Riddle of Wilamowitz' *Phaidrabild*," (supra n. 55) 219-36 (= *Antiqua* 27, 165-82). I provide evidence that any alleged influence from *Hedda Gabler* is chronologically impossible. H. Lloyd-Jones replies at *The Justice of Zeus*[2] (Berkeley 1984) 248: "This does not alter the general truth that Wilamowitz at that period of his life saw Euripides in an Ibsenian way, even if he was not directly influenced by Hedda Gabler or any other work of Ibsen." This is a *confessio fidei* and cannot be refuted by historical scholarship.

[58] *Euripides, Hippolytos* (Berlin 1891).

[59] For the *Family Chronicle* see now *Antiqua* 27, 239-65.

September 10, 1879, was the silver wedding anniversary of Theodor Mommsen, who with his wife passed it at Greifswald with the Wilamowitzes. His son-in-law had prepared a gift, a text and translation of Euripides' *Heracles*.[60] Even Wilamowitz perceived that a poem whose hero brutally murders his wife and children served awkwardly as a commemoration of twenty-five years of connubial bliss and fourteen children. He apologizes in the dedicatory epigraph.[61] The point is that wife and children did not matter. Mommsen in 1879 was the Heracles of *Wissenschaft*, the θεῖος ἀνήρ. The famous epigram easily applies to Mommsen:[62]

Mensch gewesen, Gott geworden; Mühen erduldet, Himmel erworben.

This was the fundamental meaning of the figure ("Grundbedeutung der Gestalt"). Mommsen won greatness through toil and, like Heracles, became in the Greek sense a hero after his death: on Mommsen's hundredth birthday, Wilamowitz urged young men to invoke him.[63] In the ten years that followed, Wilamowitz' disenchantment began; by the publication in 1889 of the completed Heracles, he had dethroned Mommsen and saw himself as the Heracles of Wissenschaft. This identification was made easier because Wilamowitz wrote not in the manner of a modern historian of mythology or religion, but of Plutarch's *Vita Heraclis* (= frr. 6-8 Sandbach). Similarly early Nietzsche projected a *Vita Promethei*.[64] Further, Wilamowitz documented carefully the ancient tradition of drawing contemporary parallels with Heracles (the νέος Ἡρακλῆς).[65] Placing special emphasis on a passage in Aristotle ([*Pr.*] 30. 1) where Heracles is discussed along with Plato and Socrates as the type of the "melancholic man," the unstable genius, Wilamowitz set him "in the ranks of the heroes of the mind."[66] Heracles dared to undertake tasks that would daunt the greatest contemporaries. He was the man who attained heaven through the (distinctively Prussian) ethic of hard work. After his death he became a god, as Wilamowitz said Mommsen did—and as Werner Jaeger and Eduard Fraenkel would say of Wilamowitz.[67]

---

[60] See *Euripides Herakles als Manuskript gedruckt* (Berlin 1878). For the Mommsens at Greifswald see *Erinnerungen*[2] 183.

[61] Indirectly of course: see *Elegeia*, ed. W. Buchwald (Berlin 1938) 55.

[62] *Herakles* II 38. The language recalls the Creed.

[63] *Kleine Schriften* VI (Berlin 1972) 28. See in greater detail my remarks at *50 Jahren* 95.

[64] *Nietzsche Briefwechsel: Kritische Gesamtausgabe* I. 1, edd. Giorgio Colli and Mazzino Montinari (Berlin/New York 1975) 60f (no. 70: Pforte April-May 1859).

[65] See my documentation at *50 Jahren* 96f.

[66] See *Herakles* II 93.

[67] See W. Jaeger, *Humanistiche Reden und Vorträge*[2] (Berlin 1960) 220f; Ed. Fraenkel, *Kleine Beiträge zur klassischen Philologie* II (Rome 1964) 545: in 1948 Wilamowitz remains "so immensely alive"; cf. 557, where he has the eyes of Apollo, the lips of Hermes, and on his forehead Zeus has impressed "the seal of power."

Wilamowitz took a further step. He identifies not only with the character of Heracles but with the poet Euripides. This is how Wilamowitz sums up Euripides' genius:[68]

> A restless mood, a bleak, tormented mood, that disdains gods and men, possessions and pleasures; and, along with it, a new strength to create and an audacity, a tireless striving after new tasks and new solutions, an ever-youthful receptivity to all that is new, good and bad, that comes his way—one cannot take sufficient pains to describe that human mind [*Menschenseele*] for which it was possible to create this series of contradictory works.

Wilamowitz had written his own epitaph: the enormous and varied production, the tireless energy, the intellectual curiosity, the scholar and the poet. Wilamowitz was an excellent poet, as the volume *Elegeia* proves, and a brilliant parodist.[69] He says of Euripides:[70] "Like a true scholar he left behind only one treasure that moths could corrupt: his library." His brother Hugo had inherited the estates.

This leads us to a further reason for Wilamowitz' preference for Euripides over the other two tragedians. Wilamowitz' approach, wherever possible, was biographical. He was attracted to great individuals whom he could admire, whether fictional or historical. He could never write a book on a man whom he detested, such as Demosthenes.[71] This approach was a legacy of German New Humanism, represented especially by Wilhelm von Humboldt. The quintessence of humanism was *das Menschliche*, which attains expression in the great individual, the hero. Wilamowitz tells us that Carlyle influenced him.[72] Euripidean delineations of character, especially of women—whose roles, detested by the Schlegels and Mommsen, Wilamowitz preferred to play in family productions and readings—attracted Wilamowitz because he discerned in them reflections of persons he knew. With an intelligent variation of Waldock's "documentary fallacy"[73] he could fill out the characters. That Euripides gives us in Aristotle's phrase "men as they are" is interpreted by Wilamowitz as Euripides' great achievement, not his flaw. Euripides did not hate women, as Aristophanes, Friedrich Schlegel, and Mommsen argue. "There are few poets to whom the female sex has

[68] *Herakles* II 133.

[69] For his parody of Voss see *Philologus* 124 (1980) 148 and for his parodies of Stefan George see Ulrich K. Goldsmith, *50 Jahren* 583-612 and "Wilamowitz as Parodist of Stefan George," *Monatshefte* 77 (1985) 79-87.

[70] *Herakles* I 11.

[71] See my "Wilamowitz on Demosthenes," *CW* 72 (1978/9) 239f.

[72] *AuA* 27 (1981) 47 with n. 85 (= *Antiqua* 27, 160 with n. 85).

[73] See A.J.A. Waldock, *Sophocles the Dramatist* (Cambridge 1951) 11-24; cf. R.P. Winnington-Ingram, *Gnomon* 25 (1953) 350B; Görgemanns, *50 Jahren* 148 n. 87. On the other hand the tradition should not be forgotten that Sophocles created roles with particular actors in mind: See *FGrHist* 334F36 (= *TrGF* IV T1. 27-30 Radt).

reason to be so thankful."[74] Thus Wilamowitz refuted all three. The judgment derives from one who since Pforte had preferred the tragedy of character to that of ideas.

Finally, there was an unexpected bond between poet and scholar. They shared, in Wilamowitz' opinion, the same religion:[75]

> Euripides himself did not believe at all in the gods whom he brought on stage, or rather he did not believe in them as his fellow citizens did, who prayed and brought offerings to them; but he believed in them, as I confess I also believe in them.

Wilamowitz elaborates. Aphrodite is the anthropomorphic incarnation of sexual desire. An abstraction is grey and pale. We are not so far from Nietzsche's Dionysus and Apollo.[76] For Wilamowitz Euripides, in this respect, stands in sharpest contrast to Sophocles, whose religion was base superstition.[77] He typically prefers the personal to the abstract, the concrete to the theoretical.[78] This is historicism and not *Geistesgeschichte*.

II. Professional Productions of Translations

Professor Hellmut Flashar has expertly assembled and analyzed the elusive data still available on the professional (in contrast to academic) production of Wilamowitz' translations in German-speaking lands.[79] Predictably, Wilamowitz' *Oedipus Rex* was the first of his translations to be performed, in the Berliner Theater in February 1900 under the direction of Hans Oberländer. A famous production of his *Oresteia* soon followed with a sold-out première on 24 November 1900 in the *Theater des Westens*. The director

---

[74] *Herakles* I 10.

[75] *Griechische Tragoedien* I⁴ (Berlin 1904) 120. I am grateful to Albert Henrichs, who first convinced me of the importance of this passage. Wilamowitz did not find it incompatible with *fidem profiteor Platonicam*. In this view Euripides was a precursor of Plato in his struggle against popular religion.

[76] See in general Martin Vogel, "Apollinisch und Dionysisch: Geschichte eines genialen Irrtums," *Studien zur Musikgeschichte des 19. Jahrhunderts* VI (Regensburg 1966).

[77] See *in nuce: Antiqua* 23, 279-91 and further Albert Henrichs, *50 Jahren* 298-301. There is a corrective at *Kleine Schriften* VI (Berlin 1972) 210-13, where Wilamowitz tries manfully to see Sophocles on his own terms.

[78] See briefly Werner Jaeger, *Five Essays*, tr. Adele M. Fiske R.S.C.J. (Montreal 1966) 61.

[79] "Aufführungen von Griechischen Dramen in der Übersetzung von Wilamowitz," *50 Jahren* 306-57 (= H. Flashar, *Eidola* [Amsterdam 1989] 649-702). What follows is little more than a summary of this fundamental study, which continues his pioneer work in the new subject of 'revival as reception' in "F. Mendelssohn-Bartholdys Vertonung antiker Dramen," *Berlin und die Antike: Aufsätze*, edd. Willmuth Arenhövel and Christa Schreiber (Berlin 1979) 351-61. See further his "Die Entdeckung der griechischen Tragödie für die deutsche Bühne," *Kunsterfahrung und Kulturpolitik im Berlin Hegels* (= *Hegel Studien* 22, edd. O. Pöggeler and A. Gerthmann-Siefert [Bonn 1983]) 285-308. [See now H. Flashar, *Inszenierung der Antike: Das griechische Drama auf der Bühne der Neuzeit* (Munich 1991).]

was again Oberländer, with a musical setting by Max von Schilling.[80]
Herakles, the first Euripidean translation, was not performed until 6 January
1902—not at Berlin or Vienna, but at a matinée of the Viennese Academic
Association for Art and Literature at the *Theater in der Josefstadt* (a suburb
of Vienna): an 'off-Broadway' production in a theater whose repertoire of
thirteen plays by eight authors included Euripides, Goethe, Ibsen (the first
German production of *Peer Gynt*), Hauptmann (of whom Wilamowitz
thought little), and Maeterlinck. In short, avant-garde. The impression of the
performance was powerful and lasting.[81] This was the first professional
revival of Euripides in Europe, preceding Gilbert Murray's efforts in
England.[82] *Hippolytus* followed on 7 November 1902 in Vienna.[83] Finally
in February 1904, at the instigation of Max Reinhardt, Wilamowitz' *Medea*
was performed in Berlin in the New Theater under the direction again of
Oberländer.[84] In this performance Wilamowitz himself deleted the Aegeus
scene.[85] The set, according to a surviving program, was modeled after
Heinrich Schliemann's excavations at Mycenae. Wilamowitz' reaction would
have been ambivalent.[86] Medea was played in an excessively naturalistic
manner by Rosa Bertens, who " hurled herself emotionally on the ground, in
daemonic wild passion, with petrifying features."[87] Reviews were not
favorable. Critics preferred Grillparzer's watered-down *Medea*, based largely
on Apollonius Rhodius.[88] In Wilamowitz' own lifetime only one other of
his Euripidean translations was professionally produced, *Alcestis* in 1909,
not at Berlin nor Vienna but at provincial Stuttgart. Of the 35 professional
productions of Wilamowitz' translations recorded by Flashar (including
posthumous ones), 13 are Euripidean compared with the 15 of the *Oresteia*
and only 7 of Sophocles. The influence of these performances on viewers is
difficult to assess, but occasional reactions that have survived, such as that

---

[80] Through the efforts of Hellmut Flashar and Hans Jaskulsky, Max von Schilling's score
was revived at Bad Homburg on 25 September 1981.

[81] See the contemporary evidence gathered by Flashar, *50 Jahren* 330-32.

[82] See Francis West, *Gilbert Murray: A Life* (London/New York 1984) 92-97, and my
review at *Gnomon* 57 (1985) 313-16. Murray's involvement in the productions was more
active than Wilamowitz'; but it must be remembered that at this time Murray held no job and
lived off the doles of his mother-in-law, the Countess of Carlisle. Wilamowitz was a working-
man. See now R. Ackerman, "Euripides and Professor Murray," *CJ* 81 (1985/6) 329-36. [See
Paul A. Edwards. *"Putting on the Greeks:" Euripidean Tragedy and the Twentieth Century
American Theater* (Diss. Colorado 1987).]

[83] See Flashar, *50 Jahren* 332 n. 86. A production of *Hippolytos* recorded for three
performances at Berlin in 1851 seems to have been under the influence of Seneca and
Racine.

[84] For details see Flashar, *50 Jahren* 332-35.

[85] He had early argued its superfluity: *Hermes* 15 (1880) 481-523 (= *Kleine Schriften* I 82-
109). T.V. Buttrey, *AJP* 79 (1958) 1-17, decisively defends the relevance of the scene
(without reference to Wilamowitz' discussion).

[86] See *Antiqua* 27, 229-34.

[87] Flashar, *50 Jahren* 335.

[88] For details see Flashar, *50 Jahren* 335 with n. 99.

of Theodor Gomperz to the *Oresteia*, attest to their extraordinary power.[89] One should recall here the attack on Wilamowitz by the George Circle, occasioned by the popularity of his translations and the success of their performances. Their anger became public with the publication in March 1910 of Kurt Hildebrandt's *Hellas und Wilamowitz: Zum Ethos der Tragödie*, in large part a protest against the allegedly colloquial diction of Wilamowitz' verse. The similarity to T.S. Eliot on *Euripides and Professor Murray* is striking.[90]

III. A Few Words on Influence

Wilamowitz had reacted against Friedrich Nietzsche and Theodor Mommsen, ultimately against the Schlegels. In *Herakles* (1889) Wilamowitz sought, by assembling all preserved evidence, to understand Euripides historically. He succeeded in making him respectable as well as accessible. The enthusiastic astonishment of August Nauck, as he first read the book, typifies the best of the older generation.[91]

But no seed could germinate on that ground. Nauck would remain until his end a *Wortphilolog*, albeit in the best sense. Paradoxically, the avant-garde claimed the conservative Junker as one of their own. In 1896 A.W. Verrall (1851-1912), whose work had early attracted Wilamowitz,[92] published an adulatory review of the revised *Herakles* (1895)[93] that is of greatest importance for the reception of Wilamowitz in Anglo-Saxony. The book had come as a revelation to Verrall (44):

> To me the book came at first, and doubtless to many others—for no one is really in front of his time—as just the thing that waited for utterance. In reading it again, I have seen, as already said, that it has dwelt with me more even than I knew; I have even unconsciously cited it; and in short shall readily reckon as high as anyone may think fit my debt to Professor von Wilamowitz-Möllendorff [*sic*].

---

[89] See Theodor Gomperz to his son Heinrich (Vienna, 8 December 1900), in Heinrich Gomperz and Robert A. Kann, "Theodor Gomperz: Ein Gelehrtenleben im Bürgertum der Franz-Josefs-Zeit," *SitzWien* 295 (1974) 325: "Gestern sah ich Berger in einem Zwischenact der Orestie... Der Erfolg des Theaters sei über alle Erwartungen gross..." For the reaction to Herakles see Hermann Barr, *Rezensionen Wiener Theater 1901-1903* (Berlin 1903) 112-20.

[90] For details see U.K. Goldsmith, "Wilamowitz and the Georgekreis: New Documents," *50 Jahren* 600-10.

[91] See *supra* n. 10.

[92] See his review of Verrall's *Medea* at *DLZ* 2 (1881) 1845f and of his *Ion* at *DLZ* 12 (1891) 1899-1901.

[93] A.W. Verrall, "Wilamowitz-Moellendorff's *Heracles* of Euripides," *CR* 10 (1896) 42-46. Because Hiller/Klaffenbach (*supra* n. 5) at no. 162 do not notice the review, it has been neglected.

Predictably the anti-clerical Verrall most approved Wilamowitz' view of Euripides' religion (46):

> The merit of Prof. von Wilamowitz-Moellendorff, as an expositor of Euripides, is simply this: that he, and he first, so far as I know, in modern times, has sat down to expound a religious play by Euripides upon the principle, firmly grasped and plainly stated, that the main purpose of the dramatist was to present a criticism of religion. Others may have said as much, or nearly as much in words; no one else, or none with equal energy, has acted on it; and "im Anfang war die That."

He finds what he already believed.[94] But he saw that Wilamowitz considered Euripides' abstract, intellectual sort of religion a considerable advance over cult, represented by Sophocles. In Mommsen's eyes this avoidance of the local made Euripides ungodly and un-Attic, cosmopolitan, and 'Jewish'. Only in this sphere of religion does Wilamowitz, a product of the *Aufklärung*, approve the revolutionary, the subversive. Euripides the poet, the student of human psychology—as well as the prolific hard worker—won Wilamowitz' admiration; he avoids moral judgments on Euripides' thought and ignores, rather than defends or excuses, Euripides the wrecker. Wilamowitz' disgust with Gerhart Hauptmann, whom he condemns in *Erinnerungen*[2] and sought to bar from the Order of Merit,[95] proves that with Euripides he swept a good deal under the carpet. Comparable is his portrayal of Socrates in *Platon*. He admires the ceaseless quest for truth. He ignored what caused Cato the Elder to call Socrates "a man of violence and a revolutionary."[96]

Where then did the crucial turn occur that caused those qualities of Euripides that offended Aristophanes, the Schlegels, Th. Mommsen, and Nietzsche—and which Wilamowitz largely ignored—to become his virtue? Or, when did Euripides become, in Wilhelm Nestle's words, "the poet of the Greek Enlightenment?"[97] To answer this question we must summon a towering figure in late nineteenth century German Hellenism, Erwin Rohde

---

[94] For Verrall's assertion (45) that Wilamowitz denies the divine paternity of Heracles see Wilamowitz, *Herakles* II 114, and for Verrall's own views see his "A Soul's Tragedy (*Heracles*)," in *Essays on Four Plays of Euripides* (Cambridge 1905) 134-98, largely an expansion of this review.

[95] See *Erinnerungen*[2] 256, where the piece that caused displeasure is G. Hauptmann, "Festspiel in deutschen Reimen," *Sämtliche Werke* II, ed. Hans-Egon Hass (Berlin 1965) 943-1006. For Hauptmann's generous view of Wilamowitz see his *Sämtliche Werke* XI, edd. H.-E. Hass and M. Machatzke (Berlin 1974) 1086-90, 1105f. For Wilamowitz' discussion of Hauptmann and the Order of Merit see his revealing letter of 14 June 1924 to Eduard Schwartz: Calder and Fowler (supra n. 47) 89 with n. 433.

[96] See Plut. *Cat. Mai.* 23. 1; cf. B.L. Gildersleeve, *Essays and Studies Educational and Literary*[2] (New York 1924) 240f.

[97] *Euripides der Dichter der griechischen Aufklärung* (Stuttgart 1901).

(1845-1898).[98] In *Psyche* (1894), his masterpiece, he devotes fifteen remarkable pages to Euripides.[99] His Euripides is the opposite of Nietzsche's. Euripides is the hero who struggles against his time, the restless skeptic, the nihilist, the precursor of modernism. Rohde has turned Nietzsche's condemnation upside down. This is the more striking because in 1870 he had whole-heartedly accepted his friend's view.[100] Rohde's early loyalty to the young Nietzsche is too well known to require extended notice here.[101] Only recently have we learned its cost. The alliance, against his better judgment, with Nietzsche and (worse yet) Richard Wagner, in opposition to scientific philology, permanently injured his professional career. The Establishment, ironically with exception of Wilamowitz, who never hesitated to praise his scholarship,[102] never forgave him his apostasy. He was denied an expected raise.[103] His authoritative study of the Greek novel was boycotted in the journals in 1876.[104] He secured the Heidelberg chair only through governmental intervention.[105]

What caused Rohde, some twenty-five years later, to reject his earlier opinion of Euripides, and thus required him to reject the Nietzschean Euripides of 1872—a view he had boldly defended against Wilamowitz? Otto Regenbogen called *Psyche* "etwas wie ein Totenopfer an den lebend geschiedenen Freund," the hopelessly ill Nietzsche.[106] Its composition extended until autumn 1893 and embraced, therefore, the collapse of Nietzsche at Turin in January 1889 and the receipt of the *Wahnsinnszettel*,

---

[98] The standard biography, with all its shortcomings, remains Otto Crusius, *Erwin Rohde: Ein biographischer Versuch* (Tübingen/Leipzig 1902). There is little of value in Ernest Seillière, *Nietzsches Waffenbruder, Erwin Rohde* (Berlin 1911). The most important recent contribution is by Rohde's grand-daughter: see Hedwig Däuble, "Friedrich Nietzsche und Erwin Rohde," *NSt* 5 (1976) 321-54. For a brief life with bibliography see W. Schmid, *BiogJahr* 102 (1899) 87-114, who (109) calls him "a man of the Achilles type." All earlier biographical work on Rohde has been antiquated by the exemplary study of Hubert Cancik, "Erwin Rohde: ein Philologe der Bismarckzeit," *Semper Apertus: Sechshundert Jahre Ruprecht-Karls-Universität Heidelberg 1386-1986* II, ed. W. Doer (Berlin/Heidelberg 1985) 436-505. [See now Andreas Patzer (ed.), "Franz Overbeck Erwin Rohde Briefwechsel," *Supplementa Nietscheana* (Berlin/New York 1990).]

[99] *Psyche: Seelencult und Unsterblichkeitsglaube der Griechen* (Leipzig/Tübingen 1898) 247-62 (tr. W.B. Willis [London 1925] 432-38).

[100] Crusius (*supra* n. 98) 223f.

[101] See the material I have gathered at *NSt* 12 (1983) 238f (= *Antiqua* 27, 207f).

[102] See *NSt* 12 (1983) 247 n. 242 (= *Antiqua* 27, 216 n. 242) and especially Albert Henrichs, *50 Jahren* 285f with nn. 107-09.

[103] *NSt* 5 (1976) 330 n. 25.

[104] So W. Schmid, *BiogJahr* 103 (1899) 94. *Der griechische Roman* was reviewed by F. Blass alone, later a critic of Wilamowitz: see U. von Wilamowitz-Moellendorff, *Aischylos Interpretationen* (Berlin 1914) 203ff. Blass (1843-1907) had done his dissertation under Ritschl at Bonn (1863) and was a follower of Rohde at Kiel (1876): he belonged to the other side. For Blass see Wilhelm Crönert, *BiogJahr* 32 (1909) 1-32. Wilamowitz reveals in his letters to Friedrich Althoff how little he thought of Blass.

[105] Albrecht Dihle, *NSt* 12 (1983) 246.

[106] Otto Regenbogen, *Kleine Schriften*, ed. Franz Dirlmeier (Munich 1961) 580. His statement that Nietzsche is never mentioned in *Psyche* is untrue: see *Psyche* II 200 n. 4, with Albert Henrichs, *HSCP* 88 (1984) 227 n. 48.

mailed by Nietzsche from Turin on 4 January 1889, in which he places Rohde among the gods and sets the most beloved goddess next to him[107]—a sentiment concerned with the subject of *Psyche*, the survival of the soul after death. Nietzsche signs himself *Dionysos*. The presence of Nietzsche in Rohde's mind during composition of *Psyche* is undeniable. He experienced his friend's collapse as a tragedy:[108]

> Es bleibt eine schwere und traurige Tragödie; eine *rechte* Tragödie, weil auch ihr Verlauf, wie jedes ächte Trauerspiel, *nothwendig*, durch keine Willkür, keine Reflexion, keine menschliche Güte und Liebe aufzuhalten war.

I suggest that Rohde included an epitaph for the living but departed friend in his *Psyche*, a book about the soul and immortality. His mature *Euripidesbild* of 1893 is thus no less influenced by Nietzsche than his youthful one of 1870: Rohde's picture of Euripides the poet, musician, scholar, philosopher, sophist, iconoclast, atheist, and believer is an antique *Nietzschebild*. Rohde saw a distorted portrait of Nietzsche in his Euripides. The evidence is twofold. Rohde's Euripides shares numerous traits with the historical Nietzsche. A number of the most distinctive cannot on the available evidence be proven; they are colors added by Rohde's brush. But the association becomes clear:[109]

> his [Euripides'] was a spirit that urgently desired to know the truth and he followed every available guide to knowledge and wisdom for a stage upon his[110] journey. But he was never able to continue permanently in any one direction; in the restlessness and bewilderment of search and experiment he is the true son of his age.
> His philosophical and sophistical leanings were sufficiently marked to make it impossible for him to accept any part of the belief or tradition of his countrymen without trial... He instituted an unsparing and unhesitating criticism of all accepted things, and in the process felt himself immeasurably superior to the wit and wisdom of the past. And yet he never satisfied himself. He could never rest content with a merely negative position, for all onesidedness was foreign to his nature. The tremendous honesty of his nature made it impossible for him to admit that element of frivolity which made the sophistic movement and the dialectical negation of all certainty so simple and attractive, and at the same time took away half its sting. But he could take nothing easily; and so with all his sophistic enlightenment he

---

[107] Regenbogen (*supra* n. 106) knows of the existence of the *Wahnsinnszettel*, which was first published by Hedwig Däuble, *NSt* 5 (1976) 340. That he never sent it to Elisabeth Förster-Nietzsche proves its value to Rohde.

[108] Rohde to Förster-Nietzsche, 23 April 1897, edited at *NSt* 5 (1976) 352.

[109] *Psyche* 432f (= II 247f). For Nietzsche's view of Euripides, see Albert Henrichs, *GRBS* 27 (1986) 369-97.

[110] Willis has "their," which cannot be right.

was never happy. The pupil of the Sophists would hear every other side as well; there were even moments when he longed to take refuge in the restful narrowness of old and traditional piety. But it was not given to him to settle down in any fixed set of opinions; all his convictions were provisional, mere hypotheses adopted for the purposes of experiment. Afloat on a changeful sea, he let himself be driven hither and thither by every wind of intellectual excitement or artistic necessity.

This is Rohde's epitaph for Friedrich Nietzsche. It is also the first time since the Hellenistic period that Euripides was applauded on his own terms. The use by Christian apologists of isolated sentiments as texts for homilies (the Euripides of Tennyson) is something quite apart.[111] Rohde's portrait of the vilified tragedian in *Psyche* is the turning-point in the modern rediscovery of Euripides. What since Aristophanes had been considered vices are first here considered virtues.

Thus, remarkably, the three warriors of 1872 reunite in 1894 with Euripides again at the center. Admittedly, Rohde used *Herakles* only grumpily.[112] He never reviewed it. But without Wilamowitz' achievement, Rohde could never have seen Euripides historically, a precondition of his conclusions. On the other hand, if Wilamowitz provided the bones, Rohde wrapped them in the flesh and blood of Nietzsche. His love and sorrow for his ruined friend caused Rohde to understand and admire an Athenian Nietzsche. Nietzsche—and here is the highest irony—who had sought to destroy Euripides with the weapons of Schlegel, provided the weapon that allowed the friend and defender ("Waffenbruder") to redeem the destroyer of tragedy. The weapon was Nietzsche's own tragic destiny.

The next year (1895) the Viennese Jew and liberal, Theodor Gomperz,[113] included Rohde's Euripides in his *Griechische Denker*.[114] His indebtedness to Psyche is clear. Euripides was a liberal thinker who thought, not surprisingly, much like Gomperz. He doubted received religion. He questioned the blessing of children. He was impatient with an aristocracy of birth and, like Hobbes and Rousseau, in favor of the equality of mankind. Mommsen forty years before had condemned what he felt Euripides shared with Jews, anti-nationalism and subversion. Precisely this, the cosmo-

---

[111] For the Christian reception of Euripides see Hermann Funke, "Euripides," *JbAntChrist* 8/9 (1965/6) 233-79.

[112] He cites it for disagreement: e.g. II 259 n. 1. His use of it for Euripides' treatment of traditional religion goes unacknowledged: see *Psyche* II 251f (almost Verrallian) and cf. Rohde, *Kleine Schriften* II (Tübingen/Leipzig 1901) 233 n. 1.

[113] For his biography see *supra* n. 89 and my remarks at *Antiqua* 23, 153f with notes.

[114] Theodor Gomperz, *Griechische Denker: Eine Geschichte der antiken Philosophie* II⁴ (Berlin/Leipzig 1925) 8-15; for his use of *Psyche* cf. 522 nn. 6f (= II¹ [Leipzig 1902] 534). Oddly he cites neither Rohde nor Wilamowitz' *Herakles* for Euripides.

politan and wrecker, Gomperz extolled. He first called Euripides "the poet of
the enlightenment."[115] It was the right phrase at the right time, and agreed
beautifully with Rohde.

In 1902 appeared the expected work of an epigone, a monument of
enlightened pedantry based on the work of Wilamowitz and intended to
provide Rohde's Euripides with a philological foundation; it bore a
provocative title, taken from Gomperz: Wilhelm Nestle's *Euripides der
Dichter der griechischen Aufklärung.* [116] This book's pedigree is revealing.
Nestle (1865-1959) took his doctorate at Tübingen in 1889 under Otto
Crusius (1857-1918), the biographer of Rohde, with the dissertation
Untersuchungen über Dodona (Tübingen 1889). Later with Crusius he edited
Friedrich Nietzche, *Philologika* III (Leipzig 1913). Crusius, with his
interest in Greek religion, drew Nestle to *Psyche,* of which he prepared the
posthumous edition (issued in 1910). Wilamowitz, who did not need such
things, would have dismissed Nestle's Euripides book as a *Sammelarbeit.*
With a pack of file-cards the schoolmaster Nestle dissected the preserved
work of Euripides, collecting, classifying, and publishing sentiments under
such labels as: the old faith; criticism of the old faith; criticism of particular
myths; what Euripides thought divine; psychology; human life; the family;
the state; the nobility; rich and poor; slaves; and, revealingly,
cosmopolitanism ("Weltbürgertum"). From Nestle on, Euripides was a
progressive. It was easier to accept his thesis than to read his book. With
Nestle's closing chapter (361-68), a eulogy of *Weltbürgertum* written in the
epochal year 1900, the circle begun by Mommsen was closed. His book
ends with a paean (368):

Euripides prophetically foresaw this spiritual empire of a Hellenistic
period and in his own way he aided in attaining it. If Alexander with his
weapons conquered the world for Greek culture, so Euripides was one of
the greatest and most successful leaders in the battle of minds; and the
thoughts expressed in his tragedies wandered to the most distant
frontiers of the ancient world in East and West. His own time failed to
recognize him; posterity has granted him his due. History has justified
him. He too might have said of himself what the champion of ideal
cosmopolitanism said 100 years ago:

'For my ideal the century is not ripe.
I live a citizen of a century to come'.

---

[115] Gomperz (*supra* n. 114) 15: "der Dichter der Aufklärung." At II¹ 12 he writes: "ein
Vertreter der Aufklärung."

[116] Stuttgart 1901. For the life of Nestle see H. Hommel, "Wilhelm Nestle," *Karls-
gymnasium Stuttgart* 12 (1965) 5-7. Because most of his life he was a schoolmaster, he has
never received his due. Among his students were K. Schefold, H. Gundert, W. Steidle, and
W. Hädicke. For a bibliography of his work see R. Nestle, *Bibliographie Wilhelm Nestle*
(Stuttgart 1965). [An edition of his memoirs by Hajo Smit (Amsterdam) is in preparation.]

Finally, in a masterly synthesis of Wilamowitz and Rohde, Eduard Meyer (1855-1930) in his universal history of antiquity presents an historical portrait of Euripides as revolutionary, "the great prophet of modern ideas":[117]

> No human being, not even one of the Sophists, did so much as Euripides to topple and annihilate the old way of thinking...so that within the brief span of a generation it sank into a distant past beyond recall; and he created a place for something new, for modern thought and culture.

The transformation is complete. We have Euripides fixed in stone, a creator of the modern mind.

A last word on Wilamowitz. At the end of his life—in the context of the history of religion, but influenced by Rohde and Meyer, his admired Berlin colleague—Wilamowitz wrote:[118]

> Certainly it is corrupting for the morality of the nation to spread abroad orally and in writing views that negate all morality. But it is not the Sophists who bear the blame for the brutalizing of traditional feeling. Euripides portrayed a world without *aidos* and *nemesis, because that is what he saw.*

And it is what Wilamowitz, the only conservative who led the revival of Euripides, saw in the death-throes of the Weimar Republic—as far removed from January 18, 1871, the founding of the Second Reich in the Hall of Mirrors at Versailles, as is late Euripides "von des attischen Reiches Herrlichkeit." The humiliation and decadence of Germany after World War I provided Wilamowitz with the key by which he could forgive what he had disapproved and therefore ignored in Euripides. Euripides was not a wrecker. He was an honest reporter.[119]

---

[117] Eduard Meyer, *Geschichte des Altertums* IV. 1[8]: *Das Perserreich und die Griechen bis zum Vorabend des peloponnesischen Krieges*, ed. Hans Erich Stier (repr. Darmstadt 1980) 805. Otto Crusius read proofs of the first edition of this volume (Stuttgart 1901, p. xi).

[118] *Der Glaube der Hellenen* II[2] 215.

[119] I am grateful for considerable improvement to Ernst Behler (Seattle) and Albert Henrichs (Harvard). Earlier versions of this paper were delivered at the annual meeting of the American Philological Association in Cincinnati on 29 December 1983, at the University of Washington in Seattle on 24 May 1984, as the fiftieth Hulley Lecture at the University of Colorado at Boulder on 7 March 1985, at the University of Milan on 8 May 1986, and at the University of Illinois at Urbana/Champaign on 30 March 1987. [Addendum (June 1986): Professor Dr. Klaus Heinrich (Freie Universität Berlin) suggests to me that in *Geburt* there is a self-identification of Nietzsche with Euripides. If this is the case, it makes Rohde's identification of Nietzsche with Euripides more easily explicable.]

Golo Mann on Ulrich von Wilamowitz-Moellendorff

Golo Mann, *Erinnerungen und Gedanken: Eine Jugend in Deutschland*
(Frankfurt/Main 1986) 472-73, writes the following:

> In den zwanziger Jahren war er [Bruno Snell (1896-1986)] Assistent des
> gewaltigen Philologen Ulrich von Wilamowitz-Moellendorff gewesen,
> welcher damals nicht mehr der Jüngste gewesen sein kann; hatte er doch
> zweimal eine Buchbesprechung mit dem Satz "Für die Wissenschaft
> existiert dieses Werk nicht" beendet, wobei es sich in einem Fall um
> Nietzsches *Geburt der Tragödie*, im anderen um Jacob Burckhardts
> *Griechische Kulturgeschichte* handelte. Auch meinen Vater konnte der
> Gestrenge nicht leiden, ich weiß nicht, warum. Nun waren sie beide
> Mitglieder des "Comité pour la Collaboration Intellectuelle" beim
> Genfer Völkerbund, eines Institutes, dessen Nutzen hier nicht in Frage
> gestellt werden soll. Seine Mitglieder trafen sich in Venedig und hatten
> im Goldenen Buch der Stadt sich einzutragen, wo möglich mit einem
> goldenen Wort. Sie stehen Schlange; Wilamowitz, gestützt auf seinen
> Assistenten, hinter TM. Dieser, sich im Buche der Stadt verewigend,
> zititert sich selber:[1] "Ein Schriftsteller ist ein Mann, dem das
> Schreiben schwerer fällt als allen anderen Leuten." Der große Gräzist
> liest es und murmelt dem jungen Snell zu: "Dann soll er's doch bleiben
> lassen!"

In Mann's 20 lines the following 10 errors must be corrected.

1. Bruno Snell was never *Assistent* of Ulrich von Wilamowitz-
   Moellendorff.
2. Wilamowitz ends his "review" of Friedrich Nietzsche, *Geburt der Tragödie*
   with the words: "den gehalt in ihrem busen und die form in ihrem geist."
   These words with the changes of two pronouns are Goethe, *Dauer im*
   Wechsel 39-40.
3. Wilamowitz never reviewed Jacob Burckhardt, *Griechische Kultur-*
   geschichte.
4. Wilamowitz was not a member of a "Comité pour la Collaboration
   Intellectuelle."

---

[1] Golo Mann presumably thinks of *Tristan* (1902): see Thomas Mann, *Stockholmer*
Gesamtausgabe der Werke: Ausgewählte Erzählungen, (Stockholm 1948) 88: "daß ein
Schriftsteller ein Mann ist, dem das Schreiben schwerer fällt als allen anderen Leuten."
Bruno Snell reports (*op. cit.*, 95) that what Thomas Mann wrote in the photographer's guest
book was: "Der Schriftsteller ist ein Mensch, dem das Schreiben besonders schwer fällt.
Thomas Mann." I prefer Snell's variant.

5. The meeting where Wilamowitz and Thomas Mann met took place in Florence and not in Venice.

6. Wilamowitz attended not because of any Comité but "im Auftrage des Reiches".

7. Wilamowitz never wrote in the Golden Book either of Venice or of Florence.

8. Wilamowitz never stood on line with Thomas Mann in order to sign the Golden Book of Venice.

9. Wilamowitz 9-16 May 1925 was vigorous enough at age 75 to stand unaided.

10. It was not Wilamowitz' severity but his honesty that Thomas Mann could never forgive.

This passage was earlier published in the *Frankfurter Allgemeine Zeitung* of 8 June 1986 with three further errors corrected in the later version. For an accurate report of what happened by an eyewitness see Bruno Snell, "Zwei Anekdoten zur Philologiegeschichte: 1. Wilamowitz und Thomas Mann," *Antike und Abendland* 12 (1966) 95-96. What he reports is confirmed by Wilamowitz' note of early May 1925 to Eduard Fraenkel which see with my commentary at Ulrich von Wilamowitz-Moellendorff, "Selected Correspondence 1869-1931," ed. William M. Calder III, *Antiqua* 23 (1983) 99 with nn. 31 and 32. Golo Mann could not have known that in a letter of 15 December 1898 to Georg Kaibel Wilamowitz wrote: "Heute entschliesse ich mich, das unerträgliche Buch von Burckhardt nicht anzuzeigen." Several months later in an essay dated 28 August 1899 (= 150th birthday of Goethe), Wilamowitz wrote, *Griechische Tragoedien* II (Berlin 1900) 6-7: "Schließlich würde ich es für feige halten, wenn ich es hier nicht ausspräche, daß die griechische Kulturgeschichte von Jacob Burckhardt, nach der mancher leicht greifen könnte, für die Wissenschaft nicht existiert." His disgust is visible again in a review of 1899 easily available at *KS* V. 1. 185.[2]

I have no idea if this paragraph on Wilamowitz is typical of the accuracy of Golo Mann's *Erinnerungen*. It is sobering that a professor of history in one of the great universities of Europe expends so little effort in the pursuit of truth.[3]

---

[2] Wilamowitz was not alone in his contempt for Burckhardt's posthumously published volume of what we should call undergraduate lectures. Th. Mommsen, Eduard Meyer, and J. Beloch shared his view: for details see Arnaldo Momigliano, *Essays in Ancient and Modern Historiography*, (Middletown 1977) 304 n. 4. German aesthetes and philosophers, sc. people unable to control the ancient evidence, admired the book: see E. Colmi, *Wandlungen in der Auffassung von Jacob Burckhardt*, (Diss. Köln 1936). In contrast to Beloch, Meyer, Mommsen, and Wilamowitz the philologist H. Lloyd-Jones at *CR* N.S. 36 (1986) 297 considers Burckhardt "the greatest historian of his time." *Cras credam.*

[3] I am grateful for informed aid to Ulrich K. Goldsmith and Hugo Schmidt.

The Members of Wilamowitz' Graeca

On 21 November 1950 Paul Maas wrote Günther Klaffenbach his wish that Klaffenbach would gather material on the Graeca "diesen einzigartigen Verein." In 1962 he wrote again "Who besides the both of us belonged? I vaguely remember Kranz and Malten. Could you name the rest for me?"[1] In 1979, almost fifty years after it ceased to exist, Friedrich Solmsen sought to reconstruct from memory the membership of Wilamowitz' "Graeca," a group of scholars who, under his guidance, for twelve years (1919-1931) read Greek authors together.[2] In alphabetical order the twenty members Solmsen recalled were:[3]

1. Franz Beckmann (?)
2. Karl Deichgräber
3. Eduard Fraenkel
4. Harald Fuchs
5. Rudolf Güngerich
6. Richard Harder
7. Werner Kappler
8. Günther Klaffenbach
9. Friedrich Klingner (?)
10. Walther Kranz
11. Paul Maas
12. Werner Peek
13. Rudolf Pfeiffer (?)
14. Otto Regenbogen
15. Luise Reinhard
16. Wolfgang Schadewaldt
17. Friedrich Solmsen
18. Friedrich Spiro
19. Johannes Sykutris[4]
20. Richard Walzer

Anyone working in the early twentieth century soon learns that one contemporary written source is worth 100 recollections. Shortly after its

---

[1] Published at Eckart Mensching, *Über einen verfolgten deutschen Altphilologen: Paul Maas (1880-1964)* (Berlin 1987) 112-13. Maas' idea that Ludolf Malten (1879-1969) was a member is wrong. Already in 1919 he left Berlin to become Extraordinarius at Königsberg: see Wolfhart Unte, "Das Werk Ludolf Maltens," *Jahrbuch der Schlesischen Friedrich-Wilhelms-Universität zu Breslau* 221 (1980) 320.

[2] Friedrich Solmsen, "Wilamowitz in his Last Ten Years," *GRBS* 20 (1979) 89-122 (= Friedrich Solmsen, *Kleine Schriften* III, *Collectanea* IV. 3 [Hildesheim/Zürich/New York 1982] 430-463 with corrigenda at 464). The list of members is at 91-92 (= 432-33). I cite throughout the reprint of 1982.

[3] A question-mark indicates that Solmsen himself was unsure. At *KS* 3. 464 without citing a source he writes: "Klingner and Beckmann did participate."

[4] For Johannes Sykutris (1901-1937) see Johannes Theoph. Kakridis, *BiogJahr* 275 (1941) 37-48 esp. 38: "Als er dann Wilamowitz seine gemeinsam mit E. Bickermann verfaßte Schrift über die Echtheit des Briefes des Speusippos an König Philipp (Sokratikerbriefe 30) im Manuskript vorlegte, wurde er in dessen "Graeca" unmittelbar aufgenommen, eine Ehre, die bis auf den Italiener A. Vogliano kein Ausländer jemals genossen hatte." Bickermann-Sykutris appeared in 1928. If he showed Wilamowitz the MS in 1927, he was a member until his return to Greece in 1929. This agrees with Solmsen (*KS* 3. 433): "three or four semesters in the latter half of the 1920s." For Sykutris' view of Wilamowitz see *Nea Hestia* 10 (1931) 1134-41.

publication errors were found in Solmsen's account,[5] welcome though it was. Further investigation has revealed more.[6] From the beginning his account lost much of its value because of Solmsen's prudish refusal to name scholars whom he discussed.[7] This is inconsistent with his professed aim in publishing his recollections sc. "to provide factual information" so that "speculation" need not "fill the gaps of available knowledge."[8] In fact his habit of suppressing vital facts has only encouraged further speculation. But we have been unable to control Solmsen's principle contribution, his list of the members of the *Graeca Wilamowitziana*. Now we can.

My friend, the Housman expert, Mr. Paul G. Naiditch, has recently discovered at the University of California at Los Angeles, Special Collections, Paul Friedländer File (Collection 1551), and copied for me a document, whose existence I had never suspected. On the occasion of Wilamowitz' eightieth birthday (22 December 1928) all members of his Graeca past and present drew up and published a congratulatory page which they presented to him, whether with a gift or not I am not informed. Copies were also made for the members themselves. It is Friedländer's which has survived. The document is written in Latin uncials.

P.G. Naiditch (*per litt.* 8 June 1988) describes the document as follows: "You will also want to know that, on the verso, appears: TYPIS MOMMSENIANIS IMPRESSIT TIEFFENBACH. The quarter sheet measures 399 X 258 mm. The text begins 78 mm. from the top; the lowest line is 160 mm. from the bottom. The widest line (SPIRO-WALZER) is 30 mm. from the left margin, 89 mm. from the right margin." I am grateful to D.S. Zeidberg, Head, Special Collections, University Research Library, University of California at Los Angeles, for owner's permission (6 June 1988) to publish. The text is:

---

[5] William M. Calder III, "The Berlin Graeca: A Further Note," *GRBS* 20 (1979) 393-97. My contention that there was only one Graeca is wrong. There were several of which the *Graeca Wilamowitziana* was one. His therefore was not a continuation of an earlier one but a new founding in 1919. Solmsen has accepted most of my corrections at *KS* 3. 464.

[6] Solmsen's assertion that the Graeca would meet for an hour without Wilamowitz in the University before meeting at his home is contested. The members met in a cafe near Wilamowitz' home: see Eckart Mensching, *op. cit.* (*supra* n. 1), 112 (citing Werner Peek). Solmsen's discussion of Diels and Maas and his dating of the Weimar inflation (455-56) are muddled: see Mensching, 111-12. But Maas' recollection in 1962 (Mensching, 113) that the Graeca was not called *Graeca* but perhaps *Stephanos* must be an error. Friedländer (not to speak of Solmsen) attests *Graeca*: *GRBS* 20 (1979) 395.

[7] See e.g., Solmsen, 433 n. 4 ("a rather well-known scholar"); 439 n. 12 ("the author of the dissertation"); 446 ("a brilliant young scholar"); 446 n. 17 ("a dissertation"); 447 ("an able young scholar"; "a recent Ph.D."); 448 ("iuvenis eximius"); 449 ("a student"; "a new Ph.D."); 454 ("a member of the Berlin faculty"); 457 n. 21 ("X"; "Bücheler's first and second successors"); 462 ("the editor of *Rheinisches Museum*"). I cannot see what is gained by this sort of evasion. The "able young scholar" of whose dissertation Wilamowitz wrote "a glowing review" (Solmsen 447) is Hans Oppermann: see Wilamowitz *KS* 5. 2 186-87. Why in the world does Solmsen conceal Oppermann's name?

[8] Solmsen, *KS* 3. 430.

UDALRICO
DE
WILAMOWITZ-MOELLENDORFF
OCTOGENARIO

GRAECAE WILAMOWITZIANAE SODALES
QUI SUNT QUIQUE FUERUNT
GRATULABUNDI VENERABUNDI

BECKMANN - DEICHGRAEBER - FRAENKEL
FRIEDLAENDER - FUCHS - GEISSLER - HARDER
KAMPSTRA - KLAFFENBACH - KLINGNER - KRANZ
MAAS - PFEIFFER - REGENBOGEN - SCHADEWALDT
SPIRO - SYKUTRIS - VOGLIANO - VOGT - WALZER

The document also provides twenty names. Fifteen names (Beckmann, Deichgräber, Fraenkel, Fuchs, Harder, Klaffenbach, Klingner, Kranz, Maas, Pfeiffer, Regenbogen, Schadewaldt, Spiro, Sykutris, Walzer) are attested also in Solmsen's list. They provide no problem. We can remove Solmsen's questionmarks from Beckmann, Klingner and Pfeiffer. Five names occur in the document but are omitted by Solmsen. They are:

1. Paul Friedländer (1882-1968)
2. Paul Geissler
3. J. Kampstra
4. Achille Vogliano (1881-1953)
5. Joseph Vogt (1895-1986)

Friedländer was a founding member. A card of Wilamowitz to him dated Berlin, 11 March 1919, and upon which Friedländer has written "Betr. Gründung der Graeca," provides the date of the group's founding.[9] Solmsen's date of 1921 is incorrect.[10] Friedländer left Berlin to become professor at Marburg in 1920. He participated at most two semesters in the Graeca which, therefore, began its meetings in 1919. Solmsen arrived in Berlin for WS 1922/23 and did not participate in the Graeca until 1929 when any memory of Friedländer's early participation had faded or disappeared.

Paul Geißler was a doctoral student of Wilamowitz whose dissertation in revised form appeared as: "Chronologie der Attischen Komödie," *Philologische Untersuchungen* 30 (Berlin 1925). The preface is dated "München, den 18. Juli 1925," sc. by then he had left Berlin. I can find no necrology and assume he died young, fell in WW II, or became a schoolteacher. Solmsen simply forgot him. I lack precise information on Kampstra. If he

[9] I have published the document at *GRBS* 20 (1979) 395-96.
[10] Solmsen, *KS* 3. 431: "...the Graeca began to meet in 1921." He accepts the new evidence at ibid., 464: "Projects and discussion concerning the Graeca go back as far as 1919." Yes, and also meetings.

was the Dutch Latin epigraphist, he would have been the third foreign member of the group. Through J. Vollgraff Wilamowitz had early connections with Holland. Any participation was presumably early and brief. Solmsen had never heard of him.

Vogliano was an Italian papyrologist with close ties to Germany.[11] He was in Berlin 1919-1923, where for much time he boarded at the home of Hermann Diels,[12] who was chronically in need of extra money. He, Kampstra, and Sykutris were the only foreign members of the Graeca. Presumably Solmsen refers to him as "a regular visitor from abroad, who had annoyed Jaeger by spreading an unkind remark of Diels in 1922; in Wilamowitz' home he received substantial help for his scholarly work yet never the kind of gossip which he craved."[13] While living in Diels' home, he may have overheard an unguarded remark of his landlord. Either Solmsen forgot him, or, because he did not approve of him, purposely omitted him.

Vogt, Catholic, conservative, brilliant, and, like Friedländer, a World War I veteran, after writing his dissertation and habilitation under Wilhelm Weber at Tübingen, did what we should call post-graduate work at Berlin 1923-1926, when he accepted the chair of ancient history at Tübingen. Only nine years older than Solmsen, he was one of the most productive men of his time. He became a staunch supporter of National Socialism. I cannot imagine that Solmsen forgot him. He certainly disapproved of him. Vogt may have been recommended to Wilamowitz by Eduard Meyer.[14]

Five names are adduced by Solmsen which are absent from the list of 1928. They are:

1. Rudolf Güngerich
2. Werner Kappler[15]
3. Werner Peek
4. Luise Reinhard
5. Friedrich Solmsen

Solmsen's inclusion of Güngerich, Kappler, Peek, and himself is easily explicable if they obtained their doctorates after 1928 when the list was published. Wilamowitz only invited men to join who had completed their

---

[11] See R. Keydell, *Gnomon* 26 (1954) 287-88. I am indebted to Professor Dr. Luciano Canfora (Bari), who first identified Vogliano for me. [See now Marcello Gigante, "Achille Vogliano compagno del sabato," *Quaderni di storia* 31 (1990) 129-36.]

[12] Keydell, *loc. cit.*, 287.

[13] Solmsen, *KS* 3. 439.

[14] See Karl Christ, *Gnomon* 59 (1987) 476-78 with portrait. His student Christ is loyally silent on his political activities 1933-1945.

[15] Werner Kappler went on to Göttingen where he became Privatdozent and Director of the Göttingen Septuagint Project. He fell in World War II: see Cornelia Wegeler in *Die Universität Göttingen unter dem Nationalsozialismus: Das verdrängte Kapitel ihrer 250jährigen Geschichte*, edited by Heinrich Becker, Joachim Dahms, and Cornelia Wegeler (Munich 1987) 268 n. 81, with the references there given.

doctorates. Luise Reinhard presents a peculiar problem. If she were a member, she would have been the only woman member. If in fact women members were allowed, I find it inexplicable that Luise Reinhard was one but Eva Sachs was not.[16] Typically (see n. 7) Solmsen conceals information.[17] Something serious happened in August 1927; for Wilamowitz writes Eduard Norden on 27 August 1927:[18]

> Frl. Reinhard hat definitiv mit mir und meinem Hause gebrochen. Die ist also erledigt—mag sie ihren Unsinn drucken, um unsere Rückständigkeit zu erweisen. Da hat man wieder viel zu viel Wohlwollen verschwendet, Sie auch.

She is not included in the list of 1928, which includes former members. In any case she would have ceased to attend over two years before Solmsen began to attend and so any knowledge Solmsen had was hearsay. Without her inclusion the membership was limited to men. For these reasons I do not believe that she ever was a member of the Graeca. Perhaps she attended occasionally as a guest.

In conclusion the membership of the *Graeca Wilamowitziana* was:

1. Ulrich von Wilamowitz-Moellendorff

2. Franz Beckmann	14. Walther Kranz
3. Karl Deichgräber	15. Paul Maas
4. Eduard Fraenkel	16. Werner Peek
5. Paul Friedländer	17. Rudolf Pfeiffer
6. Harald Fuchs	18. Otto Regenbogen
7. Paul Geißler	19. Wolfgang Schadewaldt
8. Rudolf Güngerich	20. Friedrich Solmsen
9. Richard Harder	21. Friedrich Spiro
10. J. Kampstra	22. Johannes Sykutris
11. Werner Kappler	23. Achille Vogliano
12. Günther Klaffenbach	24. Joseph Vogt
13. Friedrich Klingner	25. Richard Walzer

---

[16] For Eva Sachs (1882-1936) see William M. Calder III, "Eva Sachs on Ulrich von Wilamowitz-Moellendorff," *Illinois Classical Studies* 13 (1988) 203-16 (= *Further Letters*, 207-21).

[17] See Solmsen, *KS* 3. 432: "Miss Reinhard left for personal reasons." He is certainly wrong (*ibid.*) that she participated "from 1921 to 1928." She was already out in August 1927.

[18] William M. Calder III and Bernhard Huß (edd.), *"Sed serviendum officio...": The Correspondence between Ulrich von Wilamowitz-Moellendorff and Eduard Norden (1892-1931)* (Hildesheim 1997) 243.

Apocolocyntosis
The Biographers and the Archaeologists

Der Forscher findet, der Romancier erfindet, der Biograph empfindet.
Emil Ludwig

1. The Autobiographies

Presumably on the analogy of the vita traditionally appended to German doctoral dissertations, Schliemann in 1869 began what would become his dissertation with an autobiographical *Vorrede*.[1] This is not the place to discuss the veracity of what he said there. Nor for my present purposes is there need to discuss autobiographies by Schliemann written as early as 1852,[2] but published after 1931. The *Vorrede* of 1869 already introduces topoi which for 120 years have dominated Schliemann reception. I mention the most persistent, "The Dream of Troy." The ten year old boy presented his father with an essay in Latin documenting events of the Trojan War and relating the returns home of Agamemnon and Odysseus. As soon as the infant could comprehend human speech his father had related to him the deeds of Homeric heroes. Throughout the struggle from rags to riches Schliemann secretly preserved the child's desire to become a classicist. He first heard Greek as a child from a drunken miller. He learned Greek in 1856. Heaven blessed his business-affairs so that in 1864 he could set out for Greece. In 1866 he returned to Paris to devote his life to *Wissenschaft*, specifically archaeology. By 31 December 1868 he had realized "den Traum meines ganzen Lebens." He presented the world a book on Homer. Alas the edifying tale was constructed after his decision to excavate the citadel of Troy.[3]

At least one very great man read and believed. On 7 January 1874 the Prime Minister of England noted in his diary:[4] "Read Schliemann's remarkable account of his own youth." Epithets are rare in the sparse prose of the diaries. Schliemann had sent the book to him, probably the French version, which soon his daughters perused. On 13 October 1873 Gladstone had dined with Charles Newton and discussed "the Schliemann discoveries and photographs."[5] Had Newton reported the interest to Schliemann, who

---

[1] *Ithaka*, xix-xxviii. This is the first autobiography published (not written) by Schliemann during his lifetime.

[2] *America*, 3-93 and Calder, *CW* 67 (1973/74) 271-82.

[3] First doubts Calder *GRBS* 13 (1972), 343ff.; a full-scale refutation David A. Traill, *CJ* 81 (1985) 13-24.

[4] *The Gladstone Diaries* 8 ed. H.C.G. Matthew (Oxford 1982) 437.

[5] *Ibid.*, 400.

then sent on a letter and the volume? In a letter to Schliemann of 9 January 1874 Gladstone elaborates:[6] "I have read the preface to your book with an extraordinary interest. After reading it I comprehend better your energetic exertions & I the less wonder at, while still more admire, your success." Energy and success. Already Schliemann knew how to write what people approved and wanted to believe.

The success of the first version encouraged a revised and expanded edition. This appeared in 1881.[7] The autobiography would have been longer but the publisher intervened on the grounds of taste.[8] Schliemann need not discuss his divorce in public. The content of the book was controversial enough without that. The expanded version gained an admiring reader whose influence on subsequent history exceeded possibly that of Gladstone. Sigmund Freud on 28 May 1899 wrote from Vienna to Wilhelm Fleiß:[9]

> Ich habe mir Schliemanns *Ilios* geschenkt und mich an seiner Kindheitsgeschichte erfreut. Der Mann war glücklich, als er den Schatz des Priamos fand, denn Glück gibt es nur als Erfüllung eines Kinderwunsches.

Schliemann was "the man in whose life history Freud took the greatest pleasure, and whom he probably envied more than any other."[10] He saw himself as "the Schliemann of the mind."[11]

An American journalist has read the autobiography in a different way:[12]

> Schliemann's success was in mythmaking, not science. His story of his life, his discoveries, and even of Troy was simply a late-Victorian dime novel of high adventure that sold well.

Neither Freud nor the American journalist were naive. That the life appealed to something men wanted desperately to believe insured its success and immunity from disbelief for over ninety years.[13] Only several weeks after Schliemann's death F.A. Brockhaus, his Leipzig publisher, wrote the grieving widow. The autobiography in *Ilios* should be more widely available. Sophia did what she could. "Aber es gibt Zeiten, wo die Feder

---

[6] *Ibid.*, 438.

[7] *Ilios. City* 1-66.

[8] So A.H. Sayce, "who was seeing the book through the press in Schliemann's absence," to Roy C. Flickinger in January 1924: see *CJ* 27 (1931/32) 24f. Whether the uncut version still survives in the files of Murray, I do not know.

[9] Sigmund Freud, *Briefe an Wilhelm Fleiß 1887-1904*, ed. J.M. Masson (Frankfurt am Main 1986) 387 (No. 199).

[10] Peter Gay, *Freud: A Life for Our Time* (New York 1988) 172.

[11] *Ibid.*, 326. See further Jobst 1978.

[12] Neil Asher Silberman, *Between Past and Present Archaeology, Ideology, and Nationalism in the Modern Middle East* (New York 1989) 42.

[13] For the appeal of the autobiography see Calder 1986, 34-36.

versagt."[14] Dr. Alfred Brückner, who had accompanied Schliemann on his
last visit to Troy, completed the editing. By 23 September 1891, the edition
was complete.[15] It was published early in 1892. There has been a long
series of reprints and translations with only minor revisions.[16] *A tribus
disce omnes.* Over forty people have written lives of Schliemann. I shall
discuss three important but quite different examples and use Ludwig's
distinction: biographer, scholar, and novelist. For forty years the autobiographies sufficed. In 1931 a biographer arose. Who was he? What drew
him to Schliemann?

2. The Biographer

He was neither universally loved nor admired. Harry Graf Kessler noted in
his diary, Genoa, 12 April 1922:[17]

> Abends gegessen in Genua mit Ludwig Bauer (von der National-Zeitung
> in Basel), den Terwins und Emil Ludwig. Dieser machte auf mich einen
> unerfreulichen Eindruck. Äußerst affektiert, immer auf den Fußspitzen
> gehend, um größer zu erscheinen, als er ist, keinen Augenblick
> unbefangen und natürlich. Der typische kleine Literat, von Neid und
> Impotenz verbogen.

Emil Ludwig (1881-1948),[18] born in Breslau Emil Cohn, son of the
eyedoctor and professor of ophthalmology, Hermann Cohn (1838-1906),

---

[14] Schliemann 1892, iii. French (1956) and Italian (1958) translations were made of later
printings.

[15] Sophie dates her preface "Athen, 23. September 1891." (*Ibid.*). For Alfred Brückner
(1861-1936) see Rudolf H.W. Stichel, *Archäologenbildnisse. Porträts und Kurzbiographien
von Klassischen Archäologen deutscher Sprache*, ed. Reinhard Lullies and Wolfgang
Schiering (Mainz 1988) 144f. The *Nachlaß* is in the archive of the Deutsches
Archäologisches Institut, West Berlin. Stichel in his life omits all references to Schliemann. I
have no idea why.

[16] The revisions, sometimes revealing, are gathered by Lehrer 1989. H.A. Stoll, *Das
Altertum* 4 (1958) 52 n. 1, alleged editing on Meyer's part. What is needed is an annotated
edition on the analogy of Karl May, *Mein Leben und Streben; Vorwort, Anmerkungen,
Nachwort, Sach-, Personen- und geographisches Namenregister* von Hainer Plaul
(Hildesheim/New York 1982) where attention is drawn to errors and an explanation for them
sought.

[17] Harry Graf Kessler, *Tagebücher 1918-1937*, ed. Wolfgang Pfeiffer-Belli (Frankfurt am
Main 1982) 305. See further *ibid.*, 603 (5 October 1928): "Ludwig habe zu Tyrell das
Schwinden der Ehrfurcht im deutschen Volk vor großen Männer beklagt: 'Wenn Moltke mit
Bismarck über die Linden ging, da hat jeder vor ihnen den Hut gezogen. Aber meinen Sie,
daß, wenn ich mit Feuchtwanger über die Linden gehe, jemand vor uns den Hut zieht?'"
Clearly the man was difficult.

[18] The facts that follow are from Adalbert Wichert, *NDB* 15 (1987) 426-27. See also
Ludwig's memoirs: Emil Ludwig, *Geschenke des Lebens: Ein Rückblick* (Berlin 1931). For a
revealing but highly prejudiced account see Niels Hansen, *Biographie eines Biographen:
Emil Ludwig* (Oldenburg 1930), 12-20. For Ludwig and Stefan Zweig see Roden 1983, 236-
45.

took the name Ludwig in 1883, was a Lutheran 1902-1922, but returned to Judaism in 1922 to protest the murder of his friend Rathenau. He studied law and later history at Heidelberg, Lausanne, Breslau and Berlin. Among his teachers were K. Breysig and W. Sombart. He early composed poetry and dramas and after a disappointing year in business became in 1906 after his father's death a freelance-writer in Switzerland. Like Schliemann, he travelled widely—in Italy, Ceylon and Africa. During World War I he was a reporter for the *Berliner Tageblatt* in London, Vienna, Athens and Constantinople. He learned to write quickly about matters in which he was not expert. After the war he embraced pacifism and during the Weimar Republic cosmopolitan liberalism. In his fortieth year, in the ancient manner, came the publication that secured his reputation, a three volume life of Goethe. Others followed: Napoleon (1925); Wilhelm II (1926); Bismarck (1927); Jesus (1928); Lincoln (1930) Michelangelo (1930). By 1930 he had been translated into 27 languages and some 2,500,000 copies of his works were in circulation. Next came Schliemann (1931). Lives of Mussolini, Hindenburg, Roosevelt, Stalin, Beethoven and Freud would follow. Ludwig was never deterred by the need to master vast new fields of specialized knowledge.

What drew Ludwig to Schliemann? Of the men whose lives he wrote surely the excavator was the least important. He least affected the lives of those who came after. He was not a figure of Weltgeschichte. Ludwig tells us that about 1925 "the family, Frau Schliemann and her son and daughter, the inheritors of the fame and the papers of Schliemann, approached me with a request that I should write his life."[19] Schliemann deserved the most famous biographer in the world. Ludwig might have refused. Why didn't he? An attentive reader of the life soon sees affinities between author and subject.

1. Ludwig is the only biographer of Schliemann who had met Schliemann personally. As a child he was ordered to bow and shake hands with the great man:[20]

> Kommt her, verbeugt euch ordentlich und merkt euch, wem ihr die Hand geben dürft! Dieser Mann hat den Schatz des Königs Priamos in Troja ausgegraben! Wenn du groß bist, wirst du davon im Homer lesen!

His father had recounted to him anecdotes concerning Schliemann. A revealing one concerning Schliemann and Virchow at Breslau is preserved

---

[19] Ludwig, *Schliemann*, vf.
[20] Ludwig, *Geschenke*, 75. The first sentence of his biography recalls this meeting: Ludwig, *Schliemann*, v: "As a child, before I had even learned to read, I shook hands with him at my father's table."

in the biography.[21] There was another remarkable family connection. Ludwig's first cousin was an avid reader of Schliemann's books.[22] Robert Friedländer-Praechtel (1875-1950), a bellelettrist with an interest in antiquity, was an admirer and correspondent of Ulrich von Wilamowitz-Moellendorff (1848-1931), the sceptical critic of Schliemann and for Ludwig symbol of the hostile academic establishment. I suspect that Friedländer-Praechtel read Ludwig's *Schliemann* but I know no evidence that he did.

2. Both were Germans who lived in self-imposed exile, whether St. Petersburg, Paris, Athens, or Moscia, while vainly wishing that German professors honor them.

3. Ludwig saw in Sophia's sharing in the lifework of her husband a remarkable parallel to the role of his own wife, Elga Wolff:

> In meine Werkstatt blickt niemand als meine Frau. Berater sein ist schwierig; hier ist ein produktiver Mitarbeiter...Ähnlich scheinen Carlyle und Schliemann mit ihre Frauen zusammengearbeitet zu haben.[23]

---

[21] Ludwig, *Schliemann*, 282 with a rare note: "This anecdote was related to the author by his father." I should draw attention also to "Erinnerungen an Schliemann," von Professor Dr. Hermann Cohn in Breslau, *Breslauer Zeitung* 4. Januar 1891 (= Korres No. 1445). *non vidi.* I assume these were written by Ludwig's father although in 1891 he writes under the name of Cohn rather than Ludwig.

[22] See William M. Calder III and Alexander Košenina, "Poesie, Philologie, und Politik: Ulrich von Wilamowitz-Moellendorffs (1848-1931) Briefwechsel mit Robert Friedländer (1874-1950)," *Antike und Abendland* 36 (1990) 163-86 (= *Further Letters*, 7-32). For his familiarity with Schliemann see n. 33. Košenina (FU Berlin) writes (19 November 1989):

> In seinem Roman "Titanensturz"—der 1935 geschrieben aber in Deutschland verboten wurde, der nach dem Erscheinen in Österreich 1937 von der Gestapo eingestampft wurde und schließlich in England (1937), Amerika (1940), Schweden (1940) und Deutschland (1949) herauskommen konnte—erzählt Friedländer den Verkauf eines antiken Gold-Diadems der Helena an den amerikanischen Millionär Astor. Über das Schmuckstück, das in dem Roman noch zu einer schicksalhaft-mystischen und symbolträchtigen Bedeutung gelangt, erklärt der gelehrte Juwelier Halevy, der das exklusive Stück anbietet: "Bekanntlich ist der Schatz des Priamos, den Schliemann bei seinen Grabungen in Troja gefunden hat, Schmuckgut aus einer viel späteren Periode als der des homerischen Troja. In den unteren Schichten, in denen man Scherben der mykenischen Zeit fand, war keine Spur von Schmuckstücken zu entdecken; offenbar hatten schon die erobernden Griechen oder spätere antike Schatzgräber alles Wertvolle verschleppt. In alten persischen und arabischen Schriften taucht aber immer wieder die Mitteilung auf: im Kronschatz des Dareios Kodomannos habe sich ein Sonnen-Diadem befunden, das ehedem Helena getragen habe! Der Name Helena ist durchsichtig genug. Er ist von Helios abgeleitet, dem Sonnengott. Die schönste Frau der antiken Welt galt also wohl als Abkömmling des Gottes, als Sonnen-Tochter, wenn nicht als Sonnen-Göttin selbst" (*Titanensturz. Roman eines Zeitalters* [Wien/Leipzig 1937] 95)."

[23] The citation is from Ludwig, *Geschenke*, 766. For Ludwig's sole and inaccurate citation of Wilamowitz as critic of Jacob Burckhardt see *Geschenke*, 788.

4. Both won greater acclaim among English and Americans than among Germans. For Schliemann one need only recall Gladstone, the American diaries and editions of his works.[24] For Ludwig we have his own words and the figures of his booksales.[25] Like Schliemann, Ludwig repeatedly visited the United States and was amused by the antics of the natives.[26] He understood immediately Schliemann's attraction to the U.S.[27] There is an amusing detail. Schliemann alleged that he met President Millard Fillmore.[28] Ludwig believed the fiction.[29] Ludwig in fact in 1937 was entertained by President Franklin D. Roosevelt at Hyde Park.[30] Ludwig tells us why he published his life of Schliemann first in English:[31]

> Ich lasse diese erste Biographie des großen deutschen Autodidakten nach seinem eigenen Vorgange zuerst in England erscheinen, wo die Wissenschaft den Ernst seiner und meiner Arbeiten freundlicher anerkannt hat.

5. Ludwig was a freelance-writer. He lived from his publications. His chief aim in writing was to make money, *ars gratia argenti*. His choice of subjects and his popular style confirm this. He was a brilliant success. It is perfectly reasonable that Ludwig was attracted to a highly successful businessman. He was one himself. As a writer Ludwig sought to find a unity in Schliemann's seemingly disparate life, businessman and archaeologist/scholar. This need for unity was in part caused by the influence of tragedy on Ludwig's biographies.[32] He preferred five chapters (= acts). Niederland would later devise a psychological unity.[33] Ludwig

---

[24] See M.H. Chambers and John Vaio in *Heinrich Schliemann nach hundert Jahren*.

[25] Ludwig, *Geschenke*, 776: "Den produktivsten Leser habe ich in Amerika gefunden." For English language sales see *ibid.*, 867ff.: e.g. *Bismarck*: America 104,000, Germany 54,000; *Napoleon*: America 508,000, Germany 186,000; Ludwig's total sales New Year 1931 were 800,000 (German) and 1,210,000 (foreign).

[26] See especially Ludwig, *Geschenke*, 777ff. ("die komischen Zwischenfälle"). He is invited to write "1000 words on God" for a paper that has 2,000,000 readers and replies "On God I could only write 2,000,000 words for 1000 readers."

[27] Contrast Wilamowitz, who treated an invitation to be guest professor at Harvard as a joke: Ulrich von Wilamowitz-Moellendorff, *Erinnerungen*[2] *1848-1914* (Leipzig 1919) 290. The "Toynbee Syndrome" where English academics storm American campuses to collect dollars had not yet begun: see William H. McNeill, *Arnold J. Toynbee. A Life* (New York/ Oxford 1989) 221, 241-44. Schliemann's protégé, Wilhelm Dörpfeld (1853-1940), did a lecture tour of America in autumn 1896: see Peter Goessler, *Wilhelm Dörpfeld. Ein Leben im Dienst der Antike* (Stuttgart 1951) 109-12. From his profits he allegedly installed central heating in his Greek home.

[28] See Calder, *GRBS* 13 (1972) 338-39.

[29] Ludwig, *Schliemann*, 56.

[30] Wichert, *NDB* 15 (1987) 427: "Nach seiner Übersiedlung in die USA (1940) wurde Ludwig Sonderbeauftragter Präsident Roosevelts für Deutschland."

[31] Ludwig, *Geschenke*, 752.

[32] See Kienzle 1976, 230-48 (here 232: "Und diese Grundvision verlangt bei Ludwig allemal eine dramatische Verarbeitung des historischen Stoffs...").

[33] See W.G. Niederland, "An Analytic Inquiry into the Life and Work of Heinrich Schliemann," *Drives, Affects, Behavior* 2 (1965) 369-96 and elsewhere.

found the unity in the poor pastor's son's lifelong quest for gold. His American title was *Schliemann: The Story of a Goldseeker.* Four of the five chapter headings contain the word "gold." Ludwig endlessly elaborates his thesis until the last words of the biography where Schliemann dies "with a wallet of gold on his breast."[34] There is nothing subtle about Ludwig's writing; but he is not writing for subtle readers. The culmination of Schliemann's life is the discovery of the Treasure of Priam. Ludwig writes:[35]

> Now the great businessman came into action, the man of the world and adventurer too, who had spent a year among the gold-seekers in California, had had to deal with gold-seekers, had unearthed lucky finds and sold them. Here beckoned the prize, the gold beneath the earth, the gold of Homer, the culminating point of Schliemann's twin emotion.

The quest for gold provided the unity Ludwig sought. It also would provide the pretext for the most sustained criticism which his book received.

6. Ludwig's *Schliemann* was only secondarily the life of an archaeologist. It was first a passionate *apologia pro vita sua.* The extraordinary success of Ludwig's biographies—by 1930 he was the best selling German author in the world—coincided with the decline of interest by the educated laity in the work of professional historians. Theodor Mommsen did not win the Nobel Prize for Literature because doctoral students and his colleagues read him. Inevitably envy asserted itself. The life of Wilhelm II (1926) was too controversial to allow its author to go unpunished. In 1928 the Establishment sought revenge.[36] Ludwig replied without effect.[37] In 1930 came the two most famous assaults. They were: 1) Wilhelm Mommsen, *'Legitime' und 'illegitime' Geschichtsschreibung. Eine Auseinandersetzung mit Emil Ludwig,* and 2) Niels Hansen, *Der Fall Emil Ludwig.*

---

[34] I note Ludwig, *Schliemann,* 18, 19, 33, 35, 40, 46, 63, 64, 80, 81, 85, 86, 100, 102-04, 115, 126, 139, 144ff. (Priam's treasure), 148, 153, 155, 159, 163f., 169, 186f., 213, 221f., 226, 232, 236, 241, 252, 255, 271, 279, 281, 283, 289 (death).

[35] Ludwig, *Schliemann,* 145.

[36] *Historische Belletristik,* hg. von der Schriftleitung der Historischen Zeitschrift, 1928 (mit Beiträgen v. H. Delbrück, W. Mommsen, H. v. Srbik); *Emil Ludwig im Urteil der deutschen Presse* (1928); *Emil Ludwig im Urteil der Weltpresse* (1928). *non vidi.*

[37] Emil Ludwig, *Historie und Dichtung* (Berlin 1929); the expanded and revised version is: *Die Kunst der Biographie* (Paris 1936). The place of publication is revealing. Ludwig's books were burned in 1933 and he could no longer publish in Germany. I have not seen either of these books.

Wilhelm Mommsen (1892-1966)[38] was the most formidable. Grandson of Theodor Mommsen, student of Friedrich Meinecke, Ordinarius for Modern History at Marburg, habilitated on Bismarck, he posed an intelligent question unambiguously:[39]

> Sehr anders und ohne Zweifel ernster liegt das Problem, das an die geschichtlichen Bücher Emil Ludwigs anknüpft. Sie bestimmen die historisch-politische Urteilsbildung auch sehr ernsthafter Kreise und nehmen in der öffentlichen Meinumg vielfach den Platz ein, den im 19. Jahrhundert die großen Fachhistoriker besaßen. Ob mit Recht oder mit Unrecht ist eine Frage, über die noch zu sprechen sein wird, deren Beantwortung aber an dem Tatbestand nichts ändert. Wie kommt es, daß heute der Literat, oder wie Emil Ludwig selbst sagt, der Künstler die Stelle einnimmt, die einst der Fachhistoriker besaß?

Professional decorum did not restrain the second critic. Ludwig, Hansen alleged, was an unprincipled, opportunistic Jew who made money out of throwing mud at great men. He had one cheap trick, "der Held als Mensch." He was the "Lindbergh [*sic*] der Literatur," the "Kempinski der Weltgeschichte." Hansen posed a further question:[40]

> Zuletzt aber ist das Problem Ludwigs immer eine sittliche Frage. Sie lautet schlicht: ist Emil Ludwig geistig und menschlich berechtigt, Bücher zu schreiben, die auf die Meinung der Welt Einfluß üben? Besitzt der von uns entlarvte Autor das Genie und den Charakter [= the title of Ludwig's book of 1924], die seiner Bedeutung als meistgelesener Biograph der Welt entspricht?

This is not the occasion to study the charges and replies. Ludwig did not merely defend himself by defending poetical biography. It was a question of amateur against German professionals. Who was the most famous amateur in modern history who had proven all the German professors wrong? In 1930 Ludwig informed Sophia that he was prepared to write her husband's life. He went to Athens. The delighted widow granted him access to all the papers. He writes in the preface to the work:[41]

---

[38] For Wilhelm Mommsen see Wolfgang Weber, *Biographisches Lexikon zur Geschichtswissenschaft in Deutschland, Österreich und Schweiz. Die Lehrstuhlinhaber für Geschichte von den Anfängen des Faches bis 1970*, 2nd ed. (Frankfurt am Main 1987) 394. He reviewed Ludwig's *Bismarck* at *Historische Zeitschrift* 138 (1928) 614-21.

[39] Mommsen 1930, 8.

[40] Hansen 1930, 11. The antisemitic passages are at 13, 17f.; Lindberg and Kempinski at 20.

[41] Ludwig, *Schliemann*, xi.

The closer they [the experts] were to Schliemann in time, the sharper was the criticism of this dilettante of genius by the then sterile academic experts...Schliemann is an outstanding example of my repeated contention that the enlightened amateur beats the solid expert every time.

The superiority of the amateur to the expert, of Schliemann to Michaelis, of Ludwig to Mommsen, repeats itself, like a Wagnerian *Motiv*, throughout the life. Ludwig describes the last decade of his hero's life:[42]

Only occasionally does the intellectual warfare of the last ten years of his life stand out so clearly as this; more frequently it was shrouded in the poisonous vapors of envy and calumny, which ever hung in clouds round the clear path of this dilettante of genius. When all is said, he stood, and still stands, in spite of his crotchets in this controversy, before the bar of history on a higher level than his adversaries, the titular professors.

Schliemann has become Ludwig's *Wunschbild*. Later Ludwig cites a comforting letter of Virchow to Schliemann:[43] "But you should not forget that public opinion has always been entirely on your side, in spite of the difficulties which the classical experts have caused you." Schliemann was the proof that Ludwig would end superior to the German professors who criticized him. Ludwig himself admits the parallel. He writes:[44]

This example [sc. the life of Schliemann] also taught me that the expert is not always the happiest of men, nor do I deny that the problems of history and fiction, of the dilettante and the professor, which emerge later in my book, appeared strange to me personally.

Commercially the book was a success possibly as much because it bore the name of Ludwig as that it did Schliemann's. The English and American editions appeared first (1931); then the German original (1932) preserving Evans' introduction; the French translation (1933; a new edition with a new title in 1947); then the Spanish translation (1934; reissued 1958) followed by a Dutch (1954) and modern Greek one (1962).[45] Unexpectedly one may say that today it remains the best life. There is one drawback. Ludwig refused to cite his evidence precisely. That is what professors who write boring books do.[46] On the other hand Ludwig has the great advantage of

---

[42] Ludwig, *Schliemann*, 187; cf. 165 ("the guild of the experts"); 166 ("the archaeologists could not follow without envy the work of a dilettante, who far outsoared the experts in energy, naivete, and good luck"); 218 (German professors as priests closed to new truth); 270ff. (attacks on Schliemann by German experts).

[43] Ludwig, *Schliemann*, 206 (a letter of January 1876).

[44] Ludwig, *Schliemann*, x. The whole preface deserves careful reading.

[45] The dates are from the Korres bibliography. I have not seen the books themselves nor do I know the size of the tirage nor the number of printings.

[46] See Ludwig, *Schliemann*, ix:

seeing Schliemann, warts and all. He records the rumors that Schliemann salted his finds (190). He does not avoid Schliemann's shabby treatment of Calvert (191). He can use the epithet oriental of a letter by Schliemann to his wife (208). He does not hesitate to explain his excavations as an extension of his lust for gold (104). He chronicles his hysteria at the death of his cousin Sophie (97ff.). On the other hand he is blind to the cruelty of Schliemann to his 17 year old wife (125) and incapable of understanding Schliemann's capacity for self-delusion (47). By modern standards Ludwig often seems psychologically obtuse: e.g., his interpretation of Schliemann's letter of rebuke to his bride (61) or of his lifelong habit of bestowing gifts on his father (47). Nor is there ever an attempt to explain rather than document the ceaseless quest for gold.

The book's reception by those who mattered varied. Readers who confused biography with panegyric complained of the emphasis on Schliemann's venality. The family to Ludwig's credit disapproved.[47] The American Homerist, John A. Scott, was scandalized. The subtitle, *"The Story of the Goldseeker,* does the very greatest injustice to a great and unselfish man."[48] He concludes: "The things told in this book so degrade the name of Schliemann that it is impossible to believe that Mrs. Schliemann had full knowledge of its contents."[49] The provincial pastor's

---

Nevertheless, like Schliemann, I must risk incurring the displeasure of scholars by declining...to quote sources, a practice which destroys the freshness of all descriptive writing.

On the other hand one must remember that Schliemann was the first biography written by Ludwig and based on unpublished sources: see Ludwig, *Geschenke,* 752: "Eine Ausnahme bedeutet die Geschichte Schliemanns, die ich aus den bisher verschlossenen Quellen hob." The omission of specific references to printed sources is only annoying. Stoll followed Ludwig in the omission of specific documentation: H.A. Stoll, *Der Traum von Troia*[8] (Leipzig 1968) 544:

es wäre ungerecht, Tausende von Lesern durch immer wechselnden Druck oder Zitatennachweis zu verwirren und zu verärgern, um dafür einem Philologen Freude zu machen.

[47] Alex L. Melas in: Lynn and Gray Poole, *One Passion, Two Loves: The Story of Heinrich and Sophia Schliemann, Discoverers of Troy* (New York 1966) viii:

Research and refusal to accept apochryphal [*sic*] accounts have shown there is no evidence to support the theory that Heinrich's major objective in excavating Troy was to find gold. My grandfather had more gold than he needed...He did not need gold from Troy to add to his personal fortunes.

The competence of the Pooles is evident from their contention (70) that George Grote was a German.
[48] See J.A. Scott, *CJ* 27 (1931/32) 21: "Indeed I have read of few men more selfish than Schliemann. One need only recall his cruelty to his wives and children." But for Scott this is (20) "a life which has knocked off his [Schliemann's] halo." Concerning the first divorce (17) "I cannot comprehend why Mrs. Sophia Schliemann, her son, and her daughter allowed all this to be printed." Scott even compares Schliemann to Aristides the Just (18).
[49] *Ibid.,* 22.

son shows. Theodor Wiegand, who ought to have known much better, wrote to Wilhelm Dörpfeld from Pergamon on 17 May 1932:[50]

> Ich habe das Schliemann-Buch von Ludwig gelesen und finde es abscheulich. War es nötig, so viele kleine, unschöne Züge im Leben des Mannes hervorzuholen? Und auf der anderen Seite soll er doch ein Heros sein...Ganz und gar verstehe ich nicht Frau Schliemann. Sie hat dem Andenken ihres Mannes gar keinen Dienst geleistet, im Gegenteil.

That is, the scholar Wiegand prefers myth to truth. But Ludwig was used to this sort of thing. A.W. Gomme, the Thucydidean commentator, praised Ludwig: "For he succeeds in making an admirable story of this energetic, ambitious, acquisitive, romantic, overbearing, impatient and likeable man."[51] Gomme is not offended by the truth.

The two men most competent to judge the life have expressed their views. Sir Arthur Evans (1851-1941), at his own expense the excavator of Knossos and heir of two fortunes, provided a consistently laudatory introduction to the English edition, not included in the American one. There he approves the unity in Schliemann's life urged by Ludwig:[52]

> It is a strange story, and Dr. Ludwig...has done well to trace the single glittering thread interwoven with its whole tissue—in its crudest form the inborn instinct of a quest for gold that first took a practical and then an historic turn.

Five years later Schliemann's former employee, Wilhelm Dörpfeld (1853-1940), agreed with Wiegand against Evans and Ludwig:[53]

> Ich habe es zunächst bedauert, daß Heinrich Schliemann in dem Lebensbild [sc. von Emil Ludwig] hauptsächlich als 'Goldsucher' dargestellt und sogar auf dem Titel als solcher bezeichnet ist. Denn ich halte es nicht für richtig, daß er als Goldsucher in der Erinnerung der Deutschen und der ganzen Welt bleibt. Er war und ist vielmehr für uns der große und glückliche Ausgräber von Troja und Mykene und hat es verdient, als solcher auch in der Geschichte weiterzuleben...Ein Goldsucher war er als Ausgräber nicht.

---

[50] Cited in Meyer 1969, 426 n. 98. One wonders what could not be published in 1968.
[51] A.W. Gomme, *CR* 45 (1931) 219.
[52] Sir Arthur Evans in Emil Ludwig, *Schliemann of Troy: The Story of a Goldseeker* (London 1931) 9. *Schliemann of Troy* is in the tradition of Lawrence of Arabia: cf. Dennis of Etruria! Evans never questions Schliemann's most romantic assertions: dream of Troy (9f.); circumcision to visit Mecca (11); California citizenship (11); "Treasure of Priam" (17).
[53] Wilhelm Dörpfeld in *Briefe*, 7f. Much of Dörpfeld's introduction is concerned with polemic against Evans' introduction.

This did not prevent him from granting Ludwig some credit at least:[54]

> Ich erkenne zum Schluß gerne an, daß Emil Ludwig und Arthur Evans
> bestrebt gewesen sind, ein möglichst richtiges Lebensbild von
> Schliemann zu entwerfen und seiner Bedeutung für die Altertums-
> wissenschaft und besonders für die Homer-Forschung gerecht zu werden,
> und daß ihnen dies auch im allgemeinen geglückt ist.

A more formidable and persistent critic would soon attack Ludwig and most
unfairly.

3. The Scholar

The following—so far as I know—is all that has been published concerning
the life of Ernst Meyer (1888-1968):[55]

> Dr. Ernst Meyer wurde 1888 in Groß-Bieberau/Odenwald geboren. Nach
> dem Abitur 1908 studierte er bis 1912 in Gießen und München. Im
> Sommer 1912 promovierte er zum Dr. phil. Beginn des Schuldienstes
> nach Teilnahme am Ersten Weltkrieg 1919 am Gymnasium 'Carolinum'
> in Neustrelitz. 1937 wurde Dr. Meyer für die Schliemann-Forschung
> freigestellt. In den Jahren 1937-39 weilte er jeweils für mehrere Monate
> in Athen, um den Nachlaß Schliemanns durchzusehen und zu bearbeiten.

No bibliography of his publications is available; no volume of *Kleine
Schriften*; no necrology. We are not told if his dissertation was published
and whether a vita is attached. He taught at the school which Schliemann
briefly attended. 1937-39 he passed some months in Athens to look through
the papers of Heinrich Schliemann. Meyer himself provides details:[56]

> Studienrat Dr. Ernst Meyer-Neustrelitz weilt seit längerer Zeit in Athen,
> um im Auftrag des Reichsstatthalters und Gauleiters Friedrich
> Hildebrandt den Nachlaß des bedeutenden Archäologen und Troja-
> forschers Heinrich Schliemann zu ordnen...
> Aus dem gesamten Nachlaß kann ein zuverlässiges und allseitig
> begründetes Bild Schliemanns gewonnen werden, das frei ist von den
> Entstellungen, wie sie beispielsweise Emil Ludwig Cohn in seiner
> Biographie *Der Goldsucher* aus kapitalistischer Grundhaltung heraus-

---

[54] *Ibid.*, 16. One should note here the opinion of a careful reader of Ludwig, the later
biographer of Schliemann, Heinrich Alexander Stoll (Stoll 1968, 553): "Die umfänglischste
Biographie schrieb Emil Ludwig: ein spannend gestaltetes, elegantes Lebensbild." The
difference from Meyer's opinion is telling.

[55] I reproduce the sketch from the dustjacket of Meyer's Schliemann biography. See
further Bölke, *Heinrich Schliemann und Ankershagen* (Ankershagen 1988) 31f.

[56] I cite Meyer's report as published Neustrelitz Monday 31 May 1937 in: *Landeszeitung
für Mecklenburg* 1. Beilage zu Nr. 123. I am grateful for a photocopy of this important
source to Professor David A. Traill.

gebracht hat. Ziel der Bearbeitung, deren Ermöglichung in erster Linie der Interessenahme unseres Reichsstatthalters und Gauleiters Friedrich Hildebrandt verdankt wird, ist einmal, alle Quellenstücke hier an Ort und Stelle vollständig zu erfassen, zum anderen aber auch, möglichst viele Arbeitsunterlagen in Form von Abschriften und Photographien nach der mecklenburgischen Heimat dieses großen auslandsdeutschen Kaufmans [sic] und Forschers[57] zu bringen.

What this means in plain English is that the top local Nazi offical paid Meyer to rescue a heroic son smeared by a Jew interested only in money and restore him to his pristine German, indeed Mecklenburgian, perfection. Meyer accepted money to write an account of Schliemann colored by antisemitism and nationalism. That is a newspaper report. In a scholarly book intended for an international audience of experts Meyer elucidates Ludwig's *Schliemannbild*:[58]

Ohne auf Einzelheiten einzugehen, betone ich, daß ich die Tendenz des Verfassers [sc. Ludwigs], den Dargestellten in erster Linie unter dem Gesichtspunkt des Goldsuchers zu sehen, ablehne, da ich nirgends Beweise dafür finde...Dem Verfasser fehlt das Organ für das Deutsche in Schliemann, besonders für seinen romantischen Idealismus, wie ihm auch, nach den witzelnden Eingangssätzen seiner Biographie zu urteilen, das Gefühl für die Eigenart und den Wert des Mecklenburgischen Menschen und der niederdeutschen Landschaft abgeht.

Meyer was unable after 35 years of research to find evidence for Schliemann's compelling interest in making money. The Jew Ludwig lacked the organ to detect the German in Schliemann, his romantic idealism, or the feeling for the uniqueness of Mecklenburg, its people and landscape. The Neustrelitz schoolteacher will provide what the cosmopolitan biographer of Bismarck, Goethe, Wilhelm II missed. Until his own death, long after the deaths of both Hitler and Ludwig, Meyer still refused to give his predecessor his due. He would not list Ludwig's biography, the only serious effort that preceded his own, in his "Literatur zu Schliemann."[59] Once in his book does Meyer refer to Ludwig. He finds it extraordinary that Ludwig was allowed to see private family documents. His treatment of the courtship of Sophia declined "ins Seltsam-Komische." "Dies [sc. the release of documents to Ludwig] geschah gegen den Willen des Sohnes

---

[57] Thirty years later this would be the title of Meyer's biography 1969.

[58] *Briefe*, 25. Cf. *ibid.*, 49 n. 1: "E. Ludwig...der materialistischer Weltauffassung heraus kein Organ hat für die aus der sagenreichen niederdeutschen Heimat geborene Romantik S.s und aus dem Idealisten einen 'Mythomanen' macht."

[59] Ernst Meyer, *Heinrich Schliemann: Kaufmann und Forscher* (Göttingen 1969) 446f. The bibliography includes C.W. Ceram, *Götter, Gräber und Gelehrte*, whose portrayal of Schliemann derives largely from Ludwig. Competence clearly was not Meyer's criterion.

Agamemnon und führte zum Bruch innerhalb der Familie."[60] The evidence
adduced is assertion.

Meyer wrote the biography that Schliemann would have enjoyed
reading. The thread that runs through the life is not gold but Homer. This
means acceptance of the "dream of Troy" and Jerrer's *History* with a child's
signature. The petit-bourgeois world of Meyer is projected onto his portrait
of Schliemann. One finds unexpectedly "eine zweifelsfreie Gottver-
bundenheit" between Schliemann and God (117). "God in the Life of
Heinrich Schliemann"would be as profitable a subject for study as "Death in
Jane Austen." Meyer is uncomfortable with the letters of 1863 between
Schliemann and his first wife (144): "Sie [sc. die Briefe] sind keine
erfreuliche Lektüre, im Gegenteil, sie geben ein erschütterndes Bild einer
schon früh zerrütteten Ehe."[61] He concludes triumphantly (405):

> Wer die sachlichen Berichte über Mykene und über Troja in seinen
> Tagebüchern und den jeweils ersten Briefen unvoreingenommen liest,
> wird bald erkennen, daß er alles andere denn ein Goldsucher gewesen
> ist, so sehr er auch vom Glück begünstigt war.

Whatever is wrong or even noteworthy about being a "goldseeker" in
capitalism of the *Gründerzeit*?

Meyer convinced two readers.[62] The fact is that after 35 years of work
on Schliemann, Meyer never understood him. He never learned to treat
sources, especially autobiographical ones, sceptically nor to seek controls,
that is external sources, to confirm or refute what Schliemann said about
himself. His editing of letters is a scandal, comparable to Dore Hensler and
Elisabeth Förster-Nietzsche.[63] He chooses documents which confirm his
preconceived opinion and ignores or censors those which do not. He stole
documents from the Gennadeion which only now are slowly being returned.
His knowledge of foreign languages was inadequate to edit competently
letters not in German. He lacked training and even minimal competence in
Bronze Age Archaeology. On the Tacitean principle of *omne ignotum pro
magnifico* he imposed on those who could not read German or who,

[60] Meyer, *Schliemann*, 157. Stoll 1968, 543, attributed the "verzeichnetes Bild von
Schliemanns erster Frau" and the romantic courtship of Sophia to Fräulein Dr. Katzenstein,
Ludwig's helper who copied out the archival documents for him.

[61] Meyer's marriage contrarily lasted over 35 years with his wife devotedly nursing him in
his last illness: see Meyer *Schliemann*, 12.

[62] See Roland Hampe, *Gnomon* 35 (1963) 417: "Schliemann war alles andere als ein
Goldsucher oder Schatzgräber," and Wolfgang Schiering, *Gnomon* 43 (1971) 427: "Umso
lieber übernimmt man das aus den Berichten, Tagebüchern, und Briefen gewonnene Urteil
des Verf., daß Schliemann "alles andere denn ein Goldsucher gewesen ist."

[63] For the damage done by Dore Hensler, Niebuhr's sister-in-law, see Dietrich Gerhard in
Die Briefe Barthold Georg Niebuhrs, Hg. Dietrich Gerhard und William Norvin, Bd 1 1776-
1809 (Berlin 1926) cix-cxxi; and for the atrocities of Elisabeth Förster-Nietzsche see Curt
Paul Janz, *Die Briefe Friedrich Nietzsches: Textprobleme und ihre Bedeutung für Biographie
und Doxographie* (Zürich 1972) and H.F. Peters, *Zarathustra's Sister: The Case of Elisabeth
and Friedrich Nietzsche* (New York 1977).

impressed by a documentation they could not control and Meyer's protracted devotion, praised his learning and never queried his conclusions. Never trained in history, he lacked the minimal skills of his profession. He not only accepted Schliemann's *Selbstinszenierung*, he did all he could to disguise his hero's slips.

Meyer's book is far more pernicious than Ludwig's because Meyer sugars it with what Ludwig eschewed: documentation, both in his notes and in three volumes of edited correspondence. Meyer masquerades as a scholar but beneath the masque there remains the provincial Nazi schoolteacher and local chauvinist. Gauleiter Hildebrandt must be congratulated. He chose the right man. The misfortune for scholarship is that Meyer can no more be trusted than Schliemann himself. But there perhaps is the "innere Affinität" between the biographer and his hero. Meyer had as little respect for truth as did Schliemann. Written sources for Meyer, like archaeological evidence for Schliemann, were a heap of material from which one chose, or which one ignored, discarded or perverted.[64] They were there only to substantiate a preconceived opinion whether of Homer or of a Neustrelitz boy made good. The pity is that all the work must be done over again.[65] Schliemann the autobiographer provided the model that fatally flawed his biographer.

4. The Novelist

If little is known of Ernst Meyer, less is known, to me at least, of Heinrich Alexander Stoll (1910-1977), although I knew him personally and corresponded with him. We never spoke of his past. Among much else, he wrote three books about Schliemann:[66] 1) *Der Traum von Troja. Lebensroman Heinrich Schliemanns* (1956; 14th ed. 1987). The book was translated into Bulgarian, Estonian, Hungarian, Latvian, Polish, Romanian, Russian, and Spanish. 2) *Abenteuer meines Lebens. Heinrich Schliemann erzählt. Selbstzeugnisse*, edited and annotated by Heinrich Alexander Stoll with an Introduction by Georg Karo (1958; last ed. 1982). The book was translated into Hungarian. 3) *Auf den Spuren der Antike. Heinrich Schliemanns Berichte über seine Entdeckungen in der Griechischen Welt* (1974).

[64] In the biography of 1969 one finds, hidden in the notes, scepticism. Meyer declares candidly that Schliemann often falsified the presence of his wife at Troy (429 n. 148). When Meyer discusses (272-73) the discovery of the "Schatz des Priamos" he omits any reference to the presence of Sophia. On the other hand he nowhere states that Schliemann added her as witness and helper for the most dramatic of his Trojan discoveries: see Meyer *Schliemann*, 430 n. 159, where he ought to have. The denigration of Sophia's participation would serve the welcome purpose of refuting Ludwig.

[65] For details of the Meyer problem see Calder 1986, 21f. with notes.

[66] I owe the bibliographical details to the late H.A. Stoll. For a bit about his life see Bölke *Schliemann und Ankershagen*, 29-31. I know of no published bibliography of his work but

The last two books are editions and translations into German of sources. *Abenteuer* is of especial importance because it contains (223-376) the edition of Schliemann's letters to Rust (1868-1890). Valuable notes and transitional passages are included. The first, by far the best known and influential, is called by its author "a biographical novel." In his *Nachbemerkung* (540-55) Stoll explains what he has done. He invented several episodes to round out the tale. Some minor characters were invented. He inserted dialogue in direct speech. He omitted precise documentation because his book was not intended for scholars. One recalls Ludwig. But he insists that his novel is based closely on sources, the autobiographies, published letters, Ludwig, and Schliemann's own books. He writes:[67]

> Die erste Frage, die ein solcher Leser dem Autor stellen wird, dürfte dem Verhältnis von Dichtung und Wahrheit im Text dieses Buches gelten, das heißt, wieweit der Roman mit der historischen Wirklichkeit übereinstimmt. Sie ist leicht zu beantworten: der Autor hat in seinem Buche das Bild Schliemanns soweit das nur immer möglich war, direkt nach den beglaubigten authentischen Quellen gezeichnet.

Stoll was a master of the historical novel based on original sources. He preferred archaeologists as his heroes. He wrote similar novels about Winckelmann and Theodor Wiegand.[68] He lacked the patience and the books to write a carefully documented life for scholars. A novel allowed him the freedom to omit and adapt; but conscientious attention to sources kept his imagination in check. His interest in characterization caused him to draw the whole man. Because his faults make a man interesting, he did not conceal what was unwelcome:

> Schliemann ist eben kein konstruierter, sondern ein wirklicher, sehr lebendiger Mensch mit seinen Widersprüchen und Fehlern. Deshalb wäre es eine Fälschung des geschichtlichen Schliemann, wollte man seine Widersprüche glattschminken, seine Fehler verschweigen, seine Irrtümer bagatellisieren oder zu rechtfertigen und zu entschuldigen suchen.

The novelist gave a more historical Schliemann than the scholar. In his first Schliemann book he accepted uncritically what Schliemann wrote; but unlike Meyer the longer he worked with Schliemann the more sceptical he became. I sent Stoll a copy of my article of 1972 criticizing Schliemann. Stoll replied in a letter dated 8 October 1973. The original is now in

---

see: *Interview mit Heinrich Alexander Stoll* (Berlin 1981) with the "Nachbemerkungen des Verlags" 224-27.

[67] Stoll, *Interview*, 540.

[68] See Heinrich Alexander Stoll, *Götter und Giganten. Der Roman des Pergamon-Altars* (Berlin 1964) and *Tod in Triest. Leben, Taten und Wunder Johann Joachim Winckelmanns* (Berlin 1968).

Ankershagen. I cite the relevant paragraphs which reveal much of Stoll's own development between 1956 and 1973:

> Natürlich interessierte mich Ihr Schliemann-Aufsatz ganz besonders. In einigen Punkten scheinen Sie mir etwas zu weit zu gehen in anderen bin ich längst zu derselben Überzeugung gekommen wie Sie. Ich kann heute nicht auf Einzelheiten eingehen, da ich den Druck an einen Freund ausgeliehen habe. Meinen Schliemann I, den *Traum von Troja*, habe ich vor 18 Jahren in völliger Begeisterung und Unvoreingenommenheit geschrieben und auch für die bevorstehende 12. Auflage (121.-140. Tausend) nur einige Irrtümer berichtigt, besonders in puncto der ersten Ehe. Beim Schliemann II, dem Abenteuer meines Lebens, kamen mir schon kleine Bedenken, da Einzelheiten der Nachprüfung nicht standhielten, z.B. bei Schliemanns Itinerar nach Hamburg, wo er in Hotels übernachtete, die es nie gegeben hat oder Orte berührte, wo er nie gewesen ist. Der Brockhaus-Verlag kürzte leider rücksichtslos meinen Anmerkungsapparat, wahrscheinlich, um das 'image' nicht zu verderben. Beim Schliemann III, der 1974 in Berlin erscheinen wird und auf etwa 600 Druckseiten Auszüge aus Schliemanns Büchern wiedergibt, habe ich schon deutlich gesagt, daß z.B. das Ithakabuch mehr das Wunschbild ausdrückt als erlebte Wirklichkeit.[69] Sie haben mehr Platz zur Verfügung als ich, da unsere gelehrten Zeitschriften mehr eine Kalamität als eine Realität sind. Bitte, beachten Sie einmal die Eigennamen der ithakesischen Bürger, die Schliemann auftreten läßt. Mir scheint, schon dabei kann man allerhand eruieren und nicht nur, daß sie mit großer Wahrscheinlichkeit frei erfunden sind. Das ganze Buch ist hinsichtlich Ithakas kein Tagebuch, sondern ein Roman! Auch von *La Chine et le Japon* wird man wohl weithin dasselbe sagen können, müsste aber die zeitgenössische Literatur besser nachprüfen als ich es fern von Bibliotheken vermag.

The unexpected paradox is that the Schliemann of Stoll's novel and compilations is more historical with invented dialogue and minor characters than the Schliemann of Meyer with his letters and footnotes. The attraction Schliemann provided Stoll is clear. Of course there was the shared Mecklen-

---

[69] See Stoll 1974, 26 (concerning *Ithaka*):

Auch der moderne Leser...wird kritische Frage- und erstaunte Ausrufungszeichen an den Rand zu schreiben geneigt sein. Darüber hinaus wird er an mehr als einer Stelle ernste Zweifel hegen, ob hier ein 'richtiges' Tagebuch gedruckt worden oder ob nicht in einer späteren Überarbeitung der sonst so nüchterne Kaufmann der blauen Blume der Romantik nachjagte und ob der Blick auf sie ihn nicht Dinge sehen und hören ließ, die mehr in seiner Phantasie, in seiner Wunschvorstellung bestanden als in der nüchternen Wirklichkeit des ithakesischen Alltags.

That is Stoll anticipated by ten years the scepticism of David A. Traill, "Further Evidence of Fraudulent Reporting in Schliemann's Archaeological Works," *Boreas* 7 (1984) 295-316.

burgian past.[70] There was more. Stoll saw in Schliemann another historical novelist. Stoll turned diaries and letters into novels. His goal was to sell copies. Schliemann did just the same with *Ithaka* and *La Chine et le Japon*,[71] not to speak of his published autobiographies. Both were highly successful. Both were translated into foreign languages.

5. The Archaeologists

Emil Ludwig along with Schliemann himself formed the modern *Schliemannbild*. Both Ludwig's life and Schliemann's autobiography were translated into English. This insured worldwide familiarity with their texts. Only specialists, able to understand German, could read Meyer, whose influence, therefore, has been minimal. The book received only one review, albeit a favorable one, in an English-language journal and none in Schliemann's adopted country, the U.S.A.[72] Furthermore, the new *Schliemann-Forschung* began in 1972 only three years after the publication of Meyer's life. It had no time to become authoritative before every assertion in it was open to question. Stoll was a special case. He suffered also from the lack of translations into English, French or Italian. He did not write for a learned public who dismissed his work as popularization and failed to see its value. He was never reviewed in a learned journal. His two books of sources were pre-empted by an American imitation.[73]

There is no time to discuss the role of the archaeologists. Bronze Age Archaeology has not really been able to produce an historian of its discipline.[74] Review editors until recently have not understood that because a man has excavated Troy he may not be able to evaluate the editing of nineteenth century documents written in what is often a foreign language. Readers of reviews assume that a practitioner of a subject is competent to judge its history. Further, Bronze Age Archaeologists tend to read only what other Bronze Age Archaeologists write. There is fear of those outside the tribe and a reluctance or even inability to deal satisfactorily with their

---

[70] For Stoll's Mecklenburgian patriotism as his admitted motivation for his concern with Schliemann and Voss see Bölke 1988, 29f.

[71] For proof of Stoll's suspicion see Paul Keyser, *Heinrich Schliemann nach hundert Jahren*, 225-36.

[72] J.M. Cook, *CR* 84 (1970) 390-92.

[73] Leo Deuel, *Memoirs of Heinrich Schliemann: A Documentary Portrait Drawn from his Autobiographical Writings, Letters, and Excavation Reports* (New York 1977).

[74] The only exception might be Hartmut Döhl, *Heinrich Schliemann. Mythos und Ärgernis* (Munich/Lucern 1981). Döhl shared in the German excavations at Tiryns and wrote a book about Schliemann. His loyalty to his subject distorts his presentation of its founder: see the reviews by William M. Calder III, *German Studies Review* 6 (1983) 602f.; Donald F. Easton, *CR* NS 33 (1983) 286ff.; Wolfgang Schindler, *Deutsche Literaturzeitung* 104 (1983) 898-901; and David A. Traill, *Gnomon* 55 (1983) 149-52. In a nearby field there is Glyn Daniel, *The Origins and Growth of Archaeology* (New York 1967); (ed.) *Towards a History of Archaeology* (London 1981).

discoveries. One need only cite the puzzled rage invoked by L.R. Palmer's scepticism concerning Sir Arthur Evans.[75] Carl Blegen begins with a hymn his review of Meyer's first volume of *Briefe*:[76]

> In the annals of archaeological research no name stands out so enduringly mantled in romance and glamour as that of Heinrich Schliemann, the fortunate discoverer of Troy, of the royal shaft graves at Mycenae and of the palace of the Mycenaean kings at Tiryns. A truly self-made man, who by his own efforts and ability, in the face of innumerable obstacles and difficulties, raised himself from poverty to abundant wealth from obscurity to fame and to association with the great, his career possesses all the elements that appeal to the imagination of the ordinary man. The story has often been told in the past, and not long ago, with a flourish, in a Life of Schliemann by one of the most noted biographers of the day.

The Bronze Age Archaeologists canonized a patron-saint. They were unable to write dispassionately of him. But then they were never Schliemann-scholars. They were Schliemann-believers. Who is to say they are wrong? "Die einzige Form, in der man noch die volle Wahrheit sagen kann, ist die Lüge."[77]

---

[75] See easily Leonard R. Palmer, *A New Guide to the Palace of Knossos* (London 1969) esp. 11-13.

[76] Carl W. Blegen, *American Journal of Archaeology* 42 (1938) 594.

[77] Adolf Brennglas, *Pritsche und Knute* (Berlin 1851). I thank for all sorts of help but mostly bibliographical Professors Justus Cobet (Essen), Alexander Košenina (West Berlin), J. Mejer (Copenhagen), Wolfgang Schindler (Berlin, DDR), and David A. Traill (Davis, California).

Werner Jaeger
30 July 1888 - 19 October 1961

Werner Jaeger held the chairs of Friedrich Nietzsche, Ulrich von Wila-mowitz-Moellendorff, and Paul Shorey. A University Professorship, above all departments and requiring small teaching and no administrative obli-gations, was created for him at Harvard University. He enjoyed the finest education available in the history of classical studies. He founded two journals and what Eduard Spranger first called "The Third Humanism." He published widely in the fields of Greek education and philosophy and the Greek church fathers. He stressed Christianity as the continuation of Hellenism rather than its destroyer. His students included men of the rank of Richard Harder, Viktor Pöschl, and Wolfgang Schadewaldt. Today what was acclaimed as his most famous work is read only by dilettantes too naïve to perceive its defects. The Third Humanism has become a passing fashion, an aberration of the dying Weimar Republic, of as little abiding influence as its rival, the George Circle. His name is rarely cited in footnotes of the learned. Modern students of his own subject no longer recognize his name. Who was this man? What did he do? Why is he forgotten? Is there a permanent achievement?

Werner Wilhelm Jaeger was born 30 July 1888 to Karl August Jaeger and Helene, née Birschel, in the small town of Lobberich in the lower Rheinland near the Dutch border. He lived the first twenty-one years of his life there. We know almost nothing of this crucial formative period and he is our only source. He was an only child. His father, like his grandfathers, held a managerial post in a local textile factory. Jaeger's background was small-town and petit-bourgeois. It was also Protestant, not pious, but the Protestantism of the Enlightenment. This made his family distinctive, for Lobberich was overwhelmingly Catholic. The Protestant boy attended the Catholic Thomas à Kempis Gymnasium (today the Werner Jaeger Gym-nasium), but was forbidden to play with Catholic boys. He watched the Bishop of Münster visit his diocese, followed by the faithful peasantry on foot and horseback. Every house displayed the red-and-white church flag. One was a Catholic first, a Prussian second. The pattern of life and thought remained late medieval and ecclesiastical. The powerful Christian impact of the Lobberich years eroded but was never obliterated.

Precocious and intelligent, with no close friends among his contem-poraries, young Jaeger was always in the company of doting adults, the darling of parents and grandparents, and without a rival, either at home or at school. As a result, when he had grown to manhood, he found he could never abide a rival. He early learned to get his way by wheedling, for a child has no other way. The legacy was that throughout his life he lacked a strong moral sense and easily resorted to flattery. This led to accommodation with National Socialism and a loose way with women. In addition, his teaching never really agreed with the man.

"The start of my own work was History," he wrote. Growing up where Belgium, Germany and Holland meet, hearing low German, Dutch, Flemish, and French early gave him an idea of Europe. Round about him were the walls, castles, and churches of the Middle Ages and the roads and excavated forts of Rome. He enjoyed the inestimable advantage of beginning Latin at age nine and Greek at age thirteen. Latin never seemed a foreign language to him and he spoke and wrote easily what he called the "lingua angelorum." He first learned Greek the better to understand Rome and saw Greece through the eyes of Cicero and Horace. He had nothing like the intellectual conversion that Wilamowitz experienced at Schulpforte. The teaching must have been uninspired and by rote. He told me once that the Rector ordered his pupils to memorize the names of Horace's friends. When the boy Jaeger asked why, the Rector snapped, "When you are as old as I am, you will know why." Jaeger continued, "I am older than he was and I still do not know why." Such stupid mechanical drill must have provided an impulse in later years for his missionary zeal in restoring life to the classics.

Poor teaching caused him to read widely on his own. When he wrote a paper on the foolish theme, "What would have happened if Alexander had marched West?," he astounded his teachers by citing the Alexander historians in Greek. At age sixteen he read privately Wilamowitz's *Griechisches Lesebuch* and his edition with introduction and commentary of Euripides' *Herakles*. "I became from far away a student of Wilamowitz...A new world opened up for me." The stupendous erudition, the mastery of Greek, and the colorful depiction of Greek life stood in starkest contrast to the pale *epigoni* of the great period of German idealism and the philology of the first half of the nineteenth century. He learned the universality of his field by reading August Böckh's *Enzyklopädie und Methodenlehre der philologischen Wissenschaften*. In summer-semester 1907 Jaeger, age eighteen, matriculated at the University of Marburg. He could later write of his school years: "I always sought to perceive the intellectual in its connection with the reality of Greek life and Greek history. There the original, existential motive for my life operated." He had learned two difficult ancient languages well, had read far beyond the normal schoolboy's need in them, and was already a convinced historist.

Jaeger was only one semester at Marburg. It was long enough. A conversion took place there. He described it himself over fifty years later: "In my first semester at the University of Marburg, I came into close contact with philosophy which there, in the neo-Kantian school of Cohen and Natorp and under the influence of the logical insights gained from it, had turned to the study of Plato. Plato, interpreted in the neo-Kantian sense, was the very center of the intellectual life of the university—no small matter for a young man who was looking for a guide and who cherished the idea of an antiquity that was alive. This influence turned me definitively toward Greek philosophy" (*Essays*, 29). Here for the first time men of intelligence were taking an ancient author, Plato, seriously, as a guide for living, rather than a collection of syntactical peculiarities. Jaeger saw suddenly, after the arid apprenticeship of school, that his adored Greeks possessed "obvious philosophical relevance." Ironically the Marburg semester, although philosophical in its effect, intensified his philological proclivities, because the interpretation of Plato that he was given conflicted "with my historical-philological sense." This provocative misunderstanding of Plato made him an historian of ideas or, as he expressed it, turned him to *Geistesgeschichte*, not remote and antiquarian but vital and of central importance. "Quae philosophia fuit, philologia facta est." Seneca's epigram describes Jaeger at Marburg.

In the Prussia of 1907 the center of philological research was certainly not Marburg and was no longer Bonn. Usener had died in 1905. Buecheler had retired in 1906. Berlin, since the appointment of Ulrich von Wilamowitz-Moellendorff in 1897 by Friedrich Althoff, had become the center of philological science in Europe. Four Berlin scholars molded Jaeger's approach to Greek literature and thought. The aged Johannes Vahlen, who still lectured in Latin, continued the narrow word philology he had learned from Friedrich Ritschl in Bonn over fifty years before. Jaeger heard his lectures and benefited from the severe discipline of his seminar for two semesters. Vahlen taught him to beware brilliant conjectures and study the linguistic usage of an author with microscopic attention. Often a conjecture is unnecessary if only the difficult passage is correctly understood. Vahlen braked the young student's impetuosity; and Jaeger to his credit remembered what he owed Vahlen's method, while Wilamowitz contrarily was often impatient with him. Jaeger was able to share in a continuing seminar concerned with readings in Aristotle held by the lively octogenarian, Adolf Lasson, "the last Hegelian," who had heard Böckh and Lachmann and had known the learned schoolmaster, August Meineke, personally. Already Jaeger was alert to tradition. Lasson taught with fiery passion and wit. He continued the exegetical method of Trendelenburg and Bonitz. On Friday evenings he met advanced students (Jaeger was by far the youngest) in his house. There they read together select problematical Aristotelian texts. Lasson read to understand the thought, as opposed to Vahlen, who wished to understand only the word. Jaeger sought to combine the best of both.

But the two great figures remained the *dioskouroi*, Hermann Diels, and Ulrich von Wilamowitz-Moellendorff. The content of Jaeger's later work recalls often Diels' interests: Aristotelian philology and chronology, presocratic thought, and Greek medicine. His dissertation, later expanded into the book that made his reputation, was directed by Diels and colored by Vahlen's method. But it was Diels *per libros non vir* that influenced him.

The *Doxographi Graeci* and *Die Fragmente der Vorsokratiker*, volume I of which had appeared shortly before Jaeger's arrival in Berlin, provided a scientific foundation, along with his monographs on Parmenides and Heraclitus, for the transmission, authenticity, and therefore interpretation of preserved fragments of the presocratic philosophers. The edition in twenty-eight volumes of the *Commentaria in Aristotelem*, edited by Diels and younger colleagues, provided invaluable early material for the elucidation as well as variant renderings necessary for any scientific reconstruction of Aristotle's texts. Jaeger owned the set and continually cited it in publications and lectures. Of the man he reports that he did not attend his lectures *Über die Ethik des Aristoteles* and that Diels lacked any inner affinity (*innere Wahlverwandschaft*) for Plato. Jaeger would become something like an enlightened Christian Platonist and often called *Paideia* "a road to Plato." Diels's lack of interest in Plato was a defect. There is a further reason. "Papa Diels," with his long snowy beard, was a productive, thoroughly honest, hardworking scholar to whom we can only be grateful. As a man he was uninteresting; as a lecturer, dull. In later life Jaeger spoke as often of Wilamowitz as he was silent about Diels. The Berlin letters (after 1897) of Diels to Wilamowitz are loyal, correct, thoroughly to the point and eminently forgettable. The modest son of a railroad employee never had the personality of the confident Junker from east of the Elbe. Wilamowitz was a field marshal, actor, prima donna. Jaeger wanted to be all three. And Wilamowitz was a Platonist: *"Fidem profiteor platonicam."*

Jaeger had read Wilamowitz at school. At Marburg he encountered his oldest student, who was also the son-in-law of Vahlen, Ernst Maaß,who suggested that he read Belger's life of Moriz Haupt. At Berlin in the winter-semester of 1907-1908 he met the man whom he would call "master" and to whom after his death he would offer *Heroenkult*. Wilamowitz lectured with brilliance on expansive topics. In that semester: the history of Greek literature in the Attic period; next semester: exegesis of his Greek reader, a title that belies the importance of his theme; in the following semesters: the cultural history of antiquity since Nero, introduction to philology, the epic poetry of the Greeks and the Romans, Hellenistic poetry. Seminars held concurrently with the lectures were devoted to the great authors or subjects: Thucydides, Sophocles, Horace, Plato, Aristotle, *Athenaion Politeia*, Menander. Years later Jaeger described the lecturer to Americans: "He was an actor, a brilliant *conferencier*, a spectacular figure, enthusiastic, with a high tinny voice that snapped when touched by pathos."

Schadewaldt detects three abiding characteristics that Jaeger's work owed Wilamowitz: 1) expert acquaintance with texts and manuscripts that early turned him into a brilliant textual critic, emendator, and editor; 2) the conviction that *Geistesgeschichte* must be built on concrete examples; 3) the conviction that *Philosophiegeschichte* cannot be pursued in isolation but as part of what Jaeger's student, Harald Patzer, called Wilamowitz's *Totalitätsideal*, itself a legacy from Friedrich Gottlieb Welcker and Otto

Jahn. I should add three others to these: 1) the preference for great writers and little patience for the second-rate, whom he gratefully left to others; 2) the conviction, itself Platonic, that the teacher is more important than the research scholar; 3) the unshakable conviction that what he was doing was not a luxury but of supreme urgency. Jaeger became more than a student. A friendship began. He soon attended regularly the Wednesday evening at-homes at Eichenallee 12, where Wilamowitz met informally with gifted students. The preserved correspondence between the two (1911-1928) chronicles the rise and fall of the friendship.

The twenty-two-year-old's revised dissertation, *Studien zur Entstehungsgeschichte der Metaphysik des Aristoteles*, appeared in 1912. This was expanded in 1923 to *Aristoteles: Grundlegung einer Geschichte seiner Entwicklung*. The impact was immediate and dominated the interpretation and historical criticism of Aristotle for half a century. In the last quarter of the nineteenth century the Scottish Hellenist Lewis Campbell discovered that Plato's increasing avoidance of hiatus in his prose, an avoidance owed to Isocrates, provided a convincing criterion for establishing the relative chronology of his dialogues. Jaeger, after reconstructing Aristotle's earliest work, the lost *Protreptikos*, noticed its strong Platonic coloring in form and content. He went on to argue that the missing criterion for the relative chronology of Aristotle's esoteric works is his progressive distancing from his master, Plato. Necessary for this insight was his stress on the origin of the Aristotelian corpus as lecture notes (the Hegelian parallel may have given him the idea) and the need to explicate them in terms of genre as well as content. After a stay in Italy devoted to manuscripts, in 1914 he submitted his Habilitation on the church father, Nemesius of Emesa, and his indebtedness to Poseidonius. As the book concerned authors out of the classical mainstream, it never enjoyed the influence of the dissertation.

Before leaving the crucial formative years, I should note what Jaeger did not study. I know no testimony that he ever attended lectures on archaeology. He briefly heard Eduard Meyer on ancient history. Archaeologists dealt with objects and not with ideas, which are nobler. History, as Aristotle tells us in the *Poetics*, deals with the particular; poetry (one might add philosophy) with the universal. Historians were bound to use their sources for lesser ends than the philologist. Part of this aversion to *Realien* is the fact that Jaeger spent his *Wanderjahre* in libraries rather than museums and, unlike Wilamowitz, never visited Greece until old age and then largely to receive an honorary degree from the University of Athens. His idea of Greece could only be damaged by the reality. He told me on his return to Cambridge that, while driving him to Delphi, his chauffeur offered by a small detour to show him the crossroads where Oedipus slew Laius. "'No!' I said to him. 'Drive on!'" This is symptomatic of the vagueness and excessive abstraction that historians find in *Paideia*. Arnaldo Momigliano wrote of the book: "But this historiography, with its scant grip on reality, bears the mark of an epoch of political dissolution...That this historiography could degenerate into Nazism was a danger, which was confirmed by some of Jaeger's pupils who had remained in Germany."

Jaeger was never *assistent* and only briefly *dozent*. Between dissertation and habilitation he presumably survived on stipendia and maternal support. In the epochal year 1914, he habilitated (inaugural lecture at Berlin 14 June 1914), married Theodora Dammholz (28 March 1914), and at the age of twenty-six accepted the chair of Friedrich Nietzsche at Basel. He never fought for his country, so his influential discussion of Homeric military heroism in *Paideia* I is all secondhand. He was only a year at Basel and had neither influence nor doctoral students. His inaugural oration, *Philologie und Historie*, is programmatic and, seen in retrospect, anticipates the Third Humanism. He accepted an *Ordinariat* at Kiel in 1915, where Wilamowitz had advised his appointment. There he became a colleague of Felix Jacoby and there he found his first and loyal disciple, Richard Harder. The shattering experience of World War I, the trauma of being on the defeated side, and the attendant collapse of everything, convinced him of the rare value of continuity and tradition. He was an eyewitness of the November Revolution at Kiel (3 November 1918). His letter to Wilamowitz of 24 July 1917 already reveals his awakening. It is a document of fundamental biographical importance. Jaeger writes: "From week to week this war tears more deeply apart the foundations upon which until now my life was built and accordingly, because I am a young man, the more existentially and painfully I must endure and struggle with these problems, the less aware I am of anything at all about me that is solid and so I lapse all the more into silence. Doubt about everything that had become second nature to me from childhood has sometimes so brutally overmastered the initial momentum of my rather shy attempts at flight that even my philological work suffers."

Schadewaldt wrote of his teacher: "Intellectual continuities were for him what really constituted history and also what turned its changes into rational changes. For most men the fact that something persists and stays is scarcely worth notice. One takes it for granted and it requires no explanation. For Werner Jaeger the fact that in the passage of time there was any continuity at all was a marvel. The alertness to tradition had been there since boyhood. The November Revolution transformed a tendency into an obsession."

Jaeger always saw Christianity as a culmination of the Hellenic tradition rather than a rejection of it. He could never understand Tatian. On the wall of Jaeger's Harvard office hung two icons, a portrait of the aged Wilamowitz and another of one whom as a young philologist I did not recognize. It was the church historian Adolf Harnack. Jaeger saw the two great men united in himself. He was never Harnack's student at Berlin nor did Harnack turn Jaeger to Gregory. Wilamowitz vigorously maintained, in the *Kirchenväterkommission* against Harnack—who preferred theologians— that a trained classical philologist was more competent to edit a Greek church father. Hence Schwartz's Eusebius and Jaeger's Gregory of Nyssa. In a letter accompanying the first copy to Wilamowitz, dated 8 March 1921, he writes: "You are entitled to the first: you summoned me to the task when after my doctoral examination I stood for the first time without any idea of what to do and you added an important dimension to my philological education. You loyally advised me during composition and proof reading; and you placed your vast philological experience at my service. That way you often preserved me from error or set me in new directions." Four days later Jaeger was offered the Berlin chair. He could do things on time. Ironically, the endless project that in his lifetime seemed to classicists so remote, even unnecessary, may well prove his most enduring contribution. Early Christian texts, like Byzantine ones, had lagged far behind their classical counterparts in accuracy and scientific reporting of manuscript evidence. Believers usually make poor editors and often knowledge of a pagan source can determine the true reading, knowledge that a theologian usually lacks. Jaeger later discovered that the preparation of a minor work of Gregory appealed to American doctoral students, who wanted something concrete with a clear beginning and end—a text, not ideas. E.K. Rand, his Harvard colleague, dealt with Servius, not always happily, in the same way. The Kiel years had prepared the teacher and orator, provided the psychic impetus for *Paideia*, and initiated the Gregory. But Jaeger was too great for Kiel.

Wilamowitz was forced by new and unwelcome legislation to retire from his Berlin chair in 1921. This was a blessing for posterity, because it freed him for research and the last period of great creativity. By exceptionally good luck, Jaeger, who was fourth on the list, secured the post. Eduard Schwartz (*aet.* 63) and Hans von Arnim (*aet.* 62) were named by the faculty *honoris causa* and expectedly passed over by the Ministry because of their age. The Minister of Higher Education, the Orientalist Carl Becker, could not have approved their politics. Franz Boll (*aet.* 54) was asked but unexpectedly declined to stay at Heidelberg. That left Jaeger, who accepted immediately. For years, as proven by his letters, he had shamelessly flattered Wilamowitz. Here was the reward. He was entirely apolitical and, unlike Wilamowitz, had no difficulty in accommodating the Weimar liberal, Becker. The Jaegers lived at Kaiser Wilhelm Straße 11 in Steglitz. In spring 1927 his later Harvard colleague, J.H. Finley, visited him. He reports:

> In the Berlin years he and the tall, beautiful first Mrs. Jaeger...with their two sons and a daughter inhabited a square, high-ceilinged, mansard-roofed, tree-surrounded house in the suburb Steglitz. Its resemblance to certain houses on older back-streets of Cambridge suggests that German tastes accompanied German academic standards to Mr. Eliot's Harvard. I was kindly included in a Sunday-afternoon party for students which nobly stretched from tea to well past dinner. The others all wore frock coats; I thought myself lucky in a fairly new blue serge suit.

There was a garden where roses grew. Wilamowitz visited them in 1926 and transmitted to his wife "a description of your castle...which impressed me enormously." There is a hint of irony. Jaeger's wife was rich.

Except for *Paideia* I in 1934, the fifteen Berlin years yielded no great publication. The reason was that Jaeger put first things first. A thirty-three-year-old from provincial Kiel had succeeded the greatest Greek scholar of modern times, in the most prestigious chair of the subject in the world. For the first ten years of Jaeger's professorship, Wilamowitz was very much there. He taught a full schedule. He regularly visited the department that he had founded in the University's west wing, which he had built. He directed dissertations. He served tirelessly in the Academy and the German Archaeological Institute. Although deprived of his vote upon retirement, Wilamowitz regularly attended faculty meetings. Jaeger told me that members, as in the Roman Senate, were asked their opinion in order of seniority. Wilamowitz would rise, say *No* emphatically, and no one dared oppose him as he watched the vote. Jaeger either could become dispensable or he must prove his independence even if the cost was that Wilamowitz would think him disloyal. Of course he chose the latter and paid the expected price. Rather than compete vainly with Wilamowitz in research, he emphasized what age had made unwelcome or difficult for the septuagenarian. Jaeger excelled in three areas: charismatic teaching; work within the profession among colleagues and schoolmasters; popularization of his subject on a national scale. As part of this effort he founded for his students a monograph series, *Neue philologische Untersuchungen*, where they could publish dissertations written under him. For the guild he founded a journal devoted to scholarly reviews of high quality. He appointed his Kiel student, Richard Harder, managing editor of *Gnomon*. For pastoral work among the educated laity he founded *Die Antike*. Only *Gnomon* survived World War II. *Antike und Abendland* (*mutatis mutandis*) continues *Die Antike* in Western Germany; *Das Altertum* in the German Democratic Republic.

Just the fact that he was so young made him less remote to students. He was an older brother, not a grandfather. There was room for change. Since 1918 there had been impatience with the traditional unquestioning reverence for all things Hellenic. The brutality of the war and the devastation of defeat had destroyed illusions. The unspoken assumption of historicism that the innate excellence of antiquity justified the attention lavished by a nation's most brilliant men no longer went unchallenged. Paul Friedländer states the dilemma in a moving letter of 4 July 1921 to his teacher Wilamowitz:

> The war has changed me a great deal; and I could not, like other men, start in again in 1919 where I had broken off in 1914. For me now things must have far higher demands. Also I should not like to say anything any more that is not finished and of importance. I do not want

to write any more notes and articles simply because chance has cast
something in my path. I do not want to "share in the debate": that is, to
make an observation as C because A and B have made observations...
and as to editing texts: I do not have the strength, my life is simply too
short, to edit what is peripheral simply for the sake of editing it... So
you see, here are all sorts of inhibitions. But I find it good that these
inhibitions are there.

Because of his naïveté and self-assurance Jaeger lacked the self-doubt of
the Berlin Jew and war veteran, Friedländer. A return to Hellenism had
revitalized Europe twice before, in the Renaissance and the age of Goethe.
Why not a Third Humanism with Jaeger as Erasmus and Berlin as Weimar?
His energy, his organizational skill, his ability to delegate work to others
(students called him "our unmoved mover"), and his flair for showmanship
worked wonders. There were endless speeches, meetings of schoolmasters
and colleagues, scholarly conferences led by Jaeger with speeches by the
faithful. The most famous he held at Naumburg Whitsuntide 1930, a
colloquium on the spacious theme of "Antiquity and the Problem of the
Classical." There were eight addresses by men like Johannes Stroux,
Wolfgang Schadewaldt, Paul Friedländer, Eduard Fraenkel, Bernhard
Schweitzer, and Matthias Gelzer. Teubner hastened to publish the addresses
in a handsome volume. Wilamowitz thundered from Berlin: "Whenever I
read *Die Antike*, a millwheel goes round and round in my head; but the
wheel does not grind any meal; for me it does not...I have an idea what
classical Physics are, and classical music also exists. But other than these?
English literature is rich enough. Does one find the classic there? Is
Shakespeare classic?...I have never been able to make a start with the word
classic which for me is a horror; and so I do not expect that others do."
The movement was well-meant. Jaeger wanted to preserve an endangered
civilizing tradition that he believed irreplaceable. The catchword was *paideia*,
the Greek word that Cicero translated as *humanitas* (*puerilitas* was not
possible) and that meant both culture and its transmission, that is,
education. The word provided the title of what Jaeger often called his "three-
volume history of the Greek mind." Eduard Spranger early gave the
movement its name in his address "The Position of the Humanities Today
and the School," delivered at the Fifty-third Congress of German
Philologists held at Jena on 27 September 1921. He said, "But a difference
between our Humanism, which one might call the Third, and that Second
lies in the breadth of our quest and the understanding which we moderns are
able to bring to it." The friendly voice of a former believer, Wolfgang
Schadewaldt, summarizes what Jaeger tried to do: "Jaeger's new humanistic
approach is characterized by the fact that he set the Greek world of human
values as a system of rationally working formative power into the history of
Europe. It was, to state the matter epigrammatically, an historicizing of
human values or as well a humanizing of our European history."

But there was something sham about it all. The time had passed when the values of Periclean Athens would be a formative educational force in Germany. In 1935, in a famous review of *Paideia* I, the Hamburg classical scholar, Bruno Snell, with wit and learning wrote the epitaph of a Third Humanism just fourteen years old. He showed how Jaeger was forced to interpret the evidence (Homer is the obvious case) unhistorically in order to sustain his thesis that *paideia* provides the cornerstone on which to build an intellectual history of Greece. The educational function of poetry is a discovery of the Sophists, foreign to Homer. Snell corrects specific misinterpretations and then prophetically warns of the dangers of Jaegerian humanism. These he sees particularly in what Jaeger considered the superiority of his Third Humanism to the Second Humanism of Goethe and Humboldt; namely, its politicization. Greek political institutions cannot be exemplary in 1935 in the way that a Greek drama was *circa* 1800 for Goethe, a statue for Schadow, a building for Klenze. Jaeger misses the difference. Greek tolerance of slavery alone is decisive. Indeed, says Snell, Jaeger's Greek politics easily boil down to heroism and Platonic authoritarianism. The vagueness of Jaeger's humanism allows it to become the servant of any kind of politics. That means it is always in danger of becoming a literary game (*Literatentum*). It was the *Dientsbarkeit* of Jaeger's politics, the readiness to serve any master, the preference for accommodation over reform, that made them unacceptable to Bruno Snell. At the risk of making his Greeks trivial, Snell prefers the revival of Wilamowitzian historicism to Jaeger's humanistic evangelism. We scholars can do no more than describe what was Greek truthfully and without presuppositions.

In 1980 Johannes Irmscher stated clearly the dangers only implied by Snell in 1935. "Many used to speak of the Third Humanism as the correlative in educational policy to the Third Reich's theoretical vision of the state." Obviously Jaeger did not devise nor Spranger name the movement for that purpose. On the other hand, Jaeger undeniably sought, albeit unsuccessfully, accommodation with National Socialism. Of the some fifty classical scholars who fled Nazi Germany, Adolf Hitler and Hermann Göring thanked Jaeger *alone* for his German work and granted him official permission to accept the Chicago post. A secret directive of the Hitler government in 1941 forbade posthumous mention of the seventy-fifth birthday of Eduard Norden, Jaeger's Jewish teacher and colleague. Jaeger never resigned from the Berlin Academy, which had expelled Norden and many others, and continued to publish in Nazi Germany as late as 1944 (*Paideia* II), after he had become a citizen of a country at war against Hitler! The document most often cited by scholars to prove Jaeger's early attempt to reconcile his Third Humanism with the Third Reich is "Die Erziehung des politischen Menschen und die Antike" ("Antiquity and the Education of the Political Man,") *Volk im Werden* 3 (Leipzig, 1933) 43-49. Jaeger argues that the classical curriculum in the schools could be presented in a manner supportive of the new system. He draws attention to the ideal of the Spartan citizen in Tyrtaeus, the prophetic strength of Solon's political poetry, the presentation of work as heroism by the peasant poet Hesiod ("Arbeit ist keine Schande; Nichtarbeiten ist Schande"—so much for welfare programs), and the Homeric "heroism of the defender of his fatherland" (Hector, presumably, rather than Achilles). The "fateful struggle" of tragedy would strike a welcome note and we climax with Thucydides' Pericles as a *Führergestalt*. History has granted to the classicists of Germany an urgent task: "The particular task which History today has set before the German people is the forming of the political human being. We ought not of course to demand from the schools and scholarship what has not earlier grown organically within the reality of national life. But at the moment when a new type of political man is taking shape, we shall obviously have need of antiquity, as a formative force."

Jaeger nowhere perverts his sources. He simply picks, chooses, and ignores to make a welcome point. But if one recalls Jaeger's immense prestige at the time, publication of such an article at such a time in such a place must have weakened considerably the hand of any decent schoolmaster who sought in the classics approval for the democracy just lost. Hitler had become Reichskanzler on 30 January 1933. Jaeger's essay appeared a month later. The Association of German Classicists met in July. In 1933 the only high government official who dealt with classics in education was Bernhard Rust, a former student of the subject, later Reichsminister für Wissenschaft, Erziehung, und Volksbildung. At the urging of Rust, Jaeger, along with the chairman of the association, Kroymann, presented to the teachers of classics in Germany the program that the new government expected of them—that is, Jaeger, with all the prestige of his Berlin chair, agreed to act as mouthpiece to his profession for the new regime.

After a divorce from his first wife, following an unsavory trial, Jaeger married his Jewish student, Ruth Heinitz, on 29 December 1931. A child followed. In 1934 Jaeger was Sather Professor at the University of California, Berkeley. His lectures were published in 1938 as *Demosthenes: The Origin and Growth of His Policy*. German and British scholarship of the time regularly extolled Alexander the Great at the expense of Demosthenes, an unscrupulous lawyer and *laudator temporis acti* obstinately refusing to acknowledge the reality of history and urging his fellow Athenians to a suicidal struggle against the inevitable. Jaeger rejected this view. He argued that the moral tragedy of the man Demosthenes was of greater interest than the political events of the time. By stressing a passage in the third *Philippic*, he sought to show that Demosthenes felt obliged to urge his fellow citizens to preserve the outmoded city-state against Macedonian expansion, although he feared the cause had already been lost. He did this because he was convinced that it was the only right course of action. To what degree was Jaeger's *Demosthenesbild* a self-portrait of his own predicament? One must defend humanism even if the cause had already been lost. Events moved rapidly. In 1936 Jaeger resigned the chair of Wilamowitz and accepted exile in Chicago, a city of gangsters and cattlemen, rather than divorce his wife and abandon his child. He immediately wrote an English article: "Greeks and Jews: the First Greek Records of Jewish Religion and Civilisation" (1936). What could not appear in *Volk im Werden* was eagerly accepted by the *Journal of Religion*. Jaeger was not an anti-Semite.

Ernst Bickel, the Bonn *ordinarius*, in 1943 called Jaeger in his Harvard period "the swan among geese." The swan left the Chicago geese, who had provided him and his family with asylum, as soon as he could. In 1956 their bitterness still was undisguised. In 1939 he wisely declined the Laurence Professorship of Ancient Philosophy at Cambridge University (letter of F.M. Cornford to W. Jaeger 23 April 1939) and accepted the University Professorship at Harvard after Rostovtzeff had declined it. He quickly learned that there were two great differences between Cambridge, Massachusetts, and Berlin, and expectedly accommodated. From the start he was denied any political influence of the sort he had wielded from his Berlin throne. E.K. Rand informed him on arrival that Americans expected Americans to run their departments. At a time when posts were few and those few allotted on the old-boy system, only women and priests, whose futures were secure, dared write dissertations with him. He could not place them. In over twenty years he had no student, in the sense of one whose dissertation he directed, who compared with his great German ones. Within the profession he went from leader to outsider. The second difference Jaeger himself noted in his introduction to the *Scripta Minora*: "Without the continuing prestige of the ancient idea of Man in human culture, classical scholarship is just a waste of time. Anyone who does not see this ought to come to America and let himself learn from the way classical studies have developed there."

The history of Hellenism in America has yet to be written. In his epoch-making book, *Classica Americana: The Greek and Roman Heritage in the United States* (Detroit, 1984), Meyer Reinhold has meticulously documented the formative influence of the classical heritage in the colonial, revolutionary, and early republican periods. The populism, materialism, and attendant anti-intellectualism that accompanied the expanding frontier and the industrial revolution in nineteenth-century America relegated classics to a handful of underpaid professors of Greek, men not distinguished by a capacity to influence the great issues of their time. The middle twentieth century saw a revival of Greek influence on American literature and thought, not always directly but through three German thinkers, Freud, Marx, and Nietzsche. But in general Greek influence has remained in the architecture of banks, railroad stations, and plantation residences.

The classics Jaeger found at the Harvard of the thirties were a game of grammar and translation played by boys from good families who had graduated from pale American imitations of the great English public schools. No one dreamt of "believing" anything he read in an ancient author in the way Winckelmann, Wilhelm von Humboldt, Niebuhr, Wilamowitz, or Jaeger himself had. American classical scholarship derives historically from the German during its Ritschlian phase (that is, after K.O. Müller and before Wilamowitz), with its preference for the objective and technical (which too easily means the trivial and uninteresting), for what needs doing before what matters. Jaeger had no chance of influencing American thought the way he had briefly influenced German thought. Jaeger's last accommodation was resignation. Like Wilamowitz after 1921, he left the arena and wrote books: *Paideia*, three volumes in English translation (1939-1944); *The Theology of the Early Greek Philosophers* (1947); the Oxford critical edition of Aristotle's *Metaphysics* (1957); *Scripta Minora*, two volumes (1960); *Early Christianity and Greek Paideia* (1961). There was also volume after volume of the Gregory. Even so, much remained unwritten. He often called the footnotes of *Paideia* "the graveyard of projected monographs."

American students were colossally naïve. Recently a woman revealed in a national journal how, during written examinations, a friendly old man would give her and her friend chocolate cookies. This is what she remembered. He was a kindly eccentric, a man of stupendous learning and quaint ideas, harmless and liked from afar. He was sought after for doctoral examinations because he never expected American students to know anything and asked simple questions, often answering them himself. Again and again he lamented, "I have no school."

Americans did not think in terms of schools, of messiahs, apostles, and disciples. The reason was simple. The subject was not that important to them. American professors are dilettantes, Jaeger used to say, classicists from 9:00 to 5:00. You must live your *paideia*! A *vox clamantis in desertis*—for them it was just a job, not a way of life.

Hildegard von Wilamowitz-Moellendorff, in her memoirs of her father, recalls how, on his deathbed in September 1931, he delivered his final verdict on his student and successor, Werner Jaeger: "At that time Frau Jaeger came to my mother. He could not wait until my mother returned. When she brought the report of the divorce from Professor Jaeger, my father said: 'Up to now I have again and again defended him against all others. I see now; he is a bastard.'"

Dorothea Freifrau Hiller von Gaertringen said to me, "On his deathbed my father cursed Werner Jaeger." Not one member of the family attended Jaeger's memorial address to the Academy. Paul Mass noted that Wilamowitz never listed Jaeger among the editors of his *Kleine Schriften*.

Wilamowitz condemned the man. Few could dispute him. He lacked moral conviction and inner courage, the assurance that he was right. This was in part the plight of his generation. The crisis of self-doubt that we saw in Friedländer necessarily brought an end to certainty. Why can't we sunder the work from the man? Wrong scholarship is forgotten. Right scholarship is absorbed—and then forgotten. Only in their conjectures do philologists win immortality. Jaeger's Oxford *Metaphysica* remains the standard text.

Gregory has eclipsed all previous texts and provided a corpus of the genuine works and a paradigm for editions of other early Christian authors. Any history of Aristotelian scholarship in the twentieth century must evaluate Jaeger's contribution to the history of the corpus and the biography of the man. A brilliant idea, eloquently argued, led to a deeper historical understanding of the texts. Jaeger was an historian and philologist, never a philosopher.

What happened to the center of Jaeger's work during the Berlin years, "The Third Humanism"? It could not survive Bruno Snell and National Socialism. In one part of Jaeger's Germany, Marxism-Leninism replaced it; in the other part a revival of the historicism of Jaeger's teachers. In 1959 Jaeger denied ever having himself used the term, although in fact he had begun *Paideia* I with it. In America he won two influential apostles. His young Harvard colleague, John Huston Finley, Jr., learned from Jaeger that classics had something to say that mattered to young Harvard men of the forties and fifties. In a total break with his philological colleagues, most of them grammarians, paleographers, and exegetes, he delivered dazzling lectures on Greek literature in English translation to hundreds of undergraduates in the largest lecture hall of the university. He presented Homer as a text that could change our lives and won two generations of friends of classics in high places.

The other notable convert exerted a national, not a parochial, influence. Gilbert Highet, a naturalized Scot of boundless energy, translated all three volumes of *Paideia* into elegant English. That done, he began a popularization of the classics on a scale of which Jaeger never dreamed, introducing large lecture courses of classics in translation, writing endless articles and reviews for the popular press, lecturing tirelessly to schoolteachers and educated laity, and so on. But there was a striking difference from Jaeger. His message was not at all political; it was bellelettristic. Highet transformed into Anglo-Saxon terms Jaeger's profound conviction that classics had something to say to the modern world and he embodied this conviction in a comprehensive work that parallels but also productively contrasts with *Paidea, The Classical Tradition* (New York, 1949). Inspired by the failed Third Humanism, Highet returned to apolitical Second Humanism with the result that while in 1936 several thousand American students read Homer in Greek annually, in 1986 several million read the poet annually in English, and the several thousand continue to read him in Greek. The beginnings of this vast popular movement owe much to Finley and Highet, who themselves had been ultimately inspired by Jaeger.

Within the profession, by his example and by his English books, which regularly cited German scholars, Jaeger did much to revive the German tradition that had dominated American philology from 1853 to 1914. This revival, in which Jaeger was aided by some twenty other refugees from Hitler's Germany, sought to rescue American scholarship from English dilettantism and return it to German scientific professionalism. The success of the von Humboldt stipendia and the emigration of outstanding German philologists to American universities are in part a result of Jaeger's revival of what Gildersleeve called our "Teutonomania." This transplantation of the Berlin humanistic tradition to the New World may not impossibly be Jaeger's most enduring achievement.

Jane Harrison's Failed Candidacies for the Yates Professorship (1888, 1896): What Did Her Colleagues Think of Her?

I. Introduction

There are two sorts of evidence for what Jane Harrison's professional colleagues thought of her during her lifetime: published and unpublished. Of the published, most obvious are reviews of her books. She tells us in her letter of application for the Yates Chair what she had done by April 12th 1896[1]:

> In 1882 I published "The Myths of the Odyssey in Art and Literature"; in 1885, "Introductory Studies in Greek Art." I have from time to time published in the "Journal of Hellenic Studies," original monographs on special subjects connected with Mythology and Ceramography, e.g. an article on "Monuments relating to the Odyssey": on "The Judgment of Paris," &c. The work of drawing up the Report for the year 1887, on "The Progress of Archaeology in Greece," was entrusted to my care. In 1890 I published in conjunction with Mrs Verrall, "Mythology and Monuments of Ancient Athens," and in 1895[2] in conjunction with Mr. D.S. MacColl, "Greek Vase Painting."

Of the four books mentioned, the bibliographer of the Cambridge Ritualists, Shelley Arlen, lists for *Myths of Odyssey* only an anonymous notice;[3] for *Introductory Studies* six reviews, not one in a scholarly journal, four of the English first edition and two American notices of the 1892 reprint;[4] for *Mythology and Monuments* 11 reviews, four in scholarly journals, one on the continent, and a review article by a leading English authority;[5] of *Vase*

---

[1] I cite here and throughout the unpublished documents concerned with Jane Harrison's candidacy for the Yates Chair in 1888 and 1896 preserved in the Archive of the Library of University College, London (AM/C/216; Am/D/52). I am grateful to the archivist, G.M. Furlong, for copies and the permission (*per litt.* June 29 1990) to cite them here.

[2] In fact the book was published in 1894 and hence reviewed in that year.

[3] *Notes and Queries* (5 November 1881) 379. I wish to express my gratitude here to Shelley Arlen of the University of Oklahoma Libraries for generously allowing me to use an early MS of her book *The Cambridge Ritualists: An Annotated Bibliography* (Metuchen/London 1990). [See now my review at *BMCR* 2 (1991) 195-97.]

[4] Anonymous, *Athenaeum* (19 December 1885) 812-13; *New York Times* (18 January 1886) 116; *Notes and Queries* (21 November 1885) 420; *Saturday Review* (27 February 1886) 311; A.S. Murray, *Academy* (13 February 1886) 116; (of the 1892 edition): Anonymous, *Nation* (31 March 1892) 248 and Martin L. D'Ooge, *Dial* 12 (1892) 392.

[5] Apart from notices in *Athenaeum*, *Atlantic Monthly*, *Critic*, *Nation*, *Speaker*, and *Spectator*, I notice Anonymous, *American Journal of Archaeology* 7 (1892) 72-73; G.C. R<ichards>, *Journal of Hellenic Studies* 11 (1890) 218-20; F.B. Tarbell, *Classical Review* 4 (1890) 430-32; and a reviewer in *Revue des Études Grecques* 4 (1891) 410-11. The book

Painting only three anonymous notices in the semi-popular press and a signed review in *Art Journal*.[6] That is, she was never reviewed in Germany, the center of study in her subject. Her name was barely known in France. She had a reputation in America which, if anything, would have been used against her. Her reputation was in fact insular. Later there would be criticisms of her work in *Forschungsberichte*[7] and published replies to her writings[8] or citations of it by scholars working in her field. Only after her death would there be remarks about her in the memoirs of contemporaries. But for one review article and the books and articles themselves, the Yates Committee owed its decision to a second sort of evidence.

---

was not reviewed in Germany. The most important published document concerning Harrison's work available to the Yates Committee in 1896 was Anonymous, *Quarterly Review* 171 (1890) 122-49. Arlen (33) identifies the reviewer as Percy Gardner, then Lincoln and Merton Professor of Archaeology at Oxford, earlier (1880-1887) Disney Professor of Archaeology at Cambridge. Gardner was elder brother of Harrison's victorious adversary, Ernest Arthur Gardner (1862-1939), and did not encourage the higher education of women. See Percy Gardner, *Autobiographica* (Blackwell, Oxford 1933) 67-68: "...the Great War, which has shaken so many things, has led to the wider activity of women, and to their admission to the Parliamentary franchise. After that, Oxford and Cambridge were compelled to admit them on almost equal terms. But since, there has come a certain reaction. To the advocates of the admission of women, the question seemed extremely simple. There was only an unreasonable prejudice to set aside, and the question would solve itself. But simple as is such a view it is not in accord with many important facts of human nature, which all have their roots in the supremely important truth that the function of women is childbearing, and so in the whole future of humanity is not the same as that of men. In any stable condition of society this truth, with all its never-ending corollaries, must be fully recognized. So matters did not go quite as they were expected by the women's advocates to go. The phenomenon, well known in America, that the mass of the women took up less educational—though in their own way good—subjects, such as modern languages and modern history, has shewn the danger of letting women control the Oxford curriculum. Both Oxford and Cambridge have taken measures to limit the number of women admitted, and to secure male predominance." He certainly took Harrison's work seriously: see e.g., Percy Gardner, "A New Pandora Vase," *JHS* 21 (1901) 1-9.

[6] See Anonymous, *Athenaeum* (20 October 1894) 533-35; *Nation* (24 May 1894) 394-95; *Spectator* (7 April 1894) 468-70 and R.A.M. Stevenson, *Art Journal* NS 57 (1894) 208-09.

[7] Especially important because from so erudite a source is O. Gruppe, *Bursian* 137 (Leipzig 1908) 276ff. (*Prolegomena*), s.n. 648; and his dismissal of her, Durkheim and F.M. Cornford at *Geschichte der klassischen Mythologie und Religionsgeschichte während des Mittelalters im Abendland und während der Neuzeit* (Leipzig 1921) 243.

[8] Often extraordinarily damaging: see, e.g., M.R. James (1862-1936), "Some Remarks on 'The Head of John Baptist,'" *Classical Review* 31 (1917) 1-4, the lead article of the volume. Letters of congratulation poured in to James, then Provost of Kings and earlier Headmaster of Eton: see Richard William Pfaff, *Montague Rhodes James* (London 1980) 254-56. W. Ridgeway, a member of the board of management of *Classical Review*, wrote him (Pfaff, 256): "Never was such an audacious, shameless avowal of charlatanism, debauching young minds wholesale, and that too in a generation whose loose thinking has been doing immense harm to national life and international politics." Harrison replied at *CR* 31 (1917) 63 ("To me the keenest joys of science...are always perilous"). Murray loyally sought to make the best of a weak case: see *CR* 31 (1917) 63-64, where he raps James' fingers for his severity. See further *YWCS* 13 (1918/19) 191. This may have been one of the discouragements that caused Harrison to leave Cambridge and the field in 1922. Peacock never alludes to the *Auseinandersetzung*.

Then there is that which was not published in her lifetime: letters to her[9] and from her, diaries, and, perhaps most valuable, letters about her. Classical scholars often make the mistake of thinking that all that is important must be published. This is true for Plato but not for figures of the nineteenth century, where normally official versions are published and truth languishes in archives.[10] In the case of Jane Harrison, 24 letters[11] of recommendation, most written in 1888 and seven in 1896, survive and provide the most important sources extant for her contemporary evaluation by peers or indeed superiors. Who wrote these letters and for what purpose?

II. The Yates Chair

The Yates Chair of Classical Archaeology was created at University College, London in 1880. It bore the name of its founder, James Yates (1789-1871), the antiquarian, contributor to Smith's *Dictionary of Greek and Roman Antiquities*, and author of numerous articles on archaeological subjects. Its first holder was Sir Charles Newton (1811-1894), concurrently (and since 1861) the first Keeper of Greek and Roman Antiquities at the British Museum. In 1888 he was "compelled by increasing infirmity to give up the Yates professorship."[12] Percy Gardner, a friend and colleague at the British Museum, describes his tenure of the chair:

> Newton did not attempt to teach, but to lecture, and his careful but somewhat frigid style did not long attract the general public. Hence the lectures were soon delivered in the presence of only three of four auditors: but Newton never ceased to prepare them with care, and to illustrate them with drawings of great size and costliness. He thought of his own ideal rather than the class before him. Thus as a Professor he could scarcely be called successful.[13]

[9] Upon leaving Cambridge for reasons that are not clear Harrison burned a treasure of letters to her, including some 800 from Gilbert Murray: see Stewart, 12: "Unfortunately Jane made a holocaust of letters and papers when she left Cambridge in 1922."

[10] See my remarks at *Mnemosyne* 43 (1989) 256-62 (review of C.O. Brink, *English Classical Scholarship*: a book inadequate just because confined to published and censored sources).

[11] I do not include a hastily-written note, dated only Red House Hornton St. W. 5 May, to Petrie from W. Martin Conway (1856-1937), Baron Conway of Allington, Roscoe Professor of Art at University College, Liverpool (1885-1888) and a famous mountaineer: "I write to urge the claims of *Miss Harrison* to the Archaeological Chair of U. Coll. Of course you know what they amount to. I heard her lecture at Liverpool & her matter & manner were alike admirable. I am just off to explore the interior of Spitzbergen. Don't trouble to answer this." A guess would be that Harrison met him through MacColl. There are two letters by Verrall, who in 1896 updated his earlier letter of 1888.

[12] See Cecil Harcourt Smith, *DNB* II. 2450. The standard life is Percy Gardner, "Sir Charles Newton," *BiogJahr* 19 (1896) 132-42. He was the friend of Ruskin since student days: see E.T. Cook and Alexander Wedderburn, *The Works of John Ruskin* vol. 35 *Praeterita et Dilecta* (London 1908) 198, 384-85 (their disagreement on the statue of Mausolus).

A scholar was needed: but, if the new discipline were to survive, he must be a teacher as well. Jane Harrison, resident in London since 1880, living on unearned income and occasional lectures, applied. For 100 years her application has been unnoticed. In her *Reminiscences* Harrison avoids the matter.[14] Jessie Stewart in her *Portrait* says not a word about her heroine's failures.[15] Much to her credit, Sandra J. Peacock first in 1988 noted the two candidacies, although allotting them less than one page in a chapter of 35 pages covering the London years (1880-1897), some fifteen of which concern her friendship with D.S. MacColl. Peacock attributes Harrison's failed candidacies to misogyny and the hostility of classical scholars toward innovative thinking. We shall see whether the archival evidence supports these charges. She writes:

> ...her [Harrison's] expertise could not conquer the fears of those who questioned the wisdom of granting the distinguished professorship to a woman. In addition, the hidebound world of classical scholarship had no room for innovative thinking. Classicists considered Jane's work far too unconventional to merit such a prestigious position.[16]

---

[13] Gardner, *Newton*, 138-39.

[14] Jane Ellen Harrison, *Reminiscences of a Student's Life*² (London 1925). Readers of Peacock should be warned that she never cites the standard edition but a pirated reprint in a Texan journal, *Arion*: see Sandra J. Peacock, *Jane Ellen Harrison: The Mask and the Self* (New Haven/London 1988). Her book is reviewed by Mary Beard (Fellow of Newnham) at *TLS* (January 27-February 2 1989) 82; R.L. Fowler, *Classical Views* 10 (1991) 129-34; Carolyn G. Heilbrun, *The Women's Review of Books* 6 No. 8 (May 1989) 8-10; Robert A. Segal, *Journal of American Folklore* 103 (1990) 370-72; Robert Ackerman, *Victorian Studies* 32 (1990) 669-70; C.A. Stray, *LCM* 16 (1991) 103-11; and W.M. Calder III, *Gnomon* 63 (1991) 10-13. The book is henceforth cited "Peacock, *Harrison*." Although I must often criticize this book I wish to emphasize that I have learned from it and indeed found the subject for this paper in its pages. The best biography of Harrison in print is Renate Schlesier, "Jane Ellen Harrison, 9 September 1850-15 April 1928," in *Classical Scholarship: A Biographical Encyclopedia*, edited by Ward W. Briggs and William M. Calder III (New York/London 1990) 127-41 (henceforth cited: "Briggs-Calder"). Schlesier alludes only briefly to the Yates Professorship (130).

[15] Jessie Stewart, *Jane Ellen Harrison: A Portrait from Letters* (London 1959). The octogenarian Stewart, a former student of Harrison's and a friend of Hope Mirrlees, is as much a source as a biographer and her book remains indispensable. No critical review of the book ever appeared. There are notices: Anonymous, *TLS* (24 July 1959) 432; Jacquetta Hawkes, *New Statesman and Nation* (20 June 1959) 870-71; Edmund Leach, *Spectator* (31 July 1959) 145; Harold Nicolson, *Observer* (21 June 1959) 18. It was never noticed outside England. Until Schlesier, I have never seen it cited by a German.

[16] Peacock, *Harrison* 90. She earlier writes (*loc. cit.*): "her references included R.C. Jebb, Henry Sidgwick, Henry Jackson, A.W. Verrall, and Walter Leaf of Cambridge; Henry Butcher and Arthur Sidgwick of Oxford; F.H. Middleton, director of South Kensington Museum; and Sir Edward Maunde Thomson, librarian of the British Museum; and Continental archaeologists Wilhelm Dorpfeld, Ernst Curtius, Wilhelm Klein, Otto Bindorf and Cavalier Luigi Melina, among others." Correct as follows: (1) *Henry Butcher* is the Hellenist S.H. Butcher; (2) Butcher was not *of Oxford* but professor at Edinburgh; (3) for *Sir Edward Maunde Thomson* read *Sir Edward Maunde Thompson*; (4) Thompson was not *librarian of the British Museum*. He was *Principal Librarian, British Museum*; (5) For *Dorpfeld* read *Dörpfeld*; (6) for *Otto Bindorf* read *Otto Benndorf*. Correct p. 279. The name was apparently conflated with Dindorf; (7) for *Cavalier Luigi Melina* read *Cavaliere Luigi Milani*.

A word is necessary on procedure. A candidate wrote himself to scholars who, in his opinion, were competent to evaluate his work and sympathetic to his cause. The sponsors sent their letters to the candidate, not to University officials. Certainly this affected their matter and style. The candidate gathered the letters, introduced them with a letter of application and —in those pre-Xerox days—had them printed up for use by the University, distribution to the sponsors and (in Housman's case) to friends and relatives. We know most of the election of A.E. Housman in 1892.[17] He had a bit over 50 copies printed.[18] Who were Harrison's sponsors? Are we able to evaluate their competence?

III. The Twenty-Three Sponsors

The number of sponsors seems not to have been limited by statute. Housman had 17, Harrison had 23. Their names, in the elusive order in which she arranged them (neither alphabetical nor by seniority nor by prestige of position), follow:

1. S.H. Butcher, Litt.D., LL.D., Professor of Greek in the University of Edinburgh; formerly Fellow of Trinity College, Cambridge and University College, Oxford.[19]
2. R.C. Jebb, Regius Professor of Greek in the University of Cambridge.[20]
3. Professor W.M. Ramsay, D.C.L., University of Aberdeen.[21]

[17] See P.G. Naiditch, *A.E. Housman at University College, London: The Election of 1892* (Leiden 1988). This thoroughly admirable book is henceforth cited "Naiditch, *Housman*." Housman's election falls precisely between Harrison's two candidacies and sheds much light on procedure in her cases.

[18] Naiditch, *Housman*, 235: "The edition of the *Testimonials* therefore consisted of at least fifty-one copies and, since that is an improbable number, probably more." Housman sent twenty copies to UCL (*ibid.*, 234). We may assume that Harrison did the same.

[19] For S.H. Butcher (1850-1910), see his brother-in-law, G.W. Prothero, *DNB* II. 2545. For a delightful glimpse of the Butchers at Paris in 1886, see E.M. Sellar, *Recollections and Impressions* (Edinburgh/London 1907) 325-26. He is remembered by scholars today for his *OCT* Demosthenes and his edition with translation of Aristotle, *Poetics*. Peacock, *Harrison*, 52, documents "a mysterious unhappy love affair" between Harrison and Butcher, which Mirrlees unsuccessfully sought to cover up. The wretched Butcher married the daughter of Archbishop Trench and deserted Harrison. I see little more than an undergraduate crush and should be surprised if this were the reason why Butcher is placed first among the 23.

[20] For R.C. Jebb (1841-1905), see Caroline Jebb, *Life and Letters of Sir Richard Claverhouse Jebb O.M., Litt.D.* (Cambridge 1907) with the review of Ulrich von Wilamowitz-Moellendorff, *LittZentralblatt* (1907) 1469-71 and Mary Reed Bobbitt, *With Dearest Love to All: The Life and Letters of Lady Jebb* (London 1960). Full references are at Naiditch, *Housman*, 172ff. esp. n. 60-1, to which add Roger D. Dawe, "R.C. Jebb," Briggs-Calder 239-47.

[21] For Sir William Mitchell Ramsay (1851-1939), see P.G. Naiditch, "Classical Studies in Nineteenth Century Great Britain as Background to the Cambridge Ritualists," [henceforth cited "*Studies*"] 146 n. 74. He was Regius Professor of Humanity (1886-1911) at Aberdeen. His great work was his exploration of Anatolia. With Leaf, he was one of the two English-speaking sponsors competent to evaluate Harrison. He writes: "I would point to her

4. F.H. Middleton, D.C.L. Oxon.; Litt.D. Camb.; V.P.S.A.; Director of the South Kensington Museum.[22]

5. Dr. Wilhelm Dörpfeld, Prof., I. Sekretar des Kais. Deutschen Archälog. Instituts in Athen.[23]

6. Dr. Paul Wolters, Kaiserlich Deutsches Archäologisches Institut.[24]

7. Dr. Ernst Curtius, Professor of Archaeology in the University, Berlin.[25]

---

stimulating influence as a lecturer as her pre-eminent claim to recognition in the world of scholars."

[22] For John Henry Middleton (1846-1896), archaeologist, architect, art historian and museum director, see Lionel Henry Cust, *DNB* II. 2445. He was a close friend of J.G. Frazer: see J.G. Frazer, *Pausanias's Description of Greece* I (Lóndon 1913) viii. A wrong first initial is given him on the printed testimonials.

[23] For Wilhelm Dörpfeld (1853-1940), see Peter Goessler, *Wilhelm Dörpfeld: Ein Leben im Dienst der Antike* (Stuttgart 1951). The life is uncritical and must be read with caution: see A. von Gerkan, *Gnomon* 24 (1952) 166-68. For a recent *laudatio* with bio-bibliography see Klaus Herrmann, "Wilhelm Dörpfeld 1853-1940, "*Archäologenbildnisse: Porträts und Kurzbiographien von Klassischen Archäologen deutscher Sprache*, edited by Reinhard Lullies and Wolfgang Schiering (Mainz 1988) 112-13 [henceforth cited "*Archäologenbildnisse*"]. A critical life is desiderated. Dörpfeld certainly at first glance would have been the most impressive sponsor. Three points must be made: (1) Dörpfeld never earned a doctorate in archaeology. He was educated to be an architect. Schliemann went to Olympia in 1881 to hire him (they may have known each other since December 1876). He learned field archaeology working at Troy with Schliemann. In short, he was never one of the guild. Ludwig Curtius, *Deutsche und Antike Welt: Lebenserinnerungen* (Stuttgart 1958) 155, records Dörpfeld's appalling insensibility to poetry and beauty. His controversial excavations of the Theater of Dionysos at Athens exerted lasting influence on theories of fifth-century production. For Harrison's interest see her "Dr. Dörpfeld on the Greek Theatre," *Classical Review* 4 (1890) 274-77. (2) Wilamowitz saw to it that Dörpfeld never became a member of the Prussian Academy. On 24 June 1900 he wrote of "the infantilities" of Dörpfeld and declared his work "rubbish [Blödsinn]," adding "In comparison spiritualism is harmless." See William M. Calder III and David Traill (editors), *Myth, Scandal, and History: The Heinrich Schliemann Controversy and a First Edition of the Mycenaean Diary* (Detroit 1986) 31. That is, the highest authorities in the field queried his competence. Robert Ackerman reminds me that Harrison's *Primitive Athens as Described by Thucydides* (Cambridge 1906; reprinted Chicago 1976) is dedicated to Dörpfeld and defends him throughout against his detractors. E.A. Gardner reviews the book at *CR* 21 (1907) 114-16 and W. Judeich at *Wochenschrift für Klassische Philologie* 13 (1907) 173-74. (3) Ca. 1890 Harrison gave Dörpfeld £100 to be used for his excavations (Goessler, 98). Dörpfeld's letter is dated Athens 28 March 1896. Harrison's gift substantiates Beard's contention (*supra*, n. 14) of Harrison's wealth against Peacock. She called Dörpfeld "my most honoured master" (*Reminiscences*, 65).

[24] For Paul Wolters (1858-1936), see Reinhard Lullies, *Archäologenbildnisse*, 124-25 (with portrait and bio-bibliography). Wolters (1887-1900) was Second Secretary (= Vice-Director) of the German Institute in Athens. He worked closely with Dörpfeld and presumably Harrison met him in Athens through Dörpfeld. His letter is dated Athens, 24 October 1888. In 1908 he succeeded Furtwängler in Munich.

[25] For Ernst Curtius (1814-1896), see his son's, Friedrich Curtius', *Ernst Curtius: Ein Lebensbild in Briefen* (Berlin 1903). There is a recent bio-bibliography at Reinhard Lullies, *Archäologenbildnisse*, 40; also see M.H. Chambers at Briggs-Calder 37-42. For the archaeological importance of Curtius, see Adolf Heinrich Borbein, "Ernst Curtius, Alexander Conze, Reinhard Kekulé: Probleme und Perspektiven der Klassischen Archäologie zwischen Romantik und Positivismus," in "Die Antike im 19. Jahrhundert in Italien und Deutschland," *Jahrbuch des italienisch-deutschen historischen Instituts in Trent* Beiträge 2 (Bologna/Berlin 1988) 275-302. For Wilamowitz' famous dismissal of the man see *Aristoteles und Athen* I (Berlin 1893) 377-78, repeated at *Geschichte der Philologie*[4] (Leipzig 1959) 69. His only book of permanent value was his description of the Peloponnesus. Wilamowitz underestimates Curtius' direction of the Olympia dig, possibly because of his distaste for the site. Harrison had met Curtius in Berlin and he "took me round the museums of Berlin"

8. Dr. Wilhelm Klein, Professor of Archaeology in the University, Prague.[26]

9. Dr. Otto Benndorf, Professor of Archaeology in the University of Vienna.[27]

10. Ernest Babelon, Director of the Bibliothèque Nationale, Paris.[28]

11. Cavaliere Luigi Milani, Director of the Archaeological Museum, Florence.[29]

(*Reminiscences*, 64). She does not date the meeting. Curtius writes: "Miss Jane Harrison hat mit einem für Damen wöhnlichen Ernst und Erfolg sich in das Studium der Antike eingelebt. Sie hat durch Unterricht und durch Schriften gezeigt, daß sie die Gegenstände der Klassischen Archäologie beherrscht, und die Geschichte der Malerei und der Sculptur richtig aufzufassen versteht."

[26] For Wilhelm Klein (1850-1924), see Wolfgang Schiering, "Wilhelm Klein 1850-1924," *Archäologenbildnisse*, 98-99 (with portrait and bio-bibliography). He was an ancient art historian rather than an archaeologist. He habilitated under Benndorf in 1879 and succeeded Eugen Petersen on the Prague chair in 1876. He was one of several great Jewish scholars in the field. One thinks of Freud's friend, Emanuel Loewy. He retired in 1923. Harrison presumably met him in London. Klein draws attention to her museum work which led to the assignment of new fragments to named painters. "Ausser Ihrer literarische Arbeiten sind noch Ihrer Forschungen in den Museen zu gedenken, die der Wissenschaft hervorragende Dienste geleistet haben. Die Wiederentdeckung der Troilos Schale des Euphronios ist nur das Bekannteste aber nicht das Einzige dieser Art." Klein refers to Harrison, "Some Fragments of a Vase Presumably by Euphronios," *JHS* 9 (1888) 143-46, which he had recently read. Harrison early stated her indebtedness to Klein at *Myths of the Odyssey in Art and Literature* (London 1882) xiv, 215-19. See further *infra*, n. 44.

[27] For Otto Benndorf (1838-1907), see Hedwig Kenner, *Archäologenbildnisse*, 67-68 (with portrait and bio-bibliography). He was excavator, art historian, and organiser. He was the only sponsor who probably wrote without being asked. He writes from Vienna two days after Klein. He heard of her candidacy from Klein and hastened to wish her luck. He continues: "Ich habe leider noch nicht das Vergnügen Sie persönlich zu Kennen [*sic*], habe aber ihre [*sic*] archäologischen Arbeiten stets mit grossem Vergnügen und persönlichem Gewinn verfolgt. Wir danken Ihrem Scharfblick schon manchen glücklichen Fund und ich vergegenwärtige mir gern wie das klare, scharf getreffende [*sic*! = getroffene?], Urtheil das sich in Ihren Recenzionen <zeigt?>, und der resolute Sinn für das Thatsächliche und Wesentliche welcher überall in Ihren Untersuchungen hervortritt, Ihnen besondere Lehrerfolge sichern werde." This is one of the most authoritative as well as perceptive and intelligent of the letters. Benndorf's judgment was not clouded by Harrison's charm. Nor had she paid him one hundred pounds. He says that he had never met her. From her writings he deduces her intelligence and divines her pedagogical gifts. Are the textual errors a clue to her knowledge of German in 1888?

[28] For Ernest Babelon (1854-1923), see J. Nostos, *DBF* 4 (Paris 1948) 997-99; Peter and Hilde Zazoff, *Gemmensammler und Gemmenforscher: Von einer Noblen Passion zur Wissenschaft* (Munich 1983) 224-25, where he is considered the peer of Adolf Furtwängler; and David Le Suffleur, *Ernest Babelon* (no date) which contains a full bibliography (*non vidi*). Harrison twice calls him "Director of the Bibliothèque Nationale, Paris." In fact he was after 7 December 1897 "conservateur du Cabinet des médailles," a prominent numismatist. His letter is dated merely "Paris, le 24 Octobre." Whether written in 1888 or 1896, Babelon, although widely published, was merely something like an assistant keeper in the numismatic department of the Bibliothèque Nationale, a far cry from Director, a title which in fact was never his. I assume that Harrison carelessly or naively misrepresented his post.

[29] For Cavaliere Luigi Milani (dates unknown), see Harrison, "The Judgment of Paris: Two Unpublished Vases in the Graeco-Etruscan Museum at Florence," *JHS* 7 (1886) 196-219. The vases were published with his permission.

12. Henry Craik, C.B., LL.D., Secretary to the Scottish Education Department.[30]

13. Sir Edward Maunde Thompson, D.C.L., Principal Librarian, British Museum.[31]

14. Richard Garnett, C.B., LL.D., Keeper of the Printed Books, British Museum.[32]

15. Henry Sidgwick, M.A., Litt.D., Praelector in Moral Philosophy, Trinity College, Cambridge.[33]

16. Henry Jackson, Litt.D., Fellow and Praelector in Ancient Philosophy, Trinity College, Cambridge.[34]

17. A.W. Verrall, M.A., Litt.D., Fellow of Trinity College, Cambridge.[35]

[30] For Sir (after 1897) Henry Craik (1846-1927), see G. MacDonald, *DNB* II. 2584. He studied classics as a schoolboy and undergraduate with distinction (double first at Oxford) but he never held a professional post in classics or archaeology nor published on them. His courteous letter is worthless. He ought not to have been included.

[31] For Sir Edward Maunde Thompson (1840-1929), see G. MacDonald, *DNB* II. 2925. He was knighted in 1895 but not yet on "Oct. 19th, 1888" when he wrote for Harrison. He was a self-taught palaeographer (he never completed his Oxford B.A.). He had no professional interest in archaeology. His letter compliments Harrison's lecturing style.

[32] For Richard Garnett (1835-1906), see Sidney Lee, *DNB* II. 2646. Harrison again inflates his title. Garnett on "Oct. 20th, 1888," the date of his letter, was not "Keeper of the Printed Books, British Museum." He was appointed to that post in 1890. He was a self-educated bibliographer and belle-lettrist with no competence in Harrison's subjects. He describes her as he might a conscientious schoolgirl and enthusiastic amateur: "As Superintendent of the British Museum Reading Room while you were engaged in preparing the Lectures you delivered in this Institution, I had the opportunity of appreciating your extraordinary diligence and research. As a reader of many of your Archaeological Essays [= the *JHS* articles], I can speak with no less emphasis of your power of rendering your favourite themes luminous and attractive, and of inspiring the student with the interest you feel in them yourself."

[33] For Henry Sidgwick (1838-1900), see A.S<idgwick> and E.M. S<idgwick>, *Henry Sidgwick: A Memoir* (London 1906). He was a founder of Newnham, an ardent supporter of women's education, and so inclined to support his former pupil. His university career was hindered by his stammer: see G.P. Gooch, *Under Six Reigns*[3], (London 1960) 24: "He was better to read than to hear, for his stammer was incurable." He attests her excellence as an undergraduate, disclaims competence in her subject and writes in a future most vivid that "If she is appointed...she will prove an interesting and impressive teacher..." Harrison again muddles a title. Sidgwick had resigned the Praelectorship in 1883 to become Knightsbridge Professor of Philosophy. His letter is dated "Oct. 22nd, 1888."

[34] For Henry Jackson (1839-1921), see R. St. John Parry, *Henry Jackson O.M., Vice-Master of Trinity College & Regius Professor of Greek in the University of Cambridge: A Memoir* (Cambridge 1926) and P.G. Naiditch, *Housman*, 165-72 with the extensive collection of testimonia at n. 58-1. He praises her undergraduate work, adding, "Of Miss Harrison's Archaeological attainments I am not competent to speak."

[35] For Arthur Woollgar Verrall (1851-1912), see Naiditch, *Housman*, 211-14 with the vast bio-bibliography at n. 64-1. The standard biography is M.A. Bayfield, "Memoir," in A.W. Verrall, *Collected Essays Classical and Modern* (Cambridge 1913) ix-cii; and for his criticism of Greek tragedy see James E. Ford, *Rationalist Criticism of Greek Tragedy: A Case Study in Critical History* (Diss. Chicago 1981). Both Verralls were close friends of Harrison, who would later (1903) dedicate *Prolegomena* to them. Mrs. Verrall was also a collaborator and Newnham colleague; see Jane Harrison, "In Memoriam—Mrs. A.W. Verrall," *Proceedings of the Society for Psychical Research* 29 (1918) 376-85. Verrall's letter is among the longer; and he is the only sponsor to update a letter of 1888 with a second brief one of March 31st 1896. He is scrupulously honest, for he considered "the paraphernalia of archaeology" to be "stuffage" (Stewart, 56-57). He admits "my own acquaintance with Archaeological

18. Arthur Sidgwick, M.A., Fellow and Tutor of Corpus Christi College, Oxford.[36]
19. R.G. Tatton, Formerly Fellow and Tutor of Balliol College, Oxford; Member of the Council of the London Society for the Extension of University Teaching.[37]
20. Walter Leaf, M.A., Trinity College, Cambridge.[38]
21. Edmond Warre, D.D., Head Master, Eton College.[39]

---

subjects" is "superficial," and he reveals to the Committee that Harrison missed a First in the Classical Tripos: a miss he attributes to inadequate schooling. His generous assessment deserves citation. It is the most precise and revealing from a non-specialist and must have strengthened her case: "She has...a prudence in dealing with evidence and a clearness of perception which would secure her from avoidable error, even if her linguistic knowledge were far less than it is...Of the admiration which I feel for her industry, acuteness, and power of exposition, I could say much; but keeping to my province, I will say only that if her work had been liable to injury from inaccuracy or insufficient knowledge of the language concerned, I could not have failed to discover the fact; and I can warrant that, in this respect, she is well-equipped for her work. In her own field, it is Miss Harrison who instructs me, and she is far above any commendation of mine. Both writing and speaking she always commands my interest, and her enthusiasm has illuminated many regions into which for myself I should scarcely have looked. I can hardly conceive any one more likely to make successful the work which she proposes to undertake." I have not seen Jane Harrison, "In Memoriam—Dr. Arthur Woollgar Verrall," *Newnham College Letter* (1912) 53-55. Two of her recollections of Verrall are preserved at Verrall, *Literary Essays*, xix-xx; xciv.

[36] Arthur Sidgwick (1840-1920), a minor classicist, the lesser brother of Henry, friend of Gilbert Murray, writes about "my friend" and is not competent to speak of "Miss Harrison's technical knowledge." He repeatedly turns "never without profit" to her *Archaeology of Athens* and then praises at length her lecturing ability.

[37] R.G. Tatton (dates unknown) is called by Peacock (68) "a suitor of Jane's." He will "speak only of her teaching powers" and he seeks to anticipate "a certain prejudice amongst some of the students against being taught by a woman."[H]er command of the subject, her natural distinction, her sincerity and good sense" would dispel that. Tatton was involved in the administration of adult education and had no expertise in archaeology or classics.

[38] For Walter Leaf (1852-1927), see Charlotte M. Leaf, *Walter Leaf 1852-1927: Some Chapters of Autobiography with a Memoir* (London 1932) and Gilbert Murray, DNB II. 2745-46. With Jebb and Verrall, he was the greatest English classical scholar to write for Harrison. A banker, not an academician, he was interested in *Realien*. Persuaded by Harrison in 1890, he delivered a series of extension lectures for London University on ancient houses, dress, art and "Homeric Geography": see Leaf, *Leaf*, 154. There was a sympathy of interest. In his exegesis of Homer he used archaeological evidence and topography in a way that neither Jebb nor Verrall could and so his competence to judge Harrison's work was greater than theirs. Like Babelon, he refuses to judge her work on vases. He then writes: "In the best sense of the word, however, she has, during the last few years, popularised Archaeology in a quite extraordinary degree. The secret of Miss Harrison's success lies in the union of thorough and systematic knowledge of her subject matter with great natural endowments of clearness, fluency, and voice, all cultivated by long practice to a high pitch of perfection, and inspired by deep enthusiasm for Greek art." In June 1889, Leaf wrote a similar letter supporting William Ridgeway's candidacy for the chair of Greek at Glasgow. But for the phrase "an inspiring teacher," the whole letter concerns Ridgeway's research with citation of three specific articles: see Walter Leaf in *The Testimonials of William Ridgeway, M.A.* (Cambridge 1889) 26 No. XVIII. I am grateful to the Librarian of the University Library for a copy. For Leaf's evaluation of E.A. Gardner, see *infra*.

[39] With Edmond Warre (1837-1920) we have the first of three schoolmasters, each of whom attests Harrison's ability to impress youthful hearers, not accustomed to being lectured at by women. None of them can evaluate her archaeological competence. For Warre, see Henry Elford Luxmore, DNB II. 2949. I have not seen C.R.L. Fletcher, *Edmond Warre* (1922). A classicist devoted to *Realien*, his famous models of Odysseus' raft, Caesar's bridge, and a trireme would have enticed Harrison.

22. Rev. W.F. Fearon, D.D., Head Master, Winchester College.[40]
23. Rev. J.M. Wilson, M.A., Head Master, Clifton College.[41]

IV. Analysis of the Letters

The chair was one of archaeology. It had been the chair of Newton, arguably the most distinguished archaeologist in the English-speaking world. It was not a chair of classics. The matter was not the appointment of a University Extension Lecturer. Because Newton had been so dismal a teacher, one may safely surmise that attested teaching ability would be welcome, though not decisive. The sponsors fall easily into three groups: (A) People not entitled to a professional opinion on Harrison's archaeological work; (B) Witnesses to her lecturing ability; and (C) the Hard Core. Some straddle more than one group. I arrange sponsors alphabetically, rather than as Harrison has:

A. Persons not entitled to a professional opinion[42]

Butcher	Henry Sidgwick*
Craik*	Tatton
Fearon	Thompson
Garnett	Verrall*
Jackson*	Wilson
Arthur Sidgwick*	

B. Witnesses to Harrison's lecturing ability

Butcher	Ramsay
Craik	Arthur Sidgwick
Dörpfeld (!)	Tatton
Fearon	Thompson
Jebb	Warre
Leaf	Wilson
Middleton	

---

[40] As at Eton, so at Winchester: Harrison delivered a successful lecture, "admirably clear, attractive and stimulating." So writes William Andrewes Fearon (1841-1924). The middle initial is wrong.

[41] For J.M. Wilson (1836-1931), Head Master of Clifton 1879-1890 (sc. no longer at the time of the second election) see H.B. Mayor, *DNB* II. 2968. I have not seen James M. Wilson, *An Autobiography 1836-1931*, edited by A.J. and J.S. Wilson (1932). Peacock (61-62) calls Wilson "Archbishop." That he never was. After retirement from Clifton, he served as Archdeacon of Manchester (1890-1905). Harrison lectured twice at Clifton to 200-250 masters and senior boys. Wilson writes: "I may say at once that (with the single exception of Faraday's) I have never heard such delightful lectures." For Wilson at Clifton see O.F. Christie, *Clifton School Days* (1879-1885) (London 1930) 144 *s.n.* The frontispiece of the volume is a portrait of Wilson.

[42] An asterisk indicates those honest enough in their letters to confess their incompetence.

C. The hard core

Babelon	Leaf
Benndorf	Milani
Curtius	Ramsay
Dörpfeld	Wolters
Klein	

Who is missing? Newton may have declined to write because he was the previous holder of the chair. Percy Gardner may have pleaded conflict of interest, as his brother was a candidate. Adolf Furtwängler, arguably the greatest living archaeologist, is not represented.[43] Harrison may not have asked them. No woman writes for Harrison. Neither of her two collaborators, MacColl or Mrs. Verrall, writes for her. One would think they were best informed on her capacity for research.

Of the nine letters that count, only one is from an Englishman, and he is a banker. One is from a Scot, one from a Frenchman, and one from an Italian. Five are from German-speaking archaeologists. Two, Babelon and Leaf, declare themselves incompetent to judge her work on Greek vases. Leaf and Ramsay, the only two English-speaking sponsors competent to judge her work, call her a popularizer, a *damnatio* for a scholar. Babelon and Milani write polite phrases, but nothing specific. Of the five Germans, Curtius says little more than that she is a good student: "She has shown by her teaching and writings that she controls classical archaeological material and she knows how to interpret correctly the history of painting and sculpture." Wolters, just thirty years old, praises an older "valued colleague in the field of archaeology" for her "surety of scholarly method" and her "lucky zeal." His letter is well-intentioned and superficial.

Klein attests a European reputation and praises specifically three articles in *JHS*.[44] He wisely draws attention to the value of Harrison's museum work, because of which she has discovered a new masterpiece of Greek vase-painting. Benndorf's letter, the only unsolicited one and owed Klein, is probably the greatest. He has read her work with great pleasure and personal profit. "We already owe to your keen eye many a fortunate find and I foresee with pleasure how the clear, trenchant criticism, that is found in your

---

[43] Harrison had disagreed with his views: see *JHS* 14 (1894) xli-xlii and her "Some Points in Dr. Furtwängler's Theories on the Parthenon and its Marbles," *CR* 9 (1895) 85-92 and "The Central Group of the East Frieze of the Parthenon: Peplos or στρωμνή?" *CR* 9 (1895) 427-28. This may have made her unsure of his support. For his response, see "The Lemnia of Pheidias and the Parthenon Sculptures," *CR* 9 (1895) 269-76. See now Andreas Furtwängler's life of his grandfather at Briggs-Calder, 84-92.

[44] See *supra*, n. 26. The articles are: (1) "Monuments Relating to the Odyssey," *JHS* 4 (1883) 248-65; (2) "The Judgment of Paris: Two Unpublished Vases in the Graeco-Etruscan Museum at Florence," *JHS* 7 (1886) 196-219; (3) "Some Fragments of a Vase Presumably by Euphronios," *JHS* 9 (1888) 143-46. I think most scholars today would agree that these articles were Harrison's permanent contributions before October 1888.

reviews, and the resolute sense of the factual and essential, which comes to the fore constantly in your scholarly work, will insure for you extraordinary success as a teacher."[45] Dörpfeld, because of his spectacular finds and earlier association with Schliemann, the darling of Gladstone, was for Englishmen the most famous of the five. He writes twelve lines:

> I attest gladly here that Miss Jane E. Harrison has through long and serious studies acquired an outstanding knowledge of archaeology and has proven herself a virtuous scholar through her valuable publications of various sorts in many scholarly journals. Her book, *Mythology and Monuments of Ancient Athens*, belongs without question to the best books which have been written about Athens. Her public lectures too are known to be excellent. I can, therefore, without any hesitation, highly recommend Miss Harrison for the Yates Professorship of Archaeology.[46]

None of the German letters is cited in the recorded deliberations either of 1888 or 1896.

In 1888, Harrison was 38; in 1896, she was 46. Certainly in 1896 she ought to have made up a better dossier. Undergraduate teachers and personal friends, not to speak of the "suitor," ought to have been omitted. More care should have been given to providing accurate titles and to proofreading the German. Three, rather than thirteen, sponsors would have been sufficient to attest her lecturing ability. We have scrutinized the testimonials she provided. An equally important source must now be examined: the minutes of both elections have been preserved.

V. The Election of 1888

Two documents (AM/C/216) survive attesting the election of 1888. The first is entitled: "Yates Professorship of Archaeology. Report of Committee." It is a seven-page handwritten document, dated "Dec. 14, 1888" and signed "Alfred Church, Chairman."[47] It is a summary of the

---

[45] For the German text, see *supra*, n. 27.

[46] The German text, with corrected errors (e.g., *Ich* for *Tch*; *Ihr* for *Thr passim*) follows: "Ich bescheinige hierdurch sehr gerne, daß Miss Jane E. Harrison sich durch lange und ernste Studien hervorragende archäologische Kenntnisse erworben und sich auch durch ihre wertvollen Veröffentlichungen verschiedener Art in mehreren wissenschaftlichen Zeitschriften als tüchtige Gelehrte erwiesen hat. Ihr Buch *"Mythology and Monuments of Ancient Athens"* gehört unstreitig zu den besten Büchern, die über Athen geschrieben worden sind. Auch ihre öffentlichen Vorträge sind als ausgezeichnete bekannt. Ich kann daher Miss Harrison aus voller Überzeugung bestens empfehlen für das Yates Professorship of Archaeology."

[47] For Rev. Arthur John Church (1829-1912), since 1880 Professor of Latin at University College, see Naiditch, *Housman*, 53-54 with the material gathered at n. 14-1. Naiditch writes (*Housman*, 1-2): "But by the late 1880's, Church had lost the respect of many of his students. They circulated tales of his falling asleep whilst pupils were construing texts and of leaving

deliberations of the Committee, and served as a recommendation to the Senate, which body emended and adopted the report on December 17, 1888. It was adopted by the Council on January 12, 1889. The text falls into two parts. The first part establishes the duties of the Yates Professor. Of interest are the subjects for which he will be responsible:

> The Committee resolved to recommend...that provision must be made by the Professor for the teaching by himself, or by the aid, if necessary, of assistant lecturers of the three following branches at least, viz.
>
> (1) Classical and Oriental archaeology
> (2) Medieval archaeology
> (3) Prehistoric archaeology and the history of arts of savage races
>
> That the Professor should himself give an elementary course on General Archaeology.

There is no distinction between what we would call archaeology and art history. The professor is responsible for far more than Greece and Rome. He must give what we should call an undergraduate survey course from prehistoric times (Schliemann was still alive) through the medieval period and by no means limited to the Mediterranean basin. He is further to provide "two lectures and two demonstrations in every week of the Session." These may be held in the College or in a museum. The Committee further recommended "that with the consent of the Senate and Council, the Professor may in every year be granted leave of absence during one term for the purpose of archaeological research." On return the following term, he would be required to present three public lectures "(open to the Public without payment)" stating the results of his research. Finally, the professor will be "required to defray out of his salary the cost of adequately illustrating his lectures." One wonders if Newton had.

Next, "The Committee had to consider the qualifications of nine Candidates." Nine candidates had put in. The first two are quickly disposed of: "Mr. J.F. Hodgetts, late Professor of English in the University of Moscow"[48] and "Mr. Penrose, who has long occupied an honourable place in the Profession of Architecture."[49] They lacked credentials. An amiable

---

the classroom to consult the dictionary for the meaning of Latin words." In 1887, 29 students had submitted a letter of protest. An *ad hoc* committee was appointed. On February 9th 1889, Church resigned. The chairmanship of the Yates Committee was one of his last college functions shortly before an ignominious retirement.

[48] For the adventurer and writer J.F. Hodgetts (1828-1906), see Alexander Gordon, *DNB* II. 2698. He was the author of "Harold the Boy Earl" and "Edwin the Boy Outlaw," neither of which I have read.

[49] For the neo-classical architect, Francis Cranmer Penrose (1817-1903), see Paul Waterhouse, *DNB* II. 2832. He designed the British School at Athens in 1882 without fee and was its first Director (1886-1887).

youth, Mr. Talfourd Ely ("favourably known...both for social and intellectual qualities") is too young. Not discouraged, he would try again in 1896. They next turn down a candidate arguably superior to Harrison:

> Mr. Waldstein, University Reader in Classical Archaeology, and Director of the Fitzwilliam Museum at Cambridge, has achieved a high reputation in his subject, and has unquestionably done much to make the study of it popular in the University of Cambridge. Mr. Waldstein sent in no testimonials: but submitted a scheme for the work of the Professorship. The Committee was not satisfied that the solidity of his attainments was equal to the reputation which he enjoys.

Charles Waldstein (1856-1927), later Sir Charles Walston, educated at Columbia College, New York and at Heidelberg, was denied a career in the United States because of American anti-Semitism. Henry Bradshaw and Henry Sidgwick arranged that he be made lecturer in archaeology at Cambridge in 1880. After being unsuccessful for the Yates chair, he accepted the Directorship of the American School in Athens 1889-1893. His tactlessness offended the English. *The Times* obituary says "He was neither shy nor reserved." At a famous public occasion in Cambridge, Sir Charles Stanford had cried out in the presence of Waldstein: "I wish that German-American-Jew would go back to his respective countries."[50] In short, anti-Semitism may have been a factor.

The next three candidates are dismissed *en bloc* in spite of their virtues. "But, in view of the superior claim of two candidates now about to be mentioned, the Committee had no hesitation in passing them by." They were L.R. Farnell, Fellow of Exeter;[51] A.H. Smith, assistant in the Department of Greek and Roman Antiquities in the British Museum;[52] and E.A. Gardner, British Archaeological School [*sic*] at Athens,[53] the latter to be successful in 1896. The Committee then turned to the two finalists:

---

[50] For Waldstein (Walston), see *The Times* 23 March 1927. For the Stanford incident and the most revealing description of Waldstein, see E.F. Benson, *As We Were: A Victorian Peep-Show* (London 1930) 139-42, 146. Farnell (*op. cit., infra*, n. 51) remarks: "It is hardly to our credit that his [Brunn's] pupil Waldstein found in England a lucrative career which Germany denied him." Harrison alludes briefly to him (*Reminiscences*, 60). It is revealing that he was never included in *DNB*. [See now D.A. Traill, *An Encyclopedia of the History of Classical Archaeology* II, ed. N. de Grummond (Westport 1996) 1184.]

[51] For Lewis R. Farnell (1856-1934), see his *An Oxonian Looks Back* (London 1934) 281, where he writes: "the writings of the gifted Jane Harrison, the leading woman scholar of the time, were marred by the spirit of feminist propaganda." See further Naiditch, *Classical Studies*, 148 n. 80.

[52] For the distinguished career of Arthur Hamilton Smith (1860-1941), see F.G. Kenyon, *DNB* II. 2890.

[53] For Ernest Arthur Gardner (1862-1939), see Naiditch, *Classical Studies*, 149 n. 84, to which for his activities at the British School add Helen Waterhouse, *The British School at Athens: The First Hundred Years* (London 1986) 167 s.n.

Miss Jane Harrison comes recommended by testimonials of the very weightiest kind. Her large attainments (though the Committee did not [grant?] that she is eminent in scholarship properly so called), her enthusiasm in the study to which she has given herself, her unselfish devotion to the pursuit of knowledge, and her singular success in imparting that knowledge to her hearers, were described in terms of the heartiest praise by persons who had every right to speak with authority. The Committee were agreed in thinking that her claims were of the very first order, and would indeed have been irresistible (the question of sex being supposed to be set aside), but for the competition of a candidate of European reputation in the person of Mr. R.S. Poole. [So strongly, however, did the Committee feel the strength of Miss Harrison's claims that they resolved that it would be advantageous if her acknowledged ability as a teacher could be utilized by her acting as an occasional lecturer for the Professor.][54]

Finally, the winner:

Mr. R.S. Poole,[55] Keeper of Coins in the British Museum, has scarcely a rival in the breadth & profundity of his archaeological knowledge. He is an Egyptologist of high repute, an expert in Oriental archaeology, not less proficient in the archaeology of Greece and Rome, and, in his special occupation of Numismatology, an authority second to none. The Committee had also evidence of his efficiency as a lecturer, and they were satisfied that he had wise and liberal views of the work which the Professor should do. They have therefore no hesitation in recommending him to the Choice of the Council. They also recommend the acceptance of Mr. Poole's offer to spend £200 per annum out of the endowment of the Chair in providing instruction in those branches of the study in which he is not himself expert.

The evidence substantiates the Committee's preference for Poole. His biographer writes: "...he converted what had been a special chair of Greek archaeology into a centre of instruction in a wide range of archaeological studies. His own stimulating teaching of Egyptian, Assyrian, and Arab art and antiquities, and numismatics, was supplemented by the co-operation of specialists in other branches."[56] Poole resigned the chair in 1894 because of declining health.

A second document, a minority report, is attached to the Report of the Committee. It is the following:

---

[54] A later hand has bracketed the paragraph and adds "See Senate Minutes Dec. 17. 88 for the paragraph substituted for this." *Non vidi.*

[55] For Reginald Stuart Poole (1832-1895), see Naiditch, *Housman*, 93-94 with the rich material at ñ. 32-1. He was a numismatist and Egyptologist of prominence, and 18 years senior to Harrison.

[56] Anonymous, *DNB* II. 1687.

The undersigned disagree with that part of the report which recommends that the Professor of Archaeology should be assisted by Miss Harrison. They think it undesirable that any teaching in University College should be conducted by a woman.

E.S. Beesly[57]
G.D. Thane[58]

Dec. 15, 1888.

Beesly, although opposing women on the teaching staff, was no conservative. M.L. Clarke reports[59] that he was "a strong supporter of the cause of Labour, and aroused much criticism by a speech he made in defence of Trades Unions after some acts of violence in Sheffield. A move was made in Council to have him dismissed from his professorship, but Grote, though he was by no means pleased with Beesly's conduct, used his influence to ensure that no action was taken." That is, a leftist, indeed, a friend of Karl Marx, opposed Harrison's appointment on the grounds of her sex, as did an anatomist.

VI. The Election of 1896

Harrison added seven letters to her testimonials of 1888 (Butcher, Dörpfeld, Jebb, Middleton, Ramsay, Tatton and Verrall 2). The document for what follows (AM/D/52) is in the hand of W.M. Flinders Petrie,[60] and dated June 1, 1896. The second covering page contains the following:

Report of Committee of Senate
on Candidates for the Yates Professorship
of Archaeology

Candidates
J. Romilly Allen
Prof. W.C.F. Anderson
Talfourd Ely

---

[57] For Edward Spencer Beesly (1831-1915), then Professor of Ancient and Modern History at University College and concurrently Professor of Latin, Bedford College, London, see Naiditch, *Housman*, 73-74 with the material at n. 29-1. The minority report is written in the hand of Beesly.

[58] Sir George D. Thane (1850-1930) was Professor of Anatomy at University College (P.G. Naiditch). Beesly, Church and Thane are the only Committee members identified. There may have been six others.

[59] M.L. Clarke, *George Grote: A Biography* (London 1962) 158-59.

[60] For the great field archaeologist and Egyptologist W. Flinders Petrie (1853-1942), see Flinders Petrie, *Seventy Years in Archaeology* (New York 1932; repr. New York 1969) and Margaret S. Drower, *Flinders Petrie: A Life in Archaeology* (London 1985).

E.A. Gardner
Miss Jane Harrison
J. Stanley Rogers

Committee (10)
Professors
Barker
Bendall Brown
Rhys Davids
Ker[61]
Housman (Chair)[62]
Petrie
Platt[63]
Roger Smith
Strong

Attendance at first meeting 7
at interview of candidates 9

Two candidates did not submit printed testimonials and their fields were considered remote from the advertisement of "a chair where Classical Studies are a first requirement." There has been a change since 1888. These candidates were T. Stanley Rogers (legal institutions) and J. Romilly Allen (British Archaeology). Talfourd Ely was not up to the other candidates.[64] The first candidate seriously considered was W.C.F. Anderson.[65] His testimonials impressed the Committee. It was twice debated whether to invite him for an interview, but his lack of experience in archaeology decided them against it. "Accordingly, Miss Jane Harrison & Ernest A.

---

[61] For William Paton Ker (1855-1923), then Quain Professor of the English Language and Literature, University College, London, see Naiditch, *Housman*, 57-64 with the material collected at 57-58 n. 22-1.

[62] The bibliography on A.E. Housman (1859-1936) is *fast unübersehbar*: see Naiditch, *Housman*, 100 ff. and Briggs-Calder, 192-204, which is certainly the safest guide. Mr. Naiditch informs me that because he was Dean, Housman was Chair.

[63] Arthur Platt (1860-1924), Professor of Greek at University College, has been immortalized by A.E. Housman in one of the finest necrologies in the English language: see Arthur Platt, *Nine Essays*, with a Preface by A.E. Housman (Cambridge 1927) v-xi.

[64] P.G. Naiditch informs me that Ely was Professor of Greek at Bedford College (1891-1893), later Secretary of University College School, London. A trip to Greece in 1889 is attested. He lectured occasionally at the South Kensington Museum. He seems to have been an amiable amateur.

[65] Elusive, Anderson published reviews in *CR*, and an occasional article and schoolbook. From the two testimonials cited by Petrie, he seems to have been Professor of Classics at Firth College, Sheffield. J. Arthur Munro, Tutor of Lincoln College, Oxford, writes of him: "...we studied together at Oxford ten years ago under Professor W.M. Ramsay...We have done practical work together at excavations in Montenegro and exploration in Asia Minor." The Committee overestimated him.

Gardner were invited to see the Committee." The comparison of Harrison and Gardner is preceded by the following:

> Before considering the respective position of these candidates an allusion was made in the Committee to the question involved of the position of women on the teaching staff. It was unanimously agreed that such a question did not enter in any way into the reference to this Committee; that the sole business before this Committee was to decide which candidate appeared to be the most able, irrespective of sex; and that it rested rather with the Senate and the Council to consider if such a matter should have any weight. No prejudice was hinted at by any member against a woman holding such a post, and several members were in favour of it. It should be remembered that in the following deliberation the general question of a mixed professoriate is not touched on in any way; and any views for or against that order of things are external to the present report.[66]

What Petrie did—after the interviews—was to arrange the credentials of the two finalists under six headings. He cut up sets of their testimonials and pasted relevant bits onto his pages, interspersing them with handwritten comments. The headings are: (1) Scholarship; (2) Lecturing; (3) Work with Students; (4) Breadth & Originality; (5) Work Abroad; (6) Official Business [= Administrative Experience]. Verrall (twice), Jebb and Butcher are cited for Harrison's scholarship: none of the foreigners! Her four books are noted, and her papers in *JHS*. For Gardner, Sandys, Jebb and Henry Pelham, Camden Professor of Ancient History, are cited. Then Gardner's letter of application is quoted:

> I was placed in the First Division of the First Class in the First Part of the Classical Tripos in 1882, and in the Second Part of the same Tripos I obtained in 1884 a First Class with Distinction in Section D (Greek and Roman Archaeology).

His principal publications are listed:

> "Naukratis II" (and a chapter on inscriptions in Naukratis I) 1886-8
> "Excavations at Megalopolis" 1892
> "Handbook of Greek Sculpture" 1896 (part 1)
> and many papers in Journ. Hellen. Studies.

---

[66] Whether this reflects the minority report of 1888, I do not know. The passage is briefly summarized at Naiditch, *Housman*, 63 n. 22-10, where he cites a letter of Harrison to her undergraduate teacher, Henry Jackson (TCC Add. Ms. c 32.10), dated 1 May 1896. In the letter, Harrison alleges that one member of the Committee was averse to appointing a woman and she names W.P. Ker as the misogynist. (1) There is no other evidence that Ker was a misogynist. (2) Petrie writes that the Committee was unanimous in not making sex an issue.

Petrie then writes:

> Questions were asked of both candidates as to the study of Roman
> archaeology & Latin authors. Miss Harrison had a general acquaintance
> with this time, but had not made it a detailed study. Mr. Gardner had
> necessarily grounded himself on this branch in order to pass (First
> Class with Distinction) in Greek and Roman Archaeology; but his
> subsequent work had thrown him on the Greek examples of Roman age,
> more than on Italian work. Another scholastic branch—that of
> epigraphy—was Mr. Gardner's principal subject before he went to
> Athens.

> It was generally felt that although Miss Harrison's abilities might be
> equal to Mr. Gardner's, she had not enjoyed the same opportunities for
> a thorough scholarly grounding in the details of the various branches.
> And the testimonials bear witness mainly to her natural ability,
> insight, & artistic impulse, while Mr. Gardner's testimonials notice
> especially his accuracy & distinction in scholarship & close practical
> acquaintance with the facts of his science. The balance of intuition may
> be on Miss Harrison's side, while the balance of knowledge may be on
> Mr. Gardner's side.

Under lecturing, Petrie records: "This subject was felt by the Committee to
be that in which Miss Harrison undoubtedly had most advantage." Gardner
was helped by a valuable testimonial from Nathaniel Wood,[67] Fellow of
Kings College, Cambridge, who heard Gardner lecture successfully in the
open air to a mixed crowd in Greece. Petrie noted that "Mr. Gardner's
position at Athens has been more connected with individual than collective
teaching." That is, Harrison never had "students." Petrie then reports (8-9):

> Some of the Committee were mainly influenced by the importance of
> securing the most popular lecturer, who would draw large classes and
> make the subject as widely followed as possible in the interests of the
> College; while others attached more weight to the founding of a school
> of studies, & the encouragement of a wide grasp of the whole subject.
> Varying weight was therefore given to the claims of Miss Harrison on
> the ground of proved success in popular lecturing.

Under the rubric "Working with Students," Harrison suffered. "Miss
Harrison does not appear to have had so much opportunity of close work
with students, as she has of lecturing. Hence there are not many allusions to

---

(3) I doubt that the Committee had even met by 1 May. The final report is dated 1 June 1896;
only two meetings are recorded. Things were done with dispatch.

[67] For Nathaniel Wood (1864-1940), editor of Euripides, *Orestes*, tutor and friend of E.M.
Forster, see *Selected Letters of E.M. Forster*, Volume 1 (1879-1920), edited by Mary Lago
and P.N. Furbank (Cambridge 1983) 26 n. 1 and P.N. Furbank, *E.M. Forster: A Life* II
Polycrates' Ring 1914-1970 (New York/London 1978) 347 *s.n.* His unpublished memoirs
survive.

this branch of work." The anti-Harrison, Ridgeway, lauded "Mr. Gardner's unselfish devotion to the interests of his students" and adduced "the testimony of brilliant young men trained by him to his zeal and ability as a teacher." Gardner was astute enough to submit a "Joint testimonial of former students of the School at Athens." The students write:

> As Director of the School, Mr. Gardner has always placed his knowledge and his services ungrudgingly at the disposal of the students; and the generous interests which he has taken in their several studies, however remote from those in which he has been himself engaged, is very remarkable.

Petrie summarizes the discussion (11):

> This ability to discuss questions with students, & help them personally in their original work has been a specialty of Mr. Gardner's at Athens, & constitutes one of his strongest claims.

Comparison under this heading may have been decisive. Petrie summarizes the discussion (10-11):

> The Committee feel that in this branch of work across the study-table there is an advantage with Mr. Gardner; and how essential such work is, was shown by the lack of any school of archaeology being formed from the lectures of Prof. Newton & Prof. Poole. It appears that in this line of the formation of future scholars Mr. Gardner has much the same superiority that Miss Harrison has in popular lecturing & interest. In neither case is the proficiency of one candidate any reflection on the abilities of the other.

The next rubric is Breadth & Originality. Here Harrison has only Ramsay:

> Her successive books show that steady growth in width of knowledge and in the power of applying knowledge, which proves freedom of mind, and gives hope of a continuance of similar work and still further development.

David Hogarth[68] wrote for Gardner:

---

[68] For the distinguished field archaeologist David George Hogarth (1862-1927), see David G. Hogarth, *The Wandering Scholar* (Oxford 1925); Janet E. Courtney (Hogarth's sister), "David George Hogarth 1862-1927," in *An Oxford Portrait Gallery* (London 1931) 3-48; and F.G. Kenyon, *DNB* II. 2699. In the tradition of Colonel Leake, he combined archaeological surveying with intelligence work, and thus assured the financing of his digs: see Richard Symonds, *Oxford and Empire: The Last Lost Cause?*[2] (London 1991) 141; Jeremy Wilson, *Lawrence of Arabia: The Authorized Biography of T.E. Lawrence* (New York 1990) 1173 *s.n.*; and H.V.F. Winstone, *Woolley of Ur: The Life of Sir Leonard Woolley* (London 1990) 27-28, 61, 286-87. In 1897 he succeeded Gardner as Director of the British School at Athens.

I was intimately connected with Mr. Ernest Gardner in archaeological work four years ago, and had full opportunity of learning how genuine is his sympathy for archaeological study and how extraordinarily wide and comprehensive his knowledge. We, who worked with him in Cyprus, though no younger than he, always regarded him as possessed of an archaeological experience which placed a gap of years between us: and in the publication of our results we relied greatly on his acute and critical judgement. He has as much acquaintance with many subjects in Archaeology, as most specialists on each subject severally possess: and I do not believe that anyone in the United Kingdom is better qualified to fill a chair of Archaeology.

Under the last two rubrics, Work Abroad and Official Business, Harrison does not even appear. Of the first qualification, Leaf, identified here as "Treasurer, British School at Athens," writes of Gardner:

There is perhaps no English archaeologist with the single exception of Sir C. Newton, certainly there is not one of the younger generation, who can approach his experience in practical study of the subject in its home in Greece.

Finally, George A. Macmillan,[69] "Hon. Sec. British Sch. at Athens," writes: "I have much pleasure in bearing my testimony to his business capacity, and his conscientious discharge of the duties of his position." It may have been that at this point in the deliberations Gardner's triumph was not yet assured. For, thirty-six years later, Petrie recalls:

On the death of Reginald Stuart Poole, the Yates Chair of Archaeology was vacant at the College. A Committee was appointed to see candidates, and the two considered were Jane Harrison and Ernest Gardner. It was my duty to draw up the report, which I did as impartially as I could. The committee were on the point of naming Jane Harrison, but I remarked that, though an authority on religion,[70] she had not as wide a view and knowledge as Gardner, and that carried the day.[71]

The final summation (14) deserves citation:

The issue between the two candidates appeared to the Committee to rest much on the kind of work that was to be expected in the Chair. If the main object were to be the spread of a general interest in Greek Art and Mythology, undoubtedly Miss Harrison is a specialist in this branch, whose abilities appear to be pre-eminent. But on looking to the other questions,—of well grounded scholarship & high accuracy,—work with

---

[69] For George Macmillan's work for the British School, see Waterhouse, *British School*, 168 *s.n.*

[70] She was in fact not an authority on religion until 1903.

[71] Petrie, *Seventy Years*, 174.

students in their own special researches, & the founding of a school of general archaeology,—breadth of interests outside of the very specialised branch of Greek Art,—power of independent work,—the interpretation of evidence from actual discovery,—& general business capacity,—the evidence was all in favour of Mr. Gardner, as being the fittest person to forward the interests of archaeology in a position in which too great specialisation would be a misfortune. The general scope of the position has been already much limited by the requirement of particular capacity in one branch: and the main object after satisfying the first requirement of a high position in Greek work, would be to preserve as much breadth, & sympathy with all branches of Archaeology, as possible. In view of these considerations the Committee by a final vote recommend that Ernest A. Gardner be appointed to the Yates Professorship of Archaeology.

Notice is found on the first covering page that the recommendation was adopted by the Senate on 1 June 1896 and by Council on 7 June 1896. "E.A. Gardner appointed for 5 years."

VII. What have we learned?

Peacock attributed Harrison's failures to "fear...of granting the distinguished professorship to a woman" and alleged that "the hidebound world of classical scholarship had no room for innovative thinking." Only two members of the Committee of 1888, one a friend of Karl Marx, objected to Harrison's sex. The Committee of 1896 explicitly stated that sex played no role in their deliberations. The Committee of 1888 placed her before seven men; the Committee of 1896, before four men. Harrison's "innovative" books did not begin to appear before 1903. As late as 1896, her work was conventional. None of her 24 testimonials even raise the question of "innovative thinking." Harrison failed because in both cases there was a stronger candidate.[72]

---

[72] I am grateful for valuable help to Robert Ackerman (Philadelphia), Alexander Košenina (FU Berlin) and P.G. Naiditch (Los Angeles).

How did Ulrich von Wilamowitz-Moellendorff Read a Text?

Udalrico K. Goldsmith
collegae atque amico
sed magis amico

To the disadvantage of both, the disciplines of German Studies and Classics have drifted apart. Today only a handful of American classicists are able to read a German book through, as B.L. Gildersleeve, William Abbott Oldfather and Paul Shorey did; and I know only some dozen who can easily lecture in German. On the other hand how many professors of German under the age of fifty know the Greek alphabet, let alone can read a page of Homeric Greek? I have often seen the doctrine of eternal return, a commonplace of late Hellenistic philosophy, attributed to Nietzsche. And how many know that the laughing Zarathustra is Herodotean? It was not always so. Germanistik as a separate discipline sprouted from classical philology, in good part through the efforts of two men, Karl Lachmann (1793-1851) and Moriz Haupt (1808-1874).[1] Moriz Haupt directed the doctoral dissertation of the greatest Hellenist who ever lived.

Ulrich von Wilamowitz-Moellendorff (1848-1931)[2] was born on the estate of his father, Arnold, at Markowitz near Inowroclaw in the province of Posen. To save money his father agreed that the young boy be sent to Schulpforte, the finest humanistic gymnasium of the time[3] (only the Johanneum at Hamburg was comparable) rather than the Ritterakademie at Brandenburg which his three brothers dutifully attended. Wilamowitz had only one rival at Pforte, the pastor's son, Friedrich Nietzsche (1844-1900).

---

[1] For Lachmann see Martin Hertz, *Karl Lachmann: Eine Biographie* (Berlin 1861; repr. Osnabrück 1972) and Sebastiano Timpanaro, *Die Entstehung der Lachmannschen Methode* (Hamburg 1971[2]); for Haupt see Christian Belger, *Moriz Haupt als academischer Lehrer* (Berlin 1879). For the descent of Romanistik and Anglistik see Hans Helmut Christmann, "Romanistik und Anglistik an der deutschen Universität im 19. Jahrhundert: Ihre Herausbildung als Fächer und ihr Verhältnis zu Germanistik und klassischer Philologie," *Akademie der Wissenschaften und Literatur Mainz: Abhandlungen der Geistes- und Sozialwissenschaften Klasse*, Jahrgang 1985, Nr. 1 (Stuttgart 1985).

[2] See above all Ulrich von Wilamowitz-Moellendorff, *Erinnerungen 1848-1914* (Leipzig 1929[2]) and further Ulrich von Wilamowitz-Moellendorff, "Selected Correspondence 1869-1931," ed. William M. Calder III, *Antiqua* 23 (Naples 1983) and *Wilamowitz nach 50 Jahren*, edd. William M. Calder III, Helmut Flashar, Theodor Lindken (Darmstadt 1985) with the review by Bernhard vom Brocke, *HZ* 243 (1986) 101-36. There is an English translation, occasionally bowdlerized, of the *Erinnerungen*: see Ulrich von Wilamowitz-Moellendorff, *My Recollections 1848-1914*, translated by G.C. Richards (London 1930).

[3] See Hans Gehrig, *Schulpforte und das deutsche Geistesleben* (Darmstadt 1942); Fritz Heyer, *Aus der Geschichte der Landesschule zur Pforte* (Darmstadt 1944); and Wilamowitz, *Erinnerungen*[2] 62-83.

From this schoolboys' rivalry grew the famous struggle in 1872 over *Geburt*.[4] Pforte, not the university, won Wilamowitz for philology and caused him to abandon his aristocratic heritage.

Bonn and Berlin disappointed the young student. Of his university instructors, only Otto Jahn (1813-1869) and the orthodox Jew and uncle of Freud, Jacob Bernays (1824-1881), had a lasting influence. In 1878 he married the daughter of Theodor Mommsen (1817-1903), the first in his family in four hundred years to marry a bourgeois woman. The wedding was boycotted by his family. His three ordinariats were at Greifswald (1876-1883), Göttingen (1883-1897), and Berlin (1897-1931). His bibliography is itself a book.[5] He wrote over seventy volumes ranging from Homer to Libanius, each of which has exercised incalculable influence on subsequent scholarship. Among Germanists whom he knew well were his influential Pforte teacher, August Koberstein (1797-1870); his younger Pforte contemporary and later Berlin colleague, Erich Schmidt (1853-1913), the rediscoverer of Kleist; and his close friend, and Charlottenburg neighbor, Gustav Roethe (1859-1926),[6] who followed Wilamowitz from Göttingen to Berlin to become part of what Friedrich Meinecke called "the Göttingen clique" there.[7]

Students of modern languages must be reminded that the great difference between what we do and what they do is caused by the lamentable lack of source material for ancient authors in comparison for example with nineteenth century Europe. Far, far more has been written about Thucydides' view of Pericles than about Theodor Mommsen's view of Bismarck or Friedrich Nietzsche's of Richard Wagner. No letters of Thucydides to friends confiding his view of Pericles, no diary survive. No trustworthy ancient biography based on trustworthy sources survives. Any work on this problem necessarily is based on a microscopic analysis of the words applied to Pericles by Thucydides in his *History*. The result of course is the injection of a considerable amount of pure presupposition. Likewise one finds diametrically opposed versions of *Antigone*, propounded by good scholars arguing from the same text. Wilamowitz, using an Homeric figure, wrote that we must pour our own blood into the ghosts of the past to make

---

[4] See William M. Calder III, "The Wilamowitz-Nietzsche Struggle: New Documents and a Reappraisal," *Nietzsche-Studien* 12 (1983) 214-54, and Jaap Mansfeld, "The Wilamowitz-Nietzsche Struggle: Another New Document and Some Further Comments," *Nietzsche-Studien* 15 (1986) 41-58. Both these papers see the struggle from Wilamowitz' rather than from Nietzsche's side. *Audiatur et altera pars.*

[5] Michael Armstrong, Wolfgang Buchwald, William M. Calder III, *Ulrich von Wilamowitz-Moellendorff Bibliography 1867-1900* (Hildesheim 1991).

[6] See Julius Petersen, *Gustav Roethe: Ansprache bei der Trauerfeier des Ostbundes am 10. Oktober 1926 in der Neuen Aula der Universität Berlin mit einem bibliographischen Anhang* (Leipzig 1926) and for a selection of writings that reveal the man; Gustave Roethe, *Deutsche Reden* (Leipzig s.d.).

[7] Friedrich Meinecke, *Autobiographische Schriften* (= *Werke* 8), edited by Eberhard Kessel (Stuttgart 1969) 249, citing a remark of the historian, Max Lenz.

them alive.[8] That is, exegesis inevitably becomes *Rezeption*. Consider the reception of an important Greek text of the first century, the *New Testament*. I should go so far as to say the text is not a constant but a variable. The remoteness of Greek texts, the difficulty of their language and a lack of contemporary exegetical material, led to the rise of *Wortphilologie*, the attempt to squeeze the most elusive nuance from a word by comparing it with other occurrences of the same word and then arguing from analogy. Later lexica when extant could be used with caution, as could ancient exegetes, called *scholia*, and the ancient grammarians. The great proponent of *Wortphilologie* in the first half of the nineteenth century was Gottfried Hermann (1772-1848),[9] Leipzig Ordinarius in Greek, editor of the tragedians, and father-in-law of Moriz Haupt. He died the year Wilamowitz was born. Wilamowitz never forgot what he owed Hermann in Greek and Hermann's contemporary, Karl Lachmann.[10] What good is any generality if not founded on the *Sprachkenntnis* of a *Wortphilologe*? Hermann wrote commentaries and emended corrupt texts. He never once interpreted a whole play. This was the tradition of the English *Wortphilologen* who emended words in tragedy but never deleted or transposed verses because their competence never went so far as to trace the thought through a whole speech.[11] Still this *Wortphilologie*, as revived by Hermann Fränkel (1888-1977) and Bruno Snell (1896-1986), provides the best tool for understanding the early lyric poets preserved only in fragments.[12] Sappho is an excellent example of an author who responds to this approach. The method requires a mastery of ancient Greek unattainable in the modern world. Schoolboys no longer enjoy the advantage of learning the ancient languages well before the university; and today men of genius appear to avoid the humanities.

Wilamowitz wrote that the time came when *Wortphilologie* was not enough. In his third semester at Bonn he followed a coffin to the grave. Friedrich Gottlieb Welcker (1784-1868)[13] died 17 December 1868.

---

[8] Ulrich von Wilamowitz-Moellendorff, *Greek Historical Writing and Apollo: Two Lectures Delivered Before the University of Oxford June 3 and 4, 1908* (Oxford 1908; reprinted Chicago 1979) 25.

[9] See Otto Jahn, "Gottfried Hermann," *Biographische Aufsätze* (Leipzig 1866) 89-132.

[10] He states this clearly in the Latin Autobiography of 1928: see William M. Calder III, *Antike und Abendland* 27 (1981) 43 (= *Antiqua* 23 [1983] 156): "*Hermannum* et *Lachmannum* praeceptores monstrabant; debeo utrique philologica multa. sed venit dies qui docebat, neutrum mihi satis facere.*"

[11] See Ulrich von Wilamowitz-Moellendorff, *Euripides Herakles* I: *Einleitung in die griechische Tragödie* (Darmstadt 1969³) 230-31.

[12] I do not find the objections of Professor Fowler in his otherwise excellent book convincing: see Robert L. Fowler, "The Nature of Early Greek Lyric: Three Preliminary Studies," *Phoenix Supplement Volume* 21 (Toronto 1987) 1-13. I see no reasonable alternative for the Fränkel-Snell method when working with archaic fragments that lack an historical context.

[13] See *Friedrich Gottlieb Welcker: Werk und Wirkung*, edd. William M. Calder III, Adolf Köhnken, Wolfgang Kullmann, Gunther Pflug, *Hermes Einzelschrift* 49 (Stuttgart 1986). For Wilamowitz' view of Welcker see William M. Calder III, "Ulrich von Wilamowitz-Moellendorff to Kekule von Stradonitz on Friedrich Gottlieb Welcker," *Studi Italiani di*

Wilamowitz never met the man whom he called "the forgotten unforgettable,"[14] but his influence on the young student was decisive. From Welcker's books Wilamowitz learned the *Totalitätideal*. This is the conviction that the particular can only be understood out of a knowledge of the whole. August Boeckh (1785-1867) implies it when he says that our goal must be *totius antiquitatis cognitio*.[15]

Only a bit of Greek epic and a very small bit of Greek tragedy have been preserved from antiquity. To try to understand Sophocles' *Lebenswerk* from his seven preserved tragedies would be as fruitful as to understand Shakespeare's on the basis of some three quarters of *Macbeth*. Welcker to his credit saw that the preserved tragedies could only be understood within the context of the total *oeuvre*, and Homer within the context of the epic cycle. Paradoxically it is far more difficult to understand the few preserved verses of a lost tragedy than the 1530 verses of *Oedipus Tyrannus*. To reconstruct a lost tragedy Welcker needed to gather the scattered fragments and the testimonia for the action from throughout Greek literature and even early Byzantine. Often he needed to consult Latin authors who had translated the lost Greek originals or at least read them. Often the evidence for a lost tragedy is archaeological: contemporary Athenian vase-painting, later Italian imitations of it, sculpture (e.g., the Niobids), and frequently Roman sarcophagi and Etruscan urns.[16] This use of archaeological artifacts to elucidate literary texts came to be called "monumental philology"[17] and was practiced to great effect by Welcker's colleague and student, Otto Jahn (1813-1869), known to Germanists as the biographer of Mozart, who taught Wilamowitz for four semesters at Bonn. The fact that many of the wall-paintings and mosaics excavated at Pompeii concerned Hellenistic themes and that the archaeologists asked philologists what they meant and the

---

Filologia Classica NS 3, 2 (1984) 116-33. The standard biography is Reinhard Kekule, *Das Leben Friedrich Gottlieb Welcker's nach seinen eignen Aufzeichnungen und Briefen* (Leipzig 1880). A modern biography using the extensive *Nachlass* at Bonn is desiderated.

[14] Ulrich von Wilamowitz-Moellendorff, *Sappho und Simonides: Untersuchungen über griechische Lyriker* (Berlin 1913) 16.

[15] August Boeckh, *Enzyklopädie und Methodenlehre der philologischen Wissenschaften*, edited by Ernst Bratuscheck (Darmstadt 1966³) 25: "Die Erkenntniss des Alterthums in seinem ganzen Umfange" (= August Boeckh, *On Interpretation and Criticism*, translated by John Paul Pritchard [Norman, Oklahoma, 1968] 22). For Wilamowitz and the *Totalitätsideal* see Harald Patzer, "Wilamowitz und die klassische Philologie," *Festschrift Franz Dornseiff zum 65. Geburtstag*, ed. Horst Kusch (Leipzig 1953) 244-57.

[16] See Stefan L. Radt, "Welcker und die verlorene Tragödie," in Calder *et al.*, *Hermes Einz.* (n. 13 above) 157-78.

[17] See Wolfgang Schindler in Calder-Flashar-Lindken (n. 2 above) 244-46. The term is usually attributed to Otto Jahn; but Rudolf Kassel contends that it is a formulation of Eduard Gerhard (1795-1867), citing C.B. Stark, *Systematik und Geschichte der Archäologie der Kunst* (Leipzig 1880) 5, 11-12. *Non vidi.*

philologists did not know, began the serious study of later Greek poetry. Jahn himself was one of the pioneers. Wilamowitz wrote the single most influential book ever written on the subject.[18]

Welcker's Achilles heel was that in order to gain great breadth, he had to sacrifice the precise knowledge of the Greek language that Hermann possessed. The young Wilamowitz boldly sought to combine the *Wortphilologie* of Hermann with the *Totalitätsideal* of Welcker. Any number of his books are proof of his success. A famous example is his *Platon* of 1919. His knowledge of Greek make the second volume of interpretations indispensable to this day for anyone interested in the precise meaning of what Plato wrote. His knowledge of history, *Sittengeschichte*, and archaeology enables him to provide the Athenian background for his main characters, Socrates and Plato. We learn how they lived, what they wore, and what they ate; how they went to school or fought in battle. Just these details caused Gundolf to dismiss the book as "Plato for chambermaids."[19] Paul Shorey, always jealous of the greater man, called it "a historical novel."[20] But just these details make Plato a man rather than a name on a title-page. In a letter to Wilamowitz, Werner Jaeger greeted the book with the sentence: "You have restored the man Plato to the world."[21]

This leads us to what is often called Wilamowitz' historicism, whatever that word means. I take it to mean Wilamowitz' desire to see Greeks in their historical context, and I do not consider it a *Schimpfwort*. His famous statement on the matter is in the introduction to his edition of *Aristophanes, Lysistrate*:[22]

---

[18] Ulrich von Wilamowitz-Moellendorff, *Hellenistische Dichtung in der Zeit des Kallimachos*, 2 vols. (Berlin 1924). For Wilamowitz' contribution to Hellenistic Poetry see Ernst-Richard Schwinge in Calder-Flashar-Lindken (n. 2 above) 151-77, with the devastating criticism of Rudolf Kassel, *Göttingen Gelehrte Anzeigen* 239 (1987) 201-4.

[19] Friedrich Gundolf quoted by K. Hildebrandt, *Erinnerungen an Stefan George und seinen Kreis* (Berlin 1965) 55 n. 11; see *contra* E.R. Dodds, *Plato, Gorgias: A Revised Text with Introduction and Commentary* (Oxford 1959) 31 n. 2. The German is "Platon für Dienstmädchen." For the autobiographical elements in the book see William M. Calder III in Calder-Flashar-Lindken (n. 2 above) 101-7. Philosophers have regularly denigrated the book because it attributes Plato's philosophy in large part to traumatic experiences in his life: see the excellent remarks of E.N. Tigerstedt, "Interpreting Plato," *Acta Universitatis Stockholmiensis: Stockholm Studies in the History of Literature* 17 (1977) 47-48. The authoritative treatments of Wilamowitz and the George Circle are Ulrich K. Goldsmith, "Wilamowitz and the Georgekreis: New Documents," in Calder-Flashar-Lindken (n. 2 above) 583-612 and "Wilamowitz as Parodist of Stefan George," *Monatshefte* 77 (1985) 79-87.

[20] Paul Shorey, *What Plato Said* (Chicago 1967[7]) 2. For an honest analysis of Shorey's problems with Wilamowitz see E. Christian Kopff in Calder-Flashar-Lindken (n. 2 above) 569-76.

[21] *Antiqua* 23 (Naples 1983) 190. For the romantic background of this sort of historiography see H.R. Trevor-Roper, "The Romantic Movement and the Study of History," *The John Coffin Memorial Lecture 1969* (London 1969) [and Ernst Behler, *German Romantic Literary Theory* (Cambridge 1993)].

[22] Ulrich von Wilamowitz-Moellendorff, *Aristophanes, Lysistrate* (Berlin 1927) 5.

In the end the poem, meant for an hour, first has to be understood as what it intended to be on that occasion. Only then does one treat it for its absolute worth.

We must seek to become a member of the original audience, to have read what they did, to have experienced what they have, to see the theater, the actors, the costumes, which they saw. Several months before his death he writes to the interpreter of Greek philosophy, Julius Stenzel (1883-1935):[23]

But the thinkers were men of flesh and blood with inner contradictions, such as we all have, with love and hate. The poets were that too; and they too are squeezed today into an *Entwicklungsreihe*. If historicism means that one wants to grasp men as individuals in their time, then I confess that I belong to the allegedly *victa causa*.

We see here the famous Wilamowitzian axiom that an ancient Greek was "ein Mensch wie Du und Ich." To phrase it differently, Wilamowitz in contrast to the classicistic tradition of Winckelmann and of Nietzsche stressed similarities rather than differences. He wrote to Warren, the President of Magdalen College Oxford, that what he most liked in the Lateran Sophocles was the pot-belly. That was the only trace of the individual that the classicizing copyists could not remove.[24]

In a series of letters which I shall soon publish of Wilamowitz to his Berlin colleague, the universal historian, Eduard Meyer (1855-1930), Wilamowitz sought to distinguish between the work of a philologist and an ancient historian. The distinction is never as clear as today's between an historian and an ahistorical, even antihistorical, literary critic. The philologist pays far closer attention to the text. He stresses *Quellenforschung*, whose importance the historian is apt to underestimate. Meyer replies that the historian stresses *Entwicklung* (e.g., constitutional history) while the philologist interprets das *Gegenwärtige*, e.g., a poem, that is a text that one can hold in one's hand. The distinction is not flawless. Wilamowitz replies that the *Iliad* is *Entwicklung*. Any informed Homerist would agree. One might also remind the historian of Judaism and Christianity of the Bible. But we find that what the philologist, the man of literature and ideas, deals with is concrete, even tactile (one can hold the book), in a way that what the historian deals with is not, e.g., the Battle of Marathon. We find also that the *Universalhistoriker*, who covers the Orient, Israel, Egypt, Greece, and Rome, despite his astonishing breadth, just because he is a *Realhistoriker*, is confined to that part of a civilization that is less important because it has

---

[23] *Antiqua* 23 (Naples 1983) 278.
[24] *Antiqua* 23 (Naples 1983) 285, 291 n. 84.

vanished. Wilamowitz, who knows Greek and Latin and not the languages of the Orient, as a *Kulturhistoriker*, unexpectedly has a far greater breadth, one that includes politics, arts, literature, religion and philosophy.[25]

From Barthold Georg Niebuhr (1776-1831) Wilamowitz took his goal *die Antike wieder lebendig zu machen*, "to make antiquity alive again." That is to make it say something important to schoolboys and students. At Pforte Wilamowitz read Tacitus with K. L. Peter, the Headmaster, in order to strengthen his moral character by studying the tragedies of the Julio-Claudian house. One must *believe* the ancient authors as men had earlier Scripture and be convinced that one may be improved by them. This is clear in everything that Wilamowitz wrote about Euripides or Plato. One sees the seeds of Jaeger's Third Humanism in Jaeger's teacher. One of the sins of Friedrich Ritschl (1806-1876), the teacher of Friedrich Nietzsche and mortal enemy of Otto Jahn, was that he turned students from authors who could change their lives (as Plato did Wilamowitz') to authors where there were problems. Plautus has nothing to say to an educated man of intelligence. Humanism as a formative influence in a young man's life had become the higher crossword. Unfortunately it was the philology of Ritschl, not Welcker, that influenced American philology in its formative stage. In more recent times the disastrous legacy of New Criticism has been that by emphasizing technique of composition above content, it has trivialized ancient literature.

In revolt against the stifling methodology of the Ritschl School Wilamowitz was reluctant to discuss method. His student, Wolfgang Schadewaldt, records that in 1919 he once remarked on philological method:[26]

> Then colleagues Harnack and Roethe come to me and say: "You are in good shape; you have the 'Philological Method.'" Why, this prized "philological method"? There simply isn't any—any more than a method to catch fish. The whale is harpooned; the herring caught in a net; flounders are stomped upon; the salmon speared; the trout caught on a fly. Where do you find *the method* to catch fish? And hunting? I suppose there is something like method there? Why ladies and gentlemen, there is a difference between hunting lions and catching fleas.

---

[25] See my "'Credo gegen Credo; Arbeit gegen Arbeit; Anschauung gegen Anschauung': Ulrich von Wilamowitz-Moellendorff contra Eduard Meyer," *Eduard Meyer: Leben und Leistung eines Universalhistorikers*, edited by William M. Calder III and Alexander Demandt (Leiden 1990) 41-73 (= *Further Letters* 105-35).

[26] See Wolfgang Schadewaldt, *Hellas und Hesperien: Gesammelte Schriften zur Antike und zur neueren Literatur in zwei Bänden*, edd. Klaus Bartels, Reinhard Thurow and Ernst Zinn II (Zürich 1970²) 606-7, with my note at *Rheinisches Museum* NF 126 (1983) 191. The simile well reveals Wilamowitz' impatience with tiresome blithering about method.

The famous remark was part in fun. He imitates Ovid on the lack of method in love (*AA* I. 763-64). But he reveals his practical disgust with endless talk on method. Rather, with Aristotle, sit down and get on with it. One may adduce A.E. Housman's famous comparison of philological method to a dog hunting fleas.[27]

I shall end on a less frivolous note. On two famous occasions (1891 and 1928) Wilamowitz criticized two great contemporaries, Paul de Lagarde (1827-1891)[28] and Friedrich Nietzsche (1844-1900). Both, he said, confused the role of the scholar with that of the prophet. He approved de Lagarde:[29]

> He was more than a scholar. He was a prophet. As a prophet he has raised his voice on State and Church, on the education of youth and the worship of God, on society and morality. Nor did it disturb him that the voice of the one crying remained in the wilderness: he felt himself as a prophet. He had a right to that; for his was a prophetic nature.

He did not approve Nietzsche:[30]

> He did what I demanded of him. He gave up teaching and scholarship and became a prophet—for an irreligious religion and an unphilosophical philosophy.

In a private letter of 1 July 1920 to the Zürich Germanist and classicist, Ernst Howald, he is more precise:[31]

> They are prophets. One must believe them. The prophet has as much right to the lecture platform as the journalist does.

The prophet does not argue his case. He imposes it. Journalists are persons paid to deliver opinions on matters they do not understand. Neither is a scholar. In just this vein some fifteen years later Bruno Snell would criticize

---

[27] *The Classical Papers of A.E. Housman:* III *1915-1936*, collected and edited by J. Diggle and F.R.D. Goodyear (Cambridge 1972) 1059.

[28] See William M. Calder III, "Wilamowitz' Call to Göttingen: Paul de Lagarde to Friedrich Althoff on Wilamowitz-Moellendorff," *Studi Italiani di Filologia Classica* NS 3, 3 (1985) 136-60.

[29] Ulrich von Wilamowitz-Moellendorff, *Erinnerungen*[2] 233. He uses prophet precisely in the sense that Goethe applied the word to Mohammed: see *Goethes Werke* II, ed. E. Truntz (Munich 1984[14]) 143. I owe the reference to Professor Jaap Mansfeld (Utrecht).

[30] *Erinnerungen*[2] 130. These words have given rise to absurd misrepresentations usually by people who know them third-hand. See lately Golo Mann, *Erinnerungen und Gedanken: Eine Jugend in Deutschland* (Frankfurt 1986) 472-73, with my "Golo Mann on Ulrich von Wilamowitz-Moellendorff," *Quaderni di Storia* 26 (1987) 137-39 (10 errors of fact in 20 lines).

[31] See Jaap Mansfeld, *Nietzsche-Studien* 15 (1986) 52.

Werner Jaeger's Third Humanism.[32] The philologist was something different in Wilamowitz' mind. At the end of the first volume of his greatest work, purposely published in his fortieth year, his *akme*, *Herakles*, he states a profound conviction:[33]

> It is far more to the point that the ancient poet speak, not some modern professor. We perform our task correctly only when we don't force our own mind into every ancient book that falls into our hands; but rather read out of it what is already there. That is precisely the specifically philological task of comprehending a different individual. It is a matter of one's sinking into another mind, whether that of an individual or of a people. In the self-sacrifice of our own individuality lies our strength. We philologists as such have nothing of the poet nor of the prophet, both of which to a certain degree the historian should have. On the other hand we ought to carry something of the actor in ourselves, not of the virtuoso who sets his own idiosyncratic touches onto the role; but of the true artist, who gives life to the dead words through his own heart's blood.

We have here the quintessence of Wilamowitz' hermeneutic. From Lachmann's "Nur wer sich willig ergibt, befreit sein Urteil" ("only he who willingly submits, frees his judgment")[34] derives the sacrifice of our individuality. Here is the Homeric metaphor of pouring our own heart's blood into a figure of the remote past in order to make him speak. Here is Niebuhr's *wieder lebendig zu machen*.[35] The concept of the philologist as the great actor was suggested to Wilamowitz by Diderot's *Paradoxe sur le comédien*.[36] Hamlet must remain Hamlet and not become Sir Laurence

---

[32] See my "Werner Jaeger and Richard Harder: an *Erklärung*," *Quaderni di storia* 17 (1983) 99-121 (= "Studies in the Modern History of Classical Scholarship," *Antiqua* 27 [Naples 1984] 59-81 [esp. 65-66]).

[33] Ulrich von Wilamowitz-Moellendorff, *Euripides, Herakles* I (Darmstadt 1969³) 257.

[34] See Hertz, *Lachmann* 180, and Wilamowitz, *Erinnerungen*² 103.

[35] See G.B. Niebuhr, *The History of Rome* I, translated by Julius Charles Hare and Connop Thirlwall (Philadelphia 1835) 1-4; especially (4):

> He who calls departed ages back again into being, enjoys a bliss like that of creating: it were a great thing, if I could scatter the mist that lies upon this most excellent portion of ancient story, and could spread a clear light over it; so that the Romans shall stand before the eyes of my readers, distinct, intelligible, familiar as contemporaries, with their institutions and the vicissitudes of their destiny, living and moving.

[36] For an English translation with introduction and notes see Denis Diderot, *The Paradox of Acting*, translated by Walter Herries Pollock (London 1883); and William Archer, *Masks or Faces?* (New York 1967⁴) 1-71. I owe the suggestion that Wilamowitz here was indebted to Diderot to Professor Domenico Musti (Rome).

Olivier wearing a Hamlet costume. There is a remarkable parallel in Wilamowitz' younger contemporary, the influential English philosopher and archaeologist, R.G. Collingwood (1889-1943):[37]

> History did not mean knowing what events followed what. It meant getting into other people's heads, looking at their situation through their eyes, and thinking for yourself whether the way in which they tackled it was the right way.

It was an easy jump from interpretation of this sort to biography. Deeply impressed by a suggestion of Eduard Meyer,[38] Wilamowitz later formulated his view that biography was the highest form of philological interpretation:[39]

> The classical scholar fundamentally is interpreter but not of the words alone. These he will never fully understand if he does not understand the mind from which they come. He must also be the interpreter of his mind. Biography then which is wholly based on interpretations is essentially the work of a philologist, only raised to a higher power. His task turns out after all to be no more than understanding an author's development, intention, thought and influence.

One must present literature and ideas through the men that created them. One must put on their mind just as an actor does a role. Just as Plato recreated the historical Socrates in his dialogues; so will Wilamowitz recreate the historical Plato in his biography.[40]

---

[37] R.G. Collingwood, *An Autobiography* (Oxford 1967[5]) 58.

[38] Eduard Meyer, *Kleine Schriften zur Geschichtstheorie und zur wirtschaftlichen und politischen Geschichte des Altertums* I (Halle 1910) 66.

[39] Ulrich von Wilamowitz-Moellendorff, *Platon* I (Berlin 1920[2]) 4.

[40] An earlier version of this paper was delivered as part of the panel "The Genesis of Literaturwissenschaft" at the eleventh annual conference of the German Studies Association in St. Louis on 16th October, 1987. A later version with slides was delivered at the annual meeting of the Classical Association of the Middle West and South at New Orleans, Louisiana, on 7th April, 1988. I am grateful to my colleague, Professor Ulrich K. Goldsmith, who has beneficially read the earliest version and removed a number of embarrassing inaccuracies. For authoritative brief lives and extensive bio-bibliographies of B.L. Gildersleeve, G. Hermann, A.E. Housman, O. Jahn, W. Jaeger, K. Lachmann, Ed. Meyer, W.A. Oldfather, F. Ritschl, P. Shorey, and Wilamowitz see now Ward W. Briggs and William M. Calder III (edd.), *Classical Scholarship: A Biographical Encyclopedia* (New York 1990).

Moses Hadas
1900-1966

Moses Hadas never produced a school. He never wrote a book that was "epochmaking," one that caused its subject never to be the same again, like Beazley's book on vases, or Ronald Syme on Augustus, or Wilamowitz on the *AthPol*. He wrote few learned articles. He was interested in the periphery—Hellenistic Judaism or the Greek novel, Plutarch or Seneca. He was never Sather Professor. He was never president, not even a director of APA. He spent most of his life at one institution. He did not have a European reputation. But those who knew him will never forget him. He may have saved American Classics. When he died, his death was noticed on page 1 of the *New York Times*. Who was Moses Hadas? What was his achievement? Why is he remembered 25 years after his death?

Moses Hadas was born in Atlanta, Georgia, son of Russian-Jewish immigrant parents. His father David, a shopkeeper, published works in Hebrew and Latin on the rabbinical exegesis of the Pentateuch. He first studied Greek and Latin at Boys High School in Atlanta. He took his BA at Emory University in 1922. He received his MA (1925) and his PhD (1930) from Columbia and a rabbinical degree from the Jewish Theological Seminary (1926). The teacher to whom he owed most was Charles Knapp. His dissertation, *Sextus Pompey* (1930), is still authoritative. Hadas taught two years (1928-1930) at Cincinnati. He then returned to Columbia where he served in the Department of Greek and Latin, except for brief war service, until his death at age 66. I shall not append a bibliography. This would omit what was most important—the teacher, the colleague, and the man.

I first met him in September, 1958, when I was aged 25 with a new Chicago PhD and a first job as instructor in Greek and Latin at Columbia. I think what was most inspiring about him for a young scholar was that he utterly loved what he was doing—teaching intelligent young men the wisdom of the Greeks and Romans. This was an urgent task and an inestimable privilege. He said once that he was ashamed to be paid for what he did, and from the start he had his check sent to his bank so that he would never have to see it or to touch it. His office door was always open and there was always time for a colleague, a visitor, or, best of all, a puzzled freshman. He much preferred undergraduate teaching and he most enjoyed a senior colloquium on great books that he long taught with a colleague, sometimes with Jacques Barzun, or Andrew Chiappe, or Herbert Deane, or Joseph Mazzeo. Undergraduates were interviewed before admission. Alumni told me that it changed their lives. Both teachers of the course read the papers and often gave them different marks. Students learned that gods could disagree. Hadas, unlike most Americans but like the great Germans, believed what he taught. Hellenism was not peripheral. It was central.

Hadas was what the Germans call a *Menschenfreund*. That made him a patient teacher. He liked to quote an American humorist (Will Rogers?): "People are better than anybody." He was a kindly marker, sometimes to the disgust of C. H. Kahn and myself in our first years of teaching. He said we would change when we grew older, and he was right. His sense of humor won him friends everywhere. He liked jokes that were decently off color, especially if they were at the expense of organized religion.

He detested pretension and could be devastating. Gilbert Highet was deluged with invitations to speak and told the secretary that any invitation for less that $500 (one ninth my annual salary) should receive the reply: "Professor Gilbert Highet regrets that because of the pressure of research and teaching he is unable to accept your kind invitation." As the secretary was preparing the cards, Hadas whispered to her: "Add: 'P.S. You can have Moses Hadas for $150.'" At an annual dinner of the University Seminars, chairman after pompous chairman related how useful for the nation was the work of physicists, chemists, Slavists, the Law School. It was late when Hadas was called on to speak for the Seminar on Classical Civilizations. What he said was never forgotten: "We are utterly useless. That is why we are indispensable."

For the history of Classics in the United States, his most important contribution was his introduction of courses on Classics in translation. Following World War II, thousands of veterans returned whose college education was to be paid for under the G. I. Bill of Rights. They had not gone to the good schools. Their fathers had never been to college. They knew neither Greek nor Latin. Hadas saw that if they were to be taught at all they must be taught in translation. His senior colleagues accused him of betraying his trust. He obtained permission to teach Euripides in translation as an extra course without additional salary. He taught the same plays in two classes—one in Greek and one in English—but gave the same final examination to both. Those who read the plays in Greek flunked the examination. He showed both sets of papers to his senior colleagues. Thereafter, he taught at least two courses a year in translation.

After 1945 Hadas found Jewish orthodoxy embarrassing and dogmatic, Christianity pretentious and hypocritical. He called his religion the Religion of Hellenism and he found its apostle and his closest spiritual companion in Plutarch. He stated his creed in an address delivered on Mt. Parnassus on 6 Nov. 1945 and published in the *South Atlantic Quarterly* 46 (Jan. 1947): 84-92. In appearance an article, it is probably his most revealing autobiographical statement, a *confessio fidei*. In such Hellenism Hadas sought the moral salvation of his own age. To students he was a revered figure but always accessible. To colleagues he was an urbane despot, an aristocratic liberal, erudite, elegant, and always ironic. He began his autobiographical essay: "I am a teacher. Except for wars and holidays I have never been out of the sound of a school bell. I have written books and given public lectures, but these I have regarded as part of my teaching. The life I lead is the most agreeable I can imagine." He died shortly after his retirement from Columbia. There was nothing left to live for.

The Role of Friedrich Althoff in the Professorial Appointments of Ulrich von Wilamowitz-Moellendorff

I. Introduction

Alpha men choose alpha men. Beta men choose gamma men. That is the algebra of appointments. Everything I have studied and everything I have experienced has convinced me that this adage is true. Only exceptionally are institutes or faculties competent or willing to choose the best candidate available. Regularly factors that militate against excellence prevail. Ulrich von Wilamowitz-Moellendorff (1848-1931) by universal consent is the greatest Hellenist of modern times, comparable only to his father-in-law in Roman history, Theodor Mommsen. His publications fill some eighty volumes. His students include the leading classicists of the twentieth century. His influence on subsequent work in the field of ancient studies is incalculable.[1] Attention must also be drawn to the more important role played by classical philology at universities during his professional career (1874-1921) than today. Classics was central not marginal.

During his lifetime Wilamowitz held three ordinary professorships: Greifswald (1876-1883); Göttingen (1883-1897); Berlin (1897-1921). I shall treat all three appointments on the basis of all evidence available to me. The moral of my tale will be clear. Althoff played the decisive role in the last two appointments. Wilamowitz entered the *Weltbühne* not thanks to his Prussian colleagues, those men most competent to judge his titanic achievement; rather in spite of them and because of Althoff's uncompromising commitment to excellence.

II. The Greifswald Call (December 1875)

Wilamowitz was briefly Privatdozent at 'Berlin (autumn 1874 until Easter 1876). The *venia legendi* followed h.s successful habilitation. We are informed of his work there in his *Erinnerungen* and by the fortunate find of

---

[1] The best introduction to the man and his work is the essays in *Wilamowitz nach 50 Jahren*, edited by William M. Calder III, Hellmut Flashar, and Theodor Lindken (Darmstadt 1985). For a brief, authoritative, recent biography see Robert L. Fowler, "Ulrich von Wilamowitz-Moellendorff 22 December 1848—25 September 1931," *Classical Scholarship: A Biographical Encyclopedia*, edited by Ward W. Briggs and William M. Calder III (New York/London 1990) 489-522 and for a bibliography of his writings and writings about him see *Ulrich von Wilamowitz-Moellendorff Bibliography 1867-1990*, revised and expanded after Friedrich Freiherr Hiller von Gaetringen and Günther Klaffenbach by Michael Armstrong, Wolfgang Buchwald (†), William M. Calder III (Hildesheim 1991).

notes taken during a seminar by one of his first students.[2] In 1875 he was offered an Extraordinariat at Breslau, which he declined. On 22 December 1875 by his own testimony he received at his father's estate in Markowitz the offer of an Ordinariat at Greifswald. On 21 December during his last hours in Berlin he writes to Wilhelm Henzen (1816-1887) in Rome, mentor and revered friend. In a letter bubbling with academic gossip there is not one word on Greifswald. The call would come the next day, if we believe him, and as a complete surprise. He accepted and on 15 January 1876 Kaiser Wilhelm signed his patent.[3]

In fact much had been going on about which the 26 year old Wilamowitz was unaware. Th. Mommsen was rector of the Friedrich-Wilhelms-Universität 1874-1875. On 15th May 1875 Wilamowitz had prudently dedicated his Habilitationschrift, although on a Greek subject, to the Roman historian.[4] That Althoff paid attention to what Mommsen said is known. 5 November 1875 a request for an Extraordinariat in classical philology at Berlin was forwarded to the Minister der Geistlichen, Unterrichts- und Medicinal-Angelegenheiten, Ritter hoher Orden, Dr. Falk. I have no evidence that Wilamowitz ever in his life knew of this request. The letter is signed Nitzsch and Zeller, that is the historian, Karl Wilhelm Nitzsch (1818-1880) and the historian of ancient philosophy, Eduard Zeller (1814-1908).[5] The candidate after a tactful reference to the Nietzsche affair is praised in the highest terms:[6]

> Abgesehen von einzelnen kleineren polemischen Aufsätzen war seine erste größere philologische Arbeit eine Ausführung seiner Habilitationschrift, die unter dem Titel Analecta Euripidea im vorigen Jahre[7] erschien. Dieses Buch hat sofort in dem weiten Kreis aller Fachgenossen die Aufmerksamkeit und das Interesse auf diese frische und selten gebildete Wissenschaftliche Kraft gelenkt. Wir können zum Beweis dafür erwähnen, daß eine Reihe von Facultäten bei betreffenden

---

[2] See Ulrich von Wilamowitz-Moellendorff, *Erinnerungen 1848-1914*[2] (Leipzig 1929) 170-77. One may add that the *Probevorlesung* was 30 July 1874 and the *Antrittsvorlesung* 7 August 1874. See also Ernst Vogt, "Ein Neues Zeugnis zur Lehrtätigkeit des Jungen Wilamowitz," *Festschrift für Franz Egermann zu Seinem 80. Geburtstag am 13. Februar 1985*, edited by Werner Suerbaum and Friedrich Maier (Munich 1985) 171-80.

[3] *Erinnerungen*[2], 177. No information on the Greifswald call is preserved in *Briefe Mommsen*. The unpublished letter to Henzen is in the archives of the DAI Rome. If Wilamowitz had known of the Greifswald appointment he would certainly have alluded indirectly to it.

[4] Ulrich von Wilamowitz-Moellendorff, *Analecta Euripidea* (Berlin 1875) iii-iv. Haupt was dead and Wilamowitz had no respect for either Kirchhoff or Vahlen. We shall see how they repaid the slight in 1897 by resisting his Berlin call.

[5] For Wilamowitz and Zeller, whom he had early admired, see William M. Calder III, "Wilamowitz to Zeller: Two Letters," *GRBS* 19 (1978) 177-84 (= *Antiqua* 23 [Naples 1983] 297-304, 310).

[6] Zentrales Staatsarchiv Merseburg Rep. 76 Va Sek. 2 No. 51 vol. VI. 195 A-196. I am grateful to the kindness of the Merseburg staff for allowing copies and to Emeritus Professor Dr. Ulrich K. Goldsmith (University of Colorado at Boulder) for aid in transcribing them.

[7] An error. It had only appeared several months before.

Vacanzen der letzten Zeit nur durch die Rücksicht auf die Jugend des gennanten verhindert wurde, ihn für denselben in Vorschlag zu bringen. Das Anerbieten einer außerordentlichen Professur an der Universität Breslau hat er, wie bekannt sein wird, abgelehnt, da er für die Förderung seiner Gesamtstudien und seiner einzelnen speciellen Arbeiten auf einen noch längeren Aufenthalt in Berlin ein besonderes Gewicht legt.

The document bears an unexpected marginal note:[8]

> Erledigt durch die in Aussicht genommene Ernennung des v. Wila-
> mowitz zum ordentl. Professor in Greifswald, von welcher seiner Zeit
> auch der hies. philosoph. Facultät Kenntniß zu geben sein wird.
> daher
>   zu den Acten.
> Berlin 5/1 76
>   F. A.

The initials mislead. Althoff was not yet in Berlin. There was no other official with these initials. The scholium is dated 5 January 1876. The petition arrived at the Ministry on 8 November 1875. What happened at Greifswald?

The archivist of the Ernst-Moritz-Arndt-Universität Greifswald kindly wrote me 7 April 1986 the following:

> Nach der Versetzung von Prof. Dr. Hiller[9] von Greifswald nach Halle wandte sich die Philosophische Fakultät unserer Universität unter dem 15. 12. 1875 an den zuständigen Minister mit einer Vorschlags-liste, die drei Namen enthielt: 1) Oberlehrer Dr. von Bamberg,[10] Berlin, 2) Gymnasialdirektor und Professor Dr. Lipsius[11] in Leipzig und 3) Privatdozent Dr. von Wilamowitz-Moellendorff, Berlin.

Über diesen heißt es im letzten Absatz dieses Schreibens:

> Der dritte Gelehrte, den wir Ew. Excellenz nennen, Dr. von Wila-
> mowitz, steht freilich noch in einem sehr jugendlichen Alter: durch
> seine ungewöhnliche Begabung, sein glänzendes Lehrtalent, seine
> bedeutenden literarischen Leistungen hat er sich aber so rasch und
> unbestritten eine hervorragende Stellung in der Gelehrtenwelt

---

[8] Sig. vol. VI. 195 (see *supra.* n. 6).

[9] For Eduard Hiller (1844-1891) see C. Haeberlin, *BiogJahr* 14 (1891) 83-113 and *Berufungspolitik innerhalb der Altertumswissenschaft im wilhelminischen Preußen: Die Briefe Ulrich von Wilamowitz-Moellendorffs an Friedrich Althoff (1883-1908)*, edited by William M. Calder III and Alexander Košenina (Frankfurt am Main 1989) 16f., 67, 70, 73 henceforth cited *Berufungspolitik.*

[10] Eduard Heinrich Albert von Bamberg (b. 1844) became schoolmaster in Eberswalde. His publications are negligible and his name is forgotten.

[11] For Justus Hermann Lipsius (1834-1920) see Franz Poland, *BiogJahr* 202 (1924: published 1925) 1-36. He was a distinguished scholar in Greek law whose writings remain authoritative.

erworben, daß wir uns nur freuen können, wenn er zu uns berufen würde, selbst auf die nahe liegende Gefahr hin, daß seinem Wirken unter uns nicht längere Dauer wie der Thätigkeit seiner beiden Vorgänger beschieden sein sollte" (Phil. Fak. Nr. 26, S. 258/259).

In ihrem Begleitschreiben bei der Übersendung dieser Liste an den Minister vom 20. 12. 1875 schreiben die Kuratoren:

"...Seit dem Herbst 1838 sind zur zweiten Professur dieses Faches 11 Personen angestellt worden...," sie nennen dann die Namen, klagen über den häufigen Wechsel und fahren dann fort: "...so ist jedoch ein so häufiger und rascher Wechsel in der Besetzung der Professuren ein Übelstand, unter welchem das Studium unausbleiblich leidet. Wir glauben daher Ew. Excellenz ehrerbietigst bitten zu müssen, zur Wiederbesetzung der erledigten Professur Hoch ihre Wahl auf einen Gelehrten richten zu wollen, dessen Wirksamkeit eine längere Dauer in Aussicht stellt. Diesen Zweck scheint uns in erster Linie Professor Lipsius und in zweiter Oberlehrer Dr. von Bamberg, der Dr. v. Wilamowitz am wenigsten unter den Vorgeschlagenen zu entsprechen" (Pers.-Akte 191, v. Wilamowitz-Moellendorff).

Wilamowitz' excellence boded a short stay at Greifswald. Hence he is third. His youth did not disqualify him. Bamberg and Hiller were only four years older than he. Hiller had known him in Bonn.[12] He may well have influenced the faculty. I do not know that Mommsen had a man at Greifswald. Fear that Wilamowitz would quickly leave was unfounded. He taught seven years at Greifswald, "in spite of or rather because of his success and production," as Ed. Schwartz would bitterly remark.[13] 53 years after the event Wilamowitz recorded that "die entscheidende Nachricht, daß ich als Ordinarius nach Greifswald berufen würde,"[14] reached him at Markowitz on 22 December 1875, sc. his twenty-seventh birthday. A letter dated Markowitz, 1 January 1876 of Wilamowitz to *Hochverehrender Herr Geheimrath* survives, presumably to Falk. Wilamowitz writes:[15]

Auf die am gestrigen Tage von Ihnen in betreff der Greifswalder Professur an mich gerichtete Anfrage beehre ich mich ganz ergebenst zu erwidern, dass ich keine Bedenken trage, dem Antrage Folge zu leisten,

---

[12] For Wilamowitz' critical view of Hiller see *Erinnerungen*[2], 95, 239. A brief but friendly correspondence survives.

[13] Eduard Schwartz, *Gesammelte Schriften* I: *Vergangene Gegenwärtigkeiten* (Berlin 1938) 372: "Trotz diesen Erfolgen, trotz—man kann auch sagen, wegen—seiner Produktion, die stets Aufsehen erregte, dauerte der Greifswalder Anfang länger, als zu erwarten war." For classics at Greifswald see Jürgen Kroymann, "Geschichte der Klassischen Philologie an der Universität Greifswald," *Festschrift zur 500-Jahrfeier der Universität Greifswald 17. IV. 1956*, edited by Wilhelm Braun *et al.*, II (Greifswald 1956) 120-35; for Wilamowitz: 132-35.

[14] *Erinnerungen*[2], 177.

[15] Sig, 208, a typed copy of the original is preserved in Darmstadt (Verf. v. 26, Okt. 1912 B, Nr 1659 U1. U1K).

denn mit der Sammlung der Hauptlisten [*sic*] kleinere Schriften wird es mir möglich sein bis Ostern wenigstens im Manuscript zum Abschlusse zu kommen,[16] und persönliche Neigungen müssen zurücktreten: muss es doch selbst das etwas karge Gefühl mit einer im gleichen Masse ehrenvollen wie schwerwiegenden Verantwortung bekannt zu werden.

Gestatten Sie mir, hochzuverehrender Herr Geheimrath, neben dem lebhaften Danke für das in mich gesetzte Vertrauen und dem entschiedenen Vorsatze diesem so weit meine Kräfte reichen zu entsprechen auch die ausgezeichnetste Hochachtung und vollste Verehrung auszusprechen in welcher ich die Ehre habe zu zeichnen als Ihr

ganz ergebenster
Ulrich v. Wilamowitz-Moellendorff

The official invitation to Greifswald arrived 31 December 1875 at Markowitz. Wilamowitz replied the next day. There is no hesitation nor does he enquire whether his colleagues wanted him. In 1883 he will be more circumspect.

III. The Göttingen Call (July 1883)

Eduard Hiller was only two semesters at Greifswald and today is forgotten. His successor, the greatest Hellenist of modern times, was seven years there. Why? Wilamowitz was a victim of his own integrity. His aristocratic birth, no matter how much he might wish to deny it, gave him a self-confidence that the sons of pastors and village schoolmasters lacked. This meant that in his writings he was fearless in the pursuit of truth, intolerant of pretension, sloth and fraud, and willing, if need be, to gain implacable enemies in high places. The myth is that Göttingen rescued Wilamowitz from provincial Greifswald and placed him on the *Weltbühne*. The facts are otherwise.

Meanwhile Althoff was there. The evidence available to me is not complete (I have never seen the Althoff-Th. Mommsen correspondence) but even so is revealing. Hermann Sauppe (1809-1893) is regularly credited with initiating the call to Göttingen with a letter to Wilamowitz dated ca. 18 April 1883. This is the version Wilamowitz himself provided in 1928:[17] "In Frühjahr 1883 fragte Sauppe bei mir an, ob ich an die Stelle von E. v. Leutsch nach Göttingen kommen wollte." The crucial role of Sauppe is insured by the fact that Wilamowitz named his second son, born in Göttingen, Hermann after Sauppe. Sauppe's inquiry is lost but I found and

---

[16] *Maurici Hauptii opuscula* I (Leipzig 1875): vol. II (Leipzig 1876). The preface, notes and addenda are by Wilamowitz: for the difficulty of the task, imposed upon him by Mommsen, see *Erinnerungen*[2], 176.

[17] *Erinnerungen*[2], 197.

published in 1985 Wilamowitz' reply.[18] The reply is dated Greifswald 20 April 1883. Wilamowitz could not be sure how much Sauppe knew. It was better to play safe. Wilamowitz refers to a recent visit to Althoff in Berlin. He writes:[19]

> ich war anfang dieses monats in Berlin, und Geh. r. Althoff bestellete mich zu sich, zunächst einer anderen sache wegen; dabei fragte er mich rundweg, was ich selbst wünschte, auch Göttingen streiffend, was für mein urteil gänzlich außerhalb des bereiches der möglichkeit lag. ich habe ihm da zwar nicht verhelt, was ja auch am tage liegt, daß Greifswald meinen persönlichsten wünschen freilich in keiner weise genüge, daß ich es eher im intereße der sache für angezeigt hielte, mich vor der hand hier zu laßen. ich habe das als meinen wunsch bezeichnet, und nur ein, allerdings sehr wesentliches motiv dieses wunsches ist durch Ihren brief beseitigt. ich glaubte in Berlin betonen zu sollen, daß ich nur an einen ort gienge, wo meine specialcollegen selbst mich haben wollten.

Althoff invited Wilamowitz to his Berlin office in early April 1883. At first he spoke about another matter. This probably was whether Wilamowitz would be willing to succeed Karl Wilhelm Nitzsch (1818-1880) as ancient historian in Berlin. Wilamowitz was unwilling and Ulrich Köhler (1838-1903) gained the post. Althoff then unexpectedly questioned him indirectly about Göttingen. Wilamowitz would only go if his closest colleagues wanted him. About a week later the outstanding closest colleague at Göttingen writes Wilamowitz that he did want him. We know now that Althoff not Sauppe had initiated the matter.

Wilamowitz' father-in-law could not take a visible part in the negotiations. Not only because of nepotism but Mommsen had deadly enemies both at Göttingen and at Berlin. Sauppe, however, had long been a friend of Mommsen.[20] The conflict with Jahn had damaged but not destroyed their friendship. We know that until *der Fall Spahn* Mommsen was a trusted adviser of Althoff. My guess is that Mommsen learned from Althoff and Wilamowitz of the chance for a chair at Göttingen and, possibly at the

---

[18] William M. Calder III, "Ulrich von Wilamowitz-Moellendorff to Hermann Sauppe: Two Unpublished Letters," *Philologus* 129 (1985) 286-98: esp. 294-98 (= *Further Letters*, 223-35).

[19] *Ibid.*, 296. For Wilamowitz' admission that Mommsen had seriously tried to convince him to take the post that went to Köhler see *Erinnerungen*[2], 239.

[20] For Mommsen's long friendship with Sauppe see Lothar Wickert, *Theodor Mommsen Eine Biographie* IV *Grösse und Grenzen* (Frankfurt am Main 1980) 8-9. Mommsen through Henzen had asked Sauppe in 1868 to arrange his appointment in Göttingen. The affair with Jahn had shaken the friendship but not destroyed it and now Jahn was long dead. For the Bonn "Philologenkrieg" (Jahn against Ritschl concerning the appointment of Sauppe) see Paul Egon Hübringer, "Heinrich v. Sybel und der Bonner Philologenkrieg," *HistJahrbuch* 83 (1964) 162-216.

instigation of Althoff, intervened with Sauppe, who was himself already well-disposed to Wilamowitz.[21] Certainly in a letter of 22 May 1883 to his brother Tycho, Th. Mommsen is fully informed on the negotiations.[22]

With Althoff, Mommsen, and Sauppe for him, the rest ought to have been easy. But as Wilamowitz laconically observed:[23] "Der offizielle Ruf ließ bis Ende Juli auf sich warten..." What delayed more than three months the appointment of the greatest Hellenist in Prussia to the chair most obviously fit for him in a university that needed him? The answer is two men, one a great but unbalanced scholar: the other a *Null*.

Paul de Lagarde (1827-1891) was a brilliant Old Testament scholar and one of the most rabid and influential antisemites of the nineteenth century.[24] Later he became the most embarrassing friend whom Wilamowitz ever had, but in April 1883 Wilamowitz' father-in-law was among his most hated enemies. Mommsen reciprocated the hatred. This was particularly unfortunate in 1883 because Lagarde was Dean of the Philosophical Faculty. There were several reasons why he detested Mommsen. Most obvious was politics. Mommsen was irresponsibly and dangerously liberal. Bismarck's libel suit against him in 1882 had been widely publicized. There was a more personal reason. On 12 July 1880 through Mommsen's carelessness fire had destroyed the library in his home in Charlottenburg. Several ancient manuscripts on loan to Mommsen from European and English libraries were burnt up and as a result of the loss the libraries refused to lend original manuscripts to scholars. This was a disaster for Lagarde's work on the *Septuaginta*. In short the dean was ready to keep Mommsen's son-in-law, a Junker who had renounced his class and married the daughter of a bourgeois liberal in a wedding boycotted by all his family, out of Göttingen if asked.

---

[21] See my remarks at *Philologus* 129 (1985) 294 n. 72.

[22] Published at Wickert, *Mommsen* IV. 252. For Althoff's trust in Mommsen see Arnold Sachse, *Friedrich Althoff und sein Werk* (Berlin 1926) 181: "Auf Mommsens Urteil legte Althoff großen Wert." This made Mommsen's betrayal in the *Fall Spahn* all the more painful both for Althoff and for Wilamowitz.

[23] *Erinnerungen*[2], 197.

[24] The best modern discussion of Lagarde is Fritz Stern, *The Politics of Cultural Dispair: a Study in the Rise of the Germanic Ideology* (Berkeley/Los Angeles/London 1961: repr. 1974) 3-94. Objective and informative is Robert W. Lougee, *Paul de Lagarde 1827-1891: A Study of Radical Conservatism in Germany* (Cambridge, MA 1962). For what follows see my "Wilamowitz' Call to Göttingen: Paul de Lagarde to Friedrich Althoff on Wilamowitz-Moellendorff," *Studi italiani di filologia classica* NS 3, 3 (1985) 136-60 (henceforth cited *SIFC*). This paper was forbidden publication in a prominent West German scholarly (!) journal on the grounds that "es geht gegen die Ehre Göttingens." I then published it in Italy. In a recent volume devoted to the history of classical philology at Göttingen the editor includes no chapter on Wilamowitz. One might compare a history of Physics at Berlin without Einstein. The official explanation is that too much has already been written about him. I should suppose rather a reluctance to state in a jubilee volume that if it had been up to Göttingen their greatest classical scholar would never have been hired.

He was asked by a loser, the second rate, embittered brother, brother-in-law and colleague of greater men. Karl Dilthey (1839-1907) was a failure as philologist and archaeologist.[25] At the most he had written a competent doctoral dissertation. Dilthey had left Zürich for Göttingen in 1877 and languished there under the shadow of Sauppe. To further languish under the shadow of one eleven years younger than he would be intolerable. Further since 1869 Dilthey had been a friend of Erwin Rohde, the defender of Nietzsche and victim of Wilamowitz. He had habilitated under his sister's husband, Hermann Usener, whose view of Wilamowitz was at best problematical.

Althoff had been in Göttingen in early April and called on Lagarde who was not at home. Lagarde wrote him on 4 April 1883:[26]

> In den Akten des Ministeriums beruht [sic] eine von mir und Genossen zu Gunsten des Professors Alfred Schöne in Paris gemachte Eingabe. Ich halte diesen Gelehrten für sehr geeignet, an die Stelle des Herrn von Leutsch zu treten, wie ich andrerseits überzeugt bin, daß von Wilamowitz, der einzige, auf den wir greifen könnten, da Hartel aus Wien nicht weggelassen werden wird, der rechte Mann für uns aus einem ganz bestimmten Grunde doch nicht ist.

Lagarde has the audacity to write Althoff that for a particular reason which he will not reveal he prefers the nonentity, Alfred Schöne (1836-1918).[27] Schöne had one great virtue which Wilamowitz notoriously lacked. He was a threat to no one on campus. There were also reasons why de Lagarde could count on the loyalty of Schöne.

The files concerning Wilamowitz' call to Göttingen in 1883 are preserved in the University Archives there. The decisive document is a further letter of de Lagarde, dated 21 May 1883 (the day before Th. Mommsen's letter to his brother Tycho), to von Gossler. The list de Lagarde submitted as Dean of the Philosophical Faculty is:

1) Wilhelm Ritter von Hartel (1839-1907)[28]

---

[25] For Dilthey's hostility to Wilamowitz see my discussion at *SIFC* NS 3, 3 (1985) 147ff. and *Berufungspolitik*, 184 *sub nomine*, Dilthey, K. Wilamowitz' correspondence with Althoff about him reveals how much time an incompetent extorts from great men. I simply summarize here what I said there.

[26] Text with notes at *SIFC* NS 3, 3 (1985) 145-46.

[27] For the standard biography of Schöne, an amiable dilettante and misfit, brother of the famous Museologer, see Rudolf Ehwald, *BiogJahr* 181 (1919) 87-112 and my remarks at *SIFC* NS 3, 3 (1985) 145ff. This attempt to appoint Schöne is a prime example of the inability of faculties to govern themselves.

[28] For Wilhelm von Hartel see *SIFC* NS 3, 3 (1985) 145 n. 61 to which add S. Frankfurter, *Wilhelm von Hartel, Sein Leben und Werk zur Enthüllung des Denkmales in der Universität am 9. Juni 1912* (Wien/Leipzig 1912). The volume is of great value because it contains the correspondence between Althoff and Hartel on the matter (28-29, 93-99). For Hartel's encouragement of modern art and his support of a professorship for Sigmund Freud see Carl E. Schorske, *Fin-de-Siècle Vienna: Politics and Culture* (New York 1981) 237-45.

2) Rudolf Schoell (1844-1893)[29]
3) Ulrich von Wilamowitz-Moellendorff.

Schöne had been vetoed by Althoff. The Latinist Schoell, friendly to the Ritschl group, was inserted and Wilamowitz retained third place. De Lagarde's assessment of Wilamowitz is unexpectedly fair. Was he writing what he had learned to know that Althoff wanted to hear? He writes:[30]

> Er besitzt eine für sein jugendliches Alter höchst ausgedehnte Gelehrsamkeit und eine Energie der Forschung, die überall den Kern der Sache zu erfassen bemüht ist, in kühner Verbindung von Thatsachen und kecken Folgerungen nicht selten das Maß überschreitet, aber immer durch Scharfsinn und lebensvolle Behandlung fesselt und anregt...Aber besondere Hervorhebung verdient bei ihm die ausgezeichnete Art u. Weise, in welcher er die Studierenden zu selbstständiger Forschung anzuregen, mit Liebe zu angestrengter Tätigkeit zu erfüllen und ihre Studien mit Hingebung zu leiten versteht, wie dies alle, die seine Wirksamkeit zu beobachten Gelegenheit haben, bezeugen und eine Anzahl von Promotionsschriften zeigt, die, seit er in Greifswald ist, dort erschienen sind. Die Gegenstände seiner Vorlesungen sind Homer, Pindar, Euripides, Aristophanes, Thukydides, Catull, Ovidius; griechische Dialekte, Quellenkunde der griechischen Geschichte, grammatische Literatur der Griechen.

The next evidence we have is Althoff's letter of 5 June 1883 to Hartel, two letters of Hartel to Althoff (8 June 1883 and 15 June 1883) and a curt reply of Althoff to Hartel, acknowledging his decline of the post and dated Berlin, 18 June 1883. De Lagarde's confidence (4 April 1883) that Hartel would not leave Vienna seems to reflect Dilthey and Sauppe.[31] He was not offered the Göttingen post by Althoff until 5 June 1883. I do not know why there was a two-month delay. An obvious explanation is that Althoff was against the appointment but was pressured by someone, probably Hermann Bonitz

---

[29] For Rudolf Schoell's influence on Wilamowitz see William M. Calder III, *Nietzsche-Studien* 12 (1983) 220-21. Schoell in 1872 for selfish reasons convinced Wilamowitz to review Friedrich Nietzsche's *Geburt der Tragödie*. Schoell must have been approached for this position. See Fr. Schoell, *BiogJahr* 20 (1897) 36:

> Schon in vorhergehenden Jahre [1883] war R. in Göttingen vorgeschlagen und hatte ausgesprochene Neigung, dahin zu gehen. Die Verhandlungen wurden aber in einer für die damalige und dermalige Praxis charakteristischen Weise so geführt, daß R. sich in Strassburg halten ließ.

Apparently Althoff offered him the post in a way that would cause him to decline it. Easter 1885 he went to Munich, that is, he left Prussia and Althoff.

[30] The text was first published at *SIFC* NS 3, 3 (1985) 160 n. 149.

[31] See Karl Dilthey to Hartel 27 June 1883 (Frankfurter, 98): "...mein College Sauppe... und ich selber, schon von Haus aus mit nicht allzu großem Vertrauen auf Verwirklichung <haben> Sie beim Ministerium vorgeschlagen, so mußten wir Ihre Ablehnung vollends voraussehen..."

(1814-1888) with whose name he closes the letter, to invite Hartel. His curt second letter reveals his irritation. The invitation reflects Althoff's international niveau:[32]

> Wir fassen unsere Aufgabe vor allem so auf, daß wir zunächt der Wissenschaft im allgemeinen, ohne alle Rücksicht auf staatliche Grenzen, zu dienen haben. Und von diesem Standpunkte aus betrachten wir Sie, den Führer der klassischen Philologie in Österreich, als einen unserer liebsten und besten Mitarbeiter, obwohl wir Sie nicht als den unserigen im engeren Sinne betrachten dürfen. Das war unsere *ratio dubitandi.*

Hartel replied 8 June expressing interest and requesting before his decision to visit Göttingen 16-18 June. He included a detailed account of his Austrian income. Probably on the same day he wrote the great Austrian Germanist Wilhelm Scherer (1841-1886), since 1877 professor at Berlin and a close friend from student days, for advice. Scherer in his reply of 11 June had little good to say of provincial Göttingen ("Wie weit man sich von der dummen Fressgesellschaft ausschließen kann, weiß ich nicht."). He recalls the stifling atmosphere of Strassburg after Vienna.[33] His remarks would be decisive.

We learn "daß Hartel in Göttingen ein Jahresgehalt von 9000 Mark geboten wurde und daß sich seine fixen Gesamtbezüge auf mehr als 12000 Mark belaufen hätten."[34] The sum is immense. On 15 June 1883 Hartel wrote Althoff. He would not visit Göttingen. He declined the flattering offer not on grounds of stipend but because of his committment to Austrian gymnasial education and because after 21 years in Vienna his family could not survive "in einer kleinen Stadt." Althoff replies in seven lines on 18 June wishing him success "in der schönen Kaiserstadt Wien." On 16 June the Austrians raised Hartel's salary by 800fl. Schoell seems to have been asked with the assumption that he would refuse. By 30 July Wilamowitz had received a telegram from Althoff and informed the Greifswald dean of his intent to resign.[35] That is the end of it.

---

[32] Cited from Frankfurter, 28.

[33] The letter is at Frankfurter, 95-96.

[34] So Frankfurter, *Hartel*, 97 n. His source is "Aus dem Vortrag des Ministers Freiherrn von Conrad vom 14. V. 1883." This is an extraordinary high salary and, if accurate, proves how eager the Prussians were to win the Austrian. He was the son of a linenweaver but had been knighted in 1882 and in 1900 became Austrian Minister of Education. He defended Arthur Schnitzler and Sigmund Freud against antisemitism and opened university study in Austria to women. I am not so certain now as I was in 1985 that "He could only have been asked *honoris causa.*" Correct *SIFC* NS 3, 3 (1985) 145 n. 61.

[35] See Wilamowitz' letter to Althoff of 30 July 1883 edited with commentary at *Berufungspolitik*, 1-2. If further correspondence between Wilamowitz and Althoff survives I have not seen it. For the contact with Schöll see *supra.* n. 29.

IV. The Berlin Call (21 August 1896)

We are best informed on the Berlin call. The four principal sources are all published. They are Wilamowitz, *Erinnerungen*, the *Briefe Althoff, Briefe Diels* and *Briefe Mommsen*.[36] The brief account in *Erinnerungen* is useless and the Mommsen letters have been heavily censored or omitted so as to be of almost no value. There are literally no letters between 14 December 1895 and 27 October 1896. 1935 was too close to 1895. Further a daughter and son-in-law are not the best editors. The intrigues resorted to by Mommsen and Wilamowitz ought not to be made public. Here I need only summarize what occurred. For details the documents are easily consulted and do not require republication here.

Althoff wanted Wilamowitz in Berlin because of the imminent reform of the Prussian Gymnasium.[37] Wilamowitz was the best possible defender of the traditional humanistic gymnasium. Althoff had been impressed by the famous dedication of *Reden und Vorträge*. There had been political repercussions.[38] He had two powerful allies, Wilamowitz' father-in-law Theodor Mommsen and his lifelong friend from student years in Bonn, Hermann Diels (1848-1922).[39] Mommsen's support was always liable to incur opposition as well as do good. Mommsen too was at a disadvantage in supporting a close relative. He could only work behind the scenes. Diels carried relatively little weight in university politics. He was more an Academy man. Three powerful senior colleagues opposed the appointment: Ernst Curtius (1814-1896), Adolf Kirchhoff (1826-1908) and Johannes Vahlen (1830-1911). Their reason was one calculated to infuriate Althoff, *Konkurrenzfurcht*.[40]

[36] See Wilamowitz, *Erinnerungen*[2], 239; Wilamowitz' letters to Althoff (= *Berufungspolitik*, 112-121 [six letters 16 November 1895 to 15 August 1896]); for the Diels-Wilamowitz letters see Maximilian Braun, William M. Calder III, and Dietrich Ehlers, *"Lieber Prinz:" Der Briefwechsel zwischen Hermann Diels und Ulrich von Wilamowitz-Moellendorff (1869-1921)* (Hildesheim 1995) 104-69. See further *Mommsen und Wilamowitz Briefwechsel 1872-1905* edited by Friedrich and Dorothea Hiller von Gaertringen (Berlin 1935) 510-16 (ten months of letters are "lost" and only highly censored bits of the rest are published: see *Berufungspolitik*, 112 n. 475). [A new, annotated edition of the Mommsen-Wilamowitz letters with Wilamowitz' uncensored texts is being prepared by W.M. Calder and Robert Kirstein.]

[37] The authoritative treatment, based on archival material, is James C. Albisetti, *Secondary School Reform in Imperial Germany* (Princeton 1983).

[38] See Sachse, *Althoff*, 326: "Die Anerkennung der Bedeutung der Gymnasiallehre war Wasser auf Althoffs Mühle."

[39] The standard life is Otto Kern, *Hermann Diels und Carl Robert. Ein biographischer Versuch* (Leipzig 1927) and recently Eckart E. Schütrumpf, "Hermann Diels 18 May 1848— 4 June 1922," *Biographical Encyclopedia*, 52-60, to which add a reference to Hildebrecht Hommel, "Berliner Erinnerungen 1920-21 Hermann Diels zum Gedächtnis," *Symbola* II (Hildesheim 1988) 442-56. Of greatest value is D. Ehlers (ed.), *Hermann Diels, Hermann Usener, Eduard Zeller: Briefwechsel* 2 vols. (Berlin 1992).

[40] See Bernhard vom Brocke, *Das System Althoff*, 83: "Wenn er [Althoff] den Eindruck hatte, daß in einer Fakultät Konkurrenzfurcht oder verwandschaftliche Beziehungen und Cliquenwirtschaft den Berufungsvorschlag bestimmt hatten, konnte er sehr hart sein." Here it was precisely *Konkurrenzfurcht*.

Since his student days Wilamowitz had only contempt for Ernst Curtius. He was a shallow moralist whose lectures had nothing to do with scholarship. He often said that Curtius' only book worth reading was his *Peloponnesos* (1851/52).[41] In *Aus Kydathen* (1880), without mentioning his name Wilamowitz repeatedly corrected Curtius, whose anger is expressed in letters to his brother Georg at Leipzig. Ever the *enfant terrible* Wilamowitz in 1893 as an eightieth birthday present delivered the epitaph for Curtius' *Griechische Geschichte*.[42]

> es ist ein werk der isokrateischen stilrichtung, welche die geschichte unter die epideiktische beredsamkeit zählt, bestimmt das edle zu loben, das schlechte zu tadeln, und zu dieser panegyrischen haltung gesellt sich ein weicher oft elegischer ton, die leise trauer um die verlorene schönheit.

Obviously Curtius would do everything to keep Wilamowitz from Berlin. Althoff found an unexpected ally. Death removed Curtius 11 July 1896 and freed the chair that Wilamowitz would fill.

Wilamowitz' aversion to Kirchhoff stems from his student days and was intensified because he often published in Kirchhoff's fields (epigraphy and Homer). As a student he disliked him.[43] He disapproved his personal life.[44] He was later to be distressed by the incompetence with which Kirchhoff directed *Inscriptiones Graecae* for the Academy.[45] He could never forgive Kirchhoff's public admission that he was second rate.[46] On the other hand he was too honest not to value his Homeric work.[47] The reluctance that Kirchhoff revealed toward Wilamowitz' appointment grew from his fear of Mommsen. Wilamowitz would be a loyal and powerful ally of his father-in-law both in the University and the Academy. Hence the false letter. Kirchhoff must be convinced that Mommsen had no hand in the *Ruf*.

---

[41] See Ulrich von Wilamowitz-Moellendorff, *Geschichte der Philologie*[4] (Leipzig 1959) 69. For Curtius' rage at Wilamowitz because of *Aus Kydathen* see Heinrich Gelzer, *Ausgewählte Kleine Schriften* (Leipzig 1907) 286.

[42] Ulrich von Wilamowitz-Moellendorff, *Aristoteles und Athen* I (Berlin 1893) 377. The whole passage deserves reading.

[43] See *Erinnerungen*[2], 97: "Kirchhoffs Art ertrug ich nicht."

[44] See *Erinnerungen*[2], 165, 174.

[45] See *Erinnerungen*[2], 306 and William M. Calder III and Robert L. Fowler. "The Preserved Letters of Ulrich von Wilamowitz-Moellendorff to Eduard Schwartz: Edited with Introduction and Commentary," *SitzBAkW* Heft 1 (1986) 59-60.

[46] See Ulrich von Wilamowitz-Moellendorff, *Kleine Schriften* VI (Berlin 1972). What Kirchhoff had said publicly was: "gerechtfertigt ist das Gefühl der Wehmut, daß die Heroen uns verlassen und das Zeitalter der Epigonen begonnen hat: ich gehöre zu diesen Epigonen."

[47] See Ulrich von Wilamowitz-Moellendorff, "Homerische Untersuchungen," *Philologische Untersuchungen* 7 (Berlin 1884) 405 and (more generally) *op. cit.* (*supra*. n. 41) 64, where credit is given his history of the alphabet.

Wilamowitz wrote a letter to Diels. Its only purpose was that Kirchhoff
would read it. He summarizes the history of the call in a way he thought
would be welcome to Kirchhoff. Wilamowitz wrote:[48]

> Lieber Diels,
> Du fragst nach der Vorgeschichte meiner Berufung, die für mich immer
> noch lediglich ein Plan des Ministers ist. Es ist mir sehr lieb, Dich von
> dem was ich weiß in Kenntis zu setzen: vermutlich wirst Du manches
> genauer wissen oder beurteilen können.
> Bei mir ist vor Jahren schon wiederholt angefragt worden, ob ich
> nicht in irgend einer Form kommen wollte; es war damals, als ich die
> Professur für griechische Geschichte zu besetzen war. Ich war damals
> gerade nach Strassburg und Heidelberg berufen, hatte auch um hiesiger
> Dinge öfter zu verhandeln, so daß die Gelegenheit sich öfter bot, davon
> anzufangen. Ich habe damals rund und entschieden abgelehnt. Nach
> Andeutungen, die mir später einmal Treitschke gemacht hat, scheint
> mir jetzt, daß Mommsen damals den Plan gefasst oder verfolgt hat; das
> würde mich ja schon allein zur Ablehnung bestimmt haben, aber ich
> übersah das nicht und die sachlichen Rücksichten reichten aus.
> Als ich 1890 den Ruf nach Bonn ausschlug, brachten die Zeitungen
> das Gerücht, ich käme nach Berlin. Das verfolgte mich bis nach Athen
> und so veranlasste ich meinen ältesten Bruder, der im Staatsrat war, den
> Minister Gossler zu befragen, ob das Ministerium an dem Plane und dem
> Gerüchte beteiligt wäre. Die Norddeutsche hat darauf das Gerücht
> officiös desavouirt, und Gossler hat mich beruhigen lassen, zur Zeit
> sollte ich meinem Wunsche gemäß in Göttingen bleiben; es gäbe nur
> Leute, die nicht warten möchten.
> Jetzt spielt die Sache seit 3/4 Jahren, da ich immer gegengehalten
> habe. Ich weiß ganz gewiß, daß es ein Plan aus der Initiative einzig des
> Ministeriums ist, aber allerdings ein ernster Plan. Denn ich sollte
> schon Östern den Minister selbst darüber sprechen, habe das aber
> vermieden, weil ich mich fürchtete, weil mich zu tief einzulassen. Dagegen
> habe ich immer wieder erklärt, daß ich ohne die rückhaltlose Ein-
> willigung der Facultät und vor allen Dingen der Fachcollegen in eine
> wirkliche Verhandlung nicht eintreten könnte. Dass das allererste
> Deine Wünsche für mich gewesen sind und sein werden, weißt Du.
> Mit besten Grüßen
> Dein
> U. v. Wilamowitz

The tactic was a flop and Kirchhoff was only strengthened in his aversion to
Wilamowitz. Diels writes (15 November 1895 [=no. 67]):

> Aber die Erwähnung Mommsens und die wol darauf bezügliche Stelle
> Goßlers ("Leute die nicht warten können") haben seine Vermutung
> bestärkt, daß M. die ganzen Sache aus persönlichen Gründe insceniert

[48] See *Diels-Wilamowitz*, 113-14 (no. 66b 12 November 1895) with commentary.

habe, natürlich bloß um ihn zu ärgern vielleicht auch aus andern persönlichen Gründen. Da das Verhältnis zwischen M. u. K. seit Deiner Hochzeit, wie Du weißt, vollständig vergiftet ist, so scheint es mir, nachdem ich diese Woche täglich mit ihm verhandelte, unmöglich, ihm die Sache harmlos darzustellen.

This proves beyond doubt that the cause of Kirchhoff's opposition to Wilamowitz was his hatred of Mommsen.

Johannes Vahlen seems to have been the least formidable of the three. He had long worked amiably by the side of Mommsen as Sekretär of the Academy. In summer 1897 Vahlen along with Althoff, Diels, Harnack, Scholler and others, signed the subscription for Franz von Lenbach's portrait of Mommsen.[49] Kirchhoff's name was not there. Wilamowitz, as later his student and successor Werner Jaeger,[50] was not unaware of his virtues.[51] But he was pupil of Ritschl, archenemy of the deified Jahn and bore all the marks of the beast. For Theodor Wiegand, Vahlen belonged to the "scheußliche Fachphilologen."[52] He practiced the sort of "Wortphilologie" which Wilamowitz valued but early outgrew for the *Totalitätsideal* of Welcker and Jahn. He could be amused at the public embarrassment of Vahlen.[53] Nonetheless, rather than personal animosity between Wilamowitz and Vahlen there was only the less virulent intellectual disagreement on what was important.

Althoff offered a new chair in classical philology to the University intended for a scholar capable of delivering popular lectures to large audiences of non-specialists.[54] That is he would be no rival to Kirchhoff or Vahlen. Althoff wrote:[55]

Es ist meine Absicht, die philologischen Kräfte pp. durch die Berufung eines Ordinarius zu verstärken, der die Alterthumsstudien in möglichst weitem Umfange beherrscht. Es leitet mich dabei besonders der Wunsch, diese Wissenschaft an der hiesigen Universität auch in Vorlesungen vertreten zu sehen, welche auf weitere Kreise der Studenten-

---

[49] Wickert, *Mommsen* IV. 362.

[50] See Werner Jaeger, *Scripta Minora* I (Rome 1960) xii, xv, xvii.

[51] See Wilamowitz' generous memorial address to the Academy: "Gedächnisrede auf Johannes Vahlen," *Kleine Schriften* VI (Berlin 1972) 53-58.

[52] Carl Watzinger, *Theodor Wiegand Ein deutscher Archäologe 1864-1936* (Munich 1944) 47.

[53] See Henry Rushton Fairclough, *Warming Both Hands* (Stanford 1941) 229.

[54] Wilamowitz later did precisely this. Althoff's innovation is a remarkable anticipation of the modern American lectures on "classics in translation" to audiences of up to 1000 students unable to read Greek or Latin. Such lectures began in 1946 intended for returning veterans. Classics in the U.S.A. today owes its survival to them. Otherwise we should have become Egyptology.

[55] Published at *Berufungspolitik*, 115 n. 485. In fact because of Wilamowitz' intervention the document never reached the faculty. But it was intended for them.

schaft berechnet und dadurch geeignet sind, das Interesse am Alterthum auch bei Fernstehenden neu zu beleben. Die pp. ersache ich, mir geeignete Persönlichkeiten hierfür in Vorschlag zu bringen.

It was the old trick of announcing a general appointment in such a way that only one man in fact could fill the requirements. With the possible exception of Carl Robert at Halle there was no other candidate available. Wilamowitz unexpectedly protested against a chair imposed by the Ministry, all the worse because of the taint of nepotism. The offer was stopped before it reached the faculty. Negotiation ceased until the death of Curtius (11 July 1896). The eldest and most formidable of the three was dead. His chair was vacated and available. There was no need for a new one. How did Althoff handle the problem of Kirchhoff and Vahlen?

The solution was bold and innovative. It drew on an earlier suggestion of Mommsen. There was need of an Institute for the whole of antiquity, philology, ancient history and archaeology. Rather than argue endlessly with two seniores, Althoff founded a new Institute für Altertumskunde for Diels and Wilamowitz. Archaeology did not become part of it until 1912 but ancient history early did. This would become the famous complex institute covering Greek and Latin philology, ancient history, and archaeology. This realized the dream of Welcker and Jahn. Details are available elsewhere.[56]

The tale ended 20 August 1896 at Althoff's office, Unter den Linden 4. Ecke Wilhelmstraße. The contract was signed between Althoff and Wilamowitz and in the presence of Marie von Wilamowitz-Moellendorff, geb. Mommsen.[57] Excluding moving expenses and rent subsidy, the salary was 15,000 gold Marks (ca. 200,000 DM today). Wilamowitz may well have been the highest paid professor in Prussia.[58]

---

[56] See Wolfhart Unte, "Das Institut für Altertumskunde an der Berliner Universität," *Wilamowitz*, 730-734. The old Philological Seminar continued on until the deaths of Kirchhoff and Vahlen.

[57] The documents are published at *Berufungspolitik*, 120-121 n. 502.

[58] I am especially grateful to Dr. Dietrich Ehlers (Akademie der Wissenschaften der DDR) for inclusion of his careful transcriptions of the Wilamowitz-Diels Letters.

The German Reception
of J.G. Frazer:
An Unpublished Document

(with Dietrich Ehlers)

Introduction

Few contemporary texts survive that document the reception of J.G. Frazer's (1854-1941) work, and indeed that of the Cambridge Ritualists, among the Germans. Those letters written by German-speaking scholars in support of Jane Harrison's failed candidacies for the Yates Chair at University College, London in 1888 and 1896 are revealing and are now available.[1] The correspondence between Frazer and Ulrich von Wilamowitz-Moellendorff (1848-1931) has been published.[2] Wilamowitz is sometimes sceptical. We know as well that Hermann Usener during the years 1892-1895 would ask the young Georg Karo to read aloud to him from *The Golden Bough* while simultaneously translating it into German.[3] Dr. Dietrich Ehlers has recently found in the archive of the Akademie der Wissenschaften der DDR a document of first rate importance in this context. Only part of one sentence has been published.[4] The document is the proposal for the election of Frazer to corresponding membership in the Royal Prussian Academy of Sciences at Berlin.

Its author perhaps unexpectedly is Hermann Diels (1848-1922), rather than the author of *Glaube der Hellenen*. There are two reasons: (1) Diels was Sekretär der Akademie and a proposal from his pen had a greater chance for success than one from an ordinary member; (2) because Diels published

---

[1] See William M. Calder III, "Jane Harrison's Failed Candidacies for the Yates Professorship (1888, 1896): What did her Colleagues Think of Her?" in "The Cambridge Ritualists Reconsidered," *ICSSupp.* 2 (Atlanta 1991) 37-59.

[2] See Robert Ackerman and William M. Calder III, "The Correspondence of Ulrich von Wilamowitz-Moellendorff with Sir James George Frazer," *Proceedings of the Cambridge Philological Society* 204 (1978) 31-40 (= Ulrich von Wilamowitz-Moellendorff, "Selected Correspondence 1869-1931" edited by William M. Calder III, *Antiqua* 23 [Naples 1983] 117-26, 307).

[3] See Georg Karo, *Fünfzig Jahre aus dem Leben eines Archäologen* (Baden-Baden 1959) 33-34: "Usener pflegte mich zu bitten, auf ein paar Stunden zu ihm zu kommen und aus englischen oder italienischen Büchern laufend zu übersetzen: besonders Fraser's [sic] *Golden Bough* ist mir in Erinnerungen geblieben. Nach jeder solchen Übersetzung dankte er mir mit dem ihm eigenen Zauber, und ich ging fort, ohne zu gegreifen, daß in diesen Stunden ganz unauffällig reiche Belehrung gegeben hatte...durch die Bemerkungen, mit denen er immer wieder meine Übersetzung unterbrach."

[4] See Conrad Grau, *Die Berliner Akademie der Wissenschaften in der Zeit des Imperialismus, Teil I. Von den neunziger Jahren des 19. Jahrhunderts bis zur Großen Sozialistischen Oktoberrevolution. Studien zur Geschichte der Akademie der Wissenschaften der DDR*, Band 2/1 (Berlin 1975) 246.

little on *Religionsgeschichte* we often forget today that he was a loyal student and lifelong correspondent of Hermann Usener and lectured for nine years on the subject in Berlin.[5] One may also observe that Diels was a "good friend" and correspondent of Frazer.[6] This is one reason for his familiarity with the Scotsman's work. Robert Ackerman, Frazer's biographer, nowhere alludes to his election to the Prussian Academy. In 1911 an English academic could not hope for a higher honor. The British Academy, founded in 1901, at that time could not be compared whether in history, prestige or membership. Publication of this document will draw attention, therefore, to a neglected aspect of Frazer's success.

The composition of the document may be dated to early January 1911.[7] We are grateful to OAR Dr. phil. Wolfgang Knobloch of the Akademie der Wissenschaften der DDR, Zentrales Akademie-Archiv (Berlin, DDR) for permission to publish this document (= Sign. II-III-134, B1, 49, 49r, 50). Dr. Robert Ackerman has kindly and beneficially read an earlier draft of our paper. Dr. Anton Bierl (Leipzig) caught many errors.

TEXT

Wahlvorschlag für J.G. Frazer
verfaßt von Hermann Diels

Adresse: Prof. J.G. Frazer
St. Keyne [sic]
Cambridge
Engl.[8]

James George Frazer, Professor der sozialen Anthropologie in Liverpool, geb. 1854 in Glasgow, gilt jetzt als der bedeutendste Vertreter der

---

[5] See Otto Kern, *Hermann Diels und Carl Robert. Ein biographischer Versuch* (Leipzig 1927) 122 (nine times first in 1890-1891) and especially Albert Henrichs in *Wilamowitz nach 50 Jahren,* edited by William M. Calder III, Hellmut Flashar and Theodor Lindken, (Darmstadt 1985) 286-87 with the bibliography at n. 110. Diels began to lecture on *Religionsgeschichte* in 1890; Wilamowitz not until 1895 in Göttingen: see Henrichs, *ibid.,* 268 n. 2. [An edition of the Diels-Usener Correspondence by Dietrich Ehlers has now appeared (Berlin 1992)].

[6] So Robert Ackerman, *J.G. Frazer His Life and Work* (Cambridge 1987) 213. This exemplary and well informed biography will be henceforth cited Ackerman, *Frazer.*

[7] The document is dated by a passage in a letter of Ulrich von Wilamowitz-Moellendorff to Hermann Diels (No. 194; dated 4 January 1911). On that date Wilamowitz added his signature and returned the document to Diels. See *"Lieber Prinz:" Der Briefwechsel zwischen Hermann Diels und Ulrich von Wilamowitz-Moellendorff (1869-1921),* edd. by Maximilian Braun, William M. Calder III and Dietrich Ehlers (Hildesheim 1995) 260-61. The date is confirmed by the election of Frazer on 27 April 1911 to corresponding membership: see Grau, *op. cit. (supra* n. 4) 246.

[8] Frazer resided at St. Keyne's 1909-1914: see Ackerman, *Frazer,* 215ff.

anthropologischen Richtung der religionsgeschichtlichen Forschung.[9] Seine Ausbildung erhielt er als klassischer Philologe im Trinity College zu Cambridge.[10] Ein Zeugnis seiner eingehenden Studien auf diesem Gebiete legt sein mit englischer Übersetzung verbundener Pausaniascommentar ab, der 1898 in 6 Bänden erschien.[11] Die eingehende Berücksichtigung, die hier die Topographie und besonders die Sacralaltertümer gefunden haben, machte das Werk auch ausserhalb Englands bekannt.[12] Aber seine Stärke liegt auf dem anthropologischen Gebiete, das er bereits 1887 mit seinem Buche "Totemism" betrat.[13] Diese Schrift stellte über diese von dem Schotten Mac Lennan[14] und dem Amerikaner Morgan[15] zuerst einzeln beobachtete soziale Einrichtung primitiver Völker das damals bekannte Material aus vielen Gegenden der Erde zusammen und schien diese totemistisch orientierte Clanverfassung für eine allgemeine Einrichtung der primitiven Menschheit zu halten. Seitdem ist der Totemismus als Urform der Religionsauffassung populär geworden und die vorsichtig gegebenen Andeutungen des Verfassers sind unter den Händen seiner weniger vorsichtigen Nachfolger zur Universalerklärung aller Urreligionen misbraucht worden. [S.2] Dieser Erfolg war dem wahrheitsliebenden Forscher selbst sehr verdriesslich. Er arbeitete daher unter Benutzung eines seitdem ungeheuer angeschwollenen Materials, das ihm von allen Seiten, auch bisher ungedruckter, zurströmte<,> das kleine Buch zu einem umfassenden vierbändigen Werke um, das unter dem Titel "Totemism and Exogamy" 1910 erschienen ist. Das Facit seiner jetzigen Forschung hat er übersichtlich im 4. Bande zusammengestellt.[16] Es ergibt sich jetzt, dass seine ursprüngliche Ansicht von der religiösen Bedeutung des Totemismus irrig war. Die Totemtiere und -Pflanzen werden nicht als übergeordnete, göttliche, sondern lediglich als gleichgeordnete, den Clangenossen verwandte Wesen aufgefasst. Auch die bei vielen der Totemvölker sich findende Exogamie hat nach Frazer ursprünglich nichts mit dem Totemismus zu tun, wenn er auch gern zu

[9] "als...Forschung" is cited at Grau, *op. cit.* (*supra* n. 7) 246.

[10] See Ackerman, *Frazer*, 17-34 for details.

[11] *Pausanias's Description of Greece*, translated with a commentary by J.G. Frazer, 6 volumes, (London 1898; 1913²). For its composition see Ackerman, *Frazer*, 53-69. As far as classical scholars go this is Frazer's most enduring contribution.

[12] Diels stresses this point because of the existence of Hermann Hitzig and Hugo Blümner, *Des Pausanias Beschreibung von Griechenland mit kritischem Apparat* (Berlin 1896-1910). The distinction he makes is crucial. Hitzig-Blümner has remained authoritative until this day for all philological and palaeographical problems while Frazer is superior in questions of topography and cult.

[13] J.G. Frazer, *Totemism* (Edinburgh 1887). A French translation of *Totemism* appeared (Paris 1898).

[14] For the influence of John Ferguson McLennan (1827-1881) on Frazer see Ackerman, *Frazer*, 80-81 and for Frazer's admiration of the man *ibid.*, 322 n. 24.

[15] For the American Lewis Henry Morgan (1818-1881) see Thomas R. Trautmann, *Lewis Henry Morgan and the Invention of Kingship* (Berkeley/Los Angeles/London 1987). Frazer often took exception to him: see Ackerman, *Frazer*, 320 n. 18.

[16] J.G. Frazer, *Totemism and Exogamy. A Treatise on Certain Early Forms of Superstition and Society*, 4 volumes (London 1910). This includes a reprint of *Totemism* (1887).

diesem Zwecke benutzt ward. Ferner stellt der Verf. fest, dass der eigentliche
Totemismus nur bei den braunen und schwarzen Rassen Südafricas, der
Südsee und Nordamerikas vorkommt, dass dagegen bei den weissen und
gelben Rassen Europas und Asiens diese Erscheinung nicht auftritt.[17] Sowol
der ungeheure Stoff, der in diesem Buche rubriciert ist,[18] wie die
methodische Art der Untersuchung wird nicht verfehlen, eine befruchtende
und berichtigende Wirkung auf die grade auf diesem Gebiete noch oft
jugendlich sich gebende Wissenschaft auszuüben.

Ein anderes, noch bekannteres Buch Frazers trägt den etwas seltsamen
Titel "The golden bough."[19] Die erste Auflage erschien 1890, die II. 1900,[20]
die dritte auf vier selbständige Bände anwachsende ist im Erscheinen
begriffen.[21] Der Verf. knüpft an die barbarischen Cultgebräuche der Diana
Nemorensis [S.3] bei Aricia an,[22] deren Priester, der rex Nemorensis, nur
nach Ermordung des Vorgängers und zwar durch einen heiligen Zweig das
Amt erhalten konnte. Da Servius[23] diesen Zweig ohne Grund mit dem
goldnen Mistelzweig der Vergil'schen Nekyia[24] combiniert, erklärt sich der
Titel des Buchs. Es hat sich die doppelte Aufgabe gestellt, die Sitte des
befristeten Priesterkönigtums, das durch gewaltsamen Tod endet, aus den
Bräuchen primitiver Völker aufzuklären und zugleich die Bedeutung des
Zweiges und seinen Zusammenhang mit jenem Culte klar zu stellen. Man
kann nicht sagen, dass ihm dies überall überzeugend gelungen ist, obgleich
die Hauptsache, die Bedeutung des befristeten und durch gewaltsamen Tod
beendeten Amtes, durch seine Parallelen hinreichend deutlich geworden ist.

---

[17] Diels recalls an infamous passage in Frazer. See Frazer, *Totemism and Exogamy* IV. 14
(cited by Ackerman, *Frazer*, 219): "If we exclude hypotheses and confine ourselves to facts,
we may say broadly that totemism is practised by many savage and barbarous peoples, the
lower races as we call them, who occupy the continents and islands of the tropics and the
Southern Hemisphere, and whose complexion shades off from coal black through dark
brown to red. With the somewhat doubtful exception of a few Mongoloid tribes in Assam, no
yellow and no white race is totemic."

[18] Frazer's greatest contribution remains his tireless collection and classification of data:
see e.g., Ackerman, *Frazer*, 41: "Frazer recognized that his own theories and speculations
were all provisional, likely to be replaced by better ones, and hoped that his works might
endure as storehouses of data."

[19] For the *Entstehungsgeschichte* and enormous influence of this book see Ackerman,
Frazer, 95-110 and John B. Vickery, *The Literary Impact of The Golden Bough* (Princeton
1973; pb. 1976).

[20] J.G. Frazer, *The Golden Bough: A Study in Comparative Religion*, 2 volumes
(London/New York 1890); *The Golden Bough: A Study in Magic and Religion*, 3 volumes
(London/New York 1900).

[21] The third edition in fact appeared in 1915 in twelve volumes: see J.G. Frazer, *The
Golden Bough: A Study in Magic and Religion*, 12 volumes (London 1915).

[22] With this famous tale Frazer begins his great work: see Sir James George Frazer, *The
Golden Bough: A Study in Magic and Religion*, Part I, Vol. I³; *The Magic Art and the
Evolution of Kings* (New York 1951) 1ff. For Aricia (= modern Ariccia), at the foot of the
Albanus Mons and 16 miles south-east of Rome see *ibid.*, 3 with nn. and L. Richardson Jr.,
"Aricia (Arricia)," *The Princeton Encyclopedia of Classical Sites*, edited by Richard Stillwell
(Princeton 1976) 92-93. Richardson's bibliography manages to omit Frazer.

[23] Servius *ad* V. *Aen.* 6. 137 (= II. 30. 9ff. Thilo-Hagen).

[24] V. *Aen.* 6. 137.

Dadurch, dass der Verf. den dünnen Stoff des altitalischen Dianencultes zum Vorwande nahm, um darauf seine stupende folkloristische Gelehrsamkeit auszubreiten, hat der Verf. eine starke Wirkung auf die religions-geschichtliche Forschung ausgeübt. Ausser den drei englischen Auflagen hat namentlich die französische Bearbeitung[25] viel zur Verbreitung seiner Ideen und Methoden im Auslande beigetragen. Unter den zahlreichen Monographien möchte ich noch, um die Vielseitigkeit seiner Forschung zu zeigen, die "Anthropological Essays" in der Festschrift zu Ehren des Anthropologen Tylor erwähnen.[26] Er hat hier eine Reihe superstitiöser Überbleibsel im Alten Testament auf Grund seiner ausgebreiteten Kenntnis der primitiven Culturen aufgeklärt.

Es scheint an der Zeit diesen verdienten Gelehrten durch Wahl zum Correspondenten unserer Akademie auszuzeichnen und zwar, da kein besondres Fach für Anthropologie oder Religionsgeschichte besteht,[27] im Fache der klassischen Philologie, von der er in seinen Studien ausgegangen ist.

Diels
Conze[28] Wilamowitz
Dressel[29]
ESchmidt[30] Eduard Meyer[31] Harnack[32]

---

[25] J.-G. Frazer, *Le rameau d'or. Étude sur la magie et la religion*, traduit de l'Anglais par R. Stiebel: I, Paris 1903; II, Paris 1908; III, Paris 1911.

[26] J.G. Frazer, *Folk-Lore in the Old Testament, Anthropological Essays presented to Edward Burnett Tylor* (Oxford 1907) 101-74. For the composition of this essay see Ackerman, *Frazer*, 184-86.

[27] There was no chair for *Religionsgeschichte* in Germany until 1910 when at Berlin Otto Pfleiderer's chair for systematic theology was turned into one for *Religionsgeschichte*. It was long debated whether the chair belonged to the theological or philosophical faculty: see Karl-Wolfgang Tröger, "Zur Geschichte des Spezialfaches Allgemeine Religionsgeschichte," *Wissenschaftliche Zeitschrift der Humboldt-Universität zu Berlin, Gesellschaftswissen-schaftliche Reihe, Zur Geschichte der Theologischen Fakultät Berlins* 27 (1985) 577-79. Frazer's election is a further symptom of growing interest in a highly controversial subject: see further Adolf Deißmann, *Der Lehrstuhl für Religionsgeschichte* (Berlin 1914) und Eric J. Sharpe, *Comparative Religion: A History*[2] (La Salle 1987).

[28] For Alexander Conze see Adolf H. Borbein, *Alexander Conze 1831-1914. Archäologen-bildnisse: Porträts und Kurzbiographien von Klassischen Archäologen deutscher Sprache,* edited by Reinhard Lullies and Wolfgang Schiering, (Mainz 1988) 59-60, to whose bibliography one must add Wilamowitz, *KS* 6, 59-60.

[29] For the election of the numismatist and Direktor des Münzkabinetts der Berliner Museen, Heinrich Dressel (1845-1920) as OM in 1902 see Grau, *op. cit.* (*supra* n. 7) 145.

[30] Erich Schmidt (1853-1913), OM 1895, the Germanist and Schulpforte graduate, had been rector of the University for the jubilee year 1909-10. His interest in Frazer's work would have been marginal at most.

[31] For Eduard Meyer's (1855-1930) election as OM in 1903 see Christa Dirsten, *Die Altertumswissenschaften an der Berliner Akademie. Wahlvorschläge zur Aufnahme von Mitgliedern von F.A. Wolf bis zu G. Rodenwaldt* Band 5 (Berlin 1985) 125-26. For his life see Christhard Hoffmann, "Eduard Meyer," *Classical Scholarship: A Biographical Encyclopedia,* edited by Ward W. Briggs Jr. and William M. Calder III (New York 1990) 260-76.

[32] For Adolf Harnack's (1851-1930) service to the Academy see Agnes von Zahn-Harnack, *Adolf Harnack* (Berlin 1951[2]) 191-208.

ENGLISH TRANSLATION[33]

Proposal for the Election of J.G. Frazer
Composed by Hermann Diels

Address: Prof. J.G. Frazer
St. Keyne's
Cambridge
England

James George Frazer, Professor of Social Anthropology at Liverpool, born 1854 in Glasgow, today is considered the most important practitioner of the anthropological line in the study of the history of religion. He was educated as a classical philologist at Trinity College Cambridge. A proof of his continuing study in this field is provided by his commentary on his English translation of Pausanias, which appeared in 1898 in six volumes. The consistent attention which topography and particularly sacred antiquities receive here, made the work famous outside of England also. But his strength lies in the field of anthropology which he already treated by 1887 with his book *Totemism*. This publication brought together the material known at that time from all parts of the world concerning that social organization of primitive peoples first observed in detail by the Scot MacLennan and the American Morgan and which seemed to hold this totem-oriented clan form of government to be a universal organization of primitive mankind. Since then totemism has become popular as the original form of religion and the cautiously advanced suggestions of the author have been misused in the hands of his less cautious followers for the universal elucidation of all early religions. This success was very annoying to the scholar himself who loved truth. He expanded the little book into a comprehensive four volume work entitled *Totemism and Exogamy*, which appeared in 1910, using material which poured in to him from all sides (partially unpublished) and which has now reached enormous proportions. It now appears that his original view of the religious meaning of totemism was wrong. Totemic animals and plants were not considered as superior, divine beings but merely as equals related to members of the clan. Further, exogamy which is found among many of the totem peoples, according to Frazer, originally had nothing to do with totemism, although it also was gladly used to this end. As well the author made it clear that the true totemism only can be found among the brown and black races of South Africa, of the South Seas and North America. Contrarily among the white

---

[33] The translation is for those to whom the German is not available and is only a paraphrase not meant to replace the original.

and yellow races of Europe and Asia one does not meet this phenomenon. The mass of material which is organized in this book as well as the methodical manner of research will not fail to exercise a fruitful and corrective influence on a science which especially in this area is often still a bit juvenile.

Another still better known book of Frazer bears the rather unusual title *The Golden Bough*. The first edition appeared in 1898; the second in 1900, the third, expanded to four large volumes, is forthcoming. The author builds on the barbaric cult usage of Diana Nemorensis at Aricia, whose priest, the rex Nemorensis, could only hold office after the murdering of his predecessor and to be sure with the aid of a sacred bough. The title of the book is explained because Servius for no reason combined this bough with the golden mistletoe of the Vergilian Nekyia. The author has set himself a twofold task: (1) to elucidate from the customs of primitive peoples the peculiar habit of the priest-monarchy with its time limit which is brought to an end through violent death and (2) to make clear its connection with that cult. One cannot say that he has succeeded in being consistently convincing, although the main point, the meaning of the office limited to a certain time and ended by violent death, through his parallels, has become sufficiently clear. The author has exercised a powerful influence on research in the history of religion because he has taken the scanty evidence for ancient Italic Dianacult in order to apply to it his stupendous erudition in the field of folklore. Apart from the three English editions, the French revision has really contributed a good deal to the spreading of his ideas and methods in foreign countries. Among his numerous monographs I should like to mention further, in order to show the many-sidedness of his research, the "Anthropological Essays" in the *Festschrift* to honor the anthropologist Tylor. There on the basis of his wide knowledge of primitive cultures he elucidated a series of superstitious leftovers in the Old Testament.

It seems high time to draw attention to this deserving scholar through election to corresponding member of our Academy and indeed because no specific discipline for anthropology or the history of religion exists, in the subject of classical philology, from which he started off in his studies.

(Signed:) Diels, Conze, Wilamowitz, Dressel, ESchmidt, Eduard Meyer, Harnack.

12 March 1921: The Berlin Appointment

"...der kann aber durch zu viel Sonnenschein verdorben werden."
"...too much sunshine can ruin him."
Wilamowitz to Paul Wendland on Werner Jaeger (16 January 1913)

I. Hintergrund

The naval mutinies at Kiel culminated 4–5 November 1918. The November Revolution occurred in Munich and Berlin on 9 November. On that day Wilhelm II abdicated and fled to Dorn. Scheidemann proclaimed the Republic at 2 PM. Two hours later Karl Liebknecht proclaimed the Socialist Republic. Armistice came on 11 November. The Spartacist Uprising took place in Berlin 5–12 January 1919. The following month saw the Inauguration of the National Assembly at Weimar. The Treaty of Versailles was signed on 28 June. The Kapp Putsch occurred 13 March 1920 in Berlin. Wilamowitz and Eduard Meyer were involved.[1]

The Prussian Kultusministerium had flourished under the autocratic and thoroughly admirable Friedrich Althoff (1839–1908), architect of the System Althoff. That he trusted the judgment of Theodor Mommsen and Wilamowitz proves that he placed the uncompromising quest for excellence above politics. His immediate successors do not concern us here. The holder of his office in 1921 does. Carl Heinrich Becker (1876–1933),[2] son of a banker and Konsul, studied in Lausanne, Heidelberg, and Berlin. He took his doctorate in 1899, aged 23. He traveled 1900–1902 in Spain, Egypt, the Sudan, Greece, and Turkey. He was habilitated in Semitic philology at Heidelberg in 1902, where in 1906 he became Außerordentlicher Professor. In 1908, aged 32, he went to Hamburg as Ordinarius for the History and Culture of the Orient. In 1913 he became Professor for Oriental Philology at Bonn. He was seduced to administration in 1916, when he entered the Prussian Kultusministerium in Berlin as Vortragender Rat. He became Staatssekretär in 1919 and in 1921 Kultusminister in the Stegerwald

---

[1] For Wilamowitz' involvement see J. Erger, *Der Kapp–Lütwitz–Putsch* (Düsseldorf 1967) 94 with n. 5. I owe the reference to Professor A. Wasserstein (Jerusalem).

[2] See Erich Wende, *C.H. Becker Mensch und Politiker: Ein biographischer Beitrag zur Kulturgeschichte der Weimarer Republik* (Stuttgart 1959), henceforth cited: Wende, *Becker*. The briefest facts are at Adolf Grimme, *NDB* 1 (Berlin 1953) 711. Of special importance is his son's memoir: see Hellmut Becker, "Porträt eines Kultusministers: Zum 100. Geburtstag von Carl Heinrich Becker (12. April 1976)," *Merkur* 30 (1976) 365–76, reprinted with some revisions as "C.H. Becker—Porträt eines Kultusministers (1976)," *Auf dem Weg zur lernenden Gesellschaft: Personen, Analysen, Vorschläge für die Zukunft* (Klett–Cotta 1980) 31–44. [See now Guido Müller, *Weltpolitische Bildung und Akademische Reform: Carl Heinrich Beckers Wissenschafts- und Hochschulpolitik 1908-1930* (Köln/Weiman/Wien 1991).]

Cabinet; in autumn 1921 he was again Staatssekretär, and in 1925 he again assumed the office of Prussian Kultusminister, which he held until his retirement in 1930.

Upon his assumption of office in 1919 and even more clearly in 1921, Becker discovered who his enemies were, the enemies of what he thought necessary reform.[3]

> Seine bedeutendsten Gegner waren hierbei hervorragende Berliner Professoren...Männer wie Eduard Meyer, Lubarsch, Stutz, Hermann Schumacher, fachwissenschaftlich hoch angesehene Gelehrte, mit Becker einig in dem Bestreben, die auf höchste Leistung gegründete innere Selbständigkeit der Universität zu erhalten, fürchteten doch, daß der von Becker beschrittene Weg ins Unheil führen werde.

One might add "Männer wie Lüders, Roethe, Wilamowitz-Moellendorff." Diels was working class and different. Rectors like Reinhold Seeberg (1918/1919), Eduard Meyer (1919/1920), and the Roman lawyer, Emil Seckel (1920/1921) were not devoted to making matters easier for Becker. Professors in Prussia were appointed for life. Becker's support flourished among the young. The solution was unavoidable. *Zwangsemeritierung* had become law by 15 December 1920. Ninety-six professorships in Prussia became available overnight.

II. Werner Jaeger in March 1921[4]

His university career had been meteoric: promotion at Berlin on 5 July 1911, aged 23; habilitation there in 1914 (inaugural lecture at Berlin, 14 June 1914); briefly Dozent; never Assistent. In August war began. Jaeger assumed the chair of Friedrich Nietzsche in neutral Switzerland. In the same epochal year he married (28 March 1914) Theodora Dammholz, daughter of a good family. Her father was Geheimrat and lived at Nürnbergerstraße 63, two houses away from Diels. We know now that a mysterious Berlin widow, Margarete Stücklen,[5] had supported him financially through the doctorate. Now she had been replaced. Before his assumption of the Basel

---

[3] Wende, *Becker*, 112–13.

[4] For the most recent life of Jaeger see William M. Calder III, "Werner Jaeger: 30 July 1888—19 October 1961," *Classical Scholarship: A Biographical Encyclopedia*, edited by Ward W. Briggs and William M. Calder III (New York/London 1990) 211–26 with a bibliography of works about Jaeger (225–26), to which add Ruth Jaeger, "Werner Jaeger," *Germans in Boston* (Goethe Society of New England 1981) 19–22. I owe this reference to Professor J.P. Hallett.

[5] See Margarete Stücklen to Hermann Diels (Berlin 10 November 1911). In later life Jaeger never mentioned his early patroness.

Chair he had published, apart from the obligatory Latin *specimen eruditionis* from his dissertation, three books, all of which must be consulted to this day:

1. *Studien zur Entstehungsgeschichte der Metaphysik des Aristoteles* (Berlin 1912). This was the full version of the *specimen eruditionis* published in Latin the year before.

2. *Aristotelis de animalium motione et de animalium incessu*; *Ps.-Aristotelis de spiritu libellus* (Leipzig 1913). He owed the edition to the intervention of Diels with Teubner, who invited him 23 February 1912 to do the Teubner text.[6] This proved that he was a philologist, not a fraud given to ideas.

3. *Nemesios von Emesa: Quellenforschungen zum Neuplatonismus und seinen Anfängen bei Poseidonios* (Berlin 1914). This was the *Habilitationsschrift*.

There were as well fourteen outstanding articles and reviews.

For Jaeger in 1914 we have the opinion of the highest authority. Wilamowitz recommended him to Walter F. Otto to be his successor at Basel in a letter of 25 February 1914:[7]

Jäger ist unsere große Hoffnung: ein Talent, wie ich (und Diels ebenso) es bisher unter unsern Schülern nicht gehabt haben. Es genügen ja seine Bücher, dh. die Dissertation, der Aristoteles, und die Habilitationsschrift, Nemesios. Neben der constructiven Phantasie steht eine

---

[6] See Diels to Jaeger No. 10 (Berlin, 23 February 1912):
    "Nun aber eine Aristotelische Frage! Haben Sie Lust in der Bibl. Teubn. die Schriften de animalium motu u. de animalium spiritu zu bearbeiten? Es handelt sich, wie Sie wissen, nicht um kritische Ausgaben vollendeter Art, sondern um verständige Revisionen der Bekkerschen Ausgaben, ev. mit Revision der wichtigsten Hss."
    Martha Nussbaum's complaint at *JHS* 95 (1975) 207 that Jaeger reproduced incorrect readings and ignored significant omissions in Bekker's apparatus, while not untrue, is unfair because Jaeger was never asked nor sought to control Bekker. In his letter of 11 March 1912 to Diels, Jaeger thanks him for his "Verwendung für mich beim Teubnerschen Verlag." He has arranged with Teubner to do the edition.
    [7] See William M. Calder III and Christhard Hoffmann, "Ulrich von Wilamowitz-Moellendorff on the Basel Greek Chair," *Museum Helveticum* 43 (1986) 258–63 (here 260). In a letter to Werner Jaeger dated Erlangen, 3 May 1931, Otto Stählin writes (Harvard *Nachlaß*, unpublished):
    "Der andere Brief ist von Wilamowitz (vom 14.7.1913); seine Worte lauten: 'Jaeger, den Wendland und Schwartz von einem Besuche kennen, halten Diels und ich allerdings wohl für das bedeutendste Talent, das wir unter unsern Schülern gesehen haben. Sinn für Philosophie mit Sinn für Form gepaart. Er hat sich in diesen Wochen hier habilitiert. Aber er ist *sehr* jung, die Flamme des Seelenfeuers flickert und schwelt...noch stark. Weil ich ihm das Beste wünsche, wünsche ich ihm eine Weile Ruhe. Aber das kann mich nicht verhindern, über das Talent meine wahre Meinung zu sagen.'"
    He continues to cite Wendland, who calls only Wilamowitz and Jaeger *genial*.

solide Sprachkenntnis. Wie sich schickt, hat er sich mit Feuereifer auf das Ediren geworfen—um zu lernen. Aber natürlich ist alles noch in Gärung. Er ist persönlich so gut wie ganz mittellos—und heiratet doch eben jetzt; wir tun alles ihm die Existenz zu ermöglichen, aber natürlich wünschen wir ihm alles beste, er kann ja auch gar nicht lange warten. Wie sich solche Jugend entwickelt, kann niemand sagen: aber ich glaube, er wird, mag er auch noch unsicher gehen, keinen Schüler verderben.

Hermann Diels agreed. Jaeger was "die grösste Hoffnung unserer Wissenschaft zur Zeit."[8] Expectedly Jaeger was chosen. He served only a year. Basel's policy had long been the best that a small and provincial university can have. Better a brilliant young man for three years than a Null for 30. Jaeger, who later extolled military heroism in Homer, like Nietzsche, did not serve his country in war. All three brothers of his wife fell. Jaeger lived and retained until his death the medical documents that had disqualified him for service.

Siegfried Sudhaus (1863–1914), the papyrologist, also served. He fell on 23 October 1914 at Bixschote at the head of his company. A post in Greek thus opened at Kiel. The faculty on 3 March 1915 drew up their list:[9]

1. oProfessor Werner Jaeger (Basel)

2. Oberlehrer Ludolf Malten (Wilmersdorf)[10]

3. oProfessor Johannes Mewaldt (Marburg)[11]

---

[8] *Ibid.*, 262.

[9] See Karl Jordan and Erich Hofmann, "Klassische Philologie," *Geschichte der Christian-Albrechts-Universität Kiel 1665-1965: Geschichte der Philosophischen Fakultät* Teil 2 (Neumünster 1969) 121–65 (here 159). By 8 May 1915 Jaeger in a letter to Diels from Basel had decided for Kiel. Decisive were 1) return to his fatherland, 2) ten times as many students, 3) popular public lectures, 4) increase in salary. He regrets only that with his leaving Basel "Deutschtum" will cease to play a role there. He will miss his students, among whom are three doctorandi. No friends are mentioned. This will remain typical for Jaeger, who rarely had friends of his age: see *infra*. For the deaths of Jaeger's three brothers-in-law see Mensching, 69.

[10] For the Berliner Ludolf Malten (1879–1969) see Wolfhart Unte, "Das Werk Ludolf Maltens," *Jahrbuch der Schlesischen Friedrich–Wilhelms–Universität zu Breslau* 21 (1980) 319–36. He was a lifelong admirer of Wilamowitz. This may have been a factor in his dislike of Jaeger, attested now by F. Solmsen, *GRBS* 30 (1989) 138 n. 11 (on the authority of Eduard Fraenkel).

[11] For Johannes Mewaldt (1880–1964) see Herbert Hunger, *Gnomon* 36 (1964) 524–26. Solmsen alleges that he "in 1936 recommended himself as Jaeger's successor, stressing his political qualifications" and that like Körte and Malten he was "jealous of Jaeger's influential position": see Friedrich Solmsen, *GRBS* 30 (1989) 138 n. 11. But in 1935 he directed the dissertation of a Jewish student (A.E. Raubitschek), which suggests that Solmsen is mistaken about his politics. Professor Raubitschek observes to me *per litt.* (25 April 1990):
"About Mewaldt, I do not know anything about his trying to get Jaeger's chair in Berlin, nor do I really know that he and Jaeger were friends. He did praise the Aristotle and Paideia I. I knew Mewaldt quite well, and I admired him as a scholar and a teacher. He was an Epicurean, but he was also a Nazi—an aesthetic one, that means he liked to look at the clean-cut Storm troopers marching, in contrast to the dirty and disreputable communists and socialists. He lectured enthusiastically about the Classical 'Hoch-zeit' but made disparaging

The negotiations for Jaeger's appointment lasted from 24 April until 1 October 1915. That is, he began to work on his Kiel appointment only several months after he had accepted the Basel chair. He remained at Kiel six years. In July 1919 he declined a call to Hamburg, a post which in 1931 his detractor, Bruno Snell, would gain. A postcard to Diels dated 10 (?) July 1919 explains his decision:

> Es drängt mich nach unserem eingehenden Gespräch am Freitag Nachmittag Ihnen von dem Ausgang der Angelegenheit, die mich seit 2 Wochen geistig beschäftigt hat, Kunde zu geben. Ich habe mich zu dem Entschlusse der Ablehnung Hamburgs durchgerungen, um unter den übrigens auch äußerlich sehr günstigen Bedingungen, die Preußen mir stellte, lieber in Kiel der wissenschaftlichen Arbeit zu leben u. mir das weitere "Fortkommen"—im Doppelsinne dieses Wortes—erst selbst zu verdienen. Daß ich dabei das Gefühl haben konnte, auch in Ihrem Sinne zu handeln, hat mich moralisch sehr gestärkt zu meiner Entschließung.

He had consulted Diels. A letter from Unterstaatssekretär Becker dated Wilhelmstraße 68, Berlin, 23 April 1919, clarifies Jaeger's decision:

> Es kursieren hier so allerlei Gerüchte, als ob Sie mit dem Gedanken spielten, einer Berufung nach Hamburg Folge zu leisten. Ich möchte Ihnen doch sagen, daß ich das außerordentlich bedauern würde. Materielle Gründe dürfen Sie keinesfalls dazu bestimmen. Ich gönne Ihnen von Herzen den Ruf; lassen Sie sich nur günstige Bedingungen machen, aber dann bleiben Sie bei uns. Jedenfalls würde ich mich freuen, Ihnen auf Grund eines Rufes Ihre materielle Existenz erheblich bessern zu können.

The publications of the Kiel period were surprisingly meagre in comparison with his earlier production. But they are not indicative of his labors. He had completed by August 1918 an edition of Aristotle, *Metaphysica*. In a letter of 11 August 1918 to Diels he remarks:

> Meine fertiggestellte neue Ausgabe der Metaphysik will Teubner nicht drucken, ich habe sie also zu den beiden dicken Volumina des Gregorius Nyssenus in den Schreibtischkasten gelegt, die ja auch seit Jahr und Tag der Auferstehung vergeblich harren.

He omits the reason. They had no paper. There had been no injustice done Jaeger. His disappointment was a very small part of the national

---

remarks about the 'totalitarian' Republic of Plato. I learned a lot from him and he was always very kind and generous to me... He never discriminated against any student on race, sex, politics, and I only guessed that he was a Nazi, and I never saw him wearing a party button. Put it differently, before the invasion of Austria by Hitler I had no evidence that Mewaldt was a Nazi except for some favorable remarks of a general nature, and afterwards *everybody* was or claimed to be or to have been a Nazi."

catastrophe. Jaeger already thought practically. There was time for published panegyrics of both Wilamowitz and Diels. Earlier there had been the laudatory review of another Berlin professor.[12] In 1921 there appeared at last a philological masterpiece of enduring value, the two-volume critical edition of Gregory of Nyssa, *Contra Eunomium*. Wilamowitz had suggested the task to him in 1908. Much of the *Wanderjahre* had been devoted to collation in the libraries of Italy. The war and its aftermath had delayed publication. Jaeger wrote revealingly of his edition to Stroux on 9 March 1921:[13]

> Der Wert liegt gewiß nicht in der Wirkung, sondern ist ein rein transzendenter, ein idealer, also unabhängig von der Wirkung auf Menschen und nur in sich selber gegründet.

The doubt persisted. He asks "whether it would not have been better to have used the time to write a history of Greek philosophy or to have taught in the Volkshochschule." The appearance of the volumes coincided with an unexpected and welcome event. The most prestigious chair of classics in the world was free.

III. The Published Sources

Indubitably the most important single event in Jaeger's life was his appointment to Wilamowitz' chair. Both the prestige of the post and that he was 32 years old made him world famous. Jaeger once in print alluded to his call:[14]

---

[12] "Ulrich von Wilamowitz-Moellendorff," *Deutsche Allgemeine Zeitung* 58 (1918) 648 (here the most embarrassing misprint in Jaeger's published work is to be found) and "Hermann Diels. Zum goldenen Doktorjubiläum," *Internationale Monatschrift für Wissenschaft, Kunst und Technik* 15 (1920) 133–46 (= *Humanistische Reden und Vorträge* II [Berlin 1960] 31–40). Eduard Norden, *Agnostos Theos*, was reviewed at *GGA* 175 (1913) 569–610 (= *Scripta Minora* I [Rome 1960] 115–61).

[13] This is most explicit in an unpublished letter of Jaeger to Kirsopp Lake dated 16 January 1942 (carbon copy in Jaeger *Nachlaß*, Harvard):

"The idea of editing Gregory and if possible some other fathers of the Post-Nicene period goes back to Wilamowitz, who dedicated a large sum of money collected in his honor for his sixtieth birthday to this purpose and announced this plan in his *gratiarum actio* to the givers of the money. That was in 1908... I had come to Greek philosophy from the theological interests which had developed early in my life and consequently it was quite organic from my point of view to make Wilamowitz' plan my own and to agree, when I was invited, to edit Gregory's main work, the books *Contra Eunomium*. I started the work in 1911 and edited the two volumes containing that work in Berlin (1922–1923)."

In fact both volumes appeared in 1921. For a history of the Gregory project see Hadwig Hörner, "Über Genese und derzeitigen Stand der grossen Edition der Werke Gregors von Nyssa," *Écriture et culture philosophique dans la Pensée de Gregoire de Nysse. Acts du colloque de Chevetogne (22–26 Septembre 1969)*, edited by M. Harl (Leiden 1971) 18–50. For Jaeger to Stroux on *Gregor* see Mensching, 62, 64.

[14] Werner Jaeger, "Die klassische Philologie an der Universität Berlin von 1870–1945," *Studium Berolinense: Aufsätze und Beiträge zu Problemen der Wissenschaft und zur*

Als das neue Emeritierungsgesetz in Kraft trat, wurde der Verfasser dieses Aufsatzes, der jüngste Schüler von Wilamowitz und Diels, auf Vorschlag der Fakultät berufen (1921). Ich kam offiziell als Nachfolge von Wilamowitz nach Berlin, wozu Diels lächelnd bemerkte, daß ich ja in Wahrheit sein Nachfolger wäre. Ich hatte von allen gelernt, soviel ich konnte, aber es war mir eine tröstliche Definition, was ein alter freundlicher Kollege mir sagte: der rechte Nachfolger wäre stets, wer seinen eigenen Weg ginge.

In 1978 I published the Wilamowitz–Jaeger correspondence.[15] The official call is dated Berlin, 12 March 1921, and signed by Geheimer Regierungsrat Wende, the later biographer of Becker:[16]

Dem Auftrage meines Herrn Ministers entsprechend beehre ich mich, Ihnen die Nachfolge des Herrn Geheimrats von Wilamowitz von der hiesigen Universität mit dem Ausdruck meiner aufrichtigen Glückwünsche ganz ergebenst anzubieten. Es würde dem Ministerium eine besondere Freude sein, wenn es mit Ihrer grundsätzlichen Geneigtheit, diesen Ruf zu folgen, rechnen dürfte.

Jaeger is invited to Berlin for a discussion in the near future. Three days later he wrote from Kiel to Wilamowitz with information not in Wende's letter:[17]

Das Ministerium hat mich auf den Berliner Lehrstuhl der Philologie berufen, den Sie bis zum Inkrafttreten des Pensionsgesetzes verwaltet haben und mich unterrichtet, dass ich nach Schwartz u. Arnim sowie Boll an dritter Stelle genannt worden sei.

Jaeger continues to say what Wilamowitz wanted to hear. He will not use the opportunity to express himself on the nonsense of strictly applying the law in Wilamowitz' case. Wilamowitz still lives and works "in der Kraft eines Heros." His position in the world and at the university does not depend

Geschichte der Friedrichs–Wilhelms–Universität zu Berlin, edited by Hans Leussink, Eduard Neumann, and Georg Kotowski (Berlin 1960) 479.

[15] William M. Calder III, "The Correspondence of Ulrich von Wilamowitz-Moellendorff with Werner Jaeger," *HCSP* 82 (1978) 303–47 (= Ulrich von Wilamowitz-Moellendorff, *Selected Correspondence 1869–1931*, edited by William M. Calder III, *Antiqua* 23 [Naples 1983] 167–347, 307–08) [henceforth cited: *Briefe–Jaeger*].

[16] *Briefe–Jaeger* 200. Wolfgang Buchwald, Albert Henrichs, and I read *Wend*. Ernst Vogt (200 n. 178) *Wenk*. It is clear from more legible references in the new sources that the name was Wende. Mensching (86 n. 6) queries my dating of the call to 12 March 1921 on the grounds that in a letter to Stroux dated 26 March 1921 Jaeger writes that he had accepted the call "in der vorigen Woche." I prefer the date of Wende's offering the post to the date of Jaeger's accepting it.

[17] *Briefe–Jaeger* 200–03. The citation is on 200–01. We now know that knowledge of the list comes from Becker's letter of 12 March 1921 to Jaeger; see *infra*.

on his title. "No one understands more profoundly than I the feelings that must fill your heart, although for the average university teacher I consider some sort of mandatory retirement age desirable." He then thanks Wilamowitz and the faculty for the honor and trust that caused them to place him directly after von Arnim and Schwartz, who are decades older than he. No one, even they, could be a successor of Wilamowitz. Everyone knows that. Wilamowitz had only reluctantly left Göttingen for Berlin. Jaeger has very serious reservations. He was third, and Wilamowitz presumably preferred the first two, but the Ministerium for no good reason passed them over. He also admits that "meine Berufung nach Berlin eine Frühgeburt, die kaum glücklich für das Kind ablaufen wird." His third reservation is the serious one. Who will his colleague be? Boll was ideal but will certainly stay in Heidelberg. Jaeger means that he must have the decisive say in the choice of his *collega proximus*.

Wilamowitz replies on 17 March 1921 with tact and intelligence to "your letter, which is precisely what I expected from you." Schwartz was named *honoris causa*. Either von Arnim or Jaeger was acceptable to the faculty. There was small chance for Boll. The man appointed should have a say in the choice of *collega proximus*. Youth should not deter Jaeger. Böckh became Ordinarius in Berlin at age 26. Wilamowitz understands Becker's distaste for his politics. He will continue to lecture.

In two further letters to Wilamowitz, Jaeger discusses the Berlin appointment. In a letter of 12 April 1921 Jaeger thanks Wilamowitz profusely for a copy of *Griechische Verskunst*. Jaeger is still bargaining with the Ministerium. Boll will surely decline. In his letter of 30 April, Jaeger is in the last stages of discussion concerning his salary. He will join the Berlin Faculty 1 October 1921 and clearly is unhappy that a list for Boll's place may be drawn up without his participation. The Berlin call is never discussed again in the preserved letters between Jaeger and Wilamowitz.

Two new sources have become available to me since 1978. They clarify ambiguities in the Wilamowitz correspondence, and they add new information. These sources which must now be considered are the Diels–Jaeger letters and the Becker–Jaeger letters. I shall turn to these. A word should be said about a third source, namely the letters between Jaeger and Eduard Norden. Some 80 letters of Norden to Jaeger survive (22 July 1909—30 October 1939). I hope very much that Professor Dr. Bernhard Kytzler (FU Berlin) will edit them. Of these, relevant to the Berlin call are certainly No. 52 (9 March 1921) and for the replacement for Boll Nos. 53–56 (15, 19, 24, 26 May 1921). Two further letters, Norden to Becker (15 January 1921) and Becker to Norden (6 January 1921), probably concern Jaeger's appointment. The strain between Norden and Jaeger is evident from No. 53, which begins:

Mein lieber Freund, ich weiß freilich nicht, ob diese seit Jahren unter uns übliche trauliche Anrede noch Widerhall bei Ihnen findet, aber ich möchte sie doch—vielleicht als letzter—noch einmal gebrauchen, und sei es auch nur um einer schönen Illusion willen.

In 1989 Eckart Mensching published selections from the letters of Werner Jaeger to Johannes Stroux today in the possession of Dr. L. Stroux in West Berlin: see Eckart Mensching, "Über Werner Jaeger (geb. am 30. Juli 1888) und seinen Weg nach Berlin," *Nugae zur Philologie-Geschichte* II (Berlin 1989) 60–92. Stroux' letters to Jaeger are at Harvard. The whole correspondence deserves publication with commentary.

IV. The Diels–Jaeger Letters

The Diels–Jaeger Letters are preserved in the Jaeger *Nachlaß* at the Houghton Library of Harvard University. Sixty-seven letters and postcards survive: 31 of Diels to Jaeger and 36 of Jaeger to Diels. Jaeger's letters were returned to him after Diels' death on 4 June 1922. They cover the period 8 March 1910 until 30 May 1921. I doubt that even five letters need be lost. Communication by telephone rather than letter is already attested in the correspondence. All 67 letters, plus the letter of Margarete Stöckler to Diels of 10 November 1911, were accurately transcribed in January 1990 by Dr. Dietrich Ehlers (Akademie der Wissenschaften der DDR zu Berlin), the world authority on the handwriting of Hermann Diels, to whom I express here my lasting gratitude.

This correspondence is not only more extensive than Jaeger's with Wilamowitz (18 preserved letters of Wilamowitz to Jaeger by June 1922 against 31 of Diels). There is an intimacy, even affection, apparent in the Diels–Jaeger letters. Jaeger calls it (9 May 1918) "diese Freundschaft des väterlichen Lehrers." Wilamowitz was a *heros* and a god, adored from afar, too remote and Olympian to be bothered with requests for placing articles and finding jobs and arranging publishing contracts. A good part of the difference may have been class. Diels' father was a minor rural railroad official. Wilamowitz' was a Junker; his brother was President of Posen and Kammerherr of the Kaiser. Jaeger told me once that when he attended Wilamowitz' Wednesday evening soirées, Tycho would enter late with Ernst Kapp and pointedly ignore Jaeger. "I know why," Jaeger said; "it was because my father was a tradesman." This was said without bitterness. But it is revealing and not unexpected that although often the flatterer, Jaeger is far more candid in his letters to Diels than to Wilamowitz. I edit here in chronological order those parts of the Diels–Jaeger Correspondence that concern the Berlin call.

1. The earliest reference to an opening at Berlin occurs in Jaeger's letter of 9 March 1921. Jaeger tactfully avoids any suggestion that he is available. In fact he had long known that he would be considered.

Ihr Brief zu Neujahr hat mich herzlich erfreut, die Nachrichten über das schöne Gelingen der Feier Ihres goldenen Doktorjubiläums haben mir mein Fehlen, das ja kein freiwilliges war, noch hinterher besonders schwer gemacht. Nun stehen Ihnen auch äußerlich starke Veränderungen durch das Altersgesetz bevor. Niemand bedauert es tiefer als ich, daß Männer wie Sie oder auch Wilamowitz zurücktreten. Wir haben doch überhaupt keine Persönlichkeiten, die, ich rede gar nicht von Ersatz, für eine Nachfolge in Frage kämen. Die mittlere Generation ist unschöpferisch, die jüngere unfertig und ein unbeschriebenes Blatt. Und "was ist heute Berlin für eine Attraktion"? sagte mir Norden wiederholt in letzter Zeit. Er mag Recht haben, gleichviel wie er es gemeint haben mag. Ich sehe der kommenden Ära nicht ohne Gruseln entgegen.

2. This elicited the reply for which Jaeger presumably had hoped. Diels writes him on 12 March 1921, not coincidentally the day of Wende's official letter and, as we shall see, a letter from Becker. Diels had not violated confidentiality.

Inzwischen haben wir in den letzten Sitzungen unserer Fakultät mit den Nachfolgern uns beschäftigt. Es stellte sich leider betrüblich heraus, daß eigentlich kein einziger Philologe seine Vertrautheit mit der Poesie der Hellenen durch anerkannte Werke dargetan hat. Ein Nachfolger von Wilamowitz war also nicht zu finden. Denn selbst Schwartz und v. Arnim, die als erste von der Fakultät genannt wurden, haben ihre Schwerpunkte in der Prosa und sind eminent dafür begabte Köpfe. Auch Boll, der dann als der bedeutendste Philologe erschien, hat sein Schwergewicht nicht im Homer oder den Tragikern. Kurz es stellte sich heraus, daß unsere moderne Philologie ihren wissenschaftlichen Schwerpunkt nicht in der klassischen Poesie hat. Da die beiden primo loco genannten Philologen schon jenseits der 60 stehen, ist zu fürchten, was die Regierung bereits bei Besetzung des astronomischen Lehrstuhls ausgesprochen hat, daß sie von den sexagenarii absieht. Boll ferner ist so ausgesprochener Süddeutscher und hat in Heidelberg eine so hervorragende Stellung, daß er gewiß sehr schwer für Berlin zu gewinnen sein wird. So hat unsere Kommission—es ist ein offenes Geheimnis—ebenso wie unsere Regierung eigentlich nur eine Hoffnung: daß Sie, lieber Jäger, der als letzter und jüngster auf dieser Liste erscheint, uns keinen Korb geben. Sie haben zwar auch bisher wissenschaftlich nur die Prosa vertreten, aber wir haben die Überzeugung, daß wenn die Entwicklung Ihrer Anlage gemäß fortschreitet, Sie die Provinz der großen Poesie Sich erobern werden. Sie werden, wie ich glaube, die Probleme z. T. anders auffassen als Wilamowitz, aber ich hoffe, daß Sie in dem Streben, dies große Kulturgebiet allseitig nach Form und Inhalt zu erfassen, hinter ihm nicht zurückbleiben

werden. Möge Ihnen nur die körperliche Kraft und Gesundheit vor-
reichen, Sich bald dieser hohen Aufgabe mit allen Ihren Kräften zu
widmen! Ob Sie es über das Herz bringen, falls man Ihnen Berlin
anbietet, einzuschlagen, wag' ich nur zu hoffen. Es würde meine letzten
Lebenstage vergolden, Sie hier zu haben. Aber für Sie und für die
Wissenschaft wäre es wichtig, wenn Ihr Lebensweg den gewünschten
Gang gehen würde, gleichviel hier oder wo anders.

This amiable letter presumably elicited a telephone call. This is easier
than to assume that Jaeger lost or destroyed letters from Diels. He went ca.
21 April to Berlin for discussion with the Ministry and visits both to Diels
and Wilamowitz. Two further problems arose: 1) the problem of Jaeger's
successor at Kiel, which will not be treated in this paper, and 2) the choice
of Jaeger's *collega proximus*. The new sources clarify what was earlier
imperfectly known so that we learn that Boll and Jaeger were intended to
succeed Diels and Wilamowitz respectively. They were not in competition.
Boll declined. Jaeger would not become a Berlin professor until 1 October
1921 and so legally could not share in the debates of the Berlin Faculty
concerning Diels' successor. His interest in the appointment extended to the
degree that he covertly threatened to go to Heidelberg if his wishes were not
followed. He could not bear a rival and needed a colleague whom he could
bully but who was not too obviously inferior. There seems to be a number
of candidates whom he does not want but no one whom he is pushing. His
situation grew from his youth. His students were all men in their twenties,
and he distrusted his contemporaries. A decision was not made until 1927.
The following correspondence and that with Becker document the
negotiations.

3. Jaeger writes Diels on 15 April 1921 that Professor Boll will decide
at the latest by Sunday 17 April. Boll declined. Jaeger visited Berlin. He
returned to Kiel and writes to Diels 24 April 1921. Because of its
importance I edit the whole letter:

> Lieber, hochverehrter Herr Geheimrat,
>
> nachdem ich bei Ihnen war, bin ich noch zu Wilamowitz gegangen und
> habe dort den Eindruck empfangen, daß er an eine Liste Körte–Jensen–
> Schöne–Mewaldt[18] denkt und wünscht, sie bald einzureichen, um keine
> Zeit zu verlieren und selbst dabei noch mitsprechen zu können. Unter
> der Voraussetzung, daß Sie und Wilamowitz bei den Beratungen jetzt

---

[18] Wilamowitz' list was Alfred Körte (1866–1946): see T.B.L. Webster, *Gnomon* 21
(1949) 179–80; Christian Jensen (1883–1940): see Werner Hartkopf, *Die Akademie der
Wissenschaften der DDR: Ein Beitrag zu ihrer Geschichte: Biographischer Index* (Berlin
1983) 212; Hermann Schöne (1870–1941): see M. Wegner, "Altertumskunde," *Die
Universität Münster 1780–1980*, edited by H. Dollinger (Münster 1980) 416; Johannes
Mewaldt: see above, note 11.

Sitz und Stimme haben, was mir im Interesse der Fakultät unbedingt erforderlich erscheint u. ganz in der Hand der Fakultät liegt, wäre ich dafür, daß die Liste möglichst schon jetzt gemacht würde u. hoffe, daß sie im Wesentlichen so ausfallen wird, wie ich sagte. Nur wegen Schöne schien Wilamowitz noch im Zweifel.

Ich sagte Ihnen telephonisch neulich, ich hätte noch die Möglichkeit, nach Heidelberg zu kommen,[19] u. würde davon ev. Gebrauch machen, falls man einen zweiten in Berlin nähme, der mir für die gedeihliche Zusammenarbeit ungeeignet schiene, möge er an sich auch in Frage kommen. Inzwischen bin ich von der Seite Jacobys[20] hier unausgesetzt bearbeitet worden nach Heidelberg zu gehen, was mich nach dem vorher mit Norden Erlebten natürlich nicht sonderlich aufregt u. vor allem gar keinen Eindruck auf mich macht. Ich lege Ihnen nur als Stilblüte, die aus diesen Norden–Jacobyschen Bestrebungen erwächst, den beifolgenden Brief[21] ein mit der Bitte um Rücksendung, u. zwar um Ihnen anschaulich zu zeigen, daß die Aussicht, mich nach Heidelberg loszuwerden, leicht auch auf das Verhalten bestimmter Kreise bei Aufstellung der Liste einwirken könnte. Ich bitte Sie daher, niemand etwas davon zu sagen, daß mich ev. die Wahl Körtes[22] zu einem solchen Schritt bewegen könnte, da dies ja gerade die gegenteilige Wirkung haben müßte. Es wäre besser, mich ganz aus dem Spiel zu lassen oder höchstens schriftlich anzufragen: ich wäre natürlich stets gern bereit, eine Äußerung über die von der Fakultät zu nennenden Herren abzugeben, möchte mich aber grundsätzlich nicht mit eigenen Vorschlägen beteiligen. An einer raschen Erledigung läge mir deshalb, weil ich im Herbst schwerlich noch den Ausweg nach Heidelberg haben werde. Bis dahin warten die Heidelberger sicherlich nicht.

    Mit besten Grüßen stets getreulich
        Ihr ergebenster
        Werner Jaeger

  1 Einlage!

---

[19] The Heidelberg call at precisely this moment greatly strengthened Jaeger's hand with the Berlin Ministry. He also had Becker on his side. He does not hesitate to threaten.

[20] Felix Jacoby (1876–1959), his Kiel colleague: see Mortimer Chambers, "Felix Jacoby: 10 March 1876–10 November 1959," *Classical Scholarship: A Biographical Encyclopedia*, edited by Ward W. Briggs and William M. Calder III (New York/London 1990) 205–10. Chambers is preparing a book-length biography.

[21] A letter of Norden to either Jaeger or to Jacoby: see Diels' reply, *infra*. There are other examples of Jaeger sending private letters of colleagues written him to others to be read and returned.

[22] Körte's jealousy of Jaeger in the 1920s is attested by Friedrich Solmsen on the authority of Eduard Fraenkel: see *GRBS* 30 (1989) 138 n. 11. He may have learned that Jaeger had intervened against Wilamowitz to deny him a Berlin chair. In Wilamowitz' extant letters to Körte there is no mention of the matter. Jaeger may as easily have been jealous of Körte. In 1917 the alternative Körte or Jaeger was discussed at Leipzig. Körte won: see Mensching, 86 n. 5.

4. Diels replies to Jaeger 28 April 1921 and returns Norden's letter to him.

Der Brief, den ich Ihnen hier wieder zurücksende, wirkt sehr aufklärend. Ich hatte den Verf. [Eduard Norden] für klüger gehalten. Aber es ist ja gut, daß Sie so durch seine Naivität in seine Karten sehen. Ich hatte heute Gelegenheit mit den beiden Kollegen [Norden und Wilamowitz][23] die Situation zu besprechen. (Von dem Inhalte Ihres Briefes sagte ich natürlich nichts.)[24] Sie meinten, wenn der Minister auffordere zu neuen Vorschlägen, so müsste Ihre Annahme feststehen. Sonst könnten sie keine passenden Vorschläge machen, da ja doch eine passende Ergänzung erwogen werden müsse. Auch würde der Minister offenbar an die Fakultät erst schreiben, wenn Sie Sich entschieden hätten. Es wird also nichts anderes übrig bleiben, als daß Sie nun die Entscheidung treffen. Wie ich und Wilamowitz wünschen, daß die Entscheidung falle, wissen Sie.[25] Daß sie rasch falle, wünsche ich auch um dessentwillen, daß bis jetzt wir unseren Sitz und Stimme in der Facultät nicht verloren haben. Das kann aber anders werden, wenn der neue Minister die Sanktion seiner Vorschläge durch die Kollegen erlangt hat.

5. The next preserved letter is that of Diels to Jaeger of 26 May 1921. Diels had meanwhile visited Kiel and spoken with Jaeger there. Hans von Arnim, originally before Jaeger on the list but passed over by the Ministerium, is now the leading candidate for Diels' chair declined by Boll.

Norden teilte mir eben mit, daß Sie mit dem gefaßten Commissions-beschluß nicht zufrieden seien, weil Sie mit v. Arnim Sich zu nah berührten. Ich sprach mit Ihnen darüber schon in Kiel und hatte den Eindruck, daß diese Unbequemlichkeit, die Sie fast mit allen andern möglichen Candidaten teilen, nicht ausschlaggebend sei. Bequemer ist es natürlich Alleinherrscher in Graecis zu sein, aber da nun einmal seit Gründung der Universität (Böckh und Heindorff)[26] 2 Gräzisten die Regel

---

[23] The names are written in the left margin by Jaeger. [Eduard Norden] with brackets is inserted into the text by Jaeger. These insertions suggest that he had others read the letter.

[24] Diels was willing to deceive his *Du-Freund* of over fifty years in collusion with the thirty-two-year-old Jaeger!

[25] Sc. that you come to Berlin. Jaeger has underlined "ich und Wilamowitz" and added in the right margin an exclamation point in brackets.

[26] For August Böckh (1785–1867) see Max Hoffmann, *August Böckh: Lebens-beschreibung und Auswahl aus seinem wissenschaftlichen Briefwechsel* (Leipzig 1901); Bernd Schneider, *August Boeckh: Altertumsforscher, Universitätslehrer und Wissenschafts-organisator im Berlin des 19. Jahrhunderts. Ausstellung zum 200. Geburtstag 22. November 1985—18. Januar 1986* (West Berlin 1985); and Helmut Klein (editor), "August Boeckh (1785–1876) [sic!] Forscher, Hochschullehrer, Zeitzeuge," *Wissenschaftliche Zeitschrift der Humboldt-Universität zu Berlin* 36 (1987) 1–70. For Ludwig Friedrich Heindorf (1774–1816) see Wolfhart Unte in *Berlin und die Antike: Aufsätze*, edited by Willmuth Arenhövel and Christa Schreiber (Berlin 1979) 11. Heindorf, the editor of Plato, whose name Diels misspells on the false analogy of Moellendorff, was appointed professor for Greek at the newly founded University of Berlin in 1810, but in 1811, against his will and to the regret of his Berlin friends, was transferred to Breslau; for his brief work there see Richard Foerster,

sind und die Facultät mit Rücksicht auf den ungeheuren Umfang und die
Bedeutung des Hellenismus gewis [sic] nicht 2 Latinisten berufen wird,
so ist die Berufung von Arnim der z. Z. einzige Ausweg aus der Ver-
legenheit. Arnim wird 6 Jahre fungieren. Macht denn da die mögliche
Concurrenz in Platonicis (das ist doch die Hauptsache) soviel aus? Ich
habe nie Plato lesen können, da Vahlen und Wilamowitz dies taten, und
ich mich auch ohne ihren besonderen Wunsch zurückhielt. Dergleichen
kommt bei Doppelbesetzungen natürlich immer vor. Wir haben 2 alte
Historiker.[27] Sie vertragen sich ausgezeichnet, und die Universität hat
den Vorteil 2 ausgezeichnete Vertreter in ihrer Mitte zu haben. Lehnen
Sie aber einen anerkannten Meister wie Arnim ab oder beeinflussen Sie
die Regierung in diesem Sinn, die bereits, ich weiß nicht auf wessen
Anregung, die zu nahe Berührung von Arnim mit Ihnen als Grund der
Nichtbefragung angegeben hat, dann wird voraussichtlich Körte
gewählt werden müssen, denn Wilamowitz, der wegen des C.I.Gr.[28]
einen jüngeren Nachfolger mit Befähigung dieses in der Akademie zu
leiten haben möchte, findet wol keinen andern Candidaten. Er denkt ja
die 6 Jahre noch die Sache leiten zu können, falls v. Arnim berufen
würde. Dagegen wenn diese Möglichkeit wegfällt, müßte der Jüngere
wol eine derartige Qualität haben. Also bitte überlegen Sie die Sache
noch einmal!

Diels is impatient. Jaeger will brook no rival young or old. There have
always been two Berlin Hellenists. If he does not want von Arnim, he is
going to get Körte, whom he also does not want. If Eduard Meyer can work
with a colleague, Jaeger can learn to. Diels' impatience was not lost on
Jaeger. He replies by return mail and backtracks.

6. The letter is dated Kiel, 28 May 1921.

...einen bedeutenden Latinisten zu berufen habe ich nur aufgrund einer
Äußerung Nordens (19.5) vorgeschlagen, wonach man keinen
geeigneten Gräcisten finden könne. Die Berufung eines Lateiners
schien mir immer noch besser als eine endlose Vacanz. Von der
Möglichkeit, Arnim oder Schwartz nochmals zu nennen, wußte ich zwar

---

Festschrift zur Feier des hundertjährigen Bestehens der Universität Breslau, edited by Georg
Kaufmann, II: *Geschichte der Fächer, Institute und Ämter der Universität Breslau 1811–
1911* (Breslau 1911) 381. He was already a dying man when he reached Breslau.

[27] For Eduard Meyer (1855–1930) see Christhard Hoffmann, "Eduard Meyer 25 January
1855—31 August 1930," *Classical Scholarship: A Biographical Encyclopedia*, edited by
Ward W. Briggs and William M. Calder III (New York/London 1990) 264–76, and *Eduard
Meyer: Leben und Leistung eines Universalhistorikers*, edited by William M. Calder III and
Alexander Demandt, Mnemosyne Supp. Vol. 112 (Leiden 1990) *passim*. His younger
colleague was the Alexander–historian, Ulrich Wilcken (1862–1944): see Alexander
Demandt, *Berlin und die Antike: Aufsätze*, 87–88.

[28] For Wilamowitz' direction of the *Corpus Inscriptionum Graecarum* see Wolfhart Unte
in *Wilamowitz nach 50 Jahren*, edited by William M. Calder III, Hellmut Flashar, and
Theodor Lindken (Darmstadt 1985) 744–55.

durch Sie, da aber Norden nichts mehr davon schrieb, glaubte ich, dieser Gedanke sei aufgegeben worden. Inzwischen sehe ich aus einem Brief Nordens vom 24.5, daß meine Voraussetzung nicht richtig war u. daß Schwartz u. Arnim nochmals genannt werden sollen, womit ich natürlich ganz einverstanden bin.

Der Irrtum, als wolle ich nicht mit Arnim zusammenwirken, ist dadurch entstanden, daß ich an N. schrieb, Reitzenstein[29] u. Heinze[30] würden sich mit ihm noch weniger decken als Arnim mit mir, womit gemeint war, daß ich ihm *nichts Unmögliches* zumuten wolle. Denn daß ich gegen Arnim kein Veto erheben würde, hatte ich Ihnen wie der Regierung gesagt u. auch an Arnim geschrieben. Ich bitte dies Mißverständnis durch nochmalige Einsichtnahme in meinen Brief aufzuklären, da es mir im hohen Maße peinlich ist. Nur in der Annahme, daß man auf Arnim nicht zurückkommen wolle, habe ich Latinisten vorgeschlagen.[31] Natürlich liegt mir weit mehr an der Erhaltung der Professur für das Griechische, wenn die Fakultät dies zu können glaubt. Es bedarf auch keines Wortes, daß ich Arnim Körte vorziehen muß, der in einem 55jährigen Leben bewiesen hat, daß er nicht die Kraft hat, etwas Großes zu schaffen, trotz aller Rührigkeit.[32]

Daß ich mich mit Arnim decke, ist zwar nicht zu leugnen, wie Sie schreiben. Auch im Ministerium hob man das sogleich hervor. Unser Zentrum ist Plato u. Aristoteles, unsere Kollegs waren bisher auch sonst die gleichen. Er hatte mich in Frankfurt für den Fall seines Fortgangs auch als Nachfolger in Aussicht genommen, was gewiß besser oder natürlicher gewesen wäre als eine Zusammenarbeit an derselben Fakultät. Aber alle diese Schwierigkeiten lassen sich wohl überwinden, wenn beide Teile elastisch genug sind, sich nicht auf gewisse Stoffe zu kaprizieren, sondern sie in gleicher Weise in angemessenem Abstand voneinander behandeln. Ich möchte, falls A. berufen wird, schon jetzt Ihre gütige Vermittlung in diesem Sinne erbitten.

Sollte seitens des Ministeriums trotzdem nicht Arnim berufen werden, so ist es für mich natürlich um so erwünschter, die Stelle *vorläufig* offen zu lassen, als ich dann später meine Meinung bei der Wiederbesetzung als Mitglied der Fakultät vertreten kann.

---

[29] For Richard Reitzenstein (1862–1931) see Wolfgang Fauth, "Richard Reitzenstein, Professor der klassischen Philologie 1914–1928," *Die klassische Altertumswissenschaft an der Georg–August–Universität Göttingen: Eine Ringvorlesung zu ihrer Geschichte* (= Göttinger Universitätsschriften Serie A: Schriften 14 [Göttingen 1989] 178–96).

[30] For Richard Heinze (1867–1929) see Hellfried Dahlmann, *NDB* 8 (1969) 447–48 with bio-bibliography and F. Klingner, *Gnomon* 6 (1930) 58–62.

[31] Not a convincing *Erklärung*. Everything we know about Jaeger at this time shows that he could not tolerate a rival.

[32] The fundamental Menander editions of 1910 and 1912, made under the close supervision of Wilamowitz, are "nothing great." Jaeger's judgment is colored by his unspoken assumption that Menander is *Trivialliteratur*.

Jaeger delays until his last sentence what he really wants. It is neither Körte, whose work he underestimates, nor Arnim, of whose work he says not a word. His colleague should be chosen when he is able to dictate the decision. He will be the only Hellenist. Diels and Wilamowitz will after 1 October no longer have a vote. Norden will do as he is told.

7. Jaeger writes his last preserved letter to Diels on 30 May 1921. No reply survives.

...ich habe im Anschluß an unseren Briefwechsel über Arnim noch länger über die Gründe des Mißverständnisses nachdenken müssen, das in betreff meiner Stellungnahme durch Nordens Auffassung meines Briefes aufgekommen war. Sie wissen ja, daß Nordens letzte Absicht keineswegs auf Arnim gerichtet ist, sondern auf Jacoby.[33] Er wünscht daher Offenlassung des Lehrstuhls auf längere Zeit, bis die Historikerfragmente[34] vorliegen. An der Gewinnung Arnims ist ihm dagegen gar nicht gelegen, er kann nur nicht von sich aus dagegen sprechen. Ich werde den Gedanken nicht los, daß er aus meinem Brief jenes Misverständnis nur darum so eifrig aufgegriffen hat um *"mir zuliebe"* noch eine weitere Sitzung der Kommission zu veranlassen, wo beschlossen werden soll, die Offenlassung des Lehrstuhls als den vielleicht relativ glücklichsten Ausweg noch etwas stärker zu unterstreichen. Jedenfalls hat die irrige Vermutung Nordens, ich sei gegen Arnim, ihn in seinem Briefe von 26.5 zu folgendem Satz inspiriert: "Daß mir an Arnim, den ich so gut wie gar nicht kenne, *nicht das Geringste* gelegen ist, erwähnte ich neulich schon. Aber nennen Sie einen Besseren." Ich teile Ihnen das nicht zu weiterer Verwertung mit, sondern damit Sie die Stellung Nordens zu der Frage richtig sehen. Ich kann, wie ich schon schrieb, gewiß nicht von mir sagen, daß mir mit Arnims Berufung ein Herzenswunsch befriedigt würde; aber das darf ich

---

[33] Norden wished Felix Jacoby to succeed Diels. The reason was not *Judensolidarität*, for both were fully assimilated anti-semites. Jacoby had habilitated under Norden at Breslau. Norden's choice of Jacoby explains a passage in a letter of Ernst Bickel (1876–1961) to Jaeger dated 28 July 1933:
"In der Philologie aber sind Sie, lieber Jaeger, unser Führer, und gerade angesichts der jetzigen Bewegung denke ich mit tiefer Dankbarkeit daran, wie Sie mich vor Juden und Judenknechten jetzt vor 12 Jahren [sc. 1921] in Kiel errettet haben. Außerdem ist es Ihr geschichtliches Verdienst, daß Sie die Berliner Philologie vor der Verjudung in der entscheidenden Stunde gerettet haben, die durch die Einfilzung Jacobys in den Berliner Lehrkörper und die Berliner Akademie rettungslos von statten gegangen wäre."
Bickel means that thanks to Jaeger he became Ordinarius at Königsberg on 30 July 1921: see Hans Herter, *Gnomon* 33 (1961) 637. He was thus saved from his archenemy, Jacoby, but also from Eduard Fraenkel, who became Ordinarius at Kiel in 1928. The *Judenknecht* in the sense "servant of a Jew" rather than "Jewish servant" possibly is Julius Stenzel (1883–1935), a student of Jacoby at Breslau, who was married to a Jewess and became Ordinarius for philosophy at Kiel in 1925. Bickel seems not to know that Jaeger's second wife was half-Jewish. In the same year that Jaeger removed Bickel from Kiel he prevented Norden from placing Jacoby in Berlin. For these acts the sycophantic Bickel thanks him in 1933.
[34] The first volume of *FGrHist* was published in 1923. Jacoby had announced the project at the Berlin Historical Congress on 6 August 1908: correct Mensching, 90 n. 37.

doch sagen, daß ich sachlich mit Freuden bereit wäre, mit ihm
zusammen zu wirken, wenn die Regierung sich nicht bereits in anderem
Sinne festgelegt hat, mag auch manche Unbequemlichkeit für ihn und
mich dabei sein. Ich fürchte nur, daß bei der einmal vorhandenen
Stimmung Nordens ein jeder von uns dreien seinen Weg für sich allein
gehen würde. Aber daran ist wohl wenig zu ändern. Auf jeden Fall
möchte ich nicht, daß die Kommission irgend etwas "mir zuliebe"
beschließt, was ich nicht selbst klar und deutlich als meine Meinung
ausgesprochen habe. Ich wollte, ich wäre schon in Berlin u. könnte
selbst die Ansicht, die ich habe, vertreten, dann brauchte ich Ihnen
nicht so große Mühe zu machen. Solange das aber noch nicht der Fall
ist, vertraue ich mich Ihnen vollständig an und weiß, daß bei Ihnen
meine Interessen am besten aufgehoben sind.

V. The Becker–Jaeger Letters

The Carl Heinrich Becker–Werner Jaeger Briefwechsel consists of 31 letters
(11 of Becker; 1 im Auftrag von Becker; 19 of Jaeger) dated 24 September
1918 to 10 October 1932. The letters are in the possession of his son
Professor Dr. h. c. Hellmut Becker, Max–Planck–Institut für Bildungs-
forschung, West Berlin. I am grateful to him for sending me copies of them
all and to my friend Professor emeritus Ulrich K. Goldsmith (Colorado) who
first drew my attention to the existence of the letters and then interceded on
my behalf. The letters parallel the Althoff–Wilamowitz Briefwechsel.[35]
There is, however, an intimacy between Becker and Jaeger not found
between Althoff and Wilamowitz. There one finds courteous respect. Even
the *Anrede* is different: from the beginning "Lieber Herr Becker." This is not
only because they are written a generation later. I do not know when they
first met, but they were friends before Becker's political apotheosis. As early
as 20 December 1918 in a partially published letter to Stroux, Jaeger
describes[36]

die herzliche Annäherung an den ganz vortrefflichen Personalreferenten
Prof. Becker, einen großen Hochschulreformer, einen *Menschen*, der
dies Wort zu Ehren bringt.

He further notes that at this time he was invited "...in einer einfluß-reichen
Stellung ins Ministerium einzutreten. Was natürlich abgelehnt wurde." Who
invited him, how official the invitation, we are not told. Becker, however,

---

[35] See William M. Calder III and Alexander Košenina, *Berufungspolitik innerhalb der
Altertumswissenschaft im wilhelminischen Preußen: Die Briefe Ulrich von Wilamowitz-
Moellendorffs an Friedrich Althoff (1883–1908)* (Frankfurt/Main 1989), with the invaluable
review articles of Edgar Pack, *Quaderni di storia* 33 (1991) 191–241 and W.A. Schröder,
GGA 242 (1990) 211–36.
[36] See Mensching, 70.

soon trusts him and even sends him documents to read which he knows he should not send. In Steglitz they became neighbors and shared a garden. Jaeger in his letters to Becker has quite a different political stance than in his letters to Wilamowitz. He writes Becker from Kiel on 1 December 1918: "Ich kann versichern, daß ich Ihr politisches Ethos...vollkommen zu teilen glaube. Ich bejahe den Sozialismus, über die Nuance bin ich freilich noch im Unklaren u. neige zur Skepsis gegen jeden Doktrinarismus." Jaeger in general was apolitical. This is clear in his historiography. Politics rarely appear in his letters. On 20th December he wrote Stroux:[37]

> Deutschlands Zukunft hängt an der Sozialdemokratie. Was bisher Vaterland, Staat, Ehre hieß, haben wir verloren. Wir Jungen können aber bei diesem Weheruf nicht lange verweilen, wir müssen anfangen, aufzubauen, was wir im Herzen als Bild eines besseren Deutschland [sic] getragen haben.

The principal new texts are the following.

1. In a letter of great importance dated 30 June 1919, almost two years before the offer was made, Becker promises Jaeger the Berlin chair. He writes to discourage him from leaving Kiel for Hamburg:[38]

> Wie die Dinge einmal liegen, kann es sich doch nur noch um einige Jahre handeln, bis Sie dauernd nach Berlin übersiedeln und es ist wirklich nicht empfehlenswert, noch einmal von neuem mit den Aufbau zu beginnen, wenn man doch sicher weiß, dass er nur von kurzer Dauer sein wird.

The highest authority assures ("sicher") Jaeger that he will in a few years be called to Berlin. Shortly thereafter Jaeger conferred with Becker in Berlin and visited him in his home. Jaeger was never adverse to flattery. If the ends do not justify the means, what do?

2. Jaeger writes Becker 23 July 1919:

> Schon alle die Tage hatte ich Ihnen schreiben wollen, um noch einmal schriftlich meine tiefe Freude auszusprechen über das, was ich in Berlin in den zwei Tagen meines Dortseins erlebt habe. Ihnen so ganz persönlich durfte ich eigentlich nur für die erhebenden Stunden des Aufatmens und der inneren Berührung danken, die Sie mir so unverdient in Ihrem Heim beschert hatten, aber was ist letztes Endes auch die große Τύχη in meiner beruflichen Arbeit, welche die Berliner Verhand-

---

[37] *Ibid.*
[38] Cf. Mensching, 61: "...doch Jaeger bleibt in Kiel, möglicherweise im Blick auf die zu erwartenden Berliner Vakanzen..."

lungen mir offenbart und mir zugesellt haben, anders als eine Epiphanie Ihrer persönlichen Ansicht und Einschätzung meiner We<ni>gkeit. Die Griechen nannten das Göttliche, soweit sie es im eignen Schicksal wahrnahmen und aufs eigne Wohl und Wehe bezogen, Δαίμων. Nur daß ich den Δαίμων in der Begegnung mit ihnen so unleugbar empfinde, macht mich heiter und schenkt mir zu dem fast zu hohen Maß des Dankes, den ich Ihnen gegenüber dauernd fühle, die notwendige Unabhängigkeit. Ich möchte lieber noch sagen: die Unabhängigkeit des Notwendigen.

The high point of Jaeger's visit to Berlin was the epiphany of the God Becker. He did not decline Hamburg because of rumors of a new retirement law.[39] He had a promise.

3. On 12 March 1921 not only Diels and Wende wrote letters to Jaeger. Becker did too:

Lieber Herr Jaeger,

Sie werden mit gleicher Post die offizielle Berufung als Nachfolger von Wilamowitz durch Geheimrat Wende erhalten.[40] Ich kann es mir aber nicht versagen, gleichzeitig auch meiner persönlichen Freude darüber Ausdruck zu geben, dass die Fakultät Sie mit dem wärmsten Worten dem Ministerium präsentiert hat.[41] In der Vorschlagsliste sind honoris causa an der Spitze Eduard Schwartz und Arnim genannt, aber man merkt dem ganzen Tenor an, dass die Fakultät diese eigentlich für zu alt hält. Dann wurden Boll und Sie mit grösster Wärme vorgeschlagen. Es ist also diesmal genau nach unsern[42] Wünschen gegangen, und Boll und Sie werden gleichzeitig berufen.[43]

Mit Ihrer Uebersiedelung nach Berlin erfüllt sich für mich ein grosser persönlicher Wunsch. Ich heisse Sie hier von ganzem Herzen willkommen, und ich weiss, dass Sie kommen werden, wenn sich vielleicht auch mancherlei innerlich bei Ihnen gegen Berlin sträubt.[44] Immerhin werden Sie hier auch noch die Ruhe zur Arbeit finden. Was am Ministerium liegt, Ihnen die Forschertätigkeit zu erleichtern, soll geschehen. Ueber das Wissenschaftliche hinaus freue ich mich aber auch als Mensch ganz besonders, mit Ihnen in Zukunft in örtlicher

---

[39] For details of the Hamburg call see Mensching, 70–75.

[40] See above, note 16.

[41] The contrast with Wilamowitz' call in 1897 is obvious.

[42] Unless the *pluralis majestatis*, Becker and Jaeger had planned it this way.

[43] This clears up once and for all the earlier ambiguity. The list was for two posts, the chairs of Diels and Wilamowitz. There were two candidates for each. The seniores were there *honoris causa*. The lists were:
1. Schwartz and von Arnim; 2. Jaeger and Boll.

[44] This was a *topos* familiar to classical scholars from Wilamowitz: see e. g., Ulrich von Wilamowitz-Moellendorff, *Erinnerungen 1848–1914*[2] (Leipzig 1929) 239.

Gemeinschaft leben zu dürfen, und ich bitte Sie nur schon heute, recht oft den Weg zu mir zu finden. Ich freue mich auf Ihr Kommen wirklich vom ganzen Herzen.

> In bekannter Gesinnung
>   aufrichtig der Ihrige
>   [Becker]

Jaeger has a friend at the top whose office door is always open.

4. The last preserved letter in the Becker–Jaeger Correspondence concerning the Berlin appointment is Jaeger's reply.

Kiel d. 15.3.1921.
Adolfplatz 10/I

Lieber Herr Becker!

Gestern erhielt ich mit gleicher Post zwei inhalt- und entscheidungs-schwere Briefe aus Ihrem Ministerium, den offiziellen Ruf nach Berlin von Geheimrat Wende und Ihren freundlich warmen Begleitbrief, für den ich Ihnen ganz besonders herzlich danke, weil er nicht nur den Schlüssel zur Situation enthält und mir die Überlegung schon vor einer Rücksprache im Ministerium ermöglicht, sondern vor allem auch, weil er Imponderabilien von großem Wert bereits jetzt in die Wagschale legt. Wenn trotz starker Bedenken doch auch manches für Berlin spricht, so ist darunter der Gedanke, von Ihrer Nähe öfter etwas zu haben, für mich besonders tröstlich: ich würde von dieser Gelegenheit sicher soviel Gebrauch machen, wie Ihnen nur eben recht ist.

Was die Sache angeht, so ist sie freilich keine reine Freude. Der Gedanke an eine solche Beschränkung des natürlichen Willens zum Leben, wie sie Berlin für jeden Menschen von feinnerviger Konstitution bedeutet, an die unerfreuliche Fakultätspolitik, die dort zuletzt getrieben worden ist, u. schließlich die näheren Umstände der Berufung selbst machen mir die Annahme recht schwer. In ersterer Hinsicht enthält Ihr Brief nun ein wesentliches Moment des Trostes wenn Sie mir ein besonderes Entgegenkommen des Ministeriums in Aussicht stellen, um mir die Forschertätigkeit zu erleichtern. Aber die Schrecken der Fakultätsstreitigkeiten sind für mich sehr groß, da ich nicht in dieselbe Kerbe hauen kann wie Gustav Roethe.[45] Endlich ist zwar die Liste ganz ehrenvoll für mich, wenn sie nach Männern von europäischer Autorität wie Ed. Schwartz und v. Arnim und einem so hervorragenden Mann wie Boll unter Umgehung einer ganzen Generation von lebenden Forschern—ich meine des mittleren Alters—

---

[45] For Gustav Roethe (1859–1926), Berlin Ordinarius for Germanistik, neighbor and former Göttingen colleague of Wilamowitz, see *Briefe–Althoff*, 79 n. 340, and Peter Müller, "Mobilisierung der Wissenschaft: Über die Zusammenführung von Germanistik und Politik bei Gustav Roethe," *Zeitschrift für Germanistik* 9 (1988) 558–71. Jaeger knew that his German nationalist politics had not endeared him to Becker.

sofort mich den 32jährigen nennt, aber es ist doch nicht natürlich, daß sich ein Junger in <diese?> Bresche stürzen soll, der, wenigstens nach eigener Einschätzung, wohl hoffen könnte, in einem etwas angemesseneren Alter als erster berufen zu werden. Es wäre mein Wunsch, meiner Natur gemäß mich weiter zu entwickeln und keine mir fremden Aufgaben mehr auf mich zu laden. Berlin ist für eine solche Entwicklung sicher nicht der geeignete Ort.

Unter diesen Umständen, deren offne Darlegung grade Ihnen gegenüber mir ein inneres Bedürfnis ist, schon bevor ich zur Verhandlung komme, muß ich mein Augenmerk besonders auf die Frage der Besetzung des anderen Lehrstuhls richten. An Boll einen Kollegen in wahren Sinn des Wortes zu finden, würde einer der wenigen positiven Gewinne sein, der mit der Berufung für mich verbunden sein könnte. Leider ist die Aussicht nicht groß, daß er kommt, so weit ich a priori sagen zu können glaube. Ich habe ihm vertraulich u. offen geschrieben, wie ich über seine Berufung denke. Sobald ich weiß, wo ich ihn sprechen kann, werde ich hinreisen, ich habe ihm Berlin vorgeschlagen. Falls er meinen Brief vor seiner Abreise nicht mehr erhält, bitte ich mich über seine Anwesenheit in Berlin, wenn nötig telegraphisch, zu benachrichtigen. Bis dahin bin ich mit verehrungsvollen Grüßen stets aufrichtig der Ihrige

Jaeger

VI. How it Happened

My study of *Wissenschaftsgeschichte* has convinced me that although merit, that is, influential publications of value, is indispensable, it is rarely decisive in academic appointments of importance. Walter Burkert has observed *per litt.* that the Wilamowitz–Althoff letters support the unwelcome truth that departments and faculties require a ruthless tyrant devoted to excellence in charge to make them great. Wilamowitz would have been forgotten in Greifswald were it not for Althoff. Jaeger's books certainly did him no harm.

Decisive for his Berlin appointment were three friendships. He may have lost a fourth. I wish at the end to summarize briefly what happened.

The documents edited above, most for the first time, provide the evidence for Jaeger's greatest victory in his professional career. From this victory all his subsequent success derived, not least his Berkeley, Chicago, and Harvard appointments. On 12 March 1921 Jaeger secured for himself at age 32 the most prestigious chair of classics in the world. From his arrival in Berlin in autumn 1907 he played his cards right. He made no student friends. Students were distractions and rivals. Good students like Karl Reinhardt were potential enemies. Therefore, no friend of his fell in World

War I.[46] The reason is simple. Jaeger was too selfish to have friends. Women were different. They were not rivals and could be used.[47] Rather, Jaeger cultivated people in high places who could help him. This meant Diels and Wilamowitz and a lesser being, "a kind of mediator between us and the semi-divine Dioscuri,"[48] Norden. They got him grants and contracts with publishers like Teubner and Weidmann. They placed his articles. They secured for him the Basel chair in 1914, the Kiel chair in 1915, and the Berlin chair in 1921. He had less respect for Norden. Wilamowitz he flattered, feared, and respected. Diels was closest. By 1921 he had also won Becker. The young Jaeger could be extraordinarily charming.[49] And, much to his credit, he had no enemies that mattered. The hatred that Ernst Curtius, Kirchhoff, and Vahlen had borne Wilamowitz in 1896 was the obvious contrast. Curtius died at the right moment. Althoff literally had to form a new Institute for Diels and Wilamowitz and order Vahlen to write Wilamowitz a Liebesbrief before the appointment was final.[50]

Semper idem. The Berlin professor, as earlier the student, could not abide a rival. While we have no evidence that anyone at Berlin opposed his appointment (Boll was intended for the second chair), Jaeger opposed Arnim, Jacoby, Körte, Malten, Mewaldt, and Schöne and apparently every other candidate suggested between 1921 and 1927 for the second Greek chair. Diels died some eight months after Jaeger began to teach in Berlin. Norden was a Latinist and so did not matter. With Wilamowitz there was a growing estrangement documented in the letters to Drachmann, Rehm, and others. This certainly cannot be attributed entirely to Jaeger, who was always diplomatic. Seneca told Nero that no matter how many men he murdered, he could never murder his successor. Wilamowitz liked centerstage. In 1927 Jaeger at last agreed to the appointment of Ludwig Deubner (1877–1946).[51] He was older and less threatened. One sees this also in the fact that his students became his friends in a way his fellow students never could. One thinks only of Richard Harder, Viktor Pöschl, and Wolfgang Schadewaldt.

---

[46] See Mensching, 68–69. Contrast how the loss of sons drew Wilamowitz, Diels, and Eduard Meyer together, a loss all the more poignant because the war was lost. *Invictis victi victuri!*

[47] See Werner Jaeger, *Paideia* I[2] (New York 1945) 22: "The real arete of woman is beauty—naturally enough: men are valued by their intellectual and physical excellence." When Jaeger met a woman who was ugly and intelligent (Eva Sachs), he could not cope; see *ICS* 12 (1988) 206–07 with n. 16.

[48] Jaeger, *Five Essays* (Montreal 1966) 63. His contempt for Norden is proven by his betrayal of his confidence to Diels.

[49] See Friedrich Solmsen, *GRBS* 30 (1989) 128: "Once for all it must be said that to those not personally acquainted with Jaeger, it is impossible to convey the magnetism and charm of his personality."

[50] For the details of Wilamowitz' call to Berlin see William M. Calder III, "Die Rolle Friedrich Althoffs bei den Berufungen von Ulrich von Wilamowitz-Moellendorff," in *Wissenschaftsgeschichte und Wissenschaftspolitik im Industriezeitalter: Das 'System Althoff' in historischer Perspektive,* edited by Bernhard vom Brocke (Hildesheim 1991) 251–66.

[51] For Deubner see Martin P. Nilsson, *Gnomon* 12 (1949) 87–88. Jaeger did not write the necrology.

Deubner could be dismissed as an archaeologist who knew Latin and specialized in Attic cult, a thoroughly antiquarian part of the Greek past. That is: what he did was trivial.

I suggest, although I cannot yet prove it, that there may have been pressure by the Government, to which Jaeger thought best to yield, to take Deubner. Nilsson notices that the Riga German was fluent in Russian and received the iron cross for his service in World War I.[52] Jaeger spoke to me once about favoritism shown Deubner at Berlin. The reason was not a scholarly one but because he had broken the Russian military code and thereby insured the German victory at Tannenberg (26–30 August 1914). This victory saved Germany from foreign invasion during World War I and assured the political career of the victorious commander-in-chief Paul von Hindenburg. Deubner certainly received his Berlin appointment during the Hindenburg Presidency.

Jaeger's fifteen years in the Berlin chair will be treated by others, his Aristotle books, *Paideia*, and the Third Humanism. So will his subsequent American period. He resigned his Berlin post effective 1 September 1936, rather than divorce his second wife, who was half Jewish. He received a letter of thanks dated 12 November 1936:

> Ich entlasse Sie auf Ihren Antrag seit Ende September 1936 aus dem preußischen Landesdienst. Ich spreche Ihnen für Ihre akademische Wirksamkeit und dem Reich geleisteten Dienste meinen Dank aus.

It is signed by Adolf Hitler. Another name is there. I wonder if Jaeger ever knew that it belonged to the cousin-in-law of Wilamowitz.[53] It is Hermann Göring's.[54]

---

[52] *Ibid.*

[53] For prosopographical details see *CP* 66 (1971) 115. This note is not known because Mde J. Ernst forbade its inclusion in *L'AnnPhil.*

[54] I cite the transcription of Daniel Ramseier (Basel). On 26 April 1991, when Dr. Anton Bierl sought to copy the letter, it "could not be found." For the special preference granted Jaeger by the Nazi government see Volker Losemann, "Nationalsozialismus und Antike: Studien zur Entwicklung des Faches Alte Geschichte 1933–1945," *Historische Perspektiven* 7 (Hamburg 1977) 43. I wish to express my gratitude to Herr Ramseier for detailed information concerning the Jaeger *Nachlaß* at Harvard. I hope that his catalogue will soon be published. I thank again Dr. Dietrich Ehlers (Berlin), whose transcriptions of the Becker, Diels, and Jaeger letters I have used. The transcriptions from the Stählin–Wilamowitz letter (n. 7) and the Norden letter are my own. Dr. Anton Bierl (Munich) has carefully read my penultimate draft. Prof. Michael Armstrong has saved me from error. I thank both scholars.

Morton Smith[1]

With the death in New York City on 11 July 1991 of Morton Smith,
professor emeritus of ancient history at Columbia University, successor of
Elias J. Bickermann, *Religionsgeschichte* in the US has lost its most
erudite and controversial figure, an exponent of Böckh's *totius antiquitatis
cognitio*. Smith was born 28 May 1915 into a prosperous Philadelphia
family. His father was a maker of church windows. He received the Harvard
B.A. 'magna cum laude' in 1936 with his major in English not classics.
"My serious work began in 1937 at Harvard Divinity School, especially
with New Testament under Henry Cadbury and rabbinics under H.A.
Wolfson."[2] Wolfson urged that Smith learn rabbinic Hebrew as background
for the New Testament. This Smith did in a year. Wolfson convinced the
Greek historian, William Scott Ferguson, then Dean of the Graduate
School, to grant Smith a Sheldon Fellowship for study at the Hebrew
University in Jerusalem, "where the New Testament was 'hellenistic
literature.'" The outbreak of World War II stranded him there. Wolfson was
able to extend the fellowship. Smith was awarded the doctorate in 1948 with
a dissertation written in Hebrew later translated as *Tannaitic Parallels to the
Gospels* (1951). This was "the first extensive application, to rabbinic
literature, of synoptic criticism and form criticism."

At this time Smith became an Episcopalian priest and briefly in the
forties had a parish. He was never defrocked but ceased to serve in 1948. He
returned to Harvard Divinity School 1948-50 and in 1957 received the Th.D.
with a famous dissertation *Palestinian Parties and Politics that Shaped the
Old Testament* (New York 1971). "It broke with common Old Testament
studies by arguing that most Israelites were not worshippers of only one
god. Monotheism was the late achievement of a relatively small movement
whose members preserved from ancient Israelite literature only a small
selection of works they approved and—centuries later—canonized." This was
the first of many studies calculated to enrage the Establishment, Jewish or
Christian, but far too intelligent and erudite to be dismissed as simply
annoying.

His first university appointment was instructor, then assistant professor
in Biblical Literature at Brown University (1950-55). He was denied tenure
and became Visiting Professor in the History of Religions at Drew
University 1956-57. In 1957 he succeeded Elias J. Bickermann in the chair

---

[1] Citations without attribution are from a brief autobiography that Smith wrote for me on 30
May 1985.
[2] See Margaret Hope Bacon, *Let This Life Speak: The Legacy of Henry Joel Cadbury*
(Philadelphia 1987), and Leo W. Schwarz, *Wolfson of Harvard: Portrait of a Scholar* (Philadelphia 1978), esp. 121-24 for Wolfson's crucial influence on Smith.

of Ancient History at Columbia but as assistant professor. He became full professor only in 1962 aged 47, a position he held until his retirement in 1985. Bickermann's interests, like Smith's, embraced Greece, Rome and the Near East and emphasized in the tradition of Eduard Meyer the central importance of *Religionsgeschichte* in understanding the ancient world. Smith was the ideal successor.[3] He soon wrote a textbook for his undergraduate lectures in Greek history: *The Ancient Greeks* (Cornell 1960 and frequent reprints). He was an authoritative rather than eloquent lecturer.[4] In 1963 in spite of the support of Wolfson and Goodenough, Smith was personally denied a Harvard professorship by President Nathan Pusey. Goodenough wrote to Smith that Pusey "is on the side of the tinsel angels in anything to do with religion." Smith never forgave this injustice. As often he was victim of his own integrity. This decided him to remain at Columbia. With Moses Hadas, he wrote *Heroes and Gods* (New York 1965) and with Bickermann, *The Ancient History of Western Civilization* (New York 1976).

Werner Jaeger had interested Smith in hunting Greek manuscripts. In summer 1958 Smith discovered at the Monastery of Mar Saba southeast of Jerusalem bound into Voss' 1646 edition of the letters of St. Ignatius of Antioch an 18th century copy of a hitherto unknown letter of Clemens Alexandrinus. The letter contained a long quotation from what Clement claimed to be a secret gospel by Mark. What Smith called "an accidental discovery," determined the direction of his work for the rest of his life, made him world-famous, and involved him in violent controversy which he thoroughly enjoyed and did all he could to exacerbate. Public announcement of the find made page 1 of the *New York Times* (30 December 1960). The great edition appeared 13 years later: *Clement of Alexandria and a Secret Gospel of Mark* (Harvard 1973), dedicated to the memory of A.D. Nock.[5] Largely because of the subject matter which could be construed as "patient of obscenity," the book met with extraordinary hostility from believers. Smith was even accused of having himself forged the document;[6] and there were attempts to argue an 18th century forgery. The Patriarchate of Jerusalem has refused to make the manuscript available for further study.

The great majority of informed scholars accepted Clementine authorship of the letter. Smith himself denied that the new Gospel was by canonical Mark. He supposed it "a reworking of pre-Markan material," a common source for Mark and John: see his "Clement of Alexandria and Secret Mark:

[3] For Smith's necrology of Bickermann see *Gnomon* 54 (1982) 223-24.

[4] His Columbia colleague, Gilbert Highet, wrote a brutal criticism of his lecturing style: see *The Immortal Profession: The Joys of Teaching and Learning* (New York 1976) 97-98. The unnamed colleague is Smith.

[5] For a popular, autobiographical account of the find see his *The Secret Gospel: The Discovery and Interpretation of the Secret Gospel According to Mark* (New York 1973), esp. 24-25 for his teacher A.D. Nock. This was translated into German (Ullstein 1975).

[6] See Q. Quesnell "The Mar Saba Clementine: A Question of Evidence," *CBQ* 37 (1975) 48-67 with Smith's reply at *CBQ* 38 (1976) 196-99.

The Score at the End of the First Decade," *HTR* 75 (1982) 449-61. The text has elucidated, or better perhaps, complicated, the vexed *Entstehungs-geschichte* of the Synoptics and the history of the early church. Smith interpreted the text as an ancient mystery initiation by Jesus, the closest parallels to which lay in the magical papyri. This led directly to his equally controversial book, *Jesus the Magician* (San Francisco 1978) with a later German version (Paul List 1980) as well as his translations and commentaries in H.D. Betz, *The Greek Magical Papyri in Translation* (Chicago 1986). His catalogue of the British Museum's collection of magical gems and his projected *A History of Greco-Roman Magic* remain unfinished. Two volumes of *Kleine Schriften* with full bibliography have now appeared.[7] A four volume *Festschrift* appeared in 1975 with a title that delighted him: *Christianity, Judaism, and other Greco-Roman Cults.*

He was a lifelong bachelor. This allowed him the means to accumulate a private library of over 10,000 volumes, bequeathed to the Jewish Theological Seminary, and, because free of domestic distraction, to devote his whole life to scholarship. It explained the central contradiction in his life. He was an articulate conservative ("I am just an old-fashioned Anglosaxon Imperialist," he told me once), who mercilessly humiliated the Establishment. This was his revenge. His youthful mysticism was replaced by icy rationalism that allowed him, like Nietzsche, to assault religion with the knowledge of an apostate.[8] He was a fearless and honest reviewer which meant that his enemies were legion and his praise cherished. He benefited immeasurably those who sought his advice. He delighted in outraging the pretentiously pious and had a keen sense for justice that made him fearless before the foe. "Thank God I have tenure," he said to a *Times* reporter. He kindled heated discussions at scholarly gatherings and cheerfully collected threatened libel suits. His scurrilous limericks could not be reproduced here. "While there is death there is hope,' he often said. Cowards who dared not attack him while he lived, will now, as they did Housman after 1936. But in 50 years when his victims are forgotten, his greatness will be extolled. *Voluit, quiescit.*

[7] [Morton Smith, *Studies in the Cult of Yahweh:* 1 *Historical Method, Ancient Israel, Ancient Judaism*; 2 *New Testament, Early Christianity, and Magic*, ed. Shaye J.D. Cohen (Leiden/New York/Köln 1996) with full bibliography and dissertations directed at 2. 257-78.]

[8] See, e.gg., his "The Present State of Old Testament Studies," *JBL* 88 (1969) 19-35, where Yahweh becomes (21) "a North-Arabian mountain god who traveled in thunderstorms and like the smell of burning fat" or his notorious intimation of the homosexuality of Jesus at *Clement* 154, 185, a view anticipated by Jeremy Bentham on the basis of Mark 14. 51-52.

Arthur Darby Nock
1902-1963

Like most scholars, externally his life was uneventful. A.D. Nock was born at Portsmouth, England, of middle-class parents. He took his BA in 1922 at Trinity College, Cambridge, earlier the college of William Robertson Smith and Sir James Frazer, in 1926 the MA. That ended his formal education. He was Fellow of Clare (1923-30), then University Lecturer in Classics. On the recommendation of Gilbert Murray to A. Lawrence Lowell, he was visiting lecturer in the history of religions at Harvard (1929-30). In 1930 for reasons still unclear he left England permanently to become Frothingham Professor of the History of Religions at Harvard, a post he held until his death. He long edited the *Harvard Theological Review*, and was editor for Greek and Roman Religion of the *Oxford Classical Dictionary*. He delivered several prestigious lecture series (Giffords and Lowells). He was a member of several prestigious academies. He wrote several famous books and several hundred erudite and influential articles and reviews. An inveterate smoker, he died in Boston of cancer, aged 60.

What was it about Arthur Darby Nock that allowed him so to influence an undergraduate utterly incompetent to understand his contribution or even imagine the extent of his erudition? Certainly with Werner Jaeger and Sterling Dow he was one of the three Harvard teachers who made me a scholar. There were several reasons. He gave the impression that he was wholly devoted to *Wissenschaft*. Nothing else mattered. Although his lectures were hilarious, teaching seemed a pause from the more important. He lectured on Tuesday and Thursday and canceled all Saturday classes. His office hours were from 12 to 12:05 on Saturdays in the Widener Stacks, which undergraduates were forbidden to enter. He stated in his first lecture: "My telephone is for the use of my superiors, my colleagues, and my few friends." I never phoned him and until this day am startled when an undergraduate phones me.

He had an enormous private library that overflowed his Eliot House rooms. When I visited him there, he showed me books in his icebox, and told me that I must first buy critical texts, then indices and commentaries, "and, if there is room, secondary literature." He had a wall covered with framed pictures of scholars. Wilamowitz was missing. In my dark room I copied the 80th birthday portrait from *Die Antike*, framed it, and gave it to him. He was delighted, drew attention to the Slavic features of the face, and added it to his collection. Professors Dow and Hammond emphasized military and political history. Nock, in the tradition of Eduard Meyer, made the history of religion central.

In lectures he presented ancient and primitive religion, as Wilamowitz said one must, as a believer. This made him different from Frazer and gained respect for the subject. He forced us to memorize his definition of religion. "Religion is that active attitude of man toward those factors, real or imaginary, in his environment or makeup, which he of himself cannot fully comprehend or control, and what he does, says, or thinks in virtue of that active attitude." He stressed that doing (ritual) comes first. "Primitive religion is not believed. It is danced," he would say. This was the legacy of the Cambridge Ritualists. He defined classical piety as doing the traditional things in the traditional ways. Next saying (liturgy), and least important was thinking, that is theology. His brief definition was "Religion is man's refusal to accept helplessness." I later saw here the influence of Gilbert Murray.

He most admired M.P. Nilsson and said in class that *Cults, Myths, Oracles and Politics in Ancient Greece* (1951) was the only book Nilsson had dedicated to a person. We ran to see to whom it was dedicated. It was dedicated to A.D. Nock. He envied Nilsson's natural understanding of agricultural religion. His family had lived on the same farm for centuries. That way one understood Hesiod. He often cited Nilsson's "The Athenians believed that they believed in gods." At his suggestion I bought Nilsson's *Opuscula Selecta* as a senior. I have consulted it regularly for 40 years. He had an aversion to theory and thought literary criticism a waste of time. "A fact is a holy thing and ought not to be sacrificed on the altar of a generality."

Nock had a brilliant way of mixing humor with important matters to make them palatable to undergraduates. He spoke often of "*homo* facetiously called *sapiens*." He defined taboo (a Frazerian staple) as "something that is just not done, like wearing brown shoes with a tuxedo." He said: "The psyche in Homer is best defined as the small boy did salt—'that which makes the potatoes taste bad when Mother leaves it out.'" I have yet to find a better definition. He told the story of the Dean of St. Paul's on a Saturday afternoon hearing an elderly lady praying aloud to the devil in his empty church. He interrupted her and asked why. She replied: "One never knows, and it is always good to have friends on both sides." He told of a self-important anthropologist who asked an Eskimo if he believed in God. The Eskimo replied: "We do not believe. We fear." The point was clear—the old lady and the Eskimo were smarter than the Dean and the anthropologist. He cited ochre on the bones of stone age burials as evidence for "say it isn't so religion." The Anglican funeral service he declared an elaboration of this.

His loyal student, the late Morton Smith, called him "a great classical scholar with a mind enormously learned, outstandingly accurate, cautious, balanced, conservative." I learned that much later and I was ready to believe it.

Friedrich Nietzsche: "Abriss der Geschichte der Beredsamkeit" A New Edition

(With Anton Bierl for Albert Henrichs)

I. Introduction

If the sands of Egypt should yield the barest scraps of Plato's lecture notes, publication would be assured and a vast secondary bibliography would soon follow. A case certainly could be made—whether cogent or not is not at issue here—that Friedrich Nietzsche is comparable. Scraps of his lecture notes also deserve publication. The most modest addition to the corpus of so great and influential a thinker may allow posterity better to understand him. That is what three Germanists, Nietzsche specialists, thought. The Director of the Goethe-Schiller Archive in Weimar and the Oxford University Press agreed with them. And so we have:

Friedrich Nietzsche on Rhetoric and Language, Edited and Translated with a Critical Introduction by Sander L. Gilman, Carole Blair, David J. Parent, New York/Oxford 1989 (henceforth cited: GBP).

The new text in the volume that is of greatest interest to historians of Greek Literature and its reception is the brief "Anhang: Abriss der Geschichte der Beredsamkeit." The essay is entirely historical. It is written in the midst of the controversy on *Geburt* that pitted Nietzsche against the greatest Hellenist of modern times.[1] Wintersemester 1872/73 was the most discouraging in Nietzsche's brief professional career. All the students in his institute boycotted him. He writes Erwin Rohde in November 1872:[2]

---

[1] See William M. Calder III, "The Wilamowitz-Nietzsche struggle: New documents and a reappraisal," *Nietzsche-Studien* 12 (1983) 214-54 and Jaap Mansfeld, "The Wilamowitz-Nietzsche struggle: Another new document and some further comments," *Nietzsche-Studien* 15 (1986) 41-58.

[2] KGB II. 3. 85 (No. 272); for Rohde's reply of 14 November 1872 see KGB II. 4. 123-27 (No. 379). Nietzsche proposed a fuller course of lectures on ancient rhetoric for SS 1874. Because of the lack of students they were never delivered. The earlier confusion between the two sets of lectures has been clarified. Otto Crusius had earlier published the 1874 notes as though the notes for WS 1872/73: see *Nietzsche's Werke* XVIII. 3. II, *Philologica* II. *Unveröffentlichtes zur Litteraturgeschichte, Rhetorik und Rhythmik*, ed. by Otto Crusius, Leipzig 1912, 199-236. Now the recollections of one of Nietzsche's two students in 1872/73, Louis Kelterborn (1853-1910) prove that the *Abriss* must be dated to November 1872: see GBP, x-xi and Sander L. Gilman, *Begegnungen mit Nietzsche*, Bonn 1985², 111 f.

> Hier ist das nächste, mich etwas bedrückende Faktum, daß an unserer
> Universität die Philologen ausgeblieben sind, für dies Wintersemester:
> ein ganz einziges Phänomen, das Du Dir wohl eben so deuten wirst wie
> ich... Mit äußerster Noth habe ich ein Colleg über Rhetorik d<er>
> G<riechen> und R<ömer> zu Stande gebracht, mit 2 Zuhörern, dh.
> einem Germanisten und einem Juristen.

Johannes Stroux adds:[3]

> Mitteilungen etc. "Die andern angekündigten Vorlesungen sind nicht zu
> stande gekommen."

He had little reason to excel and the *Abriss* confirms this.

For classical admirers of Nietzsche, proximity to *Geburt* adds considerably to their interest in the *Abriss*. *Geburt* has exerted a lasting influence on subsequent scholarship both in Greek tragedy and the religion of Dionysos.[4] What does this new essay reveal of Nietzsche's competence in the history of Greek literature? Can its composition and content cast any light on *Geburt*? What follows is concerned with this essay solely (= GBP 166-193) and aims to provide an authoritative text with commentary and evaluate what it tells us about Nietzsche as a professional philologist.

Why is our article necessary? No *editio princeps* can be expected to be definitive. But readers of an *editio princeps*, that means by definition an edition that cannot be compared with any other printed edition but only with the autograph, to which few readers will have access, may reasonably expect that:

1. The word by word transcription is accurate with dubious readings noted.
2. Any changes made by the editors that diverge from the author's manuscript are clearly indicated so that the reader may himself judge whether they are convincing.
3. The editors are expert in the language and subject matter of the material they are editing for the first time.
4. The editors competently evaluate the new material and place it within the context of what had been known.
5. The editors, if they append a translation, are able to translate their text accurately.

---

[3] Johannes Stroux, *Nietzsches Professur in Basel*, Jena 1925, 97. This book remains authoritative for its subject and is unknown to GBP.

[4] See Martin Vogel, *Apollinisch und Dionysisch: Geschichte eines genialen Irrtums*, *Studien zur Musikgeschichte des 19. Jahrhunderts*, 6, Regensburg 1966; Albert Henrichs, "Loss of self, suffering, violence: The modern view of Dionysus from Nietzsche to Girard," *HSCP* 88 (1984) 205-40, esp. 219-34; and recently Anton Bierl, "Dionysos und die griechische Tragödie. Politische und 'metatheatralische' Aspekte im Text," *Classica Monacensia*, I, Tübingen 1991, 1-25.

In short the first printed edition should relieve the reader from any need to consult the Weimar manuscript.

How do the editors (henceforth: GBP) fulfill these reasonable expectations? Our new edition and its commentary answer this question.[5] But because we shall not in our commentary draw attention to every error in the *editio princeps*, to justify our edition we provide illustrative examples for the five criteria above:

1. "2a. VIII 57" (GBP 166) conveys precisely nothing to a reader. Nietzsche wrote "La. VIII 57" that is he refers to Diogenes Laertius 8. 57. Diogenes was the center of Nietzsche's early scholarly work (see KG II. 1. 75-245) and three editors of Nietzsche miss a reference to him. At GBP 176 we find someone called "Dionys. Laert.". What Nietzsche wrote was "Dionys<ius Halicarnaseus> Isocr<ates>." GBP (186) read: "Der Academiker Corneades [*sic*], der Richter Diogenes, der Peripatetiker Aristolaus. Die Wirkung war so gross, dass Cato die Betreuung der Gesandten antrug." What Nietzsche wrote was "Der Academ. Carneades, der Stoiker Diogenes, der Peripat. Critolaus. Die Wirkung war so gross, dass Cato die Entfernung der Gesandten antrug." (See *infra* n. 214). Errors of this sort are numerous (See e.g. *infra* nn. 53, 69, 73, 142, 187, 214, 253). One cannot trust the transcription.

2. GBP (xxi) assert: "The text is transcribed as it stands in the manuscript." This is an untruth. They add words, e.g. "sind" at GBP 172. 6, without indication. They even transpose whole passages within Nietzsche's manuscript without a word of warning or justification: see *infra* nn. 26, 30, 38, 52, 75, 154. They fill out abbreviations in Nietzsche's manuscript without any indication. At GBP 172 we have "Während des pelop-ponesischen Kriegs." If in November 1872 Nietzsche were unable to spell "peloponnesischen," that would provide revealing evidence that Wilamowitz was right to urge that Nietzsche resign his chair. In fact Nietzsche wrote "pelop" and GBP cannot spell the word. All expanded abbreviations must be indicated to avoid such confusion.

3. Do they know German? We have "Grosser Lob" (GBP 170) and at GBP 180 "...flog Demosthenes nach Calauria..." Presumably in a plane. Three American professors of German cannot distinguish between *fliegen* and *fliehen*. They do not know Latin. We have (GBP 172) the "tenue

---

[5] The text of "Darstellung der Antiken Rhetorik" (GBP 2-166) seems better, not least because there is less Greek and Latin in it; but there are errors of an ignorance that expands (GBP 47) "Dionys. de compos. verbor." to *De Composita Verborum* and gives us a new Roman rhetorician (GBP 200 n. 10) Sulpitius Victor! When Nietzsche writes (GBP 46) that biography "ist kein griechisches Wort", GBP have no idea that he is wrong (see Dam. *Isid.* 8). Expectedly they cannot distinguish *xi* from *delta* (GBP 16). And so on.

dia[poreticum] g[enus]"(!) for "tenue dic<endi> g<enus>". They do not know the simplest Greek nor indeed the Greek alphabet. On the first page (GBP 166) they write δοκεῖν for ποιεῖν and thus muddle one of the most familiar clichés in Greek (see *infra* n.19). Again and again they print unintelligible Greek.

4. The editors have no idea of the history of Greek oratory (see e.g. *infra* nn. 87, 96, 253) and they lacked the wit to ask someone who did to read their manuscript. Our commentary seeks to remedy this defect.

5. The mistranslations usually derive from the fact that the editors do not understand what Nietzsche is writing about. For example (GBP 173) we have "...he got involved in the Hemocopides [*sic*] trial" instead of "...he became involved in the trial concerned with the mutilation of the herms." Or (GBP 179) "born in the Paeania province of Athens" for "born in the Athenian deme Paeania".

Our text is based on an enlarged photocopy of the original manuscript in the Weimar archive. This copy was provided for us by Professor David J. Parent (Illinois State University at Normal, Illinois). Without this copy our edition would have been impossible. We wish to stress the magnanimity of Professor Parent, who supplied us with the documents which he knew would be used to correct an edition for which he was in part responsible. *Amicus Plato, sed magis amica veritas.*

II. Text and Commentary[6]

Anhang: Abriss der Geschichte der Beredsamkeit

Empedocles[7] soll der Gründer sein 'Αριστοτέλης ἐν τῇ σοφιστῷ[8] [*sic*] φησιν La.[9] VIII 57, wie Zeno der Erfinder der Dialektik:[10] ein grosser Volksredner im höchst bevölkerten Agrigent, der eine Demokratie dort einführt.[11] Der Syracusaner Corax hat eine τέχνη hinterlassen: der Redner müsse nach dem εἰκός, dem Wahrscheinl<ichen>, streben: er unterscheidet die Redetheile u. bezeichnet das prooem<ium> als κατάστασις.[12] Seine Definition der

---

[6] We have silently standardized punctuation and have omitted periods where abbreviations are expanded. Bars indicate the beginnings and ends of manuscript pages.

[7] For Empedocles and Corax see F. Blass, *Die attische Beredsamkeit*, I, Leipzig 1868[1], 17-20 and Empedocles frag. 1 Radermacher (henceforth: R). Blass I was until Lysias Nietzsche's principal source, and often is simply copied.

[8] An error for: ἐν τῷ σοφιστῇ.

[9] GBP 166 read "2a.", because they cannot recognize the abbreviation for Diogenes Laertius, one of Nietzsche's favorite authors.

[10] Aristotle frag. 65 Rose in Diog. Laert. 8. 57.

[11] Diog. Laert. *l.c.*

[12] Frag. 24 R.

Rhetorik: πειθοῦς δημιουργός.[13] Sein Schüler ist <u>Tisias</u>, berühmte Geschichte, dass er ihm, nach einem Pact, erst den Lohn zahlen wolle, wenn er den ersten Prozess gewonnen habe (dieselbe Gesch<ichte> von Protagoras u. Euathlos[14]). Korax verklagt ihn u. stellt den Satz auf, dass er jedenfalls das Geld erhalten müsse, im Fall des Sieges nach dem Spruch des Gerichts, in dem des Unterliegens nach dem Pakt. Tisias dreht es um: er habe in keinem Falle zu zahlen: siege er, weil ihn der Richterspruch dann entbinde, siege er nicht, so finde der Contrakt keine Anwendung. Die Richter jagen beide fort mit ἐκ κακοῦ κόρακος κακὸν ᾠόν.[15]— In Thurii ist er Lehrer des Lysias,[16] in Athen des Isocrates[17] gewesen, c. 480 geb., herumwandernd, wie ein Sophist. Hinterlässt eine τέχνη.[18] Tisias u. Corax waren wesentl<ich> Lehrer des Prozessirens. Anders steht es mit den Sophisten des eigentl<ichen> Griechenlands u. der östl<ichen> Kolonien, bei denen der eig<entliche> Name σοφιστής aufkommt. Sie geben eine enkyklopädische Bildung. <u>Protagoras</u> v. Abdera, geb. 485, durchzog etwa von 455 (von wo die Sophistik zu datiren ist) die hell<enischen> Städte. Auf die attische Beredsamkeit hatte Protag<oras> viel früher Einfluss als die Sikelioten. Er verheisst zu lehren τὸν ἥττω λόγον κρείττω ποιεῖν:[19] wie man durch Dialektik der schwächeren Sache den Sieg schaffen könne. Diese Dialektik sollte alle anderen Künste u. Wissenschaften entbehrlich machen: wie man den Geometer, ohne Geometer zu sein, niederdisputiren könne: so über die Naturphilos<ophie>, den Ringkampf, das prakt<ische> Staatsleben.[20] Die Schüler mussten Musterstücke auswendig lernen. τέχνη εριστικῶν [sic] oder ἀντιλογικὰ (aus dem Plato nach Aristoxenus den Stoff zur Politeia entnommen haben soll,[21] dh. περὶ τοῦ δικαίου). Auch die anderen grossen Sophisten kommen in Betracht. Als <u>praktisches</u> Ergebniss dieser neuen Bildung nach der Mitte des fünften Jahrhunderts: der grosse <u>Pericles</u>. Er disputirte viel mit Protagoras:[22] Plato leitet die höchste Meisterschaft in der Beredsamkeit aus der anaxagorischen Philosophie her: sie verlieh dem Geiste einen erhabenen Flug u. verstehenden Blick in das Innere der Natur u. des Menschen. Phaedr. p. 269 E. Damals schämten sich noch die mächtigsten Männer, in den Städten Reden zu verfassen u. Geschriebenes zu hinterlassen.[23] Es fehlte dem Perikles noch ganz die leidenschaftl<iche>

---

[13] Frag. 13 R.

[14] 80 A 1 (II. 255. 12-14) D-K[7]: see Plat. *Phaedr.* 272 B-C.

[15] See Corax and Tisias frag. 6 R with commentary. Nietzsche's source is Blass I 20.

[16] Frag. 3 R.

[17] Frag. 5 R.

[18] Frag. 10 R.

[19] Frag. 16 R. GBP have instead of ποιεῖν the unexpected δοκεῖν.

[20] Plat. *Soph.* 232 C-E. For Protagoras see Blass I 23-29.

[21] For the title τέχνη ἐριστικῶν see Diog. Laert. 9. 55; for the ἀντιλογικά and the *Politeia* see Diog. Laert. 3. 37.

[22] Protagoras frag. 15 R (Plut. *Per.* 36. 5).

[23] Plat. *Phaedr.* 257 D.

Form der späteren Redner, besonders des Demosthenes. Unbewegt stand er da, der umgewickelte Mantel bewahrte den gleichen Faltenwurf, der hohe Ernst der Mienen verzog sich nie zum Lächeln, die Stimme behielt dieselbe Höhe u. Stärke — alles undemosthenisch, doch wundersam imponirend.[24]— Zuerst bildet <u>Gorgias</u> in Sicilien einen künstlerischen Stil für prosaische Rede aus, der freilich seine Anwendung in Lobreden, nicht in praktischen Reden fand, u. bringt diesen nach Athen. In Athen entwickelt sich nur wenig später, aus der gleichfalls eingeführten Rhetorik des Tisias u. der Dialektik der östlichen Sophisten, in Anlehnung an die bestehende Sitte des Advokatenthums, die dem Prozessirenden dienende λογογραφία, deren erster noch alterthümlicher Vertreter <u>Antiphon</u> ist. Auch sein Stil macht den Anspruch, ein künstlerischer zu sein: daher die Veröffentlichung der geschriebenen Reden, als Muster für die Nachahmung. Weiter bildet der Rhetor <u>Thrasymachus</u> den der praktischen Rede angemessenen Stil, indem er an die Stelle von Gorgias' Prunk u. Antiphon's steifer Würde die gerundete Periode u. den gebildeten Ausdruck setzt.[25] Mitten in dieser Bewegung stehen Männer wie Kritias und Andokides, die selbst keine Sophisten sind. Endlich <u>Lysias.</u>[26] der zweite grosse Logograph: er geht noch weiter als Thrasym<achus> u. wendet ganz den Ausdruck des gemeinen Lebens an,[27] den Periodenbau u. den Schmuck der Figuren wohl kennend, doch nicht überall verwendend. Alles dies in einem Zeitraum von 30 Jahren: in denselben entstehen schon neue Richtungen, die des Isocrates.— Also <u>Antiphon</u> aus Rhamnus, zur Zeit der Perserkriege geboren, etwas jünger als Gorgias: der erste, der Reden für andere verfasste: er hatte den Beinamen Nestor als Redner, zur Auszeichnung.[28] Völliger Mangel an polit<ischem> Ehrgeiz. Grosses Lob, Thucyd. 8, 63 [*sic*],[29] viell<eicht> sein Schüler.|

---

[24] Plut. *Per.* 5. For Perikles see Blass I 33-37. Compare Blass I 37: "Unbewegt, wie es uns beschrieben wird, stand er da, der umgewickelte Mantel bewahrte den gleichen Faltenwurf; der hohe Ernst der Mienen verzog sich nie zum Lächeln, die Stimme behielt stets gleiche Höhe und Stärke. Eben dies, was mit der demosthenischen Rede unvereinbar ist und auch in den Worten alle gewaltsame Leidenschaft ausschliesst, machte auf die Zuhörer, wie Plutarch berichtet, einen wundersam mächtigen Eindruck." Here and often elsewhere the similarity of language proves that Nietzsche's source was Blass I. He did not consult the ancient sources directly.

[25] Dion. Hal. *Isae.* 20 (123. 10-12 [627 f.] Usener-Radermacher [henceforth: U-R]) = frag. 10 R.

[26] Without informing the reader GBP 174 transfer "Endlich—Isocrates" to the later discussion of Lysias. They wish to put together all passages that concern each author, assuming that this was the intention of Nietzsche himself. Here they fail to understand the adverb 'endlich'. With 'endlich' Nietzsche's first version reaches a temporary conclusion. The sentence "Endlich [ist] Lysias, der zweite grosse Logograph:" in the position where GBP 174 have moved it is only tautological. After having treated Lysias' character as a logographer in a rather detailed form, the expression "Finally Lysias is the second great logograph" (GBP 175) is superfluous. Moreover, GBP do not see the reference to what was said earlier of Thrasymachus. Nietzsche's order must be restored.

[27] Dion. Hal. *Demosth.* 2 (130. 6-10 [956] U-R).

[28] [Plut.] 832 E.

[29] Nietzsche, followed by GBP, apparently reads 63. The correct reference is 68.

IA.[30] Die Anordnung der Rede sehr regelmässig. Von Isäus ab, in raffinirter Zeit, liebt man die Kunst entgegen der Natur anzuwenden.[31] Würdevoller Ausdruck, der öffentl<iche> Sprecher musste damals gemessen auftreten, eine etwas entfernte Sprache sprechen.[32] Der erhabene Stil ist natürlich dem schlichten des Lysias weit näher als der erhabene Stil in der Geschichte oder der Tragödie.[33] Alterthümlichkeit gesucht als Mittel zur Würde: während schon Perikl<es> dem modernen Dialekt folgt, das ältere ξύν u. ἐς,[34] σσ für ττ zb. Die Komödie beweist, dass man damals nur πράττειν sprach.[35] Andok<ides>, Lysias usw. schliessen sich der neuen Ausspr<ache> an, nicht Gorgias u. Antiphon.[36] In der Composition folgt er der αὐστηρὰ ἁρμονία, entgegen der γλαφυρὰ des Isocrates.[37]— Thucydides[38] erwählte, nach Dionys<ius>, anstatt der gewöhnlichen u. schlichten Redeweise die übertragene, alterthümliche, fremdartige: anstatt der glatten Composition die rauhe u. kraftvolle: dann vielfache u. ungewöhnl<iche> Gestaltung der Worte u. Glieder: endlich mit wenig

[30] The abbreviation could stand for 'Anmerkung' or, more probably, for Antiphon. The following passage is written on a separate sheet only half filled. The order of the pages can not be exactly reconstructed and the precise method of composition is not known: see *infra* nn. 52 and 75. The reconstruction here is only *exempli gratia*. The context concerns Antiphon.

[31] An almost literal transcription from Blass I 112: "Hieraus geht denn im allgemeinen hervor, dass die Anordnung bei Antiphon eine durchaus natürliche und einfache ist. Denn was die einzige Abweichung von der gewöhnlichen Reihenfolge, die Einschaltung einer Argumentation vor der Erzählung, anbetrifft, so ist dieselbe erstlich für Antiphon nicht ungewöhnlich, sondern regelmässig, zweitens aber ist das, was in diesem Theile behandelt wird, stets der Art, dass es hier und nirgends anderswo seine natürliche Stelle hat. Jene älteren Redner—ich meine die bis zu Lysias und Isokrates eingeschlossen—waren noch nicht darauf verfallen, auch entgegen der Natur die Kunst anzuwenden, wie es die späteren von Isäos ab, als das Zeitalter raffinirter geworden war, zu thun pflegten..."

[32] See Blass I 113.

[33] See further Blass I 114: "So ist der erhabene Stil in der Beredsamkeit dem schlichten des Lysias und Isäos weit mehr genähert, als in der Geschichtsschreibung, oder in der Tragödie der Abstand der entgegengesetzten Gattungen ist."

[34] In superscript. The archaic ξύν und ἐς were replaced by σύν and εἰς in later Attic.

[35] Compare Blass I 114: "Würde und Alterthümlichkeit sind nahe verwandte und zusammengehörende Dinge; denn wenn jene in der Entfernung von der gemeinen Sprechweise besteht, so muss auch der Gebrauch veraltender Formen der Rede Würde und Feierlichkeit verleihen. Wir können uns daher nicht wundern, wenn Antiphon gleichwie Thukydides nicht den Dialekt jener und der späteren Zeit, sondern den der früheren gebraucht, was namentlich in der Anwendung des σσ für ττ, wie in πράσσειν, ἧσσον, hervortritt. Schon Perikles soll sich in seinen öffentlichen Reden dem modernen Dialekt anbequemt haben, und jedenfalls giebt uns die Komödie vollgültiges Zeugniss, dass man zu Antiphon's Zeit durchaus so und nicht anders sprach." Again here GBP do not understand the subject matter. They read (170):"weiss es schon Perikles: ξύν, ἐς. Dem modernen Dialekt folgt das ältere σσ für ττ, z.B. Die komische Ansicht dass man damals nur πράγτεω [*sic*] sprach."

[36] See Blass I 114, immediately after the last citation.

[37] Dion. Hal. *De comp. verb.* 22 und 23.

[38] In the case of the two separate pages (see *infra* nn. 52, 75) GBP remove the part concerning Thucydides and make a footnote of it (199 n. 14). Presumably they are unaware that the historian Thucydides is stylistically a rhetor. Moreover, there are many famous speeches in his work.

Worten möglichst viel auszudrücken.[39] Als χρώματα, Färbungen, gebraucht er die Herbigkeit, die Gedrängtheit, das Gewichtvolle, das Erschreckende, das Pathetische.[40] Dionys<ius> sagt: wenn es ihm gelinge, diesen Charakter nach Wunsch darzustellen, so seien seine Erfolge fast übermenschlich. Doch mache die Kürze der Rede dunkel, u. das Künstliche steht nicht immer am rechten Orte u. im rechten Masse.[41] Thucyd<ides> erschreckt, wo Lysias u. Herodot angenehm berühren: Lysias bewirkt ein Nachlassen, er ein Anspannen, jener schmeichelt sich ein u. überredet, dieser zwingt. Denn wie Herodot, Meister im Ethos, er im Pathos. Die Schönheit des Herodot ist eine heitere, die des Thucyd<ides> eine furchtbare.[42]— Thrasymachus, ein Altersgenosse des Lysias, in der Einleitungsscene der platon<ischen> Republik hervortretend, als Karikatur, anmasslich, käuflich, unsittlich, dummdreist.[43] Er ist überwiegend Techniker:[44] er ist der Begründer der mittleren Gattung des Stils,[45] er ist Erfinder der für praktische Zwecke passenden Periode,[46] endl<ich> hat er zuerst den päonischen Rhythm<us> (nach Aristot<eles>[47]) angewandt.[48] Also er erfindet die περίοδος στρογγύλη oder συνεστραμμένη,[49] die Gorgias u. Antiphon noch nicht kennen. Der Gedanke wird zu einer Einheit zusammengedrückt: bei Gorgias reiht sich lose Antithese an Antithese. Nach Cicero hat er fast allzu rhythmisch geschrieben.[50] Er ist bahnbrechend für die späteren praktischen Redner, bes<onders> Lysias, im Gegensatz zu dem panegyrischen Isocrates.[51]|

|Der[52] berüchtigte <u>Critias</u> ist sehr ausgezeichnet: es muss auffallen, dass er nicht die Stelle des Andocides im Kanon bekam, aber ihm schadet, einer

---

[39] Dion. Hal. *Thuc.* 24 (361. 4-14 [866 f.] U-R); see Blass I 204.

[40] Dion. Hal. *Thuc.* 24 (363. 12-15 [869 f.] U-R); see Blass I 204.

[41] Dion. Hal. *Thuc.* 24 (363. 18-24 and 364. 1 f. [870] U-R); see Blass I 204 f.

[42] Dion Hal. *Ad Cn. Pomp.* 775 ff. and *Demosth.* 2 (131. 3-11 [957 f.] U-R). Again Nietzsche used Blass and not the ancient sources: see Blass I 223: "Thukydides erschreckt, wo jene angenehm berühren; Lysias bewirkt ein Nachlassen, der Geschichtsschreiber [*sic*] fordert ein Anspannen des Geistes, dieser zwingt, wo jener sich unvermerkt einschmeichelnd überredet. Jener ist, wie Herodot, im Ethos, Thukydides im Pathos Meister; die Schönheit des Herodot ist eine heitere, die des andern eine furchtbare..."

[43] "dreist" stands in superscript.

[44] Plat. *Rep.* I 336 ff.

[45] After Theophrastus περὶ λέξεως frag. IV Schmidt, cited in Dion. Hal. *Demosth.* 3 (132. 3-7 [958 f.] U-R).

[46] So Theophrastus περὶ λέξεως frag. III Schmidt, cited in Dion. Hal. *Lys.* 6 (132. 3 [958 f.] and 14. 1-12 [464] U-R); see also Suda, Θ 462. 2 Adler: ὃς πρῶτος περίοδον καὶ κῶλον κατέδειξε καὶ τὸν νῦν τῆς ῥητορικῆς τρόπον εἰσηγήσατο.

[47] *Rhet.* 1409 a 2 = frag. 12 R.

[48] See Blass I 246.

[49] Thrasymachus frag. 15 R. See Suda Θ 462 Adler.

[50] Cic. *Orat.* 175: Nam neminem in eo genere scientius versatum Isocrate confitendum est, sed princeps inveniendi fuit Thrasymachus, cuius omnia nimis etiam exstant scripta numerose.

[51] There are many almost literal citations taken by Nietzsche from Blass I 248-250.

[52] The text "Der berüchtigte Critias" up to "Lysias" is on a separate page only three quarters filled. It is a short passage covering Critias to Lysias, that does not fit easily into the

der Dreissig gewesen zu sein: Würde in den Gedanken, Einfachheit in der
Form. Er ist Vertreter des jungen Atticismus. Wenig Schwung[53] u. Feuer.
Wenig gewinnender Eifer. Darum behauptend ἀλλ' ἔμοιγε δοκεῖ oder δοκεῖ δ'
ἔμοιγε.[54] Andocides kein Meister der praktischen Rede, dazu fehlt ihm
allerseits Durchsichtigkeit. Sehr wenig Schmuck, wenig Lebendigkeit.[55]
Sein Stil ist nicht gleichmässig, sondern buntscheckig.[56] Mit Entlehnungen
von selbst tragischen Wendungen. Im Allgemeinen die Sprache des
gewöhnl<ichen> Lebens.[57] In der argumentatio ist er mittelmässig, im
Erzählen von Geschichten <geschickter>,[58] weshalb er die Reden auch
zumeist mit Erzählungen füllt.[59] In der Ausprägung des Ethos ist Lysias
viel vorzügl<icher>, im Pathos beide schwach. Unter den Zehnen ist er der
geringste an Talent u. Studium: obgl<eich> es eine grosse Ehre ist,
überhaupt unter sie aufgenommen zu werden.[60]— Lysias. Im
platon<ischen> Phaedrus wird die lysian<ische> Rede scharf getadelt, die
Sache sei unphilosophisch angefasst:[61] dem Isocrates wird dagegen eine
gewisse philosophische Richtung nachgerühmt: Verschiedenheit der Stoffe
beider, da Lys<ias> ausser erotisch<en> Kleinigkeit<en> nur die von Plato
verachteten Prozessreden, Isocrates epideiktische Reden mit polit<ischen>
Hintergründen schrieb, mit mehr idealen als praktischen Gesichtpunkten.[62]
Aber es ist nicht gerechtfertigt, die Bevorzugung allein aus dem Stoffe zu
begreifen: Perikles wird als grosser Redner anerkannt. Das Fehlen
allgem<einer> Begriffsbestimmungen, sehr selten allgemeine Principien

---

main narrative. It is difficult to reestablish the order of the sheets. As far as can be deduced
from a number on the top this page was inserted after the first loose one. Why GBP put
Critias before Antiphon, remains obscure. The sequence Antiphon—Thucydides—
Thrasymachus—Critias—Andocides—Lysias derives from Blass I.

[53] GBP 170 read: "Wenig Sprung und Feuer." But see Blass I 267: "denn Feuer und
Schwung fehlt auch in den Poësien" and the parallel in the 1874 lecture notes (op. cit. supra
n. 2) p. 209.

[54] 88 B 46 D-K[7]. See Blass I 265.

[55] See Blass I 290: "Weiter zeige er sehr wenig Schmuck; ebensowenig rednerische
Lebendigkeit."

[56] See Blass I 291: "Sein Ausdruck erhält auf diese Weise etwas buntscheckiges."

[57] See Blass I 291: "Im allgemeinen ist, wie gesagt, Andokides' Sprache die des
gewöhnlichen Lebens."

[58] Compare Blass I 292. GBP's <viel besser> must be discarded.

[59] See Blass I 292: "Andokides ist in der Argumentation mittelmässig, im Erzählen dagegen
zeigt er entschieden Geschick und füllt deswegen auch seine Reden grösstentheils mit
Erzählungen."

[60] See Blass I 299: "Man wird also im ganzen sich dem Urtheile O. Müller's [Geschichte
der griechischen Litteratur bis auf das Zeitalter Alexanders II, Breslau 1841, 1856², 339]
anschliessen können, dass Andokides unter den Zehnen der geringste an Talent und Studium
sei; obwohl es ja ein grosser Ruhm ist, überhaupt mit einigem Rechte in diese Liste
aufgenommen zu sein."

[61] Plat. Phaedr. 279 A after Blass I 375.

[62] See Blass I 375: "...so kann man zunächst noch immer an die Verschiedenheit der Stoffe
beider denken, da Lysias ausser erotischen Kleinigkeiten fast nur die von Platon
geringgeschätzten Prozessreden, Isokrates hauptsächlich epideiktische Reden politischen
Inhalts schrieb, mit mehr idealen als praktischen Gesichtspunkten."

berührt.[63] Dann fehlt die richtige Ordnung u. logische Folge der Gedanken. Die kunstvolle Rede dürfe nicht eine Häufung von Argumenten sein, die beliebig so u. so gestellt werden könnten.[64] Plato lobt allein den Stil: sowohl klar als abgerundet..[65] Später, bes<onders> bei Dionys<ius>, ist er der Vertreter des χαρακτὴρ ἰσχνός, λέξις λιτὴ καὶ ἀφελής,[66] συνεσπασμένη.[67] Cicero gebraucht von solchen Rednern die Ausdrücke tenues, acuti, subtiles, versuti, humiles, summissi.[68] Die künstlerische Nachbildung[69] der gewöhnl<ichen> Rede, anscheinend für jeden leicht, sei ausserordentlich schwer. Der tenuis kann bloss belehren:[70] die Leidenschaften zu erregen, gestattet ihm die Beschränktheit der Mittel nicht. Darum ist Lysias nicht der vollkommene Meister, sondern Demosth<enes>,[71] der je nach den Umständen bald knapp, bald gewaltig, bald gemässigt spricht.[72] Das Streben nach wahrhaft Grossem ist mit einem theilweisen Misslingen verbunden, während kein grosses Genie dazu gehöre, sich bei niedriger gerichtetem Streben von Fehlern fernzuhalten. Auch erhebe sich jener oft Strauchelnde, doch sein hohes Ziel Erreichende weit über diesen:[73] die Grösse der Vorzüge, nicht die Zahl entscheide. So der Autor περὶ ὕψους bei einem Vergleich von Plato u. Lysias.[74]|

Das Alterthum hatte 60 Reden von ihm,[75] Caecilius erklärte davon 25 für unecht,[76] ferner eine angezweifelte τέχνη u. noch Samml<ung> Proöm<ien> u. Epiloge. Uns sind 15 erhalten, wovon 4[77] zu Tetralogien dreimal zusammengestellt sind. Cf. Blass p. 91.[78] Meist sind es λόγοι φονικοί, dh. in Criminalfällen, nur 3 beziehen sich auf wirkl<iche> Fälle. Er gilt neben Thucyd<ides> als der Meister der alterthümlich strengen Redekunst.[79] Besonders wichtig für den politischen Stil der Reden. Der erste

---

[63] See Blass I 375 f.

[64] See Blass I 376.

[65] Plat. *Phaedr.* 234 E after Blass I 377.

[66] Dion. Hal. *Dem.* 2 after Blass I 379 n. 3.

[67] Dion. Hal. *Dem.* 15 after Blass I 379 n. 3.

[68] Particularly in the *Orator* after Blass I 379 n. 3.

[69] See Blass I 381. GBP 174 read: "Doch eine straffe Nachbildung."

[70] Cic. *Orator* 76 after Blass I 380.

[71] Dion. Hal. *Dem.* 15 after Blass I 381 n. 1.

[72] Cic. *Brut.* 35 after Blass I 381 n. 3.

[73] GBP 174 read: "Auch so erheben sich nun oft Versuchende, doch kein hohes Ziel Erreichende weit über das Mass."

[74] Ps.-Long. *de subl.* 32. 8. Nietzsche closely follows Blass I 382.

[75] Not Lysias, but Antiphon is meant. After the two separate sheets inserted here the text returns to the bottom of the first page.

[76] [Plut.] 833 C: φέρονται δὲ τοῦ ῥήτορος λόγοι ἑξήκοντα, ὧν κατεψευσμένους φησὶ Καικίλιος [frag. 100 Ofenloch] εἶναι τοὺς εἴκοσι πέντε.

[77] "3 x 4" deleted to 4.

[78] F. Blass, *Die attische Beredsamkeit*, I. *Von Gorgias zu Lysias*, Leipzig 1868[1], 91. Nietzsche cites only here his main source for the first part of his *Abriss*.

[79] For the comparison of Antiphon with Thucydides see Dion. Hal. *de comp* 10 (36. 20-37. 2 [52.f.] U-R): ἥ γέ τοι Θουκυδίδου λέξις καὶ Ἀντιφῶντος τοῦ Ῥαμνουσίου καλῶς μὲν σύγκειται νὴ Δία, εἴ πέρ τινες καὶ ἄλλαι...οὐ μὴν ἡδέως γε πάνυ.

im Canon der 10 att<ischen> Redner, den man viell<eicht> in Alexandria anlegte.

Andocides geb. 468,[80] vornehmes Geschlecht, die Würde der Mysterienherolde für die Eleusinien vererbt.[81] Bewegtes politisches Leben während des pelop<onnesischen> Kriegs, als Heerführer u. Gesandter[82], verwickelt in den Hermokopidenprozess.[83] Wir haben 4 Reden in eigenen Angelegenheiten, nur zwei περὶ τῆς ἑαυτοῦ καθόδου u. περὶ τῶν μυστηρίων ächt [sic]. Lysias geb. 459[84] zu Athen, begüterte Eltern, die ihre Heimat Syrakus 475 verlassen u. als Metöken in Athen sich niedergelassen. Er nahm an der Gründung von Thurii 444 theil, lernt dort unter Tisias u. Nikias Rhetorik, kehrt 412 nach Athen zurück, stirbt 377. Seinen Ruf begründet die Rede gegen Eratosthenes, den Mörder seines Bruders Polemarchus, einer der 30.[85] Er stiftet eine wichtige Redeschule. Von 425 Reden hielten die Alten 230 für echt.[86] Von diesen sind 34 erhalten, doch nicht sicher ächt [sic]. Seine τέχνη verloren. Meister des tenue dic<endi> g<enus>[87] u. der gerichtl<ichen> Beredsamk<eit>. Isocrates[88] geb. 436 zu Athen, Schüler des Tisias, Gorgias, Prodikus u. Socrates, der grösste Lehrer der Bereds<amkeit>. Schüchtern, schwache Stimme. Sein Vater hatte Ende des peloponn<esischen> Kriegs sein Vermögen verloren: er schrieb Reden daher. 392 eröffnet er die Schüler, zuerst auf Chios mit 9 Schülern,[89] 388 in Athen mit 100,[90] höchst ruhmvoll. Er starb freiwillig (durch Hunger) 338

---

[80] For the date of Andocides' birth see Blass I 271. Blass regards the date of 468/7 reported in his vita as "Resultat eines falschen Schlusses," based on the misunderstood report "von des Andokides' Feldherrnschaft auf Samos." Blass claims that Andocides was born c. 440.

[81] For the context see [Plut.] 834 C.

[82] Thuc. 1. 51. Andoc. 3. 6. This must be the elder Andocides; see Blass I 270. Nietzsche ignores the genealogy.

[83] Thuc. 6. 60.

[84] Here too Nietzsche is poorly informed, although Blass I 336 takes a vehement position against 459 as the date of birth. The ancient source for 459 is based on the erroneous belief that Lysias came to Thurii in the year when the colony was founded (444); see K.J. Dover, *Lysias and the Corpus Lysiacum,* Berkeley/Los Angeles 1968, 38-42 and A. Lesky, *Gesch. d. Griech. Lit,* Bern/München 1971³, 665. Nietzsche may already base his dates and numbers on Westermann I. (see *infra* n.88), who (p. 73) also has 458.

[85] Here are meant the thirty tyrants, who formed the government after the Athenian defeat of 404 until the restoration of democracy by Thrasybulus in 401. Eratosthenes was part of this oligarchic regime.

[86] [Plut.] 836 A. Blass I 345 mentions 233 genuine speeches, taking the three additional ones from Photius.

[87] GBP 172 read tenue dia[poreticum] g[enus], whatever that means.

[88] The most recent handbook for Greek oratory in 1873, Blass I, ended with Lysias: Blass II and III were published later, 1874-1880. Therefore, Nietzsche had to resort to Blass' predecessor, A. Westermann, *Geschichte der Beredsamkeit in Griechenland und Rom,* I. *Geschichte der griechischen Beredsamkeit,* Leipzig 1833. As will be shown, Nietzsche follows the same method he used with Blass, simply excerpting Westermann for the period not included in Blass I. For Isocrates see Westermann I 77-83.

[89] See [Plut.] 837 B. "Mit 9 Schülern" stands as a superscript in small letters. See Westermann I 79 n. 6.

[90] *I.e.* Schülern. "Mit 100" stands as a superscript. See [Plut.] 837 C ff. and Westermann I 79 n. 7.

nach der Schlacht bei Chäronea, aus Schmerz über den Verlust der Freiheit.[91] Mächtiger patriot<ischer> Charakter, ideales Streben. Führt die Schule zur polit<ischen> Bereds<amkeit>. Von 60 Reden erkannte Caecil<ius> 28 als ächt [*sic*],[92] 21 erhalten, 15 panegyrische davon u. 6 gerichtl<iche>. Am berühmt<esten> der Panegyr<ikos> 382, in seinem 94. Jahre geschrieben.[93] Nicht sicher die τέχνη. Seine talentvollsten Schüler Theopomp, Ephorus, Philiscus, Androtion, dann Isaeus, Demosth<enes>, Hyperides, Theodectes usw.[94] Er ist ein Feind alles Sophistenwesens zB in κατὰ τῶν σοφιστῶν, Ἑλένης ἐγκώμ(ιον) und περὶ ἀντιδόσεως. Erst im hohen Alter wendet er sich der Theorie zu, so tadelt er in κ⟨ατὰ⟩ τ⟨ῶν⟩ σοφ⟨ιστῶν⟩ die Theoretiker, οὐ μεθόδῳ ἀλλ' ἀσκήσει χρήσασθαι[95] war in früheren Zeiten sein Satz. Er wendet sich zuerst zur grossen politischen Beredsamkeit, Dionys<ius> Isocr. I[96] sagt: πρῶτος ἐχώρησεν ἀπὸ τῶν ἐριστικῶν καὶ φυσικῶν ἐπὶ τὰς πολιτικὰς [*sic*][97] καὶ περὶ ταύτην[98] σπουδάζων τὴν ἐπιστήμην διετέλεσεν. Reiner Stil,[99] aber nicht wie bei Lysias Ausdruck der Natur, sondern künstlerisch geformt. Dionys<ius>: θαυμαστὸν γὰρ ⟨δὴ⟩ καὶ μέγα τὸ τῆς Ἰσοκράτους κατασκευῆς ὕψος, ἡρωϊκῆς μᾶλλον ἢ ἀνθρωπίνης[100] ⟨φύσεως οἰκεῖον⟩. Er ahmt die μεγαλοπρέπεια, σεμνότης u. καλλιλογία des Thucyd<ides> und Gorgias nach. Aber zu der erhaben<en> Redegewalt des Demosth<enes> verhält er sich nur wie ein Athlet zu einem Vaterlandsvertheidiger (wie Cleochares aus Myrlea gesagt hat).[101] Er besitzt mehr Eleganz als Grazie, mehr Pracht als Anmuth,[102] Dionys<ius> Is<ocrates> 3: πέφυκε γὰρ ἡ Λυσίου λέξις ἔχειν

---

[91] [Plut.] 837 E und 838 B.

[92] Caecilius frag. 117 (103. 22-24) Ofenloch.

[93] <und der Panathenaikos>. Nietzsche made a careless or even ignorant mistake. Not the *Panegyrikos*, but the *Panathenaikos*, his last speech, was written, when he was 94 years old.

[94] See Westermann I 83.

[95] [Plut.] 838 F after Westermann I 79 n. 11.

[96] 55. 12-14 (536) U-R. GBP 176 read Dionys. Laert.; they cannot distinguish between Dionysius Halicarnaseus and Diogenes Laertius.

[97] Westermann I 80 n. 12 has the right form ἐπὶ τοὺς πολιτικοὺς, agreeing with λόγοι. The error reveals Nietzsche's unsure knowledge of Greek.

[98] Nietzsche accepts F.A. Wolf's emendation after Westermann I 80 n. 12. The manuscripts have αὐτὴν.

[99] Dion. Hal. *Isocr.* 2 (56. 14-16 [537] U-R). *Lys.* 2 (9. 20 f. [455] U-R).

[100] Dion. Hal. *Isocr.* 3 (59. 16-18 [541] U-R). The Greek can only be understood with addition of the omitted words: see Westermann I 82 n. 7.

[101] Caecilius frag. 115 (102. 13-17 Ofenloch): Κλεοχάρης δὲ ὁ Σμυρλεανός, ὑπὲρ τῶν Ἰσοκρατικῶν ἁπάντων οἶμαι λέγων (τοῦτο γάρ ἐστι τὸ ἐν τῇ πρὸς τὸν Δημοσθένην συγκρίσει μὴ τὰ πόρρω αὐτοῖς παρασχεῖν), φησὶ τοὺς μὲν Δημοσθενικοὺς λόγους τοῖς τῶν στρατιωτῶν ἐοικέναι μάλιστα σώμασι, τοὺς δὲ Ἰσοκρατικοὺς τοῖς τῶν ἀθλητῶν. Compare the almost literal citation from Westermann I 81: "aber zu der erhabenen Redegewalt des Demosthenes verhält er sich doch nur wie ein Athlet zu einem Vaterlandsvertheidiger," and Westermann I 83 n. 8 for Cleochares.

[102] See Westermann I 81: "Er besitzt mehr Eleganz als wahre Grazie, mehr Pracht als Anmuth."

τὸ χαριέν [*sic*], ἡ δ᾽ Ἰσοκράτους βούλεται.[103] Gerundete Periode, viel [*sic*] Figuren, oft durch Überfülle monoton u. weitschweifig.[104] Höchst ausgearbeitet u. Lysias weit in Anordnung u. Vertheilung des Stoffes überlegen.[105] Er hat daher für sein langes Leben nur wenig geschrieben. Übrigens mehr für den Leser als den Hörer. Wahre Gerichtsreden nur wenige oder keine, dageg<en> gerichtl<iche> Muster- u. Übungsstücke.[106] Isaeus[107] lebt c. 420-348, geb. in Chalcis,[108] lernt in Athen, wo er Lysias u. Isocr<ates> zu Lehrern hat. Darauf wird er λογογρ(άφος), errichtet eine Schule u. erzieht darin bes<onders> Demosthenes. Von 64 Reden hielten die Kritiker 50 für ächt [*sic*]; nur 11, alle in Erbschaftsangelegenheiten, haben sich erhalten. Technische Schriften verloren. Er gleicht Lysias in der Reinheit u. Deutlichkeit des Vortrags:[109] dagegen nicht so naiv, sondern gekünstelt, gefeilt und geschmückt;[110] doch kräftig im Ganzen. ὅσον τε ἀπολείπεται τῆς χάριτος ἐκείνης, τοσοῦτον ὑπερέχει τῇ δεινότητι τῆς κατασκευῆς.[111] Besonders feine Zerlegung des Stoffs u. schlaue Verflechtung der Argumente: er galt als verschmitzter Betrüger bei seinen Feinden.[112] Der von Antiphon erfunden<en>, von Isocrates begründeten politischen Rede gab er schärfere Umrisse. Früher gab es nur 10 Reden. 1785[113] wurde in einem cod<ex> Laurent<ianus> noch eine 11te, περὶ τοῦ Μενεκλέους κλήρου[114] gefunden: 1815 fand Mai in einem cod<ex> Ambros<ianus> die bisher fehlende grössere Hälfte von περὶ τοῦ Κλεωνύμου κλήρου.[115]

In der macedon<ischen> Periode[116] ist Demagog und Redner fast gleichbedeutend.[117] Die antimacedonische Partei Lycurgus, Demosthenes, Hyperides u<nter> anderen, macedonisch[118] Aeschines, Eubulos,

---

[103] 59. 11 f. (541) U-R after Westermann I 83 n. 9 whence the erroneous accent for χαριέν.

[104] So Westermann I 81: "sorgfältig gerundeter Periodenbau und häufiges Figuriren macht seine Rede zwar wohllautend, aber oft durch Ueberfülle weitschweifig und monoton." See also the ancient sources in Westermann I 83 n. 10.

[105] See Westermann I 81.

[106] So Westermann I 81 and 83 n. 11 and 12.

[107] See Westermann I 87-89.

[108] Dion. Hal. *Isae.* 1 (93. 2-5 [586] U-R) does not make clear, whether Isaeus came from Athens, as Hermippus alleges, or from Chalcis, as Demetrius.

[109] See Dion. Hal. *Isae.* 2 (56. 13-16 [537] U-R).

[110] Dion. Hal. *Isae.* 4 (96. 5-18 [591] U-R) after Westermann I 87 f.

[111] Dion. Hal. *Isae.* 3 (95. 10 f. [590] U-R) after Westermann I 89 n. 12.

[112] Dion. Hal. *Isae.* 3 (95. 18-22 und 96. 1-4 [590 f.] U-R).

[113] From here to the end of the section see especially Westermann I 89 n. 9.

[114] *I. e.*, Isae. 2

[115] Λόγος περὶ τοῦ Κλεωνύμου κλήρου. *Isaei oratio de haereditate Cleonymi*, nunc primum eddidit auctior, inventore et interprete Ang. Mai, Mediolani 1815. (= Isae. 1)

[116] See Westermann I 90-95.

[117] See Westermann I 93: "*Demagog* und *Redner* ist in dieser Periode fast gleichbedeutend..."

[118] See Westermann I 95-100.

Philocrates, Demades, Pytheas. Lykurgus (der VI.[119]) aus dem alten
Geschlecht der Eteobutaden,[120] c. Ol. 96[121] geb., durch Platon u. Isokrates
gebildet,[122] früh in der polit<ischen> Laufbahn. Gewissenhaft u.
uneigennützig. Von 15 im Alterthum vorhandenen Reden ist eine gegen
Leocrates auf uns gekommen. Nach Dionys<ius> ist die moral<ische>
Tendenz hervortretend. Darstellung edel u. erhaben,[123] aber nicht gefällig.
Härte im metaphorischen Ausdruck,[124] Ungenauigkeit in der Vertheilung des
Stoffes, häufige Abschweifung.[125] Er sprach wie aus dem Stegreife.[126] οὐ
μὲν ἀστεῖος, οὐδὲ ἡδὺς ἀλλ' ἀναγκαῖος.[127] Demosthenes (VII)[128] geb. im
Gau Päania zu Athen 385, ist 7 Jahre alt, als Vater stirbt. Vormünder
Aphobos u. Onetor.[129] Gebildet von Plato, Isäus u. Isokrates, 17 Jahre
alt,[130] durch Callistratus' Rede zum Studium der Beredsamkeit
fortgerissen,[131] ersetzt durch Eifer u. Übung, was an ihm von Natur oder
durch Erziehung fehlt. 354 trat er öffentl<ich> vor dem Volke auf.[132] Sein
eigentl<ich> politischer Charakter entwickelt sich mit Philipp<'s> immer
deutlicher werdenden Plänen.[133] Als 346 Philipp zum Frieden sich geneigt
zeigte, war er es, der unter den 10 Gesandten, die von Athen zum König
geschickt wurden, fest gegen Geld blieb u. den Betrug durchschaute. Die
Unterjochung von Phocis enttäuschte die Athener; Demosth<enes> von
zwei Übeln das kleinere wählend stimmte jetzt für den Frieden.[134] Philipp
mischt sich bald in die peloponnes<ischen> Händel: die Seele der

---

[119] For the ten Attic rhetors Nietzsche begins to cite the numbers which Westermann used.
For Nietzsche's almost literal citations concerning Lycurgus see Westermann I 100-103.

[120] [Plut.] 841 AB.

[121] Nietzsche, after Westermann, gives the date of birth here in Olympiads. It is equivalent
to c. 396.

[122] [Plut.] 841 B.

[123] Dion. Hal. de imit. 5. 3 (212. 9 f. [433] U-R), after Westermann 103 n. 16: Ὁ δὲ
Λυκούργειός ἐστι διὰ παντὸς αὐξητικὸς καὶ διηρμένος καὶ σεμνός.

[124] Hermog. 416 und Blass III 2. 99 f.

[125] Digressions e. g., in the speech against Leokrates § 46, 83, 95, 98, 107 f.

[126] See [Plut.] 842 C. The sentence is a literal citation from note 15 in Westermann I 103.

[127] Dion. Hal. de imit. 5. 3 (212. 11 f. [433] U-R) after Westermann I 103 n. 16. Obviously
Nietzsche did not look up the original. He only copied important passages cited in Blass or in
Westermann. But even so he makes a slight error: Westermann reads correctly οὐ μὴν,
which Nietzsche renders οὐ μὲν.

[128] See Westermann I 103-13 from whom Nietzsche has copied much of his text.

[129] "ist 7 Jahre...Onetor" written in superscript.

[130] "17 Jahre alt" written in superscript. A further superscript, later cancelled, is illegible.

[131] Nietzsche combines two traditions: 1.) the fact that aged 17 Demosthenes sued his
guardians; see Liban. VIII 603. 3 Foerster. 2.) the anecdote that he heard Callistratus' speech
as a young boy; see Hegesias of Magnesia (FGrHist 142 F 22) in [Plut.] 844 B. Both are from
Westermann I 107 n. 7 and 103.

[132] Nietzsche means the synegoria against Leptines.

[133] Compare Westermann I 104: "Sein eigentlich politischer Charakter aber entwickelte
sich mit Philipp's immer schärfer hervortretenden Plänen."

[134] Compare e.g. Westermann I 104: "Erst die Unterjochung von Phocis enttäuschte die
Athener; doch unter zwei Uebeln das kleinste wählend stimmte jetzt auch Demosthenes für
den Frieden."

Gesandtschaft war immer Demosth<enes>, der auch gegen die Staatsverräther vorging (de falsa legatione gegen Aeschines). Philipps Gewaltstreiche im Chersones[135] und Demosth<enes'> Anfeuerung[136] führt den ruhmwürdigen Kampf in Thracien herbei, der mit dem Entsatz von Byzanz 340 endigte. Der letzte phokische Krieg rief Ph<ilipp> ins Herz von Griechenland, er besetzte Elatea. Bei dieser Schreckensnachricht verlor nur D<emosthenes> den Muth nicht, er hob, nach Theopomp, die Zahl auch der [?]gaben.[137] Es gelang ihm, Athen und Theben zum Kampfe zu vereinigen. Doch ohne Erfolg: mit Chäronea 338 ging Athen's Unabhängigkeit verloren. Mit Philipp's Tode 336 gab es eine neue Hoffnung: überall Empörung. Man kam zur Ruhe, als Alexander mit einem Heer erschien: nur Theben, vor Cadmea in Empörung,[138] wurde von Grund aus zerstört.[139] Athens Antheil zu strafen, verlangte Alex<ander> die Auslieferung der Volkshäupter, darunter Demosth<enes>, doch liess er sich von Phocion u. Demades begütigen.[140] In der folg<enden> Friedenszeit wird D<emosthenes> in den Prozess verwickelt, den Harpalos durch Bestechung anregte 325; ohne überwiesen zu sein, wird er verurtheilt. Er entkam u. begab sich nach Aegina. Da kam die Nachricht von Alexa<nder>'s Tode. Leosthenes beginnt den Lamischen Krieg. Freiwillig schloss sich D<emosthenes> der Gesandtschaft an, welche Athen zum allgem<einen> Aufgebot an alle hell<enische> Staaten schickte u. wurde ehrenvoll nach Athen zurückberufen u. glänzend empfangen.[141] Aber die Schlacht bei Crannon ging verloren 322 u. Antipater zwang zum Frieden. Vor ihm, seinem Todfeinde, floh[142] D<emosthenes> nach Calauria u. dort starb er an genommenem Gift unter den Händen der Knechte des Antipater.[143] —Er war von Natur nicht wie Aeschines mit mächtiger Stimme begabt oder wie Demades gewaltiger Stegreifredner.[144] Er musste seine Gedanken sorgfältig zusammensetzen. Seine Stimme war kurz, lispelnd, seine Gesten ohne Grazie. Es waren die gleichen Gründe, die Isocrates von der öffentl<ichen>

---

[135] A reference to Demosth. 8 Περὶ τῶν ἐν Χερρονήσῳ.

[136] This is an allusion to the third speech against Philipp, a masterpiece of Demosthenes' political rhetoric. Eratosthenes (*FGrHist* 241 F 32) compares his passion to Bacchic enthusiasm (Plut. *Dem.* 9, 850 B).

[137] The MSS have Theophrastus, emended by Bünger to Theopompus (*FGrHist* 115 F 404). See Plut. *Dem.* 17, 853 E; "er...[?]gaben" is in superscript and therefore almost illegible. Perhaps better: "Eingaben." For this information there is no corresponding sentence in Westermann. He must have known it from Plutarch. The passage does not concern Demosthenes. Nietzsche seems to have confused Plut. *Dem.* 853 E with 854 B (= *FGrHist* 115 F 328).

[138] The fortress of Kadmeia, situated to the south of the city was still occupied by the Macedonians.

[139] See Diod. 17. 14; Plut. *Alex.* 11; Arrian 1. 7 ff.

[140] Plut. *Dem.* 23, 856 D-F.

[141] Plut. *Dem.* 27, 858 C-859 A.

[142] GBP 180 read 'flog'!

[143] Plut. *Dem.* 29-30. This dash refers to Westermann's subdivision in § 56 and § 57. But here Nietzsche seems to have used a different source.

[144] Plut. *Dem.* 10, 850 C.

Thätigkeit ausschlossen. In der Gesch<ichte> der Selbsterziehung ist er höchst denkwürdig.[145] Er wird der gewaltigste Redner δυνατώτατος ῥητόρων,[146] die δεινότης der Rede hat keiner erreicht. Cic. Brut. 9: plane cum perfectum et cui nihil admodum desit dixeris.[147] Von 65 Reden[148] sind 61[149] erhalten, mehrere darunter unecht, auch zweifelhaft. 17 συμβουλευτικοί, darunter die 12 philippischen.[150] Die 7te περὶ Ἀλοννήσου ist von Hegesipp gehalten,[151] früh schon einverleibt, da die unechte 11te (πρὸς τὴν ἐπιστολὴν τὴν Φιλίππου) sie benutzt. Unecht auch die 42 <te>. Dagegen der Brief Philipps, der unter den 12 Reden die 12te Stellung nimmt, usf. Dann 42 δικανικοί, 12 davon staatsrechtlich, 30 bürgerliches Recht. Am bedeutendsten darunter gegen die Vormünder, gegen Leptines, gegen Androtion, περὶ στεφάνου, der das vollkommenste Meisterwerk aller Beredsamkeit ist. ZB., 2 ἐπιδεικτικοί, der λόγος ἐπιτάφιος auf die bei Chäronea gefallenen [sic], u. der Ἐρωτικός, beide unecht.[152] Sehr zweifelhaft 56 erhalte<ne> Proömien u. 6 Briefe. A. Schäfer, Demosthenes u. seine Zeit, Leipzig 1856-58, 3 Bände.[153]|

|Hyperides[154] an kein Muster gebunden, Mitte zwischen Anmuth des Lysias u. Kraft des Demosth<enes>.[155] Ausdruck rein attisch, doch mit einiger Manier. Behandlung des Stoffes scharfsinnig,[156] doch nicht sorgfältig, vortreffl<ich> in Beweisführung. Unnachahml<iche> Eleganz u. Grazie.[157]

---

[145] For his self-education see Blass III¹ 19-24.

[146] Ariston of Chios considers Demosthenes the greatest (μέγιστον), Phokion the most able (δυνατώτατον) speaker; see Plut. Dem. 10, 850 D.

[147] The citation is not strictly accurate; see Cic. Brut. 9 (35): nam plane quidem perfectum et cui nihil admodum desit Demosthenem facile dixeris.

[148] [Plut.] 847 E.

[149] The manuscripts give only 60 speeches; the letter to Philipp has to be excluded (6 further letters and the collection of prooemia). See Jonathan A. Goldstein, The Letters of Demosthenes, New York/London 1968.

[150] Nietzsche has 12 speeches against Philipp, because he adds the above mentioned letter to Philipp. In WS 1872 Nietzsche lectured at the Paedagogium on Demosth. Phil. I, II: see Karl Schlechta, Nietzsche Chronik, Munich 1984, 39.

[151] So Harpocr. I 146. 2-3 Dindorf.

[152] Dion. Hal. Dem. 23 (180. 15 f.) and 44 (228. 16 ff., U-R). For the Epitaphios see also A. Schäfer, Demosthenes und seine Zeit, III, Leipzig² 1887, 36 n. 1.

[153] This is only a general reference; Nietzsche did not use Schäfer as he had Blass I. Schäfer is far too detailed for his purposes. Westermann I remains his obvious source.

[154] The following text from "Hyperides" to τραχύτης is on a separate sheet, only one fourth filled. There are remarks about Hypereides, Aeschines and Deinarchos, which seem to be later notes on these men. GBP again attach them to the corresponding treatments of the various authors without indicating the transpositions. But as far as can be judged by the original page numbering, this sheet was placed here in the Abriss.

[155] See Ps.-Longinus de subl. 34, 1 ff.

[156] Inter alia Dion. Hal. de imit. 5. 6 (213. 3 f. [434 f.] U-R) after Westermann I 123 n. 9.

[157] The whole short paragraph seems to be a note belonging to the larger passage concerning Hypereides (VIII): See infra. The source is Westermann I 122: "An kein Muster streng gebunden bildet sie, selbst anmuthig und kräftig, das Mittel zwischen der Anmuth des Lysias und der Kraft des Demosthenes. Der Ausdruck ist rein attisch, obgleich nicht ganz frei von Manier. Die Behandlung des Stoffes ist mit vielem Scharfsinn durchgeführt, auch

Aeschines' Fertigkeit im Improvisiren, seine Reden der reine Erguss eines übersprudelnden Genie's.[158] Kraft, Glanz[159] u. Fülle. Bei aller Anmuth doch heftig u. stürmisch, zeigt mehr Fleisch als Muskel.[160] Sein Einfluss zeigt sich vor allem darin, dass er durch Übersiedelung der Kunst nach Asien der Stifter der verbreiteten u. mächtigen asianischen Schule,[161] nach dem Erlöschen der attischen, wurde.[162]

Dinarch<us> ist nach Dionys<ius> H<alicarnaseus> nicht originell u. hat eigentl<ich> gar keinen Charakter, er ahmt bald Lysias, bald Hyperides, bald Demosth<enes> nach.[163] Eine gewisse Rauhheit, τραχύτης.[164]|

Hyperides (VIII)[165] aus Athen, Schüler des Plato u. des Isocrates, Freund des Demosth<enes>, entging mit ihm, mit Lykurg u. Charidemus nach der Vernichtung Thebens kaum der Gefahr, ausgeliefert zu werden. Nach Alexa<nder>'s Tode am lamischen Krieg betheiligt, wurde er von der macedon<ischen> Partei zum Tode verurtheilt u. entkam nach Aegina, wo er 322 auf Befehl Antipater's hingerichtet wurde. Von 77 Reden hielten die Alten 52 für echt.[166] Wir haben nur Fragmente, darunter 3 grössere. 1847 auf Papyrus durch Harris Bruchstücke einer Rede κατὰ Δημοσθένους u. 3 Fragm<ente> gefunden, durch Arden jene Reden ἀπολογία ὑπὲρ Λυκόφρονος u. ὑπὲρ Εὐξενίππου, endlich 1857 λόγος ἐπιτάφιος.[167] Grazie, Scharfsinn, Prunk, poetische Färbung. Libanius giebt ihn für den Verf<asser> von der dem Demosth<enes> beigelegten Rede περὶ τῶν πρὸς

---

wenn zuweilen nicht sorgfältig genug, doch namentlich in Bezug auf Darlegung des Gegenstandes und Beweisführung sehr nachahmungswürdig. Vor Allem aber charakterisirt die Reden des Hyperides eine unnachahmliche Eleganz und Grazie."

[158] See Phot. cod. 61 p. 20 B Bk. after Blass III[1] 164 n. 1): ἔστι δ᾽ ὁ λόγος αὐτῷ ὥσπερ αὐτοφυὴς καὶ αὐτοσχέδιος, οὐ τοσοῦτον διδοὺς τὴν τέχνην ἀποθαυμάζειν τοῦ ἀνδρὸς ὅσον τὴν φύσιν.

[159] Cic. Or. 110.

[160] Quint. 10. 1. 77.

[161] For the classical treatment of the Asian and Attic style see U. v. Wilamowitz-Moellendorff, "Asianismus und Atticismus," Kleine Schriften III, edited by Friedrich Zucker, Berlin 1969, 223-73, possibly composed with Nietzsche's Apollonine and Dionysiac in mind.

[162] Also this paragraph is only a short note belonging to the more detailed treatment of Aeschines (IX). It derives from Westermann I 117. Compare especially: "Dem entspricht wenigstens seine Fertigkeit im Extemporiren und der Charakter seiner Rede überhaupt, welche frei von aller Manier der reine Erguss eines übersprudelnden Genies ist. Hervorstechende Eigenschaft seiner Beredtsamkeit ist Kraft, Glanz und Fülle. Eindringlich und aufregend bei aller Leichtigkeit und bei aller Anmuth doch heftig und stürmisch, zeigt er mehr Fleisch als Muskel."

[163] Dion. Hal. Dein. 1 (297. 1-14 [629 f.] U-R).

[164] Hermogenes 1. 7, 299. This is only a short note belonging to the more detailed treatment of Dinarchus (X). See infra. The material is clearly from Westermann I 157-159. See particularly 157 f.: "Dinarchus ist nicht originell und hat eigentlich gar keinen besonderen rednerischen Charakter; er ahmt bald Lysias, bald Hyperides, namentlich aber Demosthenes nach..." The reference to his τραχύτης is from Westermann I 159 n. 19.

[165] In contrast to Westermann Nietzsche changed the order and numbering of Hyperides and Aeschines. Here Nietzsche has used another source, or added material on his own.

[166] [Plut.] 849 D.

[167] Papyri 1233-1236 Pack[2].

Ἀλέξανδρον συνθηκῶν.[168] <u>Aeschines</u> (IX)[169] geb. 391,[170] niede\<rer\>
Geburt, Vorfechter im Gymnasium,[171] dann γραμματεὺς im Dienste des
Staatsmanns Aristophon,[172] dann Schauspieler,[173] trat 356 gegen Philipp
auf. Grosser Rathgeber. 347 wird er mit Demosth\<enes\> zu Philipp
geschickt, verräth sein Vaterland u. lässt sich bestechen. Jetzt wird er
Todfeind des Demosth\<enes\>. Er ist jetzt Haupt der maced\<onischen\>
Partei. Κατὰ Τιμάρχου gegen die Anklage auf Hochverrath 345. 343 περὶ
παραπρεσβείας. 314 starb er auf Samos, besiegt durch Demosth\<enes'\>
Rede περὶ στεφάνου u. für ehrlos erklärt. Reich u. klar, gewandt, wortreich,
falsches Pathos.[174] Die berühmteste Rede κατὰ Κτεσιφῶντος. Man sprach
von 3 Grazien (die erhalten\<en\> 3 Reden) u. 9 Musen des Aeschines (9
verlorene Briefe.).[175]

    <u>Dinarchus (X)</u>[176] geb. zu Corinth 361, lebte zu Athen u. schrieb Reden
für andere, bes\<onders\> für die macedon\<ische\> Partei. Sehr thätig als
Werkzeug Antipater's u. während der Herrschaft des Demetrius Phalereus.
307 nach dessen Sturz verbannt. Durch Vermittl\<ung\> Theophrast's erhielt
er nach 15 Jahren die Erlaubnis der Rückkehr.[177] Auf Befehl Polysperchon's
wurde er 70 Jahre alt getödtet.[178] 160 Reden gab es,[179] nur 64[180] oder 60[181]
echt. 3 erhalten. Er ist Nachahmer des Demosthenes Δημοσθένης ὁ
κρίθινος,[182] ordearinus rhetor,[183] "gerstene D\<emosthenes\>" genannt.

<u>Demetrios</u> ὁ Φαληρεύς[184] aus geringem Geschlecht, Zögling des
Theophrast, durch glücklichste Naturanlagen zum mächtigen Staatsmann
werdend. Beginnt die polit\<ische\> Laufbahn 325 zur Zeit der harpalischen

---

[168] Liban. VIII 629 Foerster.

[169] Here again Nietzsche is not directly based on Westermann.

[170] Only some years later Blass II 2, 130 established the date of birth 390 or 389.
Westermann I 113 has 389.

[171] [Plut.] 840 A.

[172] See *Dem.* 19. 200; 237; 249 Schäfer I² 254, n.1.

[173] Demosthenes ridicules him as a tritagonistes: see *Dem.* 18. 261.

[174] Dion. Hal. *de imit.* 5. 5; Quint. 12, 10, 23.

[175] Phot. *cod.* 61: τρεῖς γὰρ μόνους αὐτοῦ φασὶ γνησίους εἶναι, καὶ ἐννέα ἐπιστολάς· διὸ
τοὺς μὲν λόγους αὐτοῦ τινὲς Χάριτας ὠνόμασαν, Μούσας δὲ τὰς ἐπιστολάς.

[176] No immediate source for Dinarchus is known to us.

[177] Dion. Hal. *Dein.* 2 (300. 1-15 [633 f.] U-R) after Westermann I 157-59.

[178] This account derives from confusion with a Corinthian of the same name whom
Antipater made commander in the Peloponnesus (Plut. *Phoc.* 33. 3-4, 757 A). The same error
can be found earlier in G.E. Groddeck, *Initia historica Graecarum litterarum* I, Vilnas 1821,
196.

[179] This account is based on Demetrius of Magnesia frag. p. 52 Scheuerl., cited by Dion.
Hal. *Dein.* 1 (299. 2 [632] U-R). Dionysius later rejects it: see *Dein.* 2 (299. 13 [633] U-R).

[180] [Plut.] 850 E und Phot. *cod.* 267.

[181] Dionysius attributes to Dinarchus 60 genuine and 27 spurious speeches.

[182] Because of his prolixity Hermogenes *Id.* 2. 11 characterizes him in these terms: ...ὥστ'
ἤδη τινὲς καὶ προσπαίζοντες αὐτὸν οὐκ ἀχαρίτως κρίθινον Δημοσθένην εἰρήκασιν.

[183] In superscript after Westermann I 159 n. 17.

[184] This part is again dependent on Westermann I 159-61.

Händel.[185] Nach Phocions Tode verwaltet er 10 Jahre Athen 317-307, unter Kassanders Regierung, zuerst zu allgem<einer> Zufriedenheit,[186] 360 Statuen ihm errichtet,[187] dann bildet sich, bei seinem Übermuth u. seiner Ausschweifung, eine Partei Missvergnügter. Er entwich nach Theben, von da nach Aegypten: dort fand er gelehrte Musse, er lebt in vertrautem Umgange mit Ptolemaeus Soter. Ihm verdächtigt stirbt er in Oberaegypten 283. Sehr fruchtbarer Autor, <Diog.> Laert. V 80: ὧν ἐστι τὰ μὲν ἱστορικά, τὰ δὲ πολιτικά, τὰ δὲ περὶ ποιητῶν, τὰ δὲ ῥητορικά, δημηγοριῶν τε καὶ πρεσβειῶν, ἀλλὰ μὴν καὶ λόγων Αἰσωπείων συναγωγαὶ καὶ ἄλλα πλείω. Unecht die vorhandene Schrift περὶ ἑρμηνείας. Mit ihm beginnt die att<ische> Beredsamkeit zu sinken. Der Charakter der Rede war sanft, weichlich, einschmeichelnd,[188] sein Ausdruck elegant, blühend, ohne richtiges Maass. Der letzte att<ische> Redner. Höchstens noch der Demosth<enes> Schüler Cineas zu nennen, der mit Pyrrhus 280 nach Italien ging.[189]

Die rhodische Schule,[190] von Aeschines gegründet, der von Demosth<enes> überwunden nach Asien ging u. zu Rhodus eine Schule stiftete.[191] Die eigentl<iche> asianische von Hegesias aus Magnesia. Die rhodische war die Vermittlerin der attischen und der asianischen, letztere viel stärker u. kräftiger, obgleich viel verwerflicher.[192] Cic. Brut. 13. 95 unterscheidet in der asian<ischen> zwei Richtungen: genera autem Asiaticae dictionis duo sunt: unum sententiosum et argutum, sententiis non tam gravibus[193] quam concinnis et venustis— aliud autem genus est non tam sententiis frequentatum quam verbis volucre et[194] incitatum, quali est nunc Asia tota, nec flumine solum orationis sed etiam exornato et faceto genere verborum.[195] 1.) die sententische Manier, in Verschlingung anmuthiger Gedanken, 2.) die verbose,[196] immer strömend, mit zierlichen u. blumigen Worten.[197] Zu ersteren Hierocles u. Menecles aus Alabanda,[198] der zweiten

---

[185] Diog. Laert. 5. 75.

[186] See Diog. Laert. 5. 77. Cic. de leg. 3. 14.

[187] This additional note "360 Statuen ihm errichtet" is written in superscript. It comes from Westermann I 161 n. 6. Ancient sources: Nepos Milt. 6 and Diog. Laert. 5. 75. GBP 184 read "360 Statuen von ihm errichtet" without indicating an addition to the text. They fully misunderstand the matter.

[188] Cic. Brut. 38. Orat. 92 after Westermann I 160.

[189] Plut. Pyrrhus 14. 1 after Westermann I 161 n. 21.

[190] This section is modelled on Westermann I 164-66 and 175-80.

[191] [Plut.] 840 D.

[192] For a general characterization see E. Norden, Die Antike Kunstprosa I, Stuttgart 1958⁵, 132f.

[193] Nietzsche carelessly copies Cicero's words from Westermann I 176 n. 2 and omits "et severis".

[194] An error for "atque".

[195] Cic. Brut. 95. 325.

[196] I. e. "die verbose Manier".

[197] For the two-fold distinction compare the words of Westermann I 176: "die eine, die sentenziöse, gefiel sich in künstlicher Verschlingung mehr anmuthiger als inhaltsschwerer

Aeschylus aus Cnidus und Aeschines aus Milet.[199] Unter den rhodischen Rednern Apollonius, Molon genannt, aus Alabanda u. Hermagoras aus Temnos, berühmt noch mehr als Techniker. Merkwürdig, wie nun Athen von Asien wieder empfängt: es bildet sich in Athen eine asianische Beredsamkeit: Menedemus, Gastfreund des Antonius,[200] Demetrius aus Syrien, den Cicero hörte,[201] usw. Cicero selbst ist gebildet einmal durch Philosophen (Archias,[202] Phaedrus,[203] Diodotus,[204] Posidonius,[205] Philo,[206] Antiochus,[207] dann durch Redner: Xenocles,[208] Dionysius,[209] Menippus,[210] Apollonius.[211] τέλος [?] dabei: Wandlung des römischen Geistes durch griech<ische> Cultur.|

Das Ereigniss [sic], das Rom der griech<ischen> Beredsamkeit öffnete, war die Gesandtschaft der Athener 155 v. C<hr.>,[212] um die Ermässigung einer wegen der Zerstörung von Oropos aufgelegten Geldstrafe zu erwirken, der Academ<iker> Carneades, der Stoiker Diogenes, der Peripat<etiker> Cristolaus.[213] Die Wirkung war so gross, dass Cato die Entfernung[214] der Gesandten antrug.[215] 161 hatte man senatus consultum de philosophis et rhetoribus Latinis gemacht, uti Romae non [sic] essent.[216] Danach aber, 6 Jahre später, sagte der Senat Aelian V<aria> H<istoria> III 17: ἔπεμψαν

Gedankenreihen, die *andere,* die verbose, in unerschöpflichen Ausströmen eines in stattliche Zierrath eingedämmten Wortschwalles."

[198] Cic. *Brut.* 325. The brothers had been active since about 140 BC; Cicero *ibid.* dates their active period to his own youth. See in general G.V. Sumner, "The orators in Cicero *Brutus:* Prosography and chronology," *Phoenix,* Supp. 11, Toronto 1973.

[199] Cic. *Brut.* 325. Cicero heard Aeschylus 78 BC in Asia Minor; Cic. *Brut.* 316. Aeschines was of the same age as Cicero; *Brut.* 325.

[200] Cic. *de or.* 1. 19. 85.

[201] Cic. *Brut.* 315.

[202] Cic. *Arch.* 1.

[203] Cic. *Epist.* 13. 1. 2; *Fin.* 1. 5. 16; 5. 1. 3; *Leg.* 1. 20. 53.

[204] *Inter alia* Cic. *Brut.* 309; *Acad.* 2. 63. 115; *Tusc.* 5. 39. 113.

[205] Cicero heard him in Rhodes; Plut. *Cic.* 4. 5, 862 F; Cic. *Tusc.* 2. 61; see also *Fin.* 1. 6; *Nat. Deor.* 1. 6.

[206] Cic. *Brut.* 306.

[207] Cicero heard him in 79/78 at Athens; Cic. *Brut.* 315. Cicero speaks of him elsewhere with respect: *Acad.* 1. 4. 13.

[208] Cic. *Brut.* 315.

[209] Dionysios of Magnesia is meant; see Cic. *Brut.* 316.

[210] Cic. *Brut.* 315.

[211] In 81 Apollonius came to Rome, in 78 Cicero visited him in Rhodes (*Brut.* 312). Cicero praises the moderating influence Apollonius had on him (*Brut.* 316).

[212] For the report about the Athenian mission see Westermann I 167-68.

[213] For the delegation of the Greek philosophers see Gellius 6 (7), 14, 8.

[214] GBP 186 read: "Der Academiker Corneades [sic], der Richter Diogenes, der Peripatetiker Aristolaus. Die Wirkung war so gross, dass Cato die Betreuung der Gesandten antrug."

[215] Plut. *Cato* 22.

[216] Gell. 15. 11. 1. *Latinis* is regularly deleted by modern editors after Pighius comparing Suet. *de rhet.* 1. Obviously Nietzsche had copied it from Westermann I 168 n. 6. Further, he replaces Gellius' *ne* with the grammatically incorrect *non*; see Kühner-Stegmann, *Lateinische Grammatik* II, Leverkusen 1955³, § 184 2a. It is correct in Westermann.

'Αθηναῖοι πρεσβεύοντας οὐ τοὺς πείσοντας, ἀλλὰ γὰρ τοὺς βιασομένους ἡμᾶς δρᾶσαι ὅσα θέλουσιν.[217] In der ersten Kaiserzeit ändert sich der Charakter der Beredsamkeit nicht. Die Schulen in Athen verloren etwas, der Zug der röm<ischen> Jugend ging nach Massilia oder Asien, wo Tarsus von Rednern wimmelte. Die Redekunst ist die Liebhaberei der studierenden Jugend. Schule zu Mytilene auf Lesbos, Timocrates — Lesbonax — Potamon, Lehrer u. Freund des Tiberius.[218] In Asien ist Theodorus aus Gadara Stifter der Sekte der Θεοδωρεῖοι, zu Rom mit Potamon in Streit verwickelt. Apollodorus aus Pergamus,[219] Stifter der pergamen<ischen> Sekte der 'Απολλοδωρεῖοι. Berühmter als alle Dio, Chrysostomus[220] zubenannt, aus Prusa in Bithynien. In der Heimat verkannt geht er nach Rom, ist dort Domitian verdächtig (Gell. N. A. XV 11,[221] philosophi <...> Domitiano imperante senatus consulto ejecti atque urbe et Italia interdicti sunt), entweicht aus Rom u. beginnt angebl<ich> auf Rath des delph<ischen> Orakels[222] im Bettlerkleide[223] eine Wanderung durch Thracien, Illyrien, Scythien u. das Land der Geten, nichts als Platons Phaedon u. Demosth<enes'> Rede de falsa legatione in der Tasche.[224] Mit Ehren überhäuft kehrt er nach Prusa zurück.[225] Nach Domitians Ermordung 96 c. stimmt er die Grenzarmeen zu Gunsten seines Freundes[226] Coccejus Nerva (daher der Beiname [?] Cocceianus[227]) u. ging nach Rom, sehr geehrt von dort nach Prusa, das ihm bald durch Kleinstädterei verleidet wird.[228] In Rom stirbt er, in hoher Achtung bei Trajan 117 pC. Es sind 80 Reden erhalten: wenig davon gehört der ersten Periode an; seine Form ist bes<onders> nach Hyperides u. Aeschines gebildet, die er als Muster selbst Demosth<enes> u. Lysias vorzog.[229] Dionys<ius> v. Halicarn<ass>, der bedeutendste rhetor<ische> Kunstrichter,[230] in den Schulen Asiens gebildet, kam 25 Jahre alt 29 a. Ch. nach Rom,[231] hauptsächlich um römische Geschichte an der Quelle zu studieren. Es entstand seine ῥωμαικὴ [*sic*]

---

[217] 48. 7-9 Dilts. This citation is taken from Westermann I 168 n. 4.

[218] Nietzsche copies an error from Westermann I 186. In fact not Potamon, but Theodorus of Gadara was Tiberius' teacher (Suet. *Tib.* 57): see F. Susemihl, *Geschichte der griechischen Literatur in der Alexandrinerzeit* II, Leipzig 1892, 514 n. 228.

[219] Pergamon is meant. Westermann I 186 too has "Pergamus".

[220] See Westermann 189-91.

[221] 15. 11. 3-4. Citation from Westermann I 190 n. 5.

[222] Dio Chrys. 13. 9 f.

[223] Dio. Chrys. 12. 85; 13. 10.

[224] See Philostrat. *Soph.* 488. The sentence is from Westermann I 190 n. 7.

[225] A direct citation from Westermann I 189.

[226] Philostrat. *Soph.* 488 I

[227] Plin. *Ep.* 10. 85; see Westermann 191 n. 9. The reading is uncertain.

[228] See the almost literal rendering from Westermann I 189: "allein der dort herrschende kleinstädtische Geist...verleidete ihm den Aufenthalt daselbst."

[229] See Westermann I 191 n. 20.

[230] See Westermann I 192-193 and in general S.F. Bonner, *The Literary Treatises of Dionysius of Halicarnassus: A Study in the Development of Critical Method*, Amsterdam 1969.

[231] Dion. Hal. *Ant. Rom.* 1. 7.

ἀρχαιολογία in XX Bänden, die ersten 9 haben wir vollständig, von X u. XI nur den grössten Theil und Auszüge der übrigen. Eine Rhetorik unter seinem Namen ist ein Cento aus 4 Hauptpartien, theilweise von Dionys<ius>.[232] Sehr wichtige Schriften verloren, aber erhalten περὶ συνθέσεως ὀνομάτων. Πρὸς Γναῖον Πομπήιον ἐπιστολή über den Vorzug der demosth<enischen> Schreibart vor der platonischen. Ἐπιστολὴ πρὸς Ἀμμαῖον περὶ τῶν Θουκυδίδου ἰδιωμάτων. Περὶ τοῦ Θουκυδίδου χαρακτῆρος. Περὶ τῶν ἀρχαίων ῥητόρων [sic] ὑπομνηματισμοί, auf 6 Abtheil<ungen> berechnet, von denen aber nur die erste Hälfte, 1. Lysias. 2. Isocrates. 3. Isaeus, u. von der zweiten[233] nur die erste Hälfte der ersten Abtheilung, περὶ τῆς λεκτικῆς Δημοσθένους δεινότητος, vorhanden ist. Leider sind die parallelen Schriften des Rhetor Caecilius[234] aus Καλὴ Ἀκτή in Sicilien (daher Καλακτῖνος) verloren. Schriften genannt bei Suidas.[235] Echtheitsentscheidung über die älteren Redner. — Eine neue Epoche beginnt mit Hadrian:[236] Athen blüht auf. Mark Aurel gründet zwei öffentl<iche> Schulen,[237] eine philosophische u. eine rhetorische, die erstere mit 4 Kathedern[238] (nach den 4 Hauptschulen, von jeder 2 Professoren), die leztere [sic] in 2 θρόνοι, in das sophistische u. das politische Fach. Die Profess<oren> erhielten jährlich 10000 Drachmen. Später stieg für jedes Katheder die Zahl der Lehrer bis auf 6. Kraft kaiserl<ichen> Willens wird der Name Sophist wieder zu Ehren gebracht.[239] Ausserordentl<icher> Wetteifer bei grosser Entartung, hohe Koketterie der Deklamierenden. Lucian entwirft ein starkes Bild von dieser Entartung. Berühmt in Athen vor Allen Herodes Atticus, in hoher Gunst bei den Antoninen. Grosser Improvisator. Schriften verloren.[240] In Asien berühmt Aelius Aristides[241] aus Adriani in Mysien geb. 129. Noch 55 Reden u. Abhandl<ungen> erhalten, 2 rhetor<ische> Schriften von geringem Werthe.[242] Lucian[243] aus Samosata 130-200 n. Chr., früher selbst Sophist

---

[232] See Westermann I 194 n. 4.

[233] The contents of the second half: 4. Demosthenes, 5. Hyperides, 6. Aeschines.

[234] See Westermann I 193 and 197 nn. 16 and 17 and *Caecilii Calactini Fragmenta*, collegit Ernestus Ofenloch, Leipzig 1907, repr. Stuttgart 1967.

[235] K 1165 Adler.

[236] For the following see Westermann I 198-202. Note the almost literal citation from Westermann 198 f.

[237] For Marcus Aurelius' founding of the University of Athens see J.W.H. Walden, *The Universities of Ancient Greece*, New York 1909, 90-94 and the sources there cited.

[238] Luc. *Eun* . 3.

[239] See G.W. Bowersock, *Greek Sophists in the Roman Empire*, Oxford 1969.

[240] Περὶ πολιτείας, edited by E. Drerup, Paderborn, 1908, is preserved. Thrasymachus is imitated so perfectly that some wanted to date this speech to the fifth century. See K. Münscher *RE* 8 (1913) 921-54; 1308-10.

[241] See Westermann I 209-12. But from here on his excerpts get so short that there are hardly any parallels to be found.

[242] Nietzsche follows Westermann I 210. Modern opinion holds that both works were attributed to Aristeides relatively late: See Christ-Schmid-Stählin, *Geschichte der Griechischen Literatur* II 2, München 1924[6], 699 n. 8.

[243] See Westermann I 213.

u. Rhetor[244] u. wendet sich 40 Jahre alt zur Philosophie, ankämpfend gegen alles Sophistenthum.[245] Ausserordentlicher Techniker, also Kunstschriftsteller, ist <u>Hermogenes</u>[246] aus Tarsus, ingenium praecox, im 15t<en> J<ahr> öffentl<icher> Lehrer, im 17t<en> Schriftsteller, im 25<ten> unheilbare Geistesschwäche.[247] Erhalten: I) τέχνη ῥητορικὴ [sic] περὶ τῶν στάσεων, de partitionibus,[248] nach Hermagoras' Grundsätzen.[249] II) περὶ εὑρέσεως, de invent<ione>,[250] in 4 Büchern. III) περὶ ἰδεῶν, de formis oratoriis,[251] in 2 Büchern. IV) περὶ μεθόδου δεινότητος, de apto et sollerti genere dicendi methodus.[252] V) προγυμνάσματα, praeexercitamenta.[253]|

Die drei Philostrati:[254] I) <u>Flavius Philostratus</u>, Sohn des Verus aus Hierapolis, lebt noch unter Severus. II) des <u>ersteren Sohn</u>, erst Lehrer in Athen, dann in Rom, Biograph des Apollonius v<on> Tyana auf Verlangen der Kaiserin Julia,[255] Verfasser der βίοι σοφιστῶν, Heroica, Imagines (εἰκόνες). III) des zweiten Schwestersohn, in Gunst bei Caracalla, starb unter Galienus [sic][256] 264. Feiner Kunstkritiker. <u>Dionysius Cassius Longinus</u> 213-273, berühmt περὶ ὕψους.[257] Verfasser von vorhandenen προγυμνάσματα sind <u>Aphthonius</u> aus Antiochien u. <u>Aelius Theon</u> aus Alexandria.[258] <u>Himerius</u>[259] aus Prusias in Bithynien c. 315-386, berühmter Lehrer in Athen. Von 71 Reden,[260] die Photius nannte, besitzen wir noch 36 von diesem gemachte ἐκλογαί, 24 Reden vollständig u. X in Fragmenten. Prunk- u. Gelegenheitsreden. Sein Schüler ist der Kaiser

---

[244] He characterises himself as ῥήτορα Σύρον and λογογράφον Σύρον; see *Bis accus.* 14 und 25.

[245] He even compares rhetoric to a rouge painted hetaira; *Bis accus.* 31.

[246] See Westermann I 217-20.

[247] Proleg. Hermog. *de Stat.* 2. 222. 12 Walz after Westermann I 217.

[248] In superscript after Westermann I 219 n. 4.

[249] See Westermann I 218.

[250] In superscript after Westermann I 219 n. 5.

[251] In superscript after Westermann I 219 n. 6.

[252] In subscript after Westermann I 219 n. 7.

[253] See Westermann I 220 n. 8. GBP 190 read: "Ausserordentlicher Darsteller also Kunstschriftsteller ist *Hermogenes* aus Tarsus, ingenium praecox, im 15. Lebensjahr öffentlicher Lehrer, im 17. Jahre Schriftsteller, im 25. unfehlbarer Geist in der Sprache. Erhalten: (I) τέχνη ῥητορικὴ περὶ τῶν στάσεων (de partitionibus) nach Hermagoras' Grundsätzen, (II) περὶ εὑρέσεως (de inventione) in 4 Büchern, (III) περὶ ἰδεῶν (de formis rhetoricis) in 2 Büchern, (IV) περὶ μεθόδου δεινότητος de apto, (V) προγυμνάσματα (praeexercitamenta) et sollerti generi methodas."

[254] See Westermann I 223-26.

[255] Vit. *Ap.* 1. 3; the empress Julia Domna is meant.

[256] Nietzsche's error for "Gallienus."

[257] The author today is regularly called Ps.-Longinus. Nietzsche does not know Aemil. Winkler, *De Longini qui fertur libello περὶ ὕψους,* Diss. Halle 1870, who proved the whole spurious on linguistic grounds. Nietzsche uncritically follows Westermann I 229-32, who (230 and 232 n. 9) explicitly defends the work as genuine.

[258] See Westermann I 230 and 233-34.

[259] For Himerius and Julian see Westermann I 239-242.

[260] Here Nietzsche errs (after Westermann I 240). Photius still knew 73, not 71; see Phot. *bibl.* p. 107-109 and 353-377 Bekk.

Julianus 331-363. In Byzanz blüht bis auf Theodosius von Constantin<opel> u. Julianus, Themistius, wir besitzen 34 Reden.[261] In Asien blüht Libanius[262] aus Antiochien, ausserordent<lich> fruchtbar. Erhalten 66[263] Reden, 50[264] Deklamationen. Dann Musterstücke zu rhetor<ischen> Vorübungen.[265] Dann die bekannten Inhaltsanzeigen der Reden des Demosth<enes>[266] u. Biographie des Demosth<enes>;[267] das letzte grosse Talent.[268]

III. What have we learned?

Certainly nothing we did not know about the Greek orators. Otto Crusius rightly remarked:[269] "Der verkürzte Abriss der Geschichte der Beredsamkeit hinter der Darstellung der Rhetorik hat neben dieser ausführlichen Form [i.e the 1874 notes] keine selbständige Bedeutung." But we have learned that Germanists innocent of Greek and Latin ought not to edit works of Nietzsche that require Greek and Latin. We have also learned something about the man Nietzsche and about his scholarly attention to Greek antiquity. The *Abriss* is written by a man about a subject that bores him. The work is *Pflicht* rather than *Neigung*. He needs a minimum of fact to support the theory of the *Darstellung der Antiken Rhetorik*. The two students might ask questions. It was a time of disappointment and even humiliation. Presumably Nietzsche had chosen the subject, because students ought to read the orators and would not on their own. Then unexpectedly all the students who needed the orators boycotted his course. What possible reason was there to spend time and do well?

There are two revealing facts that emerge from the study of the essay: Nietzsche's grasp of Greek and Latin certainly does not equal that of his younger contemporary and fellow Pforte graduate, Ulrich von Wilamowitz-Moellendorff. One need only recall the solecism ἐν τῇ σοφιστῷ[270] and the indifference to particles.[271] He was not a master of Greek and Latin[272] grammar. As far as the composition of the essay goes, we have shown that it is almost entirely derivative from two predecessors, Fr. Blass and A.

---

[261] So Westermann I 243 and 244 n. 9. Only 33 speeches are preserved; he adds the twelfth speech, which is judged as a modern forgery in the more recent research; see Westermann 328-330, Beilage XIV.

[262] See Westermann I 244-49. For the following text see Westermann I 246.

[263] Westermann I 248 n. 28.

[264] Westermann I 248 n. 29.

[265] I.e., the προγυμνάσματα (= *Libanii opera*, VIII. 1-571). See Westermann I 248 f.n. 30.

[266] *Libanii opera*, VIII, ed. R. Foerster, Leipzig 1915, 573-681.

[267] *Libanii opera*, VIII. 600-07.

[268] See G.R. Sievers, *Das Leben des Libanius*, Berlin 1868, repr. Amsterdam 1969.

[269] *Op. cit.* (*supra* n. 2), 331.

[270] See *supra* n.8.

[271] See *supra* n. 127.

[272] See *supra* n. 216.

Westermann. Both these books were in his personal library. Neither is annotated.[273] He had little independent knowledge of the subject as his omission of Isocrates' most famous oration and his naive attribution of *de sublimitate* to Longinus prove. Nor did it trouble him to lecture to students about authors whom he had never read presenting as his own conclusions what he had merely excerpted from contemporary handbooks, assured that his students were too lazy to unmask him.

Albert Henrichs has recently demonstrated that, while Nietzsche wrote in 1872 perhaps the most influential *damnatio* of Euripides, in fact he does not reveal personal knowledge of any Euripidean tragedy other than *Bacchae* which he knew well. His entire criticism of Euripides was derived from A.W. Schlegel.[274] "The fundamentals of Nietzsche's case against Euripides are demonstrably derived from Schlegel's Vienna lectures."[275] In spite of Wilamowitz' telling refutation of the philological and historical basis of *Geburt*, Nietzsche continued with oratory, as he had earlier with Euripidean tragedy, to base his case on secondary literature rather than original sources. Probably the most important contribution of the new text is that it confirms Henrichs' discovery for *Geburt* and further illustrates the welcome truth that by November 1872 traditional historical philological scholarship bored Friedrich Nietzsche. *Incipit tragoedia.*[276]

---

[273] Max Oehler, *Nietzsches Bibliothek. Vierzehnte Jahresgabe der Gesellschaft der Freunde des Nietzsche-Archivs Weimar*, Weimar 1942, 9, 16. In November 1872 he borrowed the University Library's copy of Blass I (Oehler, 51).

[274] Albert Henrichs, "The last of the detractors: Friedrich Nietzsche's condemnation of Euripides," *GRBS* 27 (1986) 369-97, esp. 376-85 ("Euripides at Second Hand: Nietzsche's Use of A.W. Schlegel"). For Schlegel's critique of Euripides see Ernst Behler, "A.W. Schlegel and the nineteenth-century *damnatio* of Euripides," *GRBS* 27 (1986) 335-67.

[275] *Ibid.* 384.

[276] See Curt Paul Janz, *Friedrich Nietzsche Biographie* I, Munich/Vienna 1978, 494.

Nuda Veritas:
William Abbott Oldfather on Classics at Columbia[1]

I. The Document

The document consists of six typed pages of Columbia University, Department of Greek and Latin stationery with occasional handwritten corrections and additions. On the first page is written "Columbia Univ" in Oldfather's hand. The original is among the Oldfather papers at the University of Illinois. My doctoral student, Mr. Michael Armstrong, while composing a life and a full bibliography of Oldfather came upon it. The date is most easily early April 1938. Oldfather was guest professor at Columbia spring semester 1938. He had been invited 6 February 1937 by President Nicholas Murray Butler "to come to Columbia as visiting professor for the year 1937–38." The salary would be $7500.[2] Because Oldfather had already agreed to be "Visiting Professor at the American School of Classical Studies in Athens during the first semester of 1937–1938"[3] he was able to accept only for the spring semester. He accepted on 11 March 1937 "at a stipend of $3,750, together with an allowance for travelling expenses of $250."[4] Clinton W. Keyes became executive officer of the Department of Greek and Latin on 1 July 1937, succeeding Clarence Young, who retired. Kurt von Fritz and Gilbert Highet were both appointed as visitors for the full year.

The document is not a letter but an aide-mémoire, presumably composed by Oldfather for use at a conference. Its origin can be reconstructed. In his original invitation Butler wrote:[5] "We are carefully studying the future of this department and hope to be able to work out a plan that will preserve the distinction that Columbia has long held in this field. Such a study

---

[1] This paper was delivered as a public lecture at Columbia University on 21 February 1992. I am grateful for the animated discussion that followed. The paper has been much improved by the late Mrs. Moses Hadas, Dr. Donna W. Hurley, Professors Charles Rowan Beye, Ward W. Briggs Jr., Dirk Obbink, David Sider, Seth Schein, Laura M. Slatkin, and John Vaio. Most of all I am indebted to Professor Michael Armstrong (Hobart and William Smith Colleges). I cite him throughout within. I have not entirely obliterated the style of oral presentation.

[2] Nicholas Murray Butler to William A. Oldfather, 6 February 1937, William A. Oldfather Papers, 1904–1945, Record Series 15/6/20, Box 2, University of Illinois Archives. All subsequent citations of unpublished documents are from this collection. I am grateful to the Director of the Archives for permission to publish the documents they hold.

[3] Oldfather to Butler 11 February 1937. This is confirmed at Louis E. Lord, *A History of the American School of Classical Studies at Athens 1882–1942: An Intercollegiate Project* (Cambridge 1947) 360.

[4] Oldfather to Butler (11 March 1937).

[5] See n. 4 *supra*.

cannot be made hurriedly if the recommendations and decisions are to be wise." In a letter dated 714 Philosophy Hall, April 2nd 1938 to Frank D. Fackenthal, Secretary of the University, Oldfather writes:

> From the general phrasing of President Butler's letter of last spring, though not indeed from any specific statement in it, I gathered the impression that it might be part of my duties while here to prepare myself to make an informal report to some appropriate officer of the University upon the organization and personnel of the Department of Classics.
>
> Now I do not at all wish to do this, for it is an awkward and unpleasant thing to engage in, but if the making of some kind of comment is really a service that I am expected to render I am willing to see the thing through.

Fackenthal replied on 4 April 1938:

> I have your letter of April 2 and am sure the President will understand your attitude as to reporting on the Department of Greek and Latin and will be glad to excuse you from doing so.

What seems to have happened is that Oldfather correctly surmised that Butler desired him to inform on the Department in which he was a guest. Oldfather drew up ca. 2 April 1938, that is after he had been there two months, his candid opinion but demurred from communicating his views to the administration. Butler, or at least Fackenthal, let him off the hook. Oldfather preserved the document among his papers. It is first made public here.

There is further information to confirm this. We know that 1937 was a watershed for classics at Columbia. Charles Knapp died that year and three of the old guard retired: Clarence Young, Frank Gardner Moore and Nelson McCrea. Moses Hadas writes in his history of the department:[6] "A University committee was appointed to plan the reorganisation of the Department." A working hypothesis is that the Committee wanted Oldfather to present his views. This manuscript then would be what he would have taken with him to the meeting.

I invited two distinguished senior scholars, present at Columbia in the thirties, and each still fully *compos mentis* to control Oldfather's evaluations. Professor Meyer Reinhold (b. 23 August 1909), whose famous

---

[6] See Moses Hadas, "The Department of Greek and Latin," in Anonymous, *A History of the Faculty of Philosophy Columbia University New York* (New York 1957) 174–82; here 181 (henceforth: Hadas). I owe the reference to Professors Roger S. Bagnall and Ward W. Briggs Jr. For the general background of American university reform there are two excellent books: see Richard J. Storr, *The Beginnings of Graduate Education in America* (Chicago 1953; repr. New York 1969) and Laurence R. Veysey, *The Emergence of the American University* (Chicago/London 1965). They both underplay the contribution of classicists.

Columbia dissertation, *Marcus Agrippa: A Biography* (1933) is still authoritative, declined. He wrote (15 October 1991) of what he knows: "Some of it I shrank from, some of it I have swept under my memory rug." Fred W. Householder Jr. (b. 1 February 1913), M.A. Columbia 1934, Ph.D. 1941 and lecturer in classics at Columbia 1938–46, now emeritus professor at Indiana, wrote a seven page response of great value which with his permission (*per litteras* 16 June 1991) I shall cite throughout. His Columbia dissertation, written under La Rue Van Hook was the famous one: *Literary Quotation and Allusion in Lucian* (King's Crown Press, 1941). Because I am not a village pastor, I shall not deliver moral judgments on Oldfather nor shall I speculate on whether his judgment was impaired for some unattested personal reason. There exists no evidence that it was.

II. Who Was Oldfather?

Historians of American classics attribute the origin of scientific philology in this country to three great German trained men: B.L. Gildersleeve (1831–1924), Paul Shorey (1857–1934), and William Abbott Oldfather (1880–1945).[7] Together they directed the dissertations of 170 American scholars. There were several women but not a single obvious Jew among them. The one surviving is L.R. Lind. These scholars held leading positions in US classics for some 100 years and shaped the discipline. Hopkins and Chicago, where Gildersleeve and Shorey taught, were late foundations purposely modeled on Prussian research universities rather than on English boys finishing schools.[8] Oldfather turned Illinois into a third Prussian University. Many American scholars today, myself for example, are their grandstudents. Both my dissertation directors were taught by Shorey. Let us look more closely for a moment at Oldfather. I have used in what I shall say the biographies of Professors Buckler and Armstrong as well as the latter's bibliography of Oldfather's works which I hope will soon introduce a volume of selected *Kleine Schriften*.[9]

---

[7] See William M. Calder III, "Die Geschichte der klassischen Philologie in den Vereinigten Staaten," *Jahrbuch für Amerikastudien* 11 (1966) 213–40 (= "Studies in the Modern History of Classical Scholarship," *Antiqua* 27 [Naples 1984] 15–42, 301–04) [henceforth: *Studies*]. Gildersleeve had 67 doctoral students, Shorey 57 and Oldfather 46.

[8] See William H. McNeill, *Hutchins' University: A Memoir of the University of Chicago, 1929–1950* (Chicago 1992) and Hugh Hawkins, *Pioneer: A History of the Johns Hopkins University, 1874–1889* (Ithaca 1960).

[9] See John Buckler, "William Abbott Oldfather," *Classical Scholarship: A Biographical Encyclopedia*, edited by Ward W. Briggs and William M. Calder III (New York/London 1990) 346–52 (with valuable selected bibliography). He begins his life with the words (346): "There was nothing simple about William Abbott Oldfather." The book is henceforth cited: Briggs-Calder. See too Michael Armstrong, "A German Scholar and Socialist in America: The Career of William Abbott Oldfather," *CJ* 88 (1992/93) 235-53. The published account

Oldfather was born in what today is Iran on 23 October 1880. His parents were both Presbyterian missionaries. He remained a Presbyterian and a deeply religious man all his life.[10] This accounted for his strong moral convictions. He was a descendant of Daniel Boone on his mother's side and of Silesian origin (Altvater) on his father's. His nephew was Edwin O. Reischauer, American ambassador to Japan. I have called him "German Scholar in America."[11] He took a BA from Harvard in 1901 and an MA in 1902. He studied there under the grammarians, William Watson Goodwin (1831–1912), Charles Burton Gulick (1868–1962) and H. Weir Smyth (1857–1937). 1903–06 he was instructor in Classics at Northwestern in Evanston (Illinois). He used his free time to become bilingual in German and to familiarize himself with German scholarship. In 1906 he matriculated at the University of Munich, receiving the doctorate in 1908. Armstrong has rightly called the German years "the central formative experience of his life." One recalls Gildersleeve. He heard the Hellenist and biographer of Nietzsche's friend, Erwin Rohde, Otto Crusius (1857–1918),[12] the Latin text critic, Friedrich Vollmer (1867–1923),[13] the ancient historian and socialist, Robert von Pöhlmann (1852–1914)[14] and the great art historian and father of the conductor, Adolf Furtwängler (1853–1907).[15] Like Gildersleeve, he remained a Germanophile throughout his life. This has caused Americans to call him a closet Nazi. The fact is that Pöhlmann converted him to socialism and his early political writings might have cost him his career in the McCarthy period. Some of these will be published in his *Kleine Schriften*. They differ considerably from Gildersleeve's Civil War editorials. His dissertation was modeled on Karl Otfried Müller's *Aegina*. It was entitled *Lokrika* and had been suggested by Smyth but was directed by Crusius. An expanded version later became the great Pauly-Wissowa

---

that best captures Oldfather the man is C.A. F<orbes>, "William Abbott Oldfather 1880–1945," *CJ* 41 (1945) 9–11. I am grateful to Professor Forbes for a copy.

[10] The *opus classicum* is: W.A. Oldfather, *Is Religion Essential to Every Adequate Philosophy of Living?* (Young Men's Christian Association, Urbana, Illinois 1930). Pp. 37. A second slightly revised edition appeared in 1934 published by the Young Men's Christian Association of the University of California.

[11] *CW* 74 (1980–1981) 249 (= *Studies*, 11). Cf. Buckler, Briggs-Calder, 346: "...his efforts to introduce German principles of higher education influenced not only his own University of Illinois but also the general development of modern American education."

[12] For Otto Crusius (1857–1918) see William M. Calder III and Alexander Košenina, *Berufungspolitik innerhalb der Altertumswissenschaft im wilhelminischen Preußen: Die Briefe Ulrich von Wilamowitz-Moellendorffs an Friedrich Althoff (1883–1908)* (Frankfurt/Main 1989) 67–71 with literature there cited. The authoritative biography is Winfried Bühler, "De Ottonis Crusii vita et studiis paroemiographicis," *Zenobii Athoi proverbia* I (Göttingen 1987) 327–43.

[13] For Friedrich Vollmer (1867–1923) see Hans Rubenbauer, *BiogJahr* 202 (1924; publ. 1925) 68–103. He concentrated on the editing of Latin poetry.

[14] See Karl Christ, "Robert von Pöhlmann (1852–1914)," *Von Gibbon zu Rostovtzeff: Leben und Werk führender Althistoriker der Neuzeit* (Darmstadt 1979) 201–47.

[15] See Andreas E. Furtwängler, "Adolf Furtwängler," Briggs-Calder, 84–92.

article.[16] The dissertation exemplified the *Totalitätsideal* with Oldfather employing all sorts of available evidence, epigraphical, philological, archaeological, numismatic and topographical. Because of what he says of epigraphy, one should recall that he was an expert at the editing of Greek dialectal inscriptions. The article was later praised by Wilamowitz, who normally had only contempt for PW articles and people who wrote them.[17]

In 1908 Oldfather returned to Northwestern but in 1909 went to Illinois to become Czar of Classics there. He became full professor in 1915 and Head of the Department, i.e., *supremus inter inferiores*, in 1926 until his death by accidental drowning in 1945. This is no place to list his publications. Armstrong's bibliography includes 252 items and omits the some 500 articles in PW. No American approaches this. In my own library I have his Loeb of Aeneas Tacticus and the military writers, his great two volume Loeb Epictetus with the two volume bibliography to Epictetus, his *indices verborum* to Seneca Tragicus, Apuleius, and the rhetorical works of Cicero. Oldfather wrote books that last. He held that no one had the *bona fides* to write about ancient literature or thought until he had published at least one critical *index verborum* and a critical text "from the ground up" of one Latin and of one Greek author. Oldfather sensibly preferred authors off the beaten track because there were not so many manuscripts and there still was a lot to be done with the text.

He wrote much else, often articles of great brilliance as his famous one arguing that Socrates was silent on trial.[18] He seems the first to have taught Ancient Athletics.[19] His lectures survive. He was Sather professor[20] in spring 1934 and spoke on "The Decline of Culture within the Roman Empire." In 1938 the year of his guest-professorship at Columbia he was president of APA and delivered the presidential address on "Some Ancient Thoughts on Progress and Decadence." An extensive summary of the address was published in the *New York Times* of 29 December 1938. He asserted there that "gross maldistribution of wealth" had brought about the collapse of ancient civilization—a vestige of Pöhlmann. He drew parallels to the decadence of modern culture. The address received wide press coverage and Oldfather writes a friend: "...but it is frightful the way I have lost caste with my fellow classicists by saying anything that the 'public prints' could be

---

[16] *RE* 13 (1926) 1135–288. For the dissertation see *Philologus* 67 (1908) 412–72.

[17] See William M. Calder III, "Ulrich von Wilamowitz-Moellendorff to William Abbott Oldfather: Three Unpublished Letters," *CJ* 72 (1976–77) 115–27, here 123 (= *Antiqua* 23 [Naples 1983] 243–55, 308–09).

[18] "Socrates in Court," *CW* 31 (1937–38) 203–11. Oldfather's thesis was accepted by Sterling Dow and long presented as truth to Harvard undergraduates in Greek History.

[19] See David Sansone, *Greek Athletics and the Genesis of Sport* (Berkeley 1988) xiii–xiv.

[20] See Sterling Dow, *Fifty Years of Sathers: the Sather Professorship of Classical Literature in the University of California, Berkeley 1913/4–1963/4* (Berkeley/Los Angeles 1965) 62 (1933–34).

interested in."[21] He held a number of administrative posts within the University of Illinois and, as I have already observed, had time to direct 46 dissertations.[22] At his unexpected death eleven large projects were left unfinished. His active participation in American classics on the national scale is clear in his over 30 years' correspondence with A.S. Pease, preserved at The Houghton Library, Harvard. He was an eloquent speaker, an outstanding athlete, and a man of charismatic personality. His students called him "der Herr." This was the man who in 1937–38 was invited to be guest professor at Columbia and whose opinion of the Department, with suggestions on what to do, was elicited.

The aide-mémoire begins with an evaluation of departmental members. First is the Jay Professor, followed by others in the Department in alphabetical order and ending with those affiliated with classics but in other departments. He continues with suggestions for further appointments and some general suggestions for improvement. The uncensored text follows. I have documented Oldfather's comments with the remarks of Professor Householder and some exegetical scholia of my own. What he says is of interest not only for Columbia but because it reveals the opinion of America's leading classical scholar on what a good department should be.

III. The Text

Van Hook.[23] Once competent, gone lazy & superficial, popular in the bad sense, and now merely having a good time. A distinctly 2nd rate[24] man holding the titular professorship in a first class institution.

W.L. Carr.[25] Breezy and energetic; talks pedagese and probably thinks it, too; working hard for the cause, but is a small man personally with

---

[21] Letter to Carl Stephens, 20 January 1939, Oldfather Papers, University of Illinois Archives, *s.v.* Stephens. I owe the reference to Michael Armstrong.

[22] See Suzanne N. Griffiths, "Doctoral Dissertations Completed at the University of Illinois under William Abbott Oldfather," *CJ* 74 (1978–79) 149–53. In this context one should consult, W.A. Oldfather, "The Character of the Training and of the Thesis for the Degree of Doctor of Philosophy in the Classics," *CJ* 26 (1930–31) 580–88 and "The Dissertation," *CW* 32 (1938–39) 231–33.

[23] E.B. Harrison, who took courses from La Rue van Hook (1877–1953) several years later remarks: "Probably fair." Householder observes: "I agree pretty much with what Oldfather says. A nice guy, but not terribly bright." He is remembered today for his Loeb Isocrates volume. Oldfather at the time was living in Van Hook's New York apartment (39 Claremont Avenue). See the life by Meyer Reinhold, *Biographical Dictionary of North American Classicists*, ed. Ward. W. Briggs, Jr. (Westport 1994) 664 (henceforth *Briggs*).

[24] Oldfather first wrote "third" and then crossed it out replacing it with "2nd."

[25] Wilbert Lester Carr (1875–1974) never took a doctorate although a fellow in Latin at the University of Chicago (1902–05). He was professor of Latin at Teachers College (Columbia) 1930–42. He was president of the American Classical League (1931–37) and began in 1938 his long associate editorship of *Classical Outlook*. He edited or revised numerous schoolbooks. In short he successfully devoted his life to encouraging Latin in the

cheap, poor taste, and pathetically incompetent to represent, or even to understand, the high cultural values with which it is his task to deal. Should certainly be made a member of the University Department of Classics and subjected to the control of colleagues who are also scholars.

Edith Clafflin [*sic*!].[26] Not particularly productive; a weak personality.

M. Hadas.[27] Cheerful and open-minded; apt to be fanciful; unnecessarily ingratiating; has neither the bearing nor the personality of a university professor; but has a good mind, if only he would use it seriously.

G.A. Highet.[28] Brash, wise-cracking, garrulous, full of endless funny stories told in a smart-alec fashion; has never done anything of any

schools. He never existed for scholarship. On 18 June 1937 he wrote a friendly letter to Oldfather briefly in New York before sailing for Europe. See L.S. Thompson, *Briggs*, 88-89.

[26] For Edith Frances Claflin (1875–1953) see *School and Society* 77 No. 1995 (14 March 1953) and Bernard Bloch, "Edith Frances Claflin," *Language* 29 (1953) 219–20. She had taught Greek at girls' schools and was lecturer in Greek and Latin at Barnard College (1936–45) and special lecturer since 1945 at Columbia. E.B. Harrison observes that she taught C.U. Extension, later General Studies. She did not exist for scholarship. See W.W. Briggs, Jr., *Briggs* 96.

[27] For Moses Hadas (1900–1966) see William M. Calder III, *Dictionary of American Biography Supplement Eight 1966–1970* (New York/London 1988) 235–37 and "Moses Hadas 1900–1966," *CO* 69 (1991) 8–9. Oldfather's remark that Hadas was "unnecessarily ingratiating" must be seen in context. Hadas was 38 years old. He had been kept an instructor for 13 years and would not be made a member of the faculty until 1952. After James Loeb, Hadas is the most blatant example of antisemitism in American classics. How other than ingratiating could he possibly behave toward the personification of the American Classical Establishment? For the difficulties incurred by Hadas' Columbia friend and colleague in English, Lionel Trilling, see Susanne Klingenstein, *Jews in the American Academy 1900–1940: The Dynamics of Intellectual Assimilation* (New Haven/London 1991) 137–98, 232–40. The book is often superficial and poorly informed but certainly worth reading. Mrs. Hadas recalls that when Trilling was tenured he telephoned Moses Hadas to express the hope that his tenure would not adversely affect Hadas' future. Householder observes: "Hadas. I would rate him a little higher than O. did; he seemed to me to personify the virtues of a university professor. Of course he is also far and away the most productive of the lot. He and his wife (his first wife; I also knew his second wife, who had been a student in one of my classes) entertained us more than once, and we visited him at his summer place in Vermont. I would rate him as the second brightest of the lot."

[28] For Gilbert Arthur Highet (1906–1978) see William M. Calder III, *Gnomon* 50 (1978) 430–32; R. J. Ball, ed., *The Classical Papers of Gilbert Highet* (New York 1983) 1–11; and Thomas A. Suits, "Gilbert Highet," Briggs-Calder, 183–91. Highet was 32 years old at Columbia on a one-year appointment as Visiting Associate in Greek and Latin. Butler had hired him on the recommendation of C.M. Bowra, who had been offered a post but declined. Within the year he was tenured as a full professor, although six years younger than Hadas. Householder adds: "Here Oldfather was way off. Highet was indeed full of funny stories, which he used to advantage in his lectures. And he did produce some work of consequence... And he had no particular interest in Carr's specialty, teaching future high-school Latin teachers." Ball, *Papers*, 4 writes: "When the Scotsman arrived at Columbia, he joined a faculty including such senior scholars as Frank Gardner Moore, La Rue Van Hook, and Kurt von Fritz." In fact Moore had retired. La Rue Van Hook was on sabbatical and not in New York. Von Fritz was only six years older than Highet and like Highet and Oldfather a guest professor.

consequence, and never will; might perhaps succeed Carr, but is certainly not of professorial caliber.

C.W. Keyes.[29] Shrewd but timid New England Yankee; amiable but defeatist; without requisite qualities of leadership or enthusiasm<,> capable of doing fair work, but has finished very little in 25 years; lacks drive, inspiration, and willingness to accept responsibility; a fair second rate man, but not an exponent of Classical Studies of whom everyone should be proud. He is essentially a canny rustic who has quite surprised himself by appearing to make good in a great metropolitan university, and is afraid of being found out some day.

K. von Fritz.[30] Learned but fanciful, writing too much, and without adequate thoughtfulness; exaggerating the importance of slight considerations and much too confident about his conclusio<ns,> lacking in personal forcefulness and impressiveness; a distinctly second rate German professor, who might much better have stayed at home.

---

[29] Of Clinton Walker Keyes (1888–1943) Householder adds: "He was chairman when I was hired, and was always friendly and helpful. He taught the Proseminar in things like editing, papyrology, epigraphy, etc., and did it well. I learned a lot. When I went to work for Westermann, I took over Keyes' edition and translation of the Columbia papyri. It was completely finished, with six or seven interesting excursus on the arithmetic of the papyri and other topics. When Oldfather wrote, K. already had a Loeb volume in print; not all Loeb volumes are real works of scholarship but I think that Keyes' was and still is." Householder refers to *Cicero de re publica de legibus* (Cambridge/London 1928 and later reprints). Because Keyes is 50 years old and chairman, he is severely judged. See W.W. Briggs, Jr., *Briggs*, 324-25.

[30] For Kurt von Fritz (1900–1985) see *In memoriam Kurt von Fritz 1900–1985: Gedenkrede von Walther Ludwig mit einem von Gerhard Jäger zusammengestellten Schriftenverzeichnis* (Munich 1986) and Ernst Vogt, *Jahrbuch der Bayerischen Akademie der Wissenschaften 1987* (Munich 1988) 247–53. Ludwig (9) attributes without citing evidence the suggestion for von Fritz' Columbia appointment to Margarete Bieber. Householder observes: "I have no idea why Oldfather is so negative about von Fritz; I think he was undoubtedly the best classicist at Columbia, and the best scholar. I admired him very much...Perhaps I should be angry at him because, when I received an offer more than doubling my salary (from Allegheny College) he just wished me luck, but I suspect I am better off now than I would have been staying at Columbia. His article on the discovery of incommensurability struck me (and still strikes me) as a masterpiece." He means "The Discovery of Incommensurability by Hippasus of Metapontum," *Annals of Mathematics* 46 (1945) 242–64. I also find Oldfather's evaluation inexplicable. One would have thought that he would praise a representative of German *Wissenschaft* and a fellow contributor to *RE*. The idea that he should have stayed at Rostock reveals utter ignorance of the circumstances of his departure, all the more inexplicable because Oldfather had spent the previous summer in Nazi Germany: see D.W. Hurley, *TAPA* 120 (1990) 372 n. 65 and "Alfred Gudeman in Berlin, 1935–1942," *Latein und Griechisch in Berlin* 35 (1991) 121–27. Or did Oldfather disapprove of his resignation? Von Fritz was 37 years old and Visiting Associate Professor for the year. His English may have been feeble. Von Fritz certainly was the greatest classical scholar who ever taught at Columbia. Oldfather was simply wrong. Why?

An autobiographical document of great importance by Kurt von Fritz, entitled *Die Gründe, die zu meiner Emigration i. Jahre 1936 geführt haben*, now in the Institut für Zeitgeschichte in

H.T. Westbrook.[31] Has never done anything in the way of scholarship and never will. An affected accent and little mannerisms compromise seriously whatever effectiveness he might otherwise have. He is a mere teacher. No great university can afford to fill up with dainty dilettantes of that kind.

John Day.[32] Well-trained, but falling asleep; just nobody much.

Katherine C. Reiley.[33] Nobody ever heard of her.

James H. Oliver.[34] Technically adroit and learned, but feeble and ineffective personally.

W.B. Dinsmoor, W.L. Westermann, and L.H. Gray. These are the only men of truly university caliber connected with any aspect of Classical Studies. They should perhaps be consulting members of a general university Department of Classics where their joint influence could be made to count, but no one individual be allowed to drown out either the department itself or the other two consultants.[35]

Munich illuminates his departure from Rostock and his early American experience. See Appendix I *infra*.

[31] I have no idea who Westbrook was nor does Householder. He appears in contemporary catalogues as H. Theodoric Westbrook, A.M. with the title Instructor in Greek and Latin.

[32] For John Day (1902–61) see C. Bradford Welles, *AJA* 66 (1962) 411 and Deborah Hobson, *Briggs*, 128-29. Householder delivers the *Todesurteil:* "After I left Columbia, Westermann gave the papyrus job to Day, and a few years later the volume came out, without any mention of Keyes, who had done the whole thing. This is the worst case of scholarly dishonesty I have ever encountered." [R.S. Bagnall informs me that this judgement is too severe.]

[33] I know nothing of her other than that she appears in contemporary Columbia catalogues as Katherine Campbell Reiley, Ph.D. with the title Associate in Greek and Latin in Barnard College.

[34] James H. Oliver (1905–1981), a native New Yorker, was assistant professor of history in Barnard College (1936–46). He was denied tenure and went on to a distinguished career at the Hopkins. His publications were largely in Greek epigraphy. Michael Armstrong notes: "Oldfather here condemns the scholar who can't teach." Householder observes: "I never knew him well, and O.'s estimate seems reasonable." I knew him rather well and agree with Oldfather's estimate. See J.W. Poultney, *Briggs*, 461-63.

[35] Oldfather first wrote but crossed out "and no appointment or advancement of any consequence should be made without their approval." That is the greatest scholars in ancient studies were outside the department. This bizarre state of affairs continued into my time when Elias Bickermann, Morton Smith, the Roman Lawyer Arthur Schiller, O.J. Brendel and E.B. Harrison were all outside of the Department of Greek and Latin. Householder agrees with Oldfather's assessment of Dinsmoor and Westermann and remarks of Gray: "I worked with him on details of his book on linguistics (*Foundations of Language*), which I found full of mistakes of many kinds. He was a nice guy, and I spent many hours at his house going over the book. I would not count him in the same league as Dinsmoor and Westermann, or even von Fritz and Hadas." For Louis Herbert Gray (1875–1955) see *Who was Who in America?* vol III *1945–60* 341-42, *NCAB* 15. 194; *New York Times* 20 August 1955, 17. I owe these references to W.W. Briggs Jr.

In general I should judge that von Fritz, Highet, Westbrook, Hadas, and Day should be invited to seek advancement elsewhere. Older persons like Carr, Hirst,[36] Reiley, and Clafflin [sic] ought to be retired as soon as the legal age is reached. Two or three men of professorial rank should be brought in at once. The best available, who would give the institution a high standing at once, as full professors would, in my judgment be R.P. Robinson,[37] A.D. Fraser,[38] and B.E. Perry.[39] Benjamin Dean Meritt[40] is worthy of the University, but his range of interests is pathetically narrow and it is doubtful if he could properly be called a humanist at all. C.J. Kramer [sic][41] is a man of great energy and personal effectiveness. He is, however, well placed and is perhaps, if anything, a little too drastic and assertive.

Three or four men should be added of the rank of instructor or assistant professor. The choice here is rather wide, and since it is impossible to tell whether men at that age will really make good, they should be appointed for strictly limited periods, with the understanding that they must make distinctly good in a really conspicuous fashion, within five years, in order to be reappointed.

The Department is too stiff and rigid in its course offerings, puts much too heavy a burden of instruction on its older and abler men, as the pedantic notion that every course ought to be given every year makes no allowance for the particular gifts and interests of visiting professors, who are fitted rigidly to an unreasonable system, and it lays far too much emphasis upon mere erudition and examinations. It needs a great draft of fresh air to blow through it, wake it up, cause it to believe in itself again, forget its pedantry, become more elastic, devote itself to sound scholarship and stimulating

---

[36] For Gertrude Mary Hirst (1869–1962) see Gertrude Mary Hirst, *From a Yorkshire Town to Morningside Heights: Early Recollections* (New York 1957) and *New York Times* (15 January 1962) 27. Oldfather curiously ignores the most important woman who ever taught at Barnard. Hirst at *CW* 19 (1925–26) 138–39 in a modest note first established the date of Livy's birth: see Ronald Syme, *Roman Papers* I (Oxford 1979) 414 n. 4 and my life at *CW* 90 (1996/97) 149-52.

[37] Rodney Potter Robinson (1890–1950), the earliest doctoral student of Oldfather, specializing in Latin palaeography and prose authors, long professor at Cincinnati. See W.W. Briggs, Jr., *Briggs*, 533.

[38] I have not been able to identify this fellow.

[39] For Ben Edwin Perry (1892–1968) see William M. Calder III, *Biographical Dictionary of North American Classicists* ed. W.W. Briggs Jr. (494-96) and John Vaio, *American National Biography* (forthcoming). Since 1924 he had been Oldfather's colleague at Illinois. His work on the fable and the ancient novel sets him among America's greatest Hellenists.

[40] For Benjamin Dean Meritt (1899–1989) see Ronald S. Stroud, *American National Biography* (forthcoming). For a party-line necrology see *AJA* 94 (1990) 483–84. Oldfather's characterization hits the mark. He would become arrogant, vengeful and unscrupulous.

[41] He means the papyrologist C.J. Kraemer, (1895–1958), who professed at New York University (1923–1958) and chaired the department (1930–48). See Lionel Casson, *Briggs*, 333-34.

teaching, and pay some attention to what the rest of the country and even the rest of the world is actually thinking and doing. In other words, it is rigid, timid, defeatist, feeble, pedantic, provincial, unproductive, and generally old-maidish. It simply ought to be wholly reconstructed anew. On both occasions when I have been invited to teach here I have been given a schedule 50% higher than that which I taught in my own University, and courses were simply assigned me with little or no regard for my preferences or particular abilities.[42] On the present occasion I was given four different courses, three of them new to me, and asked to assume a Seminar in addition, but this last and wholly preposterous burden I managed eventually to escape, but not until I had been compelled to carry the matter almost to the limit of a point-blank refusal.

The men called here year after year for the summer session are common third raters whose repeated reappointment is nothing less than a source of wonder to outsiders. A more feeble and futile lot of appointments during the past 40 years I have never seen anywhere. The explanation is of no concern, but only the incontestability of the fact.[43]

One or two lesser matters might be considered. The full force of the best men in the Department should be turned to the new required course in the humanities, no matter if that should make it impossible to give every year a course in every subject that has ever been offered here before. Without according linguistics anything like the inordinate emphasis which it claims for itself, at least some moderate degree of attention should be devoted in a large university department to the study of the classical languages as such.[44]

---

[42] The reference is to his correspondence with Clarence Young. In his letter to Young of 11 May 1937 he agrees to teach an undergraduate course on Herodotus, one on Tacitus and Martial (selections), graduate ones on Pl. *Gorgias* and *Republic* (selections), and Terence for graduates. Of the latter he writes: "The six plays will be read, two or three being interpreted in class. Lecture on the literary history of the period in Rome, the sources, the syntax, and the dramatic technique, together with some consideration of the general social criticism of Terence and his originals." The fifth course he refused to teach was Greek composition. The courses had between two and ten students each. He was never asked what he would like to teach. He was told what he would teach.

[43] Householder adds: "Some of the outsiders brought in were of some note. I don't know who the repeated reappointees were that he found 'a source of wonder.' I taught every summer myself, and remember only one "common third rater," an Englishman whose name I forget, who was indeed not very bright. I think Keyes originally hired him out of pity, and later gave him a regular appointment." Possibly a reference to J.F.C. Richards: see my life at *Briggs*, 522-23.

[44] Moses Hadas explains (177): "But far more important [than John Erskine's Honors Course established in 1919] for the concept of general education is the fact that since 1937 virtually the same list of books has been the basis of the so-called Humanities course, which is required of all freshmen in Columbia College and occupies almost a third of their total class program. The course is administered interdepartmentally, and the Department of Greek and Latin has no special responsibility in its direction, but members of the Department do participate in the organization and in the teaching of the Humanities." Householder observes: "Hadas taught this every year, Highet taught it, eventually I taught it. We (all three) also

The Department ought also to be consolidated, reduced in size, the courses alternated, and the salaries of the younger men increased. The newly constituted department should be made up of American scholars. There is absolutely no need of going abroad when we have better men available here. If foreigners are to be imported at all, then they ought not to be second or third raters.[45]

The entire Classical collections of books ought to be brought together in some place where they can be readily reached and used by the faculty and advanced students. Under present arrangements it takes me from two to three times as many hours to do a piece of work here as in my own University, and it is not surprising that relatively little is actually produced by members of the staff, at least by those who are not able to own a large private library.[46]

I regard it as nothing less than a catastrophe that the control of appointments of the Department of Classics should be so distinctly in the hands of one single man, W.L. Westermann,[47] a competent historian,

---

taught the advanced form of this, called the Colloquium." Of Linguistics he writes: "When I was there Gray was the whole department and they had just one Ph.D. candidate. I later taught the basic course several times. Now it is interesting that Columbia has officially discontinued the program, though Bob Austerlitz was president of LSA a year or two ago."

[45] The xenophobia of an educated man of so international an outlook is unexpected. Householder writes: "The paragraph about foreigners seems to be another attack on Highet and von Fritz." But one must see the remark in context. Oldfather was 58 years old. Until the Hitler purges no first-rate European classical scholar left Europe for America. There were occasional visiting lecturers, such as Dörpfeld or Gilbert Murray, or even under the Kaiser Wilhelm-Theodore Roosevelt Exchange professorships a guest professor. Eduard Meyer at Harvard in 1909–10 was the greatest. Before the purges, in ancient studies only the archaeologist, Valentin Müller (1889–1945), emigrated to America. This is a case not yet fully explained. With the opening of the East Berlin archives I hope to be able to clarify it. There was a personal scandal possibly a homosexual one that caused Müller, extraordinarius at Berlin, to resign in 1931 and take an associate professorship at what for a German was the Mädchenpensionat, Bryn Mawr. Highet was still very young. He had been appointed by Nicholas Murray Butler (a Stalin figure at Columbia) after Bowra refused the professorship offered him and had recommended Highet to Butler. Highet as a Scot in Oxford was mutatis mutandis in the position of a Jew at Columbia. Success in New York would be easier. I have discussed von Fritz (see n. 30). We must recall that neither von Fritz nor Highet had yet published their great works.

[46] Oldfather had created at Illinois a Prussian Seminarbibliothek. He arranged the purchase of two great libraries which still form the nucleus of the collection. With the help of Wilamowitz he purchased the library of the Berlin Latinist, Johannes Vahlen (1830–1911), as he had earlier that of the Halle Hellenist, Wilhelm Dittenberger (1840–1906). For details concerning the Vahlen purchase see W.M. Calder III, CJ 72 (1976–77) 115–27. He writes the above obviously with Illinois in mind. With the building of a new library shortly after Oldfather's visit this problem was alleviated.

[47] William Linn Westermann (1873–1954), an Illinois native and Berlin Ph.D. (1902) was professor of history at Columbia (1923–48). He was the friend of Arnold Toynbee: see Arnold J. Toynbee, "Professor W.L. Westermann," Acquaintances (London 1967) 198–207 (an evaluation utterly different from Oldfather's) and William H. McNeill, Arnold J. Toynbee: A Life (New York/Oxford 1989) 155. He was the last American classicist to play a role in the political history of his time: see Marinus A. Wes, "Michael Rostovtzeff, Historian

indeed, but only in an extremely narrow and unimportant aspect of ancient history, he is utterly without understanding of or taste for the aesthetic, literary, philosophical, and linguistic aspects of Greek and Roman culture. He systematically decries and belittles those humanistic values, which alone justify the continued existence of the Classics at all, in comparison with the trivial minutiae of the price of pigs, and the methods of writing fractions, or the barbarous bookkeeping in some wholly obscure and damnable village in decadent Egypt. Such narrow-visioned specialists there must be, & of course, they must be fanatical about the value of their own work, or else nothing could possibly induce them to do it, but to allow a man of such domineering temper and such utter lack of cultural interests to control the entire future of the Classics, whose values are surely cultural if they possess any values at all, is just a kind of tragedy.[48]

There is but one thing, in my judgment, to do, and that is to turn to some classical scholar of judgment and standing, who has no personal ax to grind and absolutely nothing to gain or lose from the consequences of telling the truth—and then trust him implicitly.[49] Such a man may be

---

in Exile: Russian Roots in an American Context," *Historia Einzelschriften Heft* 65 (Stuttgart 1990) 105 *s.n.* and W.M. Calder III, *BMCR* 2 (1991) 161 with n. 1. An annotated edition of his diaries would be welcome. See also Meyer Reinhold, *Briggs*, 684-85.

[48] In defence of Westermann, he was not just interested in the price of pigs. He would publish, thanks to the intervention of Rostovtzeff, the article *Sklaverei* in Pauly-Wissowa, a masterpiece and certainly concerned with a central subject of ancient history. On the other hand Oldfather's view of papyrology, and by implication of the sister discipline, epigraphy, agrees with those of Th. Mommsen and Wilamowitz. Mommsen regularly said "Dumm wie ein Epigraphiker" and Wilamowitz "Dumm wie Hiller," a reference to his epigraphical son-in-law Hiller von Gaertringen. "DM-Wissenschaft" in the letters of Diels, Ed. Schwartz and Wilamowitz is utterly pejorative. It means the mindless preoccupation with *dis manibus* inscriptions. Such work was done in Germany by *wissenschaftliche Mitarbeiter* in the Academies, people of no importance at all in the academic hierarchy, under the leadership certainly of Mommsen for *CIL* and Wilamowitz for *IG*. Wilamowitz writes to Schwartz (30 June 1906) "Die Epigraphik als Specialität ist wirklich verdummend": see William M. Calder III and Robert L. Fowler, "The Preserved Letters of Ulrich von Wilamowitz-Moellendorff to Eduard Schwartz Edited with Introduction and Commentary," *Bayerische Akademie der Wissenschaften philosophisch-historische Klasse Sitzungsberichte* (1986) 63 (No. 21).

[49] The following year (1938–39) Giorgio Pasquali (1885–1952) was announced Visiting Professor of Greek and Latin at Columbia in *Columbia University Bulletin of Information* 38 (June 4 1938) *Announcement of the Division of Ancient and Oriental Languages and Literatures for the Winter and Spring Sessions 1938–1939* (New York 1938) 3. He was to teach Plato's letters ("textual problems and those of authorship are considered") and Greek text criticism and metrics "studied through the medium of the lyric portions of Aeschylus' *Agamemnon*" (19). In Latin he announced Horace, *Odes* (20) and a year-long seminar on Plautus, *Mostellaria*. "The seminar is largely concerned with the attempt to distinguish between the material derived from Plautus' Greek model and the Roman elements in the play. Attention is also paid to prosody and metrics" (21). If we may judge from the silence of his distinguished biographer, the visit never took place: see Luciano Canfora, "Giorgio Pasquali," Briggs-Calder, 367–75. He certainly fits Oldfather's criteria. Professor Canfora informs me *per litt.* (18 April 1992): "Pasquali wurde als 'Visiting Professor for Greek and Latin' am 4. April 1938 von der Seite der Columbia Universität eingeladen. Die Einladung war für das Jahr 1938/39 gültig. Pasquali hat die Einladung in Juli 1938 abgelehnt." The

wrong, of course, but the present set-up is without any peradventure of a doubt, utterly and hopelessly wrong, and is certain to perpetuate for at least another generation the present futile mediocrity of the Department of Classics in Columbia University.

IV. Conclusion

Why is this new document, the Oldfather evaluation, so important? I can think of four reasons.

1. Its author was in 1938 the greatest living American classical scholar. He had survived Gildersleeve and Shorey, his only competitors. There was no one more competent to judge an American department. A German scholar might arguably have been greater but he would not have known the American situation. If his judgment is wrong, it is wrong at the highest level and for revealing reasons. If it is wrong, we want to know: why is it wrong?

2. The Columbia Department was and remains a leading American department. The Columbia case expertly evaluated, therefore, is an invaluable witness to the state of US classics just before the impact of the Hitler refugees.[50]

3. The document exemplifies an extinct genre. I don't think there is any American classicist alive today with either the competence or the courage to write what Oldfather did in the style he did. A bleeding-heart liberal could not do it. Conservatives would fear litigation. They would only say this sort of thing by telephone which leaves no paper-trail.

4. A number of the problems addressed by Oldfather in this document are not limited to the 1938 Columbia Department. They are hotly debated today.[51]

A. The role of *Nebenwissenschaften*. Is it better to write a doctoral dissertation on three boring papyri or on "Justice in Aeschylus"? Is a

---

information derives from the Secretary of Columbia University through Professor P.O. Kristeller.

[50] For them see William M. Calder III, "The Refugee Classical Scholars in the USA: An Evaluation of Their Contribution," *Illinois Classical Studies* 17 (1992) 153–73. Compare in a sister discipline Hartmut Lehmann and James J. Sheehan, eds., *An Interrupted Past: German-Speaking Refugee Historians in the United States after 1933* (Washington/Cambridge 1991).

[51] See Phyllis Culham and Lowell Edmunds, *Classics: A Discipline and Profession in Crisis?* (Lanham/New York/London 1989). The book is often carelessly written with numerous errors of detail. Its value is that it is a symptom of ignorant though well-meant despair: see *contra* Karl Galinsky, "Classics Beyond Crisis," *CW* 84 (1990–91) 441–53.

papyrologist capable of competently judging scholars for whose work he often has only contempt or which he has never proven he can evaluate? Roger S. Bagnall, a papyrologist become Dean of the Graduate Faculties at Columbia, is today's Westermann.

B. Should there be a place in a large classics department for courses on the teaching of Latin? *Der Fall Carr*: he taught at Teachers College but his courses were open to classical graduate students.

C. "He is a mere teacher."[52] This is typically American. It is not German. Wilamowitz writes that he was first a teacher and his 72 books were done on the side.[53] It is the fundamental problem in the profession today. One is paid to teach but promoted on the basis of publications.

D. The problem of women professors did not exist for Oldfather and so he does not address it. Their teaching was confined to women's colleges.[54] One of the most controversial issues in the profession today is the importation of foreign, usually English, sometimes German, rarely French (Princeton!) or Italian, classical scholars. Oldfather was dead set against it. The endowment of the three Gildersleeve and Lane chairs by Gildersleeve's grand-daughter at Harvard, Hopkins, and Virginia is the largest single bequest in the history of US classical philology. It is comparable to what Loeb did for archaeology. Until now (June 1992) these chairs have only been offered to foreigners. This has caused much ill feeling. The last, current, and future president of APA were all born in Europe. The question is should American citizenship and American education rule over purely scholarly expertise? Should we buy Japanese cars because they are better made? American assistant professors to whom I have spoken agree entirely with Oldfather. *Certent philologi!*

I shall end by citing Professor Householder's eminently sane summary:

I feel also that (in his view) the Columbia Classics faculty failed to treat Oldfather with the respect and courtesy which he deserved so much

---

[52] The Oldfather biographer, Michael Armstrong, writes (2 March 1992): "I think the accent is on the adjective, not the noun. I don't know whether Oldfather thought of himself, as Wilamowitz did, as primarily a teacher, but he certainly put immense energy into teaching and his students were devoted. Oldfather clearly believed teaching to be of great importance. Wilamowitz' 72 volumes grew out of his teaching—but would we think him quite so great a man if nothing had grown out of his teaching? I suspect that to Oldfather a 'mere' teacher was one who put in his time in the classroom and then knocked off for the day."

[53] Ulrich von Wilamowitz-Moellendorff, *Erinnerungen 1848–1914 Zweite ergänzte Auflage* (Leipzig 1929) 7.

[54] *Fortunatas illas!* The Canadians had no women's colleges and hence no women professors of classics until the 1950's. See W.M. Calder III, *CW* 90 (1996/97) 83-90.

more than they did. In short, he was annoyed and angry with them all, for no clear reason.

My own view now, in comparing that group of classicists with other groups I have encountered in stays at Vermont, Cornell, Michigan, Colorado, Hawaii and Harvard and visits to Hopkins, Illinois, Dartmouth, Princeton and Michigan State, is that the 1938 Columbia Classics Department was about par for the course, with a few excellent people, a few duds and several in between.

APPENDIX I[55]

Kurt von Fritz
Professor emeritus at the University of Munich
The Reasons which led to my Emigration in 1936

The reason for my emigration was that I was dismissed from my position as extraordinary Professor at the University of Rostock[56] and entrance into any further academic position was made impossible for me, and in the end even the use of the University of Munich library was forbidden.

The immediate cause for my dismissal, but not the official stated reason, was a letter that I sent to the Mecklenburg Minister of Culture at the request of the Minister of Education and the Arts, about taking an oath of absolute obedience to serve the Führer.[57] In this letter I explained that I could only take the requested oath if it was confirmed for me in writing by the highest authorities that on the basis of this oath an order could not be placed on me to teach anything at all that would contradict my beliefs.

The question of the oath had been discussed in the circles of the higher officers at the Rostock garrison as well as in the circles of my colleagues, who were not enthusiastic supporters of National Socialism. The predominant opinion among the high officers was that it would be a great advantage if the oath would be linked personally to the Führer, and not to National Socialism. So then it would say, "We need Hitler now in order to raise arms. He is such a fool, that surely he will be assassinated someday." To me this seemed a most dangerous calculation if these gentlemen did not want to take on the assassination themselves. Incidentally, it was

[55] The German original is available at Cornelia Wegeler, *Die Selbstbeschränkung der Wissenschaft: Ein Beitrag zur Geschichte der Klassischen Philologie seit dem ausgehenden 19. Jahrhundert, untersucht am Beispiel des Instituts für Altertumskunde der Universität Göttingen (1921-1962)* (Diss. Wien 1985) 128-34. I am grateful to her for a copy of her valuable, unpublished dissertation. The first version of the translation was made by Daniel J. Kramer. I am most grateful.

[56] For earlier classics at Rostock see Otto Kern, *Die Entwicklung der klassischen Altertumswissenschaft an der Universität Rostock* (Rostock 1906).

[57] The humanist Werner Jaeger and even the Jew Eduard Norden hastened to sign the oath. Karl Barth is the only cited parallel to von Fritz for refusal on moral grounds. [Add Kurt Weitzmann (1904-93) and see W.M. Calder III *Quaderni di storia* 45 (1997) 231-36.]

characteristic of the morale and manner of the highest officers that the commander of the regiments stationed in Rostock, Colonel von Tippelkirch, allowed the Bavarian Minister of Culture, Schemm, to be arrested by a corporal and led out of the lecture hall, when at the request of the party before the garrison soldiers he gave a lecture and delivered a speech which displeased Colonel von Tippelkirch. The latter sent a report about this event to his superiors in Berlin who completely approved of his conduct.

Among my colleagues at the University of Rostock, it was suitable for someone to swear the oath of obedience without reservations of conscience because the oath was made "by God" and consequently could commit one to nothing that would contradict the laws of God. I did not challenge the correctness of this interpretation; however, I was of the opinion that one must give a loud and public expression to it; otherwise, everyone would believe that the oath by everyone who has standing and influence in the State would be made without restrictions and that, in turn, would bring to the National Socialists an increase in power against which one could no longer prevail.

In addition there was a lack of open opposition. As an example, the following is interesting. The Nazi leader of the student organization, Schinke by name, was baptized and raised as a Catholic. After the Roehm affair,[58] he went to the Catholic priest and explained that he was in a moral dilemma. In reality many more men were murdered in connection with the alleged Putsch than the Führer admitted. Here, therefore, the Führer had lied. The priest answered that he had also heard such a thing, but he could not verify it. At the insistence of Schinke, he finally admitted that the Führer could have lied. At that the student denounced him: he had called the Führer a liar. The priest was arrested and locked up. On the following day, my friend, Professor Julius Ebbinghaus,[59] who had taken the oath to the Führer, demanded that Herr Schinke leave his lecture amid the wild applause of his students. After a weak attempt at protest, he then did.

With me, who had not taken the oath, the Mecklenburg Ministry attempted to negotiate many months by giving me orally all possible reassuring explanations. I, however, insisted on a written and binding explanation from the highest authorities. Finally, Governor Hildebrand of Mecklenburg learned of the situation. He was so beside himself in rage that a professor had held lectures for more than four months without having

[58] The Röhm Putsch (= Night of the Long Knives) refers to the purge of 30 June—2 July 1934 resulting in the murder of Hitler's earlier companion, the SA leader, Röhm (1887–1934).

[59] The Ordinarius for Philosophy was also a political activist and had offered lecture courses at Rostock on controversial subjects as "Die Kriegsschuldsfrage als rechtsphilosophisches Problem" (summer 1931) and "Wehrwille und Friedenspolitik" (1937–38); see Günter Heidorn et al., *Geschichte der Universität Rostock 1419–1969* I *Die Universität von 1419–1945* (Berlin 1969) 210, 288. That he in fact sided with the church against Schinke is revealing.

taken the required oath, that the Ministry was almost brought down by this. He ordered my immediate suspension from my post and the beginnings of disciplinary proceedings "with the goal of dismissal from office." At the same time he announced my refusal in an address to the shipyard workers in Warnemünde; he claimed that I was to blame for the fact that the secondary school teachers in Mecklenburg did not want to hang the swastika flags out of the windows. He closed with these words: "And the students still support him!"

Since the National Socialists still at that time obeyed the law that disciplinary proceedings with the goal of dismissal from office must be publicly held, for the moment I was to undergo private questioning in order to find out what I would say in the public interrogation. In this private questioning they asked me all kinds of trick questions to which I gave for the most part very unpleasant answers. Unfortunately I have forgotten them, with *one* exception. This one was probably the decisive one. To the question of whether I believed the Führer could make mistakes, I answered: to my knowledge not once did the Pope claim infallibility except in questions of dogma, and whoever believed to be able to claim infallibility beyond that would certainly commit the worst mistakes.

After this pre-interrogation, the disciplinary proceedings against me were dropped—obviously because the Governor did not want to risk that such things would be said in public: a most remarkable sign of insecurity. Some three months later I received from the Federal Minister of Culture, Dr. Rust,[60] a memo that I was dismissed on the grounds of paragraph six of the law concerning replacement of civil servants with tenure. This paragraph states that a civil servant could be dismissed if his position were no longer needed. At the same time, however, the Rostock philosophical faculty was ordered to suggest a successor for me. I permitted myself to inform the Minister of Culture that it seemed illogical to me to dismiss a civil servant because his position was no longer needed and simultaneously to ask for a nomination for his successor. His answer reads: "As in all cases of dismissal on the basis of the law concerning replacement of civil servants with tenure, the reason cannot go beyond the very reference to the paragraph in question." But I did receive "temporary wages" for six months.

Since I was now officially innocent as a lamb, my former teachers, Ernst Fabricius[61] and Dragendorf,[62] persuaded the faculty at the University of Freiburg to nominate me in the first place for an available chair in Freiburg. The faculty, however, were of the opinion that I was "politically

---

[60] For Bernhard Rust (1883–1945) see Rolf Eilers, *Die Nationalsozialistiche Schulpolitik: Eine Studie zur Funktion der Erziehung im totalitären Staat* (Köln 1963) 112 ff. Werner Jaeger collaborated with him: see William M. Calder III, "Werner Jaeger," Briggs-Calder, 221. He was the only classicist at so high a level in the Nazi government.

[61] For the ancient historian Ernst Fabricius (1857–1942) see Matthias Gelzer, *Gnomon* 18 (1942) 238–40 and W. Kolbe, *HZ* 167 (1943) 666–67.

[62] The death of H. Dragendorff is noted at *Gnomon* 17 (1941) 96. I know no necrology.

intolerable." So I was forced to look for shelter abroad because I had saved little money and beyond the mentioned six months wages had nothing to live on.

Meanwhile there were however still several incidents, positive and negative, which threw a bright light on the situation at the time.

My passport was still valid for two years and was not to be confiscated in connection with my "transgressions." On the other hand, my wife's passport was about to expire; she applied immediately for a new one. As was customary then, the passport officials made inquiries of the maid concerning us. She was married to one of the shipyard workers to whom the governor had given the forementioned address. But she gave to the police an enthusiastic report about us. The passport official shared this with my wife, but then decided to ask my wife herself whether she was "politically trustworthy." My wife's answer was "no one can really know that nowadays," whereupon the official issued a new pass for her.

The notice concerning my final dismissal came in mid-summer 1935. In order to save some money, we wanted to move immediately to my wife's relatives in Upper Bavaria. But the rental agreement for our apartment in Rostock was such that we could not terminate it until December 31st. We were greatly concerned about that because the rent for an apartment in Rostock would have exhausted nearly two-thirds of my available temporary funds. Since the owner of the apartment building was an enthusiastic SA man and had to know about the reasons for my move, we did not think at all about looking for a favor. But when I informed him that we wanted to move out in a week he voluntarily informed us that he wanted no rent from us beyond the day of our move, in the circumstances of the time, a completely unexpected and overwhelming act of generosity.

I went then to Upper Bavaria and worked daily on research at the University of Munich library, until at the end of 1935 I received from the director of the library a memo—without giving any reason—that in the future entrance to the library was forbidden to me. The director refused to reveal the reason for his measures. But my revered teacher, Prof. Eduard Schwartz,[63] learned after his energetic protest that I was being denounced for having been seen together with a Jewish colleague <reading> in a French newspaper and having laughed at something in it.[64] The ban to enter the library was carried out on the recommendation of the dean of the philosophical faculty. Luckily, two days after my expulsion from the library, I received an invitation to come to Oxford for two terms at Corpus Christi College and hold lectures on the history of ancient mathematics.[65]

---

[63] For Eduard Schwartz (1858–1940) see Calder-Fowler, *supra* n. 48 with literature there cited. For von Fritz' loyalty to Schwartz see Ludwig, *Von Fritz*, 6. Because he was also President of the Bavarian Academy of Sciences, Schwartz had influence.

[64] This is confirmed at Ludwig, *Von Fritz*, 8.

[65] This was due to the initiative of Eduard Fraenkel: Ludwig, *Von Fritz*, 8.

There I also met the above-mentioned Jewish colleague, the historian Hellman.[66] Unfortunately he, although he could have remained at Oxford, returned to Munich later and after several years was gassed at Auschwitz.

During my stay in Oxford I learned that the only friend[67] whom I had in America and who shortly before had become professor at the University of California, had arranged for me the offer of an "instructorship" (with the title 'Professor') at Reed College in Portland (Oregon). In spite of the very small salary of $150.00 per month, I immediately took it. It was not easy to survive on this salary with wife and child.[68] But the college proved itself, as far as colleagues and students go, the nicest institution where I have taught in almost 50 years of teaching.[69]

---

[66] For Sigmund Hellman (1872–1942) see Wolfgang Weber, *Biographisches Lexikon zur Geschichtswissenschaft in Deutschland, Österreich und der Schweiz: Die Lehrstuhlinhaber für Geschichte von den Anfängen des Faches bis 1970 2. durchgesehene und durch ein Vorwort ergänzte Auflage* (Frankfurt/Main 1987) 228–29. Nothing is said of his being gassed at Auschwitz.

[67] Professor John Vaio after inspection in May 1992 of the von Fritz file at Reed College has identified the friend as William R. Dennes, Professor of Philosophy at Berkeley. In a letter of 26 April 1936 to the Reed philosopher Kirby-Miller, Dennes first suggests von Fritz as a one year replacement for Kirby-Miller. The suggestion was realized by D.M. Keezer, president of the college at the time. Hermann Fränkel played no role. I thank Professor Vaio for this information.

[68] His stepson was later drafted and sent to post-war Munich, where he committed suicide.

[69] This said by a scholar who had taught at Rostock, Columbia, FU-Berlin and Munich.

Harvard Classics 1950-1956[1]
Reminiscences of S. Dow, J.P. Elder, J.H. Finley, W.C. Greene, Werner Jaeger, A.D. Nock, Joshua Whatmough and C.H. Whitman

I.

I first saw Harvard when I entered the Yard as a freshman in mid-September 1950 to live in Grays Hall, where almost thirty years before my father had lived in his senior year. I had the good fortune to attend a conservative Episcopalian boys boarding school, where I was *extraneus* and lived at my parents' home. I had five years of intensive Latin and had read Caesar, *Bellum Gallicum*, select orations of Cicero, the first six books of Vergil, *Aeneid*, Plautus, *Mostellaria*, and selected poems of Catullus, Horace and Martial. My Latin master had been a demanding tyrant, who would corporally punish boys. He once beat and physically ejected from the class a friend who had been fool enough to use a trot in preparation. *Aeneid* IV. 496-97 *lectumque iugalem / quo perii* wrought the boy's ruin; for he translated the fateful words "the bed in which I was undone." These were precisely the words of the forbidden trot. I learned never, never to use a translation. We were also punished if we wrote words in the margins. There were surprise checks to detect sinners. We learned nothing about the content of the texts we read but we could identify all the uses of *ut* and recite deponents that governed the ablative. Boys liked syntax and grammar because, like plane geometry, they were straightforward. The rules were there. If one worked and could cite a rule, one knew one would be rewarded. This seemed fair in a way classes in English literature, where questions could not be anticipated, were not.

In composition a Latin sentence would be put on the blackboard by a boy and corrected before all his classmates by the master, markbook in hand. The master would humiliate boys who made stupid mistakes. At the end of each month the marks of all boys were publicly displayed. This made us work harder to avoid general ridicule. Because of William Stanley Tanner I had decided to become a classicist while still a schoolboy. Later I would understand immediately Wilamowitz' gratitude to his Pforte teachers. I was to go to Williams, a small men's liberal arts college; but, because of the

---

[1] For two earlier studies of Classics at Harvard see H.W. Smyth, "The Classics, 1867-1929," *The Development of Harvard University*, edited by S.E. Morison (Cambridge 1930) 33-63 and A.S. Pease, "The Classics at Harvard in the Nineties," *Harvard Library Bulletin* 11 (1957) 258-67.

intervention of Mr. Tanner, I went to Harvard. The change was late in the year. A classicist, Richard M. Gummere (Loeb Seneca), was Dean of Admissions and Mr. Tanner went straight to him. He accepted me in a letter of 16 June 1950. Years later I reviewed a book by him at *Gnomon* 38 (1966) 637-38.

II.

In my first semester I took Latin II, Catullus and Horace, taught by J.P. Elder. Whatever one may say of the man's later life or of his few publications, he was a brilliant teacher of undergraduate Latin in the English tutorial tradition. The class must have been about 30 composed almost entirely of boys from the élite East coast prep schools with as much Latin behind them as I had. He learned our names quickly (attendance was taken at each class) and always addressed me as "Mr. Calder." This made us think erroneously that we were men and no longer schoolboys and we worked harder. At each class we were called upon to translate. I can recall forty years later four reasons why this class was exceptional.

1. Elder pretended not to know all the answers. He could ask "How would you translate this phrase?" with the implication that he was not certain himself.

2. He made Catullus and to a lesser extent Horace human. A poem was more than a collection of grammatical and metrical peculiarities. He gave the impression that it would have been pleasant to know Catullus personally.

3. He refused to reveal the meaning of *glubit* at Catullus 58. 5. He made the matter even more mysterious by remarking "The Romans were not circumcised," a fact which would not have occurred to any of us. On the other hand he assigned obscene poems and took evident delight in the Iuventius cycle. Modern students cannot imagine the difficulties of finding out what *irrumabo et pedicabo* meant in a pre-Krenkel era.

4. He declared to our amazement that an ancient could write a bad poem. He called Horace on the ship of state trite and dull and said clearly "I don't like this poem." For one trained to criticize an ancient, if he criticized him at all, on his knees, this was a revelation.

I took two courses from him later, Lucretius in my junior year and in my senior year the history of Republican Literature. Lucretius was an extraordinary success. I gained a lifelong love for the poet from that course. It was still an undergraduate course. In autumn 1953 I took his history of

Latin Literature in the Republic. This was required for the M.A. and urged for the B.A. I took careful notes and would read articles in the Oxford Classical Dictionary to prepare for his two examinations. I then discovered that he had cribbed the lectures for the prose authors (Cicero, Sallust) and "Letters, Latin" from the *OCD*. I was appalled and brought the material to the attention of Sterling Dow. In 1953/54 he offered a graduate seminar in Lucretius. Steele Commager, a favorite of Elder's, took the course and in his report said "This verse is so, so, so,..." and sighed sensually. Elder looked at the beautiful boy from across the table and replied "I know just what you mean, Steele." The incident became famous and was often retold. If Elder had confined himself to undergraduate teaching, he would have been universally admired.

The other great teacher of my first semester was the Eliot Professor of Greek. John Houston Finley, Jr. He taught a lecture course called Humanities II, a history of the epic in English translation. We read the *Iliad*, *Odyssey*, *Aeneid*, *Divine Comedy*, and Milton's *Paradise Lost*. The course was the largest in the college, taught in the auditorium maximum, Sander's Theater. He was a theatrical lecturer who never used notes. He conveyed to the young that Greek literature was not peripheral but central and able permanently to enrich our lives. We read the *Iliad* in the translation of Lang, Leaf and Myers, an English text which American students today no longer understand. Finley presented the *Iliad* as the "proto-tragedy." Achilles was its hero and his dilemma was to reconcile the world as ideal, symbolized by silver-footed Thetis, with the world as reality, symbolized by dark Agamemnon. The clash comes in Book I with Achilles' public humiliation. Achilles retires to his tent and seeks lonely solace in recalling the glorious deeds of men through music "because he could not read." Only the death of the one whom he most loved drew him back into the struggle. He reacts with violence ending in the slaying of Hector and mutilation of his corpse. The resolution of the conflict comes in XXIV where Achilles releases the corpse to the aged Priam. Finley stressed the passage where Priam kisses the hands that slew his sons and explained that by learning that all mankind shared in sorrow he saw that he was not an exception. He had to suffer to attain this insight. The impact on young men taught from the cradle that they had the right to be happy was unforgettable and in a phrase changed our lives. Odysseus on the other hand was the protocomic hero who accepted an imperfect world as it was and like a ruthless American businessman unscrupulously pursued success. The impact that this shattering of unexamined assumptions had on 18 year old boys in 1950 can scarcely be imagined today. We learned also the importance of poetry as a teacher of what mattered. Thornton Wilder taught the second half of the course and was an anticlimax.

III.

In my third semester I first took courses from two men who would influence me for the rest of my scholarly life. I took History of Religions 101a from the Frothingham Professor of the History of Religion, Arthur Darby Nock. he was an eccentric Englishman, too eccentric even for the English, a brilliant, highly amusing lecturer, a man of stupendous erudition and great wisdom lightly imparted. He began the course by dismissing the Rev. Mr. Thwackum's definition of religion in Fielding's *Tom Jones* and presented us with his own. Until this day I require all my students in the history of religion to memorize it. He said:

> Religion is that active attitude of man towards those factors, real or imaginary, in his environment or makeup, which he of himself cannot fully comprehend or control and what he does, says and thinks in virtue of that active attitude.

Only later I learned how very Cambridge it was and how much he owed William Robertson Smith. Doing was ritual. Saying was liturgy. Thinking was theology which came late and was least important. His brief definition was "Religion is man's refusal to accept helplessness." One of his gifts was to detect great significance in a humble source. He would cite an anonymous gladiator's epitaph as evidence for the spiritual aridity of the epoch in which Christianity triumphed: *non fui fui non sum non desidero.* He translated it: "I was not; I was; I am not; and I don't give a tinker's damn." He often cited the Eskimo who answered a foolish anthropologist's question "Do you believe in God?" with "We do not believe; we fear." He admired enormously M.P. Nilsson, who dedicated a book to him, not the least because he was born into a peasant family that had cultivated the same plot of land for generations. Nilsson could understand an agricultural religion in a way Nock thought he never could. He had no interest in theory nor philosophy but often said he 'preferred the magical papyri." This did not mean that he was a dull pedant. He was an historian and required texts for everything he said. He regularly used archaeological evidence but warned us against archaeologists who held *omne ignotum pro sacro.*

He would not tolerate women in his graduate courses. I watched him drive one out by repeatedly asking her questions she could not answer. She finally fled the class in tears. Most women students knew he did not want them and never signed up. It is revealing to me now that at the appearance of E.R. Dodds, *The Greeks and the Irrational* (1951), Nock called the book in his seminar "almost consistently brilliant," adding "absolutely right— brilliant in dreams and supernatural contact, useful in Orphism, exaggerated in regard to Shamanism." Contrarily Jaeger deplored the book in conversation because Dodds emphasized what was trivial and irrelevant. We study the Greeks to learn about the rational. Nock was obsessed with conversion, Jaeger with the hellenization of the *kerugma* from *Acts* XVII to Clemens Alexandrinus. How fortunate that I could profit from both scholars.

The teacher whose influence for better or worse would form my approach to antiquity for the next fifteen years was the Hudson Professor of Archaeology, the student and successor of William Scott Ferguson, Sterling Dow.[2] I took his famous History 106, the history of Greece from the beginnings to the Roman Conquest in two semesters. His publications were largely in Greek Epigraphy, not everyone's cup of tea. But he exerted an enormous influence both on undergraduates and graduates. He was the only American comparable with the immigrants, Jaeger, Nock and the linguist Joshua Whatmough. It did not pass unnoticed that Nock respected him but when asked his opinion on Whitman's *Sophocles* replied "I have no time to read it." Later Ronald Syme became a good friend of Dow. Dow put teaching first and he was a master teacher. He taught annually the second semester of beginning Greek, Xenophon, *Anabasis*, a couse I never took. He made a holiday of March 4th, which to his own great amusement he called "ἐξελαύνω-day".

He made History 106 famous. He preferred stones and facts to ideas. Most undergraduates did too. His presentation of Bronze Age Greece was a revelation. He stressed that with Schliemann and Evans a whole new epoch in Greek history had been discovered. He contrasted Grote who began his *History* with the first Olympiad. Ventris would publish the next year his decipherment of Linear B. The evidence was largely archaeological and his lectures were illustrated with slides. He would often say "this slide has never been shown to students before." There was an atmosphere of sharing in something new and important. In his first lecture he stressed the nearness of ancient Greece and said we must not think of it as 2500 years ago but as 70 generations ago, a number we could manage. Like Wilamowitz, whom he admired, he stressed the sameness of the Greeks, "ein Mensch wie Du und ich." Alone of the professors he distributed handouts to his students on the chronology of the Bronze Age for example. The papers he required were brilliantly chosen and based on the sources which we read to supplement Bury-Meiggs. They had titles like "Why did the Persians fail?" or "Why did the Athenians condemn Socrates?" An undergraduate could not find the answers in print but must argue from Herodotus or Plato. For 35 years I have modeled my teaching on his.

In contrast to Elder and Finley, his graduate teaching was exemplary. He was one of a handful of American scholars (one can compare Gildersleeve, Oldfather, Shorey and the Russian immigrant Rostovzeff), who created a school. In seminars he took notes on students' reports and he would ask for precise references. I cannot overemphasize the affect of this. He treated us like fellow scholars, not children, and this made us work all

---

[2] See my necrology at *Gnomon* 68 (1996) 572-74.

the harder. No other professor grasped this elemental truth. Like Ritschl, he provided dissertation topics of a sort that students liked; that is with a beginning and an end. He demanded that a narrow topic be treated in depth and held that once one learns method and develops a scholarly conscience, he could go on later to treat large matters. He warned that it never worked the other way around. I have yet to find evidence that proves him wrong.

He chaired a weekly "Dow Lunch" held at the Oxford Grill for the faithful. Visiting scholars would occasionally be invited. Only scholarly matters were discussed. Women were not invited. They would trivialize the meetings. Soon brief papers were read and discussed. We learned the excitement of research and how much new there was to be found in an old field, something we never learned from the other American professors. He had heroes, who became our heroes. They were William Bell Dinsmoor, Homer Thompson and the man he called the only American art historian, Rhys Carpenter of Bryn Mawr. He also had enemies. Benjamin Meritt was the vilest. We never noticed that no Harvard colleague ever attended the lunches. As an undergraduate I had once asked him "Did you by any chance attend Professor Finley's lecture last night?" He replied typically "If I had, it would have been by chance." Finley, on the other hand, asked me at an Eliot House lunch in front of other students: "Are you interested in the big questions, the whither and the whence? Or do you prefer to know how many ships were in the Boeotian Expedition of 457?" He called Dow Cato the Elder. But Finley had only one doctoral student, his successor, C.H. Whitman.[3] All the good graduate students wrote under Dow.

Not only did he provide subjects; often they required a year in Greece at the American School. A student of Dow was guaranteed a school fellowship. He gave endlessly of his time. A student would be guided chapter by chapter with deadlines for submission of them through his dissertation. First drafts were copiously annotated. There was a barrage of letters and notes with copious bibliographical references. Dow was famous for salvaging students everyone else had given up on by finding a topic that met their abilities. 30 students wrote doctoral dissertations under him. Even a literary man, like Charles R. Beye, wrote under Dow, a dissertation on catalogues in Homer.

There was another reason why men chose Dow. His Harvard colleagues were too vain and lazy to attend the annual professional meetings of the Archaeological Institute of America and the American Philological Association. Dow did regularly. He was past president of AIA and president of the Classical Association of New England. He founded an association of teachers of classics in New England. Members were largely schoolteachers.

---

[3] D.E. Gerber, *Lustrum* 31 (1989) 162 has recently written the epitaph of Finley the Scholar, where he remarks of *Pindar and Aeschylus* (Harvard 1955): "Little attention is paid to this book now, and rightly so, for it is far too subjective to be convincing. Sweeping statements are made without sufficient argumentation and in addition Finley's language is often opaque."

At meetings he always introduced his students to senior scholars. Jobs were allotted by the Old Boy System. Dow knew everyone. Jobs were not advertised but chairmen would phone or write Dow. Dow strongly believed that it was the duty of the dissertation director to place his students and this he always did. Jaeger and Nock were international in their interests, devoted first to scholarship. Women and Jesuits, both of whom did not need jobs, wrote under Jaeger. Only they could afford the luxury.

Two examples will suffice to show the enormous good that Dow did because he had time for people who could do nothing for him in return. A letter arrived at the Harvard Classics Department addressed to "Professor of Classics." It was from a school teacher in Oklahoma. No Harvard Professor would waste time on her. Dow did. She had told her Caesar class that no one knew how to compute with Roman numerals. A boy returned the next day and showed the class how it was done. Dow replied. The teacher sent the boy's paper. Dow arranged that he be admitted to Harvard College and a freshman's paper published in *Classical Philology*: see W. French Anderson, "Arithmetical Computations in Roman Numerals," *CP* 51 (1956) 145-50. A year later, while attending a lecture by Dow, Anderson saw for the first time how one calculated in Linear A and B: see his "Arithmetical Procedure in Minoan Linear A and in Minoan-Greek Linear B," *AJA* 62 (1958) 363-68. Launched by his Harvard education, the Oklahoma schoolboy has become one of the leading genetic scientists in the United States Government. By his own admission he owes his career to Sterling Dow.

A highschool Latin teacher visited Widener 690 one day to ask Dow if there was something she could do for scholarship. She had spare time, knew Latin, Greek, some German and French and was not afraid to work hard. Dow had a project for her. She worked some fifteen years. The result was *Articles on Antiquity in Festschriften: An Index*, compiled by Dorothy Rounds (Cambridge 1962). Typically Dow refused to allow the book to be dedicated to him; rather to the president of the Guggenheim Foundation, whom the indexer had never met.

Because of his encouragement I completed at age 21 my *Index Locorum zu Kühner-Gerth* (Darmstadt 1965) and dedicated it to *Sterling Dow Praeceptori et Impulsori*. A fellow student completed an *index locorum* to Fraenkel's *Agamemnon*, unfortunately never published. No indexer received any financial aid. All was extra unpaid work inspired by one man. No Harvard colleague of Dow did anything remotely similar. We learned that while the discovery of new truth is the noblest aim of scholarship, the duty to make earlier work available must never be ignored.

A result of all this was that while Dow's students adored him, his American colleagues in the Department hated him. This leads to a general remark on Harvard classics of the period. To understand what happened one must know that *bellum civile* raged in the Department. The Dow group was devoted to detailed philological-historical research on relatively narrow topics regularly concerned with prose texts. There was a good deal of American School positivistic archaeology thrown in, often of the three- or four-bar sigma sort. The adversary was led by Finley. They were called "literary critics," a term of vilest reproach. They and their students were considered ill-trained, irresponsible and wildly subjective, devoted to "big thoughts" without having mastered details or method. It is revealing that even among undergraduates lines were drawn. The Harvard Class of 1954 included nine men who became professional classicists. With the institution of present affiliation and in alphabetical order they were:

1. William M. Calder III (Illinois)
2. Andrew Thomas Cole (Yale)
3. Henry Steele Commager Jr. (deceased 2 April 1984; earlier Columbia)
4. James A. Coulter (Columbia)
5. Robert J. Goar (Massachusetts)
6. David E. Pingree (Brown)
7. Michael C.J. Putnam (Brown)
8. Kenneth J. Reckford (North Carolina)
9. Calvert W. Watkins (Harvard Linguistics)

Only Coulter and I took courses from Dow and Jaeger and only I from Nock. The effects lasted a lifetime. The work of Commager, Putnam and Reckford has been ahistorical aperçus. They never learned even to cite *CIL* or *IG* and certainly never read *RE*. I had nothing to say to them nor they to me, and early associated with doctoral students, men older and more advanced than I: C.R. Beye, A.L. Boegehold, M.H. Chambers, Wesley Smith and the brilliant but ill-fated James Day, an Oklahoma apostle of Ezra Pound. On the other hand, the Dowians underrated literary criticism and boasted that they saw the trees and not the forest. C.R. Beye later lamented that he had been sent by his Iowa teachers, Else and Rosenmeyer, both Harvard men, to Harvard and not to Yale where one could learn both history and literary criticism. Rostovzeff's legacy was the *Totalitätsideal*. Harvard Classics refused to make William Scott Ferguson a member of the department.

IV.

There were other lesser figures. My senior tutor was William Chase Greene, known to scholarship as editor of *Scholia Platonica* (1938). We read together in private tutorial Ovid, *Fasti* with the commentary of Frazer. Greene was a Victorian gentleman who invited students to tea on Sunday afternoons. He retired when I was a senior. I attended his last lecture before his retirement. Afterwards he invited his students to his house to buy his books which he would no longer need. He sat at a table in the middle of his library with a dish of coins before him. We were allowed to have any book on the shelves for twenty-five cents. I felt enormously embarrassed giving money to a professor but among other things bought his Jebb, *Sophocles*.

He retired to the country with Mrs. Greene and devoted the rest of his long life to gardening. He became for me the type of the English dilettante. He had been an early Rhodes scholar and had seen Robinson Ellis. I took his course on Vergil, *Eclogues* and *Georgics*, which he much preferred to the *Aeneid*. We also read the early poems and he alleged that the source for the motto of the United States, *e pluribus unum*, was *Moretum* 102.[4]

Cedric Whitman, Finley's student, was the darling of the literati. He had read T.S. Eliot and was musical. He published his dissertation which he wisely dedicated to Finley: *Sophocles: A Study in Heroic Humanism* (Harvard 1951). The book was awarded the APA Award of Merit by a committee of three, two of whom were his Harvard colleagues, W.C. Greene and A.S. Pease. I took Homer, *Iliad* with him and then fragments of the Greek Lyric and Elegiac Poets. He mumbled and was unable to lecture. He was ill prepared and already the alcoholism that would drive him to an early grave was exacting its toll. He came up for tenure in 1954 and Finley supported him to the hilt. Dow delivered an impassioned speech against his promotion based on *Sophocles* 263-64 n. 31, where Whitman argued that S. *Antigone* 904-20 was an actor's interpolation. It was not what he thought a heroine should say. Finley bullied Jaeger, who normally avoided departmental politics, into speaking at the end for Whitman. When I later asked Jaeger privately how he could have supported such incompetence he replied: "They are all the same." That is, he had only contempt for his American colleagues. He underestimated Dow because he was interested only in *Geistesgeschichte* and not in history and presumably shared Wilamowitz' denigration of epigraphy. Whitman's tenure caused Dow's famous formulation: "Alpha-men choose alpha-men; beta-men choose gamma-men." I thought it peevish at 21 but age has convinced me of its boundless wisdom.

I have written of Werner Jaeger elsewhere[5] and shall not repeat myself. What is surprising today is that he bored many good students. He had learned English very well: but he had never learned to encourage discussion. His classes were always monologues. I was grateful for I'd rather hear Werner Jaeger on Aeschylus than some silly fellow student who knew no more than I. With considerable naiveté I befriended Professor Jaeger and would occasionally invite him to lunch and regularly drive him home after his seminars. No other student had dared this and he looked with some astonishment on me and a friend of mine, who later became an Anglican priest, as his "school." After the last seminar of the year I was invited to dinner at his home. He was completely apolitical without interest in contemporary affairs. In a seminar he once called World War II "a minor event that delayed the progress of the *Thesaurus Linguae Latinae*."

---

[4] I omit mention of two Harvard teachers who live still. I learned nothing from either.

[5] See especially *Classical Scholarship: A Biographical Encyclopedia*, edited by Ward W. Briggs and William M. Calder III (New York/London 1990) 211-26.

I certainly owe my interest in Wilamowitz to Werner Jaeger. He spoke as often of Wilamowitz as he said nothing of Diels. Although I could not read German, he told me to buy any book of Wilamowitz I saw and that in time I should be grateful to own it. He was right. Nock, a bachelor with a large library, gave me other good advice. "First buy texts, then lexica and indices, then commentaries and only then, if you can, secondary literature." Dow's advice was "Read the big books." Prefer, he meant, Kühner-Gerth to Smyth, which was simply derivative and without independent value, *RE* to *OCD*. My father gave me $45.00 a month for books. That meant fifteen Loebs which today would cost some $300.00. For Christmas I asked a puzzled aunt to give me Latte's Hesychius or my parents to give me the Graz reprint of Stephanus-Dindorf. Dow calculated the costs of life memberships in learned societies and urged his students to take them out: see Sterling Dow, "Life Memberships," *ACLS Newletter* 6 (1955/56) 3-17. The effect was instantaneous. In fifth semester my mother made me a life member of the Society for the Promotion of Hellenic Studies and, seventh semester, of the Roman Society at $69.00 each. They are among the most lucrative investments I ever made. I belong to a vanishing species. One must now be 65 in order to take out such life memberships. Soon came the Egypt Exploration Society with every year a free *POxy*. I owe my library to the kindly advice of my teachers. None of the literary professors ever urged acquisition of books and none of their students ever acquired a library worth looking at.

The comparative Indo-Europeanist, Joshua Whatmough, was an hilariously amusing Englishman. He detested classicists and was delighted that an architect and not a classicist deciphered Linear B, "the greatest discovery since Bentley discovered the digamma!" He often said that the only reason to read Thucydides was to find grammatical peculiarities. He insisted that Dawn in Homer was rosy-toed, not rosy-fingered. *Daktylos* could be either. He was fighting battles with colleagues who had died when we were children. He would cite an unfortunate sentence of E.K. Rand on Ovid, *Amores* 1. 6: "the tone of this poem is parody...permeating the substance like a perfume, invisible but appreciable by those who have the sense of smell"; and add: "What Rand said is, 'Ovid, *Amores* 1.6 smells,' and this I do not understand." He included the remark in his first Sather. He was better in syntax than in phonology and morphology and best when teaching Greek dialects in Solmsen's edition because he had a text. He knew Greek well, a student of Conway and Giles; but he called his teachers "criminals" because they had made him a classicist when he ought to have become a nuclear physicist. He often cited Byron's 'in manners rude, in foolish forms precise,' which the unkind applied to him. The best monument of the man is his Sathers: *Poetic Scientific and other Forms of Discourse: A New Approach to Greek and Latin Literature* (Berkeley/Los Angeles 1956). I have never found anyone who could understand the graph of *pius* in Vergil (98-99). Precisely such lunacy made him so engaging.

V.

In May 1954 I was told by the Chairman of the Harvard Classics Department, E.A. Havelock, an opportunistic English leftist for whom I had ill-concealed contempt, that I would fail my Greek translation examination for the B.A degree. Dow, whom I immediately informed, was able at the last moment to change my major from Classics to Latin because the corrector of the Latin examination, Philip Levine, was unaligned. Two years later Levine was denied tenure, became a Dean in Los Angeles, and abandoned scholarship. Until C.P. Segal in 1991 no American Jew received tenure in the Harvard Department. In May 1955 Havelock failed me in the Greek examination for the M.A. He gave me 78% when a minimum of 80% was required to pass. He did this again in May 1956. Dow had influence enough so that I could receive an M.A. in Classics, although I had failed the obligatory Greek translation examination. I withdrew and in September 1956 went on to Chicago where I took my doctorate. My literary classmates continued at Harvard and taught there for several years. But Dow had his revenge. Commager, Putnam and Reckford were all denied tenure at Harvard. No classicist from the class of 1954 ever received a tenured post at Harvard. Only the linguist Watkins did. He was unaligned and a linguist.

What was wrong was not that colleagues violently disagreed on method and teaching. Indeed, disagreement is often invigorating. They were wrong to have wreaked vengeance on the others' students, both graduates and undergraduates. The students were naive and helpless. I was not dependent financially on scholarships, and was never given one, but others were. They were often punished by being denied financial aid or being failed, as I was, in required examinations. The literary professors would always lose because they could not place their students, who in the end turned to Dow. They had not the contacts and no one outside of Harvard respected their opinions. Dow, as Wilamowitz said of Hermann, was *nicht immer Sieger, aber immer unbesiegt*. He lived to see Finley convince Nathan Pusey, a fellow-Ferguson-student and the president of Harvard, to force him into retirement at 65, while Finley and the negligible Hammond, both Dow's classmates, continued until the age of 70. He saw the Department lost to *Wortphilologie* at a time when *Wortphilologie* had become a lethal anachronism. Of great men today, that is those who see the forest and the trees, there is only one in classics at Harvard, again an immigrant, Albert Henrichs, whose appointment Finley vigorously opposed, saying to me and presumably to many others "Why import the Dutch Elm Disease?" and in History a second immigrant, Ernst Badian. When I was a student there were four.[6]

---

[6] See further my "Arthur Darby Nock 1902-1963," *Classical Outlook* 70 (1992/93) 4-5 and "The Refugee Classical Scholars in the USA: An Evaluation of their Contributions," *ICS* 17 (1992) 153-73.

"Pionier der ersten Stunde:"
Wolfgang Schindler and the Modern Study of Heinrich Schliemann

I. Introduction

Wolfgang Schindler was born on the 107th birthday of Heinrich Schliemann. This was not without effect. No archaeologist made a more lasting contribution toward the modern understanding of that most controversial man than did he. I should like first to discuss the background of his achievement in order to stress its uniqueness. Then I shall enumerate his ten contributions and end with an attempt to explain what he did.

Archaeologists evince precious little interest in their history. I suggest four reasons for this. I make no moral judgment. I merely record the conclusions that 25 years of research in the subject have suggested to me. To understand them causes us to admire all the more Wolfgang Schindler's accomplishment. First: *Wissenschaftsgeschichte* is fundamentally a philological discipline. New discoveries emerge from a critical reading of published works, with the intent of isolating not Housman's what is "new and true" but rather what A.D. Nock called "the coefficient of mendacity," that is what is unconvincing or distorted because determined not by evidence but by personal bias. This bias can be isolated through comparison with autobiographical publications if available, by the memoirs of others or interviews with them, but most especially by archival material, in particular letters to, from or about the figure studied or personal diaries. Many American Bronze Age archaeologists can scarcely read published German. They certainly cannot read unpublished nineteenth century letters written in a Gothic hand and sometimes requiring restoration. In short to write the history of archaeology requires expertise other than that associated with successful excavators.

Next to write the history of a discipline requires certainly competence in that discipline but even more *Distanz.* Theodor Wiegand upon the publication of Emil Ludwig's life of Schliemann in 1931, the most honest life ever written of the man, based throughout on material provided by the widow, wrote to Wilhelm Dörpfeld from Pergamon on 17 May 1932:[1] "Ich habe das Schliemann-Buch von Ludwig gelesen und finde es abscheulich. War es nötig, so viele kleine, unschöne Züge im Leben des Mannes hervorzuholen? Und auf der anderen Seite soll er doch ein Heros sein...Ganz und

---

[1] Cited in an effort to discredit Ludwig at Ernst Meyer, *Heinrich Schliemann Kaufmann und Forscher* (Göttingen 1969) 426 n. 98.

gar verstehe ich nicht Frau Schliemann. Sie hat dem Andenken ihres Mannes gar keinen Dienst geleistet, im Gegenteil." The scholar Wiegand preferred myth to truth.[2] The preference persists. In the standard brief modern German life of Schliemann, written by an archaeologist, who knows Schliemann well, there is no evidence that the biographer has read any of the critical work on Schliemann of the last twenty years.[3] This reluctance to see a great predecessor whole is not limited to archaeologists. I need only compare the horrified reaction of anthropologists to the publication of the diaries of Bronislaw Malinowski. In fact they revealed for the first time a brilliant and complex man and thus deepened our appreciation of his scientific writings.[4] Surely there is a difference between a funeral *laudatio* for widow and children and history.

     Thirdly, all too often the history of archaeology exposes to the glare of day skeletons long since safely interred in closets. The nature of a discipline devoted to the dating and description of great works of art, the prestige deriving from possession of a beautiful ancient vase or statue, the existence of competing museums with enormous financial resources (in recent years the Getty!), the role of nationalism in the acquisition and exhibition of antiquities,[5] all these stain scholarship with a profit motive lacking in philology except with the smuggling of papyri.[6] This is not new. I note only how Greek nationalists and non-Greeks who work in Greece endlessly revive their libels against Lord Elgin. In fact Elgin acted legally in accordance with the Turkish government of his day and his marbles ought to remain where they are.[7] It continues. One need recall only the

---

[2] There is no need to repeat what I have written elsewhere. For the reaction to Ludwig's life see William M. Calder III, "Apocolocyntosis: The Biographers and the Archaeologists," *Heinrich Schliemann nach hundert Jahren*, edited by William M. Calder III and Justus Cobet (Frankfurt/Main 1990) 362-69.

[3] See Hartmut Döhl, "Heinrich Schliemann 1822-1890," *Archäologenbildnisse: Porträts und Kurzbiographien von Klassischen Archäologen deutscher Sprache*, edited by Reinhard Lullies and Wolfgang Schiering (Mainz 1988) 45-46, where no doubt at all is expressed concerning the thoroughly discredited "Treasure of Priam."

[4] For the controversy see Raymond Firth in Bronislaw Malinowski, *A Diary in the Strict Sense of the Term*[2] (Stanford 1989) xxi-xxxi. Similar is the reluctance of economists to allow an honest life of Maynard Keynes: see Robert Skidelsky, *John Maynard Keynes: I Hopes Betrayed 1883-1920* (New York 1994) xv-xxviii. In short the problem is not restricted to archaeologists.

[5] Revealing for this world is Wilhelm von Bode, *Mein Leben* 2 vols. (Berlin 1930). Invaluable for the Rome of collectors, forgers, dishonest workmen and dealers in the second half of the nineteenth century is Count Michael Tyskiewicz, *Memories of an Old Collector*, translated by Mrs. Andrew Lang (London/New York 1898).

[6] Here too is a fundamental difference. A papyrus loses value when once published with photographs. A vase increases in value the more it is published and its authenticity vouched for by experts. In short a vase is a better investment than a papyrus.

[7] The sane and definitive treatment remains William St. Clair, *Lord Elgin and the Marbles* (London 1967); for a lawyer's view see Jeanette Greenfield, *The Return of Cultural Treasures* (Cambridge 1989) 47-105. The passage of time and legality at the time of removal provide the basis of the British claim.

Euphronius Krater acquired by the Metropolitan Museum in New York.[8] A definitive version of that tale must await the deaths of several participants.

Our archaeological forefathers held assumptions not fashionable today which historians of archaeology cannot ignore but which practicing archaeologists prefer to forget. English colonialism fostered contempt for Greeks and Turks. One of the founders of modern surface archaeology and a decisive Director of the British School at Athens, David G. Hogarth (1862-1927) argued in his memoirs that Turks were less intelligent than dogs.[9] Sir Charles Newton writes:[10] "Our party was accompanied by a Maltese gentleman, Dr. Onofrio, who found a tomb when required, with as much sagacity as a pointer finds a partridge." Many English surface archaeologists, not least Hogarth,[11] engaged in intelligence work and received funding toward their scholarly projects that way. This was already the case with Colonel W.M. Leake (1777-1860) and was carried on by Lawrence and Sir Leonard Woolly among others.[12] The American School did its part for the CIA.[13] In my opinion this makes the lives of archaeologists all the more interesting but I am not an archaeologist. I am an historian of archaeology. Archaeologists do not like to talk about their intelligence work and often resent people who do.

Nationalism plays a role still in archaeology and my experience has been that European archaeologists are often unable to deal objectively with unwelcome revelations concerning their fellow nationals. A prime example is Wolfgang Helbig (1839-1915). An American and an Italian scholar have argued that he has forged the *fibula praenestina*.[14] German scholars either refuse even to mention this unpleasantness[15] or they seek to defend a patron saint from slander.[16] Scepticism regarding the *fibula praenestina* revives doubts about the Boston Throne and all portraits in Copenhagen attested

---

[8] See recently the controversial account by Thomas Hoving, "The 'Hot Pot,'" *Making the Mummies Dance: Inside the Metropolitan Museum of Art* (New York 1993) 307-40.

[9] David G. Hogarth, *The Wandering Scholar* (Oxford 1925) 44: "In energy and intelligence he [the Turk] takes rank a grade below his dog."

[10] C.T. Newton, *Travels & Discoveries in the Levant* Vol. I (London 1865) 8.

[11] Richard Symonds, *Oxford and Empire: the Last Lost Cause?* (Oxford 1991) 141.

[12] See H.V.F. Winstone, "Secret Service," *Woolley of Ur: The Life of Sir Leonard Woolley,* (London 1990) 80. He was joined by J.L. Myres, Ronald Storrs and others.

[13] See Robin W. Winks, *Cloak and Gown: Scholars in the Secret War 1939-1961* (New York 1987) esp. 135, 505-06. Philologists as is well known played an important part in the decipherment of codes both in the US and Britain. The decipherment of Linear B was not unconnected with the methodology learned there by Ventris.

[14] See Arthur E. Gordon, "The Inscribed Fibula Praenestina: Problems of Authenticity," *University of California Publications: Classical Studies* 16 (Berkeley 1975) and Margherita Guarducci, "La Cosiddetta fibula prenestine antiquari, eruditi e falsari nella Roma dell'ottocento," *Atti della accademia nazionale dei lincei* 377 (Rome 1980) with the review of A.E. Gordon, *CJ* 78 (1982-83) 64-70 and Guarducci, *ibid.* (Rome 1984) 381.

[15] Reinhard Lullies, *Archäologenbildnisse,* 71-72 simply ignores the most exciting work ever done on Helbig. He could not bear to cite it.

[16] See especially the reasoned defence by Hannes Lehmann, "Wolfgang Helbig (1839-1915) An seinem 150. Geburtstag," *RM* 96 (1989) 7-86.

only by Helbig have come into doubt. Scholars who long have lectured or worse published about these objects without even considering their authenticity do not accept such research kindly. Wolfgang Schindler once remarked to me: "If the Copenhagen portraits are modern forgeries, *Stilanalyse* is worthless." Several well-educated Germans have expressed to me their relief that Schliemann died an American citizen!

An example of the risks inherent in studying acquisitions are the Etruscan Warriors of the Metropolitan Museum of Art in New York. Gilbert Highet, a distinguished classical scholar who commanded the attention of millions of Americans, wrote of them in a prominent place:[17] "There is one tremendous example of Etruscan sculpture in the Metropolitan Museum of New York: a warrior, or a god of war. He is much bigger than life. His body is red, with the sun-burn red which all Etruscan men possessed; his eyes glow white from his red face. He wears strong body armor: his legs are bare and agile; he has a mighty helmet on his head; and he stands in a formidable posture of attack, with a spear ready to transfix his enemy. Whenever I look at him, I hear the steady 5/4 beat of the first movement of Holst's *Planets*, the evocation in sound of the elemental crudity and relentlessness of war. I think he is the finest male statue of a pagan divinity I have ever seen." Once Gisela M.A. Richter, the curator who had purchased them through John Marshall, had retired, her successor Dietrich von Bothmer unmasked the fraud, went to Rome and spoke with Alfredo Fioravanti, who had made Highet's warrior, modeled after a small Berlin bronze.[18] Not only does such exposure embarrass the unwary, but often vain academics in positions of power. It also means the museum loses a lot of money. Such studies are in short not encouraged.

There is a final fourth difficulty that field archaeologists in contrast to art historians confront in discussing the history of their discipline. They are dependent on Greeks, Turks, or other locals for excavation permits. They cannot run the risk of enraging their hosts and having a permit withdrawn. No prehistoric archaeologist excavating in Greece has dared to support David A. Traill's and my suggestion that the "Mask of Agamemnon" is a modern forgery. Twice requests to test the mask were refused by the Antiquities Service. The "Mask of Agamemnon" is a major tourist attraction. It has appeared on postage stamps, postcards and in books endlessly. Its value would fall calamitously were it shown to have been made by Sophia's brother or by a Parisian goldsmith.

In short the difficulties that archaeologists have in treating their own history are particularly acute in the new Schliemann-Forschung. Profit is there. The newly rediscovered "Treasure of Priam" as well as the "Mask of

---

[17] Gilbert Highet, *Talents and Geniuses* (1954 and frequent reprints) 23.
[18] See Dietrich von Bothmer, *Inquiry into the Forgery of the Etruscan Terracotta Warriors* (New York 1961) and David Sox, *Unmasking the Forger: The Dossena Deception* (New York 1987) 97-98, 103-11.

Agamemnon" could both drop considerably in value if shown to be even in part modern forgeries. Both German and Greek nationalism are threatened. Schliemann, a German, lived long in Athens and his more famous second wife, widely revered as a pioneer woman archaeologist and devoted colleague of her husband, was Greek. Do we wish to know the truth about her archaeological interests?[19] One need only recall how Ernst Meyer was commanded by the *Gaulleiter* of Mecklenburg to reclaim Schliemann from the libels of the Jew, Emil Ludwig.[20] His chief sin was to call a successful businessman mercenary.

How have archaeologists reacted to the new Schliemann research? Too often they have either sought to prevent its publication, ignored it in hope that it would go away, or inveighed against those who have dared to ask questions. David A. Traill's epochmaking proof that the "Treasure of Priam" was never found as Schliemann described its finding but rather is a collection of objects found in different places at different times augmented possibly by purchased artifacts and forgeries was refused publication by American bronze age archaeologists in the *American Journal of Archaeology* and *Greek Roman and Byzantine Studies*, where I, a member of the editorial board and the American authority on Schliemann, had urged its publication. He was driven to publish it in England.[21] The then editor of *GRBS* in his choice of referees failed to distinguish between historians of scholarship and bronze age archaeologists. The latter were incompetent to judge the work and frightened by it. It was never submitted to the former. One sees a similar error often in an editor's choice of reviewers. An expert in prehistoric potsherds is not competent to review a book on the man Schliemann anymore than an historian of nineteenth century classical scholarship could review a volume on the chronology of potsherds. Only Wolfgang Schindler could do both.

If we can not prevent the publication of unwelcome discoveries, let's just ignore them. In his foreword to a reprint of Schliemann's *Bericht über die Ausgrabungen in Troja*, the current excavator of Troy is incapable of discussing Traill's challenge to the "Treasure of Priam" or indeed of mentioning his name. Without a word of warning to the reader Sophia is still at Troy gathering the treasure in her shawl, a fiction which even Schliemann later admitted.[22] A recent book by a Munich Ph.D. in archaeology entitled *Troia-Homer-Schliemann: Mythos und Wahrheit* (!) accepts all the

---

[19] For the lies concerning Sophia see David A. Traill, "The Archaeological Career of Sophia Schliemann," *Excavating Schliemann, ICCSupp.* 4 (Atlanta 1993) 235-43 (= *Antichthon* 23 [1989] 99-107). The volume is henceforth cited: *Excavating Schliemann*. For the *fable convenue* see Hans Einsle, *Sophia Schliemann: Die Frau des großen Archäologen Biographischer Roman* (Mühlacker 1989). The title is honest.

[20] See William M. Calder III, *supra* n. 2.

[21] See David A. Traill, "Schliemann's Discovery of 'Priam's Treasure': A Re-examination of the Evidence," *JHS* 104 (1984) 96-115 (= *Excavating Schliemann*, 125-53).

[22] See Manfred Korfmann in Heinrich Schliemann, *Bericht über die Ausgrabungen in Troja in den Jahren 1871 bis 1873* (Munich/Zürich 1990) xi, 217.

mythos of the "Treasure of Priam" and banishes the names of Calder, Schindler, and Traill from his bibliography![23] Prof. Dr. Hans-Günter Buchholz in a review of two hundred years of research on Homeric archaeology from Winckelmann through Schliemann published in 1991 writes as though it were 1930 and omits all reference to any of the modern critical work on Schliemann.[24]

In general the reaction of archaeological reviewers to books on the new Schliemann research is predictable. They are incapable of refuting conclusions based on philological argument from documentary evidence which they cannot or will not control and therefore resort to irrelevant invective or polemic. I provide several examples for *Myth, Scandal and History* [25] where Wolfgang Schindler's paper on the Cleopatra portrait appeared. A senior American archaeologist, recipient of a coveted gold medal award from the Archaeological Institute of America, William A. McDonald, writes against "philologist-critics":[26] "To put it mildly, this is a mean-spirited scholarly enterprise—particularly when aimed at one who can no longer defend himself." Where would scholarship be if we were forbidden to criticize the dead? I find the objection bizarre. He concludes: "And if deposits of genuine artifacts were salted with fake copies, scientific tests (not unsupported insinuations) are the constructive way to ascertain the facts." Two requests after funding had been secured to have the "Agamemnon Mask" scientifically tested were refused by archaeologists! Carol G. Thomas in a widely read review laments:[27] "Anger pervades almost every page of this book...The editors' thesis is simple. Schliemann was a bad man.[28] ...Traill and Calder seek to discredit Schliemann both as a man and as a scholar. A further essay by W. Schindler is also hostile...The case is not compelling...A proper understanding of Schliemann's role in the field of archaeology demands more than innuendo and textual criticism." Thomas fails to see that because field archaeologists through the nature of their work must destroy the evidence on which their conclusions are based any history of what they did must derive from documents, that is be philological.[29] As I

---

[23] Michael Siebler, *Troia-Homer-Schliemann: Mythos und Wahrheit* (Mainz 1990) 121-22 (Sophia is still at Troy helping her husband), 127-29 (three pages on the "Auseinandersetzung um die Echtheit des Schatzes" omits reference to Traill!), 244-46 (reference to all the new Schliemannn research after 1972 omitted).

[24] See Hans-Günter Buchholz, "Die archäologische Forschung im Zusammenhang mit Homer Gesamtüberblick," *Zweihundert Jahre Homer-Forschung Rückblick und Ausblick, Colloquium Rauricum* 2 edited by Joachim Latacz (Stuttgart/Leipzig 1991) 11-44. Contrarily without a word of warning he cites Ernst Meyer to corroborate his text. In a comprehensive review T. Krischner, *Gnomon* 64 (1992) 481-93, fails to notice the omission!

[25] William M. Calder III and David A. Traill, *Myth, Scandal and History: The Heinrich Schliemann Controversy and a First Edition of the Mycenaean Diary* (Detroit 1986).

[26] The quotations are from *Religious Studies Review* 13 (1987) 258-59.

[27] All citations are from Carol G. Thomas, *American Historical Review* 92 (1987) 946.

[28] In fact I have repeatedly stated that I make no moral judgment on Schliemann's behavior.

[29] She expands her displeasure at the "virulent hostility" that "a few scholars of the present generation" have displayed toward poor Schliemann in four pages defaced by errors and a

have elsewhere phrased it "quae archaeologia fuit, facta philologia est" (after Sen. *Ep.* 108. 23). There is worse to come. J.T. Hooker has little patience with Calder and Traill.[30] "No one can, or should, condone the behaviour of the present editors. Their animus against Schliemann, manifest on every page, robs their work of all objectivity and leads to the confusion of fact and surmise." The book is "true to the principles of a third-rate scandal-sheet." Calder cites "Wilamowitz in a private letter" to discredit Dörpfeld. The philologist Traill "rejects the suggestions of such Shaft Grave amateurs as Karo and Mylonas in favour of his own theory." Schliemann was base but had "vision and dauntless courage." Calder-Traill exhibit "baseness...not...accompanied by any redeeming virtues." Hooker in short is incapable of discussing rationally the new discoveries. His implication that private letters may not be cited when writing the academic history of the nineteenth century is as intelligent as saying domestic pottery may not be used to establish chronology in digs. Utterly different are reviews by historians of scholarship, though untrained in field archaeology.[31]

II. Ten Items

The purpose of what I have written so far is to establish the context in which Wolfgang Schindler became the only archaeologist who dared to question the deified Schliemann, the patron-saint and founder of modern field archaeology. For only against the irrational hostility of his colleagues can the courage of his contribution be understood. He was first an archaeologist in contrast to me who am first a *Wissenschaftshistoriker*. The bulk of his work is contained in ten papers of permanent value.[32] They are in chrono-logical order the following. I append to each entry brief remarks on content and value.

1. "Heinrich Schliemann: Leben und Werk im Spiegel der neueren biographischen Forschungen," *Philologus* 120 (1976) 271-289.

---

failure to cite relevant literature at "Myth Becomes History: Pre-Classical Greece," *Publications of the Association of Ancient Historians* 4 (Claremont 1993) 11-14.

[30] Citations are from J.T. Hooker, *JHS* 108 (1988) 258-59.

[31] See the review by the Victorian intellectual historian, Robert Ackerman, at *Victorian Studies* (1967) 136-37. Compare also W. Geoffrey Arnott, *LCM* 12.8 (1987) 122–26 and Justus Cobet, *Frankfurter Allgemeine Zeitung*, (29 April 1987) 35–36.

[32] Schindler refers at *ICS* 17 (1992) 150 n. 82 to "Schliemann als Zeitgenosse," *Proceedings of the Schliemann Conference at Athens* (forthcoming). The volume has not yet been published. He refers elsewhere as in the press to "Heinrich Schliemann und Till Eulenspiege." I have not included among the ten his notice of the Boulder Colloquium: see "Heinrich Schliemann: Myth or Scandal? Kolloquium, Boulder, Colo. (USA) 1983," *Ethnographisch-Archäologische Zeitschrift* 25 (1984) 567-68. Nor have I included a brilliant article in which he defends the early dating of the Trojan War by comparing the composition of the Shield of Achilles with art of Late Helladic II and IIIA: see "New Evidence for the Trojan War," *Travaux du Centre d'Archéologie Méditerranéenne de l'Académie Polonaise des Sciences* 30 *Études et Travaux* 15 (1991) 364-70.

This famous article may well be the most often cited and best known that Wolfgang Schindler ever wrote. It was the first statement in German of the new approach to Schliemann and it was published in a journal that had the widest circulation under socialism of any East European periodical in ancient studies. One must remember that DDR archaeologists suffered from the fact that there was no archaeological journal available to them. Because his article was essentially *Wissenschaftsgeschichte* publication in *Philologus* was possible. Tact was necessary. An American in a lecture forbidden by the state but permitted by the church had challenged long cherished legends not challenged by two prominent DDR Academicians. First here Schindler in a Marxist context presented Schliemann "the self-made man." Here too he first began to explain Schliemann's behavior in terms of his "Sitz im Leben" rather than psychologically. This would become in the years that followed the fundamental distinction between American and European work on the man. Schindler emphasized the remarkable parallels with Ibsen's *Peer Gynt*, first noticed by Joachim Wohlleben. Later researchers have followed him in this. He advanced also the useful concept of "productive imagination" (*Die produktive Phantasie*) and avoided the word liar. The article ended diplomatically on a positive note in recalling the *Wissenschaftsleistung* of the hero and what he owed two highly respectable friends, Rudolf Virchow and Wilhelm Dörpfeld. Just this what he owed these two men would be expanded by later scholars. In short in many ways the article was programmatic.

2. "Mykene: Homers Dichtung-Schliemanns Grabung," *Urania* 56 (1980) 8-11.

This was a concise, lucid, masterly summary of Schliemann's achievement intended for a mass audience under socialism. On the one hand he wrote: "Heute blicken wir mit Dankbarkeit auf die Energie und Tatkraft dieses Mannes zurück" (11) but then in the notes were references to the new research which the alert could pursue.

3. "Schliemanns Selbstporträt: Die Inszenierung eines Self-made-man," *Ethnographische-Archäologische Zeitschrift* 21 (1980) 655-658.

A brilliantly written sketch that argues after appropriate citations of Karl Marx and Thomas Mann with *Ideologieanalyse* that Schliemann was much a product of his age. What today may seem weaknesses are not. "Im Gegenteil, wir bewundern den Pionier der Grabungsarchäologie um so mehr, je praller der Sack der Lügen ist, den ihm seine Zeitgenossenschaft aufzubürden und zur Selbsterbauung und Selbstbestätigung gern abzunehmen bereit war" (657). His flaws were unavoidably imposed upon him by his time and he transcended them.

4. "Schliemanns Selbstporträt: Der Mythos eines self-made-man," *Antike-rezeption, Antikeverhältnis, Antikebegegnung in Vergangenheit & Gegen-wart: Eine Aufsatzsammlung,* edited by Jürgen Dummer and Max Kunze, *Schriften der Winckelmann-Gesellschaft* 6 (Stendal 1983; published 1988) 659-669.

The article was more than ten years in the press and is the original of the preceding item with precise documentation and concentration on the remarkable similarity between Peer Gynt's and Schliemann's careers. The similarities are undeniable. The *Minnaerlebnis* and the excavation of Troy are perhaps the most striking. On the other hand Schliemann could not have known Ibsen's play. How to explain the similarities? Both are fiction. *Peer Gynt* dramatised a fundamental myth, a cultural pattern, of the day, the rise of the self-made man. Schliemann could not avoid adhering to it. Hence the paradox: the more of what we too easily dismiss as his lies, the more honestly Schliemann adheres to the ideals of his time. Detection of his fictions allow us to grasp him "in seiner Historizität." One should note here too Schindler's citation of the parallel of Karl May (662).[33] One sees very much in this remarkable paper Wolfgang Schindler the poet and lover of great literature more than the archaeologist. He can treat archaeology with a humanist's feeling. He is fundamentally in the profound sense of the term the historicist.

5. Review of Hartmut Döhl, *Heinrich Schliemann: Mythos und Ärgernis* (Munich 1981) at *DLZ* 104 (1983) 898-901.

This is the most authoritative review published of Döhl's important book because Schindler controlled the matter both as *Wissenschaftshistoriker* and as archaeologist.[34] He welcomes it warmly, stresses its virtues, and places it within the context of current research. He objects to Döhl's sweeping under the carpet proven fabrications (e.g., lies in the diary become *Schulübungen*) and makes the central point that the revelation of deceit in Schliemann's writings enhances modern appreciation of the man: "Als der entheroisierte Held muß er uns Heutigen viel näher stehen." This will become a recurrent motif in his later work.

6. "Schliemann's Cleopatra," *Myth, Scandal, and History: The Heinrich Schliemann Controversy and a First Edition of the Mycenaean Diary,* edited by William M. Calder III and David A. Traill (Detroit 1986) 81-94.

---

[33] See now Bernhard Rink, "Heinrich Schliemann und Karl May: Versuch eines Vergleichs zweier außergewöhnlicher Persönlichkeiten," *Grundlagen,* 77-85.

[34] See further William M. Calder III, *German Studies Review* 6 (1983) 602-603 and especially David A. Traill, *Gnomon* 55 (1983) 149-52 (= "Excavating Schliemann," *ICCSupp.* 4 [1993] 255-59). Contrast the *laudatio* by Carol G. Thomas, *AJA* 91 (1987) 492-93, appearing six years after publication of the book.

As a DDR-*Wissenschaftler*, Wolfgang Schindler had access to Schliemann's "Cleopatra" in a way no western scholar could. The West German Hartmut Döhl had written in 1981 that it had been lost in the war.[35] Schindler found it in the storage rooms of the Pergamon Museum. He wisely chose a subject he could control with unquestioned authority rather than rule on the authenticity of Mycenaean objects he had never seen. His expertise in Greek sculpture and Roman portraiture, the Buschor legacy, made him uniquely qualified. His address to the first conference ever held on Schliemann the man was an instant success. It was delivered in English before a large audience with superb accompanying slides, the first ever seen in the US of the portrait. There was another reason to remember the occasion. For the first time a DDR scholar in ancient studies, not a party-member, addressed an international conference in the United States. The paper was published in a book that received wide circulation. On the other hand his obvious sympathy with the new Schliemann research and his inclusion in the volume aroused the wrath of the Schliemann-defenders and he was later branded by the ignorant "a member of the Calder-Traill school."[36]

There were two problems: 1) Did Schliemann, as he alleged, conduct excavations otherwise unattested twelve to sixteen meters deep in Alexandria in February 1888 and find his Cleopatra, as he had earlier said he would, at the bottom of a trench? 2) Just who is the woman if she is not Cleopatra and how was she obtained? The answer to the first question was "No." Not even the most impassioned defender of Schliemann has sought to defend the existence of a large-scale excavation near the Ramle train station, deep enough to require expensive pumping because of the high waterlevel there. All this would have been done within some three weeks; and on arrival in Alexandria friend Rudolf Virchow ignores it all in his journal. As for the portrait itself, Schindler suggested that it was a first century A.D. copy descending from a lost late fourth century B.C. archetype.[37] "Whether he purchased the head in Alexandria or elsewhere cannot be proven from the extant evidence" (91).

7. "Rudolf Virchow und Schliemanns Kleopatra," *Mitteilungen aus dem Heinrich-Schliemann-Museum Ankershagen* 1 (1987) 43-54.

This article by its use of new evidence in the Virchow Archive allows more precise statements than in the preceding one. It is a masterpiece of the use of archival documents to reconstruct history. Few archaeologists would be able to duplicate this feat. He stresses the similarity between the alleged

---

[35] Hartmut Döhl, *Heinrich Schliemann: Mythos und Ärgernis* (Munich 1981) 72: see Wolfgang Schindler, *DLZ* 104 (1983) 900.

[36] E.F. Bloedow, S. Noyes-Roberts, David Smulders, *Classical Views* NS 8 (1989) 148, adding ominously "Schindler's study follows very closely the approaches of Calder and Traill."

[37] Professor David A. Traill informs me *per coll.* that there is reason to consider the portrait a modern forgery. *Nous verrons!*

discovery of "the Treasure of Priam" and that of the Cleopatra head. In tactful consideration of the circumstances of delivery at the Schliemann Museum in Ankershagen he urges moderation on both sides of the Schliemann controversy and wishes in no way to detract from the abiding contribution of Schliemann to science.

8. "Dichtung und Wahrheit: Schliemanns Selbstbiographie im Kontext," *Heinrich Schliemann nach hundert Jahren*, edited by William M. Calder III and Justus Cobet (Frankfurt/Main 1990) 152-169.[38]

Again one sees here the trained *Wissenschaftshistoriker* and the man of letters at work rather than the archaeologist. A crucial source for Schliemann's childhood is the sixty-four page *Monsterbrief* dated Amsterdam, 20 February 1842 and addressed to his sisters Wilhelmine and Doris. Only a highly censored version had been earlier published by Ernst Meyer. Schindler edits and interprets revealing omitted passages for the first time, elucidating them by parallels from the novels of Dickens. His purpose again is to see Schliemann as a product of his time. The parallels between the letter and Charles Dickens, like those between *Peer Gynt* and Schliemann's autobiography do not reveal dependency but rather the *genius saeculi*, the *Zeitgeist* at work. The tendency, as so often with Schindler's later Schliemann work, is healing. The facts he uncovers are not meant to vilify Schliemann but to explain him and thereby forgive him. *Tout comprendre c'est tout pardonner.*

9. "Werk und Leben Heinrich Schliemanns," *Heinrich Schliemann: Grundlagen und Ergebnisse moderner Archäologie 100 Jahre nach Schliemanns Tod,* edited by Joachim Hermann (Berlin 1992) 15-21.

This is a magnanimous and eloquent attempt to reconcile the discoveries of the preceding twenty years with the need to transmit to subsequent generations enduring gratitude for Schliemann's permanent achievement. The man was a great product of his time, formed by the age in which he lived and requiring to be judged by the standards of that age. We thank the editor that he placed it first in a valuable volume. It strikes the keynote of what the conference sought to accomplish. Archaeologists and historians of scholarship are not foes. They are allies.

10. "An Archaeologist on the Schliemann Controversy," *Illinois Classical Studies* 17 (1992) 135-151.

---

[38] See W.G. Arnott, *CR* NS 42 (1992) 178 and Beat Näf, *Gnomon* 65 (1993) 262.

I sometimes think that he thought this would be his last statement on Schliemann. It parallels the preceding contribution but is for English-speaking people. There is an *historia quaestionis* with a call for temperance, enlightened tolerance and allowing both sides their say. The contributions of the Bad Homburg and the Athens Conferences are evaluated. He was always most loyal to me and, while modestly denigrating his own contributions, allowed me more credit than I deserved.

III. The Achievement

Wolfgang Schindler is the only archaeologist who from the beginning (6 January 1972) made a lasting contribution to the new understanding of Schliemann. Without his encouragement I should never have turned to Schliemann. In summer 1971 as guest of Probst i. R. Karl Timm in Bellin we learned that the 150th birthday of Schliemann was approaching. By a remarkable coincidence the son of Probst Timm was pastor at the parish where Schliemann had been born. Hence the idea of an address arose and we became guests in the pastor's house for the birthday. Wolfgang Schindler convinced me to work on Schliemann. What caused Wolfgang Schindler to do so for twenty years? Or by implication what hindered other archaeologists from so doing? Sometimes apparent disadvantages are blessings. He was in the bizarre position of being a classical archaeologist forbidden to visit Greece or Italy. He made the enormously intelligent decision of devoting his attention to socialist Europe, where he could travel, especially Hungary, Romania and Bulgaria and the museums in Poland and Czechoslovakia. Except for Hungarian he could read the languages that Westerners could not. On the other hand, as a Berlin scholar, he had an entrée into mainline scholarship of a sort that a scholar in Cluj lacked. He devoted considerable attention to photographing and interpreting finds simply unknown to Westerners, certainly to Americans and making them available in a language Westerners could read. His Schliemann work continued this policy of making the best of an unsatisfactory situation.

His position at the Humboldt University before 1990 oddly allowed him a freedom that a West German of his generation lacked. He simply could never excavate in Greece or Turkey. Hence the fear of Greek or Turkish reprisals for stating unwelcome truth about Schliemann and his finds did not exist for him. He had no fear that an excavation permit would be denied or revoked. Excavators like Korfmann, Mellinck, or the Cincinnati Kollektiv lack for perfectly understandable reasons this freedom. Nor would he ever be part of an excavation team and so did not fear being forbidden to excavate at Tiryns because he had accused Schliemann of fraud. Döhl, a member of the Tiryns team, understandably had to be cautious. Far better to defend the patron-saint from prying philologists! Next Wolfgang Schindler had no hope whatsoever of leaving the

Winckelmann-Institut. He would never be a candidate for a chair at Munich, Würzburg or Giessen. He did not have to fear stepping on the toes of vain academics on appointment committees. His training also helped. He had begun his study at Jena as Nietzsche did at Bonn with the intent of becoming a theologian. This would mean a life based on Greek texts and his training had been philological. The lectures of Alscher won him for art-history. As he once remarked to me; "I left Jesus Christ for Pericles." But he retained the skills of a philologist. He knew, as Traill and I did, the value of documents and how to read them critically in order to extract history from them. Unlike Traill and me, he brought vast archaeological expertise to his work as well. Archaeologists could not dismiss him as an ignorant intruder.

There was a further practical reason. The material to work on Schliemann was available to a DDR scholar in a way that material to work on the Athenian agora was not. All of Schliemann's books were to hand. I carried over Check Point Charley for him copies of Meyer's editions of the letters and his biography. Ankershagen, Neubukow, and Rostock could be visited easily. Of course the Gennadeion was not available but much could be done without the *Nachlaß*. Rather than divided loyalties he had universal loyalty, a tolerance for both sides. His interest in literature and his ability to write well (he was a talented poet) extended the influence of his contribution. Although cheated of his promised book on Schliemann by his untimely death, we shall long profit from what he has given us.[39] I suppose the most enduring legacy of his work will be the conviction that the modern critical attention to this controversial figure has not damaged Schliemann but in an egalitarian, almost Marxistic, sense, welcome to a "classless society," has enhanced his appeal. "Als der entheroisierte Held muß er uns Heutigen viel näher stehen." That is for better or worse the truth.

---

[39] My hope is in the near future to gather in a single volume with corrigenda and indices his papers on Schliemann. That would be a worthy companion for David A. Traill's *Excavating Schliemann*.

Sterling Dow†

With the death of Sterling Dow, Hudson Professor of Archaeology emeritus at Harvard University, in his ninety-second year in Cambridge, Massachusetts on 9 January 1995, American classics lost its most influential teacher, the mentor of a generation of influential scholars. His professional life coincided with the great period of Harvard classics. Werner Jaeger, Arthur Darby Nock, A. S. Pease and Joshua Whatmough were his colleagues. In a way comparable only with the founding fathers of U.S. philology, Gildersleeve, Oldfather, and Shorey and the immigrant Rostovzeff, Dow created a school, clearly defined, cohesive, perpetuating and itself of considerable influence.

Dow was born at Portland, Maine 19 November 1903 into an old New England family. His father, Sterling Tucker Dow, was Treasurer of the Boston and Maine Railroad. He graduated from Phillips Exeter Academy, one of the two or three finest schools in the country, and entered Harvard College in September 1921, receiving the B.A. in 1925. Two fellow students in this class would become lifelong colleagues: J. H. Finley, a newspaperman's son, and the Boston blueblood, Mason Hammond. For one year he was Fiske Scholar at Trinity College, Cambridge, returning to Harvard, where he took the M.A. in 1928 and the Ph.D. in 1936. His dissertation, *Athenian Inscriptions in the Official Lettering of 230-200 B.C.*, was written under the Canadian Greek historian, William Scott Ferguson, who had heard Wilamowitz in Berlin.[1] He respected and appreciated Ferguson but rarely spoke of him. He married Elizabeth Sanderson Flagg in 1931.

The experience that formed Dow was five years at the Agora Excavation in Athens 1931-1936.[2] These were the golden years. John D. Rockefeller, Jr., and James Loeb in his will had provided funds for the excavation. Under the direction of T. Leslie Shear, Sr., a brilliant young team shared in an enterprise that Americans had never enjoyed before. They were excavating one of the most famous sites of classical antiquity. Friendships that would last a lifetime emerged. On the team were Dorothy Burr, Virginia Grace, James Oliver, Lucy Shoe, Homer Thompson, Eugene Vanderpool. Soon there was the architect William Bell Dinsmoor. They recorded carefully what they found. Their cautious conclusions were based on concrete evidence. There was a sharing of ideas, an innocent, impassioned quest for truth and the intoxication of repeated discovery of what mattered. He learned from Rhys Carpenter, Humfrey Payne, Richard

---

[1] See Dow's necrology of Ferguson at *Gnomon* 27 (1955) 60-61.

[2] For details see Louis E. Lord, *A History of the American School of Classical Studies at Athens 1882-1942* (Cambridge 1947).

Stillwell, and the fabled Burt Hodge Hill. For Dow there was friendship with Johannes Kirchner.[3] He often spoke of him. *Prosopographia Attica* was cited again and again as the collection of objective evidence that outlasted the scores of theories based upon it. Kirchner as much as anyone turned Dow to epigraphy. At Athens he made his greatest single discovery. He identified inscrutable remains as the kleroterion, the jury allottment machine, alluded to in Aristotle, *AthPol*.[4] His conclusions have been accepted by all subsequent scholars concerned with the matter.[5] He returned to Harvard in 1936 and taught with brief interruption in the war years until his forced retirement in 1970. He was Distinguished Professor of Greek Civilization and History at Boston College 1970-1977 and Blegen Distinguished Professor of Classics at Vassar College in 1978. He was president of the Archaeological Institute of America, the American Classical League and the Classical Association of New England. He understood that university classics depend on school classics and founded the Teachers of Classics in New England. He was Annual Professor at the American School in Athens in 1966-67 and long an active member of its Managing Committee. He was one of the very few Americans to be Honorary Life Member of the Society for the Promotion of Hellenic Studies in London and he was Honorable American Secretary for both the Hellenic and Roman Societies. He was Ehrenmitglied of the Deutsches Archäologisches Institut in Berlin. He was one of the *paucissimi* to hold three Guggenheim Fellowships. Only his powerful support at the start allowed *Greek, Roman and Byzantine Studies* to survive. He founded *Archaeology*.

His teaching at Harvard was his most enduring contribution to the profession. In a sentence his feat was to make research the most exciting pursuit that life offered. Graduate teaching at Harvard before Dow was insufferably dull. One had to write a dissertation usually in Latin on a trivial subject of no interest to anyone, directed often by an incompetent, and intended solely to win the doctoral degree, the union card that gained admission to university teaching.[6] Dow transformed research from a punishment to a privilege. The Agora-Erlebnis convinced him that knowledge of antiquity was not a closed book. New evidence was always accumulating. New ideas changed old prejudices. Ventris' decipherment of Linear B in 1953 was a favorite example. His seminars stressed how much there was to do. He treated *doctorandi* as younger colleagues. He took notes

---

[3] See S. Dow, *AJA* 46 (1942) 127-28 [and Johannes Kirchner, "Aus den Erinnerungen eines Achtzigjahrigen," *Annalen und Historien: Festschrift des Vereins ehemaliger Schüler des Friedrich Wilhelms Gymnasiums zu Berlin* (Berlin 1980) 23.]

[4] See S. Dow, "Kleroterion," *RE* Supp. 7 (1940) 322-328. Original publication was at *HSCP* 50 (1939) 1-34.

[5] For a bibliography of his publications see "Studies Presented to Sterling Dow on his Eightieth Birthday," *GRBM* 10 ((Durham 1984) xvii-xxxvi.

[6] For doctoral work in Classics at Harvard before Dow see Alston Hurd Chase, *Time Remembered* (San Antonio 1994) 129-164.

on their seminar reports. He wrote articles and reviews with them. In term his weekly "Dow Lunches" turned students into professionals. He intervened with editors to have his students' first articles published. He turned the writing of dissertations into high adventure and a matter of supreme importance, carefully correcting each chapter as it was submitted and providing bibliographical references in a barrage of notes. He helped students whom no one else would and found dissertation topics suitable to their talents. He believed that making earlier work available was as urgent as adding to knowledge. Hence many of his own publications have a bibliographical character. Dorothy Rounds, *Articles on Antiquity in Festschriften* (1962) is owed Dow's direction.[7] My *Index Locorum zu Kühner-Gerth* (1965) is owed his inspiration and support. He combined professional severity with kindness and unfailing humor. He never feared students more intelligent than himself. In a time when Irish Catholics were looked upon with contempt at Harvard, Dow gladly directed their dissertations and found posts for them.

He directed over 30 dissertations. He attracted the most intelligent young men of the time in American classics.[8] Among them were C. R. Beye, A. L. Boegehold, M. H. Chambers, Thomas Drew-Bear, John H. Kroll, Jon D. Mikalson, Leslie Threatte, Jr., S. V. Tracy and John S. Traill. They respected and benefited from his loyalty to his students. They admired his rigor and valued his praise because it was never feigned. They learned to believe that nothing was more important than research and publication. His thorough dedication to excellence and his courage in stating his convictions live on in his best students and their students. Men who never met him imitate his Maine accent. He had no patience with incompetence or pretension and was often victim of his own integrity. Epigraphy was clean and straightforward. One could control all the evidence available, read all the secondary literature, and make an irrefutable conclusion that carried knowledge forward. It did not allow fraud.

The other side was his detestation of literary criticism, which he considered the pursuit of incompetents who in the end did little more than impose personal prejudices under the guise of scholarship. His contempt for his literary colleagues was undisguised and requited. An unfortunate product of this prejudice was that in his almost 30 years of retirement he never finished his book on Homer, his life of Parry, his comprehensive study of the epheboi, or his commentary on Ar. *AthPol*.[9] He wanted to control everything in the way one could for an inscription but never can for Homer. His Sather lectures (1964) on "Knossos and Mykenai: the Great

---

[7] See *Gnomon* 25 (1953) 560; 27 (1955) 64; 34 (1962) 734-35.

[8] For his brilliant teaching see my ""Harvard Classics 1950-1956," *Festgabe für Ernst Vogt, Eikasmos* 4 (1993) 39-49.

[9] This task was completed by his student, Mortimer H. Chambers, *Aristoteles Staat der Athener* (Berlin 1990).

Powers in the Bronze Age," which attracted audiences of over 500, were never completed but his history of the chair was [10] and won him an honorary doctorate from Berkeley. One can only contrast the productive emeritude of his brother-in-law, W. Kendrick Pritchett. He also encouraged a division now some fifty years old between philologists and literary critics in American classics. They became enemies rather than allies. The good part of course was that his students received from him a *wissenschaftliches Gewissen* and what they wrote lasts in contrast to the fleeting aperçus of the poorly trained. His most enduring monument is the love of his students and their passion to bequeath to their own students the treasure they gained from him. "Seinesgleichen werden wir nicht wieder begegnen."

---

[10] *Fifty Years of Sathers* (Berkeley 1965).

Index Personarum